Zambia

the Bradt Travel Guide

Chris McIntyre

D0109341

www.bradtguides.com

Bradt Travel Guides Ltd, UK
The Globe Pequot Press Inc, USA

edition
4

AUTHOR

Chris McIntyre went to Africa in 1987, after reading physics at Queen's College, Oxford. He taught with VSO in Zimbabwe for almost three years and travelled around extensively. In 1990 he co-authored the UK's first *Guide to Namibia and Botswana*, published by Bradt, before spending three years as a shipbroker in London.

Since then, Chris has concentrated on what he enjoys most: Africa. He wrote the first guidebook to Zambia for Bradt in 1996, the first edition of their Namibia guide in 1998, a new Botswana guide in 2003, and co-authored a guide to Zanzibar in 2006. Whilst keeping these guidebooks up to date, he is also managing director of Expert Africa. This UK-based specialist tour operator organises high-quality trips throughout Africa for individual travellers from around the world; it probably sends more travellers on safaris to Zambia than any other company.

Chris maintains a keen interest in development and conservation issues, acting as advisor to various NGOs and projects associated with Africa. He is a Fellow of the Royal Geographical Society and contributes photographs and articles to various publications, including *The Times*, *Wanderlust*, *BBC Wildlife* and *Travel Africa*. Based in Teddington, west London, Chris and his wife, Susan, spend two or three months each year travelling and researching in Africa. Chris can usually be contacted by email on chris.mcintyre@expertafrica.com.

PUBLISHER'S FOREWORD *Hilary Bradt*

The first Bradt travel guide was written in 1974 by George and Hilary Bradt on a river barge floating down a tributary of the Amazon. It was followed by *Backpacker's Africa*, published in 1979. In the 1980s and '90s the focus shifted away from hiking to broader-based guides to new destinations – usually the first to be published on those places. In the 21st century Bradt continues to publish these ground-breaking guides, along with guides to established holiday destinations, incorporating in-depth information on culture and natural history alongside the nuts and bolts of where to stay and what to see.

Bradt authors support responsible travel, with advice not only on minimum impact but also on how to give something back through local charities. Thus a true synergy is achieved between the traveller and local communities.

* * *

When this book was first published, an American bookseller wrote to tell me that it was '… the most comprehensive and well-organised book of the bunch and I also believe it is one of the best travel books ever published.' Over the years, Chris has expanded his guide in line with continuing developments in Zambia's tourism. This ensures that both first-time visitors and those who have a long familiarity with the country will find insightful comments about all that is new in the context of the detailed background text that is the hallmark of the book.

Fourth edition January 2008   First published 1996
Bradt Travel Guides Ltd, 23 High Street, Chalfont St Peter, Bucks SL9 9QE, England
www.bradtguides.com
Published in the USA by The Globe Pequot Press Inc, 246 Goose Lane,
PO Box 480, Guilford, Connecticut 06475-0480

Text copyright © 2008 Chris McIntyre
Maps copyright © 2008 Bradt Travel Guides Ltd
Illustrations © 2008 Individual photographers and illustrators

ISBN-10: 1 84162 226 5   ISBN-13: 978 1 84162 226 2
British Library Cataloguing in Publication Data
A catalogue record for this book is available from the British Library

Photographs Maruska Adye (MA), Heather Angel (HA), Mark Boulton (MB), Tricia Hayne (TH), Beverley Joubert/Getty Images (BJ), Chris McIntyre (CM), Ariadne Van Zandbergen (AZ)
Front cover Hippopotamus *Hippopotamus amphibius* (BJ)
Back cover Lion cub *Panthera leo* (CM)
Title page Malachite kingfisher (AZ), Detail of Tribal Textiles' throw (MB), Aloe (TH)
Illustrations Annabel Milne   **Maps** Malcolm Barnes, Steve Munns

Typeset from the author's disc by Wakewing
Printed and bound in India by Nutech Photolithographers

Major Contributors

This book, just as much as the previous editions, has been a team effort, and many have devoted their energy to it. Largest amongst the contributions to this fourth edition are those from the following.

Tricia and Bob Hayne updated most of the text for this edition, having worked extensively on the third edition, and helped to update Chris's other guides to Botswana, Namibia and Zanzibar. As former editorial director of Bradt Travel Guides, Tricia is only too familiar with the minutiae of putting together a guidebook. Now a freelance travel writer, and a member of the British Guild of Travel Writers, she has more time to devote to hidden corners of the globe, where she and Bob can indulge their interests in culture, outdoor pursuits and the environment.

Judi Helmholz provided the bulk of the information on Livingstone. She lives beside the Zambezi with her husband, Arthur, assorted Rottweilers and dachshunds, and 18,000 chickens – whilst playing host to the occasional passing elephant, hippo, VIP and itinerant author. Having explored many of Zambia's wild places, Judi remains active in tourism development and conservation. She maintains that guiding a raft through the Zambezi's white water was child's play compared with balancing the many roles that she now has, from roving travel consultant, entrepreneur, safari guide and art collector to 'fixer extraordinaire'. Judi and Arthur have also provided me with both a base for many of my explorations of southern Africa, and a generous supply of sanity and good humour there.

Contents

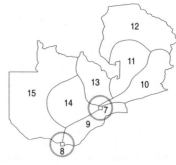

Acknowledgements   VII
Introduction   IX

PART ONE   GENERAL INFORMATION   I

Chapter I   **History, Politics and Economy   3**
                History 3, Government 13, Economy 14

Chapter 2   **People and Culture   19**
                People 19, Religion 25, Education 25, Culture 26

Chapter 3   **The Natural Environment   29**
                Physical environment 29, Flora and fauna 32,
                Conservation 36

Chapter 4   **Planning and Preparation   41**
                When to go 41, Organising a safari 45, Getting there 52,
                Red tape 54, What to take 57, Maps and navigation 59,
                Photography and optics 60, Money and budgeting 61,
                Getting around 66, Accommodation 74, Food and
                drink 75, What to buy 77, Communications and media 79,
                Giving something back 82

Chapter 5   **Health and Safety   85**
                Health 85, Safety 100

Chapter 6   **In the Wilds   103**
                Driving 103, Bush camping 108, Walking in the bush 112,
                Canoeing 115, Minimum impact 116

PART TWO   THE GUIDE   119

Chapter 7   **Lusaka   121**
                History 121, Getting there and away 121,
                Orientation 125, Getting around 125, Where to stay 129,
                Where to eat 142, Entertainment and nightlife 145,
                Shopping 146, Banks and changing money 149,
                Communications 149, Other practicalities 150, Further
                information 153, What to see and do 153

Chapter 8	**Livingstone and the Victoria Falls**	159

History 159, Geology 160, Tourist information 161,
Getting there and away 161, Getting around 163, Where
to stay 166, Where to eat 180, Entertainment and
nightlife 183, Shopping 183, Other practicalities 186,
What to see and do 188

Chapter 9	**Lake Kariba and the Lower Zambezi**	205

From Livingstone to Lusaka 205, Lake Kariba 211, From
Lusaka to Chirundu 225, Lower Zambezi Valley 228

Chapter 10	**The Luangwa Valley**	245

The Great East Road 245, South Luangwa National
Park 249, North Luangwa National Park 284, Luambe
National Park 291, Lukusuzi National Park 294

Chapter 11	**Bangweulu Area**	295

The Great North Road 295, Around Mpika 302, Kasanka
National Park 312, Around Kasanka and Bangweulu 319,
Lake Bangweulu and the wetlands 324, Isangano National
Park 332

Chapter 12	**Northern Zambia**	333

Getting organised 333, The Great North Road to
Mpulungu 333, Lake Tanganyika and environs 342,
Sumbu National Park 350, The road to Mweru Wantipa
and Kaputa 356, From Mbereshi to Kasama 363, Nyika
Plateau National Park 368

Chapter 13	**The Copperbelt**	375

The history of the copper 375, Lusaka to Kapiri
Mposhi 378, Ndola 382, Kitwe 390, Chingola 395,
Solwezi 401

Chapter 14	**The Kafue River Basin**	407

Towns around Kafue National Park 407, Kafue National
Park 413, Lochinvar and Blue Lagoon national parks 436

Chapter 15	**Western Zambia**	447

Tour operators 447, Southwestern Zambia 449,
Barotseland 458, Northwestern Zambia 477

Appendix 1	**Wildlife Guide**	491
Appendix 2	**Languages**	507
Appendix 3	**Further Information**	510
Index		514

LIST OF MAPS

Administrative areas	13	Lusaka: centre	134–5
Blue Lagoon NP	445	Lusaka, orientation	126–7
Chingola	397	Mansa	359
Chipata	247	Mbala	340
Copperbelt, the	376	Mfuwe area	264
Kabwe	380	Mongu	459
Kafue NP: Ngoma area	432	Mpika	301
Kafue, northern	419	Mpulungu	347
Kafue River Basin	406	National parks	39
Kafue: south of the lake	430	Ndola	383
Kafue, southern	427	North Luangwa NP	289
Kaoma	412	Northern Zambia	334
Kasama	336	Nsefu Sector, around the	280
Kasanka NP	313	Nyika Plateau	369
Kitwe	391	Rainfall	31
Lake Bangweulu area	296	Samfya	357
Lake Kariba & the Lower Zambezi	206	Siavonga	214
Lake Tanganyika	343	Solwezi	402
Languages	21	South Luangwa NP	251
Liuwa Plain NP	472	Southern Wetlands	326
Livingstone	168–9	Southern Zambia	158
Livingstone & Victoria Falls	165	Sumbu NP	350
Lochinvar NP	440	Topography	30
Lower Zambezi	230–1	Western Zambia	448
Luangwa Valley	244	Victoria Falls	191
Lukulu	468	Zambia	colour section ii–iii
Lusaka: Cairo Road	144		

Acknowledgements

The fourth edition of this book has been built on the first three – and like those, has been a team effort. For this fourth edition (and in many cases for help with several earlier editions, too), we would particularly like to thank Di Flynn and the team at Lechwe; Sheila Siddle; Johnny Nels and Gary Beardsley; Kim and Edmund Farmer; Charlie and Jo Harvey; Mark Harvey; Mike and Lari Merrett; Quentin Allen; Hazel and Ewart Powell; Claire Powell; Sam and Alfred at Pioneer; Chantal Pinto, Dave Bennett and the Wilderness team in Kafue; John and Carol Coppinger and Remote Africa's team; Derek, Jules and Ali from Shenton Safaris; Andy and Andrea from Bushcamps; Chris Liebenberg and the Chongwe team; Grant and the team from Chiawa; and Craig Zytkow. Thanks to Grant Gatchell both for keeping Tricia and Bob on the road and for answering endless questions, and to Gray Mitombo for putting up with Tricia for a full research trip; he deserves a medal.

Several people kindly provided bits of the jigsaw, or dropped everything to check various bits of the text, including Kerry Macfarlane and Bridget Wijnberg in the Copperbelt, Andrea at Mama Rula's, Chris and Charlotte McBride, Tom Kok, Ruth Giesner and Jan Matthew. Also in the Copperbelt, thanks to Steven Lewis for summarising 740 million years of geology in just a few hundred words. In Livingstone, Tjisse Kamstra proved to be a fount of knowledge, while in Lusaka, Chantal Pinto went way beyond the call of duty in helping with all sorts of last-minute questions. Thanks, too, to Heather Chalcraft, for her support, and for kindly allowing us access to information from *The Lowdown*.

Many others went out of their way to help with the research for earlier books, including Arthur Sonnenberg, for not only hospitality and humour, but also expert packing skills; Anne Butler, Pippa Turner, Peter and their team; Nick, Christine, Abraham and the NCS crew; Jo, Robin, Kim at RPS; Babette and Phil Berry at Kuyenda; Carol, Bryan and Stephen at Tafika; Rod and Gus – even if our timings weren't great; Bryan Jackson for great walking, and pulling my Land Rover through a few rivers; Fynn Corry, for going out of his way to help and advise us in the wild west; Lynn, Pete and Paul Fisher; Ed Smythe and his team; Tom and Viviane Heineken; Dorian Tilbury; Charlie Rae; Fil Hide; Hugo and Elsabe; Pete Leonard, who kindly shared information from his encyclopaedic new Zambian bird atlas; and Philip Briggs, for the kind use of his writings on Nyika and as the basis for the wildlife appendix.

Zambia's top birding expert, Bob Stjernstedt (see page 194) kindly reviewed the birding comments, making a number of very helpful additions and contributions. Ilse Mwanza's help over the years has been invaluable, both with general info about Zambia, and for her numerous directions and descriptions for some of Zambia's wildest waterfalls and most remote corners. And I still owe huge thanks to John Coppinger, not only for unstinting hospitality, but also for his time and many emails in the past about the Luangwa's history, wildlife and environment.

We remain indebted, too, to Stephanie Debere; Purba Choudhury; Rose-Marie Baldry; Bernie and Adrienne Esterhuyse; Lisa Harmer; Colin Louw; Karun Thanjavuvr; Laura Boardman; Jeanne and Chris Blignaut; Simon Burgess; Fr Ivo Burkhardt; Michelle Cantley; Nickson Chilangwa; Jane Dennyson; Rob Fynn; Tong Green; Adam Haines; Ros Kearney; Liesl Nel; Fr Kessel of Lundazi; Steve McCormack; Robin Miller; Helen Mills; Jake da Motta; Victoria Nash; Beryl Neilson; Map Patel; Gene Pecker and Samantha; Ron and Lyn Ringrose; Mwape Sichilongo; Oscar and Andrew Sardanis; Alistair Tough; Gwen Wawn; Derek White and Beatrice Wienand; Gerard Zytkow; David, just in case he forgets his kindness; and Philip, for his economical help; and Paul Mount and the late Sir Peter Holmes, for their photographs.

Many readers of earlier editions have helped with their news and views, and countless Expert Africa (formerly Sunvil Africa!) travellers have generously provided valuable feedback on their trips. These have given me hundreds of extra pairs of eyes and ears in Zambia every year – constantly updating me on the latest news and views of the various camps, lodges and offbeat corners. We couldn't list everyone here if we tried; most will, I hope, forgive me for not mentioning them. However, for extensive contributions I remain indebted to Sue Grainger and Peter Dolby, Val and Bob Leyland, Harvey Linehan, Roger Marston, Vikki Threlfall, Dave and Louise Armstrong; Eric and Mieke Van den Broele; and Larry Barham and Mary Earnshaw for their archaeological expertise.

Colleagues at Expert Africa – especially Claire Scott, Anna Devereux Baker and Lucy Scholte – know the country so well themselves that without their help with news and research, and support from them and the whole team there, I'd be unable to continue writing these guides.

Bradt's whole team have, as ever, been superb – including Sally Brock, Barry Kew and Malcolm Barnes. That which is good and correct owes much to their care and attention; errors and omissions are my own.

Finally my love and thanks to Susie, for company on the road, generous help in writing, map-making and proofing, and for continuous good humour through the time that this book (and all the others) have demanded.

FEEDBACK REQUEST

Every guidebook is a snapshot in time. New restaurants open, lodges change hands, tour operators come and go – and prices change. The author and publishers would appreciate any feedback you may have from your travels, whether to tell us about somewhere new that you have discovered or to share your experience of places mentioned in the guide. Such feedback will make a huge difference when it comes to the next edition, and will ensure that the guide continues to evolve and broaden its scope for future readers.

Ideally, email your feedback to Bradt at info@bradtguides.com, and copy this directly to the author at chris.mcintyre@expertafrica.com. Alternatively please write to Bradt Travel Guides, 23 High Street, Chalfont St Peter, Bucks SL9 9QE, England; ☏ +44 (0)1753 893444; f +44 (0)1753 892333; www.bradtguides.com.

Introduction

In 1995 I crossed the Zambezi with trepidation, from prosperous Zimbabwe into relatively unknown Zambia. I had been able to find little about the country's attractions, and I expected problems, but backpacking around I found kindness and friendliness in a great country. The result was the first travel guide to Zambia.

Since then I have returned often. I have grown to love the country and have been lucky enough to share it with the visitors that I send there. Researching the second edition in 1998–99 I was again travelling with my backpack, though sometimes also flying between areas. New camps had started up, but most were still small, simple bushcamps. I introduced that edition with the comment that Zambia was a country for the cognoscenti, and especially those who knew about walking safaris – it wasn't a place for everyone.

Now, for this fourth edition, I'm forced to reassess. A lot has changed in the intervening years and the options for visitors have broadened. Zambia now offers more than simply superb bushcamps: there is increasing variety – from cultural offerings to family-friendly safaris and luxury lodges. Transport is becoming much easier: internal flights make more areas accessible, whilst old Africa hands are starting to make mini-expeditions here in self-contained 4x4s. National parks that had been written off are coming back to life, as pioneers open up original camps in more offbeat areas. Levels of both quality and choice have generally increased.

Fortunately, Zambia is retaining its essence: that authentic feeling of a wilderness which is wild, beautiful and slightly unpredictable. For the cognoscenti, it remains *the* place for walking safaris. In its three main safari areas – the Luangwa Valley, the Lower Zambezi and northern Kafue – you'll find top, owner-run camps, superb game and some of the continent's best guides. In all of these you'll see few other visitors; most Zambian camps are still tiny and remote. You'll travel around using small, open-sided 4x4s seeing few, if any, other vehicles. Throughout Africa there are khaki-uniformed chauffeurs who drive through the bush, but here you still find expert guides to trust with your life.

Meanwhile new places to stay and new areas to visit are starting up outside the old, established circuits. Gradually, the rest of this huge country (twice the size of Zimbabwe) is opening up, and its less famous attractions are coming to light. Many of these lesser-known areas are gems. Consider Kafue National Park: this is a wilderness area the size of Wales, yet it receives only a scattering of visitors. The far south of this park is ideal for the adventurous and well equipped to camp on their own. It is less than a day's drive from the busy hub of Livingstone, yet most of its bush tracks were, until recently, becoming very overgrown.

In the centre of Zambia lies the huge Lake Bangweulu, surrounded by the swamp that defeated Livingstone – his heart is buried nearby. This land of islands and waterways is a permanent wetland, home to the rare shoebill stork and an endemic species of antelope, the black lechwe. It's now much easier to fly here, and the proximity of other destinations makes it more attractive than ever: Kasanka

National Park and Mutinondo Wilderness are both close by. So, also, is Shiwa Ng'andu, which remains one of the subcontinent's most extraordinary memorials to British colonial rule. Here an English aristocrat carved out a utopian estate from the untamed bush, whilst helping Zambia to achieve its own independence. Although Africa gradually defeated his dream, Shiwa, like Zambia, is being reinvented – and now tells a new story of how sheer determination can re-shape a place in the wilderness into a world-class attraction for a handful of fortunate visitors.

Far to the west, Liuwa Plain National Park is the venue for one of Africa's last great wildlife migrations: blue wildebeest in their thousands, plus zebra, tsessebe and buffalo, all converging on a vast open plain for the rains. Liuwa is one of the most amazing reserves that I've ever visited in Africa, yet it receives only a few hundred visitors per year. Getting there still requires an expedition, but that is set to change as it is rapidly put on the map by massive investment.

Surrounding Liuwa, in the remote west of the country, is the ancient Lozi kingdom of Barotseland, where the landscape has changed little since Livingstone's day. The rich cultural heritage of a monarch and his people survived colonialism almost unscathed. Their seasonal rhythm is still followed, as the whole kingdom moves by boat from the rich floodplains to higher ground in February or March, making one great, grand traditional flotilla. Now the maps and GPS locations in this guide will enable you to navigate around these areas, and explore a very lovely and remote region that's been largely unvisited by travellers.

Zambia is an amazing country if you can get to its heart. Its government encourages tourism, and foreign exchange is desperately needed to alleviate the poverty of many of its people. But for such logic, this guide might have remained unwritten. Many would prefer Zambia to stay as it is – a favourite place to visit, with superb wildlife, fascinating culture, few other visitors, and Zambians who still treat travellers with kindness and hospitality.

So now, having committed more of Zambia's secrets to paper, I again ask those who use this guide to do so with respect. Zambia's wild areas need great care to preserve them. Local cultures are easily eroded by a visitor's lack of sensitivity, and hospitality once abused is seldom offered again. Enjoy – but be a thoughtful visitor, for the country's sake.

NOTE ON DATUM FOR GPS CO-ORDINATES For all the GPS co-ordinates in this book, note that the datum used is WGS 84 – and you must set your receiver accordingly before copying in any of these co-ordinates.

All GPS co-ordinates in this book have been expressed as degrees, minutes, and decimal fractions of a minute. For further details see page 60.

NOTE ON TELEPHONE NUMBERS All Zambian telephone numbers were being changed in 2007, but the move is surrounded by considerable confusion. New numbers have been used throughout this guide, but should one of these not work, try omitting the '21' from the '021' code (see pages 79–80 for details).

Part One

GENERAL INFORMATION

Location Landlocked in the tropics at the northern edge of the region referred to as 'southern Africa'

Size 752,610km²

Climate Dec–Apr hot and wet, with torrential downpours in afternoon; May–August dry, and fairly cool; September–November dry, but progressively hotter.

Status Republic

Population 11,477,447 (2007 est)

Population growth per year 1.65% (2007 est)

Life expectancy at birth 38.4 years

Capital Lusaka (population 1 million approx)

Other main towns Livingstone, Kitwe, Ndola, Kabwe

Economy Minerals (principally copper, cobalt), agriculture, hydro-electricity, tourism

Natural resources Copper, cobalt, gemstones

GDP US$11.6 billion (2006)

GDP growth rate 5.6%

Currency Kwacha (Kw)

Rate of exchange £1 = Kw7,804, US$1 = Kw3,830, €1 = Kw5,390, ZAR1 = Kw559 (October 2007)

Language English, numerous ethnic languages

Religion Christianity

International telephone code +260 (followed by national code (0)21)

Time GMT +2

Electricity 220v, delivered at 50Hz; British-style plugs with three square pins

Weights and measures Metric

Flag Bright green background; panel lower right of three vertical bands of red, black and orange, surmounted by orange eagle in flight.

Motto 'One Zambia, One Nation'

Public holidays 1 January, Youth Day, Good Friday, Holy Saturday, 1 May, 25 May, Heroes' Day, Unity Day, Farmers' Day, 24 October, 25–6 December

Tourist board www.zambiatourism.com

History, Politics and Economy

HISTORY

ZAMBIA'S EARLIEST INHABITANTS Palaeontologists looking for evidence of the first ancestors of the human race have excavated a number of sites in Zambia. The earliest remains yet identified are stone tools dated to about 2 million years ago recovered from gravel deposits in the Luangwa Valley and probably also from Victoria Falls. It is thought that these probably belong to the *Homo erectus* species, whose hand-axes in Ethiopia have been dated to 1.75 million years. These were hunter-gatherer people, who could use fire, make tools, and had probably developed some simple speech.

Experts divide the Stone Age into the middle, early and late Stone Ages. The transition from early to middle Stone-Age technology – which is indicated by a larger range of stone tools often adapted for particular uses, and signs that these people had a greater mastery of their environment – was probably in progress around 300,000 years ago in Zambia, based on recent excavations near Lusaka and at Kalambo Falls near Mbala.

The famous 'Broken Hill Man' lived around this time. His skull and other bones and stone artefacts were unearthed from about 20m underground during mining operations near Kabwe in 1921. He has been described as being from a species called *Homo rhodesiensis*, but is more generally attributed to *Homo heidelbergensis*, the common ancestor of *Homo sapiens* in Africa, and of the Neanderthals in Europe. (His name comes from the fact that Kabwe's old name was Broken Hill.)

The late Stone Age in Zambia is normally characterised by a distinctive tradition of geometric rock art; by the use of composite tools, those made of wood and/or bone and/or stone used together; and by the presence of a revolutionary invention: the bow and arrow. This first appeared in Zambia about 25,000 years ago. Skeletons found around the Kafue Flats area indicate that some of these late Stone-Age hunters had a close physical resemblance to the modern San/Bushmen people, whose culture, relying on a late Stone-Age level of technology, survived intact in the Kalahari Desert until the middle of the 20th century.

THE IRON AGE Around 3000BC, late Stone-Age hunter-gatherer groups in Ethiopia, and elsewhere in north and west Africa, started to keep domestic animals, sow seeds and harvest the produce: they were among the world's first farmers.

By around 1000BC these new pastoral practices had spread south into the equatorial forests of what is now the Democratic Republic of Congo, to around Lake Victoria, and into the northern area of the Great Rift Valley, in northern Tanzania. However, agriculture did not spread south into the rest of central/southern Africa immediately. Only when the technology, and the tools, of iron-working became known did the practices start their relentless expansion southwards.

The spread of agriculture and Iron-Age culture seems to have been rapid. It was brought south by Africans who were taller and heavier than the existing small inhabitants. The ancestors of the San/Bushmen people, with their simple Stone-Age technology and hunter-gatherer existence, just could not compete with these Iron-Age farmers, who became the ancestors of virtually all the modern black Africans in southern Africa.

This major migration occurred around the first few centuries AD, and since then the San/Bushmen of southern Africa have gradually been either assimilated into the migrant groups, or effectively pushed into areas which could not be farmed. Thus the older Stone-Age cultures persisted in the forests of the north and east of Zambia – which were more difficult to cultivate – much longer than they survived in the south of the country.

MORE IMMIGRANTS By the 4th or 5th century AD, Iron-Age farmers had settled throughout much of southern Africa. As well as iron-working technology, they brought with them pottery, the remains of which are used by archaeologists to work out the migrations of various different groups of these Bantu settlers. These migrations continued, and the distribution of pottery styles suggests that the groups moved around within the subcontinent: this was much more complex than a simple north–south influx.

THE ORIGINS OF TRADE In burial sites dating from the latter half of the first millennium, occasional 'foreign' objects start to occur: the odd cowrie shell, or copper bangles in an area where there is no copper. This indicates that some small-scale bartering with neighbouring villages was beginning to take place.

In the first half of the second millennium, the pace and extent of this trade increased significantly. Gold objects appear (as well as the more common copper, iron and ivory) and shells from the Indian Ocean. The frequency of these indicates that trade was gradually developing. We know from European historical sources that Muslim traders (of Arab or possibly African origin) were venturing into the heart of Africa by around AD1400, and thus trade routes were being established.

As trade started, so the second millennium also saw the development of wealth and social structures within the tribes. The evidence for this is a number of burial sites that stand out for the quantity and quality of the goods that were buried with the dead person. One famous site, at Ngombe Ilede, near the confluence of the Lusitu and Zambezi rivers, was occupied regularly over many centuries. There is evidence that its inhabitants traded from the 14th century with people further south, in Zimbabwe, exporting gold down the Zambezi via traders coming from the Indian Ocean. Indications of cotton-weaving have also been found there, and several copper crosses unearthed are so similar that they may have been used as a simple form of currency – valuable to both the local people and the traders from outside.

By the middle of the second millennium, a number of separate cultures seem to have formed in Zambia. Many practised trade, and a few clearly excelled at it. Most were starting to develop social structures within the group, with some enjoying more status and wealth than others.

THE CHIEFS From around the middle of the second millennium, there is little good archaeological evidence that can be accurately dated. However, sources for the events of this period in Zambia's history are the oral histories of Zambia's people, as well as their current languages and social traditions. The similarities and differences between the modern Zambian languages can be extrapolated by linguistic experts to point to the existence of about nine different root languages, which probably existed in Zambia in the 15th century.

The latter half of the second millennium AD saw the first chiefs, and hence kingdoms, emerge from Zambia's dispersed clans. The title 'chief' can be applied to anyone from a village headman to a god-like king. However, this was an era of increasing trade, when the groups with the largest resources and armies dominated local disputes. Thus it made sense for various clans to group together into tribes, under the rule of a single individual, or chief.

One of the oldest groups is thought to have been that of the Chewa people, led by the Undi, who came to the Luangwa area from the southern side of Lake Malawi in the 16th century. By the end of that century the Ng'andu clan (clan of the crocodile) established a kingdom amongst the Bemba people. These lived mostly in woodland areas, practising simple slash-and-burn types of agriculture. Perhaps because of the poverty of their lifestyle, they later earned a reputation as warriors for their raids on neighbouring tribes.

In the latter part of the 17th century the first recorded Lozi king (or Litunga, as he is known) is thought to have settled near Kalabo, in the west of Zambia, starting a powerful dynasty which lasts to the present day. Early in the 18th century Mwata Kazemba established a kingdom around the southern end of Lake Mweru in the Luapula Valley.

THE GROWTH OF TRADE As various cohesive kingdoms developed, their courts served as centres of trade, and their chiefs had the resources to initiate trade with other communities. Foodstuffs, iron, copper, salt, cotton, cloth, tobacco, baskets, pottery and many other items were traded within Zambia, between the various tribes.

From around the 14th century, Zambia had a trickle of trade with non-Africans: mostly Muslims exporting gold through the east coast of Africa. (This trade had started as early as the 10th century on the Limpopo River, south of Zimbabwe's gold-fields.) However, by the early 17th century the Muslims had been supplanted by the Portuguese, and by the latter half of the 17th century these Portuguese merchants were operating out of Mozambique, trading gold, ivory and copper with Zambia.

Trade with the outside world escalated during the 18th century, as more and more tribes became involved, and more foreigners came to the table. Some chiefs started to barter their commodities for weapons, in attempts to gain advantage over their neighbours. Those vanquished in local conflicts were certainly used as sources of slaves – an increasingly valuable trading commodity. These and other factors increased the pressure on Zambians to trade, and the influx of foreign traders made the picture more complex still.

By the early 19th century, both traders and slavers were visiting Zambia with increasing frequency. These were responding to the increasing consumer demands of newly industrialised Europe and America. More trade routes were opening up, not just through Mozambique and Angola, but also to the north and south. Internal conflicts were increasing, as both the means to conduct these, and the incentives for victory, grew.

WESTERN REQUIREMENTS During the 19th century, the West (western Europe and North America) had traded with the native Africans to obtain what they wanted – commodities and slave labour – without having to go to the trouble of ruling parts of the continent. However, as the century progressed, and the West became more industrialised, it needed these things in greater quantities than the existing tribal structures in Africa could supply. Further, there was demand for materials that could be produced in Africa, like cotton and rubber, but which required Western production methods.

5

Given that the West wanted a wider range and greater quantity of cheaper raw materials, the obvious solution was to control the means of supply. African political organisation was widely regarded as primitive, and not capable of providing complex and sustained trade. Inward investment would also be needed, but would be forthcoming only if white enterprises were safe from African interference. Hence the solution to Western requirements was to bring Africa, and the Africans, under European rule.

Another reason for considering the acquisition of African territory was that the world was shrinking. There were no inhabitable continents left to discover. Staking a nation's claim to large chunks of Africa seemed prudent to most of the Western powers of the time, and growing competition for these areas meant they could always be traded for one another at a later date.

LIVINGSTONE'S CONTRIBUTION David Livingstone's *Missionary Travels and Researches in South Africa* excited great interest in England. This account of his journeys across southern Africa in the 1840s and '50s had all the appeal that undersea or space exploration has for us now. Further, it captured the imagination of the British public, allowing them to take pride in their country's exploration of Africa, based on the exploits of an explorer who seemed to be the epitome of bravery and righteous religious zeal.

Livingstone had set out with the conviction that if Africans could see their material and physical well-being improved – probably by learning European ways, and earning a living from export crops – then they would be ripe for conversion to Christianity. He was strongly opposed to slavery, but sure that this would disappear when Africans became more self-sufficient through trade.

In fact Livingstone was almost totally unsuccessful in his own aims, failing to set up any successful trading missions, or even to convert many Africans permanently to Christianity. However, his travels opened up areas north of the Limpopo for later British missionaries, and by 1887 British mission stations were established in Zambia and southern Malawi.

THE SCRAMBLE FOR AFRICA British foreign policy in southern Africa had always revolved around the Cape Colony, which was seen as vital to British interests in India and the Indian Ocean. Africa to the north of the Cape Colony had largely been ignored. The Boers were on the whole left to their farming in the Transvaal area, and posed no threat to the colony.

However, Germany annexed South West Africa (now Namibia) in 1884, prompting British fears that they might try to link up with the Boers. Thus, to drive a wedge through the middle of these territories, the British negotiated an alliance with Khama, a powerful Tswana king, and proclaimed as theirs the Protectorate of Bechuanaland – the forerunner of modern Botswana.

Soon after, in 1886, the Boers discovered large gold deposits in the Witwatersrand (around Johannesburg). The influx of money from this boosted the Boer farmers, who expanded their interests to the north, making a treaty with Khama's enemy, the powerful Lobengula. This in turn prompted the British to look beyond the Limpopo, and to back the territorial aspirations of a millionaire British businessman, Cecil Rhodes. By 1888 Rhodes, a partner in the De Beers consortium, had control of the lucrative diamond-mining industry in Kimberley, South Africa. He was hungry for power, and dreamt of linking the Cape to Cairo with land under British control.

His wealth enabled Rhodes to buy sole rights to mine minerals in Lobengula's territory. Thence he persuaded the British government to grant his company – the British South Africa Company – the licence to stake claims to African territory with the authority of the British government. In 1889 Rhodes sent out several expeditions to the chiefs in the area now comprising Zimbabwe, Zambia and Malawi, to make treaties. These granted British 'protection and aid' in return for sole rights to minerals in the chiefs' territories, and assurances that they would not make treaties with any other foreign powers. This effective strategy was greatly helped by the existing British influence from the missions, which were already established in many of the regions. By 1891 the British had secured these areas (through Rhodes's British South Africa Company) from the other European powers, and confirmed their boundaries in treaties with the neighbouring colonial powers.

By the closing years of the 19th century, Zambia – or Northern Rhodesia as it was called – was clearly under British rule. However, this had little impact until local administrations were set up, and taxes started to be collected.

THE MINES In the early years of the 20th century, Rhodes's British South Africa Company did little in Northern Rhodesia. Its minerals were not nearly as accessible or valuable as those in Southern Rhodesia, and little protection or aid actually materialised. It became viewed by the colonials as a source of cheap labour for the mines of South Africa and Southern Rhodesia.

To facilitate this, taxes were introduced for the local people, which effectively forced them to come into the cash economy. Virtually the only way for them to do this was to find work in one of the mines further south. By 1910 a railway linked the mine at Kimberley, in South Africa, with Victoria Falls and beyond, making long-distance travel in the subcontinent more practical.

Meanwhile the cost of administering and defending the company's interests was rising, and in 1923 Southern Rhodesia became self-governing. In 1924 the British Colonial Office took over administration of Northern Rhodesia from the British South Africa Company, though the mining rights remained with the Company. The Colonial Office then set up a legislative council to advise on the government of the province, though only a few of its members came from outside the administration.

Shortly afterwards, in 1928, huge deposits of copper were located below the basin of the upper Kafue, under what is now known as the Copperbelt. Over the next decade or so these were developed into a number of large copper mines, working rich, deep deposits of copper. World War II demanded increased production of base metals, and by 1945 Northern Rhodesia was producing 12% of the non-communist world's copper. This scale of production required large labour forces. The skilled workers were mostly of European origin, often from South Africa's mines, whilst the unskilled workers came from all over Northern Rhodesia.

Wages and conditions were very poor for the unskilled miners, who were treated as migrant workers and expected to go home to their permanent villages every year or so to 'recover'. Death rates among them were high. Further, the drain of men to work the mines inevitably destabilised the villages, and poverty and malnutrition were common in the rural areas.

WELFARE ASSOCIATIONS As early as 1929 welfare associations had formed in several of the territory's southern towns, aimed at giving black Africans a voice and trying to defend their interests. These associations were often started by teachers or clerks, the more educated members of the communities. They were small at first, far too small to mount any effective challenge to the establishment, but they did succeed in raising awareness amongst the Africans, all of whom were being exploited.

In 1935 the African mineworkers first organised themselves to strike over their pay and conditions. By 1942 the towns of the African labourers in the Copperbelt were forming their own welfare associations, and by 1949 some of these had joined together as the Northern Rhodesian African Mineworkers' Union. This had been officially recognised by the colonial government as being the equal of any union for white workers. In 1952 the union showed its muscle with a successful and peaceful three-week strike, resulting in substantial wage increases.

The unions remain a force in Zambia, especially in the state sector. In February 2004, a coalition of unions organised the country's first national strike in 16 years, protesting against tax hikes and wage freezes which were being imposed on government employees.

CENTRAL AFRICAN FEDERATION The tiny European population in Northern Rhodesia was, on the whole, worried by the growth of the power of black African mineworkers. Most of the white people wanted to break free from colonial rule, so that they could control the pace and direction of political change. They also resented the loss of vast revenues from the mines, which went directly to the British government and the British South Africa Company, without much benefit for Northern Rhodesia.

During the 1930s and 1940s the settlers' representation on Northern Rhodesia's Legislative Council was gradually increased, and calls for self-rule became more insistent. As early as 1936 Stewart Gore-Browne (founder of Shiwa Ng'andu; see *Chapter 13*, page 305) had proposed a scheme for a Central African Federation, with an eye to Britain's future (or lack of one) in Africa. This view gained ground in London, where the government was increasingly anxious to distance itself from African problems.

In 1948 the South African Nationalist Party came to power in South Africa, on a tide of Afrikaner support. The historical enmity between the Afrikaners and the British in South Africa led the British colonials in Southern and Northern Rhodesia to look to themselves for their own future, rather than their neighbours in South Africa. In 1953 their pressure was rewarded and Southern and Northern Rhodesia were formally joined with Nyasaland (which is now Malawi), to become the independent Central African Federation.

The formation of the Federation did little to help the whites in Northern Rhodesia, though it was strongly opposed by the blacks, who feared that they would then lose more of their land to white settlers. Earlier, in 1948, the Federation of African Societies – an umbrella group of welfare associations – changed its name at an annual general meeting into an overtly political Northern Rhodesian Congress. This had branches in the mining towns and the rural areas, and provided a base upon which a black political culture could be based. A few years later, it was renamed as the Northern Rhodesia African National Congress.

INDEPENDENCE Despite the Federation, Northern Rhodesia actually remained under the control of the Colonial Office. Further, the administration of the Federation was so biased towards Southern Rhodesia that the revenues from its mines simply flowed there, instead of to Britain. Thus though the Federation promised much, it delivered few of the settlers' wishes in Northern Rhodesia.

A small core of increasingly skilled African mineworkers gained better pay and conditions, whilst poverty was rife in the rest of the country. By the 1950s small improvements were being made in the provision of education for black Zambians, but widespread neglect had demonstrated to most that whites did not want blacks as their political or social equals. Thus black politics began to focus on another goal: independence.

In 1958 elections were held, and about 25,000 blacks were allowed to vote. The Northern Rhodesia African National Congress was divided about whether to participate or not, and eventually this issue split the party. Kenneth Kaunda, the radical secretary general, and others founded the Zambia African National Congress (ZANC). This was soon banned, and Kaunda was jailed during a state of emergency.

Finally, in 1960, Kaunda was released from jail, and greeted as a national hero. He took control of a splinter party, the United National Independence Party (UNIP), and after a short campaign of civil disobedience forced the Colonial Office to hold universal elections. In October of 1962, these confirmed a large majority for UNIP. In 1963 the Federation broke up, and in 1964 elections based on universal adult suffrage gave UNIP a commanding majority. On 24 October 1964 Zambia became independent, with Kenneth Kaunda as its president.

ZAMBIA UNDER KAUNDA President Kenneth Kaunda (usually known as just 'KK') took over a country whose income was controlled by the state of the world copper market, and whose trade routes were entirely dependent upon Southern Rhodesia, South Africa, and Mozambique. He also inherited a Kw50 million national debt from the colonial era, and a populace which was largely unskilled and uneducated. (At independence, there were fewer than one hundred Zambians with university degrees, and fewer than a thousand who had completed secondary school.)

In 1965, shortly after Zambia's independence, Southern Rhodesia made a Unilateral Declaration of Independence (UDI). This propelled Zambia's southern neighbour further along the path of white rule that South Africa had adopted. Sanctions were then applied to Rhodesia by the rest of the world. Given that most of Zambia's trade passed through Rhodesia, these had very negative effects on the country's economy.

As the black people of Rhodesia, South Africa and South West Africa (Namibia) started their liberation struggles, Kaunda naturally wanted to support them. Zambia became a haven for political refugees, and a base for black independence movements. However ideologically sound this approach was, it was costly and did not endear Zambia to its economically dominant white-ruled neighbours. As the apartheid government in South Africa began a policy of destabilising the black-ruled countries around the subcontinent, so civil wars and unrest became the norm in Mozambique and Angola, squeezing Zambia's trade routes further.

The late 1960s and early 1970s saw Zambia try to drastically reduce its trade with the south. Simultaneously it worked to increase its links with Tanzania – which was largely beyond the reach of South Africa's efforts to destabilise. With the help of China, Tanzania and Zambia built excellent road and rail links from the heart of Zambia to Dar es Salaam, on the Indian Ocean. However, as a trading partner Tanzania was no match for the efficiency of South Africa, and Zambia's economy remained sluggish.

During these difficult years Zambia's debt did not decrease, but grew steadily. The government's large revenues from copper were used in efforts to reduce the country's dependence on its southern neighbours, and to improve standards of living for the majority of Zambians. Education was expanded on a large scale, government departments were enlarged to provide employment, and food subsidies maintained the peace of the large urban population. Kaunda followed Julius Nyerere's example in Tanzania in many ways, with a number of socialist policies woven into his own (much promoted) philosophy of 'humanism'.

In retrospect, perhaps Kaunda's biggest mistake was that he failed to use the large revenues from copper either to reduce the national debt, or to diversify Zambia's export base – but his choices were not easy.

By 1969, the Zambian government was receiving about three-quarters of the profits made by the mining industries in taxes and duties. Because of this, they were reluctant to invest further. With the stated aim of encouraging expansion in the industry and investment in new mines, the government started to reform the ownership of the copper mines. A referendum was held on the subject and the government took control of mining rights throughout the country. It then bought a 51% share in each of the mines, which was paid for out of the government's own dividends in the companies over the coming years. Thus began ZCCM (Zambia Consolidated Copper Mines).

In the early 1970s, the world copper price fell dramatically. Simultaneously the cost of imports (especially oil) rose, the world economy slumped and the interest rates on Zambia's debt increased. These factors highlighted the fundamental weaknesses of Zambia's economy, which had been established to suit the colonial powers rather than the country's citizens.

The drop in the price of copper crippled Zambia's economy. Efforts to stabilise the world copper price – through a cartel of copper-producing countries, similar to the oil-producing OPEC countries – failed. The government borrowed more money, betting on a recovery in copper prices that never materialised.

In the 1970s and 1980s Kaunda's government became increasingly intertwined with the International Monetary Fund (IMF) in the search for a solution to the country's debt. None was found. Short-term fixes just made things worse, and the country's finances deteriorated. The West did give Zambia aid, but mostly for specific projects that usually had strings attached. What Zambia most needed was help with the enormous interest payments that it was required to make to the West.

Various recovery plans, often instituted by the IMF, were tried. In 1986 food subsidies were sharply withdrawn, starting with breakfast meal, one of the country's staple foods. This hit the poor hardest, and major riots broke out before subsidies were hastily reintroduced to restore calm. In 1988 Zambia applied to the United Nations for the status of 'least-developed nation' in the hope of obtaining greater international assistance. It was rejected. By the end of the decade Zambia's economy was in tatters. The official exchange rate bore little relation to the currency's actual worth, and inflation was rampant. Zambia was one of the world's poorest countries, with a chronic debt problem, a weak currency and at times very high inflation. A reputation for corruption, reaching to the highest levels of the government, did little to encourage help from richer nations.

Despite Kaunda's many failures with the economy, his policies did encourage the development of some home-grown industries to produce goods which could replace previously imported items. It also created systems for mass education, which were almost entirely absent when he came to power.

THE EARLY 1990S These economic problems, and the lack of obvious material benefits for the majority of Zambians, gradually fomented opposition. UNIP's tendency to become authoritarian in its demands for unity also led to unrest. Kaunda's rule was finally challenged successfully by the capitalist Movement for Multiparty Democracy (MMD) led by Frederick Chiluba. This received widespread support during the late 1980s, on a platform of liberalisation and anti-corruption measures.

Kaunda agreed to an election, apparently certain that he would win. In the event, UNIP was resoundingly defeated by the MMD (16% to 84%), and Chiluba became Zambia's second elected president, in November 1991. Kaunda accepted the results, at least on face value. However, he later claimed that the elections were unfair because many of Zambia's older people, whom he regarded as his natural constituency, didn't vote. He continued to head UNIP until 2000, and he still lives in Zambia – which, in itself, is a rare and encouraging co-existence in the volatile world of modern African politics.

When elected, Frederick Chiluba faced enormous economic problems, which he attempted to tackle. He succeeded in liberalising and privatising much of the economy. There is now a freely floating market for the kwacha, and policies to attract inward investment. However, in 1995 the country's debt stood at US$6.25 billion, and debt service payments were some 40% of the gross national product – equivalent to about US$600/£400 per capita per annum. Zambia owed US$3.1 billion to the World Bank and the IMF alone.

Initially Chiluba gained the confidence of Western donors when he came to power in 1991. However, his reforms were long term, and much of their success depended on the continued willingness of international donors to help him. Many allege that corruption grew during his time in power.

Certainly the general attitude of Zambians towards visitors changed under Chiluba: Zambia became a more welcoming country than it was under Kaunda's reign. Tourism began to be recognised as a direct and helpful source of jobs and foreign currency, and the climate of suspicion prevailing in Kaunda's Zambia was replaced with a warmer welcome.

THE LATE 1990S Presidential elections were held in 1996. However, using his enormous majority, Chiluba changed the constitution to include a clause that 'no person born of non-Zambian parents can be president'. Kenneth Kaunda, as is well known, was born of Malawian parents, and so this was a clear move to exclude him from running for the office. It was not the only such move, and caused endless furore.

As head of UNIP, KK called for all UNIP candidates to boycott the elections, believing that they could not be fair. In the event, several UNIP candidates split off and stood as independent candidates, but the overall result was another resounding win for Chiluba. (MMD won about 132 of 150 seats.) It's widely thought that he would have won anyhow, even in a fair election, so it seems a pity that he resorted to dubious tactics to achieve the victory.

With poetic justice, it later transpired that Chiluba himself is of illegitimate birth and uncertain national origin. *The Post* newspaper claimed to have researched and verified that his own parents were of DRC/Zairean descent, which led to a long-running persecution of the paper by the government for 'being disrespectful' and 'insulting' the president – both of which are punishable offences in Zambia. (Travellers take note!)

THE COUP At the end of October 1997, a small group of soldiers briefly took over the state-run radio station. They were led by Stephen Lungu, the self-styled 'Captain Solo', who claimed to represent the 'National Redemption Council'. (Neither he nor the council had been heard of before.) He announced that the group had launched 'Operation Born-again' and ousted the MMD government and Chiluba, saying later in a short broadcast that he had seen 'an angel and the message was that the Government had to be overthrown'.

Although this group transpired to have been little more than a few drunken soldiers, Chiluba used the incident as an excuse to institute a state of emergency for five months. He detained more than 70 civilians and soldiers, including opposition leaders and the former president, KK. Some detainees claimed that torture was used during interrogations, allegations which were later substantiated by the government's own human rights commission headed by Supreme Court judge, Lombe Chibesakunda. The clampdown by the state attracted heavy criticism from human rights groups and affected the international donor community's willingness to release funds for debt relief.

A year later the case against many was dropped for lack of evidence, and some sued the state for wrongful arrest. In December 2003, a further ten soldiers were freed, but the remaining 44 were convicted and sentenced to death. However, within a couple of months the current president had commuted the sentences to between ten and 20 years of hard labour, stating that he would not sign a death warrant during his tenure of office.

THE END OF CHILUBA'S REGIME Overall, many regarded President Chiluba's presidency as a disappointment, although, looking at conditions in neighbouring Zaire and Zimbabwe, most agree that the situation in Zambia could have been much worse.

Chiluba continued KK's habit of regularly reshuffling ministers (thus ensuring that none developed their own power base), was slow to take decisions and proved unable to control corruption. In earlier years he repeatedly vowed that he would stand by the constitution, and step down before the 2001 elections. Eventually he did this, but not before trying his best to arrange a third term for himself. It was only tremendous pressure from the people, and from within the MMD, that forced him to step down in favour of Levy Patrick Mwanawasa.

On a positive note, Chiluba avoided any military involvement in the conflict in neighbouring Democratic Republic of Congo (DRC) – which had already sucked in Zimbabwe, Angola, Namibia, Chad, Uganda and Rwanda – and instead played a high-profile role in brokering various peace talks.

THE 21ST CENTURY Eleven parties contested the elections in December 2001; many alleged serious irregularities. The MMD's candidate and Chiluba's chosen successor, Levy Patrick Mwanawasa, was narrowly declared as the victor, having won just 29% of the vote. These chaotic elections were criticised by international observers, and three of the opposition parties challenged the results in the High Court.

Mwanawasa is a lawyer by profession. He has practised in Zambia since 1973, and was the first Zambian lawyer to be appointed an advocate and solicitor of the Supreme Court of England and Wales. Chiluba appointed him as vice-president in 1991, but he quit the government three years later, following a row with then minister-without-portfolio Michael Sata, and returned to his successful law career.

. Mwanawasa seems to be universally respected for his integrity. As a lawyer he had a reputation for taking on cases that most wouldn't touch, and his election campaign stressed the rule of one law for everyone. His health has been a more contentious issue, with opposition politicians pointing to occasional slurs and slips, including one famous occasion when he referred to Chiluba as his sister. Taunts of 'vegetable' or 'cabbage' were used by protesters during the 2001 election, who claimed that he could not handle the heavy duties of a president.

Although many expected him to be a puppet of Chiluba, Mwanawasa proved them wrong. With his mandate of 'Continuity with Change', he launched an anti-corruption campaign in 2002 which resulted in the prosecution of his patron, Chiluba, and many of Chiluba's supporters. Chiluba has steadfastly rejected the allegations, although he was offered a pardon if he admitted the charges and repaid 75% of the money he is alleged to have stolen. Due to his ill health significant delays followed, but the prosecution stage of the trial finally took place in August

2007. A decision will be taken in February 2008 as to whether or not the former president has a case to answer.

In the meantime, following the most recent elections, held in September 2006, Mwanawasa was re-elected with a rather more convincing 43% of the vote. Opposition parties currently hold a slim majority of seats in the National Assembly.

The next elections will be held in 2011. By that time, it is anticipated that a new constitution will be in place, involving the establishment of a new Constituent Assembly, and marking Mwanawasa's final term in office.

On a less consequential note, keep your eye open for political slogans when you travel. I once saw one in Livingstone encouraging people to vote for women with the slogan: 'A government without women is like a pot on one stone.' This is, of course, immediately intelligible to any Zambian who cooks on an open fire.

GOVERNMENT

The chief of state and the head of government is the president, who appoints cabinet ministers from members of the National Assembly, a chamber of 150 elected representatives. Elections are held every four years, with all Zambian citizens of 18 years and over eligible to vote.

The country is divided into nine provinces for administration purposes: Central, Copperbelt, Eastern, Luapulu, Lusaka, Northern, North-Western, Southern and Western.

The judicial system was set up according to a British model, based on English common law and customary law. Legislative acts receive judicial review in an ad hoc constitutional council.

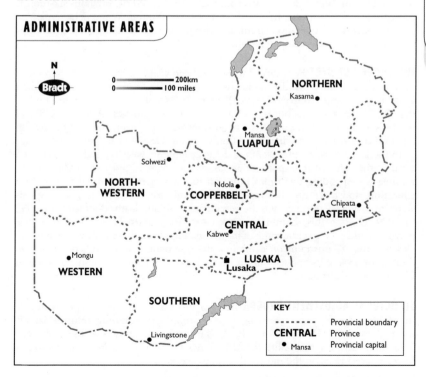

ADMINISTRATIVE AREAS

N

0 ——— 200km
0 ——— 100 miles

NORTHERN
Kasama•

•Mansa
LUAPULA

Solwezi•

NORTH-WESTERN

Ndola•
COPPERBELT

Chipata•
EASTERN

CENTRAL
Kabwe•

•Mongu

LUSAKA
Lusaka

WESTERN

SOUTHERN

Livingstone•

KEY
-------- Provincial boundary
CENTRAL Province
• Mansa Provincial capital

Despite recent improvements in the economy, Zambia remains one of the world's poorest countries, with a major national debt and a weak currency. In the mid-1990s, however, even until 1997, its prospects looked good. GDP growth was about 6.5%; inflation had been reduced to 24% (down from 187% in 1993); a prolonged decline in manufacturing was being reversed; non-traditional exports were expanding at a rate of 33% a year; and the privatisation programme was being hailed as one of Africa's most successful. Even the kwacha had been stabilised and a surge in foreign investment was being reported.

By 1998, the reversal of Zambia's economic fortunes was stark. GDP growth was minimal, manufacturing output was again in a downturn, and inflation was slowly rising. While the breakdown in the Zambia Consolidated Copper Mines (ZCCM) privatisation was a major cause of this reversal (see *Copper*, under *Zambia's mining industry*, below), part of the problem stemmed from reactions to the government's actions after the coup attempt in late 1997. On both counts, Western donors withheld aid to Zambia. A year later, in 1999, the signs improved, with aid and debt relief again forthcoming, and optimism that Zambia's economy could continue to improve.

Privatisation of government-owned copper mines relieved the government from covering mammoth losses generated by the industry and greatly improved the chances for copper mining to return to profitability and spur economic growth. An increase in copper output in 2003 has been followed by a continued rise, due to higher copper prices and resulting investment in new mines. In the agricultural sector, the maize harvest was good in both 2003 and 2005, helping to boost the economy.

On a more positive front, inflation has been brought largely under control in recent years. In August 2007, it was running at 10.7%, and the previous six-month period saw a trade surplus figure of Kw1,664,317 million. While debt remains a serious concern, co-operation continues with international bodies on programmes to reduce poverty, including debt relief.

THE BURDEN OF DEBT For years, Zambia has been visibly crippled by its burden of debt. According to UNICEF, about two-thirds of all Zambians live on less than US$1 per day; other sources observe that almost 90% of the population live on less than US$2 per day. This burden is borne out by the statistics: at around US$500 per person, Zambia had one of the highest levels of per-capita debt in the world, but a GNI (gross national income) of only around US$340 per capita.

In the late 1990s, Zambia's annual debt repayments were equivalent to about a third of the value of its exports of goods and services: to put this in perspective, Zambia was spending five times more on its interest repayments than it did on education, and three times as much as on healthcare. The consequences of this were clear: literacy declined and the percentage of infant deaths doubled from 1992 to 1999. Despite this, Zambia managed to remain current on its debt-service payments and even to clear some of its arrears. However, these commitments were clearly a major constraint on economic development. Zambia relied on foreign donors for 35% of its budget, but for every dollar Zambia received in aid, it repaid US$3 to service its debt.

STRUCTURAL ADJUSTMENT PROGRAMME For most of Chiluba's presidency during the 1990s, Zambia was following a programme of economic reforms largely dictated by the IMF and World Bank. This scheme, known as the Enhanced Structural Adjustment Facility (ESAF), allows the world's poorest nations to pay lower interest rates on the money that they owe.

In December 1995, Zambia qualified for assistance under ESAF and embarked on a series of far-reaching reforms. These centred on trade liberalisation, deregulation and exchange-rate reform. Pivotal to the whole programme was a greater role for the private sector, and the sale of state-owned enterprises. The main aim of the scheme was to encourage foreign direct investment.

Having met these requirements, and subsequently largely followed the dictates of the IMF and World Bank on its economy, Zambia found itself in the 'good books' of its donors. However the social consequences were onerous: rising unemployment, increased prices for basic necessities (including the staple mealie-meal) and cuts in healthcare and education. All of these tended to foster an increase in social unrest.

Privatisation As part of the structural adjustment programme, the Zambia Privatisation Agency (ZPA), now the Zambia Development Agency, was set up to oversee privatisation. By February 2005 it had sold 262 companies, with Zambian investment running at around 60%. A few have failed, but the majority seem to be viable. These include protracted negotiations to privatise the Zambia National Commercial Bank, which were concluded in 2007. As a result, 25.8% of the bank is to be floated on the Lusaka stock exchange, with the government retaining a share of 25%, and 49% in the hands of Dutch investors.

Debt write-offs and HIPC status In 1999, the Finnish government announced that it was writing off US$7.5 million of Zambia's debt, and later that year the IMF decided to give Zambia a much-needed boost with US$14 million of its new US$349-million ESAF loan. Also, the World Bank promised US$65 million, despite the continuing problems in selling the mines. These were crucial signals to other donors, and on 16 April of the same year the Paris Club agreed to write off US$670 million of Zambian debt, and restructure the repayments of about US$330 million of the rest. Another major step towards helping the country was to confer on Zambia the status of highly indebted poor country (HIPC), which would open the door to the World Bank and other donors relieving more of the debt.

Optimists hoped that these payments would mark the start of concerted efforts by the international community to alleviate Zambia's crippling debt, and that moves to liberalise Zambia's economy would bear fruit. However this optimism was tempered with more realism. Though Zambia had taken most of the economic medicine prescribed for it, trade liberalisation was tough on the country in the short term. A report by the World Development Movement, *Zambia: Condemned to Debt* (see *Appendix 3*, page 511), accused the IMF-backed reforms of being undemocratic and unfair and of undermining development – as well as of being counter-productive and unsuccessful. In 2003 the donors' 'Balance of Payment support' was frozen, on account of the country's weak fiscal management and inability to institute a new Poverty Reduction and Growth Facility strategy (PRGF) proposed by the IMF. Successful implementation of this PRGF strategy was one of the crucial milestone indicators needed by the IMF and World Bank before Zambia can reach the 'completion point' under the HIPC initiative, and thus trigger debt relief. Meanwhile, Zambia's external debt stood at about $6.5bn at the start of 2006 – and the repayments continued to cripple the economy.

In 2005, it was agreed at the G8 summit to write off US$40 billion of debt owed by 18 of the worlds HIPCs, of which Zambia was one, with an estimated debt of US$4 billion. The Zambian government pledged to invest the proceeds in health and education, and the following year announced that free health care would at last be restored to those living in rural areas.

STRUCTURE OF THE ECONOMY Zambia's economy is totally dependent upon its its mining sector, and particularly its copper mines, although agriculture, industry and tourism all make their contribution. The country's high, well-watered plateau means that it has about 40% of southern Africa's water resources. Hydro-electric schemes, which provide most of the country's power, make it self-sufficient in energy. Zambia already exports power to neighbouring countries.

ZAMBIA'S MINING INDUSTRY Mining as a whole accounts for around 80% of Zambia's export earnings and about 15% of its GDP. Significant investment in recent years from countries as diverse as Canada and China has resulted from a combination of high copper prices and changes in regulations that have attracted considerable overseas interest in the sector.

Copper is easily the country's most important natural resource, with cobalt second; it also has considerable reserves of silver and selenium, as well as small but significant quantities of other minerals and gemstones.

Copper Zambia has large, high-quality deposits of copper ore. Production grew by 9% in 2006, reaching 512,553 tonnes, with a figure of 800,000 tonnes predicted for 2008. This compares with an output of around 700,000 tonnes recorded in the late 1970s. The opening of several new mines is a reflection of the high copper prices on the world market, running at just below US$8,000 a tonne in 2007, and has contributed to a boom in Zambia's industrial heartland, the Copperbelt region.

Before 2000, all the mines were controlled by the parastatal Zambia Consolidated Copper Mines (ZCCM), which had long been viewed as the jewel of Zambia's economic crown. Of these, Nchanga and Nkana mines alone accounted for 65% of Zambia's total copper production. However, disuse and mismanagement caused Zambia's mines to degenerate, and by the late 1990s they were recording losses of around US$15–20 million per month.

In 2000 they were eventually privatised, and bought by a consortium led by Anglo American. The irony of the situation is that the mines had originally belonged to Anglo American before KK nationalised them.

Cobalt Zambia is the world's largest producer of cobalt, producing around 5,000 tonnes per annum of this valuable, strategic metal: some 20% of the world's total production. It is usually produced as a by-product of copper or nickel mines; and in one Zambian deal, a private mining company was granted rights to extract cobalt and copper from Nkana's slag heap. The company estimated that this still contains about 56,000 tonnes of cobalt and 86,000 tonnes of copper.

Coal Zambia's only coal mine is the troubled open-pit mine at Maamba, near Lake Kariba, where reserves are estimated at over 30 million tonnes. Production at the state-owned company has been declining for some time, from about 300,000 tonnes per annum in the late 1990s, to just 8,000 tonnes in 2006, and industrial unrest is rife. In 2007, investment of US$15 million was announced, with a view to replacing old equipment and boosting production. Plans to privatise the mine are reported to be dependent on repayment of US$20 million of debt.

Other mineral resources Zambia has natural resources of amethyst, fluorite, feldspar, gypsum, aquamarine, lead, zinc, tin and gold – as well as a variety of gemstones. All are on a small scale, and few are being commercially exploited. An exception is emeralds, which are said to be among the highest quality in the world. However, although these are being mined to the order of about US$200 million per year, about half are thought to be smuggled out of the country, so the real amounts remain uncertain. It has been estimated that if the resources were properly managed, the gemstone industry as a whole could be worth as much as US$600 million per year.

OTHER INDUSTRIAL SECTORS Zambia's manufacturing industry, including construction, chemicals, textiles and fertiliser production, accounts for about 28% of its GDP, employing just 6% of the workforce. High costs mean that the sector isn't very competitive regionally, yet the domestic market is small. Most industries need to develop larger economies of scale before they can compete with, say, competitors in South Africa. Areas with potential for this include food, cement, tobacco and textiles.

AGRICULTURE Agriculture accounts for less than 20% of Zambia's GDP, but employs perhaps 85% of its workforce. Zambia's varied topography encourages a wide diversity in the crops cultivated. Most farming is still done by small-scale subsistence farmers, although large commercial farms are gradually appearing, often financed by private investors. There remain many fertile areas that are not being exploited, largely because of the lack of infrastructure in rural parts of the country.

Zambia's main crops and agricultural products are maize (the staple food for most people), sorghum, rice, peanuts, soya beans, sunflowers, tobacco, cotton, sugarcane, cassava, cattle, goats, beef and eggs.

More recently, the 'floricultural' sector has started to bloom for export. That consists of roses, vegetables, fruit, coffee and tea. Many of these enterprises are located near Lusaka's main airport, to ensure that flowers and vegetables are freshly delivered; there's a thriving trade in export growers chartering cargo planes to Europe, though this is threatened by growing concern over the environmental impact of air-freighted goods. Processing and packaging companies are developing in parallel with this, with some companies supplying packaged vegetables to British supermarkets.

TOURISM Zambia has the (arguable) benefit of a late-developing tourism industry, which should allow it to learn from the mistakes of others. Hopes for the development of tourism lie firmly with the private sector, and the government is happy for private investors to buy into the industry. Since the mid-1990s tourism has been expanding very steadily – which is by far the best way for a tourism industry to move if it is to stay on a sustainable basis – and increasingly there is a focus on the development that tourism can bring to local communities.

Until around 2000, Zambia's annual visitor influx could still probably have been counted in the low thousands. Since then, the increase has been accelerated by the rapid demise of Zimbabwe's tourism industry, which has been all but wrecked by the country's political turmoil. The opening of two large new hotels near Livingstone had a significant impact on the town's infrastructure and flight connections, and development since then has continued apace, with accommodation options in the town broadening year on year (albeit not without considerable pressure for unsustainable development from some sectors). As a result, Livingstone has taken on the mantle of regional tourism capital, formerly held by its fading neighbour, the Zimbabwean town of Victoria Falls.

While tourism remains one of Zambia's least-developed sectors, generating an estimated 2.3% of GDP in 2007, according to the Zambian National Tourist Board, arguably it holds the greatest potential. In 2004, the number of tourists rose by 25% over the previous year to 515,000, and the tourist board is targeting a million visitors by 2010.

The praises of Zambia's national parks are sung elsewhere in this book, but here it's worth noting that the country's best camps command prices (and standards) to match their equivalents in Tanzania, Zimbabwe or Botswana. What's more, Zambia still has vast tracts of pristine wilderness, which is exactly what is needed for new safari destinations. Most importantly, visitors to Africa realise that top wildlife guides, like those found in Zambia, are few and far between.

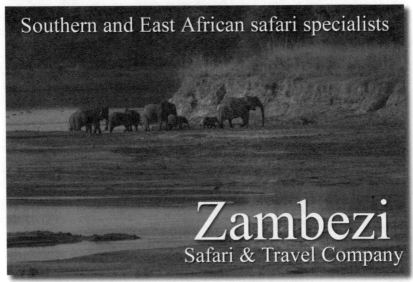

2

People and Culture

PEOPLE

THE POPULATION Recent statistics suggest that Zambia's population stands at almost 11.5 million, the vast majority of whom are of black African (Bantu) descent, though there are significant communities whose ancestors came from Europe and India. Zambia is a large country, so its population density – around 14 people per square kilometre – is relatively low: about half that of Zimbabwe, a third that of South Africa, or about a quarter the population density of Kenya. According to the United Nations, the population growth rate is about 1.7% per annum, though some sources put this higher, a reflection of the confusion on the impact of AIDS. It is estimated that around 17% of the population between the ages of 15 and 49 are affected by AIDS.

Zambia's urban population is about 40% of the total, although this has reduced in recent years due to a 'return migration' of people moving back to the land. The difficulty of life in the cities is often cited as one of the root causes. The capital, Lusaka, is home to about 10% of the country's population, whilst a further 1.5 million live in the Copperbelt Province, predominantly in the main towns of Kitwe, Ndola, Chingola and Mufulira. Thus, the rural areas generally have a low population density, and the country retains large tracts of wilderness.

Statistics indicate that infant mortality is as high as 10%, while the average life expectancy for a Zambian is 38.4 years, and the great majority of people live below the poverty line. About 46% of Zambia's population is under 15 years of age, whilst some 80% of those above age 15 are literate.

However, the statistics say nothing of the warmth that the sensitive visitor can encounter. If you venture into the rural areas, take a local bus, or try to hitchhike with the locals; you will often find that Zambians are curious about you. Chat to them openly, as fellow travellers, and you will find most Zambians to be delightful. They will be pleased to assist you where they can, and as keen to help you learn about them and their country as they are interested in your lifestyle and what brings you to Zambia.

A NOTE ON 'TRIBES' The people of Africa are often viewed, from abroad, as belonging to a multitude of culturally and linguistically distinct tribes – which are often portrayed as being at odds with each other. Whilst there is certainly an enormous variety of different ethnic groups in Africa, most are closely related to their neighbours in terms of language, beliefs and way of life. Modern historians eschew the simplistic tag of 'tribes', noting that such groupings change with time.

Sometimes the word tribe is used to describe a group of people who all speak the same language; it may be used to mean those who follow a particular leader or to refer to all the inhabitants of a certain area at a given time. In any case, tribe is a vague word which is used differently for different purposes. The term 'clan' (blood relations) is a smaller, more precisely defined, unit – though rather too precise for our broad discussions here.

Certainly, at any given time, groups of people or clans who share similar language and cultural beliefs do band together and often, in time, develop 'tribal' identities. However, it is wrong to then extrapolate and assume that their ancestors will have had the same groupings and allegiances centuries ago.

In Africa, as elsewhere in the world, history is recorded by the winners. Here the winners, the ruling class, may be the descendants of a small group of intruders who achieved dominance over a larger, long-established community. Over the years, the history of that ruling class usually becomes regarded as the history of the whole community, or tribe. Two 'tribes' have thus become one, with one history – which will reflect the origins of that small group of intruders, and not the ancestors of the majority of the current tribe.

Zambia is typical of a large African country. Currently historians and linguistics experts can identify at least 16 major cultural groupings, and more than 72 different languages and dialects are spoken in the country. As you will see, there are cultural differences between the people in different parts of the country. However, these are no more pronounced than those between the states of the USA, or the different regions of the (relatively tiny) UK.

There continues to be lots of inter-marriage and mixing of these peoples and cultures – perhaps more so than in the past, due to the efficiency of modern transport systems. Generally, there is very little friction between these communities (whose boundaries, as we have said, are indistinct) and Zambia's various peoples live peacefully together.

AFRICAN LANGUAGE GROUPS English is the official language in Zambia, and most urban Zambians speak it fluently. In rural areas it is used less, though only in truly remote settlements will you encounter problems communicating in English.

The main vernacular languages are Bemba, Kaonde, Lozi, Lunda, Luvale, Nyanja and Tonga – though more than 72 different languages and dialects are spoken in the country. Of these, the most widely recognised and understood are Nyanja and Bemba. For basic words and phrases, see *Appendix 2*, pages 507–9.

Below are detailed some of the major language groups, arranged alphabetically. This is only a rough guide to the languages and dialects of Zambia's people. Although these different language groupings do loosely correspond to what many describe as Zambia's tribes, the distinctions are blurred further by the natural linguistic ability of most Zambians. Whilst it is normal to speak English plus one local language, many Zambians will speak a number of local languages fluently.

When the colonial powers carved up Africa, the divisions between the countries bore only a passing resemblance to the traditional areas of these various ethnic groups. Thus many of the groups here are split between several countries. Note that the estimates of populations quoted below are based on surveys done during the 1980s, and average estimated population growth rates since then.

Bemba Bemba is the first language of about two and a quarter million Zambians: almost a quarter of the country's population. It is spoken in the rural areas of northern Zambia, from the Luapula River eastwards to Mpika, Kasama and beyond. Because people from these areas were the original workers in the mines of the Copperbelt, Bemba has subsequently achieved the status of *lingua franca* in the major urban areas of the Copperbelt and Lusaka.

It is recognised for administration and education purposes within Zambia, whilst outside its borders Bemba is also spoken by over 150,000 people in the Democratic Republic of Congo, and around 37,000 in Tanzania.

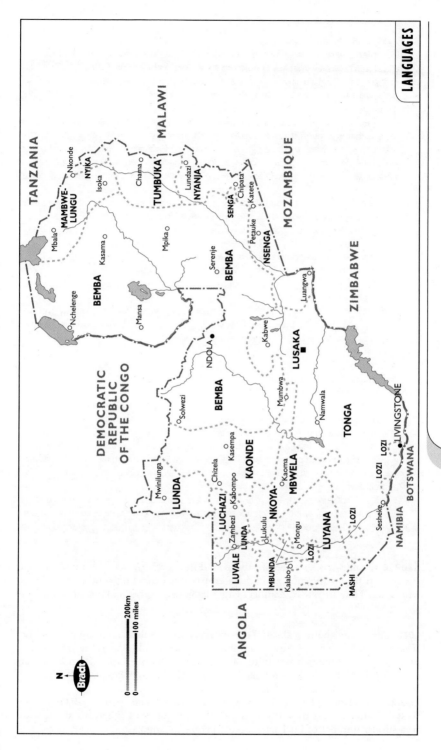

Comments here are intended to be a general guide, just a few examples of how to travel more sensitively. They should not be viewed as blueprints for perfect Zambian etiquette. Cultural sensitivity is really a state of mind, not a checklist of behaviour – so here we can only hope to give the sensitive traveller a few pointers in the right direction.

When we travel, we are all in danger of leaving negative impressions with local people that we meet. It is easily done – by snapping that picture quickly, whilst the subject is not looking; by dressing scantily, offending local sensitivities; by just brushing aside the feelings of local people, with the high-handed superiority of a rich Westerner. These things are easy to do, in the click of a shutter, or flash of a dollar bill.

You will get the most representative view of Zambia if you cause as little disturbance to the local people as possible. You will never blend in perfectly when you travel – your mere presence there, as an observer, will always change the local events slightly. However, if you try to fit in and show respect for local culture and attitudes, then you may manage to leave positive feelings behind you.

One of the easiest, and most important, ways to do this is with greetings. African societies are rarely as rushed as Western ones. When you first talk to someone, you should greet them leisurely.

So, for example, if you enter a bus station and want some help, do not just ask outright, 'Where is the bus to ...' That would be rude. Instead you will have a better reception (and better chance of good advice) by saying:

Traveller: 'Good afternoon.'
Zambian: 'Good afternoon.'
Traveller: 'How are you?'
Zambian: 'I am fine, how are you?'
Traveller: 'I am fine, thank you.' (*Pause*) 'Do you know where the bus to ...'

This goes for approaching anyone – always greet them first. For a better reception still, learn these phrases of greeting in the local language (see pages 507–9). English-speakers are often lazy about learning languages, and, whilst most Zambians understand English, a greeting given in an appropriate local language will be received with delight. It implies that you are making an effort to learn a little of their language and culture, which is always appreciated.

Occasionally, in the town or city, you may be approached by someone who doesn't greet you. Instead s/he tries immediately to sell you something, or even hassle you in some way. These people have learned that foreigners aren't used to greetings, and so

Kaonde Kaonde-speakers live mostly around the northern side of Kafue National Park, centring on the area around Kasempa, and extending southeast as far as Mumbwa. They are one of Zambia's larger language groups, and probably number about 200,000.

Lozi There are about 500,000 Lozi-speakers in Zambia, concentrated in the Western and Southern provinces, around Barotseland and Livingstone. The centre of Lozi culture is the rich agricultural floodplain around the Upper Zambezi River – and it is here that the Ku-omboka (see *Festivals*, page 26) takes place each year.

Luchazi This language has only a small number of speakers, perhaps 70,000 in the west of Zambia – less than 1% of the country's population. There are thought to be a similar number of Luchazi-speaking people in Angola.

have adapted their approach accordingly. An effective way to dodge their attentions is to reply to their questions with a formal greeting, and then politely – but firmly – refuse their offer. This is surprisingly effective.

Another part of the normal greeting ritual is handshaking. As elsewhere, you would not normally shake a shop-owner's hand, but you would shake hands with someone to whom you are introduced. Get some practice when you arrive, as there is a gentle, three-part handshake used in southern Africa which is easily learnt.

Your clothing is an area that can easily give offence. Most Zambians frown upon skimpy or revealing clothing, especially when worn by women. Shorts are fine for walking safaris, otherwise dress conservatively and avoid short shorts, especially in the more rural areas. Respectable locals will wear long trousers (men) or long skirts (women).

Photography is a tricky business. Most Zambians will be only too happy to be photographed – provided you ask their permission first. Sign language is fine for this question: just point at your camera, shrug your shoulders, and look quizzical. The problem is that then everyone will smile for you, producing the type of 'posed' photograph that you may not want. However, stay around and chat for five or ten minutes more, and people will get used to your presence, stop posing, and you will get more natural shots of them (a camera with a quiet shutter is a help).

Note that special care is needed with photography near government buildings, bridges and similar sites of strategic importance. You must ask permission before photographing anything here, or you risk people thinking that you are a spy.

If you're travelling, and seeking directions to somewhere, don't be afraid to stop and ask. Most people will be polite and keen to help – so keen that some will answer 'Yes' to questions if they think that this is what you want to hear. So try to avoid asking leading questions. For example, 'Yes' would often be the typical answer to the question, 'Does this road lead to … ?' And in a sense the respondent is probably correct – it will get you there. It's just that it may not be the quickest or shortest way.

To avoid misunderstandings, it is often better to ask open-ended questions like, 'Where does this road go to?' or 'How do I drive to … ?'

The specific examples above can only be taken so far – they are general by their very nature. But wherever you find yourself, if you are polite and considerate to the Zambians you meet, then you will rarely encounter any cultural problems. Watch how they behave and, if you have any doubts about how you should act, then ask someone quietly. They will seldom tell you outright that you are being rude, but they will usually give you good advice on how to make your behaviour more acceptable.

Lunda Not to be confused with Luunda, which is a dialect of Bemba, Lunda is the first language of about 230,000 Zambians and is spoken in areas of the Copperbelt, as well as nearby DRC and Angola. It is officially taught in primary schools, and can occasionally be heard on radio or seen in newspapers in the area.

Luvale Luvale is an important language in Angola, where it is spoken by almost one million people. In Zambia there are only about 215,000 people whose first language is Luvale, and they live in the Northwestern and Western provinces of Zambia.

Luyana The Luyana-speaking people are a small group, perhaps numbering 130,000 in total. Their language has not been well documented, though it is spoken in Zambia, Angola, Namibia and also Botswana. In Zambia it is found almost exclusively in the Western Province.

Mambwe-Lungu These are other languages that need further study – so far they appear to differ from each other only slightly, as dialects would. In total about 280,000 Zambians count them as their first language – about 3% of the population. Their stronghold is in the northeast of the Northern Province, south of Lake Tanganyika. As you might expect, they are also spoken in Tanzania.

Mashi Mashi seems to be spoken by only a tiny number of Zambians, perhaps only 25,000 people, who are often nomadic within a southwestern area of the Western Province. Little has been documented about this language – though it has been noted that virtually all the native speakers of Mashi follow traditional religious practices, rather than the more recently introduced Christian beliefs.

Mbunda The first language of about 130,000 Zambians, Mbunda is spoken in the north of Barotseland and the northern side of western Zambia – as well as in Angola.

Nkoya-Mbwela Nkoya and Mbwela are two closely related languages. Mbwela is often referred to as a dialect of Nkoya, though here we have grouped them together as equals. They also have only a tiny number of speakers – around 80,000 people – who are found around the Mankoya area, in Zambia's Western and Southern provinces.

Nsenga There are thought to be over 330,000 people speaking Nsenga as their first language, of whom the vast majority live in Zambia. These are clustered around the area of Petauke – near to the borders with Zimbabwe and Mozambique, across which the language is also spoken.

Nyanja Nyanja is the Bantu language most often encountered by visitors in Zambia. It is widely used in much of the country, including the key cities of Lusaka and Livingstone. Nyanja is sometimes described as not being a language *per se*, but rather a common skill enabling people of varying tribes living in eastern, central and southern parts of Zambia and Malawi to communicate without following the strict grammar of specific local languages. In other words, like Swahili and other 'universal' languages, Nyanja is something of a *lingua franca* for Zambia.

Nyanja is certainly the official language of the police, and is widely used for administrative and educational purposes. About a million Zambians use Nyanja as their first language – mostly in the eastern and central areas of the country – and there may be double that number using the language in Malawi. Then there are around 330,000 Nyanja-speakers in Zimbabwe, and perhaps 500,000 in Mozambique. A total of approaching four million people in the subcontinent speak Nyanja as a first language.

Nyika Also known as Nyiha, or more precisely as Chi-Nyika, Nyika is spoken most widely in Tanzania, and also in Malawi. In Zambia it is used around the Isoka and Chama areas, across to the Malawi border. (It is closely related to the language known as Ichi-Lambya in Tanzania and Malawi.)

Tonga Tonga is the language of a small minority of Zimbabweans, many of whom were displaced south by the creation of Lake Kariba (see page 211). However, in Zambia it is the first language of around one million people, about 11% of the country's population, and is widely used in the media. Tonga is distributed throughout the south of the country, with its highest concentration in the middle Zambezi Valley.

Tumbuka Zambia has about 430,000 people who speak Tumbuka as a first language, mostly living on the eastern side of the country. Outside Zambia many Tumbuka-speakers live in Malawi and Tanzania, bringing the total number to about two million.

OTHER ETHNIC GROUPS

White Zambians There are a small number of white Zambians, very different from the expat community (see below) who are often white but simply working in the country on a temporary basis. Many white Zambians will trace their families back to colonial immigrants who came over during British rule, but most will regard themselves as Zambian rather than, say, British. This is generally an affluent group of people, and many of the country's businesses and especially the safari companies, are owned and run by white Zambians.

Asian Zambians Like the white Zambians, many people of Asian origin came here during the colonial period. When the British ruled African colonies like Zambia as well as India, there was movement of labour from Asia to Africa. Now, like the white Zambians, this is generally an affluent group. On the whole, Zambians of Asian descent retain a very strong sense of Asian identity and culture, and many are traders or own small shops.

Expatriates Distinct from Zambians, there is a large expat community in Zambia. These foreigners usually come to Zambia for two or three years, to work on short-term contracts, often for either multi-national companies or aid agencies. Most are highly skilled individuals who come to share their knowledge with Zambian colleagues – often teaching skills that are in short supply in Zambia.

In the 1990s there was a migration of trained Zambian teachers and lecturers to neighbouring countries, where they are paid better, but this has now stabilised.

RELIGION

It has been estimated that there are some 200 different Christian churches in Zambia, of which the most active in the community is considered to be the Catholic Church. However, as in many other sub-Saharan African countries, many people will also subscribe to some traditional African religious practices and beliefs.

EDUCATION

In theory, primary education has been free to all children in Zambia since 2002, and statistics suggest that all children do indeed go to school. In practice, however, this is only half the story. Parents still need to find the means to pay for school uniform and books and pencils, or their children will be turned away, and the 'voluntary contribution' so beloved of state schools in the West becomes a crippling burden to impoverished Zambian families. A 'fee' of Kw50,000 for each primary-age child is not unusual, with penalties levied, for instance, if a parent fails to turn up at a school meeting. At secondary level, fees are around Kw200,000 (US$50/£25) a year. And this where the minimum wage is just US$40/£22 a month.

Typically, primary schools are run on a shift pattern, with children spending three hours in the classroom each day; the first are in school at 07.00, finishing at 10.00, when the next group starts. The secondary school day normally runs from 07.00 to 13.00. There are also 'basic' schools, which serve a wider age range than primary in areas where there is no secondary school. Class sizes are large, frequently exceeding the expected norm of 45 children, and lessons are often disrupted by strike action on the part of the teachers.

Zambia's first university was established in Lusaka as recently as 1966, shortly after independence, and has since been joined by two more, both in the north of the country: one in Kitwe, and a second in Luanshya.

CULTURE

FESTIVALS Zambia has several major cultural festivals which, on the whole, are rarely seen by visitors. If you can get to any, then you will find them to be very genuine occasions, where ceremonies are performed for the benefit of the local people and the participants, and not for the odd tourist who is watching.

Cultural celebrations were strongly encouraged during Kenneth Kaunda's reign, as he favoured people being aware of their cultural origins. 'A country without culture is like a body without a head', was one of his phrases. Thus during the 1980s one group after another 'discovered' old traditional festivals. Most are now large local events, partly cultural but also part political rally, religious gathering and sports event.

Bear in mind that, like most celebrations worldwide, these are often accompanied by the large-scale consumption of alcohol. To see these festivals properly, and to appreciate them, you will need a good guide: someone who understands the rituals, can explain their significance, and can instruct you on how you should behave. After all, how would you feel about a passing Zambian traveller who arrives, with curiosity, at your sibling's wedding (a small festival), in the hope of being invited to the private reception?

Photographers will find superb opportunities at such colourful events, but should behave with sensitivity. *Before* you brandish your camera, remember to ask permission from anyone who might take offence.

The Ku-omboka This is the most famous of the ceremonies, and takes place in the Western Province. It used to be around February or March, often on a Thursday, just before full moon. The precise date would be known only a week or so in advance, as it was decided upon by the Lozi king. Now that the ceremony attracts more visitors, it is usually held at Easter, though if water levels are not high enough, it will not take place at all.

The Lozi kingdom is closely associated with the fertile plains around the Upper Zambezi River. When dry, this well-defined area affords good grazing for livestock, and its rich alluvial soil is ideal for cultivation. It contrasts with the sparse surrounding woodland, growing on poor soil typical of the rest of western Zambia. So for much of the year, these plains support a dense population of subsistence farms.

However, towards the end of the rains, the Zambezi's water levels rise. The plains then become floodplains, and the settlements gradually become islands. The people must leave them for the higher ground, at the margins of the floodplain. This retreat from the advancing waters – known as the Ku-omboka – is traditionally led by the king himself, the Litunga, from his dry-season abode at Lealui, in the middle of the plain. He retreats with his court to his high-water residence, at Limulunga, on the eastern margins of the floodplain.

The Litunga's departure is heralded by the beating of three huge old royal war drums – Mundili, Munanga and Kanaono. These continue to summon the people from miles around until the drums themselves are loaded aboard the royal barge, the *nalikwanda*, a very large wooden canoe built around the turn of the century and painted with vertical black-and-white stripes. The royal barge is then paddled and punted along by 96 polers, each sporting a skirt of animal skins and a white vest. Their scarlet hats are surmounted by tufts of fur taken from the mane of unfortunate lions.

The royal barge is guided by a couple of 'scout' barges, painted white, which search out the right channels for the royal barge. Behind it comes the Litunga's wife, the Moyo, in her own barge, followed by local dignitaries, various attendants, many of the Litunga's subjects, and the odd visitor lucky enough to be in the area at the right time. The journey takes most of the day, and the flotilla is accompanied by an impromptu orchestra of local musicians.

John Reader's excellent book, *Africa: A Biography of the Continent* (see *Appendix 3*, page 510), comments:

> When the Litunga boards the nalikwanda at Lealui he customarily wears a light European-style suit, a pearl-grey frock coat and a trilby hat; when he leaves the barge at Limulunga he is dressed in a splendid uniform of dark-blue serge ornately embroidered with gold braid, with matching cockade hat complete with a white plume of egret feathers.

In fact, Chapter 47 of this book contains the fascinating story of some of the first Europeans to see the original Ku-omboka, and the sad narration of the gradual European subjugation of the Lozi kingdom. It also includes details of the Litunga's trip to London, in 1902, for the coronation of King Edward VII. It was here that the problem arose of what the Litunga should wear. Reader reports:

> By happy coincidence, the king [Edward VII] took a particular interest in uniforms; he was an expert on the subject and is even said to have made a hobby of designing uniforms. Doubtless the king had approved the design of the new uniforms with which Britain's ambassadors had recently been issued. Certainly he was aware that the introduction of these new outfits had created a redundant stock of the old style, which were richly adorned with gold braid. Lewanika [the Litunga] should be attired in one of those, the king ordained. And thus the Litunga acquired the uniform which has become part of the Kuomboka tradition. Not an admiral's uniform, as is often reported, but a surplus dress uniform of a Victorian ambassador; not a gift from Queen Victoria, but the suggestion of her son...
>
> When the royal barge finally arrives at Limulunga, the Litunga steps ashore in the ambassador's uniform to spend an evening of feasting and celebrations, with much eating, drinking, music and traditional dancing.

Likumbi Lya Mize The Luvale people of western Zambia have an annual 'fair' type of celebration, which takes place for four or five days towards the end of August. 'Likumbi Lya Mize' means 'Mize day' and the event is held at the palace of the senior chief – at Mize, about 7km west of Zambezi.

This provides an opportunity for the people to see their senior chief, watch the popular Makishi dancers, and generally have a good time. As you might expect, there is also lots of eating and drinking, plus people in traditional dress, displays of local crafts, and singing.

Mutomboko (also Umutomboko) This is nothing to do with the Ku-omboka, described above. It is an annual two-day celebration, performed in the last weekend of July, whereby the paramount chief celebrates the arrival of the Luunda people, the 'crossing of the river'. It is held in a specially prepared arena, close to the Ng'ona River, at Mwansabombwe (see page 361).

On the first day the chief, covered in white powder, receives tributes of food and drink from his subjects – the cause for much feasting and celebration by all. On the second an animal (often a goat) is slaughtered and the highlight is the chief's dance with his sword. See also page 361.

Shimunenga This traditional gathering is held on the weekend of a full moon, in September or October, at Maala on the Kafue Flats – about 40km west of Namwala. Then the Ila people (whose language is closely related to Tonga) gather together, driving cattle across the Kafue River to higher ground. It used to be a lechwe hunt, but that is now forbidden.

The Nc'wala On 24 February there is a festival to celebrate the first fruit, at Mutenguleni village, near Chipata. This large celebration was recently revived, after 80 years of not being practised. It consists of two parts. Firstly the chief tastes the first fruit of the land – usually sugarcane, maize and pumpkins. Secondly there is the ritual rebirth of the king (involving the king being locked up in his house) and the blessing of the fruit – which consists of a fairly gory spearing of a black bull whose blood the king has to drink. It's all accompanied by traditional dancing and beer-drinking.

Other festivals The above list of festivals is by no means exhaustive, and a few others which are known include:

Kufukwila A May celebration led by the chief of the Kaonde people, held in the Solwezi area of northwestern Zambia.

Kulamba Also a thanksgiving ceremony for the Chewa people, held in August. It's held in the Katete Province, in eastern Zambia, and here you'll be able to see lots of fascinating Nyao (secret society) dancers.

Lukuni Luzwa Buuka A celebration of past conquests by the Toka people in the Southern Province, usually held in August.

Lwiinda A ceremony celebrated by Chief Mokuni, of the Toka-Leya people near Livingstone, around February. The people honour their ancestors and offer sacrifices for rain.

Malaila A ceremony to honour past chiefs, held in July by the Kunda people. (This is currently celebrated by Chieftainess Nsefu, near Mfuwe in the Luangwa Valley.)

Tuwimba A thanksgiving festival, in October, for the Nsenga people.

3

The Natural Environment

PHYSICAL ENVIRONMENT

TOPOGRAPHY Zambia lies landlocked between the Tropic of Capricorn and the Equator, far from both the Atlantic and the Pacific oceans. It is at the northern edge of the region referred to as 'southern Africa', while sharing many similarities with its neighbours in east and central Africa. Shaped like a giant butterfly, it covers about 752,610km², That is slightly smaller than the UK and France combined, and slightly larger than California plus Nevada. In comparison with its neighbours, it is almost double the size of Zimbabwe, but only two-thirds that of South Africa.

Most of the country is part of the high, undulating plateau that forms the backbone of the African continent. Typically, it has an altitude of between 1,000m and 1,600m, deeply incised by the great valleys of the Zambezi, the Kafue, the Luangwa and the Luapula that lie below 500m.

There are several large lakes on Zambia's borders: Tanganyika and Mweru in the north, and the man-made Kariba in the south. Lake Bangweulu, and its swamps and floodplain, dominate a large area of the interior.

GEOLOGY Zambia's oldest rocks, known as the Basement Complex, were laid down at an early stage in the pre-Cambrian era – as long as 2,000 million years ago. These were extensively eroded and covered by sediments which now form the Katanga system of rocks, dating from around 1,000 to 620 million years ago. These are what we now see near the surface in most of northeast and central Zambia, and they contain the important mineral deposits of the Copperbelt. Later still, from about 300 to 150 million years ago, the karoo system of sedimentary rocks was deposited: sandstones, mudstones, conglomerates and even coal. Towards the end of this era, molten rock seeped up through cracks in the crust, and covered areas of western Zambia in layers of basalt – the rock that is seen cut away by the Zambezi River in the gorges below Victoria Falls.

About 150 million years ago, during the Jurassic era of the dinosaurs, Africa was still part of Gondwana – a super-continent which included South America, India, Australasia and Antarctica. Since then Zambia's highlands have been eroded down from an original altitude of over 1,800m (Nyika Plateau is still at this altitude) to their present lower levels.

Very recently, perhaps only a few million years ago, the subcontinent had a dry phase. Then the sands from the Kalahari Desert blew far across southern Africa, covering much of western Zambia with a covering of Kalahari sand, as still becomes abundantly clear the moment you try to drive in the region.

CLIMATE Situated squarely in the tropics, Zambia gets a lot of strong sunlight, though the intense heat normally associated with the tropics is moderated in most places by the country's altitude and its rainfall. The climate is generally moderate; only in the great valleys does it feel oppressive. It can be summarised broadly into

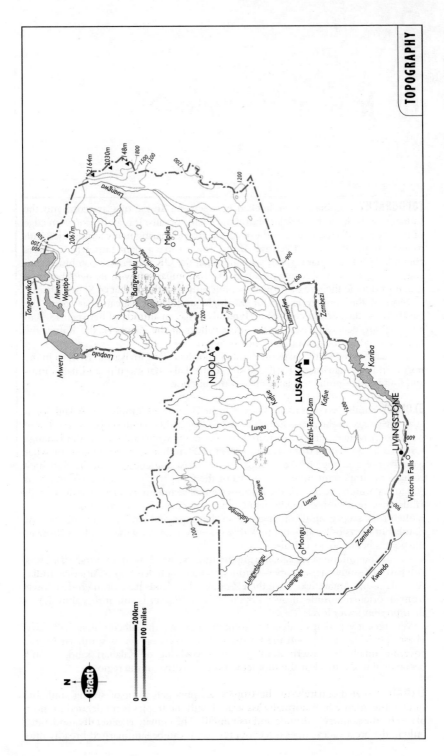

RAINFALL

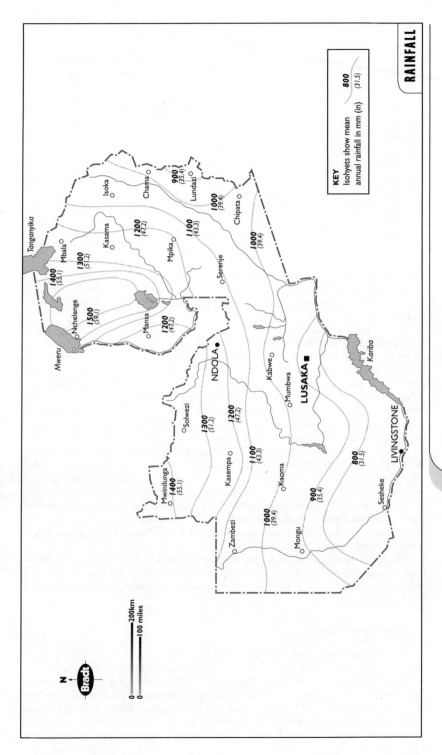

KEY
Isohyets show mean
annual rainfall in mm (in)

800
(31.5)

CLIMATE STATISTICS: LUSAKA

| | Temp °C | | Temp °F | | Humidity % | | Rainfall |
	max	min	max	min	am	pm	mm
Jan	26	17	78	62	84	71	231
Feb	26	17	78	62	85	80	191
Mar	26	17	78	62	83	56	142
Apr	26	15	78	59	71	47	18
May	25	12	77	52	59	37	3
Jun	23	10	73	50	56	32	0
Jul	23	9	73	48	54	28	0
Aug	25	12	77	53	46	26	0
Sep	29	15	84	59	41	19	0
Oct	31	18	87	64	39	23	15
Nov	29	18	84	64	57	46	91
Dec	27	17	80	62	76	61	150

three periods: from December to April it is hot and wet, with torrential downpours often in the late afternoon; from May to August it is dry, and becomes increasingly cool; and from September to November it remains dry, but gets progressively hotter.

This follows a similar pattern to that in most of southern Africa, with rainfall when the sun is near its zenith from November to April. The precise timing and duration of this is determined by the interplay of three airstreams: the moist 'Congo' air-mass, the northeastern monsoon winds, and the southeastern trade winds. The water-bearing air is the Congo air-mass, which normally brings rain when it moves south into Zambia from central Africa. This means that the northern areas, around Lakes Tanganyika and Mweru, receive the first rainfall – often in late October or November. This belt of rain will then work south, arriving in southern Zambia by the end of November or the start of December.

As the sun's intensity reduces, the Congo air-mass moves back north, leaving southern Zambia dry by around late March, and the north by late April or May. Most areas receive their heaviest rainfall in January, though some of the most northern areas have two peaks: one in December and one in March. This twin-peak cycle is more characteristic of central and eastern Africa. The heaviest total rainfall is found in the north, and the lightest in the south.

Lusaka's climate statistics are typical of the pleasant climate found in the higher areas of southern and central Zambia:

The lower-lying valleys, including the Luangwa and Lower Zambezi, follow the same broad pattern but are considerably hotter throughout the year. In October, which is universally the hottest month, temperatures there often reach over 45°C in the shade.

FLORA AND FAUNA

Zambia has many large national parks and game management areas (GMAs) where conservation and sustainable utilisation of the native wildlife are encouraged.

Miombo woodland – a mixture of grassland dotted with trees and shrubs – makes up about 70% of Zambia's natural environment, with *mopane* woodland dominating the lower-lying areas. The native fauna is classic big game found throughout east and southern Africa. Amongst the predators, leopard do exceptionally well here; lion are common but cheetah are not. Wild dog are uncommon, though seem to have increased in numbers in recent years, and there are many smaller predators. Zambia's antelope are especially interesting for the range of subspecies that have evolved. Giraffe, wildebeest, waterbuck and, especially, lechwe are notable for this – each having subspecies endemic to the country.

With rich vegetation and lots of water, Zambia has a great variety of both resident and migrant birds, over 750 species in total. Wetland and swamp areas attract some specialised waterfowl, and Zambia is on the edge of the range for both southern African and east African species.

FLORA As with animals, each species of plant has its favourite conditions. External factors determine where each species thrives, and where it will perish. These include temperature, light, water, soil type, nutrients, and what other species of plants and animals live in the same area. Species with similar needs are often found together, in communities which are characteristic of that particular environment. Zambia has a number of different such communities, or typical 'vegetation types', within its borders – each of which is distinct from the others. The more common include:

Woodlands Where they haven't been destroyed or degraded by people, woodlands cover the vast majority of Zambia, with miombo being especially common. Because the canopies of the trees in a woodland area don't interlock, you'll generally find them lighter and more open than the country's relatively few forested areas. The main types of woodland found here are:

Mopane woodland The dominant tree here is the remarkably adaptable mopane, *Colophospermum mopane*, which is sometimes known as the butterfly tree because of the shape of its leaves. It is very tolerant of poorly drained or alkaline soils, and those with a high clay content. This tolerance results in the mopane having a wide range of distribution throughout southern Africa; in Zambia it occurs mainly in the hotter, drier, lower parts of the country, including the Luangwa and Zambezi valleys.

Mopane trees can attain a height of 25m, especially if growing on rich, alluvial soils. These are often called cathedral mopane, for their height and the graceful arch of their branches. However, shorter trees are more common in areas that are poor in nutrients, or have suffered extensive fire damage. Stunted mopane will form a low scrub, perhaps only 5m tall. All mopane trees are deciduous, and the leaves turn beautiful shades of yellow and red before falling in September and October.

Ground cover in mopane woodland is usually sparse, just thin grasses, herbs and the occasional bush. The trees themselves are an important source of food for game, as the leaves have a high nutritional value – rich in protein and phosphorus – which is favoured by browsers and is retained even after they have fallen from the trees. Mopane forests support large populations of rodents, including tree squirrels, *Peraxerus cepapi*, which are so typical of these areas that they are known as 'mopane squirrels'.

Miombo woodland Without human intervention, the natural vegetation of most of Zambia (about 70%) is miombo woodland and its associated *dambos* (see below). This exists on Zambia's main plateau and its adjacent escarpments, where the acid soils are not particularly fertile and have often been leached of minerals by the water run-off.

Miombo woodland consists of a mosaic of large wooded areas and smaller, more open spaces dotted with clumps of trees and shrubs. The woodland is broadleafed

3

and deciduous (though just how deciduous depends on the available water), and the tree canopies generally don't interlock. The dominant trees are *Brachystegia*, *Julbernardia* and *Isoberlinia* species – most of which are at least partially fire-resistant. There is more variation of species in miombo than in mopane woodland, but despite this it is often known simply as 'brachystegia woodland'. The ground cover is also generally less sparse here than in mopane areas.

Munga woodland The word 'munga' means thorn, and this is the thorny woodland which occurs when open grassland has been invaded by trees and shrubs – normally because of some disturbance like cultivation, fire or overgrazing. *Acacia*, *Terminalia* (bearing single-winged seeds) and *Combretum* (bearing seeds with four or five wings) are the dominant species, but many others can be present. Munga occurs mainly in the southern parts of Zambia.

Forests In most equatorial areas further north in Africa, where rainfall is higher, forests are the norm. However, there are a few specific ecological niches in Zambia where you will find forests – distinguished from woodlands by their interlocking canopy. These are:

Teak forest In a few areas of southwestern Zambia (including the southern part of Kafue National Park), the Zambezi teak, *Baikaea plurijuga*, forms dry semi-evergreen forests on a base of Kalahari sand. This species is not fire-resistant, so these stands occur only where slash-and-burn cultivation methods have never been used. Below the tall teak is normally a dense, deciduous thicket of vegetation usually referred to as *mutemwa*, interspersed with sparse grasses and herbs in the shadier spots of the forest floor.

Moist evergreen forest In the areas of higher rainfall (mostly in the north of Zambia), and near rivers, streams, lakes and swamps, where a tree's roots will have permanent access to water, dense evergreen forests are found. Many species occur, and this lush vegetation is characterised by having three levels: a canopy of tall trees, a sub-level of smaller trees and bushes, and a variety of ground-level vegetation. In effect, the environment is so good for plants that they have adapted to exploit the light from every sunbeam.

This type of forest is prevalent in the far north of the country, especially in the Mwinilunga area. However, three more localised environments can give rise to moist evergreen forests in other areas of the country.

Riparian forests (often called riverine forests) are very common. They line many of Zambia's major rivers and are found in most of the national parks. Typical trees and shrubs here include ebony (*Diospyros mespiliformis*), mangosteen (*Garcinia livingstonei*), wild gardenia (*Gardenia volkensii*), sausage tree (*Kigelia africana*), Natal mahogany (*Trichilia emetica*) and various species of figs. But walk away from the river, and you'll find riparian species thinning out rapidly.

Montane forests are found on the lower slopes of mountains, where the rainfall is high. The Zambian slopes of Nyika Plateau are probably the best example of this kind of vegetation.

Finally **swamp** forest occurs near to some of Zambia's permanent swamps. Kasanka National Park probably has the country's best, and most accessible, examples of this.

Grasslands and open areas

Dambo A 'dambo' is a shallow grass depression, or small valley, that is either permanently or seasonally waterlogged. It corresponds closely to what is known as a 'vlei' in other parts of the subcontinent. These open, verdant dips in the landscape often appear in the midst of miombo woodlands and support no bushes or trees. In higher valleys amongst hills, they sometimes form the sources of streams and rivers. Because of their permanent dampness, they are rich in species of grasses, herbs and flowering plants, like orchids – and are excellent grazing (if a little exposed) for antelope. Their margins are usually thickly vegetated by grasses, herbs and smaller shrubs.

Pan Though not an environment for rich vegetation, a pan is a shallow, seasonal pool of water with no permanent streams leading into or out of it. The bush is full of small pans in the rainy season, most of which will dry up soon after the rains cease. Sometimes there's only a fine distinction between a pan and a dambo.

Floodplain Floodplains are the low-lying grasslands on the edges of rivers, streams, lakes and swamps that are seasonally inundated by floods. Zambia has some huge areas of floodplain, most obviously beside the Kafue River, in the Barotseland area around the Zambezi, and south of the permanent Bangweulu Swamps. These often contain no trees or bushes, just a low carpet of grass species that can tolerate being submerged for part of the year. In the midst of some floodplains, like the Busanga Plains, you'll find isolated small 'islands' of trees and bushes, slightly raised above the surrounding grasslands.

Montane grassland More common in other areas of Africa, montane grassland occurs on mountain slopes at higher altitudes where the precipitation is heavy and the climate cool. Zambia's best examples of this are on Nyika Plateau, and here you'll find many species of flora and fauna that occur nowhere else in Zambia.

FAUNA See also *Appendix 1*, page 491, for an introductory field guide to some of Zambia's larger animals.

Mammals Zambia's large mammals are typical of the savanna areas of east and (especially) southern Africa. The large predators here are lion, leopard, cheetah, wild dog and spotted hyena, although cheetah and wild dog are relatively uncommon.

Elephant and buffalo occur in large herds in protected national parks, and in small, furtive family groups where poaching is a problem. Black rhino were probably, sadly, extinct in Zambia until recent re-introduction programme in the North Luangwa National Park. A single white rhino remains in the small, well-protected, Mosi-Oa-Tunya National Park at Livingstone.

Antelope are well represented, with puku and impala numerically dominant in the drier areas. There are several interesting, endemic subspecies found in Zambia, including the Angolan and Thornicroft's giraffe, Cookson's wildebeest, Crawshay's zebra, and two unusual subspecies of lechwe – the black and the Kafue lechwe – occurring in very large numbers in some of the country's bigger marshy areas.

Because Zambia is a wet country, with numerous marshy areas, its natural vegetation is lush and capable of supporting a high density of game. The country has a natural advantage over drier areas, and this accounts for the sheer volume of big game to be found in its better parks.

Birds Much of Zambia is still covered by original, undisturbed natural vegetation, and hunting is not a significant factor for most of Zambia's birds. Thus, with a range of verdant and natural habitats, Zambia is a superb birding destination, with 750 different species recorded by 2007. A total of 42 'important birding areas'

3

(IBAs) have been identified by Peter Leonard, covering 14% of the country's total area (see *Appendix 3*, page 512).

Whilst the animal species differ only occasionally from the 'normal' species found in southern Africa, the birds are a much more varied mix of those species found in southern, eastern and even central Africa. The obvious celebrity is the ungainly shoebill stork, which breeds in the Bangweulu Swamps, and only one or two other places in central Africa. A lesser-known attraction is Chaplin's barbet, Zambia's only endemic bird species, found in southern Zambia around the south side of Kafue National Park. However, there are many other unusual, rare and beautifully coloured species that attract enthusiasts to Zambia.

In addition to its resident bird species, Zambia receives many migrants. In September and October the Palaearctic migrants appear (ie: those that come from the northern hemisphere – normally Europe), and they remain until around April or May. This is also the peak time to see the intra-African migrants, which come from further north in Africa.

The rains from December to around April see an explosion in the availability of most birds' food: seeds, fruits and insects. Hence this is the prime time for birds to nest, even if it is also the most difficult time to visit the more remote areas of the country.

FIELD GUIDES Finding good, detailed field guides to plants, animals and birds in Zambia is becoming much easier. There are now very comprehensive guides on the flora and fauna of southern Africa, which remain invaluable in Zambia. However, for total coverage there are also many smaller guides, published in Zambia by the Wildlife and Environmental Conservation Society of Zambia (see pages 51–2), covering snakes, trees, wild flowers, birds and the like, and ideal for general game viewing and birdwatching. There's even a comprehensive guide to the Zambian bird species that have been excluded from the southern Africa guides, and – at the other end of the scale – a heavy but very comprehensive guide to the birds of sub-Saharan Africa. (See *Appendix 3,* page 511, for more details.)

CONSERVATION

A great deal has been written about the conservation of animals in Africa; much of it is over-simplistic and intentionally emotive. As an informed visitor you are in the unique position of being able to see some of the issues at first hand, and to appreciate the perspectives of local people. So abandon your preconceptions, and start by appreciating the complexities of the issues involved. Here I shall try to develop a few ideas common to most current thinking on conservation, ideas to which the text in the rest of the book only briefly alludes.

Firstly, conservation must be taken within its widest sense if it is to have meaning. Saving animals is of minimal use if the whole environment is degraded, so we must consider conserving whole areas and ecosystems, not just the odd isolated species.

Observe that land is regarded as an asset by most societies, in Africa as it is elsewhere. To 'save' the land for the animals, and use it merely for the recreation of a few privileged foreign tourists, is a recipe for huge social problems – especially if the local people remain excluded from benefit and in poverty. Local people have hunted animals for food for centuries. They have always killed game that threatened them, or ruined their crops. If we now try to protect animals in populated areas without addressing the concerns of the people, then our efforts will fail.

The only pragmatic way to conserve Zambia's wild areas is to see the development of the local people, and the conservation of the animals and the environment, as inter-linked goals.

In the long term, one will not work without the other. Conservation without development leads to resentful locals who will happily, and frequently, shoot, trap and kill animals. Development without conservation will simply repeat the mistakes that most developed countries have already made: it will lay waste a beautiful land and kill off its natural heritage. Look at the tiny areas of undisturbed natural vegetation that survive in the UK, the USA or Japan. See how unsuccessful we in the northern hemisphere have been at long-term conservation over the past 500 years.

As an aside, the local people in Zambia are sometimes wrongly accused of being the only agents of degradation. Many would like to see 'poachers' shot on sight, and slash-and-burn agriculture banned. But observe the importation of tropical hardwoods by the West to see the problems that our demands place on the natural environment in the developing world.

In conserving some of Zambia's natural areas and assisting the development of its people, the international community has a vital role to play. It could effectively encourage the Zambian government to practise sustainable long-term strategies, rather than grasping for the short-term fixes which politicians seem universally to prefer. But such solutions must have the backing of the people themselves, or they will fall apart when the foreign aid budgets eventually wane.

In practice, to get this backing from the local communities it is not enough for a conservation strategy to be compatible with development. Most Zambians are more concerned about where they live, what they can eat and how they will survive, than they are about the lives of small, obscure species of antelope that taste good when roasted.

To succeed in Africa, conservation must not only be compatible with development, it must actually promote it. It must actively help the local people to improve their own standard of living. If that situation can be reached, then local communities can be mobilised behind long-term conservation initiatives.

Governments are the same. As Luangwa's late conservationist Norman Carr once commented, 'governments won't conserve an impala just because it is pretty'. But they will work to save it if they can see that it is worth more to them alive than dead.

The best strategies tried so far on the continent attempt to find lucrative and sustainable ways to use the land. They then plough much of the revenue back into the surrounding local communities. Once the local communities see revenue from conservation being used to help them improve their lives – to build houses, clinics and schools, and to offer paid employment – then such schemes rapidly get their backing and support.

Carefully planned, sustainable tourism is one solution that can work effectively. For success, the local communities must see that the visitors pay because they want the wildlife. Thus, they reason that the existence of wildlife directly improves their income, and they will strive to conserve it.

It isn't enough for people to see that the wildlife helps the government to get richer; that won't dissuade a local hunter from shooting a duiker for dinner. However, if he is directly benefiting from the visitors, who come to see the animals, then he has a vested interest in saving that duiker.

It matters little to the Zambian people, or ultimately to wildlife species, whether these visitors come to shoot the wildlife with a camera or with a gun. The vital issue is whether the hunting is done on a sustainable basis (ie: only a few of the oldest 'trophy' animals are shot each year, so that the size of the animal population remains largely unaffected).

Photographers may claim the moral high ground, but should remember that hunters pay far more for their privileges. Hunting operations generate large revenues from few guests, who demand minimal infrastructure and so cause little impact on the land. Photographic operations need more visitors to generate the same revenue, and so generally cause greater negative effects on the country.

The Zambian body responsible for conservation is the National Heritage Conservation Commission (NHCC), whose headquarters is in Livingstone (*Heritage House, Mosi-oa-Tunya Rd; PO Box 60124, Livingstone;* \ *021 3320481;* e *nhcchq@zamnet.zm*). The commission publishes a biannual magazine, *Zambia Heritage*.

TOURISM Zambia lies in the heart of sub-Saharan Africa. To the northeast lie the 'original' safari areas of east Africa: Kenya and Tanzania. Some of their best parks are now rather crowded, though their wildlife spectacles are still on a grand scale. South of Zambia are the more subtle attractions of Zimbabwe, Botswana and Namibia. Each country draws its own type of wildlife enthusiasts, and all have an element of wilderness that can seem difficult to find in east Africa today.

All have embraced tourism in different ways. Zambia is fortunate in having addressed this question later than the others, with the chance to learn from the mistakes of its neighbours. It is hoped that sustainable tourism can be a saviour of Zambia's economy as well as its wildlife, though there is a long way to go before tourism contributes a sizeable slice of the country's revenue.

Tourism is helping Zambia – both in economic terms and with conservation. It is providing employment and bringing foreign exchange into the country, which gives the politicians a reason to support the preservation of the parks. Increasingly Zambia's small-scale safari operators have mobilised themselves behind local development objectives, and in recent years we're seeing very positive initiatives for tourism to help development and sustainable land use, both inside and outside of Zambia's national parks.

The visitor on an expensive safari is generally, by his or her mere presence, making a financial contribution to development and conservation in Zambia. See pages 82–3 for ways in which you can support small local charities which directly help the people of Zambia. When on safari, one very simple thing that you can do to help is to question your safari operator, in the most penetrating of terms:

- Besides employment, how do local people benefit from this camp?
- How much of this camp's revenue goes directly back to the local people?
- What are you doing to help the people living near this reserve?
- How much control do the local people have over what goes on in the area where these safaris operate?

If more visitors did this, it would make a huge difference. If all safari operators felt that the majority of their clients wanted them to be involved with community development, then they would rapidly get involved.

At present most operators do have programmes to help their local communities. They've already realised that the mass of Zambian people must benefit more (and more directly) from tourism if conservation is going to be successful in Zambia.

HUNTING Big-game hunting, where visiting hunters pay large amounts to kill trophy animals, is practised on a number of private ranches and hunting areas. It is also a valuable source of revenue in the long term for people living in the country's game management areas (GMAs). In some this is already working, whilst in others development agencies, including the World Wide Fund for Nature (WWF), are working to start up sustainable schemes.

NATIONAL PARKS AND GMAS In practice, there is room for both types of visitors in Zambia: the photographer and the hunter. The national parks are designated for

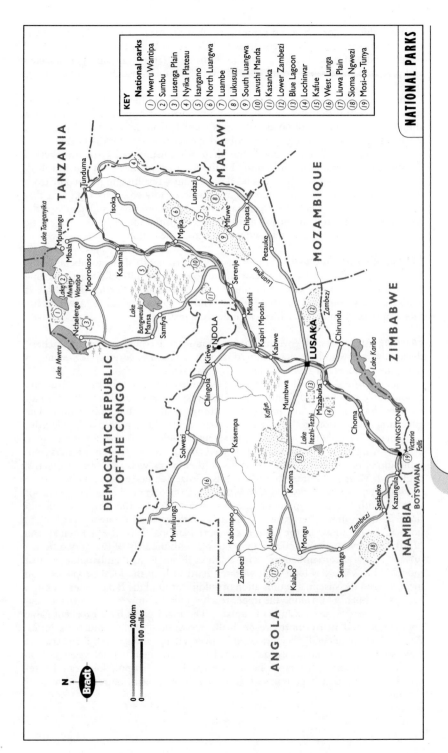

NATIONAL PARKS

KEY
National parks
1. Mweru Wantipa
2. Sumbu
3. Lusenga Plain
4. Nyika Plateau
5. Isangano
6. North Luangwa
7. Luambe
8. Lukusuzi
9. South Luangwa
10. Lavushi Manda
11. Kasanka
12. Lower Zambezi
13. Blue Lagoon
14. Lochinvar
15. Kafue
16. West Lunga
17. Liuwa Plain
18. Sioma Ngwezi
19. Mosi-oa-Tunya

photographic visitors; here no hunting is allowed. Around these are large areas designated as game management areas (GMAs). GMAs contain villages and local people, and hence small-scale farms, but hunting is (at least in theory) controlled and practised sustainably. Both local and overseas hunters use these, and the latter usually pay handsomely for the privilege.

Integral to this model is that the GMAs provide a buffer between the pristine national park and the land outside where uncontrolled hunting is allowed. This should serve to protect the national park's animals from incursions by poachers, whilst the park acts as a large gene pool and species reservoir for the GMA.

The theory of GMAs is good, but their administration has many practical difficulties. In some of them hunting by the local people has been uncontrolled, and in a few much of the game has been wiped out – resulting in no income from the wildlife, and so more pressure to hunt unsustainably. Many have projects that aim to reverse this trend, to regenerate their game resources and then set the communities off on a sustainable path. However, much more work needs to be done if there is to be a long-term effect felt across the country.

Zambia Wildlife Authority As part of the government's drive to liberalise the economy, government departments with the potential for self-sufficiency are being reformed. Several years ago the National Parks and Wildlife Service (NPWS) was disbanded, and replaced by the Zambia Wildlife Authority (ZAWA) which has more autonomy and greater financial independence.

Poaching After tales of government corruption and complicity with poachers, those travellers who have not ventured into Zambia can be forgiven for asking, 'Is there any game left in Zambia?' The answer is a definitive 'Yes'.

The 1970s and especially the 1980s saw rampant hunting in the GMAs, and considerable poaching of Zambia's national parks – partly small-scale hunting for food by local people, and partly large commercial poaching operations. The government reaction to this was a mixture of indifference and, allegedly, complicity. The only national park with an appreciable number of foreign visitors, South Luangwa, was effectively defended from all but the most persistent infiltrations of specialist rhino-poachers. Other parks were, to various extents, neglected. Most still suffer from the results of that past neglect even now.

However, various parks and GMAs are now, once again, being developed for visitors. With that development comes a reason to protect the parks (as well as a financial motivation – see page 37). Kafue's game populations are almost back to normal, as are those in the Lower Zambezi National Park. Both Kasanka and North Luangwa are being effectively protected with the help of two very different private conservation initiatives, whilst Liuwa Plain is just embarking on that model. The WWF has long been working hard to help the local people earn an income from the sustainable utilisation of wildlife around the Bangweulu Swamps. Camps are opening up along the upper reaches of the Zambezi.

So the message from Zambia is upbeat. The main parks have excellent game populations and many more are gradually recovering. Unlike much of Africa, Zambia has not generally been ravaged by overgrazing, and so even the parks that have suffered from poaching have usually retained their natural vegetation in pristine condition. This gives hope that good game populations can be re-established, and that large tracts of Zambia will once again be returned to their natural state.

4

Planning and Preparation

Tourists still come to Zambia in small numbers, and largely restrict themselves to a few of the main towns and national parks. Away from these centres, visitors are regarded with mild curiosity and often shown great warmth and hospitality. Zambia is a genuinely friendly country which (perhaps Lusaka excepted) has not yet had enough bad experiences of visitors to lower its opinion of them.

Zambia's attitude to tourism has changed considerably over the past few years, and visitors are now generally seen as good for the country because they spend valuable foreign currency and create employment. Tourism is helping both Zambia's economy and – by making a major contribution to the preservation of the national parks – its conservation policy.

WHEN TO GO

Virtually all of Zambia's tourists come during the dry season, and mostly from August to early October. Zambia's small camps and lodges ensure that it never feels busy, even when everywhere is full. (In fact, the country's capacity for tourism remains tiny compared with that of anywhere else in east or southern Africa.)

Most of those visiting outside of this season are cognoscenti, who visit early or late in the season – May to July or November – when the camps are quieter and often costs are lower. Meanwhile, only a handful of visitors come during the rains, from December to April. The camps that do open then will often be quiet for days. Their rates can be much lower, and they're often far more flexible about bringing children on safari.

Much of the blame for this 'glut or famine' of visitors lies with overseas tour operators. Many who advertise trips here just don't know Zambia well enough to organise trips in the rainy season, when there are fewer internal flights, and the connections can be more awkward. It's much easier for them to make blanket generalisations like 'it's not possible' or 'not interesting' or that 'you won't see any game' if you visit in the wet season, none of which is true – but most people don't know this in advance.

While the rains are not the ideal time for everybody's trip, they are a fascinating time to visit and should not be dismissed without serious thought.

WEATHER – THE DRY OR WET SEASON? See the section on *Climate*, pages 29–32, for a detailed description of the weather that can be expected, and note that Zambia's rainy season occurs around December to April (slightly different every year).

The **dry season** (May to November) is the easiest time to travel, as then you are unlikely to meet rain and can expect clear blue skies. This is ideal if this is your first trip to Africa, or if seeing lots of big game is top of your wish list.

Within this, you'll find June–August the coolest, and then from September onwards the heat gradually builds up. Note that where the altitude is relatively low

4

– like the Luangwa, the Lower Zambezi Valley or Lake Tanganyika – the temperature is always higher. These places, especially, can get very hot towards the end of October, and occasions of over 40°C in the shade in the middle of the day have earned October the tag of 'suicide month' amongst the locals.

November is a variable month, but many days can be cooler than October, as the gathering clouds shield the earth from the sun. On some days these bring welcome showers; on others they simply build, and with them come tension and humidity. It's always an interesting month.

The **wet season**, December to March, is totally different, and the days can vary enormously from one to the next. Even within a day, skies will often change from sunny to cloudy within minutes and then back again. Downpours are usually heavy and short, and often in the late afternoon. Even in the lower valleys, temperatures are pleasant, rising to only around 30°C, and the nights only slightly cooler (typically down to perhaps 15°C). You will need a good waterproof for the rainy season, but it seldom rains for long enough to really stop you doing anything. Except travelling on bush roads …

Travelling Travelling around Zambia in the dry season often has its challenges – but in the wet season it's a totally different game. Most untarred roads become quagmires; many are completely impassable. The rivers swell to bursting, often beyond, as their surging brown waters undermine trees and carry them downstream like Pooh-sticks. Streams that were ankle-deep in October become potential rafting challenges. Many rural areas are cut off for a few months, so getting anywhere away from the main routes can be tricky.

However, if you are planning to fly into a national park for a safari, then the South Luangwa remains a possibility. Flights there are less frequent, but still run. It is the only one of Zambia's national parks to remain open. A few camps also welcome visitors and use the park's network of all-weather roads for driving safaris. One camp, based beside the park and upriver, runs canoeing and boating safaris. If you've often been to Africa in the dry season, then this is a fascinating time to visit – like being introduced to a different side of an old friend.

Vegetation During the wet season, the foliage runs wild. The distinctive oxbow lagoons of the Luangwa and Lower Zambezi fill, while trees everywhere are deeply green. The open sandy plains become verdant meadows, often with shallow pools of water. It's a time of renewal, when a gentler light dapples Zambia's huge forests and areas of bush.

When the rains end, the leaves gradually dry and many eventually drop. More greys and browns appear, and good shade becomes harder to find. Eventually, by late September and October, most plants look dry and parched, coloured from straw-yellow to shrivelled brown.

Game From the point of view of most herbivores, the wet season is a much more pleasant time. Those in national parks live in enormous salad bowls, with convenient pools of water nearby. It's a good time to have their young and eat themselves into good condition. Val and Bob Leyland were the first visitors for whom I ever organised a trip during the rains. On returning, they commented that 'having [previously] visited Africa last dry season, there's something special about seeing all the animals when they aren't struggling with thirst and a lack of vegetation … It gives a sense of luxuriance which isn't there in the dry season.'

Visiting South Luangwa in the wet season you will see game, but probably less of it. Last trip during the rains I went on two night drives. On the first we saw a good range of antelope (including some wonderful sightings of young animals), a few elephant and buffalo and a leopard at the end of the evening. The next we found a hyena on a kill, and later followed three lionesses hunting for several hours. The birding was consistently phenomenal, far better than during the dry season.

However, if game viewing is your priority, or this is one of your first trips to Africa, then the animals are much easier to spot when it's dry, as no thick vegetation obscures the view. Further, they are forced to congregate at well-known water points, like rivers, where they can be observed. Many more tracks are navigable in the bush, and so more areas can be explored by vehicle. So if you want to see large numbers of animals, then do come to Zambia in the dry season – and later rather than earlier if possible.

A few specific animal highlights include:

Feb–May Most of the herbivores are in their best condition, having fed well on the lush vegetation.

May–Aug Leopard are generally easier to see, as they come out more during the twilight hours. Later in the year they often come out later in the evening, waiting until it is cool.

Sept–Oct Buffalo groups tend to amalgamate into larger, more spectacular herds. (They splinter again just before the rains.) Lion sightings become more frequent, as they spend more time near the limited remaining water sources.

Oct–Dec Crocodiles are nesting, so are found on or near exposed sandbanks.

Nov The great wildebeest migration masses on Liuwa Plain, in western Zambia. It's still accessible, but you'll need a small expedition to witness it.

Nov–Mar Baby warthogs and impala start to appear in November, followed by most of the mammals that calve sometime during the rainy season.

Birdlife The birdlife in Zambia is certainly best when the foliage is most dense, and the insects are thriving: in the wet season. Then many resident birds are nesting and in their bright, breeding plumage. This coincides to a large extent with the 'summer' period, from around October to March, when the Palaearctic migrants from the northern hemisphere are seen.

Certainly in terms of waterbirds – storks, herons, ducks, geese and the smaller waders – the rainy season (and just after) is an infinitely better time to visit. The birding calendar's highlights include:

March–July Large breeding colonies of storks and herons gather to breed. The only sites I know are in the Nsefu sector of the South Luangwa National Park.

August–October 'Fishing parties' of herons, egrets and storks will arrive at pools as they dry up, to feed on the stranded fish.

September–November Carmine bee-eaters form large nesting colonies in the soft sand of vertical riverbanks.

October–November Pennant-winged nightjars are in resplendent breeding plumage.

November–April Most of the weavers are in breeding plumage.

February–April Fire-crowned bishop birds, yellow-billed storks and the spectacular paradise whydahs have their breeding plumage on display.

April–June Resident African skimmers are nesting.

Photography I find the light clearest and most spectacular during the rainy season. Then the rains have washed the dust from the air, and the bright sunlight can contrast wonderfully with dark storm clouds. The vegetation's also greener and brighter, and the animals and birds often in better condition.

However, it will rain occasionally when you're trying to take shots, and the long periods of flat, grey light through clouds can be very disappointing. Sometimes it can seem as if you're waiting for the gods to grant you just a few minutes of stunning light, between the clouds. A more practical time is probably just after the rains, around April to June, when at least you are less likely to be interrupted by a shower.

The dry season's light is reliably good, if not quite as inspirational as that found during the rains. You are unlikely to encounter any clouds, and will get better sightings of game to photograph. Do try to shoot in the first and last few hours of the day, when the sun is low in the sky. During the rest of the day use a filter (perhaps a polariser) to guard against the sheer strength of the light leaving you with a film full of washed-out shots.

Walking safaris For safe and interesting walking, you need the foliage to be low so that you can see through the surrounding bush as easily as possible. This means that the dry season is certainly the best time for walking. Walking in the wet season, through shoulder-high grass, is possible – but I'd only go with a very experienced guide and it is harder than during the dry season. My favourite months for walking are June to September, as October can get hot on longer walks.

Fishing The best times to fish in Zambia depend on the area. In the north, on Lake Tanganyika, the rainy season is ideal, between November and March, but that period is off limits for fishing in many areas of the country. On Zambia's great rivers, such as the Zambezi, Kafue and Luangwa, fishing is at its best when the waters are clear. This usually happens from around May–June and lasts until the end of November. Although it is cold during those months the fish are there and will usually fall to bait and spinner, and even fly.

There is a ban on fishing during the months of December to February for all Zambian waters, with the exception of Lake Tanganyika, Lake Kariba, and private dams.

ⓘ TOURIST INFORMATION The Zambia National Tourist Board (*PO Box 30017, Lusaka Sq, Cairo Rd, Lusaka;* ✆ *021 122 9087;* f *021 122 5174; www.zambiatourism.com*) offers consumer and general information, and visa advice to potential travellers. It has a good website, and three offices overseas:

South Africa 570 Ziervogel St (off Hamilton St), PO Box 12234, Hatfield 0083, Pretoria; ✆ +27 12 3261847, 3261854; f +27 12 3262140; e tourism@zambiapretoria.net

UK 2 Palace Gate, London W8 5NG; ✆ 020 7589 6655; f 020 7581 1353, 0546; e zntb@aol.com
USA 2419 Massachusetts Av, NW Washington, DC 20008; ✆ 202 265 9717; f 202 332 0826; e zntbusa@aol.com

For details of other websites offering tourist information, see page 513.

PUBLIC HOLIDAYS

New Year's Day	1 January
Youth Day	around 11–13 March
Good Friday	
Holy Saturday	
Labour Day	1 May
Africa Freedom Day	25 May
Heroes' Day	first Monday of July
Unity Day	first Tuesday of July
Farmers' Day	first Monday of August
Independence Day	24 October
Christmas Day	25 December
Boxing Day	26 December

ORGANISING A SAFARI

Most visitors who come to Zambia for few weeks' safari stay at some of the small safari camps. Combinations of time in Kafue, the Luangwa Valley, the Lower Zambezi and a few days around the falls would be typical.

WHEN TO BOOK These trips are not cheap, but nor should they be difficult for a knowledgeable operator to arrange. If you have favourite camps, or a tight schedule, then book as far ahead as you can. Eight to ten months in advance is perfect. Bear in mind that most camps are small, and thus easily filled. They organise their logistics with military precision and so finding space at short notice, especially in the busier months, can be tricky. (The exception to this rule is usually the rainy season.)

If you are looking to travel in the next few months, then one or two of your chosen camps may be full; you'll have to accept alternatives.

HOW MUCH? Safaris in Zambia are not cheap. Expect to pay US$2,600–5,000/£1,300–2,500 per person sharing per week, plus international airfares. This would include a few of your internal transfers or flights, camp transfers, meals, activities, laundry, park fees and even drinks. It isn't cheap, so you should expect a good level of service from the operator who is arranging it for you. If you don't get it, go elsewhere.

HOW TO BOOK It's best to arrange everything together, using a reliable, independent tour operator. Many operators sell trips to Zambia, but few know the country well. Insist on dealing directly with someone who does. Zambia is changing fast, so up-to-date local knowledge is vital in putting together a trip that runs smoothly and suits you. Make sure that whoever you book with is bonded, so your money is protected if they go broke. If you're unsure, pay with a credit card. Never book a trip from someone who hasn't spent time there – you are asking for problems. Ask the person you're dealing with specifically, 'Have you been to this camp or place?'

Booking directly with most Zambian camps is easily possible; the camps are the easy bit. Once they are organised, you need to piece together the jigsaw puzzle of transfers, internal flights and stopovers to link them into your trip. Without local knowledge, this can be tricky – and you will have little recourse if anything goes wrong.

European, US and local operators usually work on commission for the trips that they sell, which is deducted from the basic cost that the visitor pays. Thus you should end up paying the same whether you book through an overseas operator, or talk directly to a camp in Zambia.

4

Perhaps because of the UK's historical links, or the high number of British safari-goers, there seems to be more competition amongst UK tour operators than elsewhere. Hence they've a reputation for being generally cheaper than US operators for the same trips.

TOUR OPERATORS Zambia is something of a touchstone for tour operators to southern Africa: those who know Zambia well are the small core of Africa specialists. Most operators can send you to Cape Town with ease. But ask them where to visit in Zambia, and you'll rapidly sort those that know southern Africa from those that haven't got a clue.

Don't let anyone convince you that there are only three first-class safari camps in Zambia, as it's rubbish. If your operator doesn't know most of the camps in this book – and offer a wide choice to suit you – then use one that does.

Here I must, as the author, admit a personal interest in the tour operating business. I run the UK operator Expert Africa (see below), which is currently the leading operator to Zambia, and also organises trips for travellers to Africa from all over the world (especially America). Booking your trip with us (or, indeed, some other tour operators) will always cost you the same as or less than if you contacted Zambia's camps directly – plus you have the benefit of independent advice, full financial protection, and experts to make the arrangements for you. Expert Africa has probably the most comprehensive choice of the best Zambian lodges, camps and destinations available anywhere. In Zambia our safaris are completely flexible, depending on where you want to go. They start at about US$4,000/£2,000 per person for a week, including flights from London, accommodation, meals and game activities.

For a fair comparison, African tour operators featuring Zambia include:

In the UK

Aardvark Safaris RBL Hse, Ordnance Rd, Tidworth, Hants SP9 7QD; ☏ 01980 849160; f 01980 849161; e mail@aardvarksafaris.com; www.aardvarksafaris.com. Small, reliable upmarket safari specialist to Africa & Madagascar.

Abercrombie & Kent St George's House, Ambrose St, Cheltenham, Glos GL50 3LG; ☏ 0845 070 0600; www.abercrombiekent.co.uk. Worldwide holidays for groups & individuals to upmarket destinations with upmarket price tags.

Acacia Adventure Holidays 23a Craven Terr, London W2 3QH; ☏ 020 7706 4700; f 020 7706 4686; www.acacia-africa.com. Adventure holidays & overland/camping safaris throughout Africa.

Africa Explorer 5 Strand on the Green, London W4 3PQ; ☏ 020 8987 8742; f 020 8994 6264; www.africa-explorer.co.uk. Tiny but knowledgeable company with unusual, large 6-wheeled self-contained vehicles for hire.

Africa Travel Centre 21 Leigh St, London WC1H 9EW; ☏ 0845 450 1520, 1541; www.africatravel.co.uk. General operator offering trips across Africa & the Indian Ocean, with emphasis on sport travel.

Audley Travel New Mill, New Mill Lane, Witney, Oxon OX29 9SX; ☏ 01993 838500; e info@audleytravel.com; www.audleytravel.com. Large tailor-made operator offering trips worldwide from Burma to New Zealand; their Africa programme was built from scratch in 2003.

Cazenove & Loyd 9 Imperial Studios, 3–11 Imperial Rd, London SW6 2AG; ☏ 020 7384 2332; f 020 7384 2399; www.caz-loyd.com. Top-end tailor-made specialists to Africa, Indian Ocean Islands, Latin America & the Indian subcontinent.

Crusader 57 Church St, Twickenham, Middx TW1 3NR; ☏ 020 8744 0474; f 020 8744 0574; www.crusadertravel.com. Large worldwide operator with a Zambian programme.

Expert Africa Upper Sq, Old Isleworth, Middx TW7 7BJ; ☏ 020 8232 9777; f 020 8568 8330; www.expertafrica.com. Specialists to southern & east Africa; the UK's main operators to Zambia, with a wide range of unusual options – run by this book's author.

Gane & Marshall 7th Floor, Northway Hse, 1379 High St, London N20 9LP; ☏ 020 8445 6000; f 020 8445 6615; www.ganeandmarshall.co.uk. Large worldwide operator with a Zambian programme.

Hartley's Safaris The Old Chapel, Chapel La, Hackthorn, Lincs LN2 3PN; ☏ 01673 861600; f 01673 861666; www.hartleys-safaris.co.uk. Long-established tailor-made specialists to east & southern Africa & Indian Ocean islands.

Journeys by Design 36 Park Cres, Brighton BN2 3HB; ☎ 01273 623790; f 01273 621766; www.journeysbydesign.co.uk. Small tailor-made operator (ground arrangements only) featuring east & southern Africa.

Kamili Safaris 3 Townend Cottages, Plumtree, Nottingham NG12 5LZ; ☎ 0115 937 7475; www.kamilisafaris.com. Represents a handful of smaller, offbeat lodges throughout southern Africa.

Nomad African Travel 14 Sharpes Hill, Barrow, Bury St Edmunds, Suffolk IP29 5BY; ☎ 01284 810101; e nomadat@onetel.com; www.nomadafricantravel.co.uk. Small UK operator specialising in set guided tours, with tailor-made options.

Okavango Tours & Safaris Marlborough House, 298 Regents Park Rd, London N3 2TJ; ☎ 020 8343 3283; f 020 8343 3287; www.okavango.com. Tailor-made specialists to Africa & Indian Ocean islands, with a good knowledge of Zambia.

Safari Consultants Africa Hse, 2 Cornard Mills, Cornard Tye, Great Cornard, Suffolk CO10 0GW; ☎ 01787 888590; www.safari-consultants.co.uk. Long-established tailor-made specialists to east & southern Africa, & Indian Ocean islands, with a good knowledge of Zambia.

Safari Drive The Trainer's Office, Windy Hollow, Sheepdrove, Lambourn, Berks RG17 7XA; ☎ 01488 71140; www.safaridrive.com. African operator specialising in self-drive trips in 4x4s.

Scott Dunn World 12 Fovant Mews, Noyna Rd, London SW17 7PH; ☎ 020 8682 5000, 5070; f 020 8682 5090; www.scottdunn.com. Worldwide coverage (everywhere except North America), with a tailor-made programme to Zambia.

Steppes Africa 51 Castle St, Cirencester, Glos GL7 1QD; ☎ 01285 650011; f 01285 885888; www.steppesafrica.co.uk. Upmarket tailor-made specialists to Africa & the Indian Ocean islands.

Tim Best Travel 4 Cromwell Pl, London SW7 2JE; ☎ 020 7591 0300; f 020 7591 0301; www.timbesttravel.com. Upmarket holidays to Africa, the Indian Ocean islands & Latin America.

Tribes Travel 12 The Business Centre, Earl Soham, Woodbridge, Suffolk IP13 7SA; ☎ 01728 685971; f 01728 685973; www.tribes.co.uk. Worldwide travel on fair-trade principles; particularly strong on cultural trips.

Wildlife Worldwide Long Barn South, Sutton Manor Farm, Bishop's Sutton, Alresford, Hants SO24 0AA; ☎ 020 8667 9158; e sales@wildlifeworldwide.com; www.wildlifeworldwide.com. Worldwide operator offering tailor-made & small-group wildlife holidays to all corners of the globe.

Zambezi Safari & Travel Company Ermington Mill, nr Ivybridge, Devon PL1 9NT; ☎ 01548 830059; www.zambezi.com. Specialist safari planners with offices in Africa & UK, concentrating on small, owner-run operators throughout Africa.

In the USA

Adventure Center 1311 63rd St, Suite 200, Emeryville, CA 94608; ☎ 510 654 1879; f 510 654 4200; www.adventurecenter.com

Adventure Travel Desk (ATD) 308 Commonwealth Rd, Wayland, MA 01778-5006; ☎ 508 653 4600; f 508 655 5672; www.otid.com

David Anderson Safaris 30 W Mission Str, #7, Santa Barbara, CA 93101; ☎ 800 733 6732, 805 884 0600; www.davidanderson.com

Geographic Expeditions 1008 General Kennedy Av, PO Box 29902, San Francisco, CA 94129-0902; ☎ 415 922 0448; f 415 346 5535; www.geoex.com

In Australia

The Classic Safari Company 109 Queen St, Woollahra, NSW 2025; ☎ 612 9327 0666; f 612 9327 0667; www.classicsafaricompany.com.au

In Malawi

Land & Lake Safaris ☎ +265 1757120, 1754303; ☎/f +265 1754560; www.landlake.net

Local tour operators Individual operators based in Zambia are listed in the chapter most relevant to their operations.

Warning One or two slippery overseas operators offer apparently inexpensive trips in small groups to Zambia. In their glossy literature, they avoid specifying exactly which camps they use for particular trips, referring simply to 'remote bushcamps'

or 'nice comfortable lodges'. They'll avoid specifying camp names, despite the fact that all Zambia's camps do have names (even the smallest bushcamps).

They do this so that they can swap around your trip without your knowledge at the last minute. They'll then bargain down the cost of the camp that they have booked, or even swap your group into a cheaper alternative. It's a shoddy way to do business.

Your group won't then get the best of what's available, and it's a particularly bad way to treat the local operators. The camp that you end up at will then cut corners, perhaps by using less experienced guides or taking you to the less interesting areas. You won't get the quality of service or catering that they'd usually give – and I know of cases where visitors have even been asked to pay extra for night drives.

Usually the operator pockets any savings, and you're left with a poorer trip. It's best to avoid any company that doesn't specify (*in writing* to you) exactly which camps are included in your trip, and how long you are going to stay at each. There's never a good reason why they can't do this.

SUGGESTED ITINERARIES Those backpacking and driving themselves around Zambia need time but have great flexibility, and part of the adventure of such a trip is having no itinerary. However, most visitors have a much shorter time available.

Fly-in trips If you're flying in, then getting your itinerary right and arranging it carefully in advance is important. For most visitors to Zambia, the four main areas of attraction are the Luangwa Valley, Kafue National Park, the Lower Zambezi Valley and Livingstone. All are parks worth visiting for a week (less than three nights in a park is really too short), and there's often a slight saving if you spend at least a week exclusively with one operator. For most people, a visit to Livingstone takes two to three nights.

When designing a trip, bear in mind that:

- Keen walkers would usually include the Luangwa, and include some of the smaller 'walking bushcamps' in their trip.
- For the variety offered by water-based activities, it's good to visit the Lower Zambezi or the Kafue.
- If you want to visit North Luangwa, then first spend a few days in the South Park before perhaps three to five nights in North Luangwa.
- Shiwa Ng'andu works really well for three or four nights, ideally as part of the trip that passes through South Luangwa (as the closest place for flights in Mfuwe).
- Kasanka, Bangweulu and Shiwa work well together, usually in that sequence.

Some combinations that work well are:

Short trips
- 7 nights South Luangwa, or Lower Zambezi, or Kafue
- 2–3 nights Livingstone plus 5–6 nights Kafue, or vice versa

Slightly longer trips
- 5–6 nights South Luangwa plus 4 nights North Luangwa
- 5–6 nights South Luangwa plus 3–4 nights Shiwa Ng'andu
- 5–6 nights Kafue plus 4 nights Lower Zambezi
- 5–6 nights Kafue or Lower Zambezi or South Luangwa, plus 2–3 nights Livingstone

Two weeks If you've got about two weeks, then the obvious option is to devote a week each to two of the main three parks. Alternatively, for something a bit more offbeat, look at:

- 8 nights South Luangwa or Kafue or Lower Zambezi, plus 3 nights Lechwe Lodge, plus 3 nights Livingstone
- For a broader view of more offbeat areas, consider 3 nights Kasanka, 3 nights Bangweulu (especially green season), 4 nights Shiwa Ng'andu, 4 nights South Luangwa
- Keen birdwatchers would be very tempted by 6 nights Kafue, plus 4 nights Nchila Reserve, plus 3–4 nights Lochinvar

4x4 trips If you're an experienced Africa hand, driving in your own self-contained vehicle in the dry season, then the choices are much wider. All such trips are long; they're effectively mini-expeditions. The country is your oyster, but there are two obvious routes, and a third that's rather more offbeat, each taking at least three weeks:

Western circuit Livingstone – Upper Zambezi – Mongu – Liuwa Plain – Mongu – Lukulu – West Lunga – Nchila Reserve – Kafue (from northern tip right through to southern tip) – Livingstone.

Eastern circuit Lusaka – Kasanka – Lake Waka Waka – Bangweulu – Mutinondo Wilderness – Shiwa Ng'andu – transit through North Luangwa – Luambe – South Luangwa – Lusaka.

Northern circuit This suggestion, perhaps for those who have already visited some of the country's highlights, could take you north, visiting some of the lesser-known waterfalls and the Lake Tanganyika area: Lusaka – Kasanka – Bangweulu – Luapula River – Sumbu National Park – Kasama – Shiwa Ng'andu – Mutinondo Wilderness – Lusaka.

NATIONAL PARKS

Head office Currently all of Zambia's national parks fall under the control of the Zambia Wildlife Authority – known simply as the ZAWA (*Private Bag 1, Chilanga, Zambia;* ❭ *021 1278524, 1278366;* f *021 1278244;* e *info@zawa.org.zm; www.zawa.org.zm*). See also *Chapter 3*, page 40. They set the rules and administer the parks from their head office near Chilanga, about 20km south of Lusaka. If you want to do anything unusual, or to go to any of the more remote parks, then it will make your trip easier if you buy your permits in advance from Chilanga. Address written requests to the Director General, and note that telephoning or calling in person is much more effective than emailing or faxing. Having cleared your trip with them, get some written permission that looks official: a letter from Chilanga and the appropriate permits work wonders at even the most remote scout camps. Failing this, the next best option is to try to get permission for your trip at one of the regional ZAWA offices – which may be easier than negotiating with the scouts on the gate.

Park entry fees Most organised trips will include park entry fees in their costs, but if you are travelling on your own then you must pay these directly, either at one of the ZAWA offices or at the park gates themselves. There is a scale of entry fees, with additional charges for taking a vehicle into the parks, and for camping. Fees vary, not just between parks, but according to the visitor, with non-residents paying significantly higher rates than residents, who in turn pay more

Gordon Rattray (www.able-travel.com)

Although Zambia's tourism infrastructure is developing fast, proper facilities for people with mobility problems are still rare. But don't let this put you off; depending on your ability and sense of adventure, most obstacles are surmountable and Africans are used to finding solutions for practical problems: if you need help, you will receive it.

PLANNING AND BOOKING Although there aren't many operators running specialised trips to Zambia for disabled people, most travel companies will listen to your needs and try to create an itinerary suitable for you. For the more independent traveller, it is possible to limit potential surprises by contacting local operators and establishments by email in advance.

ACCOMMODATION Lusaka's Holiday Inn (page 130) has one adapted room. In Livingstone, the Zambezi Sun (page 178) and the Royal Livingstone (page 177) have roll-in showers and bathroom grab-rails, and the less pricey Zig Zag Guesthouse (page 171) has fairly wide doorways and level access around the complex. I have yet to hear of completely accessible accommodation in any of Zambia's national parks.

TRANSPORT
Air travel Both Lusaka and Livingstone international airports have assistance, wheelchairs and aisle chairs for those who need help entering or leaving the aircraft. Livingstone also has accessible toilets and at the time of writing this feature is part of Lusaka's current 'five year plan'.

Buses and trains There is no effective legislation in Zambia to facilitate disabled travellers' journeys by public transport; therefore, if you cannot walk at all then both of these options are going to be difficult. You will need to ask for help from fellow passengers to lift you to your seat, it will often be crowded and it is unlikely that there will be an accessible toilet.

By car Distances are great and roads are often bumpy, so if you are prone to skin damage you need to take extra care. Place your own pressure-relieving cushion on top of (or instead of) the original car seat and if necessary, pad around knees and elbows.

than Zambian citizens. Current ZAWA fees for non-residents are as follows, per person, per day:

South Luangwa	US$35
Lower Zambezi	US$25
North Luangwa	US$20
Kafue	US$15
Mosi-oa-Tunya, Kasanka, Sumbu, Lochinvar	US$10
Other parks	US$5

On top of these, vehicles (up to 3 tonnes/50 hp) are charged at US$15 per day, and camping within the parks costs another US$5 per person per night.

In general, park offices accept US dollars, or UK pounds, euros or kwacha at the prevailing exchange rate, but they cannot take credit cards or travellers' cheques. Park offices are normally open 06.00–18.00.

If you're not sticking to the main roads, you will need to use a 4x4 vehicle, which will be higher than a normal car making transfers more difficult. Drivers/guides are normally happy to help, but are not trained in this skill, so you must thoroughly explain your needs and always stay in control of the situation.

Hemingways (see *Specialist operators*, below) can provide wheelchair accessible transport.

HEALTH AND INSURANCE Doctors will know about 'everyday' illnesses, but you must understand and be able to explain your own particular medical requirements. Zambian hospitals and pharmacies are often basic, so it is wise to take as much essential medication and equipment as possible with you, and it is advisable to pack this in your hand luggage during flights in case your main luggage gets lost. Zambia can be hot; if this is a problem for you then try to book accommodation with fans or air conditioning, and a useful cooling aid is a plant-spray bottle.

Travel insurance can be purchased in the UK from Age Concern (✆ 0845 601 2234; www.ageconcern.org.uk), who have no upper age limit, and Free Spirit (✆ 0845 230 5000; www.free-spirit.com), who cater for people with pre-existing medical conditions. Most insurance companies will insure disabled travellers, but it is essential that they are made aware of your disability.

SECURITY Although the vast majority of people will only want to help you, it is worth remembering that, as a disabled person, you are more vulnerable. Stay aware of who is around you and where your bags are, especially during car transfers and similar.

SPECIALIST OPERATORS
Hemingways ✆ +260 3 320996; m +260 97 7866492, 97 7870232; e info@hemingwayszambia.com; www.hemingwayszambia.com. Livingstone-based operator offering transfers & safaris using wheelchair-accessible vehicles.
Endeavour Safaris ✆/f +27 21 556 6114; m +27 73 206 7733; e info@endeavour-safaris.com; www.endeavour-safaris.com. Southern African specialists in accessible travel for disabled people.
Flamingo Tours ✆ +27 21 557 4496; f +27 21 556 5853; e info@flamingotours.co.za; www.flamingotours.co.za. Cape Town-based operator running trips for disabled travellers.
Titch Tours ✆ +27 21 686 5501; f +27 21 686 5506; e titcheve@iafrica.com; http://titchtours.co.za. Cape Town-based operator running trips for disabled travellers.

Guides For more adventurous trips to remote parks, hire a game scout from the nearest camp to act as your guide. This will save wasted driving time, and probably personal anguish over navigational puzzles. You may have to provide food for the scout, but even then this can be an inexpensive way to get a local guide who may be able to add a whole new dimension to your trip.

WECSZ The Wildlife and Environmental Conservation Society of Zambia (*4435 Kumoyo Rd, off Los Angeles Bd, PO Box 30255, Lusaka;* ✆/f *021 1251630;* e *wecsz@zamnet.zm; www.wcsz.org; open Mon–Fri 08.00–17.00; membership Kw250,000 pp per year*) was founded as the Wildlife Conservation Society of Zambia, changing its name in 1995 to emphasise its broader remit for the environment in its widest sense. Its work remains similar, supporting environmental education and awareness in Zambia. It sponsors various conservation activities, and runs innovative children's conservation clubs, like the Chongololo and Chipembele conservation clubs, and the related Chongololo Club of the Air (broadcast on Radio 2 each Sunday). It also publishes a number of good, inexpensive field guides specific to Zambia (see *Appendix 3*, page 511). As part of the commitment to education, the society contributes the weekly 'Environmental Notes by Warthog' that appear in Zambia's *Sunday Times*.

The WECSZ also owns several very simple camps in the national parks: Kafwala and Chibila camps in Kafue, and the Wildlife Camp at Mfuwe. Although these are managed by others, some of the revenue still comes back to the society. Bookings for these camps can be made in writing to the WECSZ, or in person at their offices in Lusaka. The society's books can also be bought here, or at one of the bookshops in town, as can its quarterly magazine, *Black Lechwe*. Well written, and with plenty of interesting articles, it is free to members, and available to non-members at Kw20,000 per issue.

GETTING THERE

✈ **BY AIR** However you get to the subcontinent, if you don't fly directly to Lusaka then do book your flight to Africa and any scheduled internal links between countries (eg: Nairobi–Lusaka or Johannesburg–Lusaka flights) at the same time. Booking the whole trip together is almost certain to save you money. Sometimes the airline taking you to Africa will have cheap regional flights within Africa; for example Johannesburg–Lusaka with British Airways is usually much cheaper if booked with a BA flight from London to Johannesburg, than it is if booked alone. At other times the tour operator you book through will have special deals if you book all the flights with them. And most importantly, if you book all your flights together then you'll be sure to get connecting ones, so you have the best schedule possible.

Departure tax Note that there is a US$25 departure tax for all international flights from Lusaka or Livingstone. Although the tax is now sometimes pre-paid on your ticket, this is not always the case, so be sure to check, ideally in advance of travel. If you're not sure, check at the airport, and ensure that you have sufficient dollars left over; credit cards will not be accepted.

From Europe The only direct flights to Zambia from Europe are run by British Airways (BA; *www.britishairways.com*), which operates three flights a week from London Heathrow. Various other airlines have connecting flights to Lusaka, usually through Nairobi, Addis Ababa or Johannesburg, but only BA flies direct.

These routes are mainly for business traffic and pre-booked holidays; finding cheap 'bucket-shop' tickets is usually difficult (if not impossible). Expect to pay about £550–650/US$1,100–1,300 for a return flight. Tour operators usually have access to slightly cheaper seats, but you will only be able to buy these if you are buying a complete holiday from them. (This often makes sense; see *Tour operators*, pages 46–8.)

If you want a cheap flight, but don't mind spending longer travelling, then consider using one of the nearby regional centres and connecting through to Zambia (see *From within Africa*, below). It used to be cheaper to fly to Harare than to Lusaka, but that's now changed, so there is no longer any advantage in taking that route. Johannesburg is certainly the busiest airport on the subcontinent, and most of the world's larger airlines have flights there, or at least connections. Other options include flying via Malawi, Dar es Salaam or Nairobi.

From within Africa Several operators have regular flights linking regional cities with Lusaka. From Johannesburg (JNB), South African Airways (SAA; *www.flysaa.com*) flies into Lusaka, and BA's subsidiary, Comair (*www.britishairways.com*)

has five flights a week to Livingstone. Zambian Airways (*www.zambianairways.com*) – a privately owned company rather than the state airline that the name suggests – has spread its wings beyond the domestic routes to offer daily flights connecting Johannesburg with Lusaka and Ndola, and also from Harare or Dar es Salaam to Lusaka at very interesting fares. Additionally, flights from Dar es Salaam are operated every day by Kenya Airways (*www.kenya-airways.com*), which also flies from Nairobi to Lusaka daily, and from Lilongwe. Another option is Ethiopian Airlines (*www.ethiopianairlines.com*), which has good fares and large luggage allowances. It's worth noting that Ethiopia is one of the few African countries from which the US government allows direct flights to and from the USA.

Between April and October, Air Malawi (*www.airmalawi.com*) has four flights a week to Lusaka from both Lilongwe and Blantyre. Flights operate on Sunday, Monday, Wednesday and Friday, returning the same day.

From North America If you are coming from the US then you will probably need to stop at London or Johannesburg to make connections to Zambia. There are no direct flights. Booking everything in the US may not save you money; investigate the flight prices in comparison with those available in London. Increasingly visitors from America are discovering that UK operators offer better-value safaris than their competitors in America. So consider buying a cheap ticket across the Atlantic, and then organising your Zambian trip through a reliable UK operator.

OVERLAND Most overland border posts open from about 06.00 to 18.00, although this is less rigidly adhered to at the smaller, more remote posts.

To/from South Africa or Namibia CR Holdings (*www.crholdings-zambia.com*) has one bus a week to Livingstone from Johannesburg, and a daily service between Lusaka and Johannesburg via Chirundu.

The South African Intercape Mainliner (*www.intercape.co.za*) has a regular bus between Windhoek and Livingstone, with onward connections through to Johannesburg. For self-drivers, there is a high-level bridge across the Zambezi. See *Chapter 15*, page 450, for more details.

To/from Zimbabwe Zambia's greatest flow of visitors comes from Zimbabwe, over the Livingstone–Victoria Falls border. Many visitors come over for just a day trip and locals come to shop, so this is usually a very relaxed and swift border crossing. The crossings over the Kariba Dam and at Chirundu are also straightforward, and the latter is especially good for hitchhiking on long-distance lorries, which ply the route from Harare to Lusaka.

To/from Botswana Despite their territories only meeting at a point, Botswana does have one border crossing with Zambia: a reliable ferry across the Zambezi linking Kazungula with the corner of Botswana, which costs about US$25/£13 per vehicle.

To/from Angola Certain areas of Angola are still not regarded as safe to visit, so do check with the Foreign and Commonwealth Office (*www.fco.gov.uk*) if you're planning to use this route. The easiest border post with Angola is near Chavuma, northwest of Zambezi town. Elsewhere in western Zambia there is a danger of accidentally wandering into Angola, as the border has few markings.

To/from Democratic Republic of Congo (formerly Zaire) There are numerous crossings between Zambia and the DRC, especially around the Copperbelt.

Otherwise there is a good track leading into DRC reached via Mwinilunga and Ikelenge. However, the DRC remains an unstable and potentially dangerous place to visit; you should check on the latest security situations before crossing the border, and be careful not to stray across by accident if you're in the Copperbelt region or heading east near Mkushi.

To/from Tanzania Many visitors from Tanzania enter Zambia by ferryboat across Lake Tanganyika, into Mpulungu (but the security situation means that ferries are not currently stopping in Burundi). The main alternative is the land border, either by road crossing or by Tanzania Zambia Railway Authority (TAZARA) train, crossing east of Tunduma. See *Chapter 13*, and the section on *Kapiri Mposhi* (pages 381–2), for more details of TAZARA's important rail link between Zambia and Dar es Salaam. There should also be good hitchhiking opportunities as there are plenty of long-distance lorries plying the route, as well as Zambian drivers who pick up cars, bought from Japan, in Dar es Salaam.

To/from Malawi The main crossing between Zambia and Malawi is east of Chipata. This would also be the swiftest way to reach the Nyika Plateau, as the roads in Malawi are better than those to Nyika in Zambia. Travellers on this route may require a certificate of inoculation against yellow fever, although this is technically no longer required.

To/from Mozambique There is a land crossing between Zambia and Mozambique south of Katete, west of Chipata, though this is not often used. A more common route would be via Malawi or Zimbabwe.

RED TAPE

VISAS AND ENTRY REQUIREMENTS Zambia's visa rules appear, on reading them, to be very complex. The Zambian Immigration Department has an informative website (*www.zambiaimmigration.gov.zm*). It's also probably essential to ask at your nearest Zambian embassy or high commission (see opposite), as they will know the latest news and how the rules are generally being interpreted.

All visitors to Zambia – including those in transit overland to Botswana – need a visa, except those from Ireland and a few selected Commonwealth countries; Commonwealth countries whose citizens do need a visa include Great Britain, Canada, Australia, New Zealand, Cyprus, Ghana, India, Bangladesh, Nigeria, Sri Lanka, Pakistan, Gambia, Mozambique, Sierra Leone and Papua New Guinea. US citizens also need visas, but most citizens of neighbouring southern African countries (including South Africa) do not. (Check *www.zhcl.org.uk* and *www.zambiaembassy.org* are good and contain information for most nationalities.)

Most visas can be obtained at border posts (including international airports) on arrival or overseas at your local Zambian diplomatic mission. You must have at least six months left on your passport, and at least two blank pages. You may be asked to show an onward ticket, or at least demonstrate that you can support yourself as you pass through the country (credit cards are invaluable), but this is unusual.

Costs for a visa vary for different nationalities and sometimes depend upon which high commission or embassy you apply through. Currently costs for single-/multiple-entry visas from the Zambian High Commission in London are £33 (single entry) or £45 (multiple entry) for British nationals, and US$100 (multiple entry only) for citizens of the USA via the Zambian Embassy in Washington or at the border. British citizens can expect to pay US$60/80 in cash for a single-/multiple-entry visa in Zambia itself, while for citizens of a number of other countries, including the Netherlands, the fee is US$25. Visas for most nationalities are generally valid for up to three months from date of issue, and for a maximum stay of 90 days.

Visa-waiver system for pre-arranged holidays Despite the above, 'bona fide tourists' who have pre-arranged trips of less than 14 days may organise a free ('fee-waived') visa through their tour operator. This is a rather complex procedure that involves communication between operator, the various lodges and the immigration department, but it does work – most of the time. It is possible to organise direct with a lodge, but it involves them taking a letter to the immigration authorities, getting it stamped, then getting the original (not a copy) to you, so it's not recommended. And do note that the maximum allowed is 14 days; if you're planning a more leisurely trip, then the rules state that the visa-waiver system will not apply.

If you're crossing into Zambia for the day from Zimbabwe, and have your name put on a list compiled by local Zambian tour operators at least 24 hours in advance, you should be able to avoid any fee at the border.

Visa extensions Visas can be extended, by personal application to the Immigration Office (*PO Box 50300, 2nd Floor, Memaco Hse, Cairo Rd, Lusaka;* ↘ *021 1251725;* f *021 1252659*). You'll need two completed application forms (each with a passport photo), a valid passport and proof of sufficient funds to cover your stay. If it's a business application then you'll also need an explanatory letter with some good reasons. Your application will take at least three working days to process.

In the 1980s, during KK's rule, visitors were routinely treated with suspicion – especially those with cameras. Fortunately this distrust has now vanished, and the prevailing attitude amongst both the government and the people is very welcoming. Visitors are seen as good for the country because they spend valuable foreign currency – so if you look respectable then you will not find any difficulties in entering Zambia.

Given this logic, and the conservative nature of local Zambian customs, the converse is also true. If you dress very untidily, looking as if you've no money, when entering via an overland border, then you may be questioned as to how you will be funding your trip. Dressing respectably in Zambia is not only courteous, but will also make your life easier.

Ⓔ ZAMBIA'S DIPLOMATIC MISSIONS ABROAD For details of foreign embassies in Zambia, see *Chapter 7, Lusaka,* page 151.

Angola (embassy) PO Box 1496, Luanda; ↘ 02 331241; f 02 393483

Belgium (embassy) 469 Av Molière, 1060 Brussels; ↘ 02 343 5649; f 02 347 4333

Botswana (high commission) Zambia Hse, 1118 The Mall, Box 362, Gaborone; ↘ 351951; f 353962

Canada (high commission) 151 Slater St, Suite 205, Ottawa, Ontario KIP 5H3; ↘ 613 232 4400; f 613 232 4410; www.zambiahighcommission.ca

China (embassy) Dongsijie, San-Li-Tun, Beijing; ↘ 6532 1554; f 6532 1778, 1891

Democratic Republic of Congo (embassy) 54–58 Av de L'Ecole, Gombe, BP 1144, Kinshasa; ↘ 243 12 23 038; f 243 12 123 151

Egypt (embassy) 25 Abdel Monein, Riad St, 10 El-Gumhuriya Muttahada Sq, PO Box 253, Mohandessine, Cairo 12311; ↘ 02 361 0282; f 02 361 0283, 0833

Ethiopia (embassy) Old Airport Area, Higher 23 Kebele 12, PO Box 1909, Addis Ababa; ↘ 01 711302

Germany (embassy) Bad Godesberg, Mittelstr 39, 5300 Bonn 2; ↘ 0228 376811, 376813; f 0228 379536

France (embassy) 76 Av O'Jena, 75116 Paris

India (high commission) F-8/22 Vasant Vihar, New Delhi 110057; ↘ 011 687 7681; f 011 687 7928

Japan (embassy) 10-2 Ebarn 1-Chome, Shinagwa-Ku, Tokyo 142; ↘ 03 349 10 121; f 03 349 10 123

Before you read this tale, it must be emphasised that the overwhelming majority of lodges and their owners in Zambia are honest and reliable, with a real commitment to good practice and responsible tourism. The events described below refer to an extreme exception, rather than the rule. Dave and Louise tell me it's a true account, and only the names have been changed.

The story begins in 1990, when a young English couple – Dave and Louise – fell in love with Africa on holiday. Nothing unusual there. Further trips heightened their affection, until the two were dreaming of swapping their England life for a new life in Africa. Neither being doctors, engineers or teachers – the professions needed most in Africa – their chances of employment seemed meagre. Until, that is, they met Stuart.

Stuart was a South African with fingers in many pies, including the construction of a safari camp. He didn't have time to supervise this, but – with their qualifications in business, finance and management, and with David also a professional chef – it seemed that Louise and David were the answer to his prayers, and vice versa. Before long, the pair had taken a year off, with a view to a permanent move if things worked out, packed their bags and flown to Zambia to oversee the building work. With qualified local builders, the couple's lack of knowledge of construction didn't seem to be a problem.

Initially, Dave and Louise had agreed to work for free, with a view to managing the camp when it was finished. Stuart promised that they would be provided with a 4x4, radio communication, a weapon, food, fuel and a tent at the camp/construction site. However, when the pair were finally dumped at the camp, 90km from the nearest town, things began to look a little less rosy. A few days after arriving, the owners of a nearby lodge warned them that Stuart was not a man to be trusted.

True, they were in the heart of Africa, in an idyllic spot overlooking the Zambezi with an abundance of the local fauna, including elephants, hippos, hyenas, lions, leopards, snakes and even the odd poacher for company. However, the promised vehicle, weapon and radio communication all failed to materialise, and the allowance to pay for their upkeep proved entirely inadequate. They were not even given enough to cover the cost of the building materials, or to buy sufficient food. Trips back to the city to see Stuart proved fruitless – he always seemed to be 'away on business'.

Though their dreams were crumbling, Dave and Louise remained determined, and resourceful. They set up an impromptu campsite to raise cash, and with the income generated they bought food to supplement the fish that Dave caught from the Zambezi.

Details were sketchy, but what Louise and Dave found out about Stuart wasn't proving positive. It involved allegations of smuggling: cobalt, diamonds and even ivory was mentioned. Stuart appeared to be using three different aliases, each with a different passport. The final straw came when a group of besuited heavies arrived at the camp, demanding money for their involvement with the 'big bwana' – Stuart's nickname. Dave and Louise successfully sent them away, but next time the couple visited Lusaka, they were arrested at a roadblock and had their visas revoked. It seemed that Stuart was behind this too. The pair were now visa-less and without work permits. They eventually fled Zambia, poorer, perhaps more cynical – but infinitely wiser.

Looking back, Dave doesn't regret the experience. He's philosophical, preferring to concentrate more on the positive aspects of the whole farrago, and the opportunity it gave them to live in the wilds of the world's most beautiful continent. Their decision to leave their jobs merely for a year proved to be a good one, and as Dave wrote at the end of his letter: 'I sincerely hope that our experience will act as some kind of warning to anyone else who is looking for the same dream.'

Kenya (high commission) City Hall Annex, Nyerere Rd, Box 48741, Nairobi; ☎ 02 724 850, 796, 799; f 02 718 494

Malawi (high commission) Box 30138, 40/2 Capital Hill, Lilongwe 3; ☎ 731911; f 784349

Mozambique (embassy) Av Kenneth Kaunda, 1286, Maputo, PO Box 4655; ☎ 01 492 452

Namibia (high commission) 22 Sam Nujoma Dr (cnr Manduma Nddemufayo Rd), PO Box 22882, Windhoek; ☎ 061 237610–11; f 061 228162

Nigeria (high commission) 430 Lobito Crescent, Wuse 11, PMB 5055, Wuse, Abuja; ☎ 02 413 1256–8; f 413 1255

Russian Federation (embassy) Prospect Mira 52, Moscow; ☎ 095 288 5001; f 095 975 2056

South Africa (high commission), PO Box 12234, Pretoria, 570 Ziervogel St, Arcadia, Hartfield 0083; ☎ 012 326 1847, 1854; f 012 326 2140; www.zambiapretoria.net

Sweden (embassy) Gardsvagen 18, Stockholm, Box 3056, 169 03 Solna; ☎ 08 6799 9040; f 08 6799 6850

Switzerland Permanent Mission of Zambia to the UN, 17–19 Chemin du Champs-d'Anier, 1209 Le Petit Sacconneux, Geneva; ☎ 022 788 5330–1; f 022 788 5340; e zamembas@algonet.se

Tanzania (high commission) Box 2525, Plots 5 & 8, Ohio St, Sokoine Dr Junction, Dar es Salaam; ☎ 051 227261–3; f 051 246389

Uganda (high commission) 20 Philip Rd, Kololo, Kampala; ☎ 041 233777

UK (high commission) 2 Palace Gate, London W8 5NG; ☎ 020 7589 6655; f 020 7581 1353; www.zhcl.org.uk

USA (embassy) 2419 Massachusetts Av NW, Washington, DC 20008; ☎ 202 265 9717–9; f 202 332 0826; www.zambiaembassy.org

Zimbabwe (high commission) Zambia Hse, 48 Union Rd, Box 4698, Harare; ☎ 04 773782; f 04 776782

WHAT TO TAKE

This depends on how you intend to travel and exactly where you are going. If you are flying in for a short safari holiday then you need not pack too ruthlessly – provided that you stay within your weight allowance. However, note that smaller, privately chartered planes may specify a maximum weight of 10–12kg for hold luggage, which must be packed in a soft, squashable bag. Once you see the stowage spaces in a small charter plane, you'll understand the importance of not bringing along large or solid suitcases.

If you are backpacking then weight becomes much more important, and minimising it becomes an art form. Each extra item must be questioned: is its benefit worth its weight?

If you have your own vehicle then neither weight nor bulk will be so vital, and you will have a lot more freedom to bring what you like. Here are some general guidelines.

CLOTHING For most days all you will want is light, loose-fitting cotton clothing. Pure cotton, or at least a cotton-rich mix, is cooler and more absorbent than synthetic materials, making it more comfortable in the heat.

For men shorts (not too short) are fine in the bush, but long trousers are more socially acceptable in the towns and rural villages. (You will rarely see a respectable black Zambian man wearing shorts outside a safari camp.) For women a knee-length skirt or culottes are ideal. Zambia's dress code is generally conservative: a woman wearing revealing clothing in town implies that she is a woman of ill repute, whilst untidy clothing suggests a poor person, of low social standing.

These rules are redundant at safari camps, where dress is casual, and designed to keep you cool and protect skin from the sun. Green, khaki and dust-brown cotton is *de rigueur* at the more serious camps (especially those offering walking trips) and amongst visitors out to demonstrate how well they know the ropes. The same cognoscenti are usually to be found wearing old and well-worn items, rather than anything straight out of the box; charity shops in the UK can be a great source of safari wear! At the less serious camps you'll see a smattering of brighter-coloured clothes amongst many dull bush colours, the former usually worn by first-time visitors who are less familiar with the bush.

A squashable hat and a robust pair of sunglasses with a high UV-absorption are essential.

No matter what your plans, you'll need something warmer, such as a thick fleece, for evenings during the cooler winter months – roughly from April until August. And in the rainy season, don't forget an umbrella if you want to avoid getting drenched; a waterproof jacket, while occasionally useful, is rarely up to the task.

Note that washing is done daily at virtually all camps, so few changes of clothes are necessary.

FOOTWEAR If you plan to do much walking, either on safari or with a backpack, then lightweight walking boots (with ankle support if possible) are essential. This is mainly because the bush is not always smooth and even, and anything that minimises the chance of a twisted ankle is worthwhile. Secondly, for the nervous, it will reduce still further the minute chance of being bitten by a snake, or other creepy-crawly, whilst walking.

Because of the heat, take the lightest pair of boots you can find – preferably go for canvas, or a breathable Gore-tex-type material. Leather boots are too hot for wearing in October, but thin single-skin leather is bearable for walking in July and August. Never bring a new pair, or boots that aren't completely worn in. Always bring several pairs of thin socks – two thin pairs of socks are more comfortable than one thick pair, and will help to prevent blisters.

CAMPING EQUIPMENT If you are coming on an organised safari, then even a simple bushcamp will mean walk-in chalets with linen, mosquito nets and probably an en-suite shower and toilet. However, if you're planning on doing any camping, then note that little equipment is available in Zambia, and see *Camping equipment* on pages 110–11 for ideas of what you should bring.

OTHER USEFUL ITEMS Obviously no list is comprehensive, and only travelling will teach you what you need, and what you can do without. Here are a few of my own favourites and essentials, just to jog your memory. For visitors embarking on an organised safari, camps will have most things but useful items include:

- Sunblock and lipsalve – for vital protection from the sun
- Binoculars – totally essential for game viewing
- A small pocket torch (see *Camping equipment*, page 111)
- 'Leatherman' tool – never go into the bush without one, but always pack it in your check-in bag; never in your hand luggage
- A small water bottle, especially on flights (see *Camping equipment*, page 111)
- Electrical insulating tape – remarkably useful for general repairs
- Camera – long lenses are vital for good shots of animals
- Basic sewing kit – with at least some really strong thread for repairs
- Cheap waterproof watch (leave expensive ones, and jewellery, at home)
- Couple of paperback novels
- Large plastic 'bin-liner' (garbage) bags, for protecting luggage from dust
- Simple medical kit and insect repellent

And for those driving or backpacking, useful extras are:

- Concentrated, biodegradable washing powder
- Long-life candles – as Zambian candles are often soft, and burn quickly

- Nylon 'paracord' – bring at least 20m for emergencies and washing lines
- Hand-held GPS navigation system, for expeditions to remote areas
- Good compass and a whistle
- More comprehensive medical kit

WHAT NOT TO TAKE There are several things worth leaving behind. Firstly, avoid anything which looks military. Leave all your camouflage patterns at home; wearing them anywhere in Africa is asking for trouble. You are very likely to be stopped by the genuine military, or at least the police, who will assume that you are a member of some militia – and question exactly what you are doing in Zambia. Few will believe that this is a fashion statement elsewhere in the world.

Secondly, even if you're going on the most expensive of safaris, leave any jewellery that you don't usually wear all day, every day, at home. It'll take a load off your mind not to have to worry about its security.

ELECTRICAL ITEMS The local voltage is 220V, delivered at 50Hz. Sockets fit plugs with three square pins, like the current design in the UK. Even the most remote safari camp nowadays can usually arrange for you to charge a camera battery, but if this is important, do make sure to check facilities in advance.

MAPS AND NAVIGATION

MAPS For general purposes, there are several reasonable road maps of Zambia, of which the best is currently the 1:1,500,000 sheet published in Germany by **Ilona HupeVerlag** (*www.hupeverlag.de*), and widely available at bookshops in Lusaka. In addition to good road and topographical detail, it features filling stations, campsites and GPS co-ordinates – though the last (and the distances) aren't always entirely reliable. There are also inset overview maps of Lusaka and Livingstone.

Other commercially produced maps, available both in Zambia and overseas, include those published by International Travel Maps, Globetrotter (New Holland), both at 1:1,500,000, and Macmillan (1:2,200,000). The **International Travel Map** shows contours and the parks, with surrounding text boxes covering topics from wildlife to Zambia's history and geography. Road detail is good, with many of the pontoons (flat, open-sided ferry boats) carefully marked, though coverage of the main points of tourist interest is less detailed. The illustrated **Globetrotter** map incorporates several regional and national park maps at a larger scale, as well as town plans of Livingstone and Lusaka, and climate charts. The smaller-scale **Macmillan** map scale is less detailed, but better at marking the points of interest for visitors, and on the reverse are many excellent 'inset' maps of the main parks, plus plans of Lusaka and Livingstone.

For **more detail**, Zambia has an excellent range of 'Ordnance Survey'-type maps available cheaply in Lusaka, from the Ministry of Lands in Mulungushi House (see page 125). A wide range of maps is kept here, including the useful 1:250,000 series, a number of town plans, some 'tourist' maps of the parks – including an excellent 1989 map of South Luangwa's landscape and vegetation – and many more detailed maps of selected areas. Some are always out of print, and many are out of date – but you can usually find at least some sort of map to cover most areas. If you are planning to drive yourself around, then buy the maps for your trip at the start.

Navigation by any of these maps becomes more difficult as your location becomes more remote, when expecting any of them to be entirely accurate is unrealistic. Thus if you're heading into the wilds, get what maps you can and compare them with reality as you go.

GPS SYSTEMS If you are heading into one of the more remote parks in your own vehicle, then consider investing in a hand-held GPS: a global positioning system. Under an open, unobstructed sky, these can fix your latitude, longitude and elevation to within about 100m, using 24 American military satellites which constantly pass in the skies overhead. They will work anywhere on the globe.

These small units will enable you to store 'waypoints' and build a simple electronic picture of an area, as well as working out basic latitude, longitude and elevation. So, for example, you can store the position of your campsite and the nearest road, making it much easier to be reasonably sure of navigating back without simply retracing your steps. This kind of function can be invaluable in remote areas with lots of bush and no signposts, but it comes with a warning: a GPS takes no account of bends in the road, or indeed of natural hazards, so both directional arrows and distances may appear to be misleading at times.

Although a GPS may help you to recognise your minor errors before they are amplified into major problems, note that such a gadget is no substitute for good map work and navigation. Try not to rely on your GPS too much, or you will be unable to cope if it fails. Always remember to have a back-up plan in case it stops working. Note, too, that all these units use lots of battery power, so bring spares with you and/or a cigarette-lighter adaptor.

Commercial units cost from around £100/US$160 in Europe or the USA, although prices are falling (and features improving) as the technology matures.

GPS positions in this book You'll note that I've given almost all of the GPS locations in this book a six-digit name. These were simply the names that I assigned to them in my system, as I recorded them, and I've used them throughout the book for ease of reference. All GPS co-ordinates in this book have been expressed as degrees, minutes, and decimal fractions of a minute.

I hope that their inclusion may enable this book's more adventurous and experienced travellers to venture safely out to Zambia's lesser-known corners, although my points don't remove the need to take up-to-date local advice on safety and conditions.

Important note For all the GPS co-ordinates in this book, note that the datum used is WGS 84; you must set your receiver accordingly before copying in any of these co-ordinates. Many maps in Zambia used the ARC 1950 datum – so you should expect a slight discrepancy between points estimated from such maps, and your GPS unit.

PHOTOGRAPHY AND OPTICS

Don't expect to find any reasonably priced or reasonably available optical equipment in Zambia – so bring everything that you will need with you. For technical tips and equipment, see pages 62–3.

CAMERA INSURANCE Most travel insurance policies are poor at covering valuables, including cameras. If you are taking valuable camera equipment abroad, then include it in your house insurance policy, or cover it separately with a specialist.

BINOCULARS For a safari holiday, especially if you are doing much walking, a good pair of binoculars are essential. They will bring you far more enjoyment than a camera, as they make the difference between merely seeing an animal or bird at a distance, and being able to observe its markings, movements and moods closely. Do bring one pair per person; one between two is just not enough.

There are two styles: the small 'pocket' binoculars, perhaps 10–12cm long, which account for most modern sales, and the larger, heavier styles, double or triple that size, which have been manufactured for years. Both vary widely in cost and quality. If you are buying a pair, then consider getting the larger style. The smaller ones are fine for spotting animals; but are difficult to hold steady, and very tiring to use for extensive periods. You will only realise this when you are out on safari, by which time it is too late.

Around 8 x 30 is an ideal size for field observations, as most people need some form of rest, or tripod, to hold the larger 10 x 50 models steady. Get the best-quality ones you can for your money. The cheapest will be about £40/US$60, but to get a reasonable level of quality spend at least £250/US$400. If you use binoculars regularly, as against for just one holiday, then try to stretch your budget above the £500/US$900 barrier. Once you do this, makes like Swarovski, Zeiss and Leica, which are considerably better than cheaper models, come within reach – and will hugely enhance your experience of viewing wildlife.

$ MONEY AND BUDGETING

CURRENCY Zambia's unit of currency is the kwacha (Kw). Theoretically each kwacha is divided into 100 ngwee, although one ngwee is now worth so little that these subdivisions are never used. Almost all currency comes in the form of notes; the smallest denomination is in fact a coin, worth Kw50, but it is extremely rare.

Over the years, the kwacha has been devaluing steadily, in line with the country's inflation rate, but in recent years the rate of devaluation has slowed and it has become more stable. The old practices of strict exchange control and unrealistic exchange rates have gone – as has the black market for currency that these policies created.

EXCHANGE RATES Inflation has varied enormously since at least 1989, but at last seems to be coming under control. In December 2000 it was quoted as being around 30%, but by mid-2007 the underlying rate of inflation was down to a more manageable 9–11%. As the kwacha has strengthened, hotels and lodges have been expected to quote their prices in kwacha, rather than the US dollar which was preferred until recently. So while in recent years it has been easier to plan a trip to Zambia in US dollars, and previous editions of this guide quoted prices in US dollars, this is no longer necessary. Thus most of the prices in this guide are given in kwacha. Those that are given in US dollars are usually for those lodges whose clientele comes primarily from overseas.

Where sterling and US dollar equivalents are given in this guide, I have assumed a notional rate of around £1 for Kw8,000, or US$1 for Kw4,000.

In mid-October 2007 exchange rates against the kwacha were:

£1	=	Kw7,804
US$1	=	Kw3,830
€1	=	Kw5,390
ZAR1	=	Kw559

BUDGETING Zambia is not a cheap country to visit, especially if you want to see some of the national parks. This isn't because of high park fees: on the contrary, US$15–25/£8–12 per day is reasonable by African standards. Rather, costs are high because most safari camps are small and seasonal, and their supply logistics are difficult and costly. However, you do generally get what you pay for: camps in remote locations and pristine environments tend to set very high standards.

Ariadne Van Zandbergen

EQUIPMENT Although with some thought and an eye for composition you can take reasonable photos with a 'point-and-shoot' camera, you need an SLR camera if you are at all serious about photography. Modern SLRs tend to be very clever, with automatic programs for almost every possible situation, but remember that these programs are limited in the sense that the camera cannot think, but only make calculations. Every starting amateur photographer should read a photographic manual for beginners and get to grips with such basics as the relationship between aperture and shutter speed.

Always buy the best lens you can afford. The lens determines the quality of your photo more than the camera body. Fixed fast lenses are ideal, but very costly. A zoom lens makes it easier to change composition without changing lenses the whole time. If you carry only one lens, a 28–70mm (digital 17–55mm) or similar zoom should be ideal. For a second lens, a lightweight 80–200mm or 70–300mm (digital 55–200mm) or similar will be excellent for candid shots and varying your composition. Wildlife photography will be very frustrating if you don't have at least a 300mm lens. For a small loss of quality, tele-converters are a cheap and compact way to increase magnification: a 300 lens with a 1.4x converter becomes 420mm, and with a 2x it becomes 600mm. Note, however, that 1.4x and 2x tele-converters reduce the speed of your lens by 1.4 and 2 stops respectively.

For wildlife photography from a safari vehicle, a solid beanbag, which you can make yourself very cheaply, will be necessary to avoid blurred images, and is more useful than a tripod. A clamp with a tripod head screwed onto it can be attached to the vehicle as well. Modern dedicated flash units are easy to use; aside from the obvious need to flash when you photograph at night, you can improve a lot of photos in difficult 'high contrast' or very dull light with some fill-in flash. It pays to have a proper flash unit as opposed to a built-in camera flash.

DIGITAL/FILM Digital photography is now the preference of most amateur and professional photographers, with the resolution of digital cameras improving all the time. For ordinary prints a 6 megapixel camera is fine. For better results and the possibility to enlarge images and for professional reproduction, higher resolution is available up to 16 megapixels.

Memory space is important. The number of pictures you can fit on a memory card depends on the quality you choose. Calculate in advance how many pictures you can fit on a card and either take enough cards to last for your trip, or take a storage drive onto which you can download the content. A laptop gives the advantage that you can see your pictures properly at the end of each day and edit and delete rejects, but a storage device is lighter and less bulky. These drives come in different capacities up to 80GB.

Bear in mind that digital camera batteries, computers and other storage devices need charging, so make sure you have all the chargers, cables and converters with you; a spare battery is invaluable. If you're flying around to small safari camps, then most camps will

To make up a trip using such camps, which are the easiest and most practical way for visitors to Zambia, budget for an all-inclusive cost of about US$400–700/£200–350 per person per day when staying in a camp. Internal flights cost varying amounts, but US$180/£100 per leg would be a good approximation.

At the other end of the spectrum, if you travel through Zambia on local buses, camping and staying in the occasional local (sometimes seedy) resthouse, then Zambia is not expensive. A budget of US$40–60/£20–30 per day for food, accommodation and transport would suffice. However, most backpackers who have some form of power, even though there is no socket in your tent. (Even the smallest bushcamp will normally have a fridge and a radio, and both will require some power.) If you bring a few sets of spare batteries, and a charger, most camps will usually be able to charge your batteries given 24 hours. Ideally, and crucially if you're camping, also bring an adaptor for a vehicle's cigarette lighter, as batteries can then be charged while you're on the road or during a game-viewing drive.

If you are shooting film, 100 to 200 ISO print film and 50 to 100 ISO slide film are ideal. Low ISO film is slow but fine grained and gives the best colour saturation, but will need more light, so support in the form of a tripod or monopod is important. You can also bring a few 'fast' 400 ISO films for low-light situations where a tripod or flash is no option. Film is difficult to find in Zambia, so bring anything you need from home.

DUST AND HEAT Dust and heat are often a problem. Keep your equipment in a sealed bag, stow films in an airtight container (eg: a small cooler bag) and avoid exposing equipment and film to the sun. Digital cameras are prone to collecting dust particles on the sensor which results in spots on the image. The dirt mostly enters the camera when changing lenses, so be careful when doing this. To some extent photos can be 'cleaned' up afterwards in Photoshop, but this is time-consuming. You can have your camera sensor professionally cleaned, or you can do this yourself with special brushes and swabs made for the purpose, but note that touching the sensor might cause damage and should only be done with the greatest care.

LIGHT The most striking outdoor photographs are often taken during the hour or two of 'golden light' after dawn and before sunset. Shooting in low light may enforce the use of very low shutter speeds, in which case a tripod will be required to avoid camera shake.

With careful handling, side lighting and back lighting can produce stunning effects, especially in soft light and at sunrise or sunset. Generally, however, it is best to shoot with the sun behind you. When photographing animals or people in the harsh midday sun, images taken in light but even shade are likely to be more effective than those taken in direct sunlight or patchy shade, since the latter conditions create too much contrast.

PROTOCOL In Zambia, as elsewhere, it is unacceptable to photograph local people without permission, and many people will refuse to pose or will ask for a donation. In such circumstances, don't try to sneak photographs as you might get yourself into trouble. Even the most willing subject will often pose stiffly when a camera is pointed at them; relax them by making a joke, and take a few shots in quick succession to improve the odds of capturing a natural pose.

Ariadne Van Zandbergen is a professional travel and wildlife photographer specialising in Africa. She runs the Africa Image Library. For photo requests, visit www.africaimagelibrary.co.za or contact her on ariadne@hixnet.co.za.

undertake such trips are simply 'in transit' between Malawi and Zimbabwe. They see little of Zambia's wildlife or its national parks, missing out on even its cheaper attractions.

If you have your own rugged 4x4 with equipment *and* the experience to use it, then you will be able to camp and cook for yourself which can dramatically cut costs: down to US$12–34/£6–17 per person per day for both park fees and camping fees. However, to hire such a vehicle and supply it with fuel would cost upwards of another US$400/£200 per day.

Although the kwacha has stabilised in recent years, its rates against the US dollar and UK pound have varied greatly over the last decade or so, providing an interesting context to the present economic climate. Rough trends have been as follows:

Date	To US$	To British £	To SA rand	To euro
1995: Jan/July	700/925	1,100/1,480	195/255	–
1996: Jan/July	975/1,270	1,500/1,970	267/289	–
1997: Jan/July	1,290/1,310	2,100/2,180	278/287	–
1998: Jan/July	1,450/1,945	2,380/3,200	295/310	–
1999: Jan/July	2,425/2,500	3,980/4,000	410/415	2,810/2,630
2000: July	3,083	4,656	448	2,710
2001: July	3,585	5,208	453	2,480
2002: July	4,720	7,340	470	4,690
2003: July	4,930	8,020	655	5,600
2004: July	4,775	8,800	785	5,870
2007: July	3,978	8,081	560	5,453

Finding a trip of medium expenditure, without your own vehicle, is difficult. One possibility is to make use of the odd medium-priced safari camp. The Wildlife Camp or Flatdogs in South Luangwa, are obvious options, as is Kasanka – especially if four or five people are travelling together. Creatively using these options, being prepared to pay where necessary, you might spend only US$200/£100 per day whilst seeing some of the very best that the country has to offer.

The cost of food depends heavily on where you buy it, as well as what you buy. If you can shop in Lusaka for your camping supplies then you will save money and have a wider choice than elsewhere. Imported foods are inevitably more expensive than locally produced items. If you are sensible, then US$12–25/£6–12 per day would provide the supplies for a good, varied diet, including the odd treat. In any event, it will be cheaper than eating out.

If you are staying in Lusaka, or one of the main cities, then the bigger hotels are about US$180–280/£90–140 for a double room, whilst a nice small guesthouse will cost around US$20–45/£10–22. Camping at organised sites on the outskirts of the cities is, again, a good bet if you have the equipment and transport. It will cost an almost universal US$5/£3 per person per night.

Restaurant meals in the towns are cheap compared with Europe or America: expect to pay US$12–25/£6–12 for a good evening meal, including a local beer or two. Imported beers are more expensive than local beer (which is perfectly adequate), and South African wines are more costly again. European wines and spirits, as you might expect, are ridiculously priced (and so make excellent gifts if you are visiting someone here). You will pay well over US$100/£55 for a bottle of champagne in Lusaka!

Finally, do be aware that prices in Zambia – as anywhere else – can and do rise. Rates quoted in this guide were correct at the time of research in 2007, but many will change during the life of the guide, so please do be sensitive to such changes.

HOW TO TAKE YOUR MONEY Although US dollars and UK pounds sterling are easily changed, you will normally need to have US dollars in cash to pay for visas at the border, and for any departure tax due at the airport. Sometimes you can pay for the larger hotels and other services in US dollars (small-denomination notes) directly, as you would with kwacha, but this becomes less common away from the bigger towns. In addition, park fees are almost always payable in cash US dollars. Travellers' cheques may be preferable from a security point of view, as they are refundable if stolen, but they are less flexible, and cannot be used as cash as they are in the USA. (And note that Amex travellers' cheques are not always welcomed, and their charge cards are seldom of use in Zambia.)

If you're going to more offbeat locations, you increasingly need kwacha – although in case of need, some places will accept cash in low denominations of US dollars, or pounds sterling. If you're driving yourself, it is crucial that you allow sufficient cash (in kwacha) to pay for fuel; credit cards will not be accepted.

I travel with mostly US$1, US$5, US$10 and US$20 bills (and a few £10 or £20 notes). Because of the risk of forgeries, people are sometimes suspicious of larger-denomination notes; conversely, some places offer a lower exchange rate for smaller-denomination notes. US$100 and even US$50 bills are often rejected in shops and even some banks. Be careful not to take the older US dollar bills (before 1996) with a small portrait on the front; only those with the larger portraits are acceptable.

South African rand are occasionally accepted, typically in the western provinces near Namibia; elsewhere they're virtually useless.

Although some safari camps accept credit cards, any park fees that are not included will usually need to be paid at the park gate in US$ cash. Don't expect to be able to pay these with travellers' cheques.

CHANGING MONEY AND BANKING If you need to change foreign currency, receive bank drafts, or do any other relatively complex financial transactions, then banks in the larger cities (ideally Lusaka) are your best option, though almost all banks will exchange US dollars. Banks open as early as 08.15–08.30, and close around 14.45–15.30 from Monday to Friday, although in small towns they may close earlier, or be open only on certain days. Some work a shorter day on Thursday, from 09.00 to 11.00. A few of the bigger banks in Lusaka also open 09.00–11.00 on Saturdays, a policy that is spreading nationwide. Cashpoint (ATM) machines are widely available in the major towns, but outside of these, they are not the norm. At a number of banks (Barclays, Standard Chartered, Stanbic) you can use European debit cards bearing the Maestro or Visa logo to withdraw up to Kw2,000,000 per day. It makes sense to take more than one credit or debit card, ideally a Visa and a MasterCard, since some banks will accept one but not the other; if in doubt, Visa is probably the more useful.

If you are changing money at one of the main banks, in Lusaka or Livingstone, then there is minimal difference in the rates between presenting a travellers' cheque, or presenting pounds sterling or US dollars in cash. If you use a bureau de change, you'll usually get better rates for cash.

Until relatively recently there was a 'black market' in foreign currency in Zambia, with US dollars worth much more if changed surreptitiously with a shady (and illegal) street dealer rather than at a bank. This was a result of the official (government-decreed) exchange rate for the kwacha not corresponding to the true market value of the currency. Financial reforms have enabled the kwacha to float at a free-market rate, wiping out the black market. Now the shady characters on the street who hiss 'Change money' as you pass are more likely to be conmen relying on sleights of hand than genuine money-changers. Give them a very wide berth.

TIPPING Tipping is a difficult and contentious topic – worth thinking about carefully. While I'm told that it's illegal in Zambia, it is done widely, and is often expected, especially in restaurants, though the amounts are generally moderate. Read the section on *Local payments* in *Chapter 6*, pages 117–18, and realise that thoughtlessly tipping too much is just as bad as tipping too little.

Ask locally what's appropriate; here I can give only rough guidance. Helpers with baggage might expect Kw1,000–2,000/US$0.25–0.50, someone looking after your car around Kw500–2,000/US$0.12–0.50, depending on the time you're away, whilst sorting out a problem with a reservation would be Kw4,000–12,000/US$1–3. Restaurants will often add an automatic service charge to the bill, in which case an additional tip is not usually given. If they do not do this, then 10% would certainly be appreciated if the service was good. Tipping a taxi driver is not normally expected.

At safari camps, tipping is not obligatory despite the assumption from some visitors that it is. If a guide has given you really good service then a tip of about US$5–8 per day per guest would be a generous reflection of this. If the service hasn't been that good, then don't tip.

Always tip at the end of your stay, not at the end of each day or activity. Do not tip after every game drive. This leads to the guides only trying hard when they know there's a tip at the end of the morning. Such camps aren't pleasant to visit and this isn't the way to encourage top-quality guiding. It's best to wait until the end of your stay, and then give what you feel is appropriate in one lump sum.

However, before you do this find out if tips go into one box for all of the camp staff, or if the guides are treated differently. Ask the managers as you're about to leave. Then ensure that your tip reflects this – with perhaps as much again divided between the rest of the staff.

GETTING AROUND

✈ **BY AIR** For those who want to fly internally in Zambia, the number of possibilities is increasing. Several local companies provide very reliable charters, although only one or two – notably Proflight (operating as Copper Air in the Copperbelt region) and Zambian Airways – operate any kind of scheduled service. Zambia Airways is the only one of those that offers internet booking opportunities with payment by credit card. None of the others is featured on any of the global flight reservations systems, so outside of Zambia (and even inside sometimes) most travel agents won't have a clue about the intricacies of Zambia's internal flights. You are strongly advised to book your internal flights through an experienced tour operator, who uses them regularly. (As an aside, this means that if the airline goes bust the tour operator loses money; you don't.) If you want to arrange something whilst you are in Zambia, or need to get in touch with an airline in a hurry, see the contact details opposite and on page 122.

The services that I have encountered are high-quality operations, so you need have few worries about safety. On the whole, the smaller charter operations are very reliable, and more flexible for individual passengers, than the larger airlines.

However, if you book an internal flight a long time in advance, be aware that its timings (and indeed existence) may change. Cancellation at short notice is unlikely, though taking a philosophical attitude towards this possibility would be wise. A good operator will always be able to make a back-up plan for you.

If you want to fly into, or out of, Mfuwe International Airport, then you can normally find a scheduled way. However, getting anywhere else is often a matter of **chartering** your own plane. This isn't for the backpacker's budget, but if you plan to stay at private safari camps then short charters may be within your price range.

It's possible to charter planes seating up to 12 passengers. If you decide to charter a plane, then expect to pay around US$2.10 per kilometre for a single-engine plane seating 3–5 passengers; US$2.6/km for a twin-engine plane for 4–5 people; or US$3/km for a pressurised twin-turbine plane seating 6–7. Use these figures as a rough guide only, as the rates fluctuate significantly according to the route travelled, the individual companies and the (increasingly high) price of fuel. When making your calculations, remember to include any mileage to/from the aircraft's base, and when booking remember that tour operators who book these trips every day will be given much better rates that individuals interested in a one-off charter. And if you do decide to charter, it's important to be aware that there is a maximum luggage allowance of 12kg per person, to be carried in soft bags only.

For rough one-way distances, in kilometres, see box on page 68.

Scheduled and charter airlines

Avocet Air Link ‿/f 021 1236437; airport ‿ 021 1233422, after hrs ‿ 021 1264866; m 097 770502; e avocet@zamnet.zm; www.avocet-charters.com. Operates twin-engine Cessna 400 planes out of Lusaka.

Copper Air ‿ 021 1271032, 1271035; f 021 1271139; m 097 335563; e proflight@iconnect.zm; www.copperair.net. The recently renamed Copperbelt arm of Proflight, Copper Air has regular scheduled flights linking Lusaka with Ndola & Kitwe in the Copperbelt, & Solwezi; the fare between Lusaka & Ndola is US$100–305 return, depending on ticket type.

Livingstone Air Safaris ‿ 021 3321248, 3323224; e livingstnair@zamnet.zm. Based in Livingstone, this is the cheapest charter operation out of that airport. Livingstone to the Lower Zambezi is US$350 pp one way (min 2 people).

NAC 2000 ‿ 021 1271012, 1271046; m 097 7883972, 095 5775577; e md@nac2000.com.zm, ops@nac2000.com.zm; www.nac2000.com.zm. NAC arranges charters for passengers & cargo both within Zambia, & throughout Africa & the rest of world.

Premier Air m 097 829722; e premierair@amanita.com. This single-plane outfit operates charters for around US$2.20/km.

Proflight ‿ 021 1271032, 1271035; f 021 1271139; m 097 7335563; e proflight@iconnect.zm; www.proflight-zambia.com. See also Copper Air. Proflight operates a range of charter aircraft linking the Lower Zambezi with Lusaka (US$150), Mfuwe (US$350) & Livingstone (US$390), all pp one way, subject to availability & a minimum of 4 passengers per flight.

Royal Air Charters ‿ 021 1261265; m 097 9486618; e royalzambezihq@iwayafrica.com; www.royalaircharters.com. Linked to Royal Zambezi Lodge in the Lower Zambezi (US$85 to Royal Airstrip), it also operates charters between Lusaka and other airstrips in the valley: Jeki (US$110) and Kulefu (US$135).

Sefofane ‿ 021 1271152, 1271157–8; m 097 640602; f 021 1271162 e reservations@sefofane.co.zm; www.sefofane.com, www.wilderness-safaris.com. A newcomer to Zambia, Sefofane is owned by Wilderness Safaris, and is already well established in the rest of the region. Flights within Zambia operate from its bases at Lusaka, Livingstone & Mfuwe, while internationally they link Mfuwe with Lilongwe in Malawi. Daily internal flights (min 2 people) connect Kalamu in the South Luangwa with Lusaka, Mfuwe and Kafue.

Sky Trails Satellite ‿ +873 762 067957; e wasa@kasanka.com. Sky Trails operates 2 planes, 1 out of Kasanka & a 2nd from Mfuwe, & specialise in northern & eastern Zambia, inc Bangweulu, Mutinondo & Shiwa N'gandu. Both planes are high-wing craft so offer good views. Rates in the sgl-engine C206, taking 4–5 passengers, are US$2/km, which works out at Lusaka–Kasanka US$1,470, or Mfuwe–Shiwa US$920. For an extra 10% (making it particularly good value), there's the option of a twin-engine C337.

Staravia ‿/f 021 1291962; airport ‿ 021 1 271332–3, m 096 6750800; e staravia@zamnet.zm; www.staraviazambia.com. Based in Lusaka, the well-established Staravia operates both 4/5-seater twin-engine Baron aircraft & the 6/7-seater pressurised twin-turbine King Air.

Star of Africa ‿ 021 1271056, 1271058; ‿/f 021 1271014; e starofafrica@zamnet.zm; www.star-of-africa.com/circuit/soaac/charter.htm. Based out of Lusaka airport.

Zambian Airways Lusaka International Airport; ‿ 021 1257655, m 095 5926247, 096 6926247, 097 7926247; e reservations@zambianairways.com; www.zambianairways.com. Regular hops connect Lusaka with Livingstone, Mfuwe, Chipata, & Ndola in the Copperbelt.

~~~ **BY RAIL** There are two totally separate rail systems in Zambia: ordinary trains and TAZARA (Tanzania Zambia Railway Authority) trains. Zambia's ordinary rail network was privatised in 2003 and is now run by RSZ (Railway Systems of Zambia) on a 20-year contract – but the system is currently worse than ever. Trains run on

ONE-WAY FLYING DISTANCES (KM)

	Bangweulu	Kafue	Kalabo	Kasanka	Livingstone	Zambezi	Lusaka	Mfuwe	Nchila	Shiwa
Bangweulu		490	885	70	810	410	435	235	650	185
Kafue (Lunga)	490		405	465	410	385	255	610	400	670
Kalabo	885	405		865	455	750	610	1,015	450	1,070
Kasanka	70	465	865		760	350	380	195	670	220
Livingstone	810	410	455	760		480	390	840	750	980
Zambezi (Jeki)	410	385	750	350	480		140	365	750	545
Lusaka	435	255	610	380	390	140		455	635	600
Mfuwe	235	610	1,015	195	840	365	455		860	230
Nchila	650	400	450	670	750	750	635	860		810
Shiwa Ng'andu	185	670	1,070	220	980	545	600	230	810	

only one line, linking Livingstone with Kitwe in the Copperbelt via Lusaka. They're painfully slow, and rarely used by travellers – one local described the journey as 'like signing a death warrant'! If you have lots of patience, and a few good books, then try them by all means – just remember to take plenty to eat and drink for the journey as nothing is available on board.

In contrast the TAZARA service is very popular with backpackers. It connects Kapiri Mposhi with the Indian Ocean, at Dar es Salaam in Tanzania. This is a reliable international transport link which normally runs to time and is by far the fastest way between Zambia and Tanzania with the exception of flying. See *Chapter 13*'s section on *Kapiri Mposhi*, page 381, for more details of this useful service.

BY BUS AND COACH Zambia's **local buses** are cheap, frequent and a great way to meet local people, although they can also be crowded, uncomfortable and noisy. In other words they are similar to any other local buses in Africa, and travel on them has both its joys and its frustrations.

In the main bus stations, there are essentially two different kinds: the smaller minibuses, and the longer, larger 'normal' buses. Both will serve the same destinations, but the smaller ones tend to go faster and stop less. They may also be a little more comfortable. Their larger relatives will take longer to fill up before they leave the bus station (because few buses ever leave before they are full), and then go slower and stop at more places. For the smaller, faster buses there is usually a premium of about 20% on top of the price. Be aware, too, that even buses said to be running to a timetable may not depart until they are full, so check carefully what service you can expect – and ideally take a look at the bus on which you'll be travelling too. A broken windscreen hints at poor overall maintenance.

Then there are a few **postbuses** which operate between the post offices in the main towns, taking both mailbags and passengers as they go. These conform to a more fixed schedule, and standards have improved in recent years. Tickets are booked in advance at the nearest post office. For details, see page 124.

Various **luxury coach services** connect most major towns and the smaller towns in between. See individual chapters for details of those that are running at the time of writing.

BY TAXI Taxis are common and very convenient in Lusaka, Livingstone and the main towns of the Copperbelt, and are starting to appear in smaller towns; Tom Kok reports that even Kaoma has several taxis. (Elsewhere they are uncommon or don't formally exist.) They can be hailed in the street, though foreign travellers may be best advised to book one through a reliable source or through your hotel. Meters are non-existent, but all drivers should have typed sheets of the 'minimum' rates to and from various local places – though charges can be higher if their customers appear affluent. Rates should always be agreed before getting into the vehicle. If you are unsure of the route then rates per kilometre, or per hour, are easy to negotiate.

BY POSTBOAT Rather like the postbuses, postboats used to operate on the Upper Zambezi and the waters of Lake Bangweulu during the rainy season, transporting cargo, passengers and even vehicles. However, this service is now being subcontracted, with information sketchy and none too reliable, even at the individual ports themselves. For the most part it's best to ask advice locally.

DRIVING Driving in Zambia is on the left, based on the UK's model. However, the standard of driving is generally poor, matched only by the quality of the roads. Most roads in the cities, and the major arteries connecting these, are tar. These vary from silky-smooth recently laid roads, to pot-holed routes that test the driver's skill at negotiating a 'slalom course' of deep holes, whilst avoiding the oncoming traffic that's doing the same. Inconveniently, the smooth kind of road often changes into the holed variety without warning, so speeding on even the good tar is a dangerous occupation. Hitting a pot-hole at 40–60km/h will probably just blow a tyre; any faster and you risk damaging the suspension, or even rolling the vehicle.

As an additional hazard, even the tar roads are narrow by Western standards, often with steep sides designed to drain off water during the rains. As a result, it's all too easy, faced with a sharp bend or an oncoming lorry, to veer off the road, a fact borne out by the regular sight of a truck lying on its side in the ditch, or to damage the sump of the vehicle. Finally, watch out for speed humps that may occur without warning, even on major roads. You might find these at the entrance and exit of a town (Kapiri Mposhi, for example), but also sometimes as you approach a level crossing.

Away from the main arteries the roads are gravel or just dirt and usually badly maintained. During the dry season these will often need a high-clearance vehicle: a 4x4 is useful here, but not vital. (The exceptions are areas of western Zambia standing on Kalahari sand, which always require 4x4.) During the wet season Zambia's gravel roads are less forgiving, and they vary from being strictly for 4x4s to being impassable for any form of vehicle. Travel on anything except the tar roads is very difficult during the rains. For more details, and particularly if you intend to hire a vehicle, read the important section on driving in *Chapter 6*, pages 103–8.

Speed limits are 120km/h on main roads and 50km/h in towns, but there are significant local variations, particularly in the approach roads to Lusaka, where they tend to be strictly enforced. Beware of speed humps, often without warning, at the approach to a town, in both directions.

All vehicles should carry two warning triangles for use in case of an accident or breakdown (although you'll often see brushwood laid out on the road at strategic intervals to warn of an accident or breakdown). They should also display reflective tape: white at the front, and red at the rear. Failure to comply with these regulations will result in a fine.

Police (and immigration) roadblocks are an occupational hazard of driving, and you can expect to be stopped regularly. They are usually indicated in advance by oil drums or traffic cones placed in the middle of the road, but some are very poorly marked, so keep an eye out for them, and do stop! For more on this subject, see *Chapter 6*, pages 104–5.

If you drive carefully in Zambia, during the day, and stick to the speed limits and sensible speeds (maximum 100–120km/h on good tar, much less on gravel or pot-holed tar), then you should never have an accident here. However, animals and people (especially cyclists) on the road can be a nightmare, so don't be shy about using your horn a lot, and well in advance, particularly in busy towns.

If you're unfortunate enough to be involved in an accident, you need to think clearly. If you've hit a dog, a goat or a chicken, then you do not have to stop. It would be courteous to compensate the owner – although you may end up in a heated situation which becomes very difficult. If you hit a wild animal, you should report it to the local ZAWA office, or police station. Always check the vehicle, too; if you have hit a goat, for example, the impact could damage the coolant system and cause a leak.

If you hit a person, then the accident must be reported. Your natural instinct will be to stop – but most Zambians will tell you that you should not to do so, for fear of being seriously assaulted by friends or relatives of the injured person. That said, if the person is injured then you may be able to help to get him or her to hospital. I've never had to make this choice, and hope I never have to. (Should you be in this situation, and decide to help, do remember to wear plastic gloves and glasses to minimise the risk of HIV infection, and don't attempt mouth-to-mouth resuscitation without a protective mask.) In any case, you must go directly to the nearest police station, or police roadblock. If a death has occurred then you will be expected to hand over your passport to the police.

In order to make an insurance claim in Zambia you will need to obtain a police report, for which you'll be expected to pay.

Fuel Availability of fuel can be a problem at the best of times, so it is important to top up whenever you can rather than to let the tank run low. Not only are fuel stations thin on the ground outside of major centres, but supplies can be erratic, so that at any given time diesel, for example, may be difficult to find throughout the country.

The price of fuel is extremely high by southern African standards, a reflection of high government taxes, which account for over 50% of the price. Despite the country's distance from the nearest port, transportation is less of an issue: crude oil is brought by pipeline from Dar es Salaam to Ndola, where it is refined then distributed both within Zambia and to the DRC. Thus the country's cheapest fuel is in Ndola, but it varies quite significantly according to the part of the country, and from one fuel station to another. In summer 2007, the price of petrol in Lusaka was around Kw6,808 a litre, with diesel at Kw5,610, which represented an increase of around 10% in just three months, and brought it close to British prices. (As an indication of potential difference, prices at the same time in Kasama, in the Northern Region, were Kw7,600 and Kw6,761 respectively.)

Vehicle hire With difficult roads, which seem to vanish completely in some of the more remote areas, driving around Zambia away from the main arteries is not easy. The big car-hire firms do have franchises in Lusaka, but most concentrate on businesspeople who need transport around the city. Even now, some will insist that foreigners hiring cars also hire a chauffeur, and only the specialists are geared up for visitors in search of recreation.

Hiring a 2WD A mid-range model like a Ford Mondeo from, say, Europcar (*www.europcarzambia.com*) will cost around US$100/£55 per day with fully comprehensive insurance, 100km 'free' per day, and a 54¢/26p charge per kilometre after that. While this is an improvement on rates even a few years ago, just add up the distances on a map and you'll realise that it still isn't viable for most trips. Further, a standard saloon vehicle just wouldn't stand up to the pot-holes found on most of the main highways – never mind the state of the dirt tracks beyond, so for exploring beyond the major towns you'll be needing either a high-clearance 2WD or – better – a 4x4.

See *Car hire* in the chapters on Lusaka (page 128), Livingstone (page 164), and the Copperbelt (pages 384, 395 and 398) for contact details of the various car-hire agencies.

Hiring a 4x4 Until recently, it wasn't possible to hire reliable 4x4 vehicles in Zambia so the only option was to bring them in from outside, or arrange for a safari company to take you around on a mobile safari. However, this has changed, and there are now a few options within Zambia itself. All the same, it's important to realise that self-drive trips around Zambia are not for the inexperienced; I think that they're suitable only for those who have previously taken several in Africa, including at least one self-drive 4x4 trip (a 4x4 trip around Botswana makes a perfect precursor). And if you have any doubts, read the box *Lessons in bush travel* on pages 262–3, then think hard about what you're planning. Bear in mind, too, that self-drive trips are expensive; it can often be cheaper to fly between major cities before collecting a vehicle.

If you're thinking of a trip just around the eastern side of Zambia, then UK-based **Safari Drive** (see page 47) has a small fleet of Land Rover 110 Tdi vehicles available out of Lilongwe, for about £135/US$250 per day. All come well equipped with sturdy kit for bush camping, including long-range fuel tanks, rooftop tents, portable fridges and satellite phone, as well as the relevant paperwork to take them into Zambia.

If you plan to explore more of Zambia, there are other obvious candidates:

Hemingways See page 166
Limohire Zambia 📞 021 1278628; 📱 097
7743145; 📧 limohire@zamnet.zm; www.limohire-zambia.com. From its origins hiring out limousines for special occasions, this company now offers a wide range of well-maintained vehicles, including 4x4 with rooftop tents. Based just south of Lusaka, they will pick you up from the airport for free if you rent a car for more then three days.
Livingstone 4x4 Hire 📞/📠 021 1254096; 📱 097
7355348; 📧 info@4x4hireafrica.com; www.4x4hireafrica.com. Despite the name, this operates out of Lusaka, albeit with the option to hire from Livingstone. They have a small fleet of good, Land Rover Defenders that come either fully equipped with long-range fuel tanks, rooftop tents & fridges, etc, or without the equipment. Satellite phones & GPS systems are also available. Mileage is unlimited, & vehicles can be driven throughout southern Africa; cross-border paperwork to allow driving to South Africa is included (clients are responsible for relevant fees, permits etc). Rates are

on application, but expect something in the region of US$150–220 per day, depending on equipment, time of year and length of hire.
Voyagers 📞 02 617062, 620604; 📠 02 620605; 📧 carrental@voyagers.com.zm; www.voyagerszambia.com/safveh.htm. Based in Ndola, but with offices in Lusaka, Livingstone and elsewhere in the Copperbelt (and also at the airports), Voyagers have fully equipped Ford 4x4s complete with long-range fuel tank, rooftop tents, cooking equipment, fridge & linen, all carefully designed to fit into the vehicle. Also available are campervans, in the shape of Toyota Land Cruisers with a sleeping/dining area behind the driver's cab, also complete with equipment. Base rates are US$230 and US$188 per day respectively, inc VAT, fully comprehensive insurance & 200km. It's an efficient operation with particularly helpful staff. If provided with a rough itinerary, they will also advise on the state of the roads (& thus the type of vehicle required), & can book accommodation en route.

Finally, there's the Johannesburg-based **Britz 4x4 Rentals** (📞 *+27 11 396 1860; +27 11 396 1937;* 📧 *britz@iafrica.com; www.britz.com*), who have an impressive fleet

Distances in kilometres (approx)

Note that distances between towns are only one part of the equation when calculating travelling times. More important are the type of road (tar, gravel, dirt), and the conditions, both of which must be taken into consideration.

	Chipata	Chirundu	Kapiri Mposhi	Kasama	Kitwe	Livingstone	LUSAKA	Mansa	Mbereshi	Mongu	Mpika	Mporokoso	Mpulungu	Mwinilunga	Sesheke	Solwezi
Chirundu	706															
Kapiri Mposhi	780	346														
Kasama	1475	996	644													
Kitwe	990	498	150	796												
Livingstone	1080	608	682	1332	834											
LUSAKA	605	136	210	860	362	472										
Mansa	1400	926	650	350	800	1262	790									
Mbereshi	1600	1126	850	386	1000	1462	990	200								
Mongu	1210	760	834	1484	986	525	624	1414	1614							
Mpika	1269	839	493	221	643	1175	703	559	759	1327						
Mporokoso	1635	1156	804	160	954	1492	1020	307	181	1644	381					
Mpulungu	1679	1210	864	210	1014	1576	1074	517	560	1698	431	370				
Mwinilunga	1470	1020	674	1324	501	1356	884	1324	1524	780	1167	1478	1538			
Sesheke	1260	741	872	1522	1024	190	662	1452	1652	335	1311	1682	1736	1115		
Solwezi	1210	744	398	1042	225	1080	608	1048	1248	896	891	1202	1262	292	1231	
Zambezi	1650	1156	810	1454	658	1150	1020	1460	1660	625	1303	1614	1674	396	960	515

of vehicles, including Land Rover Td5s, which have been custom-built for comfortable camping trips and come comprehensively equipped. It's practical to collect and drop these in Livingstone, even though they are brought up from Jo'burg.

I've used vehicles from three of these, and there are pros and cons to them all; the best choice depends on the route you're taking.

HITCHHIKING Hitchhiking is a practical way to get around Zambia – especially in the more remote areas. Most of Zambia's poorer citizens hitchhike, and view buses as just a different form of vehicle. Either way, lifts are normally paid for.

Hitching has the great advantage of allowing you to talk one-to-one with a whole variety of people, from local businesspeople and expats, to truck drivers and farmers. Sometimes you will be crammed in the back of a windy pick-up with a dozen people and as many animals, while occasionally you will be comfortably seated in the back of a plush Mercedes, satisfying the driver's curiosity as to why you are in Zambia at all. It is simply the best way to get to know the country, through the eyes of its people, though it is not for the lazy or those pressed for time.

Waiting times can be long, even on the main routes, and getting a good lift can take six or eight hours. Generally, on such occasions, the problem is not that lots of potential vehicles refuse to take you. The truth is that there are sometimes very few people going your way with space to spare. If you are in a hurry then combining hitchhiking with taking the odd bus can be a quicker and more pragmatic way to travel.

The essentials for successful hitching in Zambia include a relatively neat, conservative set of clothes, without which you will be ignored by some of the more comfortable lifts available. A good ear for listening and a relaxed line in conversation are also assets, which spring naturally from taking an interest in the lives of the people that you meet. Finally, you must always carry a few litres of water and some food with you, both for standing beside the road, and for lifts where you can't stop for food.

Dangers of drink driving Unfortunately, drinking and driving is common in Zambia. It is more frequent in the afternoon/evening, and towards the end of the month when people are paid. Accepting a lift with someone who is drunk, or drinking and (simultaneously) driving, is foolish. Occasionally your driver will start drinking on the way, in which case you would be wise to start working out how to disembark politely.

An excuse for an exit, which I used on one occasion, was to claim that some close family member was killed whilst being driven by someone who had been drinking. Thus I had a real problem with the whole idea, and had even promised a surviving relative that I would never do the same … hence my overriding need to leave at the next reasonable town/village/stop. This gave me an opportunity to encourage the driver not to drink any more; and when that failed (which it did), it provided an excuse for me to disembark swiftly. Putting the blame on my own psychological problems avoided blaming the driver too much, which might have caused a difficult scene.

Safety of hitchhiking Notwithstanding the occasional drunk driver, Zambia is generally a safe place to hitchhike for a robust male traveller, or a couple travelling together. It is safer than the UK, and considerably safer than the USA; but hitchhiking still cannot be recommended for single women, or even two women travelling together. This is not because of any known horror stories, but because non-Zambian women, especially white women, hitching would evoke intense curiosity amongst the local people. Local people might view their hitching as asking for trouble, whilst some would associate them with the 'promiscuous' behaviour of white women seen on imported films and television programmes. The risk seems too high. Stick to buses.

 ## ACCOMMODATION

Zambia boasts the full range of accommodation, from top-class safari lodges and international hotels to simple guesthouses and campsites, with an equally diverse range of standards and prices. Pricing can appear complex at first, since many of the better establishments have a two- or even three-tier structure. Typically, there will be two rates: one for local visitors, the other for international guests. In some cases, the 'local' rate will be further divided into Zambian citizens and Zambian residents; in others, these two may be lumped together, but a further category introduced: visitors from within southern Africa.

Prices quoted in this guide are for the most part international rates – those payable by visitors from Europe, America and other Western countries.

HOTELS Traditionally, hotels in Zambia have tended to fall into two categories, all geared to the business market: large concrete blocks with pretensions to an 'international' standard, or small, run-down places catering to Zambians who are not very particular about quality. They're a very uninspiring bunch on the whole, and most visitors spend as little time in them as possible. Things started to change when Sun International opened two hotels near Victoria Falls in Livingstone in 2001, and since then other investors have seized the initiative. The South African Protea chain has recently branched out with two more interesting offerings in Chingola and Livingstone, while the Royal Solwezi to the west of the Copperbelt sets an entirely new style standard for the region.

The larger hotels are restricted to Lusaka, Livingstone and the Copperbelt. They generally have clean modern rooms, good communications and all the facilities that international businesspeople expect. Their prices reflect this, at around US$200–300/£100–150 per person sharing, or US$185–275£90–140 for a single. Most still have little to distinguish them from each other, and are pretty soulless. Alternatives within reach of Lusaka are the Cresta Golf View, a few game-lodge-cum-hotels like the Protea Safari Lodge and Chaminuka, and the rather more intimate Lilayi and Lechwe Lodge. These have more character and make more interesting places to stay than the international hotels, but they're further away from town and take time to get to.

Zambia's smaller and cheaper hotels vary tremendously, but very few are good and many seem over-priced.

GUESTHOUSES In the last few years Zambia's larger towns, and especially Lusaka, have seen a proliferation of small guesthouses of varying quality spring up throughout the more spacious suburbs. These are not very practical if you need a courtesy bus to the airport, room service, or a telephone beside your bed – but they are often full of character and can be good value. Expect them to cost US$50–100/£25–50 per person sharing, or US$60–120/£30–60 for a single, though in urban areas – especially the Copperbelt – these can be considerably higher. Typically rates will include a continental breakfast, which is mostly just a roll and a cup of tea, but could be a substantial meal complete with eggs.

GOVERNMENT RESTHOUSES These are dotted around the country in virtually every small town: a very useful option for the stranded backpacker. The town or district council usually runs them and, although a few have degenerated into brothels, others are adequate for a brief overnight stop. The sheets are usually clean, and most have rooms with private facilities. These are normally clean, though rarely spotless or in mint condition.

LODGES AND BUSHCAMPS Zambia's lodges and bushcamps are a match for the best in Africa. As befits a destination for visitors who take their game viewing and birdwatching seriously, the camps are very comfortable but concentrate on good guiding rather than luxury *per se*. En-suite showers and toilets are almost universal, the accommodation is fairly spacious, the organisation smooth and food invariably good to excellent. However, a few forget that their reputations are won and lost by the standards of their individual guides.

Aside from larger operations like Mfuwe and Chichele Lodge (which are different in emphasis), expect a maximum of ten to eighteen guests, and close personal care. But beware: if you seek a safari for its image, wanting to sleep late and then be pampered in the bush; or expect to dine from silverware and sip from cut-glass goblets ... then perhaps Zambia isn't for you after all.

✗ FOOD AND DRINK

FOOD Zambia's native cuisine is based on *nshima,* a cooked porridge made from ground maize. (In Zimbabwe this is *sadza,* in South Africa *mealie-pap.*) This is usually made thin, perhaps with sugar, for breakfast, then eaten thicker – the consistency of mashed potatoes – for lunch and dinner. For these main meals it will normally be accompanied by some tasty relish, perhaps made of meat and tomatoes, or dried fish.

Do taste this at some stage when visiting. Safari camps will often prepare it if requested, and it is always available in small restaurants in the towns. Often these will have only three items on the menu: nshima and chicken; nshima and meat; and nshima and fish – and they can be very good.

Camps, hotels and lodges that cater to overseas visitors will serve a very international fare, and the quality of food prepared in the most remote bushcamps amazes visitors. Coming to Zambia on safari your biggest problem with food is likely to be the temptation to eat too much.

If you are driving yourself around and plan to cook, then get most of your supplies in Lusaka or the larger towns. Shoprite stores have revolutionised what's available, and really have all that you will need. Away from Shoprite, in the smaller towns, availability is usually limited to products that are popular locally. These include bread, flour, rice, soups and various tinned vegetables, meats and fish, though locally grown produce such as tomatoes or sweet potatoes will be available in season. This is fine for nutrition, but you may get bored with the selection in a week or two.

ALCOHOL Like most countries in the region, Zambia has two distinct beer types: clear and opaque. Most visitors and more affluent Zambians drink the **clear beers**, which are similar to European lagers and always served chilled. Mosi, Castle and Rhino are the lagers brewed by South African Breweries' Zambian subsidiaries. They are widely available and usually good. There is one craft brewery in Zambia which makes Dr Livingstone's Lager, Zikomo Copper Ale, Safari Stout and Baobab White, which is brewed with the fruit from the baobab tree.

Note that all beer produced in Zambia has a deposit on its bottles, like those of soft drinks. The contents will cost about US$1/Kw4,000 from a shop, or about US$2/Kw8,000 in a hotel bar. Imported lagers such as Windhoek, Holsten and Amstel will cost almost double this.

Judi Helmholz

November typically marks the beginning of the rainy season in Zambia. The first rains bring vast swarms of termites out of their nests to find mates and reproduce. Termites are a once-a-year delicacy not to be missed for culinary adventurers. And capturing them is half the fun!

Termites are attracted to light, so it's easiest to catch them when they are swarming around in the evening. Get a large bowl and fill it with water. Catch live termites with your hand as they fly around and drop them into the water (which keeps them from flying or crawling out). Or you can wait until the morning and collect them off the ground after they have dropped their wings (then you don't have to pull the wings off yourself). Gather as many as you need, live ones only.

PREPARATION Remove any wings from termites and throw wings away. Place wingless termites in a colander or bowl to rinse. Rinse them under running water. Heat a frying pan with a dash of cooking oil until sizzling temperature. Drop in live termites and sauté until they are crisp and golden brown (about one minute). Add salt to taste. Serve in a bowl as you would peanuts. *Bon appétit!*

Less affluent Zambians usually opt for some form of the **opaque beer** (sometimes called Chibuku, after the market-leading brand). This is a commercial version of traditional beer, usually brewed from maize and/or sorghum. It's a sour, porridge-like brew, an acquired taste, and is much cheaper than lager. Locals will sometimes buy a bucket of it, and then pass this around a circle of drinkers. It would be unusual for a visitor to drink this, so try some and amuse your Zambian companions. Remember, though, that traditional opaque beer changes flavour as it ferments and you can often ask for 'fresh beer' or 'strong beer'. If you aren't sure about the bar's hygiene standards, stick to the pre-packaged brands of opaque beer like Chibuku, Chinika, Golden, Chipolopolo or Mukango.

SOFT DRINKS Soft drinks are available everywhere, which is fortunate when the temperatures are high. Choices are often limited, though the ubiquitous Coca-Cola is usually there at around US$0.50/Kw2,000 – perhaps a little cheaper in a supermarket, and a little more in a decent café. Diet drinks are rarely seen in the rural areas – which is no surprise for a country where malnutrition is a problem.

Until recently, all soft drinks were sold in glass bottles, though increasingly plastic bottles are in use. If you're faced with glass, try to buy up at least one actual bottle (per person) in a city before you go travelling: it will be invaluable. Because of the cost of bottle production, and the 'deposit' system (typically around US$0.30/Kw1,500 per bottle), you will often be unable to buy full bottles of soft drinks in rural areas without swapping them for empty ones in return. The alternative is to stand and drink the contents where you buy a drink, and leave the empty behind you. This is fine, but can be inconvenient if you have just dashed in for a drink while your bus stops for a few minutes.

WATER Water in the main towns is usually purified, provided there are no shortages of chlorine, breakdowns or other mishaps. The locals drink it, and are used to the relatively innocuous bugs that it may harbour. If you are in the country for a long time, then it may be worth acclimatising yourself to it – though be prepared for some days spent near a toilet. However, if you are in Zambia for just a few weeks,

Willard Nakutonga and Judi Helmholz

There are several types of beer or *mooba* ('beer' in Nyanja) produced in Zambia. The bottled Mosi lager reflects the local name for Victoria Falls – 'Mosi Oa Tunya', meaning the 'Smoke that Thunders' and is one of the most popular beers in Zambia. Rhino lager is another bottled beer, produced and distributed throughout Zambia. You can ask for it in Nyanja by saying '*Nifuna mooba wa Rhino*' – 'I want Rhino beer'.

Chibuku or Shake-Shake is a much cheaper, opaque beer. Resembling an alcoholic milkshake, it is an acquired taste and a favourite amongst more traditional and less affluent Zambians.

Kachusu is the name for the main illicit beer – akin to 'moonshine'. It is brewed in villages or at shebeens, and best avoided. Not only is it illegal, so you may be arrested just for drinking it, but it may also damage your liver and kidneys.

Cigarettes, or *fwaka* in Nyanja, can be purchased almost anywhere. In local markets, you can find big bins of raw tobacco, or tobacco shavings, on sale for those who like to roll their own. The most popular cigarette brand available in Zambia is Peter Stuyvesant, affectionately referred to as 'Peters'. Don't even think about trying *mbanje* or *dagga* (marijuana); if you're arrested there is no bail, and the penalty is five years in prison with hard labour.

then try to drink only bottled, boiled or treated water in town – otherwise you will get stomach upsets. Bottled water can be bought almost anywhere, although if you want it cold you may often find it's frozen! Expect to pay around US$0.60/Kw2,500 for a half-litre in a supermarket, more in a smaller outlet or garage.

Out in the bush, most of the camps and lodges use water from boreholes. These underground sources vary in quality, but are normally free from bugs so the water is perfectly safe to drink. Sometimes it is sweet, at other times a little alkaline or salty. Ask locally if it is suitable for an unacclimatised visitor to drink, then take their advice.

WHAT TO BUY

CURIOS Zambia's best bargains are handicrafts: carvings and baskets made locally. The curio stall near Victoria Falls close to the Zimbabwean border has a good selection, but prices are lower if you buy away from tourist areas, in Lusaka (try Kabwata Cultural Centre, page 155), or at some of the roadside stalls.

Wherever you buy handicrafts, don't be afraid to bargain gently. Expect an eventual reduction of about a quarter of the original asking price and always be polite and good-humoured. After all, a few cents will probably make more difference to the person with whom you are bargaining than it will mean to you.

Note that you will often see carvings on sale in the larger stalls which have been imported from Kenya, Tanzania, DRC and Zimbabwe. Assume that they would be cheaper if purchased in their countries of origin, and try to buy something Zambian as a memento of your trip.

Occasionally you will be offered 'precious' stones to buy – rough diamonds, emeralds and the like. Expert geologists may spot the occasional genuine article amongst hoards of fakes, but most mere mortals will end up being conned. Stick to the carvings if you want a bargain.

For a more practical and much cheaper souvenir get a *chitenje* for about Kw30,000–40,000 – there are shops in the smallest of towns. You will see these 2m-long sections of brightly patterned cotton cloth everywhere, often wrapped around local women. Whilst travelling use them as towels, sarongs, picnic mats or – as the locals do – simply swathed over your normal clothes to keep them clean. When back home, you can cut the material into clothes, or use them as wall-coverings or tablecloths. Either way, you will have brought a splash of truly African colour back home with you.

IMPORTS AND EXPORTS There is no problem in exporting normal curios, but you will need an official export permit from the Department of National Parks to take out any game trophies. Visitors are urged to support the letter and the spirit of the CITES bans on endangered species, including the ban on the international trade in ivory. This has certainly helped to reduce ivory poaching, so don't undermine it by buying ivory souvenirs here. In any case, you will probably have big problems when you try to import them back into your home country.

SUPPLIES In the past decade or so Zambia's shops have emerged from a retailing time-warp, where cramped corner shops had the monopoly. Until then, most of the country's residents were innocent of consumer-friendly hypermarkets where wide, ergonomically designed aisles are lined with endless choice.

Then, in 1996, Shoprite/Checkers arrived promoting a largely alien practice of high volume, low margin superstores using good levels of pay to reward honest employees. This rocked Lusaka's existing, mainly Asian, shop-owning community who had always gone for the high-margin corner-shop approach. Rumours were rife of the ways in which Shoprite's arrival was resisted, and even blocked by the capital's existing business community. Now, though, Shoprite has found a very solid footing. Within just a few years, it has opened stores in most of Zambia's major towns, and these are normally the best and cheapest places to shop for supplies. Increasingly you'll also find the chain's fast-food subsidiary, Hungry Lion, next door, selling chips, burgers and similar sanitised bites.

However, all is not rosy. To many it seems that while the state is dismantling many of its own monopolies, the private sector is being allowed to generate new ones. Many aggressive South African companies, from Shoprite to Game, and HI-FI to Electric City, have moved into Zambia and started to dominate it, causing resentment from local businesspeople. Critics say the success of these is down to South Africa's policy of lucrative tax breaks, which effectively subsidise exports. They fear that by allowing these new companies to build monopolies, local entrepreneurs are losing out. They point to the import bills generated by such stores, which often source more of their stock from outside Zambia than from inside. However, supporters point to the increased availability of goods, and the small Zambian businesses which are improving their standards and starting to supply to these stores.

Whatever the arguments, you can now buy most things in Zambia (and in kwacha) at a price, and if you have the money then this will seem like a good thing. Perhaps the best advice for the careful visitor is to try to buy Zambian products wherever possible, for the sake of the local economy.

✉ COMMUNICATIONS AND MEDIA

POST The post is neither cheap nor fast, though it is fairly reliable for letters and postcards. The charges are increased to keep pace with devaluations of the kwacha, but currently it costs around Kw2,700 to send a letter to the UK, or Kw3,300 to the US, while a postcard costs Kw1,600 to either destination. It's worth noting that Zambia has some lovely stamps for sale, a favourite of stamp collectors.

The best way to send mail quickly within Zambia is via EMS (Expedited Mail Service), a reasonably priced service where letters are hand delivered (no postbox mail). It is also available to overseas destinations and is generally less expensive than a courier company. For express mail services, there are several choices, some of which also offer phone, fax and internet as well. With any you can send letters, parcels and small packets to destinations within Zambia and worldwide. This is costly but reliable. If you need important documents sent from overseas, couriers such as DHL or FedEx (see pages 150 and 187 for contact details in Lusaka and Livingstone) are the quickest way to be assured of them reaching you safely. Packages take about a week from Europe or the USA.

Post offices in large towns are normally open Monday to Friday, 08.00–17.00, Sat 08.00–1200, but you can expect shorter hours in more out-of-the way places.

✆ **TELEPHONE** The Zambian telephone system is overloaded and has difficulty coping. Getting through to anywhere can be hard, and this difficulty generally increases in proportion to the remoteness of the place that you are trying to contact. If you must use the phone, then persistence is the key – just keep on trying and eventually you should get a line that works.

Telephone codes In 2007, the entire landline system in Zambia was being overhauled, to give a single access code – 021 – for the whole country. As a result, all telephone numbers are changing. Prior to this, there were 12 regional codes, most covering large regions of the country, but based on the following towns:

01	Chilanga, Chirundu, Chisamba, Chongwe, Kafue, Luangwa, Lusaka, Mumbwa, Namalundu Gorge, Nampundwe, Siavonga
02	Chambishi, Chililabombwe, Chingola, Itimpi, Kalulushi, Kawambwa, Kitwe, Luanshya, Mansa, Masaiti, Mufulira, Mwense, Nchelenge, Ndola, Samfya
03	Livingstone
032	Choma, Gwembe, Itezhi-Tezhi, Kalomo, Maamba, Mazabuka, Monze, Namwala, Pemba
04	Chinsali, Isoka, Kasama, Luwingu, Mbala, Mpika, Mporokoso, Mpulungu, Mungwi, Nakonde
05	Chibombo, Kabwe, Kapiri Mposhi, Mkushi, Serenje
062	Chadiza, Chipata, Katete, Mfuwe, Sinda
063	Nyimba, Petauke
064	Chama, Lundazi
07	Kalabo, Kaoma, Lukulu, Mongu, Senanga
08	Kabompo, Kasempa, Mufumbwe, Mwinilunga, Solwezi, Zambezi

In order to work out the new numbers, preface the original number and code with 021, delete the next 0, then add the remaining numbers to the beginning of the number. Thus, the Lusaka number 01 123456 becomes 021 **1**123456. The same will apply for all other landlines, so that Livingstone 03 320145 will be 021 **3**320145, or for the Copperbelt 02 232145 will become 021 **2**232145. When dialling from a landline within Zambia, there is no need to dial the 021. If – like most Zambians – you're using a mobile phone, then you will need to include 021 in the number. All mobile phone numbers were also changed (see below).

Phone numbers in this guide have been changed in line with the new system, but there remains considerable confusion in Zambia itself, with many subscribers unaware of the changes. Should the new number not work, try omitting the '21' from the '021' code, thus reverting to the old number.

To dial into the country from abroad, the international access code for Zambia is +260. From inside Zambia, you dial 00 to get an international line, then the country's access code (eg: 44 for the UK, or 1 for the USA).

New lines are difficult to acquire from the state-owned company, Zamtel, which has a monopoly over the phone system, and old ones take time to repair. Thus for local people or companies to have four or five different numbers is still common, though increasingly both business and personal users rely on mobile phones.

Mobile phones The use of mobile phones, or 'cells' as they're usually called in Zambia, has grown very rapidly to counter the problems with the country's landline network. Coverage is surprisingly widespread, although in rural areas you can expect it to be patchy at best, or non-existent. The major networks are Celtel (*www.celtel.com*), MTN and Cellz, as well as the state-owned Zamtel.

During 2007, all mobile phone numbers throughout Zambia were changed, as follows:

Celtel Celtel prefixes 097, 098 and 099 will all now be 097. The last digit of the old prefix will then be added to the main number, to give a 7-digit number. So:

097 770945 will be 097 **7**770945
098 986234 will be 097 **8**986234
099 926752 will become 097 **9**926752

MTN and Zamtel All MTN (Telecel 096) and Zamtel (095) numbers will retain their original code, but the final number of the prefix will now also be added to the old number, to give a new 7-digit number:

096 763232 will be   096 **6**763232
095 752836 will be   095 **5**752836

Top-up cards for each of the mobile networks are available in even the smallest towns, or from touts at major road junctions. If you're in the Livingstone area, be careful of picking up Zimbabwean networks, as prices may be based on official Zimbabwean exchange rates, and hence be much more expensive than their Zambian equivalents.

If you're planning to use your own mobile phone in Zambia, it's almost certainly going to be cheaper to buy a local SIM card for the duration of your visit. Celtel in particular have numerous outlets, with a SIM card costing just Kw5,000 (about 60p/US$1), and top-up cards available in denominations from Kw5,000 to Kw500,000. According to the package you select, calls are payable either by the second (which works out cheaper for short calls up to a minute) or by the minute – in which case you'll be looking at around 30p/US$0.50 per minute to a Zambian landline (16p/US$0.32 off-peak), or US$1.81/1.36 per minute to the UK, with texts (including international messaging) at US$0.13.

Payphones The old payphones used always to be out of order, but newer cardphones are now the norm. Phonecards, available from Zamtel offices and many other outlets, cost Kw10,000 initially, but are then rechargeable by buying scratchcards in units from Kw10,000 to Kw100,000. You can dial internationally from these, and there is no time limit placed on their use.

Local calls are cheap; those within Lusaka, for example, cost Kw200 (approx £0.025/US$0.05) per minute.

FAX If you are trying to send a fax to, or within, Zambia then always use a manual setting to dial (and redial, and redial ...) the number. Listen for a fax tone on the line yourself. Only when you finally hear one should you press the 'start' button on your machine to send the fax.

🔵 EMAIL AND THE INTERNET Contrary to what you may have expected, the email community in Zambia is quite large, and there are fairly reliable and high-speed internet cafes in Lusaka and other bigger towns, although don't expect the latest hardware.

In the early days, virtually all Zambian websites and addresses were accessed through the Zamnet server, which was associated with the University of Zambia. This eventually split from the university to become a separate company, but not before users encountered numerous problems using it, earning it a wide variety of nicknames; 'Damnet' was one of the less offensive. Because of these problems, many email subscribers changed their addresses, some to alternative service providers within Zambia and others to providers outside (usually linked by satellite telephone systems, in order to avoid the telephone problems). Nevertheless, significant problems remain, so if you're emailing someone in Zambia and don't get a reply within 48 hours, it would be wise to resend the email. Note that although increasing numbers of people and businesses in Zambia are getting email, far fewer have access to the internet.

MEDIA
The press The main daily papers are *The Post*, which is privately owned and fairly independent, and the *Times of Zambia* and the *Daily Mail*, both of which are owned by the government. The *Financial Mail* is part of the *Daily Mail*, as are the *Sunday Mail* and the *Sunday Times*. On the whole, *The Post* is the most outspoken and interesting paper.

There are also several weekly papers, including the *National Mirror, Monitor* and *Mail & Guardian*, which despite its independent status tends to be strongly pro-government. There are also a few good monthlies, including *Mining Mail*, and the indispensable Lusaka-based guide, *The Lowdown*.

Zambia claims to have a free press, and most issues are debated openly. However, when the more sensitive ones are skirted around, only *The Post* tries to take a more investigative approach. Often this is respected, but see Zambia's most recent history in *The late 1990s* in *Chapter 1*, page 11, for an example of an incident when the authorities were less than respectful in their approach.

You can find the very the latest news from *The Post* in Zambia at www.postzambia.com, or from the *Times of Zambia* at www.times.co.zm. Some of the stories can be fascinating, so it's well worth having a look before you go.

In addition to these, there are three magazines that are targeted directly at the visitor. Newest of these is *Travel Zambia*, launched in 2007 by the team from the well-respected *Travel Africa* (*www.travelafricamag.com*) and available both in the UK and throughout Zambia. The more established *Zambian Traveller* is published bi-monthly, and is distributed through hotels and lodges in Zambia. It features a range of articles covering everything from mining and conservation to hotel reviews. Tighter in focus is *Zambia Heritage*, issued twice a year by the National Heritage Conservation Commission, and geared to promoting their sites.

Radio and television Radio is limited, as Zambia National Broadcasting Corporation (ZNBC) runs three channels which are all used as government communication tools: Radio 1, Radio 2 and Radio 4. (Radio 4 used to be the rather fun Radio Mulungushi, until it was swallowed up.)

There is some good news though, as in the cities – especially Lusaka – you'll find smaller commercial stations. The obvious one is probably Radio Phoenix, which broadcasts popular music and Zambian news, though it's worth scanning the airwaves. Outside of the large cities, you'll find little, although those with short-wave radios can always seek the BBC World Service, the Voice of America and Radio Canada.

The public television stations are also run by ZNBC, broadcasting during the week from midday through to midnight, with programmes at weekends starting at around 07.00. They stick to the official party line on most issues, but do tune in – some of their panel debates can be fascinating. Most hotels with in-room televisions subscribe to satellite channels, often including BBC World, CNN and/or the South African cable network, M-Net, with its multitude of sports and movie channels.

GIVING SOMETHING BACK

HELPING ZAMBIA'S POORER COMMUNITIES Visiting Zambia, especially the rural agricultural areas and the towns, many visitors are struck by the poverty and wish to help. Giving to beggars and those in need on the street is one way. It will alleviate your feelings of guilt, and perhaps some of the immediate suffering, but it is not a long-term solution.

There are ways in which you can make a positive contribution, but they require more effort than throwing a few coins to someone on the street. My favourite is the ZOCS (Zambia Open Community Schools) project, which provides a basic education to young Zambians who could not otherwise afford school at all. Education is vital for Zambia's future, while in the present it gives children some hope. Deaths from AIDS have left increasing numbers of orphans, many of whom end up on the streets. This project is making a difference on a local level, helping communities to organise their own schools.

There are many other charities equally worthy of your help, trying to provide sustainable solutions at a local level. Some are part of CHIN (Children in Need Network) – a group of non-governmental organisations, community-based groups and government departments working with children in need. Their website (*www.chin.org.zm*) will give you some idea of the scale of the help required. All welcome donations – so make a resolution now to help at least one of them as an integral part of the cost of your trip.

LOCAL CHARITIES WORKING IN ZAMBIA Your best source of up-to date local info is probably www.chin.org.zm, but three organisations are worthy of special mention:

Habitat for Humanity PO Box 34987, 1st Floor, Impala Hse, Chachacha Rd, Northend, Lusaka 10101; ➦ 021 123 2249; f 021 123 2250; e hfhzam@ zamnet.zm; www.habitatzam. This is a non-profit,

Christian NGO trying to solve the housing problems of the poor. Since 1984 they have built over 1,300 houses in different projects throughout the country. Families pay back the loan over a period of 10 years into a revolving fund, enabling more houses to be built in the same community. Volunteers provide most of the labour.

Zambia National Association for the Physically Handicapped (ZNAPH) PO Box 72908, Buteko Av, Ndola; ☏ 021 262 2226; f 021 262 2226; e znaph@zamtel.zm; www.add.org.uk/. ZNAPH runs a carpentry workshop for physically handicapped people, training them to be carpenters & to produce furniture that is sold to raise funds for the workshop.

Zambili d'Afrique PO Box 38540, 5087 Luanshya Rd, Lusaka 10101; ☏ 021 122 7286, 122 9691; f 021 122 9691; e zcraft@zambili.co.zm; www.catgen.net/zambilicraft. An NGO working with Traidcraft Exchange, a UK-based organisation that promotes ethical & effective business in support of fair trade, Zambili helps small & medium-sized businesses to start exporting their goods.

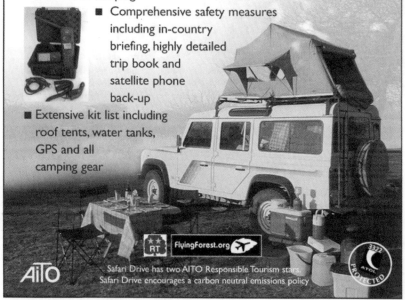

5

Health and Safety

There is always great danger in writing about health and safety for the uninitiated visitor. It is all too easy to become paranoid about exotic diseases that you may catch, and all too easy to start distrusting everybody you meet as a potential thief – falling into an unjustified us-and-them attitude towards the people of the country you are visiting.

As a comparison, imagine an equivalent section in a guidebook to a Western country – there would be a list of possible diseases and advice on the risk of theft and mugging. Many Western cities are very dangerous, but with time we learn how to assess the risks, accepting almost subconsciously what we can and cannot do.

It is important to strike the right balance: to avoid being either excessively cautious or too relaxed about your health and your safety. With experience, you will find the balance that best fits you and the country you are visiting.

✚ HEALTH with Dr Jane Wilson-Howarth and Dr Felicity Nicholson

BEFORE YOU GO

Travel insurance Visitors to Zambia must take out a comprehensive **medical insurance policy** to cover them for emergencies, including the cost of evacuation to another country within the region. Such policies come with an emergency number (often on a reverse-charge/call-collect basis). You would be wise to memorise this – or indelibly tattoo it in as many places as possible on your baggage.

Personal effects insurance is also a sensible precaution, but check the policy's fine print before you leave home. Often, in even the best policies, you will find a limit per item, or per claim – which can be well below the cost of a replacement. If you need to list your valuables separately, then do so comprehensively. Check that receipts are not required for claims if you do not have them, and that the excess that you have to pay on every claim is reasonable.

Annual travel policies can be excellent value if you travel a lot, and some of the larger credit-card companies offer excellent deals. However, often it is better to get your valuables named and insured for travel using your home contents insurance. These year-round policies will try harder to settle your claim fairly as they want your business in the long term.

Immunisations Having a full set of immunisations takes time, normally at least six weeks, although some protection can be had by visiting your doctor as late as a few days before you travel. Ideally, see your doctor or travel clinic (see pages 88–9) early on to establish an inoculation timetable.

Legal requirements No immunisations are required by law for entry into Zambia. Yellow fever is no longer considered to be endemic to the country, and Zambia in turn no longer asks for proof of vaccination from those crossing its borders. That said, recent reports suggest that this information hasn't always filtered down to individual border crossings, and those entering from Malawi may still be asked to provide evidence of yellow fever vaccination.

Recommended precautions Preparations to ensure a healthy trip to Zambia require checks on your immunisation status: it is wise to be up to date on **tetanus**, **polio** and **diphtheria** (now given as an all-in-one vaccine, Revaxis, that lasts for ten years), and hepatitis A. Immunisations against meningococcus and rabies may also be recommended. Immunisation against cholera is not required for trips to Zambia.

Hepatitis A vaccine (Havrix Monodose or Avaxim) comprises two injections given about a year apart. The course costs about £100, but may be available on the NHS; it protects for 25 years and can be administered even close to the time of departure. **Hepatitis B** vaccination should be considered for longer trips (two months or more) or for those working with children or in situations where contact with blood is likely. Three injections are needed for the best protection and can be given over a three-week period if time is short. Longer schedules give more sustained protection and are therefore preferred if time allows. Hepatitis A vaccine can also be given as a combination with hepatitis B as 'Twinrix', though two doses are needed at least seven days apart to be effective for the hepatitis A component, and three doses are needed for the hepatitis B.

The newer injectable **typhoid** vaccines (eg: Typhim Vi) last for three years and are about 85% effective. Oral capsules (Vivotif) are currently available in the US (and soon in the UK); if four capsules are taken over seven days it will last for five years. This is encouraged unless you are leaving within a few days for a trip of a week or less, when the vaccine would not be effective in time. **Meningitis** vaccine (ideally containing strains A, C, W and Y, but if this is not available then A+C vaccine is better than nothing), is recommended, especially for trips of more than four weeks (see *Meningitis*, page 97).

Vaccination against **rabies** is unnecessary for most visitors, but would be wise for those who travel for extended periods (four weeks or longer), or stay in rural areas (see *Rabies*, page 98). Ideally three injections are taken over a minimum of 21 days, though even taking one or two doses of vaccine is better than none at all. Contrary to popular belief these vaccinations are relatively painless.

Experts differ over whether a BCG vaccination against **tuberculosis** (TB) is useful in adults: discuss this with your travel clinic.

In addition to the various vaccinations recommended above, it is important that you should be properly protected against malaria. For detailed advice see below.

Ideally you should visit your own doctor or a specialist travel clinic (see pages 88–9) to discuss your requirements if possible at least eight weeks before you plan to travel.

Malaria Malaria is the most dangerous disease in Africa, and the greatest risk to the traveller. It occurs throughout Zambia, all the year round, so it is essential that you take all possible precautions against it.

Malaria prevention Prophylaxis regimes aim to infuse your bloodstream with drugs that inhibit and kill the malaria parasites which are injected into you by a biting mosquito. This is why you must start to take the drugs *before* you arrive in a malarial area – so that they are established in your bloodstream from day one. Unfortunately, malaria parasites continually adapt to the drugs used to combat them, so the recommended regimes must adapt and change in order to remain effective. None is 100% effective, and all require time to kill the parasites – so unless there is a medical indication for stopping, it is important to complete the course after leaving the area as directed (usually one to four weeks depending on the regime). Falciparum (cerebral) malaria is the most common in Africa, and usually fatal if untreated, so it is worth your while trying to avoid it.

Seek current advice on the best antimalarials to take: usually mefloquine, Malarone or doxycycline. If mefloquine (Lariam) is suggested, start this two and a half weeks (three doses) before departure to check that it suits you; stop it immediately if it seems to cause depression or anxiety, visual or hearing disturbances, severe headaches, fits or changes in heart rhythm. Side effects such as nightmares or dizziness are not medical reasons for stopping unless they are sufficiently debilitating or annoying. Anyone who has been treated for depression or psychiatric problems, has diabetes controlled by oral therapy or who is epileptic (or who has suffered fits in the past) or has a close blood relative who is epileptic, should probably avoid mefloquine.

In the past doctors were nervous about prescribing mefloquine to pregnant women, but experience has shown that it is relatively safe and certainly safer than the risk of malaria. That said, there are other issues, so if you are travelling to Zambia while pregnant, seek expert advice before departure.

Malarone (proguanil and atovaquone) is as effective as mefloquine. It has the advantage of having few side effects and need only be continued for one week after returning. However, it is expensive and because of this tends to be reserved for shorter trips. Malarone may not be suitable for everybody, so take advice from a doctor. The licence in the UK has been extended for up to three months' use and a paediatric form of tablet is also available, prescribed on a weight basis.

A third alternative is the antibiotic doxycycline (100mg daily). Like Malarone it can be started one to two days before arrival. Unlike mefloquine, it may also be used in travellers with epilepsy, although certain anti-epileptic medication may make it less effective. In perhaps 1–3% of people there is the possibility of allergic skin reactions developing in sunlight; the drug should be stopped if this happens. Women using the oral contraceptive should use an additional method of protection for the first four weeks when using doxycycline. It is also unsuitable in pregnancy or for children under 12 years.

Chloroquine and proguanil are no longer considered to be effective enough for Zambia but may be considered as a last resort if nothing else is deemed suitable.

All tablets should be taken with or after the evening meal, washed down with plenty of fluid and, with the exception of Malarone (see above), continued for four weeks after leaving.

Despite all these precautions, it is important to be aware that no anti-malarial drug is 100% protective, although those on prophylactics who are unlucky enough to catch malaria are less likely to get rapidly into serious trouble. In addition to taking anti-malarials, it is therefore important to avoid mosquito bites between dusk and dawn (see *Avoiding insect bites*, pages 93–4).

There is unfortunately the occasional traveller who prefers to 'acquire resistance' to malaria rather than take preventative tablets, or who takes homeopathic prophylactics thinking these are effective against killer disease. Homeopathy theory dictates treating like with like so there is no place for prophylaxis or immunisation in a well person; bone fide homeopaths do not advocate it. Travellers to Africa cannot acquire any effective resistance to malaria, and those who don't make use of prophylactic drugs risk their life in a manner that is both foolish and unnecessary.

TRAVEL CLINICS AND HEALTH INFORMATION A full list of current travel clinic websites worldwide is available from the International Society of Travel Medicine on www.istm.org. For other journey preparation information, consult www.tripprep.com. Information about various medications may be found on www.emedicine.com. For information on malaria prevention, see www.preventingmalaria.info.

UK

Berkeley Travel Clinic 32 Berkeley St, London W1J 8EL (near Green Park tube station); ☎ 020 7629 6233

Cambridge Travel Clinic 48a Mill Rd, Cambridge CB1 2AS; ☎ 01223 367362; e enquiries@ travelcliniccambridge.co.uk; www.travelcliniccambridge.co.uk; ⊕ 12.00–19.00 Tue–Fri, 10.00–16.00 Sat.

Edinburgh Travel Clinic Regional Infectious Diseases Unit, Ward 41 OPD, Western General Hospital, Crewe Rd South, Edinburgh EH4 2UX; ☎ 0131 537 2822; www.link.med.ed.ac.uk/ridu. Travel helpline (*0906 589 0380*) ⊕ 09.00–12.00 weekdays. Provides inoculations & antimalarial prophylaxis, & advises on travel-related health risks.

Fleet Street Travel Clinic 29 Fleet St, London EC4Y 1AA; ☎ 020 7353 5678; www.fleetstreetclinic.com. Vaccinations, travel products & latest advice.

Hospital for Tropical Diseases Travel Clinic Mortimer Market Bldg, Capper St (off Tottenham Ct Rd), London WC1E 6AU; ☎ 020 7388 9600; www.thehtd.org. Offers consultations & advice, & is able to provide all necessary drugs & vaccines for travellers. Runs a healthline (☎ *0906 133 7733*) for country-specific information & health hazards. Also stocks nets, water purification equipment & personal protection measures.

Interhealth Worldwide Partnership Hse, 157 Waterloo Rd, London SE1 8US; ☎ 020 7902 9000; www.interhealth.org.uk. Competitively priced, one-stop travel health service. All profits go to their affiliated company, InterHealth, which provides health care for overseas workers on Christian projects.

Liverpool School of Medicine Pembroke Pl, Liverpool L3 5QA; ☎ 051 708 9393; f 0151 705 3370; www.liv.ac.uk/lstm

MASTA (Medical Advisory Service for Travellers Abroad) Moorfield Rd, Yeadon, Leeds LS19 7BN; ☎ 0870 606 2782; www.masta-travel-health.com. Provides travel health advice, anti-malarials & vaccinations. There are over 25 MASTA pre-travel clinics in Britain; call or check online for the nearest. Clinics also sell mosquito nets, medical kits, insect protection & travel hygiene products.

NHS travel website www.fitfortravel.scot.nhs.uk. Provides country-by-country advice on immunisation & malaria, plus details of recent developments, & a list of relevant health organisations.

Nomad Travel Store/Clinic 3–4 Wellington Terr, Turnpike La, London N8 0PX; ☎ 020 8889 7014, travel-health line (office hours only) ☎ 0906 863 3414; e sales@nomadtravel.co.uk; www.nomadtravel.co.uk. Also at 40 Bernard St, London WC1N 1LJ; ☎ 020 7833 4114; 52 Grosvenor Gdns, London SW1W 0AG; ☎ 020 7823 5823; and 43 Queens Rd, Bristol BS8 1QH; ☎ 0117 922 6567. For health advice, equipment such as mosquito nets & other anti-bug devices, & an excellent range of adventure travel gear.

Trailfinders Travel Clinic 194 Kensington High St, London W8 7RG; ☎ 020 7938 3999; www.trailfinders.com/clinic.htm

Travelpharm The Travelpharm website, www.travelpharm.com, offers up-to-date guidance on travel-related health & has a range of medications available through their online mini-pharmacy.

Irish Republic

Tropical Medical Bureau Grafton Street Medical Centre, Grafton Bldgs, 34 Grafton St, Dublin 2; ☎ 1 671 9200; www.tmb.ie. A useful website specific to tropical destinations. Also check website for other bureaux locations throughout Ireland.

USA

Centers for Disease Control 1600 Clifton Rd, Atlanta, GA 30333; ☎ 800 311 3435; travellers' health hotline 888 232 3299; www.cdc.gov/travel. The central source of travel information in the USA. The invaluable *Health Information for International Travel*, published annually, is available from the Division of Quarantine at this address.

Connaught Laboratories PO Box 187, Swiftwater, PA 18370; ☎ 800 822 2463. They will send a free list of specialist tropical-medicine physicians in your state.

IAMAT (International Association for Medical Assistance to Travelers) 1623 Military Rd, 279, Niagara Falls, NY 14304-1745; ☎ 716 754 4883; e info@iamat.org; www.iamat.org. A non-profit organisation that provides lists of English-speaking doctors abroad.

International Medicine Center 920 Frostwood Dr, Suite 670, Houston, TX 77024; ☏ 713 550 2000; www.traveldoc.com

Canada
IAMAT Suite 1, 1287 St Clair Av W, Toronto, Ontario M6E 1B8; ☏ 416 652 0137; www.iamat.org

TMVC Suite 314, 1030 W Georgia St, Vancouver, BC V6E 2Y3; ☏ 1 888 288 8682; www.tmvc.com. Private clinic with several outlets in Canada.

Australia, New Zealand, Singapore
IAMAT PO Box 5049, Christchurch 5, New Zealand; www.iamat.org
TMVC ☏ 1300 65 88 44; www.tmvc.com.au. Clinics in Australia, New Zealand & Singapore, including: Auckland Canterbury Arcade, 170 Queen St, Auckland; ☏ 9 373 3531

Brisbane 6th Floor, 247 Adelaide St, Brisbane, QLD 4000; ☏ 7 3221 9066
Melbourne 393 Little Bourke St, 2nd Floor, Melbourne, VIC 3000; ☏ 3 9602 5788
Sydney Dymocks Bldg, 7th Floor, 428 George St, Sydney, NSW 2000; ☏ 2 9221 7133

South Africa & Namibia
SAA-Netcare Travel Clinics P Bag X34, Benmore 2010; www.travelclinic.co.za. Clinics throughout South Africa. TMVC 113 D F Malan Dr, Roosevelt Pk,

Johannesburg; ☏ 011 888 7488; www.tmvc.com.au. Consult website for details of other clinics in South Africa & Namibia.

Switzerland
IAMAT 57 Chemin des Voirets, 1212 Grand Lancy, Geneva; www.iamat.org

MEDICAL KIT Pharmacies in the main towns in Zambia generally have good supplies of medicines, but away from these you will find very little. If you're venturing deep into the wilds, then you should take with you anything that you expect to need. If you are on an organised trip, an overlanding truck, or staying at hotels, lodges or safari camps, then you will not need much, as these establishments normally have comprehensive emergency kits. In that case, just a small personal medical kit might include:

- alcohol-based hand rub or bar of soap in plastic box
- antihistamine tablets
- antiseptic, eg: iodine or potassium permanganate (don't take antiseptic cream)
- aspirin or paracetamol
- blister plasters (if you plan any serious walking)
- condoms or femidoms and contraceptive pills
- impregnated bed-net or permethrin spray
- insect repellent
- lipsalve (ideally containing a sunscreen)
- malaria prophylaxis
- Micropore tape (for closing small cuts – and invaluable for blisters)
- moisturising cream
- sticking plaster (a roll is more versatile than pre-shaped plasters)
- sunscreen

However, if you are likely to end up in very remote situations, then you should also consider taking the following – and know how to use them:

Dr Jane Wilson-Howarth

Long-haul air travel increases the risk of deep vein thrombosis (DVT). Although recent research has suggested that many of us develop clots when immobilised, most resolve without us ever having been aware of them. In certain susceptible individuals, though, clots form on clots and when large ones break away and lodge in the lungs this is dangerous. Fortunately this happens in a tiny minority of passengers.

Studies have shown that flights of over five and a half hours are significant, and that people who take lots of shorter flights over a short space of time can also form clots. People at highest risk are:

- Those who have had a clot before – unless they are now taking warfarin
- People over 80 years of age
- Anyone who has recently undergone a major operation or surgery for varicose veins
- Someone who has had a hip or knee replacement in the last three months
- Cancer sufferers
- Those who have ever had a stroke
- People with heart disease
- Those with a close blood relative who has had a clot

Those with a slightly increased risk are:

- People over 40
- Women who are pregnant or have had a baby in the last couple of weeks
- People taking female hormones, the combined contraceptive pill or other oestrogen therapy
- Heavy smokers
- Those who have very severe varicose veins

- burns dressings (burns are a common problem for campers)
- antibiotics: ciprofloxacin or norfloxacin, for severe diarrhoea
- antibiotic eye drops, for sore, 'gritty', stuck-together eyes (conjunctivitis)
- injection swabs, sterile needles and syringes
- lint, sterile bandage and safety pins
- oral rehydration sachets
- steristrips or butterfly closures
- strong painkiller (eg: codeine phosphate – also use for bad diarrhoea)
- tweezers (perhaps those on a Swiss army knife)
- water purification equipment (2% tincture of iodine and dropper is ideal)
- a good medical manual (see *Appendix 3*, page 512).
- tinidazole for giardia or amoebic dysentery (see below for regime)
- malaria diagnostic kits (5) and a digital thermometer (for those going to remote areas)

If you wear glasses, bring a spare pair. Similarly those who wear contact lenses should bring spare ones, also a pair of glasses in case the dust proves too much for the lenses. If you take regular medication (including contraceptive pills) then bring a large supply with you – much easier than hunting for your usual brand in Zambia. Equally, it's worth having a dental check-up before you go, as you could be several painful days from the nearest dentist.

- The very obese
- People who are very tall (over 6ft/1.8m) or short (under 5ft/1.5m)

A deep vein thrombosis is a blood clot that forms in the deep leg veins. This is very different from irritating but harmless superficial phlebitis. DVT causes swelling and redness of one leg, usually with heat and pain in one calf and sometimes the thigh. A DVT is only dangerous if a clot breaks away and travels to the lungs (pulmonary embolus). Symptoms of a pulmonary embolus (PE) include chest pain that is worse on breathing in deeply, shortness of breath, and sometimes coughing up small amounts of blood. The symptoms commonly start three to ten days after a long flight. Anyone who thinks that they might have a DVT needs to see a doctor immediately who will arrange a scan. Warfarin tablets (to thin the blood) are then taken for at least six months.

PREVENTION OF DVT Several conditions make the problem more likely. Immobility is the key, and factors like reduced oxygen in cabin air and dehydration may also contribute. To reduce the risk of thrombosis on a long journey:

EXERCISE BEFORE AND AFTER THE FLIGHT
- Keep mobile before and during the flight; move around every couple of hours
- Drink plenty of water or juices during the flight
- Avoid taking sleeping pills and excessive tea, coffee and alcohol
- Perform exercises that mimic walking and tense the calf muscles
- Consider wearing flight socks or support stockings (see *www.legshealth.com*)
- Ideally take a meal each week of oily fish (mackerel, trout, salmon, sardines, etc) ahead of your departure. This reduces the blood's ability to clot and thus DVT risk. It may even be worth just taking a meal of oily fish 24 hours before departure if this is more practical.

If you think you are at increased risk of a clot, ask your doctor if it is safe to travel.

IN ZAMBIA
Hospitals and dentists Zambia's public-health system is overstretched and under-funded, presenting a risk of coming away with something worse than you had when you arrived. In the main cities – Lusaka, Livingstone and the Copperbelt – there are better-funded private hospitals that cater for both affluent Zambians and expats/diplomatic staff. These are much better, and will accept payment from genuine travel health insurance schemes.

For situations that are more serious, and may require immediate evacuation, **Speciality Emergency Services MedRescue (SES**; ⌇ *021 1273302–7, 1212663–4;* m *097 770302–5;* f *021 1273301, 273181;* e *med@zamnet.zm; www.ses-zambia.com*) operates throughout Zambia, with bases in Lusaka, Livingstone and Kitwe. If offers ambulances and in-patient care, as well as emergency cover. They can also arrange short-term insurance cover for visitors, either prior to arriving in Zambia or at their local offices. Most tour operators, and many lodges, include SES cover in their rates, but it's important to have good travel insurance – costs for evacuation are extremely high.

Pharmacies Pharmacies in main towns have a basic range of medicines, often at considerably lower prices than in their Western counterparts; they also stock malaria-test kits. That said, not all of these outlets are reliable, so stick to one that has been recommended, such as Jubilee Chemists in Lusaka.

As you might expect, specific brands are often unavailable, so bring with you all that you will need, as well as a repeat prescription for anything that you might run out of. Outside of the main centres, you will be lucky to find anything other than very basic medical supplies. Thus you should carry a very comprehensive medical kit if you are planning to head off independently into the wilds.

Staying healthy Rural Zambia is often not a healthy place to be. However, visitors using the better hotels, lodges and camps are unlikely to encounter any serious problems. The standards of hygiene in even the most remote bushcamps are generally at least as good as you will find at home.

The major dangers in Zambia are car accidents (especially likely if you drive at night) and sunburn. Both can also be very serious, yet both are within the power of the visitor to avoid.

The following is general advice, applicable to travelling anywhere, including Zambia.

Food and storage Throughout the world, most health problems encountered by travellers are contracted by eating contaminated food or drinking unclean water. If you are staying in safari camps or lodges, or eating in restaurants, then you are unlikely to have problems in Zambia.

However, if you are backpacking and cooking for yourself, or relying on local food, then you need to take more care. Tins, packets and fresh green vegetables (when you can find them) are least likely to cause problems – provided that clean water has been used in preparing the meal. In Zambia's hot climate, keeping meat or animal products unrefrigerated for more than a few hours is asking for trouble.

Water and purification Whilst piped water in the major towns is unlikely to harbour any serious pathogens, it will almost certainly cause upset stomachs for overseas visitors. In more rural areas, the water will generally have had less treatment, and therefore will be even more likely to cause problems. Hence, as a general rule, ensure that all water used for drinking or washing food in Zambia is purified.

To purify water yourself, first filter out any suspended solids, perhaps passing the water through a piece of closely woven cloth, or something similar. Then bring it to the boil, or sterilise it chemically. Boiling is much more effective, provided that you have the fuel available.

Tablets sold for purification are based on chlorine, iodine or silver, and are normally adequate. Just follow the manufacturer's instructions carefully. Iodine is most effective, especially against the resilient amoebic cysts that cause amoebic dysentery and other prolonged forms of diarrhoea.

A cheaper alternative to tablets sold over the counter is to travel with a small bottle of medical-quality tincture of iodine (2% solution) and an eye dropper. Add four drops to one litre of water, shake well and leave to stand for ten minutes. If the water is very cloudy – even after filtering – or very cold, then either double the iodine dose, or leave to stand for twice as long.

This tincture of iodine can also be used as a general external antiseptic, but it will stain things deep purple if spilt – so seal and pack its container exceedingly well.

Heat and sun Heatstroke, heat exhaustion and sunburn are often problems for travellers to Zambia, despite being easy to prevent. To avoid them, you need to remember that your body is under stress and make allowances for it. First, take things gently; you are on holiday, after all. Next, keep your fluid and salt levels high: lots of water and soft drinks, but go easy on the caffeine and alcohol. Third, dress to keep cool with loose-fitting, thin garments – preferably of cotton, linen or silk. Finally, beware of the sun. Hats and long-sleeved shirts are essential. If you must expose your skin to the sun, then use sun blocks and high-factor sunscreens (the sun is so strong that you will still get a tan). Be especially careful of exposure in the middle of the day and of sun reflected off water, and wear a T-shirt and lots of waterproof suncream (at least SPF15) when swimming. The glare and the dust can be hard on the eyes, too, so bring UV-protecting sunglasses and, perhaps, a soothing eyebath.

Prickly heat A fine pimply rash on the trunk is likely to be heat rash; cool showers, dabbing dry and talc will help. Treat the problem by slowing down to a relaxed schedule, wearing only loose, baggy, 100%-cotton clothes and sleeping naked under a fan; if it's bad you may need to check into an air-conditioned hotel room for a while.

Eye problems Bacterial conjunctivitis (pink eye) is a common infection in Africa; people who wear contact lenses are most open to this irritating problem. The eyes feel sore and gritty and they will often be stuck together in the mornings. They will need treatment with antibiotic drops or ointment. Lesser eye irritation should settle with bathing in salt water and keeping the eyes shaded. If an insect flies into your eye, extract it with great care, ensuring you do not crush or damage it otherwise you may get a nastily inflamed eye from toxins secreted by the creature. Small elongated red-and-black blister beetles carry warning colouration to tell you not to crush them anywhere against your skin.

Skin infections Any mosquito bite or small nick in the skin gives an opportunity for bacteria to foil the body's usually excellent defences; it will surprise many travellers how quickly skin infections start in warm humid climates and it is essential to clean and cover even the slightest wound. Creams are not as effective as a good drying antiseptic such as dilute iodine, potassium permanganate (a few crystals in half a cup of water) or crystal (or gentian) violet. One of these should be available in most towns. If the wound starts to throb, or becomes red and the redness starts to spread, or the wound oozes, and especially if you develop a fever, antibiotics will probably be needed: flucloxacillin (250mg four times a day) or cloxacillin (500mg four times a day). For those allergic to penicillin, erythromycin (500mg twice a day) for five days should help. See a doctor if the symptoms do not start to improve within 48 hours.

Fungal infections also get a hold easily in hot, moist climates so wear 100%-cotton socks and underwear and shower frequently. An itchy rash in the groin or flaking between the toes is likely to be a fungal infection. This needs treatment with an antifungal cream such as Canesten (clotrimazole); if this is not available try Whitfield's ointment (compound benzoic acid ointment) or crystal violet (although this will turn you purple!).

Avoiding insect bites The most dangerous biting insects in parts of Zambia are mosquitoes, because they can transmit malaria, yellow fever and a host of other diseases.

Research has shown that using a mosquito net over your bed, and covering up exposed skin (by wearing long-sleeved shirts, and tucking trousers into socks) in the evening, are the most effective steps towards preventing bites. Bed-net treatment kits are available from travel clinics; these prevent mosquitoes biting through a net if you roll against it in your sleep, and also make old and holey nets protective. Mosquito coils and chemical insect repellents will help, and sleeping in a stream of moving air, such as under a fan, or in an air-conditioned room, will help to reduce your chances of being bitten.

DEET (diethyltoluamide) is the active ingredient in many repellents (Repel have an excellent range), and the current guidance is to use one containing around 50–55%. It is also fine to use for children and pregnant women. You need to reapply the repellent about every six hours and again if you have been in water. It will dissolve some plastics and synthetic materials, and may irritate sensitive skin. Because of this, many people use concentrated DEET to impregnate materials, rather than applying it to themselves. An alternative to this is to use Bug Guards – wrist and ankle bands containing 100% DEET in capsule form. The capsules break on movement, but the chemical never touches the skin. One pack contains four bands, which when used, last for two weeks. Mosquito nets, socks and even cravats can be impregnated and used to deter insects from biting. Eating large quantities of garlic, or cream of tartar, or taking yeast tablets, are said to deter some biting insects, although the evidence is anecdotal – and the garlic may affect your social life.

Mosquitoes and many other insects are attracted to light. If you are camping, never put a lamp near the opening of your tent, or you will have a swarm of biters waiting to join you when you retire. In hotel rooms, be aware that the longer your light is on, the greater the number of insects will be sharing your accommodation.

Aside from avoiding mosquito bites between dusk and dawn, which will protect you from elephantiasis and a range of nasty insect-borne viruses, as well as malaria (see pages 86–7), it is important to take precautions against other insect bites. During the day it is wise to wear long, loose (preferably 100%-cotton) clothes if you are pushing through scrubby country; this will keep off ticks and also tsetse and day-biting *Aedes* mosquitoes which may spread viral fevers.

Tsetse flies hurt when they bite and it is said that they are attracted to the colour blue; locals will advise on where they are a problem and where they transmit sleeping sickness.

Minute pestilential biting blackflies spread river blindness in some parts of Africa between 190°N and 170°S; the disease is caught close to fast-flowing rivers since flies breed there and the larvae live in rapids. The flies bite during the day but long trousers tucked into socks will help keep them off. Citronella-based natural repellents (eg: Mosi-guard) do not work against them.

Tumbu flies or putsi, often called mango flies, are a problem where the climate is hot and humid. The adult fly lays her eggs on the soil or on drying laundry and when the eggs come into contact with human flesh (when you put on clothes or lie on a bed) they hatch and bury themselves under the skin. Here they form a crop of 'boils' each with a maggot inside. Smear a little Vaseline over the hole, and they will push their noses out to breathe. It may be possible to squeeze them out but it depends if they are ready to do so as the larvae have spines that help them to hold on.

In putsi areas either dry your clothes and sheets within a screened house, or dry them in direct sunshine until they are crisp, or iron them.

Jiggers, or sandfleas, are another flesh-feaster, which can be best avoided by wearing shoes. They latch on if you walk barefoot in contaminated places, and set up home under the skin of the foot, usually at the side of a toenail where they cause a painful, boil-like swelling. They need picking out by a local expert.

Snakes, spiders and scorpions ... Encounters with aggressive snakes, angry spiders or vindictive scorpions are more common in horror films than in Zambia. Most snakes will flee at the mere vibrations of a human footstep whilst spiders are far more interested in flies than people. You will have to seek out scorpions if you wish to see one. If you are careful about where you place your hands and feet, especially after dark, then there should be no problems. You are less likely to get bitten or stung if you wear stout shoes and long trousers. Simple precautions include not putting on boots without shaking them empty first, and always checking the back of your backpack before putting it on.

Snakes do bite occasionally, and you ought to know the standard first-aid treatment. First, and most importantly, *don't panic*. Most snakes are harmless and even venomous species will only dispense venom in about half of their bites. If bitten, you are unlikely to have received venom; keeping this fact in mind may help you to stay calm.

Even in the worst of these cases, the victim has hours or days to get to help, and not a matter of minutes. He/she should be kept calm, with no exertions to pump venom around the blood system, whilst being taken rapidly to the nearest medical help. The area of the bite should be washed to remove any venom from the skin, and the bitten limb should be immobilised. Paracetamol may be used as a painkiller, but never use aspirin because it may cause internal bleeding.

Most first-aid techniques do more harm than good: cutting into the wound is harmful and tourniquets are dangerous; suction and electrical inactivation devices do not work. The only effective treatment is antivenom. In case of a bite, which you fear may be both serious and venomous then:

- Try to keep calm. It is likely that no venom has been dispensed.
- Stop movement of the bitten limb by applying a splint.
- If you have a crêpe bandage, wrap it around the whole limb (eg: all the way from the toes to the thigh), as tight as you would for a sprained ankle or a muscle pull.
- Keep the bitten limb *below* heart height to slow spread of any venom.
- Evacuate the victim to a hospital that has antivenom.
- *Never* give aspirin. You may offer paracetamol, which is safe.
- *Do not* apply ice packs.
- *Do not* apply potassium permanganate.

If the offending snake can be captured without any risk of someone else being bitten, take it to show the doctor. But beware, since even a decapitated head is able to dispense venom in a reflex bite.

When deep in the bush, heading for the nearest large farm or camp may be quicker than going to a town: it may have a supply of antivenom, or facilities to radio for help by plane.

DISEASES AND WHEN TO SEE A DOCTOR

Travellers' diarrhoea There are almost as many names for this as there are travellers' tales on the subject. Firstly, do resist the temptation to reach for the medical kit as soon as your stomach turns a little fluid. Most cases of travellers' diarrhoea will resolve themselves within 24–48 hours with no treatment at all. To speed up this process of acclimatisation, eat well but simply: avoid fats in favour of starches, and keep your fluid intake high. Bananas and papaya fruit are often claimed to be helpful. If you urgently need to stop the symptoms, for a long journey for example, then Lomotil, Imodium or another of the commercial anti-diarrhoea preparations will do the trick. They stop the symptoms, by paralysing the bowel, but will not cure the problem. They should be used only as a last resort and never if you have bad abdominal cramps with the diarrhoea.

If the diarrhoea persists for more than two days, or the stools contain blood, pus or slime, and/or you have a fever, you must seek medical advice. There are as many possible treatments as there are causes, and a proper diagnosis involves microscopic analysis of a stool sample, so go straight to your nearest hospital. The most important thing, especially in Zambia's climate, is to keep your fluid intake up. If it is not possible to reach medical help quickly then a dose of norfloxacin or ciprofloxacin repeated twice a day until reaching medical help may be appropriate (if you are planning to take an antibiotic with you, note that both norfloxacin and ciprofloxacin are available only on prescription in the UK). If the diarrhoea is greasy and bulky and is accompanied by sulphurous (eggy) burps the likely cause is giardia. This is best treated with tinidazole (four x 500mg in one dose, repeated seven days later if symptoms persist).

The body's absorption of fluids is assisted by adding small amounts of dissolved sugars, salts and minerals to the water. Sachets of oral rehydration salts give the perfect biochemical mix you need to replace what is pouring out of your bottom but they do not taste so nice. Any dilute mixture of sugar and salt in water will do you good so, if you like Coke or orange squash, drink that with a three-finger pinch of salt added to each glass. The ideal ratio is eight level teaspoons of sugar and one level teaspoon of salt dissolved in one litre of water. Palm syrup or honey make good substitutes for sugar, and including fresh citrus juice will not only improve the taste of these solutions, but also add valuable potassium.

Drink two large glasses after every bowel action, and more if you are thirsty. If you are not eating you need to drink three litres a day *plus* whatever you are sweating *and* the equivalent of what's going into the toilet. If you feel like eating, take a bland diet; heavy greasy foods will give you cramps.

If you are likely to be more than a few days from qualified medical help, then come equipped with a good health manual and the selection of antibiotics which it recommends. *Bugs, Bites & Bowels* by Dr Jane Wilson-Howarth (see *Appendix 3*, page 512) is excellent for this purpose.

Malaria You can still catch malaria even if you are taking anti-malarial drugs so you should do everything possible to avoid mosquito bites. Untreated malaria is likely to be fatal, but even strains resistant to prophylaxis respond well to prompt treatment. Because of this, your immediate priority upon displaying possible malaria symptoms – including a rapid rise in temperature (over 38°C), and any combination of a headache, flu-like aches and pains, a general sense of disorientation, and possibly even nausea and diarrhoea – is to establish whether you have malaria, ideally by visiting a clinic.

A definite diagnosis of malaria is normally possible only by examining a blood sample under the microscope. It is best to get the problem properly diagnosed if possible, so don't treat yourself if you can easily reach a hospital first. Even if you test negative, it would be wise to stay within reach of a laboratory until the symptoms clear up, and to test again after a day or two if they don't. It's worth noting that if you have a fever and the malaria test is negative, you may have typhoid or paratyphoid, which should also receive immediate treatment.

If (and only if) medical help is unavailable, then self-treatment is fairly safe, except for people who are pregnant or under 12 years of age. Should you be travelling to remote parts of Zambia, you would be wise to carry a course of treatment to cure malaria, and a rapid test kit. With malaria, it is normal enough to go from feeling healthy to having a high fever in the space of a few hours (and it is possible to die from falciparum malaria within 24 hours of the first symptoms). In such circumstances, assume that you have malaria and act accordingly – whatever risks are attached to taking an unnecessary cure are outweighed by the dangers of untreated malaria.

There is some division about the best treatment for malaria, but either Malarone or Coarthemeter are the current treatments of choice. Discuss your trip with a specialist at home or in Zambia.

Dengue fever This mosquito-borne disease – and other similar arboviruses – may mimic malaria but there is no prophylactic medication available to deal with it. The mosquitoes that carry this virus bite during the daytime, so it is worth applying repellent if you see any mosquitoes around. Symptoms include strong headaches, rashes and excruciating joint and muscle pains and high fever. Dengue fever only lasts for a week or so and is not usually fatal. Complete rest and paracetamol are the usual treatment. Plenty of fluids also help. Some patients are given an intravenous drip to keep them from dehydrating. It is especially important to protect yourself if you have had dengue fever before. A second infection with a different strain can result in the potentially fatal dengue haemorrhagic fever.

Sexually transmitted diseases AIDS is spread in exactly the same way in Africa as it is at home, through body secretions, blood and blood products. The same goes for the dangerous hepatitis B. Both can be spread through sex.

Remember that the risks of sexually transmitted disease are high, whether you sleep with fellow travellers or locals. About 80% of HIV infections in British heterosexuals are acquired abroad. If you must indulge, use condoms or femidoms, which help reduce the risk of transmission. If you do have unprotected sex, visit a clinic as soon as possible; this should be within 24 hours, or no later than 72 hours, for post-exposure prophylaxis. And if you notice any genital ulcers or discharge, get treatment promptly.

Hepatitis This is a group of viral diseases which generally start with Coca-Cola-coloured urine and light-coloured stools. It progresses to fevers, weakness, jaundice (yellow skin and eyeballs) and abdominal pains caused by a severe inflammation of the liver. There are several forms, of which the two most common are typical of the rest: hepatitis A (or infectious hepatitis) and hepatitis B (or serum hepatitis).

Hepatitis A, and the newly discovered hepatitis E, are spread by the faecal-oral route, that is by ingesting food or drink contaminated by excrement. They are avoided in the same ways you normally avoid stomach problems: by careful preparation of food and by drinking only clean water. But as there are now excellent vaccines against hepatitis A it is certainly worth getting inoculated before you travel. See *Recommended precautions* on page 86.

In contrast, the more serious but rarer hepatitis B is spread in the same way as AIDS (by blood or body secretions), and is avoided the same way as one avoids AIDS. There is a vaccine which protects against hepatitis B, but three doses are needed over a minimum of 21 days. It is usually considered necessary only for medical workers, people working closely with children or if you intend to travel for six weeks or longer. There are no cures for hepatitis, but with lots of bed rest and a good low-fat, no-alcohol diet most people recover within six months. If you are unlucky enough to contract hepatitis of any form, use your travel insurance to fly straight home.

Meningitis This is a particularly nasty disease as it can kill within hours of the first symptoms appearing. The telltale symptoms are a combination of a blinding headache (light sensitivity), a blotchy rash and a high fever. Immunisation (see page 86) protects against the most serious bacterial form of meningitis. Although other forms of meningitis (usually viral) exist, there are no vaccines for these. Local papers normally report localised outbreaks. A severe headache and fever should make you get to a doctor immediately. There are also other causes of headache and fever; one of which is typhoid, which occurs in travellers to Zambia. Seek medical help if you are ill for more than a few days.

Rabies Rabies is contracted when broken skin comes into contact with saliva from an infected animal. The disease is almost always fatal when fully developed, but fortunately there are excellent post-exposure vaccines. It is possible, albeit expensive, to be immunised against rabies before you travel (see page 86). You are advised to take this if you intend working with animals or you are travelling for four weeks or more to remote areas. Rabies is rarely a problem for visitors, but the small risk is further minimised by avoiding small mammals. This is especially true of any animals acting strangely. Both mad dogs in town and friendly jackals in the bush should be given a very wide berth, as should ground squirrels.

If you are bitten, scratched or licked over an open wound, clean and disinfect the wound thoroughly by scrubbing it with soap under running water for five minutes, and then flood it with local spirit or diluted iodine. This helps stop the rabies virus entering the body and will guard against wound infections, including tetanus.

Seek help immediately, ideally within 24 hours, though it is never too late, as the incubation period for rabies can be very long. Those who have not been immunised will need a full course of injections. The vast majority of travel health advisors including WHO recommend rabies immunoglobulin (RIG), but this product is expensive (around US$800) and may be hard to come by – another reason why pre-exposure vaccination should be encouraged. Tell the doctor if you have had pre-exposure vaccine, as this should change the treatment you receive. The later stages of the disease are horrendous – spasms, personality changes and hydrophobia (fear of water). Death from rabies is probably one of the worst ways to go.

Tickbite fever African ticks are not the rampant disease transmitters they are in the Americas, but they may spread tickbite fever and a few dangerous rarities in Zambia. Tickbite fever is a flu-like illness that can easily be treated with doxycycline, but as there can be some serious complications it is important to visit a doctor. It is most prevalent in Zambia between November and January.

Ticks should ideally be removed as soon as possible as leaving them on the body increases the chance of infection. They should be removed with special tick tweezers that can be bought in good travel shops. Failing that you can use your fingernails: grasp the tick as close to your body as possible and pull steadily and firmly away at right angles to your skin. The tick will then come away complete, as long as you do not jerk or twist. If possible douse the wound with alcohol (any spirit will do) or iodine. Irritants (eg: Olbas oil) or lit cigarettes are to be discouraged since they can cause the ticks to regurgitate and therefore increase the risk of disease. It is best to get a travelling companion to check you for ticks; if you are travelling with small children, remember to check their heads, and particularly behind the ears.

Spreading redness around the bite and/or fever and/or aching joints after a tick bite imply that you have an infection that requires antibiotic treatment, so seek advice.

Bilharzia or schistosomiasis Bilharzia is an insidious disease, contracted by coming into contact with contaminated water. It is caused by parasitic worms which live part of their lives in freshwater snails, and part of their lives in human bladders or intestines. A common indication of an infection is a localised itchy rash – where the parasites have burrowed through the skin – and later symptoms of a more advanced infection may include passing bloody urine. Bilharzia is readily treated by medication, and only serious if it remains untreated.

The only way to avoid infection completely is to stay away from any bodies of fresh water, which in Zambia includes Lake Kariba. Obviously this is restrictive, and would make your trip less enjoyable. More pragmatic advice is to avoid slow-moving or sluggish water, and ask local opinion on the bilharzia risk, as not all water is contaminated. Generally bilharzia snails do not inhabit fast-flowing water, and hence rivers are free of it. However, dams and standing water, especially in populated areas, are usually heavily contaminated. If you think you have been infected, don't worry about it – just get a test done on your return at least six weeks after your last possible exposure.

Avoiding bilharzia If you are bathing, swimming, paddling or wading in fresh water which you think may carry a bilharzia risk, try to get out of the water within ten minutes.

- Avoid bathing or paddling on shores within 200m of villages or places where people use the water a great deal, especially reedy shores or where there is lots of water weed.
- Dry off thoroughly with a towel; rub vigorously.
- If your bathing water comes from a risky source try to ensure that the water is taken from the lake in the early morning and stored snail-free, otherwise it should be filtered or Dettol or Cresol added.
- Bathing early in the morning is safer than bathing in the last half of the day.
- Cover yourself with DEET insect repellent before swimming: it may offer some protection.

Sleeping sickness or trypanosomiasis This is really a cattle disease, which is rarely caught by people. It is spread by bites from the distinctive tsetse fly – which is slightly larger than a housefly, and has pointed mouth-parts designed for sucking blood. The bite is painful. These flies are easily spotted as they bite during the day, and have distinctive wings which cross into a scissor shape when they are resting. Note that not all tsetses carry the disease.

Prevention is easier than cure, so avoid being bitten by covering up. Chemical insect repellents are also helpful. Dark colours, especially blue, are favoured by the flies, so avoid wearing these if possible.

Tsetse bites are nasty, so expect them to swell up and turn red – that is a normal allergic reaction to any bite. The vast majority of tsetse bites will do only this. However, if the bite develops into a boil-like swelling after five or more days, and a fever starts two or three weeks later, then seek immediate medical treatment to avert permanent damage to your central nervous system. The name 'sleeping sickness' refers to a daytime drowsiness which is characteristic of the later stages of the disease.

Because this is a rare complaint, most doctors in the West are unfamiliar with it. If you think that you may have been infected, draw their attention to the possibility. Treatment is straightforward, once a correct diagnosis has been made.

RETURNING HOME Many tropical diseases have a long incubation period, and it is possible to develop symptoms weeks after returning home (this is why it is important to keep taking anti-malaria prophylaxis for the prescribed duration after you leave a malarial zone). If you do get ill after you return home, be certain to tell your doctor where you have been. Alert him/her to any diseases that you may have been exposed to. Several people die from malaria in the UK every year because victims do not seek medical help promptly or their doctors are not familiar with the symptoms, and so are slow to make a correct diagnosis. Milder forms of malaria may take up to a year to reveal themselves, but serious (falciparum) malaria will usually become apparent within three to six months, and can start as early as one week into a malarial area.

If problems persist, get a check-up at one of the hospitals that specialise in tropical diseases: the Hospital for Tropical Diseases (see page 88), or in the US to the Centers for Disease Control (see page 88). Note that to visit such a hospital in the UK, you need a letter of referral from your doctor.

SAFETY

Zambia is not a dangerous country. If you are travelling on an all-inclusive trip and staying at lodges and hotels, then problems of personal safety are exceedingly rare. There will always be someone on hand to help you. Even if you are travelling on local transport, perhaps on a low budget, you will not be attacked randomly just for the sake of it. A difficult situation is most likely to occur if you have made yourself an obvious target for thieves, perhaps by walking around, or driving an expensive 4x4, in town at night. The answer then is to capitulate completely and give them what they want, and cash in on your travel insurance. Heroics are not a good idea.

The British Foreign and Commonwealth Office currently advises against all but essential travel to rural parts of the country bordering the Democratic Republic of Congo (DRC), especially after dark, a reflection of ongoing cross-border raids. The advice does not relate to main roads, or to towns along the routes, including those between Kapiri Mposhi and Serenje, Serenje and Mansa, and the main routes through the Copperbelt. However, those proposing to travel north from Ndola to Mufulira should be cautious.

For women travellers, especially those travelling alone, it is doubly important to learn the local attitudes, and how to behave acceptably. This takes some practice, and a certain confidence. You will often be the centre of attention but, by developing conversational techniques to avert over-enthusiastic male attention, you should be perfectly safe. Making friends of the local women is one way to help avoid such problems.

THEFT Theft is a problem in Zambia's urban areas. Given that a large section of the population is living below the poverty line and without any paid work, it is surprising that the problem is not worse. Despite Lusaka's reputation, in my experience theft is no more of a problem here than it is in Harare – while the centre of Johannesburg is significantly more dangerous than either. However, car jacking is on the increase, so it is wise to take sensible precautions to protect your vehicle – and you.

How to avoid it Thieves in the bigger cities usually work in groups – choosing their targets carefully. These will be people who look vulnerable and who have items worth stealing. To avoid being robbed, try not to fit into either category – and certainly not into both. Observing a few basic rules, especially during your first few weeks in Zambia's cities, will drastically reduce your chances of becoming a target. After that you should have learnt your own way of assessing the risks, and avoiding thefts. Until then:

- Try not to carry anything of value around with you.
- If you must carry cash, then use a concealed money-belt for your main supply – keeping smaller change separately and to hand.
- Try not to walk around alone. Move in groups. Take taxis instead.
- Try not to look too foreign. Blend in to the local scene as well as you can. Act like a streetwise expat rather than a tourist, if you can. (Conspicuously carrying a local newspaper may help with this.)
- Rucksacks and large, new bags are bad. If you must carry a bag, choose an old battered one. Around town, a local plastic carrier bag is ideal.

Janice Booth

When attention becomes intrusive, it can help if you are wearing a wedding ring and have photos of 'your' husband and children, even if they are someone else's. A good reason to give for not being with them is that you have to travel in connection with your job – biology, zoology, geography, or whatever. (But not journalism – that's risky.)

Pay attention to local etiquette, and to speaking, dressing and moving reasonably decorously. Look at how the local women dress, and try not to expose parts of yourself that they keep covered. Think about body language. In much of southern Africa direct eye-contact with a man will be seen as a 'come-on'; sunglasses are helpful here.

Don't be afraid to explain clearly – but pleasantly rather than as a put-down – that you aren't in the market for whatever distractions are on offer. Remember that you are probably as much of a novelty to the local people as they are to you; and the fact that you are travelling abroad alone gives them the message that you are free and adventurous. But don't imagine that a Lothario lurks under every bush: many approaches stem from genuine friendliness or curiosity, and a brush-off in such cases doesn't do much for the image of travellers in general.

Take sensible precautions against theft and attack – try to cover all the risks before you encounter them – and then relax and enjoy your trip. You'll meet far more kindness than villainy.

- Move confidently and look as if you know exactly what you are doing, and where you are going. Lost foreigners make the easiest targets.
- Never walk around at night – that is asking for trouble.

If you have a vehicle then don't leave anything in it, and avoid leaving it parked outside in a city. One person should always stay with it, as vehicle thefts are common, even in broad daylight. Armed gangs doing American-style vehicle hijacks are on the increase, though still rare – and their most likely targets are new 4x4 vehicles. When driving in urban areas, and especially at night, keep the doors locked, and ensure that you're not using a mobile phone within easy reach of a passer-by. Scams to get you to stop include faking an accident, so be on the alert. And if you are held up then just surrender: you have little choice if you want to live.

Reporting thefts to the police If you are the victim of a theft then report it to the police – they ought to know. Also try to get a copy of the report, or at least a reference number on an official-looking piece of paper, as this will help you to claim on your insurance policy when you return home. Some insurance companies won't act without it. But remember that reporting anything in a police station can take a long time, and do not expect any speedy arrests for a small case of pick-pocketing.

ARREST To get arrested in Zambia, a foreigner will normally have to try quite hard. During the Kaunda regime, when the state was paranoid about spies, every tourist's camera became a reason for suspicion and arrest. Fortunately that attitude has now vanished, though as a precaution you should still ask for permission to photograph near bridges or military installations. This simple courtesy costs you nothing, and may avoid a problem later.

One excellent way to get arrested in Zambia is to try to smuggle drugs across its borders, or to try to buy them from 'pushers'. Drug offences carry penalties at least as stiff as those you will find at home – and the jails are a lot less pleasant. Zambia's police are not forbidden to use entrapment techniques or 'sting' operations to catch criminals. Buying, selling or using drugs in Zambia is just not worth the risk.

Failing this, arguing with any policeman or army official – and getting angry into the bargain – is a sure way to get arrested. It is essential to control your temper and stay relaxed when dealing with Zambia's officials. Not only will you gain respect, and hence help your cause, but also you will avoid being forced to cool off for a night in the cells.

If you are careless enough to be arrested, you will often only be asked a few questions. If the police are suspicious of you, then how you handle the situation will determine whether you are kept for a matter of hours or for days. Be patient, helpful, good-humoured and as truthful as possible. Never lose your temper; it will only aggravate the situation. Avoid any hint of arrogance. If things are going badly after half a day or so, then start firmly, but politely, to insist on seeing someone in higher authority. As a last resort you do, at least in theory, have the right to contact your embassy or consulate, though the finer points of your civil liberties may be overlooked by an irate local police chief.

BRIBERY Bribery is a fact of life in Zambia, though it is a difficult subject to write about. If you're visiting on an organised holiday, then it's unlikely to become an issue – you'll not come across any expectation of bribes. However, independent travellers ought to think about the issue before they arrive, as they are more likely to encounter the problem, and there are many different points of view on how to deal with it.

Some argue that it is present already, as an unavoidable way of life, and so must be accepted by the practical traveller. They view using bribery as simply practising one of the local customs. Others regard paying bribes as an unacceptable step towards condoning an immoral practice, thus any bribe should be flatly refused, and requests to make them never acceded to.

Whichever school of thought you favour, bribery is an issue in Zambia that you may need to consider. It is not as widespread, or on the same scale, as countries further north – but on a low level is not uncommon. A large 'tip' is often expected for a favour, and acceptance of small fines from police for traffic offences often avoids proceedings which may appear deliberately time-consuming. Many pragmatic travellers will only use a bribe as a very last resort, and only then when it has been asked for repeatedly.

Never attempt to bribe someone unsubtly, or use the word 'bribe'. If the person involved hasn't already dropped numerous broad hints to you that money is required, then offering it would be a great insult. Further, even if bribes are being asked for, an eagerness to offer will encourage any person you are dealing with to increase their price.

Never simply say 'Here's some dollars, now will you do it?' Better is to agree, reluctantly, to pay the 'on-the-spot-fine' that was requested; or to gradually accept the need for the extra 'administration fee' that was demanded; or to finally agree to help to cover the 'time and trouble' involved ... provided that the problem can be overcome.

6

In the Wilds

🚗 DRIVING

Driving around Zambia isn't for the novice, or the unprepared. Long stretches of the tarred roads are extensively pot-holed, most of the secondary gravel roads are in very poor repair, and many areas rely on bush tracks maintained only by the passage of vehicles. If you plan on exploring in the more rural areas, and remote parks, then you will need at least two sturdy, fully equipped 4x4 vehicles. It says something of the roads in general that until very recently most of Zambia's car-hire companies would rent vehicles only if you took a local driver – and even then only for use in towns.

Those planning to drive themselves around Zambia should read this section in conjunction with the general details on driving in *Chapter 4*, pages 69–73.

EQUIPMENT AND PREPARATIONS

Fuel and fuel consumption Petrol and diesel are available in most of the towns (see page 70), but elsewhere diesel is generally more widely available. Although shortages are relatively rare, but they do still occur, and you'll need to be prepared for them. For travel into the bush in particular you will need long-range fuel tanks, and/or a large stock of filled jerrycans. It is essential to plan your fuel requirements well in advance, and to carry more than you expect to need.

Remember that using the vehicle's 4x4 capability, especially in low-ratio gears, will significantly increase your fuel consumption. Similarly, the cool comfort of a vehicle's air conditioning will burn your fuel reserves swiftly.

Spares Zambia's garages do not generally have a comprehensive stock of vehicle spares – though bush mechanics can effect the most amazing short-term repairs, with remarkably basic tools and raw materials. Spares for the more common makes are easiest to find, so most basic Land Rover and Toyota 4x4 parts are available somewhere in Lusaka, at a price. If you are arriving in Zambia with a foreign vehicle, it is best to bring as many spares as you can, though be aware that you could be charged import duty. Spares for both Toyota and Ford are available in Lusaka and Kitwe, Southern Cross in Lusaka and Chingola stock Mercedes and Jeep parts. For more general spares, there are branches of Autoworld in several major cities, including Lusaka and Ndola.

Navigation See the section on *Maps and navigation* in *Chapter 4*, page 59, for detailed comments, but there are good maps available – and for this there's no alternative to visiting the Surveyor General's office in Mulungushi House, in Lusaka. You should seriously consider taking a GPS system if you are heading off the main roads in the more remote areas of the country.

Often in Zambia you'll come across a police or immigration roadblock. You'll find them on all the main roads around the larger towns, and randomly placed on other tar roads and arteries also. It's vital that you stop for them, and it'll speed your journey if you know how to deal with them. I usually slow down on my approach, turn off any music or air conditioning, take off any sunglasses and roll down my window. Then greet the officer with a broad smile and a traditional greeting, or at least a polite 'Good morning, how are you?' (See *Cultural guidelines* in *Chapter 2*, pages 22–3, for more on these.)

Foreigners will often be waved through. Sometimes you'll be asked a few questions – typically about where you are going and what you are doing. Keep your answers simple, honest and clear. You may be asked to test your lights, or indicators, or to show your insurance or identification, so it's important to have your passport, driving licence and vehicle documentation to hand. Answer politely with good humour and keep cool.

Like any country, Zambia has occasional radar traps, and there are rules of the road; if you contravene these, then you may be fined. If so, then it's best to fill out the official forms, pay the official fine as swiftly as possible, and keep the receipt. Fines vary from Kw18,000 for driving without a seatbelt to Kw65,000 for speeding.

SPURIOUS CHARGES The vast majority of roadblocks are fair and friendly, but occasionally you may find one where the officers are really looking to levy a fine. This is rare, but it happens! Then the officers will either find a problem, or make one up, to try to get you to pay an on-the-spot fine – and they won't be using official forms.

Some of their favourite excuses may be the finer, real or fictitious, points of the law of the road. These might include claiming that you haven't got two six-inch white strips of reflective tape on your front bumper, or two in red on the back bumper; or that you should have two steel triangles (a favourite is to fine people with plastic ones!) and make sure they are easy to get at; or that your reversing lights don't work. Another ploy is to charge a fine, but one that's lower than it should be – if you're

COPING WITH ZAMBIA'S ROADS

Tar roads Many of Zambia's tar roads are excellent, and a programme of tarring is gradually extending these good sections. However, within them there are occasional patches of pot-holes. These often occur in small groups, making some short stretches of tar very slow going indeed. If you are unlucky, or foolish, enough to hit one of these sections after speeding along a smooth stretch of tar, then you are likely to blow at least one tyre and in danger of a serious accident. For this reason, if for no other, even tar roads that look good are worth treating with caution. It is wiser never to exceed about 80km/h.

At the beginning of the rainy season, in October and November, take particular care. During the dry season there can be a considerable build up of diesel and oil on tar roads, so after the first rains water tends to lie on this layer and can create a surface akin to black ice.

Strip roads Occasionally there are roads where the sealed tar surface is only wide enough for one vehicle. This becomes a problem when you meet another vehicle travelling in the opposite direction … on the same stretch of tar. Then local practice is to wait until the last possible moment before you steer left, driving with two wheels on the gravel adjacent to the tar, and two on the tar. Usually, the vehicle coming in the opposite direction will do the same, and after passing each other asked for, say, Kw20,000 for speeding, the likelihood is that no receipt will be forthcoming.

Whatever the charge, however unreasonable, it's vital that you keep your cool, take your time, and don't appear at all bothered. Act as if you've all the time in the world, keep smiling and stay helpful and cheerful. Never get angry; always keep it amiable. However, do politely insist on a few of Zambia's basic road laws:

- You should always, very pleasantly and politely, record the officer's name and number – I'd be casual about this – but make it clear that you have done it.
- Note that higher police officers and authorities try hard to stamp out this sort of corrupt behaviour. For this reason you should always find a way to report dodgy behaviour to a higher officer at the local station, though obviously don't imply that the officer(s) in question is doing anything wrong.
- You never need to give your car keys or licence to a police officer; they have the right to see your licence – but not to take it off you.
- If you are charged with anything, then you have the right to insist that the officer accompanies you to the local police station, to discuss the charge with his superior. So, basically, you say politely that you're happy to pay the fine … but you wish to do so at the local police station.
- Never threaten to 'report' an officer – but instead you might innocently insist that you need a receipt with a stamp – and you'll have to take it to the station for one, even after they let you go.
- Finally, I'd never admit to being late, or having to be anywhere too quickly; it's tantamount to admitting that you'll be willing to pay a bribe to get away faster.
- If you willingly pay bribes then your corruptness is perpetuating the practice. Don't do it.

Stick to these rules, take your time, remain patient and they'll eventually let you go – or at least the price of the 'fine' will reduce to being insignificant!

both vehicles veer back on to the tar. If you are unused to this, then slow right down before you steer on to the gravel.

Gravel roads Gravel roads can be very deceptive. Even when they appear smooth, flat and fast (which is not often), they still do not give vehicles much traction. You will frequently put the car into small skids, and with practice at slower speeds you will learn how to deal with them. Gravel is a less forgiving surface on which to drive than tar. The rules and techniques for driving well are the same for both, but on tar you can get away with sloppy braking and cornering which would prove fatal on gravel.

Further, in Zambia you must always be prepared for the unexpected: an animal wandering onto the road, a rash of huge pot-holes, or an unexpected corner. So it is verging on insane to drive over about 60km/h on any of Zambia's gravel roads. Other basic driving hints include:

Slowing down If in any doubt about what lies ahead, always slow down. Road surfaces can vary enormously, so keep a constant lookout for pot-holes, ruts or patches of soft sand which could put you into an unexpected slide. If you do find the vehicle wandering having hit a corrugated section, always steer into the direction in which you are travelling.

Passing vehicles When passing other vehicles travelling in the opposite direction, always slow down to minimise both the damage that stone chippings will do to your windscreen, and the danger in driving through the other vehicle's dust cloud.

Using your gears In normal driving, a lower gear will give you more control over the car – so keep out of high 'cruising' gears. Rather stick with third or fourth, and accept that your revs will be slightly higher than they normally are.

Cornering and braking Under ideal conditions, the brakes should only be applied when the car is travelling in a straight line. Braking whilst negotiating a corner is dangerous, so it is vital to slow down before you reach corners. Equally, it is better to slow down gradually, using a combination of gears and brakes, than to use the brakes alone. You are less likely to skid.

DRIVING AT NIGHT Never drive at night unless you have to. Both wild and domestic animals frequently spend the night by the side of busy roads, and will actually sleep on quieter ones. Tar roads are especially bad as the surface absorbs all the sun's heat by day, and then radiates it at night – making it a warm bed for passing animals. A high-speed collision with any animal, even a small one like a goat, will not only kill the animal, but also cause very severe damage to a vehicle, with potentially fatal consequences. A word of caution about other road users, too: there's a prevalence for both drivers and pedestrians to be under the influence of alcohol at night. Finally, watch out for drivers with poorly maintained vehicles, who tend to drive between dawn and dusk to avoid contact with the police.

4X4 DRIVING TECHNIQUES You will need a high-clearance 4x4 to get anywhere in Zambia that's away from the main arteries. However, no vehicle can make up for an inexperienced driver – so ensure that you are confident of your vehicle's capabilities before you venture into the wilds with it. You really need extensive practice, with an expert on hand to advise you, before you'll have the first idea how to handle such a vehicle in difficult terrain. Finally, driving in convoy (preferably with some reasonably strong people) is an essential precaution in the more remote areas, in case one vehicle gets stuck or breaks down. Some of the more relevant techniques include:

Driving in sand If you're in 4x4 and are really struggling in deep sand, then stop on the next fairly solid area that you come to. Lower your tyre pressure until there is a small bulge in the tyre walls (having first made sure that you have the means to re-inflate them when you reach solid roads again). A lower pressure will help your traction greatly, but increase the wear on your tyres. Pump them up again before you drive on a hard surface at speed, or the tyres will be badly damaged.

Where there are clear, deep-rutted tracks in the sand, don't fight the steering wheel – just relax and let your vehicle steer itself. Driving in the cool of the morning is easier than later in the day because when sand is cool it compacts better and is firmer. (When hot, the pockets of air between the sand grains expand and the sand becomes looser.)

If you do get stuck, despite these precautions, don't panic. Don't just rev the engine and spin the wheels – you'll only dig deeper. Instead stop. Relax and assess the situation. Now dig shallow ramps in front of all the wheels, reinforcing them with pieces of wood, vegetation, stones, material or anything else which will give the wheels better traction. Lighten the vehicle load (passengers out) and push. Don't let the engine revs die as you engage your lowest-ratio gear. That probably means using '4x4 low' rather than '4x4 high'. Use the clutch to ensure that the wheels don't spin wildly and dig themselves further into the sand.

Sometimes rocking the vehicle backwards and forwards will build up momentum to break you free. This can be done by the driver intermittently applying the clutch and/or by getting helpers who can push and pull the vehicle at the same frequency. Once the vehicle is moving, the golden rule of sand driving is to keep up the momentum: if you pause, you will sink and stop.

Navigation note Remember that your fuel consumption when driving in sand is much higher than on harder surfaces. Also, when navigating on sandy roads observe that your wheels slip and spin, and so your milometer will register a much greater distance than you have actually travelled. I've generally used a GPS to track distances for this book – not a vehicle's milometer.

Driving through high grass After the rains, many of Zambia's tracks are often knee-high in seeding grass. As your vehicle drives through, stems and especially seeds can build up in front of and inside the radiator, and get trapped in crevices underneath the chassis. This is a major problem in the less-visited areas of Kalahari sand. It's at its worst in March to June, after the rains, and in western Zambia and Kafue.

This causes a real danger of overheating (see below) and fire. First, the build-up of seeds and stems over the radiator insulates it. Thus, if you aren't watching your gauges, the engine's temperature can rocket. It will swiftly seize up and catch fire. Secondly, the grass build-up itself, if allowed to become too big, can catch fire due to its contact with the hot exhaust system, underneath the vehicle.

In addition to the obvious precaution of carrying a fire extinguisher, there are several strategies to minimise these dangers; best apply them all. Firstly, before you set out, buy a few square metres of the tightly woven window-meshing gauze material used in the windows of safari tents. Fix one large panel of this on the vehicle's bull-bars, well in front of the radiator grill. Fix another much closer to it, but still outside of the engine compartment. This should vastly reduce the number of seeds reaching your radiator.

Secondly, watch your vehicle's engine-temperature gauge like a hawk when you're travelling through areas of grassland.

Thirdly, stop every 10km or so (yes, really, that often) and check the radiator and the undercarriage for pockets of stems and seeds. Pay special attention to the hot areas of the exhaust pipe; you should not allow a build-up of flammable material there. Use a stick or piece of wire to clean these seeds and stems out before you set off.

When driving through the grass, take particular care to avoid hidden obstacles, which can inflict considerable damage to your vehicle. Watch out too, for bush fires, which can move rapidly and make some roads impassable for a while.

Driving in mud This is difficult, though the theory is the same as for sand: keep going and don't stop. That said, even the most experienced drivers get stuck. Many areas of Zambia (like large stretches of the Kafue, Luangwa and Lower Zambezi valleys) have very fine soil known as 'black-cotton' soil, which becomes impassable when wet. This is why many of the camps close down for the rains, as the only way to get there would be to walk.

Mud can also have the same overheating effect as grass seed, so it's important to wash it away from the radiator once you stop.

Push-starting when stuck If you are unlucky enough to need to push-start your vehicle whilst it is stuck in sand or mud, there is a remedy. Raise up the drive wheels, and take off one of the tyres. Then wrap a length of rope around the hub and treat it like a spinning top: one person (or more) pulls the rope to make the axle spin, whilst the driver lifts the clutch, turns the ignition on, and engages a low gear to turn the engine over. This is a very difficult equivalent of a push-start, but it may be your only option.

On rocky terrain Have your tyre pressure higher than normal and move very slowly. If necessary, passengers should get out and guide you along the track to avoid scraping the undercarriage on the ground. This can be a very slow business, but often applies in some of Zambia's mountainous areas.

Crossing rivers The first thing to do is to stop and check the river. You must assess its depth, its substrate (type of riverbed) and its current flow; and determine the best route to drive across it. This is best done by wading across the river (whilst watching for hippos and crocodiles, if necessary). Beware of water that's too deep for your vehicle, or the very real possibility of being swept away by a fast current and a slippery substrate.

If everything is OK then select your lowest gear ratio and drive through the water at a slow but steady rate. Your vehicle's air intake must be above the level of the water to avoid your engine filling with water. It's not worth taking risks, so remember that a flooded river may subside to safer levels by the next morning.

Many rivers in Zambia have hand-operated pontoons – usually wooden platforms tied on top of buoyant empty oil cans and kept in line by steel cables stretched across the river. There are often, but not always, local people around who man these, for either a large official charge or a handsome tip. You need to take great care (everybody out, use first gear) when driving on and off these, and make sure that the pontoon is held tightly next to the bank on both occasions.

Overheating If the engine has overheated then the only option is to stop and turn it off. Don't open the radiator cap to refill it until the radiator is no longer hot to the touch. Even then, keep the engine running and the water circulating while you refill the radiator – otherwise you run the risk of cracking the hot metal by suddenly cooling it. Flicking droplets of water onto the outside of a running engine will cool it.

And see *Driving through high grass* above.

DRIVING NEAR BIG GAME The only animals which are likely to pose a threat to vehicles are elephants – and generally only elephants which are familiar with vehicles. So, treat them with the greatest respect and don't 'push' them by trying to move ever closer. Letting them approach you is much safer, and they will feel far less threatened and more relaxed. Then, if the animals are calm, you can safely turn the engine off, sit quietly, and watch as they pass you by.

If you are unlucky, or foolish, enough to unexpectedly drive into the middle of a herd, then don't panic. Keep your movements, and those of the vehicle, slow and measured. Back off steadily. Don't be panicked, or overly intimidated, by a mock charge – this is just their way of frightening you away. Professionals will sometimes switch their engines off, but this is not for the faint-hearted.

⚐ BUSH CAMPING

Many 'boy scout'-type manuals have been written on survival in the bush, usually by military veterans. If you are stranded with a convenient multi-purpose knife, then these useful tomes will describe how you can build a shelter from branches, catch passing animals for food, and signal to the inevitable rescue planes which are combing the globe looking for you – whilst avoiding the attentions of hostile forces.

In Zambia, bush camping is usually less about survival than comfort. You're likely to have much more than the knife: probably at least a bulging backpack, if not a loaded 4x4. Thus the challenge is not to camp and survive, it is to camp and be as comfortable as possible. With practice you'll learn how, but a few hints may be useful for the less experienced.

WHERE YOU CAN CAMP In frequently visited national parks, there are designated campsites that you should use, as directed by the local game scouts. Elsewhere the rules are less obvious, though it is normal to ask the scouts, and get their permission, for any site that you have in mind.

Outside of the parks, you should ask the local landowner, or village head, if they are happy for you to camp on their property. If you explain patiently and politely what you want, then you are unlikely to meet anything but warm hospitality from most rural Zambians. They will normally be as fascinated with your way of life as you are with theirs. Company by your campfire is virtually assured.

CHOOSING A SITE Only experience will teach you how to choose a good site for pitching a tent, but a few points may help you avoid a lot of problems:

- Avoid camping on what looks like a path through the bush, however indistinct. It may be a well-used game trail.
- Beware of camping in dry riverbeds: dangerous flash floods can arrive with little or no warning.
- In marshy areas camp on higher ground to avoid cold, damp mists in the morning and evening.
- Camp a reasonable distance from water: near enough to walk to it, but far enough to avoid animals which arrive to drink.
- If a lightning storm is likely, make sure that your tent is not the highest thing around.
- Finally, choose a site which is as flat as possible – you will find sleeping much easier.

CAMPFIRES Campfires can create a great atmosphere and warm you on a cold evening, but they can also be damaging to the environment and leave unsightly piles of ash and blackened stones. Deforestation is a major concern in much of the developing world, including parts of Zambia, so if you do light a fire then use wood as the locals do: sparingly. If you have a vehicle, consider buying firewood in advance from people who sell it at the roadside.

If you collect it yourself, then take only dead wood, nothing living. Never just pick up a log: always roll it over first, checking carefully for snakes or scorpions.

Experienced campers build small, highly efficient fires by using a few large stones to absorb, contain and reflect the heat, and gradually feeding just a few thick logs into the centre to burn. Cooking pots can be balanced on the stones, or the point where the logs meet and burn. Others will use a small trench, lined with rocks, to similar effect. Either technique takes practice, but is worth perfecting. Whichever you do, bury the ashes, take any rubbish with you when you leave, and make the site look as if you had never been there. (See *Appendix 3*, page 511, for details of Christina Dodwell's excellent *Travel, Survival and Bush Cookery*.)

Don't expect an unattended fire to frighten away wild animals – that works in Hollywood, but not in Africa. A campfire may help your feelings of insecurity, but lion and hyena will disregard it with stupefying nonchalance.

Finally, do be hospitable to any locals who appear – despite your efforts to seek permission for your camp, you may effectively be staying in their back gardens.

USING A TENT (OR NOT) Whether to use a tent or to sleep in the open is a personal choice, dependent upon where you are. In an area where there are predators around (specifically lion and hyena) then you should use a tent – and sleep *completely* inside it, as a protruding leg may seem like a tasty take-away to a hungry hyena. This is especially true at organised campsites, where the local animals are so used to humans that they have lost much of their inherent fear of man.

Outside game areas, you will be fine sleeping in the open, or preferably under a mosquito net, with just the stars of the African sky above you. On the practical side, sleeping under a tree will reduce the morning dew that settles on your sleeping bag. If your vehicle has a large, flat roof then sleeping on this will provide you with peace of mind, and a star-filled outlook. (Hiring a vehicle with a built-in rooftop tent would seem like a perfect solution, until you want to take a drive whilst leaving your camp intact.)

CAMPING EQUIPMENT If you are taking an organised safari, you will not need any camping equipment at all. However, for those travelling independently very little kit is available in Zambia. So buy high-quality equipment beforehand as it will save you a lot of time and trouble once you arrive. Here are a few comments on various essentials.

Tent During the rains a good tent is essential in order to stay dry. Even during the dry season one is useful if there are lion or hyena around. If backpacking, invest in a high-quality, lightweight tent. Mosquito-netting ventilation panels, allowing a good flow of air, are essential. (Just a corner of mesh at the top of the tent is not enough for comfort.) Don't go for a tent that's small; it may feel cosy at home, but will be hot and claustrophobic in the heat.

I have been using the same Spacepacker tent, manufactured by Robert Saunders Ltd (*Five Oaks Lane, Chigwell, Essex IG7 4QP, UK; www.robertsaunders.co.uk*) for over ten years. It's a dome tent with fine mesh doors on either side which allow a through draught, making all the difference when temperatures are high. The alternative to a good tent is a mosquito net, which is fine unless it is raining or you are in a big game area.

Sleeping bag A lightweight, 'three-season' sleeping bag is ideal for Zambia, unless you are heading up to the Nyika Plateau in winter where the nights freeze. Down is preferable to synthetic fillings for most of the year, as it packs smaller, is lighter, and feels more luxurious to sleep in. However, when down gets wet it loses its efficiency, so bring a good synthetic bag if you are likely to encounter much rain.

Ground mat A ground mat of some sort is essential. It keeps you warm and comfortable, and it protects the tent's groundsheet from rough or stony ground. (Do put it underneath the tent!) Closed cell foam mats are widely available outside Zambia, so buy one before you arrive. The better mats cost double or treble the cheaper ones, but are stronger, thicker and warmer – well worth the investment. Therm-a-Rests, the combination air-mattress and foam mats, are strong, durable and also worth the investment – but take a puncture repair kit with you just in case of problems.

Sheet sleeping bag Thin, pure-cotton sheet sleeping bags (eg: YHA design) are small, light and very useful. They are easily washed and so are normally used like a sheet, inside a sleeping bag, to keep it clean. They can, of course, be used on their own when your main sleeping bag is too hot.

Stove 'Trangia'-type stoves, which burn methylated spirits, are simple to use, light, and cheap to run. They come complete with a set of light aluminium pans and a very useful all-purpose handle. Often you'll be able to cook on a fire with the pans, but it's nice to have the option of making a brew in a few minutes while you set up camp. Methylated spirits is cheap and widely available, even in the rural areas, but bring a tough (purpose-made) fuel container with you as the bottles in which it is sold will soon crack and spill all over your belongings.

Petrol- and kerosene-burning stoves are undoubtedly efficient on fuel and powerful – but invariably temperamental and messy. Gas stoves use pressurised canisters, which are not allowed on aircraft and are difficult to buy in Zambia.

Torch (flashlight) This should be on every visitor's packing list. Find one that's small and tough, preferably water- and dust-proof. Head-mounted torches leave your hands free (useful when cooking or mending the car) but some people find them bulky and uncomfortable to wear. The small, strong and super-bright torches (eg: Maglites) are excellent, but their bulbs are difficult to buy in Zambia. Bring several spares with you.

Those with vehicles will find that a strong spotlight, powered by the car's battery (perhaps through the socket for the cigarette lighter), is invaluable for impromptu lighting.

Water containers For everyday use, a small two-litre water bottle is invaluable, however you are travelling. If you're thinking of camping, you should also consider a strong, collapsible water-bag – perhaps 5–10 litres in size – which will reduce the number of trips that you need to make from your camp to the water source. (Ten litres of water weighs 10kg.) Drivers will want to carry a number of large containers of water, especially if venturing into the Kalahari sand in western Zambia, where good surface water is not common.

See *Planning and preparation*, page 58, for a memory-jogging list of other useful items to pack.

ANIMAL DANGERS FOR CAMPERS Camping in Africa is really very safe, though you may not think so from reading this. If you have a major problem whilst camping, it will probably be because you did something stupid, or because you forgot to take a few simple precautions. Here are a few general basics, applicable to anywhere in Africa and not just Zambia.

Large animals Big game will not bother you if you are in a tent – provided that you do not attract its attention, or panic it. Elephants will gently tiptoe through your guy ropes whilst you sleep, without even nudging your tent. However, if you wake up and make a noise, startling them, they are far more likely to panic and step on your tent. Similarly, scavengers will quietly wander round, smelling your evening meal in the air, without any intention of harming you. Bear the following precautions in mind:

- Remember to use the toilet before going to bed, and avoid getting up in the night if possible.
- Scrupulously clean everything used for food that might smell good to scavengers. Put these utensils in a vehicle if possible, suspend them from a tree, or pack them away in a rucksack inside the tent.
- Do not keep any smelly foodstuffs, like meat or citrus fruit, in your tent. Their smells may attract unwanted attention.
- Do not leave anything outside that could be picked up – like bags, pots, pans, etc. Hyenas, amongst others, will take anything. (They have been known to crunch a camera's lens, and eat it.)

111

- If you are likely to wake in the night, then leave the tent's zips a few centimetres open at the top, enabling you to take a quiet peek outside.

Creepy-crawlies As you set up camp, clear stones or logs out of your way with great caution: underneath will be great hiding places for snakes and scorpions. Long moist grass is ideal territory for snakes, and dry, dusty, rocky places are classic sites for scorpions.

If you are sleeping in the open, it is not unknown to wake and find a snake lying next to you in the morning. Don't panic: your warmth has just attracted it to you. You will not be bitten if you gently edge away without making any sudden movements. (This is one good argument for using at least a mosquito net!)

Before you put on your shoes, shake them out. Similarly, check the back of your backpack before you slip it on. Just a curious spider, in either, could inflict a painful bite.

WALKING IN THE BUSH

Walking in the African bush is a totally different sensation from driving through it. You may start off a little unready – perhaps even sleepy – for an early morning walk, but swiftly your mind will awake. There are no noises except the wildlife, and you. So every noise that isn't caused by you must be an animal, or a bird, or an insect. Every smell and every rustle has a story to tell, if you can understand it.

With time, patience and a good guide you can learn to smell the presence of elephants, and hear when a predator alarms impala. You can use ox-peckers to lead you to buffalo, or vultures to help you locate a kill. Tracks will record the passage of animals in the sand, telling what passed by, how long ago and in which direction.

Eventually your gaze becomes alert to the slightest movement, your ears aware of every sound. This is safari at its best: a live, sharp, spine-tingling experience that's hard to beat and very addictive. Be careful: watching game from a vehicle will never be the same again for you.

WALKING TRAILS AND SAFARIS One of Zambia's biggest attractions is its walking safaris, which can justly claim to be amongst the best in Africa. The concept was pioneered here, in the Luangwa Valley, by the late Norman Carr. He also founded Nsefu Camp and Kapani Lodge, and trained several of the valley's best guides. It was he who first operated walking safaris for photographic guests, as opposed to hunters. The Luangwa still has a strong tradition of walking – which, in itself, fosters excellent walking guides. Several of the camps are dedicated to walking safaris, and guiding standards are generally very high.

One of the reasons behind the valley's success is the stringent tests that a guide must pass before he, or she, will be allowed to take clients into the bush. Walking guides have the hardest tests to pass; there is a less demanding exam for guides who conduct safaris from vehicles.

The second major reason for excellence is Zambia's policy of having a safari guide and an armed game scout accompany every walking safari. These groups are limited (by park rules) to a maximum of seven guests, and there's normally a tea-bearer (carrying drinks and refreshments) as well as the guide and armed scout.

If a problem arises with an aggressive animal, then the guide looks after the visitors – telling them exactly what to do – whilst the scout keeps his sights trained on the animal, just in case a shot is necessary. Fortunately such drastic measures are needed only rarely. This system of two guides means that Zambia's walks are very safe. Few shots are ever fired, and I can't remember hearing of an animal (or a person) ever being injured.

Contrast this with other African countries where a single guide (who may, or may not, be armed) watches out for the game *and* takes care of the visitors at the same time. The Zambian way is far better.

Etiquette for walking safaris If you plan to walk then avoid wearing any bright, unnatural colours, especially white. Dark, muted shades are best; greens, browns and khaki are ideal. Hats are essential, as is sunblock. Even a short walk will last for two hours, and there's no vehicle to which you can retreat if you get too hot.

Binoculars should be immediately accessible – one pair per person – ideally in dust-proof cases strapped to your belt. Cameras too, if you decide to bring any, as they are of little use buried at the bottom of a camera bag. Heavy tripods or long lenses are a nightmare to lug around, so leave them behind if you can (and accept, philosophically, that you may miss shots).

Walkers see the most when walking in silent single file. This doesn't mean that you can't stop to whisper a question to the guide; just that idle chatter will reduce your powers of observation, and make you even more visible to the animals (who will usually flee when they sense you).

With regard to safety, your guide will always brief you in detail before you set off. S/he will outline possible dangers, and what to do in the unlikely event of them materialising. Listen carefully: this is vital.

Face-to-face animal encounters Whether you are on an organised walking safari, on your own hike, or just walking from the car to your tent in the bush, it is not unlikely that you will come across some of Africa's larger animals at close quarters. Invariably, the danger is much less than you imagine, and a few basic guidelines will enable you to cope effectively with most situations.

First of all, don't panic. Console yourself with the fact that animals are not normally interested in people. You are not their normal food, or their predator. If you do not annoy or threaten them, you will be left alone.

If you are walking to look for animals, then remember that this is their environment and not yours. Animals have evolved in the bush, and their senses are far better attuned to it than yours. To be on less unequal terms, remain alert and try to spot them from a distance. This gives you the option of approaching carefully, or staying well clear.

Finally, the advice of a good guide is far more valuable than the simplistic comments noted here. Animals, like people, are all different. So whilst we can generalise here and say how the 'average' animal will behave, the one that's glaring at you over a small bush may have had a really bad day, and be feeling much grumpier than normal.

That said, here are a few general comments on how to deal with some potentially dangerous situations.

Buffalo This is probably the continent's most dangerous animal to hikers, but there is a difference between the old males, often encountered on their own or in small groups, and large breeding herds.

The former are easily surprised. If they hear or smell something amiss, they will charge without provocation – motivated by a fear that something is sneaking up on them. Buffalo have an excellent sense of smell, but fortunately they are short-sighted. Avoid a charge by quickly climbing the nearest tree, or by side-stepping at the last minute. If adopting the latter, more risky, technique then stand motionless until the last possible moment, as the buffalo may well miss you anyhow.

The large breeding herds can be treated in a totally different manner. If you approach them in the open, they will often flee. Sometimes though, in areas often used for walking safaris, they will stand and watch, moving aside to allow you to pass through the middle of the herd.

Neither encounter is for the faint-hearted or inexperienced, so steer clear of these dangerous animals wherever possible.

Black rhino If you are both exceptionally lucky to find a black rhino, and then unlucky enough to be charged by it, use the same tactics as you would for a buffalo: tree climbing or dodging at the last second. (It is amazing how even the least athletic walker will swiftly scale the nearest tree when faced with a charging rhino.)

Elephant Normally elephants are a problem only if you disturb a mother with a calf, or approach a male in musth (state of arousal). So keep well away from these. Lone bulls can usually be approached quite closely when feeding. If you get too close to any elephant it will scare you off with a 'mock charge': head up, perhaps shaking – ears flapping – trumpeting. Lots of sound and fury. This is intended to be frightening, and it is. But it is just a warning and no cause for panic. Just freeze to assess the elephant's intentions, then back off slowly.

When elephants really mean business, they will put their ears back, their head down, and charge directly at you without stopping. This is known as a 'full charge'. There is no easy way to avoid the charge of an angry elephant, so take a hint from the warning and back off very slowly as soon as you encounter a mock charge. Don't run. If you are the object of a full charge, then you have no choice but to run – preferably round an anthill, up a tall tree, or wherever.

Lion Tracking lion can be one of the most exhilarating parts of a walking safari. Sadly, they will normally flee before you even get close to them. However, it can be a problem if you come across a large pride unexpectedly. Lion are well camouflaged; it is easy to find yourself next to one before you realise it. If you had been listening, you would probably have heard a warning growl about 20m ago. Now it is too late.

The best plan is to stop, and back off slowly, but confidently. If you are in a small group, then stick together. *Never* run from a big cat. First, they are always faster than you are. Secondly, running will just convince them that you are frightened prey, and worth chasing. As a last resort, if they seem too inquisitive and follow as you back off, then stop. Call their bluff. Pretend that you are not afraid and make loud, deep, confident noises: shout at them, bang something. But do not run.

John Coppinger, one of Luangwa's most experienced guides, adds that every single compromising experience that he has had with lion on foot has been either with a female with cubs, or with a mating pair, when the males can get very aggressive. You have been warned.

Leopard Leopard are very seldom seen, and would normally flee from the most timid of lone hikers. However, if injured, or surprised, then they are very powerful, dangerous cats. Conventional wisdom is scarce, but never stare straight into the leopard's eyes, or it will regard this as a threat display. (The same is said, by some, to be true with lion.) Better to look away slightly, at a nearby bush, or even at its tail. Then back off slowly, facing the direction of the cat and showing as little terror as you can. As with lion – loud, deep, confident noises are a last line of defence. Never run from a leopard.

Hippo Hippo are fabled to account for more deaths in Africa than any other animal (ignoring the mosquito). Having been attacked and capsized by a hippo whilst in a dugout canoe, I find this very easy to believe, but see *Appendix 1* (page

501) for an alternative comment on this. Visitors are most likely to encounter hippo in the water, when paddling a canoe (see *Canoeing*, below) or fishing. However, as they spend half their time grazing on land, they will sometimes be encountered out of the water. Away from the water, out of their comforting lagoons, hippos are even more dangerous. If they see you, they will flee towards the water – so the golden rule is never to get between a hippo and its escape route to deep water. Given that a hippo will outrun you on land, standing motionless is probably your best line of defence.

Snakes These are really not the great danger that people imagine. Most flee when they feel the vibrations of footsteps; only a few will stay still. The puff adder is responsible for more cases of snakebite than any other venomous snake in Zambia because, when approached, it will simply puff itself up and hiss as a warning, rather than slither away. This makes it essential to always watch where you place your feet when walking in the bush.

Similarly, there are a couple of arboreal (tree-dwelling) species which may be taken by surprise if you carelessly grab vegetation as you walk. So don't.

Spitting cobras are also encountered occasionally, which will aim for your eyes and spit with accuracy. If one of these rears up in front of you, then turn away and avert your eyes. If the spittle reaches your eyes, you must wash them out *immediately* and thoroughly with whatever liquid comes to hand: water, milk, even urine if that's the only liquid that you can quickly produce.

CANOEING

The Zambezi – both above the Victoria Falls and from Kariba to Mozambique – is in constant use for canoeing trips. One good operator, Remote Africa Safaris (see page 260), even features canoeing on the Luangwa whilst it is high and in flood. Canoeing along beautiful, tropical rivers is as much a part of Zambia's safari scene in the Lower Zambezi as are open-top Land Rovers. Generally you either canoe along the river for a set number of days, stopping each night at a different place, or paddle for a short stretch as an activity at one of the camps – as an alternative to a walk or a game drive.

Most operators use large, two- or three-person Canadian-style fibreglass canoes. Three-person canoes usually have a guide in the back of each, while two-person canoes are often paddled in 'convoy' with a guide in just one of the boats. Less confident (or lazier) paddlers might prefer to have a guide in their own canoe, while the more energetic usually want to have the boat to themselves.

ZAMBEZI CANOE GUIDES Most of the Zambezi's specialist canoeing operations are run by large companies on a very commercial basis. On these you can expect to join a party of about seven canoes, one of which will contain a guide. S/he should know the stretch of river well and will canoe along it regularly. The actual distances completed on the two-/three-night trips are quite short. All the trips run downstream and a day's canoeing could actually be completed in just three hours with a modicum of fitness and technique.

Like other guides, the 'river guides' must possess a professional licence in order to be allowed to take paying guests canoeing. Note that only a few of the best river guides also hold licences as general professional guides (ie: are licensed to lead walking safaris). These all-rounders generally have a far deeper understanding of the environment and the game than those who are only 'river guides'.

However, their greater skill commands a higher wage – and so they are usually found in the smaller, more upmarket operations. Given the inexperience of some of the river guides, I would always be willing to pay the extra. Although the safety record of river trips is good, accidents do happen occasionally.

THE MAIN DANGERS

Hippo Hippos are strictly vegetarians, and will usually attack a canoe only if they feel threatened. The standard avoidance technique is first of all to let them know that you are there. If in doubt, bang your paddle on the side of the canoe a few times (most novice canoeists will do this constantly anyhow).

During the day, hippopotami will congregate in the deeper areas of the river. The odd ones in shallow water – where they feel less secure – will head for the deeper places as soon as they are aware of a nearby canoe. Avoiding hippos then becomes a fairly simple case of steering around the deeper areas, where the pods will make their presence obvious. This is where experience, and knowing every bend of the river, becomes useful.

Problems arise when canoes inadvertently stray over a pod of hippos, or when a canoe cuts a hippo off from its path of retreat into deeper water. Either is dangerous, as hippos will overturn canoes without a second thought, biting them and their occupants. Once in this situation, there are no easy remedies. So – avoid it in the first place.

Crocodiles Crocodiles may have sharp teeth and look prehistoric, but are rarely a danger to a canoeist while in the boat, although the larger, wilier animals can pose a serious threat. If you find yourself in the water, the situation is considerably worse. Then the more you struggle and the more waves you create, the more you will attract their unwelcome attentions. There is a major problem when canoes are overturned by hippos – then you must get out of the water as soon as possible, either into another canoe or onto the bank.

When a crocodile attacks an animal, it will try to disable it, normally by getting a firm, biting grip, submerging, and performing a long, fast barrel-roll. This will disorient the prey, drown it, and probably twist off the limb that has been bitten. In this dire situation, your best line of defence is probably to stab the reptile in its eyes with anything sharp that you have. Alternatively, if you can lift up its tongue and let the water into its lungs whilst it is underwater, then a crocodile will start to drown and will release its prey.

Jo Pope reports that a man survived an attack in the Zambezi when a crocodile grabbed his arm and started to spin backwards into deep water. The man wrapped his legs around the crocodile, to spin with it and avoid having his arm twisted off. As this happened, he tried to poke his thumb into its eyes, but with no effect. Finally he put his free arm into the crocodile's mouth, and opened up the beast's throat. This worked. The crocodile left him and he survived with only a damaged arm. Understandably, anecdotes about tried and tested methods of escape are rare.

MINIMUM IMPACT

When you visit, drive through, or camp in an area and have 'minimum impact' this means that that area is left in the same condition as – or better than – when you entered it. Whilst most visitors view minimum impact as being desirable, spend time to consider the ways in which we contribute to environmental degradation, and how these can be avoided.

DRIVING Use your vehicle responsibly. If there's a road, or a track, then don't go off it – the environment will suffer. Driving off-road can leave a multitude of tracks that detract from the 'wilderness' feeling for subsequent visitors. Equally, don't speed through towns or villages: remember the danger to local children, and the amount of dust you'll cause.

HYGIENE Use toilets if they are provided, even if they are basic longdrop loos with questionable cleanliness. If there are no toilets, then human excrement should always be buried well away from paths, or groundwater, and any tissue used should be burnt and then buried.

If you use rivers or lakes to wash, then soap yourself near the bank, using a pan for scooping water from the river – making sure that no soap finds its way back into the water. Use biodegradable soap. Sand makes an excellent pan-scrub, even if you have no water to spare.

RUBBISH Biodegradable rubbish can be burnt and buried with the campfire ashes. Don't just leave it lying around: it will look very unsightly and spoil the place for those who come after you.

Bring along some plastic bags with which to remove the rest of your rubbish, and dump it at the next town. Items that will not burn, like tin cans, are best cleaned and squashed for easy carrying. If there are bins, then use them, but also consider when they will next be emptied, and if local animals will rummage through them first. Carrying out all your own rubbish may still be the sensible option.

HOST COMMUNITIES Whilst the rules for reducing impact on the environment have been understood and followed by responsible travellers for years, the effects of tourism on local people have only recently been considered. Many tourists believe it is their right, for example, to take intrusive photos of local people – and even become angry if the local people object. They refer to higher prices being charged to tourists as a rip-off, without considering the hand-to-mouth existence of those selling these products or services. They deplore child beggars, then hand out sweets or pens to local children with outstretched hands.

Our behaviour towards 'the locals' needs to be considered in terms of their culture, with the knowledge that we are the uninvited visitors. We visit to enjoy ourselves, but this should not be at the expense of local people. Read *Cultural guidelines*, pages 22–3, and aim to leave the local communities better off after your visit.

LOCAL PAYMENTS If you spend time with any of Zambia's poorer local people, perhaps camping in the bush or getting involved with one of the community-run projects, then take great care with any payments that you make.

First, note that most people like to spend their earnings on what *they* choose. This means that trying to pay for services with beads, food, old clothes or anything else instead of money isn't appreciated. Ask yourself how you'd like to be paid, and you'll understand this point.

Second, find out the normal cost of what you are buying. Most community campsites will have a standard price for a pitch and, if applicable, an hour's guided activity, or whatever. Find this out before you sleep there, or accept the offer of a walk. It is then important that you pay about that amount for the service rendered – no less, and not too much more.

As most people realise, if you try to pay less you'll get into trouble – as you would at home. However, many do not realise that if they generously pay a lot more, this can be equally damaging. Local rates of pay in rural areas can be very low, and a careless visitor can easily pay disproportionately large sums. Where this happens, local jobs can lose their value overnight. (Imagine working hard to become a game scout, only to learn that a tourist has given your friend the equivalent of your whole month's wages for just a few hours guiding. What incentive is there for you to carry on with your regular job?)

If you want to give more – for good service, a super guide, or just because you want to help – then either buy some locally made produce (at the going rate) or donate money to one of the organisations working to improve the lot of Zambia's most disadvantaged (see pages 82–3). ZOCS is one such charity, working for some of Zambia's poorest children, but if you ask locally you'll often find projects that need your support. Some lodges and camps also assist with community projects, and will be able to suggest a good use for donations.

Part Two

THE GUIDE

Bradt Travel Guides

www.bradtguides.com

Africa

Africa Overland	£15.99
Algeria	£15.99
Benin	£14.99
Botswana: Okavango, Chobe, Northern Kalahari	£15.99
Burkina Faso	£14.99
Cape Verde Islands	£13.99
Canary Islands	£13.95
Cameroon	£13.95
Congo	£14.99
Eritrea	£15.99
Ethiopia	£15.99
Gabon, São Tomé, Príncipe	£13.95
Gambia, The	£13.99
Ghana	£15.99
Johannesburg	£6.99
Kenya	£14.95
Madagascar	£15.99
Malawi	£13.99
Mali	£13.95
Mauritius, Rodrigues & Réunion	£13.99
Mozambique	£13.99
Namibia	£15.99
Niger	£14.99
Nigeria	£15.99
Rwanda	£14.99
Seychelles	£14.99
Sudan	£13.95
Tanzania, Northern	£13.99
Tanzania	£16.99
Uganda	£15.99
Zambia	£17.99
Zanzibar	£12.99

Britain and Europe

Albania	£13.99
Armenia, Nagorno Karabagh	£14.99
Azores	£12.99
Baltic Capitals: Tallinn, Riga, Vilnius, Kaliningrad	£12.99
Belarus	£14.99
Belgrade	£6.99
Bosnia & Herzegovina	£13.99
Bratislava	£6.99
Budapest	£8.99
Bulgaria	£13.99
Cork	£6.99
Croatia	£13.99
Cyprus see North Cyprus	

Czech Republic	£13.99
Dresden	£7.99
Dubrovnik	£6.99
Estonia	£13.99
Faroe Islands	£13.95
Georgia	£14.99
Helsinki	£7.99
Hungary	£14.99
Iceland	£14.99
Kiev	£7.95
Kosovo	£14.99
Krakow	£7.99
Lapland	£13.99
Latvia	£13.99
Lille	£6.99
Lithuania	£13.99
Ljubljana	£7.99
Macedonia	£14.99
Montenegro	£13.99
North Cyprus	£12.99
Paris, Lille & Brussels	£11.95
Riga	£6.95
River Thames, In the Footsteps of the Famous	£10.95
Serbia	£14.99
Slovakia	£14.99
Slovenia	£12.99
Spitsbergen	£14.99
Switzerland: Rail, Road, Lake	£13.99
Tallinn	£6.99
Ukraine	£14.99
Vilnius	£6.99
Zagreb	£6.99

Middle East, Asia and Australasia

China: Yunnan Province	£13.99
Great Wall of China	£13.99
Iran	£14.99
Iraq	£14.95
Iraq: Then & Now	£15.99
Kyrgyzstan	£15.99
Maldives	£13.99
Mongolia	£14.95
North Korea	£13.95
Oman	£13.99
Sri Lanka	£13.99
Syria	£14.99
Tibet	£13.99
Turkmenistan	£14.99
Yemen	£14.99

The Americas and the Caribbean

Amazon, The	£14.99
Argentina	£15.99
Bolivia	£14.99
Cayman Islands	£12.95
Colombia	£15.99
Costa Rica	£13.99
Chile	£16.95
Dominica	£14.99
Falkland Islands	£13.95
Guyana	£14.99
Panama	£13.95
Peru & Bolivia: Backpacking and Trekking	£12.95
St Helena	£14.99
USA by Rail	£13.99

Wildlife

100 Animals to See Before They Die	£16.99
Antarctica: Guide to the Wildlife	£14.95
Arctic: Guide to the Wildlife	£15.99
Central & Eastern European Wildlife	£15.99
Chinese Wildlife	£16.99
East African Wildlife	£19.99
Galápagos Wildlife	£15.99
Madagascar Wildlife	£14.95
Peruvian Wildlife	£15.99
Southern African Wildlife	£18.95
Sri Lankan Wildlife	£15.99

Eccentric Guides

Eccentric America	£13.95
Eccentric Australia	£12.99
Eccentric Britain	£13.99
Eccentric California	£13.99
Eccentric Cambridge	£6.99
Eccentric Edinburgh	£5.95
Eccentric France	£12.95
Eccentric London	£13.99
Eccentric Oxford	£5.95

Others

Your Child Abroad: A Travel Health Guide	£10.95
Something Different for the Weekend	£12.99

7

Lusaka

Despite the assertions of the tourist board, Lusaka is still not high on Zambia's list of major attractions. Its wide, tree-lined boulevards can be pleasant, but the traffic is chaotic and many of the suburbs are sprawling and dirty. However, Lusaka is no worse than London, New York or any number of other big cities. Like them, it has a fascination because it is unmistakably cosmopolitan, alive and kicking. As home to one-tenth of Zambia's people, it has a discernible heartbeat which smaller or more sanitised cities lack. So if you go to Zambia with an interest in meeting a cross-section of its people, Lusaka should figure on your itinerary.

In my experience, the city's bad reputation is exaggerated. It is certainly unsafe for the unwary – but much less risky than Nairobi or Johannesburg. Walking around at night is stupid and potentially dangerous, and during the day pickpockets will strike if you keep valuables obvious or accessible. However, visitors to Lusaka who allow their paranoia to elevate the city's dangers to the dizzy heights of Lagos are deluding themselves. It isn't that dangerous, if you are careful.

HISTORY

Lusaka's status as a capital city dates only from 1935. Until then, the capital of Northern Rhodesia had been Livingstone, but as the country's mines were developed it was felt that the town was too far away from the industrial heartland in the Copperbelt.

The site of the new capital was chosen both for its central location and for its position high on a plateau, resulting in a relatively cool climate. There was already a permanent settlement here: Lusaka owes its establishment to construction of the railway at the beginning of the 20th century, when a camp was needed for the workers. The decision to site the new state buildings on the ridge a couple of kilometres to the east of the railway was linked to the frequency with which the lower-lying land was flooded during the rains. While it was anticipated that Lusaka's heart would eventually shift east, the capital has remained firmly divided, with its spacious new administrative area contrasting with the bustle of the business area focused on Cairo Road.

GETTING THERE AND AWAY

BY AIR Lusaka (airline code LUN) is reasonably well served by international flights. Currently British Airways is the main intercontinental airline connecting Europe direct with Zambia, but other carriers are possible if you use Nairobi or Johannesburg as gateways to the continent. See *Planning and Preparation*, page 52, for more details of the best fares to Zambia, and page 67 for local airlines, and general comments on getting around the country by air.

International airlines Airlines represented in Lusaka include:

✈ **Air Botswana** ✆ 021 1227739/40, 1227285;
f 021 1223724; www.airbotswana.co.bw
✈ **Air France** ✆ 021 1227739–40, 1227285; airport
✆ 021 1271212; f 021 1225178; www.airfrance.com
✈ **Air India** ✆ 021 1229563, 1226349, 1223128;
f 021 1228124; www.airindia.com
✈ **Air Malawi** ✆ 021 1228120/–1; f 021 1228124;
www.airmalawi.com
✈ **Air Tanzania** ✆ 021 1251189, 1252499;
www.airtanzania.com
✈ **British Airways** ✆ 021 1254444; f 021 1250623,
1255328; www.britishairways.com

✈ **Kenya Airways/KLM** ✆ 021 1228908/886; f 021
1228902; airport ✆ 021 1271042; f 021 1271478;
www.kenya-airways.com
✈ **South African Airways** Tel: 021 1254350; f 021
1254064; airport ✆ 021 1271101; f 021 1271170;
www.flysaa.com
✈ **TAAG-Angolan Airways** ✆ 021 1222401,
1221684; f 021 1238633–4
✈ **Zambian Airways** ✆ 021 1271230/342; f 021
1271054; www.zambianairways.com

Local airlines and charter companies The charter companies and local airlines based in Lusaka have had a chequered past, with companies forming and disappearing with monotonous regularity. The current contenders wisely stick mainly to domestic routes. Zambian Airways have the best planes; their 19-seaters are so shiny and new they make you wonder who found the money to buy them. For details of services and operators, see *Chapter 4, Planning and preparation*, page 67.

Lusaka Airport The airport is well signposted, if isolated, at 25km from the city's major hotels, off the Great East Road. Transport there is either by shuttle bus from one of the big hotels (InterContinental, Holiday Inn or Taj Pamodzi), by the new Platinum Shuttle (m *099 069571, 096 6249299;* e *platinumshuttleservices@yahoo.com*) or by private taxi. The Platinum service runs up to six times a day between the airport and the Cresta Golf View, Arcades, InterContinental, Taj Pamodzi and Holiday Inn, with one-way fares at Kw40,000 per person. This slightly undercuts the hotel shuttles which cost about US$12 per person one way, while a taxi for the same journey should cost around US$20 for up to 4 passengers (though this is the route for which the drivers will charge most imaginatively). At weekends, the journey takes only about 20 minutes, but during the week – and especially at peak periods – you should allow at least double that time because of the traffic. If you're driving yourself, note that the speed limit between Lusaka and the airport is 80km/h, rising to 100km/h, and there are frequent speed traps. Parking at the airport costs Kw5,000 per day, though rates are higher in the secure area, where you'll need to book.

In addition to offices for all the main airlines, facilities at the airport include a post office, and desks for the major car-hire companies: Avis and Voyagers (representing both Imperial and Europcar). There are also two banks, one with a 24-hour ATM, and a couple of gift shops.

In the departure lounge upstairs it's well worth the cost of a drink to take advantage of the comfortable seating in the bar/café. Also on hand are a couple of duty-free shops selling textiles and curios, and an internet café with somewhat sporadic opening hours.

Departure tax A departure tax of US$25 is levied on all international flights, and of US$8 on domestic flights. This may be included in the price of your ticket; if in doubt check at the information office on the ground floor and pay any outstanding tax there before going through the departure gate. In the departure lounge upstairs, a clerk will check that this has been done, so there's no escape!

BY BUS

Long-distance coaches and buses Zambia's buses fall broadly into two categories. Comfortable, long-distance coaches, often with air conditioning, ply the longer routes, operating to a timetable and generally keeping good time. Rather less well-maintained vehicles may cover the same ground, but may wait until they're full before leaving. The two used to operate out of different bus stations, but today they all operate out of the Intercity Bus Terminal on the western side of Dedan Kimathi Road, near the railway station. It's a noisy, bustling station sheltering under a large purpose-built roof, and the place to catch a bus to virtually any of Zambia's provincial or district capitals, even those that are quite isolated such as Nakonde or Kashikishi.

Locals are paranoid about thieves who frequent the area, so expect warnings about safety. It is certainly not a place to go idly strolling at night, or to display your valuables, but if you keep your wits about you, and keep a firm eye on your belongings, then you should have no problems. Be aware, though, that ticket touts can be quite aggressive in their bid for your custom, so be firm if you haven't made up your mind.

Despite the apparent confusion that greets you, there is some order to the terminal's chaos. The buses sitting in bays are grouped roughly by their eventual destinations, as indicated on the boards displayed next to the driver. If you can't see the name you want, then ask someone – most people will go out of their way to help, and the staff on the information desk are usually very helpful.

Coach operators tend to come and go, so it's best to ask around the city's travel agents or at the bus station itself for the latest news, including details of services to South Africa. Carriers include Euro-Africa, RPS and CR (*www.crholdings-zambia.com*) buses, but there are numerous regional variations, some better than others. The first departures tend to be early in the morning, around 05.00, and are fairly punctual; it's advisable to be there half an hour ahead of the listed departure time. The best are well maintained and comfortable, with air conditioning and on-board toilet, and they tend to reach their destinations in good time – albeit sometimes at high speed. That said, recent reports suggest that standards on internal (as against international) routes operated by CR buses have declined, and we have even heard that their licence was suspended for a while in 2007.

For most (but not all) long-distance buses, you will need to buy a ticket at the terminus in advance. Generally there are two different prices for any given place: a higher one to travel in a smaller, faster minibus, and a lower rate for the larger, slower normal buses. Expect about a 20% premium for a minibus. Tickets are on sale the day beforehand, and the buses run to a timetable – in theory. In reality, many buses (big or small) may not leave until they are full, which can take hours. Try to avoid paying until the bus has started on its way, as you may want to swap buses if another appears to be filling faster and hence is likely to depart earlier.

Buses to some destinations leave frequently, others weekly – according to demand. The only way to find out is to go to the bus station and ask. There are regular services between Lusaka and Livingstone, and Lusaka and the Copperbelt, as well as east to Chipata. Just a few of the many options, with one-way fares, include:

To/from Livingstone Several buses a day run between Livingstone and Lusaka, some of them fast, modern coaches which run to a timetable. The journey takes about six hours, and a ticket costs about Kw75,000. There is also usually at least one operator running fast, air-conditioned coaches between Livingstone and Kitwe, via Lusaka. Operators change regularly, so ask locally before you travel; they include Euro-Africa Coaches, RPS and CR.

To/from Kitwe and beyond Several buses a day, mostly in the morning and early afternoon, head from Lusaka to Kitwe via Kabwe, Kapiri Mposhi and Ndola, taking approximately six hours. Some services then continue on to Chingola and Solwezi. Approximately Kw30,000 to Kapiri Mposhi; Kw50,000–65,000 to Ndola, Kw75,000 to Kitwe.

Other destinations
To Chipata CR has two buses a day, leaving at around 05.00 and 12.00; Kw95,000

To Kashikishi via Kabwe, Kapiri Mposhi, Serenje, Samfya, Mansa and Nchelenge; also to Kawambwa. Buses are operated by Zamsaf, Sierra, Jordan Motors and Germins. Four buses a day, departing around midnight. Serenje Kw50,000, Mansa Kw95,000, Kashikishi Kw120,000.

To Mongu Normally two buses per day, at 09.30 and 13.30; Kw85,000

To Mpulungu via Kasama and Mbala. Operators include the recommended Juldan Motors. Depart around 16.00. Kw120,000.

To Sesheke Departures at 06.30; Kw90,000

A few **international buses** also leave from here, travelling to Johannesburg, Harare, Lilongwe and Blantyre in Malawi, and Dar es Salaam.

Postbuses The post office has recently expanded its scheduled passenger service, on which vehicles stop only at post offices. These are generally quicker (they run to a timetable) and less crowded than the normal buses, and some are brand-new vehicles. Seats must be booked in advance at the 'postbus' counter in the main post office on Cairo Road, ideally two to three days before departure. Buses leave from the area just behind the post office.

Services currently run on the following routes, with fares quoted here being those for the full journey:

Lusaka to Chipata Lusaka – Katete – Sinda – Petauke – Nyimba – Luangwa – Chipata. Depart Tuesday and Saturday at 07.00, arriving in Chipata at 14.00. Kw75,000 one way.

Lusaka to Ndola Lusaka – Kabwe – Kapiri Mposhi – Ndola. Depart Monday to Saturday at 07.30 and 13.00; arrive in Ndola 11.00 and 17.00 respectively. Kw40,000 one way.

Lusaka to Kasama Lusaka – Kabwe – Kapiri Mposhi – Mkushi – Serenje – Mpika – Kasama. Depart Monday, Wednesday and Friday at 06.30, arriving at Kasama at 17.00. Kw85,000 one way.

Fares are reduced proportionately if you alight at a town en route. The buses return to Lusaka on the day following their outward journey. Tickets can be booked at local post offices where they stop, but note that postbuses cannot be hailed from the roadside unless pre-booked.

BY TRAIN Trains connect Lusaka with Livingstone, and with Kitwe in the Copperbelt, but for most travellers they are far too slow and totally impractical.
Trains to Livingstone leave Lusaka at 05.00 on Tuesday, Thursday and Saturday, arriving in Livingstone the next day at 20.00. The return train leaves Livingstone at 22.00, arriving back in Lusaka at 16.30, so is slightly quicker. In the other direction,

trains to Kitwe leave Lusaka at 18.02 on Tuesday, Thursday and Saturday, reaching Kitwe the next day at 14.00. Fares are Kw16,500 to Livingstone and K13,000 to Kitwe, so at least it's cheap.

The regular, efficient TAZARA trains to Tanzania are different. They leave from Kapiri Mposhi, not Lusaka, so see pages 381–2 for details. Although tickets can be purchased at the station in Kapiri Mposhi, they are also available with rather less hassle at Tazara House in Lusaka (⊕ *08.30–12.30 Mon–Fri, and 13.00–15.30 Mon, Wed, Thu*). To get there, take Independence Avenue from the south end of Kafue Road, cross the bridge over the railway line, and you'll see it on your left. The current timetable is usually displayed on a noticeboard outside, to the left of the door.

DRIVING FROM LIVINGSTONE For details of getting to Lusaka by road from Livingstone, see page 205.

ORIENTATION

Lusaka is very spread out, so get hold of a good map when you first arrive (see *Maps*, below). Its focus is the axis of Cairo Road, which runs roughly north–south. This is about six lanes of traffic wide, 4km long, and has a useful pedestrian island which runs like a spine down its centre. Parallel to Cairo Road, to the west, is Chachacha Road – a terminus for numerous local minibuses and home to a lively market, variously known as Central Market, City Market or Town Centre Market. Cairo Road is the city's commercial centre and the location for most large shops, so it bustles with people during the day.

Completely separate, about 2km to the east, is the much larger, more diffuse 'Government Area'. It is linked to Cairo Road by Independence Avenue, and centres on the areas of Cathedral Hill and Ridgeway. Here you will find the big international-standard hotels, government departments and embassies set in a lot more space. It has a different atmosphere from the bustle of Cairo Road: the quiet and official air that you often find in diplomatic or administrative corners of capitals around the world.

MAPS Detailed maps covering the whole of Zambia can be bought cheaply from the main government map office at the Ministry of Lands (*basement of Mulungushi Hse, by the corner of Independence Av and Nationalist Rd;* ⊕ *08.30–12.00 & 14.00–16.30 Mon–Fri*). Prices are very good, at around Kw20,000–30,000 per map. Aside from the normal 'Ordnance Survey'-type maps, special tourist maps are available on request. To see what's in stock, browse through the maps in the entrance area before choosing. The detailed street map of Lusaka held by the office is dated 1986, so has now been superseded by commercial mapping, although as it comes complete with an alphabetical street index it could still be useful. For trips venturing beyond Lusaka, however, and particularly off the main roads, you'll simply have to come here and buy up a selection of the 1:250,000 series, or for serious expeditions, the more detailed 1:50,000 sheets. They're generally very good, though their information is inevitably dated.

A limited selection of Zambia's most commonly used maps can be found at one of the city's bookshops (see page 148), which – more importantly – also sell the recommended street atlas of Lusaka and Livingstone published by Streetwise.

GETTING AROUND

Lusaka is very spread out, so if you don't have your own vehicle you'll probably want to use taxis, and/or the small minibuses that ply between the outer

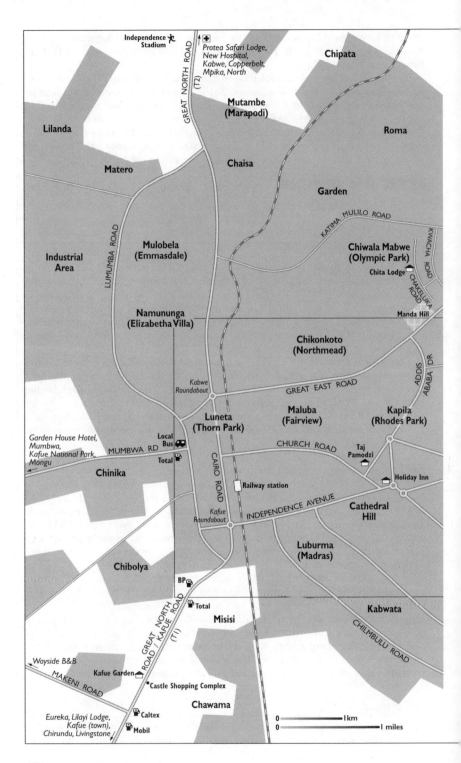

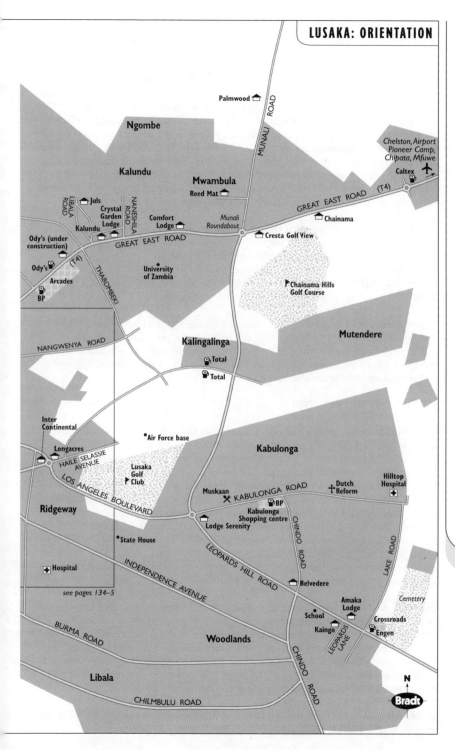

suburbs/townships and the centre. If you are careful, then these are very useful and quite safe. The other possibility is to note that car-hire firms usually supply their cars with a driver – who can act as a convenient guide for a short business trip.

BY TAXI Lusaka's taxis have traditionally been small, decrepit Datsun 120Y or 1200 models, held together by remarkable roadside mechanics and lots of improvisation; today, however, these are outnumbered by rather less run-down Toyota Corollas. The licensed ones are light blue and white in colour, and will have a large number painted on their side, but even these will have no fare meter. When taking a taxi, you should agree a rate for the journey before you get into the vehicle. If you know roughly what it should cost, then most drivers recognise this and don't try to overcharge. As a last resort when bargaining, all licensed taxis should have a rate-sheet, giving the 'standard' prices for waiting time and various common journeys – though drivers will not admit to having one if the bargaining is going their way. Typical fares are:

Kw15,000	between Ridgeway (international hotels) and Manda Hill/Arcades
Kw20,000	between Ridgeway and Cairo Road
Kw80,000	between the airport and town
Kw30,000–40,000	between the centre of town and the inner suburbs
Kw20,000	per hour of additional waiting time

If you need a vehicle all day, then consider hiring a taxi with its driver. Start by making a clear deal to pay by the hour or the kilometre, and record the time or the mileage reading. Around Kw20,000 per hour, or Kw2,000 per kilometre, is fair, though a tough negotiator would pay less. Drivers inevitably change, but there's one consistent taxi service that can be booked by phone:

Dial a Cab m 096 222222, 097 773937

BY MINIBUS These are the packed transport that the city's poorer commuters use to travel between the outer, satellite suburbs and the centre of town. The blue-and-white vehicles dominate the local traffic scene, fanning out from their base at City Market, to the west of Cairo Road. The buses are all privately owned, and cover many different routes, so competition between them is fierce. Minibuses are an especially good way to reach the farther-flung suburbs, or to get a lift along one of the main routes out to a good hitching spot. Fares are relatively low, reflecting the cramped seating and general lack of timetable – for the most part, buses leave only when they are full. You can expect to pay around Kw1,800 for a journey between Cairo Road and the international hotels, or Kw2,000 to Manda Hill shopping centre. Minibuses usually have regular stops, but if you're lucky they can sometimes just be flagged down if they're not full.

CAR HIRE See *Vehicle hire* in *Chapter 4*, pages 70–3, for advice and a guide to typical rates. Lusaka's car-hire companies cater more for businesspeople visiting the city than for tourists. Many will insist on foreign drivers using a chauffeur, and will usually only have time-and-mileage rates rather than the 'unlimited-mileage' rates normally expected by those hiring cars for fly-drive trips. (Which makes sense as you'd have to be insane to hire a 2WD for a fly-drive trip around Zambia.) The larger companies, including two offering 4x4 hire, are:

🚗 **Avis** Holiday Inn, Lusaka; ➚ 021 1251652; 24hr emergency m 097 434495; f 021 1252201; e avis@zamnet.zm; www.avisworld.com. Min age 23. Rentals include free mobile phone.

🚗 **Julo Car Hire** 5507 Libala Rd, Kalundu; 📞 021 1292979, 1293972; **f** 021 1291246; **e** julscar@zamnet.zm; www.julscar.com. Minibuses & 4x4s only, either self-drive or chauffeur-driven.

🚗 **Livingstone 4x4** 📞 021 1254096; **e** info@4x4hireafrica.com; www.4x4hireafrica.com. Self-drive & chauffeur-driven vehicles. See page 71.

🚗 **New Ace Car Hire** Zimco Hse, Ground Floor, Cairo Rd; 📞 021 232654; **m** 097 704368

🚗 **Voyagers/Imperial/Europcar** 6941 Suez Rd; 📞 021 1253064; airport 📞 021 1271221–3; **f** 021 1271239; **e** carrental@voyagers.com.zm; www.voyagerszambia.com. Reliable agents for both Imperial and Europcar, with both 2WD and 4x4 vehicles, with or without a driver. For 4x4 hire, see page 71.

🚗 **Zédash** 📞 021 1271116; **m** 097 857891; **e** zedash@coppernet.zm

🚗 **Zungulila** Zambia PO Box 31475, TAZ Hse Annex, cnr Chiparamba and Chachacha roads; 📞 021 227730, 223234, 220251; **f** 227729

DRIVING YOURSELF Traffic in and around Lusaka can be chaotic at the beginning and end of a working day, and accidents are not infrequent. Speed limits on the roads around the city are strictly enforced, with an on-the-spot fine of Kw67,500 for infringements. The limit of 65km/h on the Great East Road towards the airport is something of a black spot in this respect; be warned. For the most part, drivers in the city centre would be hard pushed to get anywhere near the urban limit of 50km/h.

Parking on the streets is not a good idea unless you leave someone trustworthy in charge of the vehicle. Far more sensible is to use one of the guarded private car parks. In the vicinity of Cairo Road, this means either the large free area at Central Park, or in front of Shoprite, where there's a fee of Kw1,000 an hour. Most hotels and guesthouses have secure parking, as do shopping complexes and many restaurants.

It is not advisable to drive at night in or around the city. Aside from the risk of car-jackings, you're likely to encounter vehicles without lights (especially around the time of the full moon), and even people sleeping on the warm tarmac, a hazard that's said to be particularly common on the Great North Road.

There are numerous fuel stations throughout the city. However, even here unleaded petrol is not always easy to come by; if there are shortages, and your vehicle runs on unleaded, your best bets are at the BP station on the left as you're coming in from Livingstone, or at Longacres.

🏠 WHERE TO STAY

There is an increasing level of choice between Lusaka's international-standard hotels, with improving levels of service and design, although they can often be soulless. You might ask yourself if you need to be near the centre, or can afford to stay beyond the suburbs, at somewhere like Lilayi, Pioneer, Protea Safari Lodge, or even Lechwe Lodge (see page 226). These are more pleasant than being in town, but transport (with the exception of Pioneer, which is close to the airport) can be a costly issue.

Those on a budget should choose their lodgings with care. Price is often a poor guide and the quality of the budget hotels varies considerably. Ask around if you can, as new places are opening all the time. If your budget is very tight then head for a backpackers' dorm or a campsite. Lusaka's cheap hostels are often seedy.

A word of warning: if you plan to make international phone calls from any hotel, find out their charges first, or – better – buy a local phonecard or a SIM card for your mobile phone. Hotel phone bills can run into hundreds of dollars for just a few minutes.

INTERNATIONAL HOTELS If you're passing through Lusaka, perhaps between flights, or are here for a few days' business, then look no further. Three of these hotels have been established in Lusaka's central area for many years; the fourth –

the Cresta Golfview – is east of town towards the airport. None of them deserves prizes for atmosphere or originality, but all organise reliable airport transfers, and have pleasant comfortable rooms and communications that work efficiently. You can rely on them; that's what you need.

🏠 **Taj Pamodzi Hotel** (193 rooms) Addis Ababa Dr; ☏ 021 1254455; f 021 1224005/25; e pamodzi@zamnet.zm; www.tajhotels.com. Opposite the Holiday Inn, on the cnr of Church Rd, the 5-star Pamodzi is a member of the Indian-owned Taj group of hotels, & the level of service is impressive. Its rooms, slightly less corporate than most, have AC, bath/shower, DSTV, fridge/minibar, safe & phone. Each has a proper balcony, with those on the higher of the Pamodzi's 9 floors affording some fine views.

There's a comfortable lobby downstairs, with soft piano music played in the comfortable lounge, the open-plan Marula bar with discreet sports TV, a car-hire centre, & a couple of classy shops, though the business centre struggles with outdated hardware. Adjacent to the hotel is its own fitness centre with 2 squash courts, plus sauna, steam room, hair salon & spa; the gym is one of the best in town, popular with many of Lusaka's more affluent residents. Outside, lawns surround a good-size swimming pool under jacaranda trees. This is overlooked by an informal restaurant with a large terrace area, & the more formal Steak & Grills restaurant, open for dinner only with live music every night. A good, varied buffet b/fast is part of the deal, while dinner menus include some very good Indian dishes. I've often stayed here, & always found the staff to be courteous & helpful. Airport transfer US$12 pp. $$$$$

🏠 **Hotel InterContinental** (200 rooms, 21 suites) Haile Selassie Av; ☏ 021 1250000, 1250149, 1250661; f 021 1251880; e reservations@ interconti.com.zm; www.ihg.com. This is the second of Lusaka's 5-star hotels. When last visited, staff seemed to have been to charm school, and standards of service have improved. A display of masks in the lobby is complemented by other examples of African art.

Rooms, which were renovated in 2007, are reasonably big, with enough space to include both a couch & a desk; you can expect an en-suite bath/shower, DSTV, fridge & phone. For meals there's the Savannah Grill & Restaurant, which has both a buffet & a daily à-la-carte menu served either indoors or on a pleasant covered terrace over the pool. More upmarket is the Olive Grove, a Mediterranean-style venue open Mon–Sat for dinner only. There's also a rather soulless bar, typical of those in large hotels.

The InterCon's lobby is a good meeting place, with huge windows looking out to the front & a café whose piano is sadly only for show. There is also an expensive jewellery shop, & some smart gift shops. The more active can take advantage of the hotel's gym (and attendant health facilities), attractive oval swimming pool & floodlit tennis courts. There's also a 24hr business centre. $$$$$

🏠 **Holiday Inn** (155 rooms) Cnr Independence Av & Church Rd; ☏ 021 1251666; f 021 1253529; e reservations@holidayinn.co.zm; www.holidayinn.co.zm. The rather less upmarket Holiday Inn occupies the site of the old Ridgeway Hotel. Its rooms are similar to those of the InterCon, & show little more imagination, though they were being refurbished in 2007. Each is functional & clean with shower & bath, AC, phone, DSTV, razor plug, & tea/coffee-making facilities. Beds are queen-size double or twin.

On the ground floor there's the main Musuku restaurant, serving buffet (Kw80,000) or à-la-carte meals from b/fast through to dinner. Alongside is McGinty's Irish Pub (🕙 10.00–23.00), which serves salads & more substantial pub grub against a backdrop of TV screens featuring an unrelenting diet of news & sport – a cool, dark retreat from the heat. However, instead of gazing into your pint here, try stepping outside into the central courtyard & studying the colony of masked weavers nesting in a tree over the ornamental pond, where a few small crocs bask on the sheltered rocks.

In front of either side of the entrance to the Holiday Inn you'll find the office for Avis & a very useful Barclays ATM in the bank's on-site lobby. There's also a shop: books, curios, carvings & gemstones. Airport transfer U$12 pp. $$$$$

🏠 **Cresta Golfview** (60 rooms) 10247 Great East Rd; ☏ 021 1290770, 1291490, 1291822, 1291858, 1291896, 1290718; f 021 1292049; e reservations@cresta.co.zm; www.cresta-hospitality.com. Well placed some 16km from the airport, & 13km from the centre of Lusaka, Cresta's first foray into Zambia was opened in 2005 on the south of the road, adjacent to Chainama Hills Golf Club. Although technically a 3-star establishment, the hotel's rates put it in the top bracket.

It's an earthy terracotta & cream complex that

blends nicely into the surroundings. En-suite dbl & twin rooms, typical of business hotels the world over, share the neutral approach, with AC, minibar, tea-/coffee-making facilities & phone. Half have views over an attractive pool & the golf course, so do ask for one of these: rates are the same for all. If the entrance is rather soulless, this doesn't extend to the bar & traditional restaurant which overlook the pool, enclosing a small courtyard with umbrella shade. There's also a business centre. The hotel is affiliated to the golf club, where residents can play free of charge except for club rental (Kw50,000–60,000) and caddy fees (Kw20,000). 16 self-catering chalets were under construction in 2007. Airport transfer US$10 pp one way. $$$$

MID-RANGE HOTELS

⌂ **Ody's** Great East Rd. The long-promised new hotel & casino opposite The Arcades is set to open in 2008.

⌂ **Protea Hotel** (75 rooms) Cnr Cairo & Katondo rds; ✆ 021 1238360; f 021 1238317; e phcairord@proteahotels.co.zm; www.proteahotels.com/cairoroad. While it won't win any prizes for design, the new 7-storey Protea on Cairo Rd, opposite the Lusaka Hotel, has certainly raised the standard for business hotels in the area. Sgl, dbl or twin rooms are clean, smart & functional, with all the accoutrements of a decent business hotel, inc AC, safe & wireless internet access, & some good views of the city from the top floors. The restaurant is in the same mould – light and airy – & the internet centre (open 08.00–22.00) has some of the best rates in town at Kw60/minute. Crucially, the hotel has its own secure multi-storey car park. (*Lunch/dinner* $$$$$) $$$.

⌂ **Chrismar Hotel** (47 rooms) Los Angeles Bd; ✆ 021 1253036, 1253605; f 021 1252569; e chrismar@zamnet.zm; www.chrismar.co.zm. In extensive grounds next to the Lusaka Club, with secure parking, the Chrismar was opened in 1999. Rather small dbl rooms are all carpeted, with blue walls & matching bedcovers, tea-/coffee-making facilities & an en-suite bath/shower. Some overlook the courtyard, others the swimming pool. 12 newer suites are more spacious, with leopard-print covers & colourful African wall-hangings; these have a bath & shower, satellite TV, phone & AC. It's simple, light & modern, & certainly a cut above most of Lusaka's cheaper hotels, though it can be noisy at weekends.

Outside a rather over-elaborate stone bridge leads across a fishpool with fountain, half hidden by an overgrown bamboo. Umbrella-shaded tables surround the large swimming pool with its own bar, next to the popular Cattleman's Grill (see page 143), a favourite for meat-eaters & a venue for live bands on Fri & Sat nights. Indoors, the warm yellows of the brasserie bring a real sense of location. Fitness fanatics can use the gym, & in the front is a children's play area. The business centre upstairs opens Mon–Fri 08.00–17.00, & w/ends 08.00–12.00. $$$$

⌂ **Fairview Hotel** (31 rooms) Church Rd; ✆ 021 1222604/5, 1239637; f 021 1239741; e fairview@zamnet.zm, fairview@zamtel.zm; www.fairview.co.zm. Significantly cheaper than the Chrismar, and more central, the Fairview is on the left past the fire station if you're coming from Cairo Rd, opposite the Rachel Lumpa Memorial Health Centre. It is a hotel training centre, and as such you can expect very attentive service from its young personnel. En-suite rooms are old-fashioned but spotlessly clean, with heavy wooden bedsteads & ornate mirrors; satellite TV & tea-/coffee-making facilities introduce a more modern touch. The public rooms include a terrace bar overlooking Church Rd & a restaurant that serves traditional Zambian food at lunchtime Mon–Fri for up to Kw50,000, with a Western à-la-carte menu in the evenings. Outside is a beer garden, & there's also a small business centre with internet, open w/days only. $$

GUESTHOUSES AND BUDGET HOTELS Even 'budget' hotels aren't that cheap in Lusaka, but if you have upwards of Kw160,000 (US$40) per night to spend on a double room, then there is a choice of smaller hotels. However, many are used extensively for conferences and few shine. Most visitors prefer the city's smaller guesthouses, which are often much friendlier and start at the same kind of price, though the range is considerable. The last few years have seen a real boom in the numbers, and the quality, of such guesthouses throughout Zambia, but especially in Lusaka. Some are simply restaurants that offer a few rooms for guests as a legal convenience, others are dedicated entirely to their guests, with prices to match. A few are old favourites, but beware of the speed with which these open up and then close down again. The selection below is listed alphabetically by area.

Centre and Cairo Road

⌂ **Endesha Guest House** (6 rooms) Parirenyatwa Rd; ☎ 021 1225780–1; f 021 1225781. Very close to the Cairo Rd area, but in a quiet location, Endesha (the name means 'Hurry up'!) opened early in 1999 & is clearly marked. Leave town on Church Rd, take a left onto Makishi Rd, just after the fire station, then turn first right; Endesha is on your right. It is owned by Mohamed Ali Hanslot, whose brother owns a similar guesthouse in Ndola. All its rooms have the luxury of a dbl & a sgl bed, though their décor is perhaps a little stark, with just the odd picture. Each room has a TV, small fridge & fan. More expensive rooms have en-suite showers/toilets, while standard rooms have private facilities just across the corridor. All are clean if quite dark.

Endesha's communal areas are less stark than the rooms, & outside is a thatched bar, used by residents & guests only, within sight of the private parking area & protected by high walls & a security gate. There's a Friday *braai*, with other meals available on request, or guests may use the kitchens to cook for themselves. $$ inc cont b/fast.

⌂ **Longacres Lodge** (58 rooms) Los Angeles Bd; ☎ 021 1254847; f 021 1251761. This government-run establishment is often used for conferences, & is unique for its labyrinth of long corridors, some of which are open to one side. It's located 100m north of the junction with Haile Selassie Av, or about 600m east of the InterContinental Hotel. Carpeted rooms are reasonably clean & have basic twin beds, or a dbl, with perhaps a dressing table or wardrobe; suites have a sitting area as well, with the option of linking rooms for families. Some have fridges; some have DSTV. Each also has a simple en-suite tiled bathroom with a toilet, bath & basin. There's secure parking & an on-site restaurant. $$ inc cont b/fast.

⌂ **Lui Holiday Homes** 1134 Church Rd; ☎ 021 1223809; e luiguesthouse@zamtel.zm. This basic place just round the corner from Endesha is pretty cheap, so if money is very tight, it could be an option. Rooms are en suite, though pretty basic, & it's all a bit rough round the edges. $ inc cont b/fast.

⌂ **Lusaka Hotel** (77 rooms) Cairo Rd; ☎ 021 1229049–52; f 021 1225726; e lushotel@zamnet.zm; www.lusakahotel.com. Some decades ago the Lusaka Hotel was the only hotel in Lusaka, right at the centre of town. Now competition is fierce, not least from the new Protea Hotel opposite. The area around the hotel's entrance tends to be busy with people loitering suspiciously &, though there's a security guard on the entrance, you should be careful with both your belongings & your vehicle if you stay here.

Despite a recent change of ownership, the hotel still feels old & cramped, though it's perfectly clean. Budget rooms have tea/coffee makers, M-Net TV, a phone, fan, mosquito nets, fridge & en-suite toilet/shower. Standard rooms are a little larger with bath & shower, & AC instead of fan. Décor is simple, the sombre carpet tiles giving a rather drab appearance. On the plus side, the restaurant spills outside alongside a new swimming pool which is very much a first for this part of Lusaka, & bodes well. $$–$$$

⌂ **Marble Inn** (10 rooms) Makanta Cl; ☎ 021 1230617; e marbleinn@gmail.com. Next to Kuomboka Backpackers (see page 139) this new place was opened at the end of 2006. Its dbl rooms are tiled & light, with pine furniture, mosquito nets, fans & en-suite shower. It's early days, but when visited it was clean, pleasant & good value. $$, b/fast extra.

⌂ **Ndeke Hotel** (47 rooms) Chisidza Cres; ☎ 021 1251734; f 021 1253881; e gardengroup@zamtel.zm; www.gardengroupzambia.com. Near the roundabout of Haile Selassie Av & Los Angeles Bd, the Ndeke is an old hotel that's had a welcome facelift. The spacious, light entrance with original artwork & wooden sculptures is a far cry from its rather institutional past. The newly kitted-out rooms, in a sgl block, have cane furniture offset by cream-painted brickwork, although some of the older-style rooms remain too. All except 4 sgl rooms have TV & en-suite toilet & bath; the sgls have en-suite shower, but share a toilet. At the front is a slightly sunken dining area with a lounge above, & outside is a courtyard. (*Lunch & dinner* $$$–$$$$) $$

⌂ **Nena's Guest House** (4 rooms) 126 Masansa Cl, Rhodes Pk; ☎/f 021 1239541; m 097 773213; e nenaguesthouse@zamnet.zm; www.nenaguesthouse.co.zm. Yugoslavian-born Nena opened her eponymous guesthouse & restaurant in 2002. Its clean rooms with en-suite showers & dbl or twin beds have been upgraded with DSTV & AC, while outside a small area has been set aside for camping, with a couple of pre-erected tents. Guinea fowl & hens forage in the garden around a large pool with its own terrace, & a nearby bar; there's also secure parking. The restaurant is open daily for meals, including Yugoslav specialities cooked by Nena; on Fri evening & for Sun lunch there's a spit roast. Main courses average around Kw50,000. Airport transfer Kw100,000 per trip. $$. *Camping Kw25,000 pp, with b/fast on request.*

⌂ **Oriental Garden Guesthouse** (3 rooms) United Nations Av (opposite Netherlands Embassy); ☎ 021 1252163; m 096 6457275. This is primarily an oriental restaurant (see page 143), but also has a few simple rooms for guests, one of which is en-suite. Outside is a small pool & bar, and there's secure parking. $$$

⌂ **Pearl Haven Inn** (8 rooms) Twikatane Rd, off Addis Ababa Dr, Rhodes Pk; ☎ 021 1252455; f 021 1251126; e pearl@zamnet.zm. Run by Malcolm Jhala, Pearl Haven is in a commercial residential area, 5 mins' walk from Manda Hill, though with Johnny's close by it could be quite noisy at night. To get there from the Great East Rd, turn right before Manda Hill then take the first right. Rooms are extraordinarily ornate, with floral curtains & heavy carved furniture — and brown pile carpets. Each has an en-suite bath & shower, AC, satellite TV, fridge, minibar, tea & coffee-making facilities & direct-dial phones. The guesthouse is surrounded by its own gardens where a thatched bar on stilts looks down on a good-size swimming pool, & there's an attractive restaurant, complete with chandeliers, for residents (mains $$$$). $$$ inc cont b/fast.

East towards the airport

⌂ **Chainama Hotel** (31 rooms) Great East Rd; ☎ 021 1290073; f 021 1223309; e chahotel@zamnet.zm. On the south side of the Great East Rd, about 7km from the city centre, the basic but friendly Chainama has a motel feel. Rooms, each with table & chairs, fan, & DSTV, are quite spacious. In most, a picture window takes up one wall, & the en-suite facilities have baths rather than showers. (*Evening meal* $$–$$$) $$ inc cont b/fast.

⌂ **Chita Lodge** (10 rooms) 25 Chakeluka Rd; ☎ 021 1293779; f 021 1290814; e chitalodge@microlink.zm; www.chita.co.zm. The stylish and professionally run Chita Lodge was opened in 2001. To find it, turn left immediately after Manda Hill onto Kwacha Rd, take the 2nd left, follow this to the end, turn right & it's on the left. Indoors, a wildlife theme is reflected in the décor & touches of original artwork. Spotless dbl & twin rooms are spacious, with smart tiled floors scattered with warm rugs, & comfy chairs; each has an en-suite shower or bath, phone, AC/heating, fridge, hot drinks facilities, DSTV, & a DVD player (there's a DVD library for guests to use). A large upstairs veranda offers a cool spot to relax away from the heat of the day.

Friendly, modern & very well looked after, the lodge boasts secure parking, a crystal-clear swimming pool with soft grassy surround & a poolside bar. There's a small dining area & bar with tables on a shaded terrace by the pool. The restaurant is open all day for both light lunches & à-la-carte dinner — when we visited, the menu ranged from Indian dishes through traditional Zambian fare such as oxtail & fried bream to a range of grills (mains Kw32,000–40,000). This is without doubt one of Lusaka's best places to stay. $$$

⌂ **Comfort Lodge** (10 rooms) Great East Rd, Jesmondine; ☎ 021 1290314; f 021 1291631; e info@comfortlodgezambia.com, comfortinn@zamtel.zm; www.comfortlodgezambia.com. Just east of the university, on the north side of the road, this light, airy lodge is marked by a bright yellow signboard. From the comfy chairs in the lounge/reception to the dining area overlooking the pool with a thatched bar, it's a pleasant & relaxed place, if suffering a little from traffic noise. Rooms have TV, AC, en-suite bath or shower, fridge & kettle; more interestingly, wrought-iron furniture is adorned with leopard-print fabrics. There's an à-la-carte menu for lunch & dinner (mains Kw30,000–38,000). $$

⌂ **Crystal Garden Lodge** (10 rooms) 11789 Kabompo Cl, Kalundu; ☎ 021 1290044. Near the university, Crystal Garden has taken over where Arabian Nights left off — with the addition of a further 3 rooms. Find it by taking the Great East Rd from Addis Ababa Dr & turn north opposite the university on Naneshila Rd; take the first left, & it's on the left. En-suite rooms are large & carpeted, with dark-wood furnishings inc a dbl bed, plus phone, TV & fridge. Outside, there's a good-size pool in a walled garden, & safe parking. The restaurant is pleasant, geared to residents but open to outsiders as well: the menu is primarily Indian, but there are grills too ($$$–$$$$). $$

⌂ **Juls Guesthouse** (13 rooms, 2 cottages) 5508 Lusiwasi Rd, Kalundu; ☎ 021 1292979/1293972; f 021 1291246; e julscar@zamnet.zm; www.julscar.com. Juls's accommodation in this quiet residential area now boasts 2 self-catering cottages as well as its en-suite rooms, although most are let out to long-stay visitors, such as NGO staff. To find it, head along the Great East Rd, and turn left after the Arcades, then left again. Simple, modern décor, with twin beds & stone floors, makes a pleasant change from that of most of Lusaka's guesthouses;

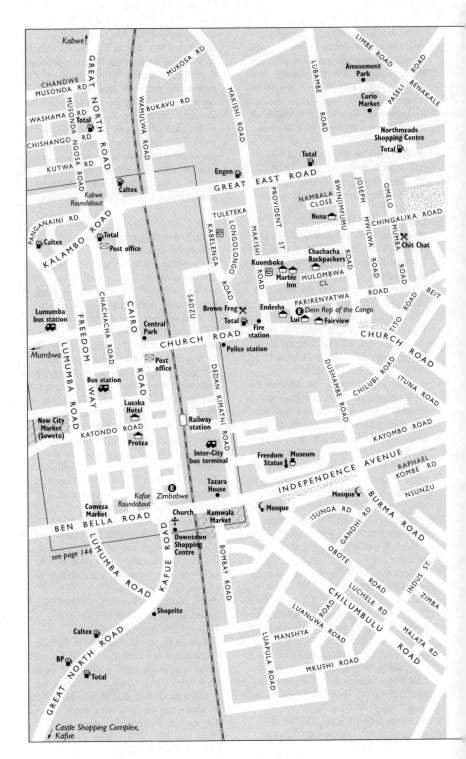

Kabwe

CHANDWE
MUSONDA RD

WASHAMA

CHISHANGO

KUTWA RD

MUKOSA RD

GREAT NORTH ROAD

MUSONDA RD

WAMULWA ROAD

BUKAVU RD

MAKISHI ROAD

NGOSA ROAD

Total

Caltex

Kabwe
Roundabout

PANGANAINI RD

Caltex

KALAMBO ROAD

Total
Post office

CHACHACHA ROAD

CAIRO ROAD

Lumumba
bus station

FREEDOM WAY

Mumbwa

LUMUMBA ROAD

Bus station

Lusaka
Hotel

New City
Market
(Soweto)

KATONDO ROAD

Protea

Central
Park

Post office

SADZU

KABELENGA ROAD

TULETEKA

Engen

LONGOLONGO ROAD

MAKISHI ROAD

Brown Frog
Total

CHURCH ROAD

DEDAN KIMATHI ROAD

Railway
station

Inter-City
bus terminal

Tazara
House

Kafue
Roundabout

Zimbabwe

Comesa
Market

BEN BELLA ROAD

see page 144

LUMUMBA ROAD

KAFUE ROAD

Church
Downtown
Shopping
Centre

Kamwala
Market

BOMBAY ROAD

GREAT EAST ROAD

PROVIDENT ST

Total

NAMBALA
CLOSE

Nena

Kuomboka

Marble
Inn

Endesha

Fire
station

Police station

BWINJIMFUMU

JOSEPH MWILWA ROAD

Chachacha
Backpackers

MULOMBWA
CL

PARIRENYATWA

Dem Rep of the Congo

Lui
Fairview

DUSHAMBE ROAD

Freedom
Statue

Museum

INDEPENDENCE AVENUE

Mosque

Mosque

Shoprite

Caltex

BP
Total

GREAT NORTH ROAD

Castle Shopping Complex,
Kafue

LIMBE ROAD

PASELI ROAD

BENAKALE

Amusement
Park

Curio
Market

Northmeads
Shopping Centre

Total

LUBAMBE ROAD

OMELO

CHINGALIKA ROAD

MUMBA ROAD

Chit Chat

ROAD

BEIT

TITO ROAD

CHURCH ROAD

CHILUBI RD

ITUNA ROAD

KAYOMBO ROAD

RAPHAEL
KOMBE RD

NSUNZU

BURMA ROAD

ISUNGA RD

GANDHI RD

OBOTE ROAD

LUCHELE RD

INDUS ST

ZIMBA

CHILUMBULU ROAD

MALATA RD

LUANGWA ROAD

MANSHYA ROAD

LUAPULA ROAD

MKUSHI ROAD

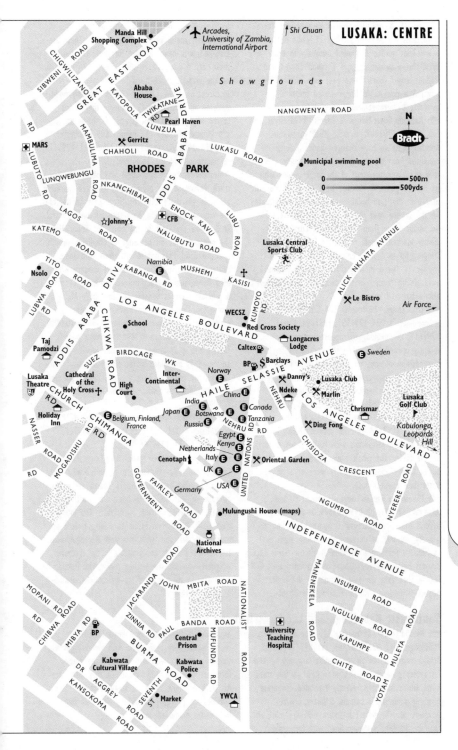

LUSAKA: CENTRE

Manda Hill
Shopping Complex

✈ Arcades,
University of Zambia,
International Airport

↑ Shi Chuan

SIBWENI ZANO ROAD

CHIGWILIZANO ROAD

GREAT EAST ROAD

KATOPOLA

Ababa
House

TWIKATANE RD

LUNZUA

Pearl Haven

✗ Gerritz

CHAHOLI ROAD

MAMBULIMA ROAD

MARS

LUBUTO RD

LUNQWEBUNGU

NKANCHIBAYA

Showgrounds

NANGWENYA ROAD

N

Bradt

LUKASU ROAD

● Municipal swimming pool

0 ━━━━━━ 500m
0 ━━━━━━ 500yds

RHODES   PARK

ADDIS ABABA DRIVE

ENOCK KAVU

☆Johnny's

CFB

LAGOS ROAD

KATEMO ROAD

NALUBUTU ROAD

LUBU ROAD

Lusaka Central
Sports Club

TITO ROAD

Nsolo ●

LUBWA RD

KABANGA RD

Namibia

MUSHEMI

KASISI

✝

ALICK NKHATA AVENUE

Air Force →

DRIVE

ADDIS ABABA

CHIKWA ROAD

LOS ANGELES BOULEVARD

School ●

WECSZ

KUMOYO RD

Red Cross Society

✗ Le Bistro

Taj
Pamodzi

BIRDCAGE

WK

Caltex

Longacres
Lodge

SUEZ

Inter-
Continental

Norway

BP $ Barclays

Sweden

Lusaka
Theatre

Cathedral
of the
Holy Cross ✝

High
Court

CHURCH RD

HAILE   SELASSIE   AVENUE

China

Danny's ✗

Lusaka Club

NEHRU

Ndeke

Marlin

Chrismar

Lusaka
Golf Club

Holiday
Inn

CHIMANGA RD

Belgium, Finland,
France

India

Japan

Botswana

Russia

Canada

Tanzania

NEHRU RD

✗ Ding Fong

LOS ANGELES BOULEVARD

Kabulonga,
Leopards
Hill

NASSER ROAD

MOGADISHU RD

Netherlands

Egypt
Kenya

Italy

CHISIDZA CRESCENT

NGUMBO ROAD

NYERERE ROAD

Cenotaph ⚑

UK

UNITED NATIONS

✗ Oriental Garden

Germany

USA

GOVERNMENT   ROAD

FAIRLEY ROAD

● Mulungushi House (maps)

INDEPENDENCE   AVENUE

National
Archives

NATIONALIST ROAD

JACARANDA

JOHN MBITA ROAD

ZINNIA RD PAUL

BANDA ROAD

MANENEKELA ROAD

NSUMBU ROAD

NGULUBE ROAD

MULEYA ROAD

MOPANI ROAD

CHIBWA RD

MIBYA RD

BP

BURMA ROAD

Central
Prison ●

MUFUNDA RD

University
Teaching
Hospital

KAPUMPE RD

CHITE ROAD

YOTAM ROAD

DR AGGREY ROAD

Kabwata
Cultural Village ●

Kabwata
Police ●

KANSOKOMA ROAD

SEVENTH ST

● Market

YWCA

Lusaka **WHERE TO STAY**

7

all have AC, & 'executive' rooms have phones. There's a spacious lounge with satellite TV, while outside is a well-kept garden & shaded terrace with braai area, plus a swimming pool & sauna. There's also a floodlit tennis court (bring your own racquets & balls) & a pool table. Home-cooked meals are available by arrangement. $$–$$$

🏠 **Kalundu Guest House** (6 rooms) 5493 Great East Rd; ☎ 021 1293009; e meri_db@yahoo.com. Another place to have changed hands, Kalundu has benefited from the ownership of Croatian-born Meri, who is making the most of the large garden with its mature guava & avocado trees (great if you visit in Feb or Mar!) to build an outside bar. It's situated on the service road to the north of the Great East Rd, about 12km from the centre of Lusaka, & is clearly marked. Simple rooms, inc family rooms sleeping up to 6, have en-suite bath or bath & shower, TV, fan & mosi net. Meals ($$$$) are available on request in the small dining area; there's also a bar and lounge. $$

🏠 **Mika Lodge** (29 rooms) 106 Central St, Jesmondine; ☎ 021 1291557, 1291494; f 021 1291617; e mikalodge@coppernet.zo.zm The recently opened Mika is on the cnr of 1st St. The juxtaposition of cool, tiled entrance with heavy armchairs & arrangements of fresh flowers suggests a modern approach tempered with tradition – a reflection of the lodge as a whole. Each cream-painted room, with tiled floor & dbl bed, has a good desk, AC, TV & en-suite shower. There's a bright, modern restaurant with funky chairs & roses on the tables. The whole atmosphere is one of businesslike efficiency: definitely more of a small hotel than a guesthouse. $$

🏠 **Mwambula Garden Lodge** (9 rooms) Mwambula Rd; m 097 897020, 095 767979. If you can get beyond the unprepossessing entrance, you'll find a friendly welcome at this new guesthouse, right next to Hibiscus restaurant. Turn north off the Great East Rd just before the roundabout at Chainama Hills Golf Course, then take the first left; it's on the right. Attractive gardens with an enormous stand of

bamboo, & a pool, form the focus of the lodge, whose best rooms overlook the garden. These are L-shaped, with heavy wooden furniture, TVs, fans & mosi nets, & adequate en-suite showers. Wicker chairs on the veranda make for a peaceful place to relax – except on Fri & Sat nights when it's BBQ night, open to all comers. That's assuming they're not scared off by the garden gnomes at the front. $$

🏠 **Palmwood Lodge** (32 rooms) 609 Chudleigh; ☎ 021 1290828; m 097 521123; f 021 1295411; e palmwoodlodge@yahoo.com; www.palmwoodlodge.com. Some way off the beaten track, Palmwood has been greatly enlarged in recent years. To get there, take the Great East Rd out of the city for about 7km, then turn left onto Central St & follow the signs to the north for about 3km; the guesthouse is on the edge of Chudleigh suburb, near farmland. Pleasant rooms, albeit with some rather tired en-suite bathrooms, are modern with tiled floors, simple, metal-framed furniture, TV, phone & wireless internet connectivity. Dbls have AC, sgls just a fan. Outside, set on lawns with flower gardens, are 2 restaurants (dinner from Kw30,000), a large terraced bar area & a swimming pool. There's also a TV lounge, & car hire can be organised. As an added attraction, gemstones are for sale on the premises; perhaps the hotel's relatively rapid expansion is linked with the mining industry. $$$

🏠 **Reed Mat Lodge** (19 rooms, 3 chalets) 9718 5th St, Munali; ☎ 021 1293426; m 097 7854768, 9180339; f 021 1295196; e info@ reedmatlodge.com; www.reedmatlodge.com. This Zambian-run lodge with a strong cultural ethic is about 15 mins from the airport. Rooms are either en suite or with shared facilities, set in attractive gardens & decorated with local crafts. Two lounges have DSTV, & email access is on hand. Children are particularly welcome, with cots and play equipment. Home-cooked meals are available in the restaurant, or guests can use the kitchen themselves. Outside is a pool – in the shape of the African continent! – & secure parking.

Southeast: Kabulonga and Leopards Hill

🏠 **Amaka Lodge** (31 rooms) 375 Leopards Hill La, Kabulonga; ☎/f 021 1262868; m 097 78766338. Amaka means 'power' in the Bemba language – and it's rather gone to the designer's head in this small hotel, which has been recently expanded. Elaborate furnishings, deep-pile carpets, & heavy, ornate furniture are the hotel's hallmark, nowhere more so than in the formal lounge lined with large, plush

armchairs & dominated by a huge TV. En-suite rooms (some with bath, some with shower) get a similar treatment, with size dictating the grade (ordinary dbls are rather cramped); they also have AC, DSTV & phone. There's a small restaurant, and outside is a plunge pool, incongruously surrounded by life-size model animals. $$

Belvedere Lodge (21 rooms) Leopards Hill Rd; \/f 01 263079. On the east side of the city, close to Kabulonga shopping centre, Belvedere stands at the cnr of Chindo Rd. Rooms are small & uninspiring, but reasonably modern & clean. Each has a fan, mosquito nets, fridge, TV & an en-suite toilet & bath or shower. $$ inc cont b/fast.

Kaingo Executive Guest House (12 rooms) 35D Leopards La, Kabulonga; 021 1263231; e kaingo@zamtel.zm. To reach Kaingo, take Leopards Hill Rd out of town from the roundabout on Los Angeles Bd. After St Mary's, but before the Spar complex, take a right turn onto Leopards Hill La. A little way down here there's an alley on the right, & Kaingo is the first gate on the right; the sign is very small.

This well-kept guesthouse, deep in the suburbs, is run by Jesmine & David Thompson, who clearly aim mainly for business visitors & NGO personnel sent to Zambia for short postings. A further 6 rooms were added to the original 6 in 2004, & although each one is different, all are en suite with dbl beds, internet access, fridge & TV. The communal areas are relaxed; there's a comfy TV lounge/bar & a self-catering kitchen, although b/fast, lunch & dinner are available. Jesmine is planning to introduce traditional Zambian dishes at lunchtime. Outside is a good swimming pool, surrounded by fountains & with a sunken bar. $$$

Lodge Serenity (9 rooms, cottage) 2 Leopards Hill Rd, Kabulonga; 021 1262182; m 095 195500; f 021 1262239; e serenity@coppernet.zm. Opened in 2001, Serenity is aptly named: a 2-storey lodge with large, clean, carpeted rooms, albeit rather randomly furnished. Rooms also boast DSTV, a kettle for hot drinks, AC, fridge, phone & en-suite bath or shower (or both). A 2-bedroom cottage provides further choice. Guests have the use of a small, neat dining room, & outside are a pool & a tennis court that's seen better days. $$, cottage $$$

South along the Kafue Road

Andrews Motel (110 rooms) Kafue Rd; 021 1272017, 1272026, 1273575; f 021 1272276; e andymotel@zamnet.zm. About 8km south of the Kafue roundabout, Andrews is a sprawling complex, typical of motels everywhere, with a security guard on the gate & parking bays in front of rooms — reassuring for those concerned about the safety of vehicles. Rooms are functional but clean, with fans, TVs, twin beds & bath or shower. The motel is popular with locals — perhaps because its facilities include 2 tennis courts & a spacious pool, with adjacent bar & restaurant serving everything from snacks to steaks. If you stay here, ask for a new or renovated room; the price is the same and they're much nicer. B/fast consists of cereals & fruit. $$

Comfort Zone (10 rooms) Casanova Rd; 021 1272610; f 021 1225617; e czone@coppernet.zm; www.comfortzone.com.zm. Not to be confused with the Comfort Lodge towards the airport, Comfort Zone was opened in 2000, in pleasant gardens with secure parking. It is located 7km south of Lusaka, down a dirt road to the right almost opposite the eye hospital. All rooms have en-suite toilet & shower or shower/bath, plus TV & floor fan. Tables are set around the small pool (open to non-residents) with a pool bar that gets quite busy at weekends, & there's a restaurant serving light meals & grills (up to $$$). $$

Kafue Garden Hotel (23 rooms) Kafue Rd, Makeni; 021 1274987; e gardengroup@zamtel.zm; www.gardengroupzambia.com. Some 2–3km south of town, this is set in its own gardens, opposite the Castle shopping complex. To find it, turn right just after the shopping centre, then dbl back on a rough track & turn immediately left. Bare corridors contrast with large, quite plush rooms, each with en-suite shower or bath, & toilet, plus TV, fridge, kettle & fan. (Lunch/dinner buffet Kw42,000) $$ inc cont b/fast.

Wayside B&B (8 rooms) 40 Makeni Rd; \/f 021 1273439; m 096 765184/758936; www.wayside-guesthouse.com. This oasis of calm just south of Lusaka has been run with flair & meticulous attention to detail by Beverley Horn since 1998. Take the Kafue Rd for about 4km, go past the Castle shopping complex, then turn right onto Makeni Rd opposite Caltex. The Wayside is on the left about 2km from the main road.

It's clear that a lot of thought & hard work has gone into Wayside, with its tranquil flower gardens, well-tended lawns & hardwood mukwa doors. Along one side of the garden is a row of self-contained rooms, each with a covered porch & proper table & chairs fronting the garden. Solid-wood furniture, Zambian wall-hangings & curtains of local fabric give a sense of place; amenities include a fan, fridge, tea-/coffee-making facilities, safe, wireless internet connection, & an en-suite bathroom; 5 rooms have a TV & larger rooms have a small study. There's also a small TV lounge & attractive dining room (meals available on request), with a small meetings/exercise room opening in 2007. Luggage can be stored for those heading out of town for a few days. A self-contained cottage with 2 en-suite rooms & a dining/kitchen area is tucked away in another part of the garden, while an entirely separate walled garden secludes a pool set in attractive lawns.

Behind this again, Beverley is busy planting a huge plot with plans for a campsite & a jogging/exercise track. For now, though, this is without doubt one of Lusaka's best B&Bs. $$–$$$

West towards Mumbwa & Kafue National Park

⌂ **Garden House Hotel** (50 rooms) Mumbwa Rd; ↘ 021 1213004; f 021 1251760; e gardengroup@zamtel.zm; www.gardengroupzambia.com. About 6km west of the city, this is well situated if you arrive late from Kafue National Park. Dbl or twin rooms have AC, fan, DSTV, fridge, & en-suite toilet & shower or bath.

The institutional feel of the corridors is relieved by plenty of original Zambian artwork on the walls, and there's a pool in the otherwise unadorned gardens. The hotel is noteworthy as the place where the MMD political party was started in 1990. Lunch/dinner ($$$$) is available. $$

HOSTELS AND CAMPING If you're visiting on a tight budget, then look towards one of the campsites on the edge of town, which are surprisingly attractive, or one of the backpackers' dorms in the centre. Excellent camping is also available at Pioneer Camp, just east of the airport (see page 140), and – rather more basic – at Fringilla (see page 378).

⌂ **Chachacha Backpackers'** (28 dorm beds, 6 cabins, chalet, camping) 161 Mulombwa Cl; ↘/f 021 1222257; e info@chachachasafaris.com; www.chachachasafaris.com. Off Bwinjimfumo Rd, which runs between the Great East Rd & Church Rd, Chachacha (the name was given to the period leading up to independence) is two-thirds of the way down Mulombwa Cl on the right-hand side (useful to know if you arrive after dark). It has recently been taken over by Fawlty Towers in Livingstone. Clean & well-kept dorms have 4, 6 or 8 beds, while for a little more privacy there are private rooms in an A-frame chalet or cabin in the garden. If they're full, you can rent a tent (US$8), plus the camping fee. All showers, toilets & kitchen facilities are communal, & there are safes to store your valuables.

A set meal is usually available (around Kw30,000) each evening, as is b/fast each morning (Kw25,000). If you wish to cook for yourself then head for the 'campers' kitchen' at the back, where hotplates, a fridge & various cooking utensils are supplied. Inside, a large wall map of Zambia sets the tone for a place where there's a lot of coming & going. To contact the outside world, there's a payphone (with phonecards on sale), or you can use the internet for Kw1,500 per 10 mins. If you're planning to explore beyond Lusaka, Chachacha can organise a number of trips within Zambia & will store your backpack free of charge; they'll even rent you a tent to help you on your travels. Airport transfers cost US$30 for up to 3 people, or you can take a taxi for around Kw200,000; a taxi into Cairo

Rd will cost about Kw20,000. Chachacha is relaxed & fairly spacious, & is still the best place in Lusaka for independent backpackers, though it's all slightly less personal than in the past. *Dorm bed US$12, cabin or A-frame chalet US$25, camping US$5 pp.*

⋏ **Eureka** (camping, 4 A-frames, 13 chalets, 5-bed cottage, 6-room bunkhouse) Kafue Rd; ↘/f 021 1272351, 278110; e eureka@zamnet.zm; www.eurekacamp.com. Lusaka's best campsite is on a private farm within a game area, owned & run since 1992 by Henry & Doreen van Blerk, & all protected by an electric fence. Expect to see the ghostly stripes of zebra by moonlight, or to be woken by antelope at b/fast!

The site is clearly signposted on the eastern side of Kafue Rd, opposite Baobab College, about 10km south of the Kafue Rd roundabout. For campers, there's an extensive area of beautiful lawn under trees, with electric hook-ups available. There are also simple thatched A-frame chalets, each with 2 or 3 beds, whose occupants share well-kept toilets & showers with the campers. For more privacy, get one of the 2- or 3-bed chalets, each with en-suite shower & toilet & worth booking in advance. There's also a 5-bed cottage with toilet & shower. The latest addition, a rather incongruous-looking corrugated-iron 6-room dormitory with 26 beds, stands on the edge of the grounds & is primarily intended for school groups.

Most people bring their own food & cook on one of the outside BBQs, but b/fast, good burgers & pies are available from a thatched bar that is central to the campground, & they'll sell you fresh meat for the braai (wood & charcoal are available too). Here you'll also find easy chairs, a dartboard & pool table & DSTV. In the grounds, a fenced swimming pool & a volleyball court offer more active pastimes, while internet facilities under construction in 2007 will be a useful addition.

Eureka has maintained its position as the city's best place for budget travellers. If you don't have a vehicle, get here from town by going to Kulima Tower bus stop (on south side of Lusaka on Freedom Way between Katunjila Rd and Ben Bella Rd) & taking the Chilanga bus. Ask to be dropped at Eureka; the fare is about Kw3,000. Similarly, picking up lifts from minibuses heading into town is fairly easy, by just waiting outside the gates; the fare is roughly the same. A taxi from the centre of town will cost about Kw30,000–40,000 pp. *Camping US$5 pp (overlanders & backpackers US$2.50 pp), A-frame US$35/40 2-bed/3-bed, chalet US$45/60 2-bed/3-bed, cottage US$95, dorm bed US$10 pp.*

🏠 **Kuomboka Backpackers** (11 rooms, 30 beds in 3 dorms) 9965 Makanta Cl; \/f 021 1222450; m 096 430867; e kvkirkley@zamtel.zm. Carole Kirkley's easy-going place is modern & clean, with colourful murals depicting Zambian life & attractions, & secure parking. Expansion in the last few years means that it's all a bit cramped now, but facilities

are good. Dbl & trpl rooms share a bath & toilet (the trpls have a fan & facilities to make hot drinks). There's also a guest kitchen & a dining area; meals from a surprisingly broad menu average Kw25,000, or you can order a take-away from the local Indian at 61 Great East Rd. There's a small curio shop &, outside, an equally small bar & TV, while next door is an internet café. Laundry can be done for Kw20,000. Despite the name, it's proving as popular with the volunteer market as with backpackers. Airport transfer Kw90,000 per vehicle. *Dorm bed Kw30,000, dbl Kw100,000.*

🏠 **Pioneer Camp** See page 140 for details of this popular campsite, now with lodge accommodation too.

🏠 **YWCA** Nationalist Rd; \ 021 1252800, 1255204; e ywca@zamnet.zm. Opposite the University Teaching Hospital, the YWCA is easy to find. It accepts both men & women to stay overnight, & women as long as required. Rooms are small & very basic, & the communal cooking, washing & toilet facilities are none too clean. There's a restaurant for simple meals, a craft shop, & the hospital's morgue across the street, so you can expect plenty of noise when mourners collect their dead in the early mornings. *Kw80,000/100–150,000 per room, or Kw40,000 per bed.*

LODGES OUTSIDE TOWN If you've more than a night and want somewhere to relax away from the city, then try one of these. All have lots of space and are set in large areas of greenery, often stocked with game. Because of this, all are out of the centre, so communications can be less easy. Also, because they are smaller, most of them organise transfers to/from the airport (or the city) on an individual basis, and this is reflected in their rates or in transfer charges. However, for an extended stay all are very pleasant and worth seeking out. Listing them by area:

North and northeast

🏠 **Chaminuka Lodge** (19 suites) \ 021 1233303–5; f 021 1222815; e information@ chaminuka.com or reservations@chaminuka.com; www.chaminuka.com. Chaminuka is about 50km northeast of town, conveniently close to the airport. To get there, head towards the airport, go under the arch, then turn left straight after the police roadblock; the lodge is signposted. From here it is about 28km, or 30 mins' drive, along a gravel road, but allow longer during the rains, when you will need a 4x4. Many guests are effectively in transit, & the lodge usually provides transfers; it also caters for day visitors, though its plethora of hunting trophies or high costs may discourage some.

Once the private home of one of Lusaka's most affluent citizens, the lodge stands atop a small rise

overlooking Lake Chitoka. This is one of 4 small, manmade lakes in the 100km² Chaminuka Nature Reserve, which has a variety of different woodland & savanna habitats, lots of wetlands, & plenty of game. Lion & hyena are kept in their own fenced enclosures.

Chaminuka is said to house the country's largest collection of traditional & contemporary Zambian art in the country. At the top is a spacious lounge, adorned with original art, animal skins, hunting trophies & leather sofas. Its walls are large sliding glass doors, leading onto a wide terrace. It's all very grand; some would say soulless. Around the main building are square, red-brick chalets, with en-suite facilities & lots of space. Rooms have solid wood queen- or king-size beds, & their own music systems, phones, AC & patio doors onto the surrounding lawns; some interconnect to make family rooms. There are a few *insakas* (small lounges), plus a sunken TV lounge (the only TV on the premises), a dining room, a sauna, a small library including a section on African history, & a snooker room (with full-size table). Outside are 2 swimming pools, with adjacent terrace, tennis court, sauna & jacuzzi.

Activities are flexible. In addition to 4x4 game drives, walks, & fishing sorties on the lakes, horseriding is available for all levels. The lodge's simple bushcamp, Munano Camp, was closed at the time of research, but may be reopening in future. Airport transfer US$40 pp return. *US$325 pp sharing, FB, inc tours & activities. Day visitor US$125 inc meals, drinks & house wine, fishing & use of all facilities.*

🏠 **Fringilla Lodge** (46 rooms, 5 chalets, 2 flats, 2 houses, camping) Great North Rd, Chisamba; \/f 021 1213885, 1214364; f 021 1213638; e fringill@zamnet.zm; www.fringillalodge.com. Situated about 50km north of Lusaka on the Great North Rd towards Kabwe. See page 378.

🏠 **Pioneer Camp** (11 chalets, cottage, camping) Palabana Rd; m 096 432700; e info@ pioneercampzambia.com; www.pioneercampzambia.com. The popular Pioneer was taken over in 2005 by Sandie & Neil Robinson, who have moved the emphasis more towards that of a safari lodge, although campers remain welcome & the atmosphere remains friendly & relaxed. Pioneer is about a ¹/₂hr drive from the centre of Lusaka or – crucially – a similar distance from the airport. To get there, drive east on the Great East Rd, then turn right 3km after the turn-off to the airport, just after the roadblock It's a further 5km from there on (sometimes very uneven) gravel roads, & is clearly signposted. If you don't have transport, take a minibus from Manda Hill to Chelston, by the water tower (approx Kw2,800), from where you can get a taxi for about Kw45,000. Taxi transfers to/from town or the airport cost Kw100,000 for up to 4 people. If the owners are going into town, they're happy to offer a free lift.

Pioneer has 2 simple 3-bed thatched chalets which share a toilet & separate shower; a family chalet of a similar standard with its own facilities, a large, self-contained 2-bedroom cottage sleeping up to 6, & 4 brand-new 'safari' chalets, located on the edge of the site & facing east to catch the sunrise. These last are a cut above the others: spacious & well designed, each with an en-suite bathroom; one is built of natural stone under high thatch, cool & dark, with a toilet & stone bath discreetly tucked

behind a solid screen of the same material. There is also a large grassy camping site with plenty of shade, a clean ablution block, & a small, fenced pool – all in about 30 acres of woodland surrounded by a discreet electric fence, beyond which is a 6km walking trail. The camp's rural location means that you'll wake to the sound of Heuglein's robin rather than the blare of a horn.

The large, thatched bar area is the focus for a real mix of travellers, which makes for plenty of interesting conversation. There are comfy chairs aplenty, & a small satellite TV. Snacks & meals are on hand, with a full b/fast (*around US$5*), & dinner (*US$10*). Fridge/freezer space is available, as are laundry facilities. With its rural location close to the airport, Pioneer is a good choice for the first or last night of a safari holiday. *2-bed chalet US$120, 3-bed chalet US$30 pp, both B&B. Camping Kw25,000 pp, cottage US$120 (6 people, exc b/fast). Safari special US$125 pp sharing, inc DBB & airport transfers.*

🏠 **Protea Hotel Lusaka Safari Lodge** (40 rooms) Chisamba; \ 021 1212843–6; f 021 1212853; e chisamba@zamnet.zm; www.proteahotels.com. Protea stands in a 12km² private game reserve of rolling bush about 45km north of Lusaka. To get there take the Great North Rd for about 38km, then turn right & follow the signs for a further 7km. Note that during the rainy season this road can be uneven & very wet in places, barely suitable for a low-clearance saloon vehicle.

The lounge, bar & dining room are all set beneath a large, curved, thatched roof that's been cleverly constructed. Inside the main thatched area is a deceptively spacious restaurant that manages to remain quite intimate. In one corner you'll find the 'Trading Post', a small shop with books & curios; in another, a comfy sofa & chairs. The food is good, gaining it a reputation amongst the more affluent residents of Lusaka as an excellent venue for the buffet Sunday lunch (*Kw130,000 for all you can eat*), while the rest of the week, there's an à-la-carte menu. A smaller 'sister' building hosts a cosy bar with plenty of seating for relaxing with a beer in hand.

The original bedrooms are stunning: high, thatched ceilings, lots of style & space, & views across the lawns. All have en-suite bathrooms with marble tops, bath & separate (powerful) shower, as well as phones, tea/coffee makers, & DSTV. Mosi nets cover the king-size dbls or twins. Larger suites or family rooms are constructed in pairs, each with 2 bunks in a separate area, & with the option of interlinking the rooms as required. These are more

Christine Coppinger (age 10) and Jenny Coppinger (age 9)
When we got Imphamvu she was an orphan; her mother had died from anthrax.
We found her on the way to North Luangwa quite close to Chibembe. She was
standing on her own, too weak to run away. Our friends Dup and Rambo put her
in the car and took her back to Chibembe, with the help from the guests. We had
an elephant called Moto and a zebra called Ebba.

They made friends for a while but after a time they caught anthrax from
Imphamvu and died. After that we got another pet zebra but she also died. After
many years at Chibembe we left to make our own camp called Tafika. Imphamvu
came with us. She lived many happy years with us but she started raiding the local
villagers' fields and drinking their beer. Now she had to go to a game ranch outside
Lusaka and that's where she still is today.

conventional but still very comfortable, their
colourful headboards & mirror frames embellished
with zany African patterns.

Outside, beautiful herbaceous borders surround a
figure-of-8 swimming pool & a network of lawns.
Beyond lies a wilderness area, including a lake (in
the rainy season), which is home to a wide range of
wildlife. The author can testify to watching a
memorable flock of Abdim's stork during the wet
season here, but the grass was too high (& lunch
too good) to go out searching for game. You'd
expect to find zebra, warthogs, reedbuck, puku, kudu
& impala, amongst other common game. More
surprising is the presence of Lichtenstein's
hartebeest, tsessebe, oribi, sable, Kafue lechwe, eland
& sitatunga. Clearly it's worth exploring during the
dry season, either driving or on one of 2 short

walking trails. A large lion enclosure houses 4
resident lions, 2 males & 2 females, while even more
prominent are various antelope that have been hand
reared, including a bushbuck, Safari, with her foals.
Finally, there is a 19-year-old elephant named
Imphamvu, who is occasionally seen on drives. If she
seems friendly it's because she was rescued &
brought up in the Luangwa by John Coppinger of
Remote Africa Safaris (see box above). After attempts
to release her back into elephant groups in South
Luangwa, she was walked up to North Luangwa
National Park, in the hope of reintroducing her
there, further from people. That failed & she ended
up at Shiwa Ng'andu, before finally coming to
Protea. Now she's a star attraction, though guests
should of course keep their distance.

$$$-$$$$

South of Lusaka

🏠 **Lechwe Lodge** (6 rondavels) ➘ 021 1212578;
📱 095 704803; **f** 032 30707; **e** students@
zamnet.zm; www.lechwelodge.com. Though 90 mins'
drive south of Lusaka, Lechwe is a super spot if
you've 2 or 3 days to relax & don't need to come
into town at all. It's very simple, natural &
unpretentious. See page 226 for details.
🏠 **Lilayi Lodge** (12 rondavels) ➘ 021 1279022/5;
f 021 1279026; **e** lilayi@zamsaf.co.zm;
www.lilayi.com. If you can arrange the transport, then
Lilayi is the most pleasant, & the best value, of the
more upmarket options close to Lusaka under the
watchful eye of general manager Cathy Miller who is
overseeing a rolling programme of refurbishment. The
lodge is on a 600ha game farm, criss-crossed with
game-viewing roads, about 20 mins' drive south of
the city. To get there from Lusaka, head south from
the Kafue roundabout at the end of Cairo Rd. Turn

left after about 11km, signposted to Lilayi & the
lodge, then right at the T-junction, where the police
training college is in front of you. Take the next left
turn & continue straight to the lodge, which is about
10km off the main road.

Lilayi means 'place of rest', & the name is apt.
Accommodation is in comfortable, well-furnished brick
rondavels spread out over green lawns. 6 of the
rondavels are suites, with a bedroom, spacious
lounge, & en-suite bath, shower & toilet, all recently
refurbished. The other 6 each have 2 bedrooms, both
with en-suite shower & toilet, & these share a small
lounge.

The main building has a spacious bar & dining
area overlooking a large pool, plus another upstairs
lounge & a small library for reference. Attached is a
new conference room for up to 120 people. The
restaurant is excellent, with an à-la-carte menu &

daily specials, which include venison (*Kw65,000*); this is often complemented by a popular outdoor braai.

The farm has been well stocked with most of Zambia's antelope, including some of the less common species like roan, sable, defassa waterbuck, tsessebe and giraffe, & boasts around 300 species of birds. So if you failed to sight something in one of the parks, walk around here for a few hours before you leave or ask to be taken on a game drive or guided walk (free to residents; non-residents US$5). For experienced riders, horseriding is another option, at US$25 pp per hr; hard hats are available. There are also facilities for badminton & volleyball, & a small curio shop. $$$–$$$$

✖ WHERE TO EAT

In the past few years fast-food places have sprouted up at the various shopping complexes that are beginning to characterise the city, not to mention individual fuel stations, and a few along Cairo Road. Here, Creamy Inn, Zamchick and Curry in a Hurry jostle for business with the more internationally known pizza chains and the likes of Subway and Hungry Lion. There's far more to the city's culinary offerings than these, though, so don't despair.

With quite a high turnover of restaurants, it's inevitable that my recommendations are soon obsolete, so do ask around for what's new, or buy a copy of *The Lowdown* for the best of the latest restaurants. And remember that menu prices are frequently quoted without VAT (17.5%) and service (10%); prices quoted here are as given on individual menus.

If you're on a tight budget, then you will want to buy supplies from the shopping centres and cater for yourself. See *Shopping: food and drink* (page 147) for details of these. The surprising lack of street food stalls is the result of a controversial policy introduced in 1999 banning all vendors from the streets of the city.

CAFÉS, PUBS AND LIGHT MEALS

📇 **Chit Chat** 5A Omelo Mumbwa Rd (Omela Rd on some maps) between Great East & Church roads; m 097 7774481; www.chitchat-lusaka.com; ⏱ 09.00–22.00 Tue–Sat, 09.00–20.00 Sun, 12.00–15.00 Mon. The smart set with withdrawal symptoms might head for the designer beverages of Chit Chat. Although under new ownership it's not quite the place it used to be, it still serves a trendy choice of drinks on its L-shaped veranda, plus substantial breakfasts, light salady lunches & more. It's also developed into a venue for live music & art exhibitions. *from* $$
📇 **Ababa House** Twikatane Rd; ⏱ 09.00–17.30 Mon–Sat, Not far from Chit Chat, at the gallery boutique of the same name (see page 148), salads & pitta wraps are served in the garden. $$
📇 **Le Bistro** At the Alliance Française, Alick Nkhata Av; ⏱ to 19.00 lunchtime. Somewhat smarter, this specialises in quiche, salads, etc. Not licensed. $$
📇 **Black Knight** Cnr Chindo & Kabulonga rds, up from Tukanka Mall. Toasted sandwiches & pastries. $
📇 **Kilimanjaro Café** Manda Hill; ✆ 021 1255830; ⏱ 07.30–18.00 Mon–Fri, 08.00–17.00 Sat,

08.00–14.00 Sun. As one of Manda Hill's best cafés closed, another opened. With its wicker furniture & colourful artwork pinned up around the walls, it's a buzzing, barn-like place that feels distinctly at odds with the formulaic approach of a shopping mall. B/fast, salads & light lunches are on offer, & at the back there's an internet café & travel agent. $$
📇 **La Mimosa** Arcades; ✆ 021 1257264; ⏱ 08.00–22.30. This rather more conventional coffee shop with sports TV serves b/fasts, baguettes, crêpes & salads. $$
📇 **Times Café** Arcades; ✆ 021 1256811; ⏱ 11.00 till very late Mon–Sat. A generally younger crowd heads for this minimalist but loud sports bar offering eat-in or take-away snacks, steaks, grills & salads. $$
📇 **Coffee Talk** Farmers House, Cairo Rd; ⏱ 07.00–17.45 Mon–Fri, to 13.00 Sat. Just by Barclays Bank, this is Cairo Rd's best bet. Light & airy, it's popular for salads & sandwiches. There's a range of fresh breads & croissants as well, while hot drinks include a selection of herbal teas. $

If you're staying to the **south of town**, try Pizza Island (⏱ *08.00–23.00*) at the Castle shopping centre, on the left after the third set of lights on the Kafue Road.

RESTAURANTS In recent years, the number and variety of restaurants in Lusaka has all but exploded, with almost every ethnic cuisine catered for (frequently in the same venue), and a range of standards to match. Nobody walks in Lusaka at night, so unless you stick with your hotel's restaurant you'll probably take a taxi to eat somewhere. In this case, arrange with your driver to collect you at the end of the evening as well. For those with their own vehicle, most restaurants and shopping complexes offer secure or guarded parking. If you're looking for somewhere special, then a consensus of informed opinion gives Lusaka's top spots for foodies as Marlin's (formerly Jaylin's) and Rhapsody's. In most places, it's perfectly acceptable to take your own wine, although you may be charged corkage in the more upmarket establishments. Finally, do remember that restaurants can get very busy, so at the classier places – especially on Friday and Saturday nights – it's wise to book.

For competent but unimaginative food, the big **hotels** – the InterCon, Taj Pamodzi and Holiday Inn – all have their own restaurants. The Taj Pamodzi also does a good line in Indian cuisine, with a popular Indian buffet on Friday nights. The location and generally good service of these hotels make them popular with visitors, but there are more interesting alternatives within relatively easy reach.

Centre and Cairo Road

✘ **Brown Frog** Kabelenga Rd; ☎ 021 1225756; ⏰ Mon–Thu 10.00–23.00, Fri–Sat 10.00– 04.00. A lively bar that also serves food, & has regular functions, the Brown Frog is a 'happening' 20-to-30-somethings' place, relaxed & mixed. You'll find a variety of good beer on tap & a range of grills on the menu, as well as the local nshima. Fri night is disco night & live bands take to the stage on Sats. **$$**
✘ **Cattleman's Grill** Los Angeles Bd; ☎ 021 1253036/1253605. ⏰ daily. The thatched outdoor restaurant at the Chrismar Hotel, with its African friezes decorating the walls, has recently been extended. Specialising in steaks & grills, it comes well recommended. Fri & Sat nights are particularly popular, with regular live bands, from around Kw42,000, **$$$**
✘ **Dong Fang** Dunduza Chisidza Crt; ☎ 021 1250328. Set in a red-brick colonial building in the quiet Longacres area of the city, this pleasant restaurant offers large portions of traditional Chinese fare. **$$$**
✘ **Engineers** Central Pk, Cairo Rd; ☎ 021 1223445, 📱 097 829604; ⏰ Mon–Thu 10.00–23.00, Fri–Sat 10.00–late. The pub-like atmosphere here is slightly at odds with the décor, which makes imaginative use of steel girders & old sleepers, in keeping with the location close to the railway. The open-plan kitchen is the source of everything from homemade pasta to substantial grills, with some vegetarian options, though standards are not what they were. Secure parking. **$$$**

✘ **Gerritz** Chaholi Rd; ☎ 021 1253639; www.gerritzrestaurant.com; ⏰ 12.00–21.00 Mon–Fri, 12.00–16.00 Sun; closed Sat. Off Addis Ababa, this German restaurant is owned & run by the eponymous chef, who serves reliable & original dishes from a mixed menu. The atmosphere is casual, with regular theme evenings usually advertised in *The Lowdown*. **$$$**
✘ **Marlin's** (formerly Jaylin's) Lusaka Club, Longacres; ☎ 021 1252206. This old favourite, near the cnr of Los Angeles Bd & Haile Selassie Av, is based in the old sports club with its colonial, almost seedy atmosphere. Walk past the doorman, though, and towards the back of the clubhouse you'll find what seems like an uninspiring café. However, it serves some of the best (and best-value) food in town. The menu isn't fancy, but the food is good quality. The sizeable pepper steaks are a renowned, & consistently good, speciality. Don't miss them. The salads are always good, as are the chow meins & stir-fried dishes – & the proprietor is invariably around to keep an eye on things. If there's a drawback, it's that it gets quite noisy. Booking essential. **$$$$**
✘ **Oriental Garden** United Nations Av (opposite Netherlands Embassy); ☎ 021 1252163; 📱 096 6457275; ⏰ lunch & dinner daily. 'Oriental' is only half the story for this Indian-owned restaurant that serves Chinese as well as Zambian & Continental dishes – although its speciality is Indian cuisine. Secure parking. **$$$**

Manda Hill, Arcades, Showgrounds and suburbs Lusaka's shopping complexes are more like cities in themselves, with good-quality restaurants jostling for

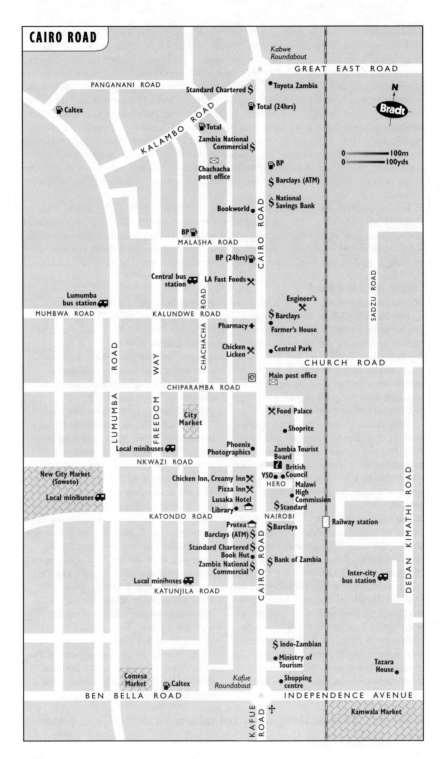

CAIRO ROAD

Kabwe Roundabout

GREAT EAST ROAD

PANGANANI ROAD

Standard Chartered $

● Toyota Zambia

🅿 Caltex

⛽ Total (24hrs)

KALAMBO ROAD

⛽Total

Zambia National
Commercial $

⛽ BP

✉️
Chachacha
post office

$ Barclays (ATM)

$ National
Savings Bank

Bookworld
●

CAIRO ROAD

BP ⛽

MALASHA ROAD

BP (24hrs)⛽

Central bus
station 🚌

LA Fast Foods ✕

CHACHACHA ROAD

Engineer's
✕

Lumumba
bus station 🚌

MUMBWA ROAD

KALUNDWE ROAD

$ Barclays

● Farmer's House

Pharmacy ✚

● Central Park

Chicken
Licken ✕

CHURCH ROAD

SADZU ROAD

ℯ

Main post office
✉️

CHIPARAMBA ROAD

LUMUMBA ROAD

FREEDOM WAY

City
Market

✕ Food Palace

● Shoprite

Local minibuses 🚌

Phoenix
Photographics ●

Zambia Tourist
Board

NKWAZI ROAD

🅵 British
Council

New City Market
(Soweto)

Chicken Inn, Creamy Inn ✕

VSO ●●

Malawi
High
Commission

Local minibuses 🚌

Pizza Inn ✕

HERO

Lusaka Hotel

Library ● 🏠

$ Standard

KATONDO ROAD

NAIROBI ROAD

Railway station

Protea 🏠

Barclays (ATM) $

$ Barclays

Standard Chartered $
Book Hut ●

Zambia National $
Commercial

$ Bank of Zambia

DEDAN KIMATHI ROAD

Local minibuses 🚌

Inter-city
bus station 🚌

KATUNJILA ROAD

$ Indo-Zambian

● Ministry of
Tourism

Comesa
Market

⛽ Caltex

*Kafue
Roundabout*

Tazara
House ●

● Shopping
centre

BEN BELLA ROAD

INDEPENDENCE AVENUE

KAFUE ROAD

✝

Kamwala Market

N
Bradt

0 ——— 100m
0 ——— 100yds

position alongside the banks and supermarkets. The Showgrounds, near Manda Hill on the Great East Road, is worth an evening visit in its own right, when its restaurants and bars come to life. And then there are several restaurants that are worth exploring tucked away in the suburbs.

✕ **Arabian Nights** Arcades; ☎ 021 1257085; m 097 789300; ⏲ 12.00–14.00, 18.00–22.30 Mon–Sat. From its new, rather more formulaic home at the Arcades, complete with Middle Eastern brass artefacts, Arabian Nights continues to serve high-quality Pakistani cuisine, plus a few Cajun specialities & more universal dishes including game. There are also several vegetarian options. $$$

✕ **Dil Restaurant** 153 Ibex Hill Rd; ☎ 021 1262391; f 021 1224515. East of Kabulonga, this is sometimes cited as Lusaka's best restaurant for high-quality Indian cuisine (& some Chinese dishes). The food is good, but it's not cheap. $$$

✕ **La Gondola** Arcades; ☎ 021 1280250; ⏲ 12.00–22.00 daily. All things Italian can be found here, including pizza & pasta – as well as more standard fare of wraps & steaks. $$$

✕ **Hibiscus** 40 Central St, Jesmondine; ☎ 021 1295011; m 097 461521; ⏲ closed Mon. About 5km from Manda Hill, to the left of the Great East Rd beyond the university, Hibiscus has been taken over by owner-chef David Semple. Gone is the drama instilled by its French owner; in its place is a peaceful restaurant that spills over onto a cool, covered veranda surrounded by hibiscus. The menu ranges from tiger prawns & quails with port sauce to more regular grills. $$$$$

✕ **Muskaan** Chindo Rd, Kabulonga; ☎ 021 1265976. A relative newcomer to the capital's Indian restaurants, Muskaan is rated highly by locals both for quality & – at around Kw100,000 for 2 people – value for money. $$$

✕ **Ocean Basket** Arcades; m 097 7755368. A branch of the popular South African fish chain that's gradually making inroads across southern Africa. $$$$–$$$$$

✕ **O'Hagans** Manda Hill; ☎ 021 1255555; ⏲ 10.30–late, last food orders 22.30; occasional happy hours. The popular O'Hagans has upgraded its menu, now boasting a range of specials from Irish pancakes to calamari curry. If it's the staples you're craving, though, never fear: main meals of bangers & mash or steaks (Kw40,000–50,000) continue to dominate, and they still do their half & full portions of salads (Kw9,000–29,000). $–$$$$$

✕ **Rhapsody's** Arcades; ☎ 021 1256705/6; www.rhapsodys.co.zm; ⏲ 12.00–late. With its large circular bar area, varnished brickwork, & blue & terracotta décor, this relative newcomer has quickly established a reputation for interesting food & a lively atmosphere – especially on Fri nights. The restaurant, set slightly higher than the bar, is fronted by a courtyard with umbrellas that is popular at lunchtime, when there's a separate menu. Evening options range through steaks, salads, fish & veggie dishes, with sufficient innovation (such as chicken wrapped with bacon, peppers & chilis) to lift it above Lusaka's norm. Note that no shorts are allowed after 18.00. Credit cards accepted. $$$$

✕ **Sichuan Chinese Restaurant** Showgrounds, Great East Rd; ☎ 021 1253842. One of countless Chinese restaurants in the city. Recommended. $$$

✕ **Le Triumph Dolphin** Northmead; ☎ 021 1292133. Reliable Creole & seafood specialities. $$$$$

ENTERTAINMENT AND NIGHTLIFE

BARS AND NIGHTCLUBS The period that a nightclub remains in fashion, and hence remains in business, is even shorter than the life of most restaurants, so recommendations in this section will, by their very nature, be out of date quickly. It's better to ask the locals about the best places, and follow their recommendations. Always be mindful of your safety: don't take much cash to a club with you, and don't linger anywhere that feels uncomfortable.

For live music, you'll need to be in town on a Friday or Saturday night, when there are bands at the **Cattleman's Grill** (see page 143). The easy-going **Brown Frog** (see also page 143) on Kabelenga Road, has a disco every Friday night (*entrance Kw10,000*), and features live bands on Saturdays (*entrance Kw30,000*).

The bar at O'Hagans (see above) is open till very late, and consistently popular, as is the friendly **Johnny's** (*9 Lagos Rd, off Addis Ababa; ☎ 252197; safe parking*) in the leafy suburbs of Kapila (Rhodes' Park). At the Arcades, Rhapsody's bar attracts a mixed, fairly upmarket crowd, while a rather more local clientele is to be found at the **Times** (see page 142) in the Arcades.

Several popular clubs are found around **Northmeads** shopping centre. Be warned, though, that there is a security problem at night, so go with a local, and don't even think about taking a vehicle or anything valuable. **Zenon** is a crowded, no-smoking disco, from where the crowds tend to move on to **HQ** just in front of the **Alpha Bar.** This last is open 24 hours a day, 365 days a year, and is the final venue on the club circuit when all the others have turned out the lights.

Hooligans, in the Light Industrial Area just off the Lumumba Road behind Micmar hardware shop, has sports television and a pool table, and serves good food; it's particularly popular among the farming fraternity. At the other end of the scale is the **Majestic Casino** on the Kafue road, in the Makeni area, with a heavily used pool table. For rave music, try **The Cage** in the Industrial Area, while rather more traditional is **Chez Ntemba**, behind the Kamwala Market, which has a small cover charge and plays mainly rumba. The bar is good and on Friday and Saturday nights partying continues until dawn – but there's no food available.

More upmarket, the Steaks & Grills restaurant at the Taj Pamodzi features live music every night.

ENTERTAINMENT Lusaka at last has a permanent cinema (℡ *021 1256719*) in the form of a modern five-screen multiplex at the Arcades. Films are mostly fairly up to date, and tickets cost Kw22,000, or half price from Monday to Thursday. Opposite the cinema is a ten-pin bowling alley, charging Kw,20,000/10,000 per adult/child.

The Lusaka Playhouse, opposite the Holiday Inn and Taj Pamodzi hotels in the centre of town, features a variety of local theatrical productions. For details, check the current edition of *The Lowdown,* or just turn up to see what's on. Note, though, that parking in the area isn't great, so you'd be well advised to leave your vehicle in the car park of the Holiday Inn.

If the city is hosting a concert, the most likely venue is the Mulungushi International Conference Centre opposite the Arcades, out towards the airport.

SHOPPING

Lusaka's main shopping centre used to be Cairo Road which, before 1996, was full of small, cramped private trader's shops where it was very difficult to find the right place to buy what you wanted. Then Shoprite opened its flagship store in the centre (see *Supplies*, page 78), followed shortly afterwards by the city's first shopping mall. Since then, the city's shopping opportunities have marched on apace.

The complex at **Manda Hill**, on the corner of the Great East Road and Manchichi Road, revolutionised shopping in Lusaka when it was first opened. Modern and clean, with plenty of parking and a conspicuous security presence, it's the preferred place to shop for most visitors and, increasingly, local people. In addition to branches of the major banks with plenty of ATMs, and several fast-food outlets, there are a pharmacy, two bookshops, a large branch of Shoprite and an even larger Game supermarket. Alongside these sit various fashion and clothes shops.

Competition stormed onto the scene in 2004 from the brand-new **Arcades** complex, a stone's throw to the east, on the other side of the road. While this has more of an entertainments bias, it also offers a range of shops, including music and video stores and a Superspar supermarket (☉ *08.00–20.30 Mon–Fri, 08.00–17.30 Sat–Sun*). There's also an internet café, several ATM machines, a BP filling station and a tour operator – Safari Par Excellence. Round-the-clock guarded parking has space for up to 750 vehicles.

In the wealthier suburbs, smaller shopping complexes include Crossroads at Leopards Hill, and the more established Kabulonga. Nevertheless, Lusaka's traditional, vibrant markets (see pages 153–4) continue to thrive, and are well worth a visit if you have the time.

Shops at Lusaka's malls are open Monday to Friday, from around 09.00 to 18.00, but on Saturday and Sunday most shops close earlier, especially on Sunday when midday or early afternoon is the norm. Shops elsewhere in the city are usually closed on a Sunday.

FOOD AND DRINK For food and supplies, most of Lusaka's visitors now stick to one of the shopping centres, the larger supermarkets at Manda Hill and the Arcades and the smaller but still modern outlets at both Kabulonga and Leopards Hill as mentioned above. For details of markets, see pages 153–4.

Most central is the original **Shoprite**, on the eastern side of Cairo Road. This was Shoprite's pioneering store in Zambia. It is huge and very successful with guarded parking (Kw1,000) outside. Inside you'll find a wide range of fresh vegetables and all kinds of food plus clothes and plastic containers – very much like what you'd find in a large supermarket in Europe or America. There's an in-store bakery, a deli counter, a butchery, etc. Perhaps more surprising, it also stocks a range of tools, some bicycle parts, engine oil and a few basic motor spares including a very limited range of car tyres!

Outside of Lusaka's centre, there are a couple of smaller (but still sizeable) supermarkets, supplying good-quality produce. **Melissa minimarket** is one of the best, its original branch situated just off the Great East Road in Northmead, behind the Mobil petrol station. It isn't cheap compared with its larger rivals, but several delis and a bakery or two have sprung up around it and opposite it is a small craft market selling some good malachite bracelets, necklaces and a wide selection of carvings.

Kabulonga shopping centre is similar, though not quite as upmarket. Found at the corner of Kabulonga and Chindo roads, it is very convenient for those staying at Belvedere Lodge. Next to it, on Chindo Road, is a larger branch of Melissa supermarket, flanked on the other side of the road by an informal gathering of local vendors of fruit and vegetables. Not far from here, along Leopards Hill Road next to the Engen fuel station, is the smart new **Crossroads** mall, where there's a large Superspar among other offerings.

Fresh fruit and vegetables can also be picked up from various street-sellers, like the excellent stall at the BP station on the south side of the Great East Road. **Bizzie Bee**, on Sable Road, by the El Toro coffee shop is equally good for fresh vegetables. If you're shopping on a Saturday morning, then the **Lusaka Garden Club** in the Showgrounds is open until 14.00. It's a popular and quite genteel social affair, where you can have tea and cakes as well as buy your vegetables.

For those staying to the south of the city, perhaps at Eureka, the Castle supermarket is a good alternative, and offers a reasonable choice. Also in this direction, some 8km from the Kafue roundabout, is the small new Farmers' Market, though it's early days and there's a lack of variety as yet.

If you're buying in bulk, head for the Shoprite Wholesale Outlet on the Kafue road, about 2–3km after the Cairo Road roundabout, on the left-hand side. You don't need to purchase vast quantities, though buying just one or two of something is not usually allowed. It's certainly the cheapest place to shop.

BOOKS AND MUSIC For books on Zambia or wildlife, new novels, maps and reference books of all kinds, try the Book Cellar (✆ *021 1255475/6*) at Manda Hill or Planet Books (✆ *021 1256715*) at the Arcades. For a wider range of literary interests, including Zambian literature and poetry, check out Bookworld (✆ *021 1255470*) which has branches at Manda Hill, at the north end of Cairo Road and in both Kabulonga and Crossroads shopping centres. The Video Shop, on Bishop's Road in Kabulonga, also stocks a small selection of second-hand books – which tends to be a more interesting and eclectic range than the new books which are available.

A reasonable selection of **music** CDs can be found at Sounds, which has branches both at the Arcades and at Crossroads.

OTHER SUPPLIES You'll find most other supplies, including cosmetics, toiletries and suncreams, at one of the supermarkets or in shops at the shopping complexes, especially at Manda Hill and the Arcades. There are **pharmacies** all over the city, though the best is Jubilee Chemist, which has branches on Cairo Road opposite Farmers House, and at Manda Hill, Crossroads and Kabulonga. More expensive, but still reliable, is the Link chain.

Basic **camera supplies** can be found at Phoenix Photographics on Cairo Road; Phoenix also has a branch at Manda Hill (✆ *021 1255469;* ⊕ *10.00–14.00 daily, inc Sun*). Don't expect to find a great range of anything, though they do stock film, and can arrange camera repairs.

General **outdoor equipment**, including camping, fishing and riding gear, can be found at Reflections (✆ *021 1268317*) at Crossroads on Leopards Hill Road.

For **car spares**, see page 150.

SOUVENIRS AND CURIOS For typical African carvings, basketware and curios, you probably won't get better value or a wider selection than at Kabwata Cultural Centre, on Burma Road (see *What to see and do*, page 155), although there's a good range of baskets for sale at the shop in the National Museum. Slightly less central is the craft market the back of the outdoor market at Northmead, opposite Melissa minimarket (park at the supermarket), while every Sunday there's a regular curio market held at the Arcades.

Specialist shops afford the opportunity to browse at leisure. Of these, one of the best is **Ababa House** (*Twikatane Rd;* ⊕ *09.00–17.00 Mon–Sat*), the brainchild of Serena Ansley who has converted a private house into a showcase for handmade Zambian (and to a lesser extent, Zimbabwean and South African) art and crafts. Don't rush a visit here: browsing through the pottery, sculptures, furniture, jewellery, textiles and much more besides makes for a very enjoyable hour or so, particularly if combined with coffee or lunch in the garden. Serena's suppliers number over 80 artists and craftworkers, from AIDs orphans and the Malambo Women's co-operative at Monze to professionals, and much of their work is very affordable – and transportable.

More conventionally, there's also **Kubu Crafts** (✆ *021 1256644*) at Manda Hill, and **Optimana** at Kabulonga, while the colourful artwork around the walls at the complex's Kilimanjaro Café (see page 142) is also for sale. For last-minute purchases, you could also try one of the shops at the airport.

Gems and jewellery can be found in expensive shops at the InterContinental, Taj Pamodzi or Holiday Inn, though don't expect any bargains. A good place to start is Jagoda (*1 Luano Rd, Fairview;* ✆ *021 1223131; www.jagodagems.com*).

For a much cheaper souvenir in the form of a *chitenje* (see page 77), try one of the smaller local shops, or take a trip to one of the markets (see pages 153–4). Even if you come away empty-handed, you'll have seen a far more authentic side to Zambian shopping culture than that offered by upmarket shops.

BANKS AND CHANGING MONEY

Use a bank or bureau de change to change money wherever possible; otherwise stick to a hotel. Changing money on the street is of no advantage, as the rates are the same, but opens you to a much greater risk of being ripped off. Be aware, too, that counterfeit US$100 and Kw50,000 notes are in circulation. Wherever you change money, don't forget to take some ID with you.

When changing travellers' cheques, you will – somewhat controversially – need to take the 'proof of purchase' slip that you were given when you bought the cheques. American Express cheques can be cashed at branches of Standard Chartered Bank.

BANKS The main banks have their head offices along Cairo Road, but most have branches with ATMs at Manda Hill, the Arcades and other shopping complexes, where security is far better than on Cairo Road. There is also a well-guarded ATM at the Holiday Inn.

These are the head offices of the major banks:

$ **Barclays Bank Zambia** Kafue Hse, Cairo Rd; ☎ 021 1220933
$ **Citibank** Citibank Hse, Chachacha Rd; ☎ 021 1229025
$ **Finance Bank** Chanik Hse, Cairo Rd; ☎ 021 1226457
$ **Indo-Zambia Bank** Cairo Rd; ☎ 021 1224653, 1225080, 1224652, 1228074, 1227194

$ **Stanbic Bank** Woodbank Hse, Cairo Rd; ☎ 021 1229071–3
$ **Standard Chartered Bank** Standard Hse, Cairo Rd; ☎ 021 1229242
$ **Zambia National Commercial Bank** Cairo Rd; ☎ 021 1229539

BUREAUX DE CHANGE While Cairo Road remains the stronghold of Lusaka's bureaux de change, usually with the best rates, they are now to be found in shopping complexes across the city. With the slight decrease in rates comes a conspicuous improvement in security. There is also a bureau de change upstairs at the main post office on Cairo Road (⊕ 08.00–17.00 Mon–Fri, 08.00–12.00 Sat). Bureaux de change usually deal only with cash and will not exchange travellers' cheques.

In many places you can expect a surcharge if you're changing less than US$50. For small amounts of currency, consider Runnymede in Kabulonga or Castle shopping complex (⊕ Mon–Sat); their rates are relatively low, but there's no surcharge.

Most of the larger hotels will change money, including travellers' cheques, though they generally offer poor rates of exchange, or charge steep commissions – and may insist that you are a guest of the hotel.

COMMUNICATIONS

INTERNET CAFÉS While Lusaka doesn't seem to have quite the same proliferation of internet cafés as other African capitals, there are certainly several around. Charges vary considerably, but are generally Kw1,500–3,000 for ten minutes, depending on the location. If this seems relatively accessible, be warned that you'll often be faced with outdated hardware, so even the simplest email can take a significant time to write and send. The large hotels also have business centres with internet facilities, though up-to-date fast hardware is like gold dust. As you might expect, venues open and close with almost alarming frequency; those listed here are reasonably accessible and reliable. There's also an internet café at the Arcades complex, and another at Northmead.

E **Foresight** Crossroads, Leopards Hill; ⏰ 09.00–21.00 daily. Kw1,500 for 10 mins. E **I-Zone** Central Park, Cairo Rd; ⏰ 07.30–19.30 Mon–Sat. Kw150/min.

E **Kilimanjaro Café** Manda Hill. At the back of this popular café (see page 142), internet facilities cost Kw1,000 for 5 mins. There's also WiFi access. E **Post office** Cairo Rd; ⏰ 08.30–16.30 Mon–Fri, 08.00–12.00 Sat. Kw1,500/10 mins.

POST AND TELEPHONE Lusaka's busy main **post office** is in the centre of Cairo Road, on the corner with Church Road. The main hall on the ground floor has a row of assistants in cubicles – above which the occupant's responsibilities are detailed. There is a telegraph office (⏰ *08.30–16.30 Mon–Fri, 08.00–12.00 Sat*). Here you can send a fax, use the internet or make an international phone call. It is often crowded and conversations are anything but private, but they can be accomplished surprisingly fast. Time is metered in three-minute units, and a call will be cut off automatically unless you instruct the operators otherwise. Both the main post office and the one at Ridgeway have a philatelic counter for purchasing Zambia's colourful stamps, including first-day issues and blocks. Upstairs you will find a bureau de change where rates are on a par with those of the banks.

If you're just looking for stamps, it's probably quicker to go to one of the smaller post offices around the city.

The major **mobile-phone** providers have countless branches throughout the city – with Celtel offices particularly prominent at Manda Hill, the Arcades, Crossroads and on the Cairo Road.

COURIERS If you need to send something valuable then do not trust the postal service; a courier is by far the best way. The main couriers in Lusaka are:

DHL (Zambia) ☎ 021 1229768/71; www.dhl.co.zm
Fedex ☎ 021 1252189, 1252191; www.fedex.com

Mercury Express/UPS ☎ 021 1257361–4; www.ups.com
Skynet Couriers ☎ 021 1224047; www.skynet.net

OTHER PRACTICALITIES

BRITISH COUNCIL If you are in Lusaka for any length of time then the British Council (☎ *021 1228332;* ⏰ *10.00–18.00 Mon, Tue, Thu, Fri, 09.30–13.00 Sat*) runs a good library, with lending and reference sections, from its offices in Heroes Place off Cairo Road. Membership costs Kw200,000 a year.

CAR REPAIRS Repairs used to be difficult to arrange as spare parts were in poor supply. However, in the last few years this has changed considerably as (particularly) Toyota have moved into Zambia, with others following suit. The main Toyota centre (☎ *021 1229109/13, 221635;* f *021 1223846*), for parts, sales and service, is at the north end of Cairo Road, while further out is a Nissan dealership 2km north of the Kabwe roundabout on the Great North Road. For Mercedes, Jeep and Mitsubishi, head for Southern Cross Motors on the Kafue Road (☎ *021 1214778, 1214780, 1214287*), just before the Castle shopping complex.

One of the most highly recommended places for car repairs in general is Brian Vermaak at World of Wheels (☎ *021 1227256*).

For spares and tyres in general, try the Impala Service Station (*Great North Rd;* ☎ *021 1238275, 1238284*) just past the roundabout at the end of Cairo Road, Autoworld (*Kafue Rd;* ☎ *021 1230740–1; www.autoworldzm.com*), next to the Downtown shopping centre (you could get an ice cream from the Italian gelateria here while you wait!), or TS Tyre Services opposite the Arcades.

EMBASSIES AND HIGH COMMISSIONS IN LUSAKA There's often a list of Lusaka's diplomatic missions, including those in neighbouring countries when necessary, in the front of the telephone directory.

Ⓔ Angola (embassy) 6660 Mumana Rd, Olympia Pk, PO Box 31595, Lusaka; ✆ 021 290346/1291142; f 021 1292592–5

Ⓔ Botswana (high commission) 5201 Pandit Nehru Rd, Diplomatic Triangle, PO Box 31910, Lusaka; ✆ 021 1250555, 1250019, 1252058; f 021 1253895

Ⓔ Britain See United Kingdom, below

Ⓔ Canada (high commission) 99 United Nations Av, PO Box 31313, Lusaka; ✆ 021 1250833; f 021 1254176; e lsaka@international.gc.ca

Ⓔ China (embassy) 7430 United Nations Av (cnr of Haile Selassie), PO Box 31859, Lusaka; ✆ 021 1253770, 1252410; f 021 1251157

Ⓔ Cuba (embassy) 5574 Magoye Rd, Kalundu, PO Box 33132, Lusaka; ✆ 021 1291308/80, 1291586

Ⓔ Denmark (embassy) 5219 Haile Selassie Av (opp. InterContinental Hotel), PO Box 50299, Lusaka; ✆ 021 1254277, 1254182, 1253750; f 021 1254618; e lunam@um.dk

Ⓔ DRC (Zaire) (embassy) Mpelembe Hse, Broadway Rd, Ndola; ✆ 02 614247

Ⓔ Egypt (embassy) Plot No 5206, United Nations Av, Longacres, PO Box 32428, Lusaka 10101; ✆ 021 1250229; f 021 1254149

Ⓔ Finland (embassy) Haile Selassie Av (opp. Ndeke Hse), Longacres, PO Box 50819, Lusaka; ✆ 021 1251988, 1251234; f 021 1253783; e sanomat.lus@formin.fi

Ⓔ France (embassy) 4th Floor, Anglo American Bldg, 74 Independence Av, PO Box 30062, Lusaka; ✆ 021 1251322, 1251340; f 021 1254475

Ⓔ Germany (embassy) 5209 United Nations Av, PO Box 50120, Lusaka; ✆ 021 1250644, 1251259, 1251262; f 021 1254014

Ⓔ India (high commission) 1 Pandit Nehru Rd, PO Box 32111, Lusaka; ✆ 021 1253159–60; f 021 1254118; e chancery@india.zm

Ⓔ Ireland (embassy) 6663 Katima Mulilo Rd, Olympia Park Extension, PO Box 34923, Lusaka; ✆ 021 1290650, 1291124, 1292288482; f 021 1290482

Ⓔ Italy (embassy) 5211 Embassy Pk, Diplomatic Triangle, PO Box 31046, Lusaka 10101; ✆ 021 1250755; f 021 1254929; e ambasciata.lusaka@esteri.it

Ⓔ Japan (embassy) 5218 Haile Selassie Av, PO Box 34190, Lusaka; ✆ 021 1251555; f 021 1253488

Ⓔ Kenya (high commission) 5207 United Nations Av, PO Box 50298; Lusaka; ✆ 021 1250722, 1250742, 1250751; f 021 1253829

Ⓔ Malawi (high commission) 5th Floor, Woodgate Hse, Cairo Rd, PO Box 50425, Lusaka; ✆ 021 1228297; f 021 1265765

Ⓔ Mozambique (embassy) Plot 9592, Kacha Rd, Northmead, PO Box 34877, Lusaka; ✆ 021 1220339; f 021 1220345

Ⓔ Namibia (high commission) 30B, Mutende Rd, Woodlands, PO Box 30577, Lusaka; ✆ 021 1260407, 1250968; f 021 1263858

Ⓔ Netherlands (embassy) Plot 5208, United Nations Av, PO Box 31905, Lusaka; ✆ 021 1253819; f 021 1253733; e lus@minbuza.nl

Ⓔ Nigeria (high commission) 17 Broads Rd, Fairview, PO Box 32598, Lusaka; ✆ 021 1253177, 1229860–2; f 021 1223791

Ⓔ Norway (high commission) 65 Birdcage Wk, Haile Selassie Av, PO Box 34570, Lusaka; ✆ 021 1252188, 1252625; f 021 1253915

Ⓔ Portugal (embassy) 23 Yotam Muleya Rd, Woodlands, PO Box 33871, Lusaka; ✆ 021 1253720; f 021 1253896

Ⓔ Russia (embassy) Plot No 6407, Diplomatic Triangle, PO Box 32355, Lusaka; ✆ 021 1252120, 1252128, 1252183; f 021 1253582

Ⓔ Saudi Arabia (embassy) 4896 Los Angeles Bd, PO Box 34411, Lusaka; ✆ 021 1227829, 1277830; f 021 1222334

Ⓔ Somalia (embassy) 377A Kabulonga Rd, PO Box 3251, Lusaka; ✆ 021 1262119, 1263944

Ⓔ South Africa (high commission) 4th Floor, Bata Hse, Cairo Rd, P Bag W369, Lusaka; ✆ 021 1260999; f 021 1263001; e sahc@zamnet.zm

Ⓔ Sweden (embassy) Haile Selassie Av (opposite Ndeke Hse), PO Box 50264, Lusaka; ✆ 021 1251711; f 021 1254049; e ambassaden.lusaka@foreign.ministry.se

Ⓔ Tanzania (high commission) Ujamaa Hse, 5200 United Nations Av, PO Box 31219, Lusaka; ✆ 021 1253222; f 021 1254861; e tzreplsk@zamnet.zm. ⏲ for visas 08.00–12.00 only.

Ⓔ United Kingdom (high commission) Diplomatic Triangle, 5210 Independence Av, PO Box 50050, Lusaka; ✆ 021 1251133; f 021 1253798

Ⓔ United States (embassy) Independence Av (cnr United Nations Av), PO Box 31617, Lusaka; ✆ 021 1250955; f 021 1252225; e BHC-lusaka@fco.gov.uk

Ⓔ Zimbabwe (high commission) 4th Floor, Memaco Hse, Cairo Rd (south end, next to Findeco Hse), PO Box 33491 Lusaka; ✆ 021 1254006

EMERGENCIES For a serious medical condition, see *Chapter 5, Health and safety*, page 91, and don't hesitate to use the emergency number given with your medical insurance. As a failsafe, many adventure/safari companies, lodges and camps also subscribe to an emergency medical evacuation service. Good travel insurances will also cover you for use of their service, although authorisation for this in an emergency can take time. Their regional offices are:

Health International/Medical Air Rescue Service (MARS) Great East Rd, PO Box 35999, Lusaka; emergency ➲ 021 1236644, 1702664, general enquiries ➲ 021 1231175–6; f 021 1231081, 1224833; e marsintl@zamnet.zm

Specialty Emergency Services MedRescue (SES) The Grove, Kafue Rd, PO Box 31500, Lusaka; ➲ 021 1273302–7, 1212663–4; m 097 770302–5; e med@zamnet.zm

For less life-threatening conditions, either your embassy or hotel should be able to recommend a doctor. A sick foreign traveller will usually be accepted by one of the well-equipped clinics used by the city's more affluent residents without too many questions being asked at first, though proof of comprehensive medical insurance will make this all the more speedy.

Care for Business (CFB) The Medical Centre, Addis Ababa Bd; ➲ 021 1255727–30, 1291489 **Corpmed Clinic** 3236 Cairo Rd (behind Barclays Business Centre); ➲ 021 1222612, 1236643; ⏲ 08.00–16.00 Mon–Fri, 09.00–11.00 Sat. This is probably Lusaka's best-equipped hospital & is managed by MARS (see above). It has a very modern trauma centre, its own ambulance service & a laboratory. There's a doctor on duty 24hrs, though the clinic routinely opens for non-emergencies.

Health Centre Lusaka 8238 Nangwenya Rd; ➲/f 021 1254819; m 097 7773012; www.corpmedzambia.com **Hilltop Hospital** Plot 148 Kabulonga Rd, Ibex Hill; ➲ 021 1263407, 1263452; f 021 1264949; m 095 5767471 **Monica Chiumya Memorial Clinic** Off Buluwe Rd, near Lake Rd, Kabulonga; ➲ 021 1261247

The government-run **University Teaching Hospital** on Nationalist Road has a department for emergencies (➲ 021 1254113), though it is sadly overstretched and best avoided if possible.

RELIGIOUS SERVICES Lusaka is well served both for churches and mosques. The city's Anglican Cathedral of the Holy Cross is close to the international hotels in the Ridgeway district. Regular services are held here every Sunday at 08.00, 10.00 and 17.00, while those on weekdays vary; for details, see the noticeboard outside the church.

TRAVEL AGENTS There's no shortage of travel agents in the capital, but attentive and efficient service isn't so common, and at present only a few, such as Voyagers, are used to the demands of overseas clients. In addition, many have their own favourite properties or trips, and will recommend those, regardless of what would suit you best.

Most safari arrangements are best made as far in advance as possible. Unless you are travelling totally independently (driving or hiking, and camping everywhere), you should book with a good specialist tour operator before you leave home (see pages 45–8). This will also give you added consumer protection, and recourse from home if things go wrong; most importantly, it'll get you into the places you want to visit.

If you are in Lusaka and need to arrange something urgently, try one of Lusaka's better travel agents – or one for which you have been given a personal recommendation. You will almost certainly have to accept that there is little choice in the camps that are left.

Bush Buzz Kilimanjaro Café, Arcades; 📞 021 1256992; www.bush-buzz.com
Juls 📞 021 1292979, 1293972; f 021 1291246; e julscar@zamnet.zm; www.julscar.com
Silverline Travel & Tours Great East Rd, Northmead; 📞 021 1294523, 1294528, m 095 800003; e silverlinetravel@microlink.zm
Steve Blagus 24C Nkwazi Rd; 📞 021 221445, 224320, 229560; f 225178; e sblagus@zamnet.zm. Also the office for American Express.

The Travel Shop Arcades; 📞 021 1255559, 1253194; f 021 1250746; e travelshop@microlink.zm. Owned by Safari Par Excellence.
Voyagers Suez Rd (100m from the Holiday Inn); 📞 021 1253064–5; f 021 1253048; e travel@voyagers.com.zm; www.voyagerszambia.com
Zambian Safari Co Farmers Hse, Cairo Rd; 📞 021 1231450; f 021 1224915; m 095 5782698, 096 6764433, 097 7782698; e reservations@zamsaf.co.zm; www.zambiansafari.com

FURTHER INFORMATION

There are few really useful sources of information about Lusaka, except for the excellent monthly *The Lowdown* (*www.lowdown.co.zm*). Each issue of this super booklet approaches 100 pages in length and has independent reviews of restaurants, lots of topical articles, letters and the occasional travel feature, and a fair sprinkling of humour. At only Kw3,000 per copy, you can't afford not to buy a copy if you see one – even if you're only passing through the capital. Seek them out at hotels, supermarkets, service stations, craft and bookshops in Lusaka and Shoprite outlets across the country.

For information on Zambia as a whole, drop into the **Zambian National Tourist Board** (📞 *021 1229087–90;* f *021 1225174; www.zambiatourism.com;* ⏰ *08.00–13.00 & 14.00–17.00 Mon–Fri, 08.00–12.00 Sat*) on Cairo Road, just to the side of Shoprite. The staff here are helpful, but the service is limited to supplying leaflets and brochures about Zambian attractions.

WHAT TO SEE AND DO

Perhaps the most fun to be had around town is simply people-watching, and talking with those who live here. From the poor street-vendors (when the police haven't chased them away!) to taxi drivers and the aid-agency expats in the larger hotels, you'll find that people are usually happy to chat. They will comment freely on politics and the issues of the day, and probably ask you how you view things as a foreigner.

These conversations can be fascinating, but be mindful that there aren't debating points to be earned, just new points of view to learn. Try not to expound your prejudices and you'll have much longer and more interesting conversations. Other ways to spend your time in Lusaka include:

LOCAL MARKETS Several of the markets are fascinating to wander around, but pay attention to your safety and don't take anything valuable with you. Think twice before wandering around with a backpack, which is inviting theft, and if you have a safe place to leave your money-belt, then don't take that either.

Most of the market stalls concentrate on vegetables and fresh and dried fish, plus new and second-hand clothes. There'll be plenty of others, though, selling everything from baskets to tobacco, bicycle parts to an assortment of hardware. Of particular interest may be the traditional-healer stalls, tinsmiths and furniture makers.

The more relaxed of the two main markets for visitors is Kamwala Market on Independence Avenue; if you're heading west, it's just before the railway on the left-hand side of the road. Stalls here are predominantly owned by the city's Chinese and Lebanese communities, and have a reputation for poor quality, though the difference between this and other markets is none too clear to the casual observer.

On the western side of Cairo Road, the New City Market – widely known as 'Soweto' Market , although the location and name were changed some years ago – is on Lumumba Road (⊕ 06.00–18.00 daily), which in itself is lined with street-vendors peddling their wares. This is the city's biggest market, lively and interesting – it's even popular with adventurous expats on Saturday mornings. Here in particular it's important to dress down for a visit, and don't even think of taking those valuables with you.

There are two other large markets in the centre, though both are smaller than the New City Market. The Central Market is on Chachacha Road, and Comesa (or Luburma) Market, also open daily 06.00–18.00, is off Independence Avenue near the Kafue Road fly-over bridge. Comesa is the preserve of traders from across the region, importing goods from Botswana, Zimbabwe, Namibia, Mozambique and Angola. In all of these you'll find clothing donated by charities from the West, with shoes piled up in great heaps. This trade, known as *salaula*, has badly affected Zambia's indigenous clothes industry – which previously thrived on the production and sale of printed cotton fabrics, like the common *chitenjes*. This is why *salaula*'s long-term value as a form of aid is hotly debated.

BAZAARS Somewhat different in character from the markets are a couple of genteel, upmarket bazaars, although their atmosphere is equally interesting.

The Dutch Reformed Church has a bazaar (*entry Kw3,000 pp*) on the last Saturday of each month (⊕ 08.30–12.30). Find it about 4km east of Ridgeway on Kabulonga Road, past Bishop's Road and towards Ibex Hill. Once *the* place to go for high-quality gifts and crafts, from jewellery to hand-made clothing, it's now more focused on plants, furniture and books, with any crafts on offer likely to be little more than trinkets for the most part. It is, though, a good place for various foodstuffs – from good biltong to Indian snacks, and is a friendly and relaxed place to have coffee and cakes.

There are occasional indoor flea markets held at the National Sports Development Centre, near the Showgrounds (⊕ 09.00–13.00 Sat). They normally have about 50 stalls with a variety of handmade craft There is secure parking, refreshments are always available, and there's a nominal entry fee.

SPORT AND ACTIVITIES The National Sports Development Centre has Lusaka's cheapest and best **squash** courts (glass-backed) here, as well as **tennis** courts and a bar. The bigger hotels have their own fitness suites, featuring gyms, saunas and spas, as well as one or two very good private pools. The municipal Olympic-size **swimming pool** on Nangwenya Road, near the International School, is usually open between October and April. Entry is around US$1.

The city has all the normal sports clubs, including the rugby club at the Showgrounds, and golf clubs both at Longacres and at Chainama, towards the airport. More accessible to most visitors is the ten-pin **bowling** centre at the Arcades.

Adventure City (*off Leopards Hill Rd;* m *097 779666;* ⊕ *09.00–18.00 Tue–Sun. Entry Kw20,000/10,000 adult/child; supervised play for younger children Kw5,000 per child, per hr*) About 9km down Leopards Hill Rd, Adventure City is 2km down a bumpy track to the left, clearly signposted. Very popular with children and families, its main attractions are the swimming pools and waterslides, but there is also plenty of play equipment, from sandpits to trampolines. For little ones, Jungle Monkeys is a great place to let off steam, under supervision, while for adults, a bar is set well away from the rest of the complex. With attractively landscaped gardens, this is also a good spot for a family picnic.

PLACES TO VISIT

Kabwata Cultural Centre (⊕ *07.00–18.00*) On Burma Road, just west of Jacaranda Road, are the rondavels of the Kabwata Cultural Village. These are all that remain of 300 similar huts, which were built in the 1930s and '40s by the colonial government to house Lusaka's black labour force. They were designed with just one room, to house single men, whose families were expected to remain in the rural areas rather than become permanent urban settlers.

Between 1971 and '73 the government demolished most of them to construct the flats now seen nearby. Fortunately, in 1974, 43 rondavels were saved and turned into a 'cultural centre' with the aim of preserving the country's cultural heritage. Today, many of the rondavels house artists from all over Zambia, who live and work here. In addition to wood- and stone-carvers, you'll find jewellery and other crafts, much of it the work of a women's co-operative based at the centre, as well as some interesting textiles. Sadly, though, with little money spent on it, the centre isn't in a great state of repair, and plans to upgrade and revitalise it have so far come to nothing. Nevertheless, it probably remains the city's best spot for buying hand-carved crafts and curios. Large wooden hippos are cheaper than equivalent carvings at the craft centre near Victoria Falls in Livingstone.

National Museum (⊗ *09.00–16.30 daily, exc Christmas and New Year's Day. Entry US$2/1 adult/child. No cameras*) Off Independence Avenue, Lusaka National Museum officially opened its doors to the public in October 1996, more than ten years after its inception. It was to have been part of the UNIP Party complex on Independence Avenue but, after Kaunda's electoral defeat in 1991, the plans came to naught and the complex remained an unfinished eyesore until the government stepped in.

The museum houses several galleries on two storeys, and is well worth a visit. Upstairs is the museum proper, currently in the throes of a major and ongoing reorganisation, subject to securing appropriate funding. The eventual aim is to focus individually on Zambia's history, culture and urban culture, with a separate children's corner. As part of the first phase, on culture, a new exhibition nearing completion features a rural village complete with full-size rondavels and life-size models, set against a painted mural, all depicting traditional village life. It's well thought out and executed, and bodes well for the future.

For now, the rest of the museum has sections devoted to archaeology and ethnography, political and social history, and an area where artwork by children is displayed. Of these, the ethnography section is probably the most interesting, with exhibits of the material culture of various Zambian ethnic groups, including musical instruments, pottery and basket work, and a popular display of artefacts relating to witchcraft and initiation ceremonies. Don't miss the display of masks, particularly the Makishi masks of the North-Western Province. By contrast, the archaeology section is very small, essentially showing only a cast of 'Broken Hill Man', Zambia's contribution to early hominid finds. The political-history displays feature colonial, independence-era and present-day leaders, with the emphasis on Kaunda's liberation struggle.

On the ground floor, work by contemporary Zambian painters and sculptors is displayed around the walls, while in the central area a handful of traders have jewellery and clothes for sale. This is also where short-term exhibitions take place, as well as occasional special functions like book launches or film premieres (for details check the local press). Students of Zambian history will find the small library useful, but visitors may be more likely to head for the well-stocked shop selling a good range of baskets, and a few relevant books. There's also a simple snack bar.

Freedom Statue This memorial to fallen freedom fighters is on Independence Avenue, just west of the National Museum. The statue, of a man breaking his chains, symbolises Zambia's liberation from the colonial yoke.

Henry Tayali Visual Art Centre (↘ *021 1254440;* ⊕ *08.00–17.00 Mon–Fri, 10.00–16.00 Sat; entry free*) In the middle of the Agricultural Showgrounds, opposite Manda Hill shopping centre, this interesting art gallery has permanent as well as changing exhibitions of contemporary Zambian art. Items on display are for sale, at prices negotiated with the artist. The centre is probably the best place in Lusaka from which to buy paintings, and sometimes carvings and sculptures.

Namwane Art Gallery (*Leopards Hill Rd;* ↘ *096 6750694.* ⊕ *09.00–12.00 & 14.00–16.30 Tue–Fri; Sat & Sun 09.00–12.00; closed Mon*) Those interested in Zambian painting and sculpture might also try this gallery, which is about 15km from the centre of Lusaka, just past the American School. Expect oil paintings by prominent Zambian artists as well as watercolours, wood and stone carvings, and some delicate ceramics by over 150 Zambian artists. There are also pieces from other African artists.

National Assembly buildings Guided tours are organised around the National Assembly, on Nangwenya Road (off Addis Ababa Drive), on the last Thursday of the month.

The Showgrounds Known more formally as the Agricultural Society Showgrounds, this is an enclosed area on the south side of the Great East Road, just past the Manda Hill complex.

This area has its own network of little roads which, once a year, fill to overflowing with visitors to stalls and displays for an annual exhibition of many aspects of Zambian industry and commerce. For most of the rest of the year it's quieter and reduces to an eclectic mix of restaurants, bars and businesses, from Barclays Bank to a canine vet and a primary school to fast-food outlets. Note that many of its entrances and exits close around sunset.

Outside the city
Kalimba Reptile Park (↘ *021 1213272;* m *097 7623788, 7474849;* ⊕ *09.00–17.30 daily. Entry Kw20,000/10,000 adult/child under 12*) This well-established attraction has good displays of crocodiles, snakes, chameleons and tortoises, including the rare African slender-nosed crocodile, *Crocodilus cataphractus*. These occur from the DRC to west Africa, but are endangered because of the degradation of their habitat and because they are hunted for food in the DRC. In Zambia, *C. cataphractus* are found only in the Luapula River system, where they were (erroneously) thought to be extinct until recently.

Kalimba also has fishing ponds for anglers, stocked with bream, as well as crazy golf, a children's playground and a volleyball court. Drinks and snacks are available, with croc-burgers a major attraction – though note that these are derived from farmed animals.

To get there, head out of town on the Great East Road, then turn left onto District Road at the Caltex station, about 1km before the Chelston Water Tower. Follow this road, the D564, for about 11km to a T-junction, turn right and park about 1km later on the right. (There's also an alternative access road that's clearly signposted from the airport.)

Munda Wanga Wildlife Park & Sanctuary (☏ *021 1278456;* m *097 790883;* f *021 1278529;* e *sanctuary@zamnet.zm; www.mundawanga.com;* ⊕ *09.00–18.00 daily. Entry Kw20,000/10,000 adult/child*) About 20 minutes' drive from the centre of town, in the Chilanga area, Munda Wanga's botanical gardens and wildlife sanctuary are now firmly back on the map. To get there, take the Kafue road south out of the city for about 15km (and watch your speed – there's a limit of 80km/h along this road). The park, with its bright red and yellow gates, is on the right.

The park's recent history has been depressing, but since privatisation in 1998, both the sanctuary and the botanical gardens have been revitalised, with the help of volunteer workers. Now, environmental education is the watchword, with the aim of helping Lusaka's citizens (and the wider public, too) to understand and appreciate the importance of their natural heritage. There's an educational centre for local schoolchildren, many of whom will not have seen these animals in their natural habitat. For visitors who have no time to travel to one of the national parks, this is one way to see the wide variety of Zambian fauna at close quarters.

Local sponsors have helped to achieve the park's aim to specialise in native Zambian species, for which specialist environments have been created. In the wetlands area, the Kafue lechwe shares space with the puku, while impala and crowned crane are clearly visible in the grassland zone – and waterbuck move between the two. Predators, which include two cheetahs, a couple of wild dogs and seven lions, are housed in large, natural enclosures, as is the sanctuary's Bengal tiger which, like the brown bear, is living out its years in peace having been brought here when the place was an old-fashioned zoo.

These, and Phoenix the baby elephant, are among the most popular attractions. On Friday–Sunday and public holidays, feeding time at 14.00 is particularly popular – though it's suggested that you should arrive at 12.00 to take full advantage of this. There's also a bird sanctuary that's home to illegally traded or damaged birds, such as African grey parrots and black kites.

Alongside the animal park, the botanical gardens have been redeveloped with an interpretation centre, and will eventually be extended to include an indigenous forest. The work of young Zambian sculptors – all for sale – is displayed in a natural setting in the gardens, which are a super venue for a picnic (drinks and snacks are available) or a laze in the sun. Children, though, are likely to head for the recreational village, with its swimming pool and waterslide. Nearby is a licensed bar where lunch is served.

For visitors without transport, the park authorities are discussing with travel agent Bush Buzz the possibility of scheduling a day trip to Munda Wanga, to include lunch.

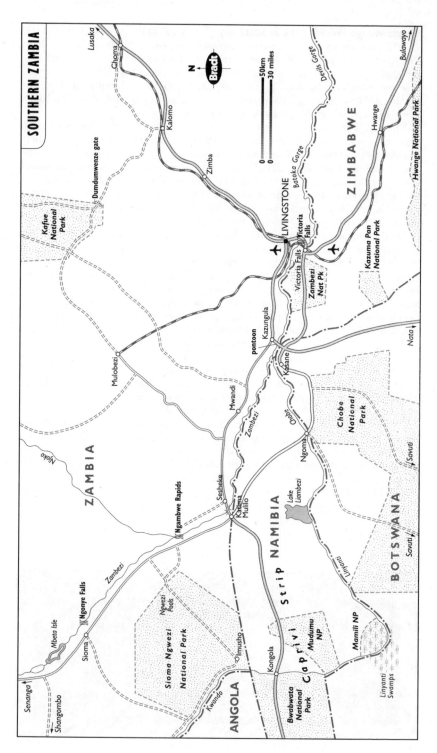

SOUTHERN ZAMBIA

8

Livingstone and the Victoria Falls

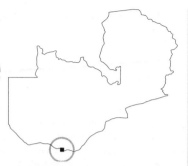

Livingstone is probably better oriented towards visitors than any other corner of Zambia. In spite of this, visitors travelling north from Zimbabwe are attracted simply by the Victoria Falls. Until recently the town of Livingstone often remained unseen. In the past, some have even viewed it with suspicion, being bigger and less well known than the small Zimbabwean town which shares the name of the waterfall. As a result of Zimbabwe's political instability, however, much of this has changed in recent years. Zimbabwe is now considerably more expensive than Zambia, and the requirement for high-priced visas has not helped. Add to this concerns over safety, and fuel and food shortages, and it's not hard to see why Livingstone, and the lodges on the Zambian side of the river, are going from strength to strength.

The Zambian and Zimbabwean sides offer different views, and if you have time it is worth seeing both sides to appreciate the whole waterfall. While this chapter aims to give details of both, it incorporates far more information on Livingstone, reflecting the situation on the ground. Livingstone has developed and become popular in its own right; it's now the destination of first choice for most people visiting the Victoria Falls. Historians might note that most adventure activities like rafting, bungee jumping and microlighting originally started on the Zambian side of the falls, before being taken over by more commercial Zimbabwean companies.

HISTORY

We can be sure that the falls were well known to the native peoples of southern Africa well before any European 'discovered' them. After the San/Bushmen hunter-gatherers, the Toka-Leya people inhabited the area, and it was probably they who christened the falls *Shongwe*. Later, the Ndebele knew the falls as the *aManza Thunqayo*, and after that the Makololo referred to them as *Mosi-oa-Tunya*.

However, their first written description comes to us from Dr David Livingstone, who approached them in November 1855 from the west – from Linyanti, along the Chobe and Zambezi rivers. Livingstone already knew of their existence from the locals, and wrote:

> I resolved on the following day to visit the falls of Victoria, called by the natives
> Mosioatunya, or more anciently Shongwe. Of these we had often heard since we
> came into the country: indeed one of the questions asked by Sebituane [the chief of
> the Makololo tribe] travelling was, 'Have you the smoke that sounds in your
> country?' They did not go near enough to examine them, but, viewing them with
> awe at a distance, said, in reference to the vapour and noise, 'Mosi oa tunya' (smoke
> does sound there). It was previously called Shongwe, the meaning of which I could
> not ascertain. The word for a 'pot' resembles this, and it may mean a seething
> cauldron; but I am not certain of it.

Livingstone continues to describe the river above the falls, its islands and their lush vegetation, before making his most famous comment about sightseeing angels, now abused and misquoted by those who write tourist brochures to the area:

> Some trees resemble the great spreading oak, others assume the character of our own elms and chestnuts; but no one can imagine the beauty of the view from anything witnessed in England. It had never been seen before by European eyes; but scenes so lovely must have been gazed upon by angels in their flight. The only want felt is that of mountains in the background. The falls are bounded on three sides by ridges 300 or 400 feet in height, which are covered in forest, with the red soil appearing amongst the trees. When about half a mile from the falls, I left the canoe by which we had come down this far, and embarked in a lighter one, with men well acquainted with the rapids, who, by passing down the centre of the stream in the eddies and still places caused by many jutting rocks, brought me to an island situated in the middle of the river, on the edge of the lip over which the water rolls.

From the autobiographical *Journeys in South Africa*

Those who bemoan the area's emphasis on tourism should note that there must have been sightseeing boat trips ever since David Livingstone came this way.

Being the most eastern point reachable by boat from the Chobe or Upper Zambezi rivers, the area of the falls was a natural place for European settlement. Soon more traders, hunters and missionaries came into the area, and by the late 1800s a small European settlement had formed around a ferry crossing called the Old Drift, about 10km upstream from the falls. However, this was built on low-lying marshy ground near the river, buzzing with mosquitoes, so malaria took many lives.

By 1905 the spectacular Victoria Falls Bridge had been completed, linking the copper deposits of the Copperbelt and the coal deposits at Wankie (now Hwange) with a railway line. This, and malaria, encouraged the settlers to transfer to a site on higher ground, next to the railway line at a place called Constitution Hill. It became the centre of present-day Livingstone, and many of its original buildings are still standing. A small cemetery, the poignant remains of Old Drift, can still be seen on the northern bank of the Zambezi within the Mosi-oa-Tunya National Park.

In 1911 Livingstone became the capital of Northern Rhodesia (now Zambia), which it remained until 1935, when the administration was transferred to Lusaka.

GEOLOGY

The falls are, geologically speaking, probably a very recent formation. About a million years ago, the Zambezi's course is thought to have been down a wide valley over a plateau dating from the karoo period, until it met the Middle Zambezi rift – where the Matetsi River mouth is now.

Here it fell about 250m over an escarpment. However, that fast-falling water would have eroded the lip of the waterfall and gouged out a deeper channel within the basalt rock of the escarpment plateau – and so the original falls steadily retreated upstream. These channels tended to follow some existing fissure – a crack or weakness – formed when the lava first cooled at the end of the karoo period. At around the Batoka Gorge these fissures naturally run east–west in the rock, parallel to the course of the valley.

By around the Middle Pleistocene period, between 35,000 and 40,000 years ago, this process had formed the Batoka Gorge, carving it out to within about 90km of the present falls. However, as water eroded away the lip of the falls, the valley gradually turned north, until it was almost at right angles to the basalt fault lines which run east–west. Then the water began to erode the fissures and turn them into walls of rock stretching across the valley, perpendicular to it, over which gushed broad curtains of water.

Once such a wall had formed, the water would wear down the rock until it found a fault line behind the wall, along which the water would erode and cause the rock subsequently to collapse. Thus the new fault line would become the wall of the new falls, behind the old one. This process resulted in the eight gorges that now form the river's slalom course after it has passed over the present falls. Each gorge was once a great waterfall.

Today, on the eastern side of the Devil's Cataract, you can see this pattern starting again. The water is eroding away the rock of another fault line, behind the line of the present falls, which geologists expect will form a new waterfall a few thousand years from now.

TOURIST INFORMATION

The Zambia National Tourist Board or ZNTB (\ *021 3321404/87;* e *zntblive@ zamnet.zm; www.zambiatourism.com;* ⊕ *08.00–13.00* & *14.00–17.00 Mon–Fri, 08.00–12.00 Sat*), has an office at the tourist centre next to the Livingstone Museum, where you can expect pleasant, friendly staff working with limited resources. You can pick up brochures and get referrals, but agents and tour operators (see pages 189–90) are usually better geared to assist you with actual bookings.

GETTING THERE AND AWAY

BY AIR Livingstone's international airport, code LVI (\ *021 3321153, 3323322;* m *0977 790733;* f *021 3324235;* e *nacliv@zamnet.zm*), is just 5km northwest of the town centre on Airport Road. It is currently going through a further phase of upgrading and redevelopment, which will transform its current facilities and service, including extending the airport runway to accommodate flights direct from Europe. As it stands, it has pleasant waiting rooms, airline offices, a bank, car hire and Bushtracks desk, as well as a snack bar in the main terminal. You can buy sundries such as sweets, postcards, stamps, etc and there are curio shops for last-minute purchases. Be warned, though, that once you've passed through to the departure side of passport control, the only bar has no catering facilities (aside from sweets and crisps) and there is nowhere to purchase books or magazines, though there is someone selling daily Zambian newspapers, stamps and postcards. There is, though, a small private lounge, for which entry – open to all – costs US$15, to include unlimited drinks (with rather basic snacks).

Departure taxes (US$25 per person for international flights, or US$8 on domestic routes) are payable in the main terminal building *before* going through security and proceeding to check-in. Airport personnel are friendly and helpful.

Airlines The airport is served by a number of scheduled airlines and charter companies.

Scheduled airlines One-way fares between Livingstone and Johannesburg fares are around US$155–200, and slightly more expensive in the opposite direction; the flight normally takes 1½ hours.

✈ **British Airways/Comair** \ 021 3322827; f 021 3322873; e bamnvfa@mweb.co.zw. Flights 5 times weekly on Johannesburg–Livingstone route, Mon, Wed, Thu, Fri & Sun. Flights typically depart Johannesburg mid-morning & return early afternoon.

✈ **Nationwide Airlines** ✆ 021 3322251, Sun's Activity Centre ✆ 021 3323360; f 021 3324575; e nationwide@zamnet.zm, reslvi@nationwideair.co.za; www.flynationwide.co.za. This South Africa-based carrier has daily flights from Johannesburg at competitive prices, sometimes several flights a day. Nationwide was the 1st major carrier to come into Livingstone & remains the only carrier to fly every day of the week.
✈ **South African Airways** ✆ 021 3323033/2/1; f 021 3323034; e saalivingstone@zamnet.zm. Flies

Mon, Thu, Sat. The most recent newcomer to Livingstone, SAA flies between Livingstone & Johannesburg on Mon, Thu & Sat.
✈ **Zambian Airways** ✆ 021 3322967 or Lusaka 01 257655; f 021 3323080; e livingstone@zambianairways.com, reservations@zambianairways.com; www.zambianairways.com. Daily scheduled flights to Lusaka, departing midday with connections around Zambia and to Johannesburg, though time keeping is not the best.

Charter airlines Of the charter companies that fly into Livingstone, the following have offices here. Remember that luggage must be carried in soft bags, and is restricted to 12kg per person. For more details of individual charter airlines, see *Chapter 4*, page 67:

✈ **Livingstone Air Safaris** ✆/f 021 3323224/321248; m 097 7707967; e livingstnair@zamnet.zm. Offers charter flights for groups and individual passengers from Livingstone to numerous camps throughout Botswana, Zambia, Namibia & Zimbabwe in 3-seater C182 & 5-seater C210 aircraft.
✈ **NAC 2000** ✆/f 021 3323498; m 097 7718840, 095 5718840; e nac2000@zamnet.zm; www.nac2000.com.zm. Although they don't have their own aircraft, NAC's are experienced in organising charter flights for groups of all sizes.

✈ **Proflight** Lusaka ✆ 021 1271032/5; f 021 1271139; m 097 335563; e proflight@iconnect.zm; www.proflight-zambia.com (shares offices with Livingstone Air Safaris). A reliable company offering a charter between Livingstone & the Lower Zambezi for US$390 pp each way, min 4 persons. Flights are scheduled to connect to international flights whenever possible.

BY BUS The main terminus for local buses is on the corner of Akapelwa Street and Mosi-oa-Tunya Road, opposite Barclays Bank. Some also leave from around the post office, where a range of buses gather in the early morning, most heading towards Lusaka. This trip takes around five to six hours, depending on the company, with a one-way fare costing around Kw75,000.

If you want to go west to Sesheke or Kazangula you'll need to get a minibus from the Mingongo bus station down Nakatindi Road. Alternatively, you could take the daily Mazhandu Family Bus that goes to Mongu via Sesheke. This leaves from in front of the Hungry Lion.

Expect the first buses to leave at around 06.30, with others to follow according to demand (and note that music played may be at ear-splitting levels). Tickets are bought on the bus; if you're backpacking, you can expect the attentions of bus touts. Since buses leave when they're full, they may leave early, so ideally you should buy tickets the day before.

A number of private coaches also run scheduled services to Lusaka. Again, you'll need to book a ticket several hours in advance, and preferably the day before, at the point of departure. Each coach operates from a different place, so be sure to get to the right stop.

🚌 **CR Carriers** The largest of the local coach services, albeit with very mixed standards, has 5–6 buses a day to Lusaka. Services operate from the cnr of Mosi-oa-Tunya Rd & Akapelwa St, opposite Barclays Bank. The first departs from Livingstone

at 06.00, & the last at 14.00. There are also onward services to Chipata (5–6hrs), Ndola (4–5hrs) & Kitwe (5–6hrs).
🚌 **RPS** 2 buses a day leave for Lusaka from their depot next to the Hungry Lion. Onward

services connect to Mongu (6–7hrs) & Mansa (11–12hrs).

🚌 **Euro Coaches** Usually 1 coach a day for Lusaka, leaving from outside the post office.

In addition to these, Intercape Mainliner runs a return service from Windhoek in Namibia to Victoria Falls, stopping at Kasane in Botswana, right on the Zambian border. This is a popular option for those travelling to or from Namibia, as you can avoid paying the visa fee for Zimbabwe by travelling via Botswana. The journey from Kasane to Livingstone takes an hour or so, and costs about Kw12,000 by minibus or Kw100,000 by taxi. Tickets must be booked in advance, either online at www.intercape.co.za, or at the Intercape Mainliner offices in Windhoek or Victoria Falls.

BY TRAIN The railway station (*reservations* ✆ *021 3321001, ext 336*) is well signposted about 1km south of the town centre on the way to the falls, on the eastern side of Mosi-oa-Tunya Road. However, most trains are geared to freight nowadays, and travelling by train from Livingstone is rarely viable. If you're not to be put off, check with the railway station to see if any passenger trains are going to Lusaka but beware: this is the slowest and most unreliable method of transport between the two cities. Even the cheap fare is unlikely to make up for the very lengthy journey and the delays that are commonplace en route.

DRIVING For details of the road between Lusaka and Livingstone, see page 205.

Driving west For those heading west, into Namibia's Caprivi Strip, Botswana or western Zambia, then Nakatindi Road – signposted as the M10 – continues past the lodges by the river and, after about 60km, to Kazungula – where Namibia, Botswana, Zimbabwe and Zambia all meet at a notional point. Here you can continue northwest within Zambia to Sesheke, or take the ferry across the Zambezi into Botswana, near Kasane.

IMPORTANT NOTE ON VISAS In recent years both Zambia and Zimbabwe have changed their rules on visas, requiring more payments for crossing the borders. Zimbabwe's visas proved the major problem, seeming excessive to the operators in the falls area, who relied for their livelihood on a free flow of people across the border. (Visitors may stay on one side, but would want to take part in activities on both sides.)

For information on visas required for Zambia, and the visa waiver scheme, see pages 54–5.

GETTING AROUND

ORIENTATION Livingstone town itself is fairly compact and surrounded by several small township suburbs, sprawling out from its centre. It has an estimated population of 140,000. Much bigger than the Zimbabwean town of Victoria Falls, on the other side of the river, the town has two main business areas, concentrated along its main street, the all-important Mosi-oa-Tunya Road. Sections of this are lined with classic colonial buildings with corrugated-iron roofs and wide wooden verandas, some beautifully restored and others in a state of disrepair. The larger and busier central business district begins atop a small hill just past the museum, while in the lower part of town is a smaller but growing retail area known as '217'. Navigation is easy, even without a map, though signposts are often missing or may point to establishments no longer in existence.

Drive north out of the city, and the main street leading to the capital becomes Lusaka Road. Head south for about 10km and you reach the Zambezi River and the Victoria Falls themselves, and the border post to cross into Zimbabwe via Victoria Falls Bridge. Many visitors choose to stay here at the border post, most at one of Sun International's two hotels which are close to the falls.

Travel west from town on the M10. Nakatindi/Kazungula Road and you soon find yourself parallel to the Zambezi, following its north bank upstream towards Kazungula and the ferry to Botswana. Signposts to the left point to small, exclusive lodges, perched at picturesque spots on the river's bank.

BY TAXI OR TOUR GUIDE Livingstone town is small enough to walk around, as is the falls area. However if you are travelling between the two, or going to the airport, or in a hurry, then use one of the plentiful – if battered – light blue taxis that congregate near Shoprite at the main taxi stand or on Mosi-oa-Tunya Road near the main bureaux de change. All taxis are supposed to carry a fare chart, though you may be lucky to see one. A taxi between town and either the falls or the airport will cost around US$8–10/Kw30,000–40,000 per person depending upon the number of passengers. From the airport to town is about US$8/Kw32,000, from the airport to the falls/border is about US$10–12/Kw40,000–50,000 or more, and out to the riverside lodges will cost from around US$15/Kw60,000. Taxi drivers are not allowed into the game park. Competition amongst taxi drivers can be fierce, so be sure to negotiate for the best deal and agree on the price in advance.

Tour operators While you can negotiate to hire a taxi for the day to take you around town, to the falls and into the game park, you'll have a more informative trip with the licensed and more knowledgeable tour operators. For details, see pages 189–90.

BY BUS The best way to get around is the **Bus that Thunders**, a tourist bus that cruises back and forth from the town centre to the falls all day long with key stops along the way. Departing from the Livingstone Museum, this 19-seater vehicle offers convenient hop-on, hop-off transport for Kw10,000 per person along the following route: Museum–Ngolide Lodge–Falls Park shopping centre–Chrismar–Waterfront–Crocodile Park–Maramba River Lodge–Sun International Hotels–Victoria Falls (Zambian side). In theory, there's also a minibus to the falls from the market in the centre of Livingstone but service is pretty haphazard.

DRIVING YOURSELF Most lodges and hotels in and around Livingstone have secure parking, as do many restaurants. If you're parking on the street in town, you're likely to come across any number of volunteers to look after your car or to wash it for you. There's nothing organised about this; but if you're prepared to trust someone then – in spite of considerable protestations to the contrary – a tip of about US$0.30–0.50/Kw1,000–2,000 should be about right, depending on the length of time you're away. There are several 24-hour petrol stations on the main Mosi-oa-Tunya Road; the only ones with unleaded fuel are the newly built Engen at the entrance to Falls Park shopping centre, and Vuma complex just past Tunya Lodge to the south of town.

Car hire If you don't have a vehicle and wish to explore the area at your own pace, you can hire a car with or without a driver – the former can even be a cheaper option. Alternatively, you can hire a 4x4 with full kit if you wish to do a self-drive safari (see page 71 for further details).

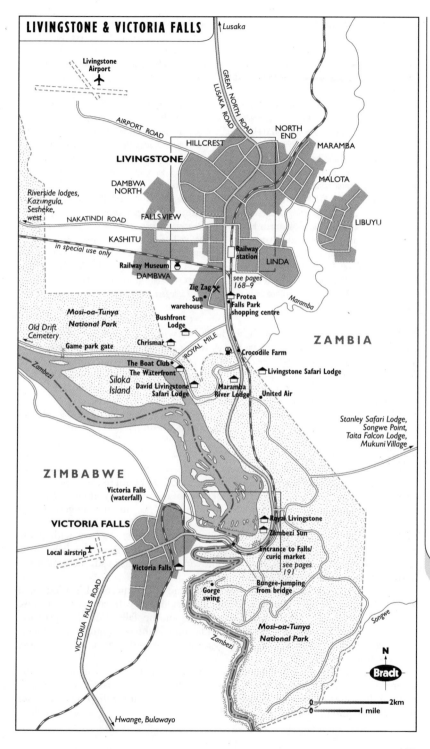

LIVINGSTONE & VICTORIA FALLS

↑ Lusaka

Livingstone Airport

AIRPORT ROAD

GREAT NORTH ROAD

LUSAKA NORTH ROAD

NORTH END

HILLCREST

MARAMBA

LIVINGSTONE

DAMBWA NORTH

MALOTA

Riverside lodges, Kazungula, Sesheke, west

NAKATINDI ROAD

FALLS VIEW

LIBUYU

KASHITU

in special use only

Railway station

LINDA

Railway Museum

DAMBWA

see pages 168–9

Maramba

Zig Zag ✕
Sun● warehouse

Protea
Falls Park
shopping centre

ZAMBIA

Mosi-oa-Tunya
National Park

Bushfront Lodge

Old Drift Cemetery

Game park gate

Chrismar

ROYAL MILE

Crocodile Farm

The Boat Club ●
The Waterfront

Livingstone Safari Lodge

Zambezi

Siloka Island

David Livingstone Safari Lodge

Maramba River Lodge

United Air

Stanley Safari Lodge,
Songwe Point,
Taita Falcon Lodge,
Mukuni Village

ZIMBABWE

Victoria Falls (waterfall)

VICTORIA FALLS

Royal Livingstone

Zambezi Sun

Local airstrip ✈

Entrance to Falls/
curio market
see pages
191

VICTORIA FALLS ROAD

Victoria Falls

Bungee-jumping
from bridge

Gorge
swing

Mosi-oa-Tunya
National Park

Songwe

Zambezi

N

Bradt

0 _____ 2km
0 _____ 1 mile

Hwange, Bulawayo

Livingstone and the Victoria Falls GETTING AROUND

8

🚗 **AJ Car Hire & Tours** Liso Hse (room 306), Mosi-oa-Tunya Rd; ℣/f 021 3322090. Vehicles for self-drive or chauffeured hire include 5-seater Toyota saloons (US$40/day plus US$0.50/km), an 8-seater Toyota Hiace minivan (US$55/day plus US$0.50/km) & a 26-seater Mitsubishi bus (US$100/day plus US$1/km). Prices are subject to taxes & possible extra charges. Transfers, tours & activity bookings are also available.

🚗 **Botrek Car Hire & Tours** m 097 7875113, 7870486, 095 5870456, 096 6923799. Chauffeur-driven & self-drive vehicles both within Livingstone & beyond. Also do tours to museums, Mukuni village, craft markets & Victoria Falls.

🚗 **Hemingways** ℷ 021 3320996; m 097 7866492, 7870232; e info@hemingwayszambia.com; www.hemingwayszambia.com. Specialist vehicle hire for day tours or safaris, inc disabled-accessible transport. Has 16-seater VW minibus, Land Rover Defender 110, 12-seater Game Viewer & Super stretched Land Rover 150 300 Tdi. Can also provide vehicles fully-outfitted with camping gear & requisites for self-contained travel, inc fridge/freezer & generator.

🚗 **Monomotapa** Falls Trading (turn off Mosi-oa-Tunya Rd onto Nakatindi Rd & it's one block up on the left-hand corner); ℷ 021 3320771, 097 806459; f 021 3320678; e solankis@zamnet.zm. A wide range of vehicles for hire from 4-seater Lexus to 60-seater Mitsubishi coach at competitive rates.

🚗 **Thunderbird Investments** Mosi-oa-Tunya Rd; ℷ 021 3320331; f 021 3323422; e thunderbird@microlink.zm. New on the scene, & well signposted across from 217, Thunderbird rents cars, 4x4s & minibuses, & can arrange taxis, other transport & tours. (It also has an internet café & business centre.)

🚗 **Voyagers** ℷ/f 021 3323454; e carrental@voyagers.com.zm; www.voyagerszambia.com; www.europcarzambia.com. From its base at the airport, Voyagers is the local agent for Europcar, with self-drive & chauffeured-driven vehicles in all price ranges and styles. They can also arrange trips throughout the region, inc pick-ups from Kazungula.

BY BICYCLE Bikes can be hired individually, or with a guide, from outlets that include Cliff Sitwala (the 'Zambezi Cowboy') at the shop next to Mo-Money on Mosi-oa-Tunya Road (m *097 7747837*). Prices for a half day are around US$20 per person for a guided tour, depending on the distance: options include riverside rides, market and village tours and birdwatching; part of the fee goes towards community initiatives which include training in bicycle maintenance.

Bikes may also be hired from Voyagers (see *Car hire*, above) or The Waterfront. Expect to pay around US$10 per half day, or US$20 full day.

🏠 WHERE TO STAY

Since the late 1990s years, Livingstone has experienced a boom in tourism and now offers a great variety of places to stay for all types of travellers and budgets. Whereas accommodation used to be limited to a handful of luxury lodges, a few backpackers' hostels and guesthouses and several hotels of widely varying standards, now you will find excellent choices in all price ranges, with many providing the service, standards and amenities that international visitors have come to expect. If the choice is overwhelming, knowing the options in advance will make finding the right place much easier.

The Zambian side of the falls is spread out and has numerous bush lodges in lovely situations on the Zambezi River, a short distance from town yet close enough to enjoy the attractions and activities of the falls. Further upstream, towards the Botswana border, the lodges and camps of the Kazungula area are ideal for those seeking a more remote getaway with river-based diversions. Zimbabwe has very few equivalents.

At the cheaper end of the market, staying in a guesthouse or in-town lodge, where you may meet African travellers or volunteers from overseas, adds a multi-cultural dimension to your visit, while backpacker accommodation tends to cater strictly to the international budget traveller.

IN TOWN
Hotels

🏠 **New Fairmount Hotel** (73 twin rooms, family rooms, 3 suites) Mosi-oa-Tunya Rd; 📞 021 3320723/8, 321136, 320075; **f** 021 3321490; **e** nfhc@zamnet.zm. In the centre of town, between Mose & Mwela streets, this is a large, old hotel of Moorish design in sparkling white plaster that was once the town's focal point. The hotel was refurbished a few years ago & its upgraded rooms – ranging from sgls through to the presidential suite – are clean with en-suite facilities, AC, mini fridge, satellite TV & even a DVD/video player. These are set around white-painted concrete courtyards at the back, where there's a swimming pool & plenty of shady sitting places. The hotel has a restaurant serving Zambian & international dishes, plus a casino & disco, both popular local nightspots at weekends. It also has one of Livingstone's only squash courts. A desk for Bwaato Adventures occupies a corner of the cavernous entrance lobby, while a small arcade with beauty salon & shops hides in a courtyard behind. In front is ample covered parking under the watchful eye of 24hr security. $$

🏠 **Ngolide Lodge** (16 rooms) 110 Mosi-oa-Tunya Rd; 📞 021 3321091/2; **f** 021 3321113; **e** ngolide@zamnet.zm. On the south side of town, as the main road leaves Livingstone for the falls, this lodge has a large thatched roof & small gardens in front with a secure car park. It's more of a mini-hotel than a lodge, well built & compact, but a bit austere. Its rooms all lead off a central quadrangle. Each has a high thatched ceiling, polished floors, stone bathrooms, twin or dbl beds with mosi nets & AC. Rooms are comfortable, & each has its own tea/coffee maker & satellite TV. There is

a licensed bar, & the Indian restaurant, tucked away at the back, is among the best in Livingstone. $$

🏠 **Protea Hotel Livingstone** (80 rooms) Mosi-oa-Tunya Rd; 01 212843; **f** 01 212853; **e** mauro@zamnet.zm; www.proteahotels.com. Adjacent to the Falls Park shopping centre (about 0.5km past railway line crossing on left side as you head towards the falls), this new hotel, part of the South African Protea Hotels group, is scheduled to open in 2008. It promises good 3-star accommodation of modern African design with a swimming pool, indoor & outdoor dining, conference rooms & secure car park. Half the rooms contain 2 queen beds for a maximum of 2 adults & 2 children; each of the rest will have a king-size bed. All rooms will have luxury bathrooms, AC, safes, electronic door locks, tea-/coffee-making facilities & phone. $$$

🏠 **Wasawange Lodge** (18 rondavels, 2 rooms) Airport Rd; 📞 021 3324066, 324141/2; **f** 021 3324067; **e** waslodge@zamnet.zm; www.tourvicfalls.com. Situated 2km from the town centre & the same distance from the airport, Wasawange Lodge is a comfortable small hotel with a few ethnic touches. Its spacious rooms are individual rondavels with en-suite facilities, AC, a fridge/minibar, in-room coffee/tea, mosquito repellers & satellite TV. Clean & well serviced, they have high wooden ceilings, large mirrors & rugs to cover nice stone floors. The place is popular with business visitors for its in-house conference rooms & has a good restaurant, bar, swimming pool, sauna & Jacuzzi. Because of its popularity & small size, you will often need to book in advance to get a room. Transfers & all activities can be arranged. $$$

Guesthouses Even the most unobservant visitor in Livingstone can't help but notice the multitude of signs pointing to guesthouses all over town, but standards vary immensely. Many are new to tourism and others cater to the local market rather than to overseas visitors. One thing is for certain, the Western image of a guesthouse – a charming bed and breakfast inn – is not to be found here … yet. Rather, a 'guesthouse' can be anything from a small, rustic hostel (or worse) to a converted house or quasi-mini-hotel. Some are old, converted homes with smallish rooms, limited facilities and lower prices; others are newly constructed with restaurant, bar, pool, air conditioning and other mod-cons, priced accordingly. Interior decorating leans towards the basic and functional (a few have ethnic touches), or tends to be overblown, with an abundance of velvet, chrome and multi-patterned fabrics. Although few can be described as charming or quaint, they are functional and offer yet another alternative in the budget and mid-range category. Inevitably new places crop up all the time so it's worth looking around to see which place catches your eye and which location suits you best. Always make sure you ask to see the room and facilities before booking in, as there's no shortage of choice – it's a buyer's market.

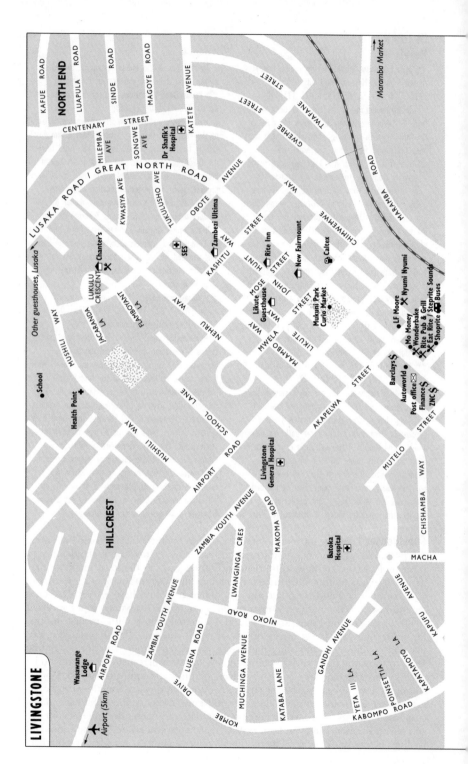

LIVINGSTONE

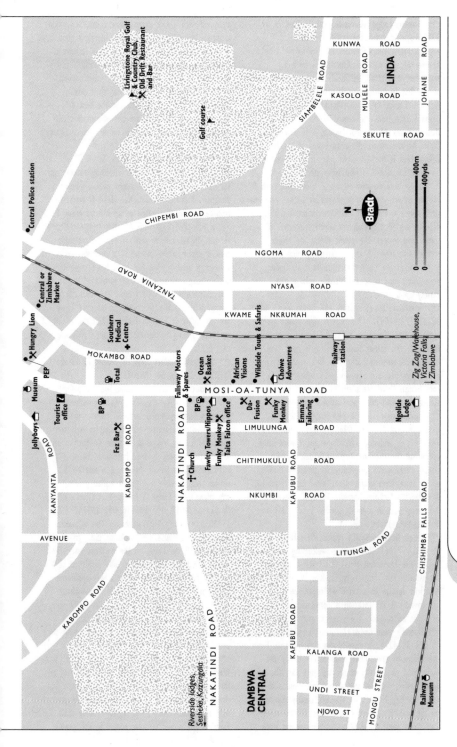

LINDA

KUNWA   ROAD

KASOLO   ROAD

SEKUTE   ROAD

MULELE ROAD

JOHANE ROAD

SIAMBELELE ROAD

Livingstone Royal Golf & Country Club, Old Drift Restaurant and Bar

Golf course

Central Police station

CHIPEMBI ROAD

NGOMA   ROAD

NYASA   ROAD

KWAME   NKRUMAH   ROAD

TANZANIA ROAD

Central or Zimbabwe Market

Southern Medical Centre

Hungry Lion

PEP

Museum

Jollyboys

Tourist office

BP

Fez Bar

MOKAMBO ROAD

Total

Fallsway Motors & Spares

Ocean Basket

African Visions

Wildside Tours & Safaris

Cholwe Adventures

Railway station

Zig Zag/Warehouse, Victoria Falls Zimbabwe

Bradt

N

0   400m
0   400yds

MOSI-OA-TUNYA   ROAD

BP

Church

Fawlty Towers/Hippos

Funky Monkey

Taita Falcon office

Da-Fusion

Funky Monkey

Emma's Tailoring

Ngolide Lodge

LIMULUNGA   ROAD

CHITIMUKULU   ROAD

NKUMBI   ROAD

NAKATINDI ROAD

KABOMPO ROAD

KANYANTA ROAD

AVENUE

KABOMPO ROAD

KAFUBU ROAD

LITUNGA ROAD

CHISHIMBA FALLS ROAD

Riverside lodges, Sesheke, Kazungula

NAKATINDI ROAD

DAMBWA CENTRAL

KAFUBU ROAD

KALANGA ROAD

UNDI STREET

NJOVO ST

MONGU STREET

Railway Museum

☐ **Chanters Lodge** (10 rooms) Lukulu Cres; ☎ 021 3323412; e richard.chanter@yahoo.co.uk; www.chanters-livingstone.com. Run by former Lusaka hotelier Richard Chanter, Chanters is both a restaurant & a small, personally run guesthouse, one of the first in Livingstone. It stands in a leafy residential area on the northern side of town, perhaps 2km from the centre. To reach it, follow Mosi-oa-Tunya Rd towards Lusaka, & turn left onto Obote Av just before the road bends to the left. Lukulu Cres is the 4th right turn; it is not named on some maps, but is well signposted.

Comfortable en-suite rooms — some with bath & shower, others with just a shower or bath — vary in size from sgls to family accommodation, but all have AC, satellite TV & broadband wireless internet, & some have fridges. The public rooms are more stylish, with tables & chairs extending onto a patio & garden at the back that includes a swimming pool. Good food is served all day, with a nice variety on offer. $$

☐ **Guestmate Inn** (5 rooms) 394 Obote Av; ☎ 021 3323939; m 097 777 520. The sign at the entrance says, 'Come as a guest, leave as a mate!' Rooms in this rather basic guesthouse have twin or dbl beds & en-suite bathrooms. Neither AC nor mosi net is provided, but you do get satellite TV & a cont b/fast. There are plans to construct some chalets & a swimming pool at the back. $

☐ **Limbo Lodge** (10 thatched chalets) 205/206 Lusaka Rd; ☎ 021 3322096; m 095 5780330, 097 7881567; e limbolodge@zamnet.zm. A good-value option on the road heading north out of town, Limbo offers warm hospitality. Its thatched chalets, all en suite, have ethnic décor, mosi nets; a minibar & coffee/tea facilities, satellite TV & AC. There's a swimming pool in a lovely garden setting, & a bar & conference room. $$

☐ **Likute Guesthouse** (14 rooms) 62 Likute Way; ☎ 021 3323661. This clean & welcoming guesthouse behind the Fairmount Hotel offers self-contained rooms with fans, mosi nets, satellite TV, alarm clocks & a nice lounge in a small walled complex. The staff are friendly & the location is convenient. Meals are available on request. $

☐ **Namel's Guest Lodge** (7 rooms) Lusaka Rd; ☎ 021 3324274; e namelslodge@zamnet.zm. From the centre of town, head towards Lusaka up the main road to the top of the hill. Just past the water tower, you will see several guesthouses in a row, including Namel's on the left, clearly signposted on the wall. It's about a 10-min walk from town. This clean guest lodge offers en-suite rooms, each

equipped with a safe deposit box, coffee-/tea-making facilities, fridge, satellite TV & AC. There's a good swimming pool in the grounds, & 24hr security is provided in the ample parking area. Namel's caters to Lusaka business travellers, but is also a good choice for couples & families with their own transport. Rooms at the back are the best & quietest. Lunch & dinner are not offered, but self-catering facilities are available for a nominal charge. $$

☐ **Rite Inn** (9 rooms) 301 Mose St; ☎ 021 3323264; f 021 3324201; e riteinv@zamnet.zm. Set in a small, secure courtyard within walking distance of town, Rite Inn has clean & attractive twin-bed rooms decorated in an African motif. Each has a well-tiled bathroom, AC, mini-fridge, coffee/tea service, digital safe & satellite TV. The reception area & rooms are adjacent to a sparkling swimming pool, surrounded by a large concrete patio, though without poolside furniture. The street-side carport is patrolled around the clock, or you can park inside the courtyard on request. There are no meals or kitchen facilities, but the rooms here are among the nicest we've seen. $$ inc cont b/fast.

☐ **Southern Comfort Lodge** (8 rooms) 75 Lusaka Rd; ☎ 021 3323103, 097 895088; e cliffbanda2003@yahoo.co.uk. Situated along 'guesthouse row' by Namel's & Wane guesthouses, Southern Comfort has a large & spacious main building with decorative tiles leading to well-sized rooms with fans, fridges & satellite TV. Each is en suite with a creatively tiled bathroom. There is a large, rather flamboyant lounge, & a kitchen & dining area. Parking is inside a walled gate. $

☐ **Wane Guest Lodge** (7 rooms, hse) Lusaka Rd; ☎ 021 3324058, 097 881536, 096 755742; f 021 3324058; e wangull@zamnet.zm. This is another lodge on 'guesthouse row'; look for the sign on the main road & the name on the entrance gate. The en suite bedrooms & separate, fully furnished, self-catering family house are clean & well-appointed. Each has AC, with a bath, satellite TV, telephone, mini-fridge & tea/coffee. There is a full restaurant (US$5) & bar, serving international & Zambian dishes, as well as 24hr room service, round-the-clock security & courtesy bus service. $$

☐ **Zambezi Ultima Guesthouse** (14 rooms) 36 Likute Way; ☎ 021 3323534. Situated on a large plot in the residential section of town, this guesthouse has dbl & twin rooms, & 2 suites, all apparently painted with the same colour as Livingstone's blue taxis. Even so, the newer en-suite rooms in the garden area are nice enough & the hotel has a pool, dining room, satellite TV, & kitchen facilities. All rooms have baths & fans, 9 have AC, but none has mosi nets & there are no phones. $$

⌂ **Zig Zag** (12 rooms) Industrial Rd; ⍁ 021 3322814; m 095 780180; e zigzag@zamnet.zm; www.zigzagzambia.com. Near the railway crossing just off Mosi-oa-Tunya Rd, look for the signpost indicating the turn to Zig Zag, which is on the edge of town. Originally a coffee house, restaurant & craft market

(see page 183), Zig Zag now includes accommodation in its spacious garden complex in the form of a block of en-suite twin/dbl & family rooms, with wheelchair access. These are nicely furnished with tiled bathrooms & ethnic décor. Zig Zag's private 0.5ha compound has an enticing pool surrounded by gardens & shady green trees, a children's play area & satellite TV lounge. Its on-site restaurant serves excellent cappuccinos, extensive b/fasts & freshly prepared meals 08.00–20.00 daily. $-$$

Backpackers For the budget-minded, nothing beats Livingstone's popular backpackers' hostels. Generally clean, convenient and cheap, they are ideal for independent travellers – but can be crowded at times. As a one-stop shop, they offer shared and private rooms, camping, booking agency, restaurant, bar, kitchen, laundry, pool and even a built-in social life.

⌂ **Fawlty Towers Lodge & International Backpackers** (42 dorm beds, 13 rooms, camping) 216 Mosi-oa-Tunya Rd; ⍁/f 021 3323432; e ahorizon@zamnet.zm; www.adventure-africa.com. Just south of the turn-off to Nakatindi/Kazungula Rd, you can't miss this popular international backpackers' place. Look for the colourful wrought-iron burglar bars shaped like rising suns. Enter through the large gates covered by straw mats, & you come to the reception & lounge with satellite TV, free internet facilities & a pool table. Upstairs in the main building are 4 dorms sleeping 6, 1 sleeping 4, 1 trpl & 1 dbl, all sharing toilets & showers. There's also a reading lounge, self-catering kitchen & dining room serving a full English b/fast for about US$4. Behind the main building, you'll find a spacious private garden area shaded by mango trees & coloured with bougainvillea where you can relax in the hammock or go for a dip in the inviting swimming pool surrounded by lawns. Campers on the lawns share toilets & showers, all clean with hot & cold running water. Also in the garden area are 8 dbl en-suite rooms, 3 twins, a new dormitory wing with 2 4-bed rooms & yet another dorm – this one with AC – sleeping 6. There is a 2nd communal kitchen (all accessories provided) & shared showers & toilets, as well as a washing machine. Everything is neat & clean, all rooms come with mosi nets, desk fans & bed linen, & showers have both hot & cold running water. Tea & coffee are on hand all day, & free pancakes are offered poolside each afternoon. Dinner is available at the popular Hippo's restaurant & bar with direct access from the garden. Fawlty Towers is quiet, secure, well run & tremendously convenient for the centre of Livingstone. They offer free transport & transfers to Victoria Falls daily at 10.00, & you can

avoid paying Zambian entry visas if you book at least 48hrs in advance. And to help with organising your stay, there's an in-house booking office (⏰ 07.30–16.30 Mon–Fri, 07.30–13.00 Sat). *Private room $, Dorm bed US$10, camping US$5 (own tent). No children under 10.*

⌂ **Jollyboys Backpackers** (8 chalets, 5 rooms 40 dorm beds, camping) 34 Kanyata Rd; ⍁ 021 3324229; f 021 3322086; e jollybs@zamnet.zm; www.backpackzambia.com. In 2003, the ever-popular Jollyboys moved to new & improved premises to the west of Mosi-oa-Tunya Rd, just behind the museum, a 2-min walk from the town centre. Owner-operated & managed by the helpful Kim & Sue, its reputation as the quintessential backpackers' lodge remains undimmed. The convenient purpose-built complex has 8 individual thatched chalets (6 dbl/twins with shared ablutions & 2 dbl en suite) in the back garden where there is also ample camping space. A further 5 en-suite rooms all have AC. The main facilities are set within a large, central thatched quadrangle, with the dorms, reception area & ablutions around the perimeter. Dorms come with 4 beds, 8 beds (& AC!), or the cheapest with 16 beds, all with fans & sharing a well-sized toilet & shower block with endless hot water. In the middle of this 'quad' is a wonderful sunken lounge with firepit & pillows – a perfect spot to chill out, read & meet fellow travellers. Above is a wooden deck from which you can see the spray from the falls. A pool table, table tennis & sitting area are also under cover looking out to an enticing rock swimming pool, lawns & gardens. Adjacent are the open-plan bar with satellite TV & the restaurant, where you can sip a cold beer (or several) & enjoy a home-cooked meal at reasonable prices. There's also a separate kitchen for those who wish to self-cater. Internet/email is on site & they also have short- & long-term baggage storage. Secure parking is part of the package & a laundry service is available. Kim & Sue offer friendly, first-hand advice on what to see & do; there are free lifts to the falls at 10.00 daily, & they can book any & all activities. The atmosphere is relaxed & unpretentious, if busy, & with the bar shut by 23.00 noise isn't a major issue. All in all it's a fun place to stay. Book at least 2 days ahead to get your Zambian entry visa fees waived. *Chalet/room* $, 4/8/16-bed dorm US$12/10/8 pp, camping US$5 pp.

🏠 **Cholwe International Backpackers** (4 rooms, 6 tents, camping) 141 Mosi-o-Tunya Rd; ☏ 021 3321044; m 097 7586803; e cholweadv@zamtel.zm, cholwerc@zamtel.zm; www.cholweadventures.com. The newest of

Livingstone's backpackers' places, Cholwe is in the centre of town, close to the railway station & near to several restaurants, & has its own activities centre (see page 189). Although it's relatively small, it's frequented by the big overland groups as well as independent travellers, so this isn't a place to come for peace & quiet.

Large mango trees shade the complex, whose focus is a thatched bar overlooking an irregular-shaped pool. Accommodation ranges from 4- & 6-bed dorms through sgl & dbl rooms (all with bedding & mosquito nets) to pre-erected dome tents with basic beds & bedding available. For campers, there's a grassy site with showers & toilets, and a few electric sockets. There's a fully equipped kitchen for guests' use, but meals are at present provided only for groups on a pre-arranged basis. $ exc b/fast; dorm bed US$7 pp; camping US$5 pp.

BESIDE THE ZAMBEZI: UPRIVER
Livingstone's riverside lodges are for the most part spread along the shores of the Zambezi leading west from the town off Nakatindi Road. The number of places opening to visitors has multiplied in recent years, so this is just a selection, listed as if heading west out of Livingstone.

🏠 **Toka Leya** (12 rooms) Contact via Wilderness Safaris, page 417 (⊕ 17°51.651'S; 25°46.591'E). Taking the name from a local tribe, this newcomer to Livingstone is scheduled to open in May 2008. It will be situated inside the Mosi oa Tunya National Park, approximately 5km from Livingstone, along the river. All rooms will be en suite, built of canvas & timber on raised platforms, & with a river frontage. Most will have twin beds, but 2 suites are to have 2 individual en-suite rooms adjoining a small lounge. The rooms will also have fans & AC, & will be wheelchair friendly. There will be a spa and reasonable-sized pool. Activities from the lodge will include a river cruise on its own boats, or a game drive into the national park, as well as tours of the falls, and a visit to the museum & curio shops. *Rates on application, to inc FB, local drinks, laundry, & 2 activities a day.* ⊕ *all year.*

🏠 **Sussi & Chuma** (12 chalets, 2 luxury houses) Contact via Sanctuary Lodges & Camps, page 261. Built in 2001 by Star of Africa, the property was sold in 2007 to Sanctuary Lodges & Camps, & has since undergone total renovation, with the final 6 chalets to be completed in Jul 2008. Just 10 mins' drive from Livingstone, it lies within the outer section of the Mosi-oa-Tunya National Park, on a highly prized site which, historically, was known as 'Fairyland'. The lodge is named after the 2 Zambian bearers who carried David Livingstone's body from

Zambia to the British Embassy at Dar es Salaam.

If you've a yearning to act out a childhood fantasy of living in a tree house, this could be your chance. Set amongst the riverine forest, Sussi's large, almost circular chalets are set quite high up on raised wooden platforms, & command fabulous views over the Zambezi. Large glass doors fold out onto a sizeable balcony with comfortable chairs. Furnishings are stylish & tasteful — lots of natural fabrics, woven matting on dark wooden floors, & a walk-in mosquito net around the bed(s) — while thoughtful touches include a minibar, a whistle & an umbrella. Each en-suite bathroom is open plan, housing a bath with a view; only the toilet is private.

Raised walkways connect the chalets to a large dbl-storey thatched boma, the repeated use of a circular design affording a sense of relaxation. Upstairs is the sitting room with comfortable sofas, as well as a bar, both offering fantastic views over the river. Below, the dining area extends out to a deck where meals may be taken with other guests, or individually, as you prefer. A short walkway leads to the river's edge where a swimming pool & a sundowner deck with firepan are set on a sheltered bend of the river. There's even an elephant-viewing area overlooking a small waterhole. The reception building, which also houses a gift shop, has historical significance (& a preservation order), though it has been extensively & thoughtfully refurbished. Activities include game drives or boat cruises, a village tour, & visits to the falls & the museum. *US$350–480 pp sharing, inc FB & 2 guided activities a day. House US$1,500–2,000.* ⊕ *all year.*

⌂ **Thorntree River Lodge** (9 chalets) ☎ 021 3327480; reservations: +27 31 310 3333; f +27 31 310 6939; e ceres@threecities.co.za; www.threecities.co.za. Thorntree is located 15km from the falls on private land within the broader confines of the national park, about 10 mins' drive from town along Nakatindi Rd. It is clearly signposted to the left, well before the national park exit gate, so if you get that far, turn back.

Accommodation is along the riverbank in brick-under-thatch chalets with electricity, en-suite bath, small riverside veranda & simple but attractive interiors. Most chalets also feature an outdoor bath or shower, set in a private enclosure. Two well-appointed honeymoon suites are raised on teak decking with open sides overlooking the river. There's a comfortable bar, lounge & dining area, recently refurbished, with a riverside deck from which you can watch elephants moving between the islands in the Zambezi. A figure-of-8 swimming pool lies next to a thatched boma fronted by a waterhole where buffalo, elephant, hippo, waterbuck & bushbuck often come to drink — one of the advantages of being in the national park. The boma has recently been renovated into a spa, inc steam & massage rooms (the latter overlooking the waterhole), & a Jacuzzi; there's a qualified beauty therapist on site.

Set a little way along the river (though entirely separate from the lodge) is the base for SafPar's elephant-back safaris (the only one in Zambia), & guests can meet their resident herd. In addition, they operate their own river cruises from the lodge, as well as offering other activities (see SafPar page 190). *US$250 pp FB, inc 1 daily activity (sunset cruise, game drive or falls tour), drinks (local beverages) & transfers, exc US$10 pp per day park fee. B&B & DBB rates on request.*

⌂ **The River Club** (10 luxury chalets) ☎/f 021 3327457; m 097 7892179; lodge e riverclub@iconnect.zm; contact via Wilderness Safaris, page 417. For reservations, contact your tour operator. With the atmosphere, décor & service reminiscent of the colonial era, the River Club was opened in 1998, perched on a rise beside the Zambezi. Guests are driven from town to a launch site upstream, & then brought downriver by boat, a scenic 10-min ride. For those driving themselves, the turn-off from Nakatindi Rd is signposted at the same junction as Tongabezi.

Thatched, en-suite chalets, each named after an explorer or colonial figure, are cleverly designed & constructed on stilts, amidst indigenous riverside trees. All are high up with stunning views, their open fronts (most are fully screened) facing over the Zambezi below. Two honeymoon suites have dbl beds, plus gardens with sunloungers in front. There is 1 wheelchair-friendly family room with dbl bed & 2 sgls; the other chalets have 2 sgls. All are large with good decoration, quality fabrics, canopied mosquito nets & many nice touches (like the claw-foot bathtubs). The beautifully polished floors tend to be slippery so be careful. Creature comforts inc duvets & hot water bottles in winter, a ceiling fan inside the mosquito nets, international electric sockets, & room safes.

The main lodge building is also constructed in the colonial style with tin roof & wide verandas (which looks better than it sounds), boasting magnificent views of the river. Here you can sit & enjoy traditional high tea or watch the sun slip beneath the horizon with a cocktail in your hand. Inside are the reception, a small gift shop, cloakrooms, a formal dining room (with a magnificent teak table), a comfortable lounge, a massive dbl-sided fireplace & a well-stocked library, plus wireless internet connection. Antiques, colonial pictures & many decorator touches add to the lodge's Edwardian ambience. Meals are elegant affairs featuring pre-set dinner menus that change daily. (Typically guests dine together, although tables can be arranged.)

Overlooking the river is a stunning infinity swimming pool with rock fountain surrounded by patios with plenty of sunloungers to soak up the sun, & over-sized umbrellas for shade. Walkways (illuminated at night) are set amongst the sweeping lawns, while palms, brightly coloured bougainvillea & gardens complete the picture. Croquet, boules & bush golf are on hand, & for the more active, a nature-walk/running track spans the 20ha property that will soon feature an all-weather tennis court & maze. Included in the price is a choice of fishing, sundowner boat trips, game-park drives, museum & falls visits, & trips to local villages & schools, Stone-Age sites & Livingstone town. A tented gazebo provides the perfect venue for riverside massages, which can be arranged at extra cost, & all other activities can be booked direct from the lodge. This exclusive & intimate lodge is set in a securely fenced compound which also has a heli-pad. *US$475 (Jan–15 Jun), US$615 (16 Jun–Dec), all pp sharing, inc FB & activities; sgl supplement US$125.* ⊕ *all year.*

🏠 **Tongabezi** (5 cottages, 5 hses) ➘ 021
3327450/68; f 021 327483; e reservations@
tongabezi.com; www.tongabezi.com. Set on a sweeping
bend of the Zambezi, Tongabezi has set the region's
standard for innovative camp design since it opened
well over a decade ago. It remains one of the most
exclusive places to stay on the north side of the
Zambezi, its setting matched by excellent service
from a team of first-class local Zambian staff.

Beautiful thatched cottages overlook the river, 3
with king-size beds, the others twin; all are tastefully
decorated & have large tiled en-suite bathrooms
complete with river-view bathtubs, & their own
private sitting area. Even more exclusive are the
spacious houses: the Bird House, the Tree House, the
Dog House or the Honeymoon House (once cited as
'worth getting married for'). Each is individually
designed, with a king-size dbl bed, impressive en-suite
bathrooms with inviting bathtubs & one side
completely open to the river. Tucked away from the
river in its own private enclosure is the Garden
House with master bedroom, small twin room &
living room ideal for families. Both cottages & houses
are carefully secluded from their neighbours; all have
the services of a private valet dedicated solely to
looking after the guests in that cottage or house.

There is a lovely riverside thatched boma, shaded
by ebony trees hung with trailing creepers, where
you'll find the bar, dining room & a spacious lounge
with fireplace & small library. In the evenings,
everyone gathers for sundowners & hors d'oeuvres
that are served around a roaring campfire — a
perfect vantage point to watch the sun set. The
swimming pool is set against a rock wall, under a
tumbling waterfall, while sunloungers wait on a large
wooden deck over the Zambezi, while further
relaxation comes in the form of massages, manicures
& pedicures. Meals are sumptuous affairs, cooked to a
high standard & served outdoors on the riverside
deck, in the dining room, or even in the privacy of
your own cottage. By special arrangement, couples can
dine under the stars on Tongabezi's floating 'sampan'
moored offshore, where each course is hand delivered
by canoe — a romantic & memorable occasion.

The lodge's ethos is confirmed by its school,
Tujatane, run for over 100 children of Tongabezi
staff & from local villages. Visits to the school are
popular, with many guests choosing to contribute to
its upkeep & future development.

Guided boat trips from the lodge's own jetty,
canoeing, birdwatching trips, fishing, game drives (to
Mosi-oa-Tunya National Park), picnics on Chundu
Island, village visits, shopping excursions, museum

tours & gorge walks are all included (aside from
national park & museum entrance fees, at US$10 &
US$5 pp, respectively). The more energetic can take
mountain bikes to visit Simonga village & explore
the area. There are also options to sleep on
Sindabezi, one of the islands in the river (see
below), or to have a special meal on Livingstone
Island (see page 193), beside the falls. These options
are not inc in the price &, like the lodge itself,
should be booked well in advance. *Cottage
US$400/485, hse US$475/590 pp sharing, low/high
season (Nov–May/Jun–Oct), 40% sgl supplement in
high season; inc FB, most drinks (not premium wines,
champagne & liqueurs), laundry, levies & all
activities, exc transfers, park fees . No children under
7.*

🏠 **Sindabezi Island** (5 chalets) Contact via
Tongabezi, above. Sindabezi Island is a short, 2km
boat (or canoe) trip downstream from its parent
lodge, Tongabezi. This small sandy island has just 5
thatched en-suite chalets, beautifully appointed with
twin or dbl beds, & carefully spaced around the
shores of the island for max privacy. A relaxed bar
area with teak decking, surrounded by tall ebony
trees, is the setting for sumptuous meals cooked by
the island's own chef. It's an island hideaway with
no electricity from which you can explore the river
& surrounding islands with your own guide or
simply relax & enjoy the beautiful setting. Elephants
& hippos are frequent visitors, & game is often
sighted on the banks of Zambezi National Park, a
stone's throw away. Sindabezi is the closest you can
come to being a castaway in luxurious comfort.
Activities inc canoeing, boating, walking, fishing &
birdwatching, as well as all activities run at
Tongabezi itself. *US$365/385, low/high season
(Nov–May/Jun–Oct), inc meals, drinks, laundry,
transfers to/from the island, & all activities. 4 or
more people booking together can reserve the whole
island for their own exclusive use. No children under
14.*

🏠 **Tangala House** (sleeps up to 8) Contact via
Tongabezi, above, or direct: e ben@tongabezi.com.
Right on the Zambezi about 15km upstream of
Victoria Falls & 1km from Tongabezi, this luxury
private house is certainly worth considering for
families, not least because it's well protected against
insects, or for those seeking a greater degree of
privacy & freedom than is possible in a lodge.
Accommodation for 4–8 people is in 3 en-suite
bedrooms with river views (1 is a much larger
master suite) & a 4th bedroom with a separate
bathroom & garden view. Beautifully furnished &

equipped living & dining areas lead out onto a large swimming pool overlooking the Zambezi, with views in both directions. The house is available either for rental only, or on a FB basis with food & drinks but without activities, or on a fully inclusive basis serviced by Tongabezi with a chef, waiters, housekeeping staff, pool attendant, private guide & even a trained nanny, plus private use of vehicles & boats. On that basis all meals & drinks plus Tongabezi's river & land activities are included in the cost. *US$600 pp, inc use of boat & vehicle, & 3 friendly dogs. Min 4 adults, 3 nights.*

⌂ **Natural Mystic Lodge** (10 chalets) Nakatindi Rd; ⑊/f 021 3327436; m 097 7408024; e nmlodge@zamnet.zm; www.naturalmysticlodge.com. Opened in 2002, Natural Mystic is 20km from Livingstone. The statue at the entrance to the lodge, of Namatama (Mother Earth) with her water pot, depicts the philosophy that underpins Natural Mystic, that the source of life comes from the earth. The low-lying, often wet site is crossed by a walkway with strategic points from which visitors can watch visiting hippos or the occasional elephant. Eight of the simple thatched chalets are grouped close together, 4 of them fronting the river, although the design means that you can see the river only if the front door is left open. The other 2 are set further back on the site. Some have bath & shower, others just a shower, & there's a small porch area by the door. With 2 dbl beds in each, they're quite cramped, but reasonably priced for a riverside location if you plan to spend most of your time out & about.

Right on the river is a large decked bar/restaurant area which is the lodge's best feature & is open to non-residents. Dinner costs US$10 pp, sometimes accompanied by cultural dancing & marimba bands. There's also a small swimming pool, a curio shop & lounge with satellite TV, plus an internet service. River cruises, game drives & other tours/activities can be organised direct at the lodge. *US100/150 sgl/dbl B&B inc transfers from Livingstone; extra guest US$25 up to max 4; reduced rates for Peace Corps & VSO volunteers.*

⌂ **Waterberry Zambezi Lodge** (3 chalets) ⑊ 021 3327455; enquiries +44 1379 783392; e info@waterberrylodge.com; www.waterberrylodge.com. About 35 mins' drive from Livingstone, Waterberry Lodge was fully refurbished in 2007 from the former Mwala Lodge. Set on a secluded position on the banks of the Zambezi, it offers a range of activities from island picnics & sunset cruises to birding & fishing, as well as —

more unusually — wilderness awareness, photographic workshops & bush training courses.

Accommodation is in dbl, twin or sgl rooms in thatched cottages with private bathrooms, grouped around the main lodge area & swimming pool. Downstairs in the dbl-storey main lodge is the dining area & ground-floor terrace, while upstairs the main bar & lounge is open to the high thatch with magnificent views over the river & the game park beyond. Here there is plenty of seating, a small reference library, & a well-stocked bar. Meals are served at times to fit in around individual activities, either in the dining area, on the sun deck or on the terrace overlooking the pool. Tea & coffee are always available & the bar is open at all reasonable times. *US$200–250 pp FB inc airport transfer, exc bar & activities.*

⌂ **Islands of Siankaba** (6 chalets, 1 honeymoon/VIP chalet) ⑊/f 021 3327490; m 097 7791241; e siankaba@zamnet.zm; www.siankaba.com; reservations ⑊/f 021 1260279; m 097 7720530. One of the newer lodges on the Zambezi, Siankaba is a considerable 45km from Livingstone, down a 7km track through open bush, followed by a 5-min boat ride. The mood is set as you leave the jetty with its small gift shop & chug along a peaceful back channel of the Zambezi before joining the main river. Shortly upstream, Siankaba lies on 2 separate islands linked by suspension bridges (great fun to walk across). On one, spacious chalets reached along raised wooden walkways nestle like bird hides among the trees that overhang the banks, their decks an ideal vantage point from which to watch the river in complete privacy. In contrast to the half-canvas walls & roof, everything about the accommodation oozes luxury & comfort. Polished teak furniture sits on polished teak floors, offset by thick oriental rugs. Stately comfortable beds with an integral ceiling fan are hung like 4-posters with pristine white mosquito nets, & good reading lights complement the otherwise subdued lighting. Set on a platform to the rear are a regal claw-footed bathtub & twin pedestal china basins with views towards the river, as well as a modern shower & separate toilet. Tucked discreetly away, a safe & fridge are almost incidental.

Those in search of greater luxury or privacy can choose the honeymoon/VIP chalet, which boasts its own deck with views across the river & loungers in the shade of a pergola, as well as a minibar, games compendium, 'his & hers' aromatherapy products & reference bookcase. Private meals can be set up on the deck & b/fast in bed is offered as standard.

The adjacent island serves as the epicentre of the camp. Here you'll find the spacious restaurant & comfortable bar/lounge area, with natural décor & tables out on the deck for al fresco dining. Among the trees nearby is a secluded pool with stylish sunloungers, & running round the island is a 1.5km marked nature trail. In addition to this, activities include a sundowner cruise, birding & fishing excursions, & a trip via mokoro among the islands. You can also do a village walk, which takes in a visit to the local school, with the return trip by mokoro. The school, Mandia, is a government-run establishment that — along with other community projects like tree planting & a clinic — is supported by a trust fund operated by the lodge. Siankaba is an exclusive lodge that offers considerable attention to detail & superb cuisine. *Chalet Jun–Oct*

US$410/492, Nov–May US$345/414; honeymoon suite Jun–Oct US$465/558, Nov–May US$400/480, all pp sharing/sgl, inc FB, drinks, transfers to/from Livingstone airport, & their own activities. No children under 12.

Royal Chundu Zambezi River Lodge (10 suites) \ +267 716 46064; e reservations@ royalchundu.com; www.royalchundu.com. Reopening in 2008, the new Royal Chundu will have rooms on stilts in the river, each with AC & a private deck. In addition to a restaurant, boma, lounge & bar, there will be a library, internet facilities, TV lounge, gym, spa, 2 swimming pools & 3 separate decks.

Island Lodge (4 suites) Contact via Royal Chundu above. An exclusive lodge on a private island, with all its own facilities.

GAME PARK, FALLS AND GORGE ENVIRONS
The development by Sun International of a prime spot close to the falls has introduced a whole new style of accommodation to Livingstone. Other accommodation to the south of town has in recent years been augmented by lodges built away from the river, affording the advantages of open bush but without the high prices associated with a riverside location. Many of the following are actually much closer to the falls than those situated on the upper river to the west of Livingstone, and are listed as if heading south from Livingstone towards the falls, then out towards the gorges.

⌂ **Chrismar Hotel** (51 rooms, 8 suites) Sichango Rd; \ 021 3323141; f 021 3323142; e guestrelations@livingstone.chrismar.co.zm; www.chrismarhotels.com/livingstone. The newly built Chrismar, a mid-market hotel offering good value for money, is located near the entrance to the game park. While it is not on the river, its bush setting is enhanced by numerous fountains & water features, inc the largest swimming pool in town complete with a bar in the middle. Rooms are cottages in a range of styles up to executive suites are spaced around the grounds with new gardens gradually taking shape. The hotel is tastefully furnished with splashes of ethnic colour. Rooms are comfortable and have AC, wireless internet & TV. Already the hotel has become a popular place to stay & with good rates it's important to book in advance. $$$$

⌂ **The Zambezi Waterfront** (21 rooms, 24 tents, camping) off Sichango Rd, near the Boat Club. Contact Safari Par Excellence, \ 021 3320606/7; m 097 7693147; f 021 3320609; e waterfront@safpar.com; www.safpar.net. This large, secure & affordable riverside complex, within the unfenced area of Mosi-oa-Tunya National Park, incorporates a range of facilities on a beautiful spot, one of the best places around to view the

spectacular Zambezi sunset. To get here, head south from Livingstone towards the falls, then turn right at the signpost by Tunya Lodge (Sichango Rd) towards the river. Secure & private, the complex has a stunning setting & is.

The main thatch-&-pole building has a magnificent view over the river & contains the reception, booking office, internet café & a small souvenir shop. A spacious restaurant & teak bar (with satellite TV) both have plenty of seating indoors & out. Outside, amongst palm trees, is a sunken pool surrounded by teak decking, with lounge chairs set overlooking the river. Nearby, 8 large A-frame thatched chalets contain separate en-suite dbl or twin rooms, at ground level, with a patio & choice of river or garden views. The upper level comprises the larger executive suites with a queen bed, separate lounge area, good-size bathroom, & deck offering sweeping river views. Also up here are 3 spacious family rooms with 4 sgl beds & a deck, overlooking the garden. The rooms are all very comfortable, light & airy, with teak furniture, quality fabrics & ethnic touches.

Beyond the main building is the Adventure Village which has a large natural-style rock pool, another bar & a thatched auditorium where daily activity briefings are given & rafting videos are shown in the evening accompanied by a BBQ. Here, permanent tents are perched on wooden platforms along the river, each with 2 beds with bedding & linen (or you can bring your own). Nearby ablutions are clean & spacious, with flush toilets & hot & cold showers. Further along is a separate grassed camping area, with its own ablutions, BBQ & washing-up area, that can take about 75 campers.

The Waterfront is SafPar's one-stop shop, where their own Adventure Centre booking office offers a full range of activities & excursions, many of which they operate themselves (see page 190). Among these are 2 boats offering b/fast, lunch, sunset or dinner cruises from the Waterfront's own jetty. The Mambushi is the more upmarket, taking 25 passengers max, while trips on the larger Makumbi can turn into traditional 'booze cruises'. Both include snacks or dinner & unlimited drinks. *Chalet room* $$$$, *tent* $$$, *camping US$8 pp*.

⌂ **The Bushfront Lodge** (13 chalets, camping) Zambia reservations, ✆ 021 3322446; f 021 3320609; e bushfront@safpar.com; www.safpar.net. The former Nyala Lodge, now owned & operated by SafPar and offering good value, is about 5km from town, bordering the Mosi-oa-Tunya National Park. To get there, head south towards the border & turn right at Tunya Lodge (Sichango Rd) towards the river & park entrance. The lodge is a few kilometres upriver from Victoria Falls, set amongst indigenous vegetation with abundant birdlife.

Chalets are all under African thatch, & each has an en-suite bathroom with with potted plants & rock walls, from where water cascades off a small ledge that serves as the shower tap. There is also a private campsite with modern ablutions & a braai area. The main lodge area is well designed & maintained, & has satellite TV, a large bar/lounge & a restaurant. Meals are served daily & snacks are always available. Guests can relax by the swimming pool or explore Livingstone — all activities can be booked at the lodge. $$$$; *camping US$10 pp*.

⌂ **David Livingstone Safari Lodge** (72 rooms, 4 suites) www.threecities.co.za. This new 4-star lodge, adjacent to The Waterfront on the banks of the Zambezi, is scheduled for completion at the end of 2007. All its rooms will have balconies overlooking the river, while 4 suites will each have a lounge/bar area and a private jacuzzi. Facilities will include a large tropical pool with water feature by the river, a spa & wellness centre, & a restaurant & a bar, as well as state-of-the-art conference facilities & an on-site activity centre. On offer will be daily river cruises

aboard the specially designed 144-seater MV *David Livingstone*, while all local activities that can be booked via their in-house activity centre. $$$$$

⌂ **Royal Livingstone** (173 rooms) Mosi-oa-Tunya Rd; ✆ 021 3321122; f 021 3324558; e falls@sunint.co.za; www.suninternational.com. Opened by the president in 2001, this opulent 5-star hotel situated in extensive grounds is owned by the South African Sun International group. If its broad, low, white frontage is rather disappointing at first glance, inside all is spacious & elegant, with an old-world attention to detail & service. Step outside onto extensive verandas, where sweeping lawns lead to an unparalleled frontage along the Zambezi, the 'smoke' from the falls rising tantalisingly close. A 15-min walk along the river brings you to the falls themselves via the direct access point that is the preserve of the two Sun International hotels, or visitors can be transported on one of the hotel's 'club cars' (golf-cart style). The hotel is in the national park; zebras & giraffe are often seen grazing on the grounds.

All rooms have twin or king-size beds & are fitted with AC, satellite TV, radio, video, safe & phone; 2 rooms are fully equipped for the disabled. Tasteful & comfortable, but on the small side, each room has its own private balcony, & guests have the services of an individual butler. Should all this not be sufficient, there are also 4 suites.

Meals are served either in the excellent à-la-carte restaurant (see page 182), or outside on the veranda, while for a special occasion individual candle-lit dinners on the lawns can be arranged at extra cost. The long, wood-panelled bar has a relaxed, colonial air. Elsewhere on the property is an African boma, crafted in the traditional Zambian manner with seating for up to 350 people, with a smaller riverside boma adjacent for special functions (including weddings) & small groups. The grand swimming pool overlooks the Zambezi & is surrounded by sunloungers. This is a great spot to relax, as are the massage tents along the river frontage (massages approximately US$65 pp; manicures, pedicures & facial treatments also available). On the practical side, the concierge can organise activities from white-water rafting to game drives.

Considerably more expensive than the adjacent Zambezi Sun, the Royal Livingstone caters for a very different market — those seeking traditional standards of décor & service in a truly gracious setting. If you'd like to indulge without the high price of accommodation, consider sundowners on their magnificent riverside deck or taking afternoon tea in the lounge; at about US$20 pp for tea. With a lovely selection of cakes & finger sandwiches on offer, it's highly civilised — though be warned: vervet monkeys are a nuisance, & might try to steal food off your table or balcony, & don't approach the zebras in the grounds. $$$$$

⌂ **Zambezi Sun** (212 rooms) 393 Mosi-oa-Tunya Rd; ⤷ 021 3321122; f 021 3322930; e falls@sunint.co.za; www.suninternational.com. This is the lively 3-star sibling of the Royal Livingstone, & what a contrast. Crenellated walls are more reminiscent of a north African mosque than of southern Africa, their deep desert red contrasting with the Zambian sky. Vervet monkeys, the bane of the staff, cavort through the colourful grounds as if through a children's playground. Although it's close to the falls, there are no views of the river, though all the rooms have a balcony overlooking the extensive lawns. The rooms are very comfortable — the standard of a good international business hotel — but with considerably more flashes of ethnic colour & individuality. Well designed, if rather compact, each has AC, satellite TV, safe, minibar & phone, with a bath & shower in the en-suite bathroom. 2 rooms are adapted for paraplegics.

In addition to the extensive buffet restaurant, there's a relaxed al fresco grill beside the pool that snakes through the grounds, or Squire's Grillhouse adjacent to the activity centre, or Fegos, a simpler Italian café. (You can always book into the posh restaurant next door if you want to feel more formal for a while.) The complex also includes a conference centre, a business centre & a children's club & playground. Ultimately, though, everything hinges on the location. Just a few hundred metres' walk from the lip of the falls & the curio market, & with unrestricted access, the hotel's position is unbeatable. $$$$$; all major credit cards accepted.

⌂ **Songwe Village** (8 thatched huts) m 097 7783053; e reservations@kwando.co.za; www.kwando.co.za. For an entirely different experience, Songwe Village, a joint venture between the local community & what is now Kwando Safaris, promises the cultural experience of staying in an African village-style setting with the service & comfort of a lodge. The 'village' is poised on the edge of 1 of the gorges downstream of the falls, 120m above the Zambezi between Rapids 10 & 12. It's a breathtaking location.

As the crow flies, it's only 5km downstream from the falls, but the road winding through the bush, past small villages & out to the gorge is a 30–45-min drive. Accommodation is in comfortable, thatched huts built in the traditional style. Each has its own

bathroom (showers, flush toilet & washbasin), & commanding views of the gorge. Accentuating the view, 3 huts also have bathtubs overlooking the gorge, & a communal shower & bath facility is available for those that don't.

Zambian hosts welcome visitors into the 'village family' & explain local customs, beliefs & history of the area. Meals, served in the traditional style, allow guests to sample African cuisine like mealie-meal & relish as well as standard fare, & are shared in a central thatched enclosure, called a Ntantaala. There is traditional singing & dancing in the evenings & guests are encouraged to participate if the mood strikes them. Everything tries hard to be authentic, right down to an ox-wagon journey to a small field museum displaying Stone-Age artefacts, some more than 700,000 years old. It's the closest that the visitor can come to experiencing African culture first hand, but with a higher level of comfort.

The area is steeped in archaeological history, & the emphasis is on sharing African culture with visitors. Guided visits are offered to early Stone-Age sites, the 700-year old Mukuni village, the tree where David Livingstone first met the local chief, & various other local historical & cultural sites. The fine balance between authenticity & comfort is well executed & Songwe is ideal for those with a keen interest in experiencing African culture. If that is not your cup of tea, staying at one of the luxury riverside lodges may be better value for money, given that prices are comparable. Kwando Safaris also has 3 tented safari camps in Botswana's Okavango Delta, linking up with Songwe Village to form a popular regional safari circuit. US$350/475 pp sharing/sgl Apr–Nov, US$385 pp Dec–Mar, inc FB, drinks, all cultural activities, drinks, Zambezi River cruise, guided tour of the falls, Mosi-oa-Tunya National Park visit & transfers to/from Livingstone Airport.

⌂ **Taita Falcon Lodge** (6 chalets) ⤷/f 021 3321850; m +263 11 208387; e taita-falcon@zamnet.zm; www.taitafalcon.com. Perched atop the Batoka Gorge, this lodge overlooks Rapids 16 & 17, downstream of the falls. It is a 45-min drive from Livingstone, along the road normally used to bring rafters back from the river. To get there, take the main road from town towards the falls, & then take the well-signposted left turning opposite the entrance to Zambezi Sun. From here it's about 11km of long, winding track through the Mukuni village area. Near the end, you'll pass a turn on the right to Songwe Village. You'll want a 4x4 for this trip during the rains.

The lodge is named after the rare Taita falcon that frequents cliffs & gorges, especially in the Zambezi Valley, & this area is one of the best in Africa for spotting them. They are small (less than 30cm long) with cream to brown underparts – no bars or markings – & a strong, fast style of flight. Look for them especially in the evenings, perhaps trying to catch swallows or bats on the wing. Verreaux's (black) eagles, peregrine falcons & many other raptors & small birds are also resident.

Run by Faan & Anna-Marie Fourie, the lodge is a pleasant, friendly place surrounded by indigenous gardens. Its comfortable, en-suite chalets, named after birds, are open-plan using stone, reeds & local furnishings throughout, & the three-quarter walls, providing light & flow-through ventilation, can be raised to full height if preferred. Thatched roofs with beams, mosi nets draped over beds & a small patio in front blend seamlessly with the natural bush environment. Two can be made up as family rooms, sleeping up to 5; the rest are dbls or trpls.

The camp is particularly notable for a lovely deck beside the bar, overlooking the gorges & river below. Perched on the very edge of the gorge with the raging waters below, Taita's view is breathtaking to say the least. It's a great place to watch rafters from a very safe distance. Despite the fact that the chalets have been set back from the precipice, I'd be wary of letting children run wild here because of the cliffs nearby. The lodge's electricity is from a generator; it also has its own heli-pad, & there's a nice small pool for a dip, encompassed by a tiled patio with adjacent small lawn. Small pathways weave through the bush linking the chalets to the pool, bar & restaurant. The setting is casual & informal; the service friendly & personable.

Activities include guided bush & bird walks, village tours to Nsongwe (which come particularly well recommended), hiking trails in & around the gorge (equipped hikers can do 2–3-day hikes), fishing & mountain biking. Taita Falcon's a good place if you want a remote spot away from it all, & the attention to detail is excellent, but if you want to pop in & out of the falls for activities, it can feel cut off from the epicentre of things. *US$260/312 pp sharing/sgl Apr–Oct, US$216 pp Nov–Mar, all FB. US$345/414 pp Apr–Oct, US$288 pp Nov–Mar, fully inclusive.*

⌂ **Maramba River Lodge** (9 chalets, 6 luxury tents, 10 safari tents, camping) ✆/f 021 3324189; e maramba@zamnet.zm; www.maramba-zambia.com. This well-established lodge & campsite, founded in 1995, is located just 4km from the Victoria Falls

(between the falls & Livingstone town) in the Mosi-oa-Tunya National Park. Situated on the banks of the Maramba River, it is a real oasis in the bush, with green lawns & mature trees, hippos, elephants & birds aplenty. The lodge is excellent for families & individuals, with an activity booking office, pool, children's play area, craft shop, fully licensed bar, restaurant, braai stands & picnic tables. There are also 2 ablution blocks with hot showers for campers.

There are 4 types of accommodation to choose from. The thatched chalets (with 2, 3 or 4 beds) are bright & airy, in a pretty location under the mopane & mahogany trees. Each is en suite & has treated mosquito nets & ceiling fans. Luxury (Landela) safari tents combine lodge comfort with the pleasures of camping. Each of these spacious tents is en suite (with tiled bathroom & open-air shower) & has handcrafted furniture & a small veranda; BBQ facilities are available outside. For campers without their own tents, standard twin-bedded safari tents set under a thatched roof are ideal, with beds, chairs, clothes storage, electricity, BBQs & shared ablutions provided. There's also plenty of space to pitch tents on the manicured lawns, sharing 2 ablution blocks with hot showers & laundry facilities. *Chalet/Landela tent US$105/130 dbl, standard tent US$45/60 dbl, low/high season. Camping US$10 pp, & US$3 per vehicle if power required. No credit cards.*

⌂ **Livingstone Safari Lodge** (11 chalets, camping) m 095 5832168, 097 7403881; e livingstone-lodge@microlink.zm; www.livingstonebushlodge.com. This rambling lodge set amid 8.5ha of open bush is 6km from the centre of Livingstone, & a similar distance from the Falls. To get there, follow Mosi-oa-Tunya Rd towards the falls, & turn left after the Crocodile Park. From here, take the first left-hand track, then it's clearly signposted, almost 1.5km on a good gravel road.

The laid-back approach of this 'love-it-or-hate-it' lodge is epitomised by its eccentric Dutch owner, Tjisse Kamstra, a fount of local knowledge, stories & forthright views. Spurwing geese, 'the most stupid birds in the world', greet the newly arrived. The rustic bar includes a pool table & braai area, & xylophones & drums are temptingly displayed on the terrace. While guests are welcome to try their hand, musicians may be brought in on request: a 3-course dinner costs US$15–17, the latter price including entertainment.

Chalets are secluded & cool, most with high thatched roofs & colourful stencilling on the exterior walls. Six have large tiled en-suite facilities with bath, separate shower & a second shower in a private garden. A further 3 have an en-suite bath or shower, & 2 tin-roofed budget chalets share a bathroom. Families or friends travelling together can choose a chalet with a second smaller bedroom above the bathroom. All have good mosquito nets, coffee- & tea-making facilities, & private verandas Three chalets have a second smaller bedroom above the bathroom ideal for families or friends travelling together but wishing privacy. Asphalt roads link the chalets to the main building where the restaurant, bar & reception are located.

The main campsite has open grassy pitches with electric hook-ups, & plenty of water points. Ablution & laundry facilities are tiled & clean, with hot & cold showers. Two 'deluxe' stands have private shower & toilets. Unusually, the complex is fully accessible to wheelchair users.

A large, secluded swimming pool with waterslide is set away from all buildings. *Standard* $$$, *executive* $$$$. *Cabin US$35. Camping US$6/12 pp (standard/en-suite).*

Stanley Safari Lodge (10 cottages) +33 870 440575 (reservations), m 097 7848615 (lodge emergency no); f +1 206 350 0259; e reservations@stanleysafaris.com; www.stanleysafaris.com. This Belgian-owned luxury lodge was opened in the autumn of 2002. To get there, turn off the main road to the falls almost opposite the Zambezi Sun & continue straight past the large baobab; follow the road round towards Mukuni village. The turning is almost hidden, on the rise of a hill

where you can see the village in the distance; it's a sandy track for which a 4x4 is advisable.

The lodge is set behind a high electric fence, but once inside all is calm & spacious. Large, fairly formal gardens with a central pool face west with sweeping views down towards the Zambezi & the falls in the distance. Behind is the main building, a beautifully designed thatched affair with an open-aspect lounge, bar & dining area, & a 'map room' that deserves to be very popular with guests. Above is a further sitting area, while an innovative wine cellar on a mezzanine floor should be ready soon, allowing candle-lit wine tastings of a range of South African, French & Italian wines.

Stylish open 'cottages', each with a view, are built in a half-moon shape, with king-size or twin beds, a 'loo with a view' & an outside shower & bath. The honeymoon suite has its own plunge pool & fireplace, & those with children will love the family room, with a shallow paddling pool, & a bucket shower set outside around a tree, giving younger children the opportunity to experience in safety the fun of living in the bush. Throughout, the décor is both stylish & comfortable, with good use of wood, stone & natural fabrics, & plenty of space.

The lodge is best suited as a place to chill out, relax & unwind. Activities, excursions & transport are all at extra cost, which can add up quickly if you venture out a lot. *From US$370/400/460 pp sharing, FB, Mar–Feb/Apr, Jun & Nov/Jul–Oct..*

✖ WHERE TO EAT

TAKE-AWAYS AND FAST FOOD There are several take-aways in town, including Wonderbake, one of the best and most popular, plus Kaazmein across the road near the post office and the Hungry Lion on the corner. For a few thousand kwacha, these serve the usual fare of pre-packaged chips, burgers, samosas, sandwiches and soft drinks. They are all in the centre of town, along Mosi-oa-Tunya Road. The new Falls Park shopping centre is a useful source of fast food, too, with branches of Subway and Debonair's Pizza.

If you prefer to sit down, then try Wonderbake itself. Spacious and clean with ample seating, it has a good selection of cool drinks, cakes, pastries, fresh bread and baguettes, soft ice cream, meat pies, samosas, sandwiches and other staples to eat in or take away. Though often crowded, it's convenient, cheap and good. Several of the restaurants below also offer take-aways.

✖ **Nyumi Nyumi Takeaway & Restaurant** m 097 7520699; ⊕ 10.00–20.00 daily. Recently opened place serving good battered hake 'n' chips at Kw14,500, as well as chicken, burgers & pizzas.

⌨ **Wonderbake** In the centre of town next to the Rite Pub & Grill. Serves fresh breads, samosas,

drinks, chicken, cakes, sandwich rolls & ice cream; plus coffees, expressos & cappuccinos should you need a jolt of caffeine. One of the few places in the area with WiFi. A convenient location for a quick snack & a great spot to rendezvous.

RESTAURANTS For a long time most of Livingstone's better places to eat were in the upmarket lodges and hotels, which still remain fine choices though lodges usually cater only to their guests. However, recently more dedicated restaurants have opened up, offering better variety (Indian, Chinese, seafood, etc) at fairly decent prices; this is just a selection. Don't expect to find haute cuisine, as food tends more towards standard pub fare and sustenance rather than fine dining. Here's a small selection of the current favourites, though it's also worth remembering restaurants in the main hotels, which often cater to foreign tastes and have more to offer, albeit at higher prices. For authentic Zambian fare, **Ngoma Zanga** along Mosi-oa-Tunya Road, down in 217 area, is highly recommended for a memorable meal with a great ambience.

✗ **African Visions Café** 125 Mosi-oa-Tunya Rd; ☎ 021 3323668. This gift shop also doubles as a vegetarian restaurant with nice variety & daily specials, inc great lentil wraps, tostadas, salads, vegetable curries & freshly made fruit smoothies. The site has secure parking, plus a garden setting & playground for kids; funky, rustic & recommended.

✗ **Chanters** Lukulu Cres; ☎ 021 3323412; www.chanters-livingstone.com. ⏲ all day. Chanters has one of the most varied & comprehensive menus in town, offering something for everyone, from steaks & bream to a range of pasta & vegetarian dishes. It also serves local specialities. The food is good, & the garden setting attractive. **$$$–$$$$**

✗ **Da-Fusion** Mosi-oa-Tunya Rd; ☎ 021 3322259; ⏲ 10.00 until late. Opposite the post office, near Mini Market (& with a second branch out of the centre), this is a small, family-run restaurant/takeaway. It serves good curries, naan breads, samosas & tandoori chicken, & also pies. It is pleasantly air-conditioned, & usually has special meals designed to suit impecunious backpackers.

✗ **Fez Bar** Kabompo Rd. From Mosi-oa-Tunya Rd, turn at the sign onto Kabompo Rd opposite Afric Trading, a block down from the Total service station. Fez Bar serves snacks, lunch & dinner daily, with standard meals of chicken, burgers, steaks & chips, etc. It has a full satellite TV, & is a popular hang-out in the evenings.

✗ **Funky Munky Pizza Bistro** 214 Mosi-oa-Tunya Rd (within 217 area, half block down from Fawlty Towers); ☎ 021 3320120; ⏲ 07.30–20.30 daily. Funky Munky serves great pizzas (eat in or takeaway), & a variety of low-priced snacks throughout the day. Its casual atmosphere makes it a good place to pop in for a quick bite or cool drink, or to start your day with a full English b/fast.

✗ **Hippos** Behind Fawlty Towers; ☎ 021 3323432. Hippos is a popular spot for visitors & local tour operators who come to unwind after a hard day's rafting, touring or guiding. There are signs for it at the cnr of the Mosi-oa-Tunya & Kazungula roads. Hippos has undergone a complete refurbishment: it now has a bar with plasma screen satellite TV & tables set under a gigantic thatched roof. Its atmosphere is unpretentious & friendly, & there are lots of choices on the menu catering for every taste (try the deep-fried mozzarella with blue cheese, or the crispy chicken wings). *Lunch US$10, dinner US$15.*

✗ **Laughing Dragon** John Hunt Way; m 097 846919; ⏲ daily 11.00–23.00. Set behind the museum, Laughing Dragon serves authentic Szechuan Chinese food, has a full alcohol licence & will also do takeaways. Run by a family of Chinese origin, it has a detailed menu, though much depends on what ingredients are available for them to buy on the day in Livingstone. However, what they do cook is good, & the quantities are generous. Their chow mein is delicious, & one very reliable correspondent described their deep-fried oyster mushrooms as 'too yummy for words'. Expect dinner with several dishes to share to be around US$8–10 each, which is good value for the quantity & quality of the food.

✗ **Ngolide Lodge's Indian Restaurant** ☎ 021 3321091/2; ⏲ daily for lunch 12.30–14.00; dinner 18.30–22.00. Closed Mon. One of the better places to eat in town is this small Indian tandoori restaurant, tucked away at the back of Ngolide Lodge. They boast a chef from Mumbai & offer a good variety of tasty Indian dishes (and a few continental ones as well) — everything from naan bread to lamb curry — & you can also order takeaway. A dinner for 2 with a couple of dishes to share, without drinks, averages about US$30. As it only has a few tables & is popular, do book in advance.

✗ **Ngoma Zanga Zambian Restaurant** Mosi-oa-Tunya Rd, next to Ocean Basket; m 097 9390458; ⏲ lunch & dinner daily. For an authentic taste of Zambia & a meal to remember, you shouldn't miss this delightful restaurant with distinctive African faces along its roadside perimeter. The adventurous can sample the surprisingly tasty fried locusts & mopane worms amongst other seasonal delights. For the more conventional, there are grilled steaks & chicken dishes like 'village' chicken or coconut chicken, & a variety of fresh vegetables prepared the Zambian way. Order a selection of dishes to share (US$9–15 pp), & be sure to try the deep-fried fresh kapenta (tiny sardine-like fresh fish from Lake Kariba) served with lime as a starter. Ngoma Zanga's friendly staff are beautifully attired in African costumes, food is served the traditional way & the restaurant's innovative décor completes the picture. It's not 'staged' as a tourist attraction, the food is delicious & the atmosphere authentic. On evenings & weekends, there is often live music & African dancers providing entertainment. With advance notice, they can even specially arrange for traditional dancers to perform for you during your meal. For a taste & experience of something different, Ngoma Zanga is the place to go.

✕ **Ocean Basket** 82 Mosi-oa-Tunya Rd; ✆ 021 3321274; ◷ 12.00–22.00 daily. A branch of the South African chain, this fish restaurant is located in a restored historical building near the junction of Kazungula Rd. It opened in May 2002 to instant local acclaim – quite an accolade in a landlocked country. One shouldn't forget that the freshest seafood is invariably found closest to the ocean; but still, if you have a hankering for fish or prawns, this is the place. Set inside a large secure courtyard with sprawling lawn & ample parking, it offers dining either inside or out on the wide veranda. Staff are efficient & very friendly & the food, served in large frying pans, is good. Expect to pay US$8–15 pp for dinner.

✕ **Old Drift Restaurant and Bar** Livingstone Royal Golf & Country Club; ✆ 021 3323052; m 0979 374308. ◷ daily. From the town centre, turn onto Akapelwa St, cross the railway line, turn left at the junction towards the police station & then immediate right. Follow the signs. À-la-carte restaurant & bar in the newly renovated, colonial-style clubhouse at the historic Livingstone golf club (see description under activities). Serves excellent food at b/fast, lunch & dinner in a beautiful setting overlooking the golf course. Full English/cont b/fasts cost around US$6.50; main meals (pizzas, sandwiches, burgers, steaks, samosas) **$$–$$$**. Dinners are more extravagant & consequently slightly more expensive but good value overall. There are free snacks & happy hour prices 17.30–18.30 every Fri.

✕ **Rhapsody's** Falls Park Shopping Centre; ✆ 021 3322015; ◷ restaurant 08.30–22.30 daily, bar till late. Standard fare is on offer here: steaks, chicken, vegetarian dishes, salads, & a few oddities such as snails. Generally the food is good, but the service is very slow even when the place is empty. **$$$$**

✕ **Rite Pub & Grill** Mosi-oa-Tunya Rd. Diagonally opposite Barclays Bank, across from Mini Market, this is a pleasant enough place to stop for lunch, dinner or a drink. Individual booths with their own thatched roof are a bit on the dark side, but nevertheless cosy. A fairly standard menu includes pizzas & chips (**$$**), & there's a full bar.

✕ **Royal Livingstone** Sun's flagship hotel has a fabulous restaurant with surprisingly reasonable prices, particularly when compared with the Zambezi Sun next door. It's not cheap but worth splashing out. The setting is lovely – old-world elegance & comfort – the service excellent, & the food certainly the best in town. However, be sure to book in advance; if the hotel is full they don't take outside reservations. Dinner from about US$40 each; lunch about US$30, exc drinks. If you feel like a bit of refined luxury, try the very genteel afternoon tea (about US$20), which includes finger sandwiches & tea cakes.

✕ **Squire's Grillhouse & Action Bar** Located behind the casino in The Falls (alongside the Zambezi Sun), right off Mosi-oa-Tunya Rd; ◷ 11.00–22.00 daily. Squire's is a South African restaurant chain serving decent but standard fare, mostly grilled meat, chicken & fish. It's not terribly cheap, for the quality & quantity provided, though they have a 'happy hour' in the early evening, & some lunch specials, which are better value. Its unprepossessing location is an obvious drawback, & there's noise from the road, but the service is friendly & efficient.

✕ **Zambezi Sun** Off Mosi-oa-Tunya Rd. The buffet restaurant here is wide ranging with a selection of grilled kebabs, burgers, omelettes to order, salads & desserts. (Though it's not cheap at US$25 pp for dinner, there is a big variety on offer.) Alternatively, there's an al fresco grill located alongside the entertainment area at the pool, ideal for light lunches & snacks. It has a fun atmosphere, especially in the afternoons, & tables are set inside & out around a large pool. When there's live music, it's good value for an evening out, but don't expect cordon bleu standards. Within the same complex are Squire's (see above) & Fegos, a small Italian café serving coffees/teas, snacks & light lunches.

✕ **The Zambezi Waterfront** Sichango Rd. The magnificent setting of SafPar's riverside complex (see page 176) makes this a good place to dine. You can enjoy b/fast, lunch or dinner (or a snack) overlooking the Zambezi at affordable prices. The food is good & plentiful with the usual variety of chicken dishes, burgers & chips, soups, sandwiches & daily specials served by friendly staff. There is also a full bar. While it is out of town, it's the kind of place you might go for a meal & stay for hours to savour the riverside ambience.

✗ **Zig Zag** Industrial Rd; 🎧 021 3322814; e zigzag@zamnet.sm; ⏱ 08.00–20.00 daily. Zig Zag is a welcome respite from the hustle & bustle of town. Look for the signpost indicating the turn. Large & inviting, with shady guava, lemon & mango trees, it's a popular place for coffee & cakes, lunch,

or an evening meal. Tremazini – toasted filled pitta bread – makes a welcome change from the usual run of fast food, as do quiches, pasta, nachos & daily specials, all at reasonable prices. There's also a full children's menu, a range of desserts & milkshakes, & a fully licensed bar.

The multi-purpose site was formerly a textile warehouse, & the space is being used to advantage. There's an enticing pool with grassy surround & a changing area for a nominal charge, & a children's play area, useful if you want to keep the kids entertained as you sip your cappuccino.

ENTERTAINMENT AND NIGHTLIFE

Livingstone's nightlife centres largely around dancing and drinking, although the bars at various restaurants (Hippos, The Waterfront, Sun Hotel, Zig Zag, etc) offer a pleasant atmosphere if you simply want to relax and chat. For live music, there's a band at the Zambezi Sun most evenings and at weekends, or at the Rite Pub at weekends only. Traditional dancing can be seen at The Waterfront, though you'll need to check times and dates with them, while at Ngoma Zanga restaurant you can expect music and singing on Friday and Saturday nights, and sometimes also during the week.

Those wishing to dance and partake of the local nightlife should try Eat Rite's open-air disco on Kapondo Street, which moonlights as a nightclub – Steprite Sounds – on Fridays and Saturdays. The New Fairmount Hotel has a popular disco/dance club (and casino), generally jam-packed on weekend nights. In all of these places, the music is loud, you can dance until you drop and, because they can become very rowdy later in the evenings, it's advisable to venture out in a group.

The Fez Bar (see page 181) on Kabombo Road is a lively venue most nights – a favourite hangout for local expats letting off steam after a tough day looking after visitors.

SHOPPING

Bear in mind when paying by credit card that you'll usually be charged 3–5% commission. Be sure to enquire, prior to using your card, about any commission charges.

FOOD AND DRINK There is no shortage of grocers and shops in Livingstone and you can find most things, though you may have to visit several shops, and imported gourmet items are harder to come by and expensive. The Spar Super Store (*Falls Park shopping centre*) is definitely the best choice: clean, bright and well stocked with local and imported produce (from gourmet cheeses to rice-wine vinegar), it has made grocery shopping in Livingstone far easier. Mini Market (*Mosi-oa-Tunya Rd; 🎧 021 3320633*) across from the post office stocks a good supply of fresh fruits and vegetables in addition to all the basics like eggs, milk, cheese, chickens, meats and dry goods. Shoprite (*Kapondo St*) is a large South African supermarket chain with a wider variety of goods, but often at higher prices and with some past the expiry date – and parking is a nightmare. Furthermore, their fruit and vegetables are not very fresh since most have travelled up from South Africa via Lusaka and down to Livingstone. Spar is a better option for a big shop; if you're buying fruits and vegetables only, try the Zambian open-air markets or wheelbarrow marketeers.

Positioned around town and in front of Shoprite, these have fresh tomatoes, onions and other basic fruits and vegetables, and are generally cheaper. Further down the road is Parma Meats with a selection of beef, poultry and pork. Shopper's Butchery (*John Hunt Way*), behind the post office, is also a good choice for meat, and Wonderbake sells lovely fresh-baked bread and staples. For speciality and hard-to-find items, try the new Spar or Sun International Warehouse (*2652 Linda Rd; ℄ 021 3324290*), off Mosi-oa-Tunya Road in the industrial area, beyond Zig Zag, which stocks a wide range of imported goods – from wines and spirits to meat and dairy produce and many canned goods – all highly priced in US$ and some only in bulk.

SOUVENIRS AND CURIOS If you like bargaining and have lots of patience, try the Mukuni Park Curio Market in town, where local artisans, craftsmen and traders sell their wares from makeshift stalls. The entire park is under restoration, receiving a much-needed facelift to include permanent structures for curio vendors. In the meantime, don't be put off by the market's ramshackle appearance. They have a great, if not intriguing, selection of wooden carvings, baskets, souvenirs, curios and crafts – priced according to your negotiating skills. Expect to be bombarded with vendors vying for your attention and business. But with perseverance and good humour you can walk away with some fantastic deals. On weekends look for the informal craft market at Falls Park shopping centre where curio vendors lay out their goods in the parking lot on a more ad hoc basis.

The largest curio market is at the Zambian side of the falls (beside the Falls Museum) with a wider selection of items and even more aggressive salesmen. It can be fun if you have time and enjoy haggling over prices, but frustrating if you are in a hurry. Failing those, one of the following might suit you much better:

African Visions 125 Mosi-oa-Tunya Rd; ℄ 021 3323668; e alishenton@zamnet.zm. Two blocks down from Ocean Basket, opposite 217 in a historical railway house, you'll recognise this shop by its distinctive burglar bars of African faces at the entrance gate. Alongside a selection of textiles, baskets, jewellery, artefacts & Zambian-produced souvenirs you'll find a well-stocked bookshop, selling mainly second-hand books, & a small café that serves filter coffee, milkshakes, homemade cakes, vegetarian meals & light snacks. The playground in the garden provides a welcome diversion for children, giving parents a chance to relax or browse.
Bobbli Gems, Falls Park Shopping Centre; ℄ 021 3323210. If bling is your thing, look no further. Bobbli Gems designs its own jewellery, much of it fashioned from Zambian silver, beads, semi-precious stones & gemstones. Necklaces, earrings & other items are beautifully, if not temptingly, displayed in illuminated glass cabinets. Friendly staff are on hand to answer your questions & help you find that special souvenir, or the resident artisan will work with you to create your own signature piece.
Museum Curio Shop & Art Gallery at the Livingstone Museum. The museum's curio shop showcases Zambian handicrafts & basketware. Art collectors will

enjoy the wide selection of Zambian paintings & art by local artists for purchase – everything from wildlife to people to abstract.
River Gallery, Falls Park shopping centre; ℄ 021 3320069; e rivergallery@zamnet.zm. Opened in 2006, the gallery has a variety of decorative items, gifts & collectables inc paintings & photographs from some of Zambia's best artists, many of them not available elsewhere in town.
Savannah Wood, Falls Park shopping centre; ℄ 021 3320085; www.savannawood.com. Hand-crafted teak furniture, interior furnishings & decorative items.
The Shop that Thunders Between the curio market & Field Museum on the Zambian side of the falls; e theshopthatthunders@zamnet.zm. This shop stocks the usual collection of souvenirs & memorabilia – wall-hangings, basketware, carvings, postcards & gifts. It's convenient if you are at the falls & doesn't involve the haggling required at the adjacent curio market. They also sell cool drinks & snacks.
Studio Africa ℄ 021 3327458; e info@ bushbling.com. If you are a serious collector of or interested in Kuba textiles or artefacts from the DRC, Zambia and Angola, then you should contact this company. They specialise in upmarket & unusual items & also design and make high-quality soft

interior furnishings, using traditional African textiles & artefacts. Buyers can make an appointment to view the wide selection at their private gallery 20km west of town.
The Whole in the Wall 217 area, next to Fawlty Towers; ↘ 021 3324189; e tambao@zamnet.zm.

This small but well-outfitted shop has a good variety of fun & innovative locally produced souvenirs, tending towards smaller & easy-to-carry items like wire animals, keyrings, postcards, maps, T-shirts, handicrafts & gifts.

PHARMACIES For cosmetics, toiletries or medicines there are four good pharmacies with a selection of items as well as insect repellents, beauty products, suncreams, medical supplies, baby supplies, batteries, film and more. Each has a trained pharmacist, who can also offer advice on medications and fill prescriptions. Otherwise, the Spar Super Store in the new Falls Park shopping centre and Shoprite in the centre of town sell a variety of beauty products and the basics.

L F Moore Chemists Akapelwa St; ↘/f 021 3321640; ⊕ 08.00–18.00 Mon–Fri, 08.00–13.00 Sat, 09.30–12.30 Sun/public holidays. Located across from the High Court & bus depot, L F Moore was established in 1936 & is a Livingstone institution. It remains one of the best-stocked chemists in town & with friendly, helpful service; they will go out of their way to assist you.
Link Pharmacy Falls Park Shopping Centre; ↘ 021 3324222; ⊕ 09.00–18.00 Mon–Fri, 09.00–17.00 Sat, 09.00–13.00 Sun. Well-stocked chemist & if they don't have it, they can usually get it for you from their Lusaka store.

Musamu Chemist Mosi-oa-Tunya Rd, between Wonderbake & Rite Pub; ↘ 021 3 323226; after-hours m 0979-276839; e zulunet@microlink.zm; ⊕ 08.00–20.00 daily. Stocks all the requisites.
HK Pharmacy & Photo Studio Mosi-oa-Tunya Rd, near post office; el: 021 3324296; ⊕ 08.30–18.00 Mon–Fri, 08.30–13.00 Sat, 09.00–13.00 Sun. Here, you can get your prescriptions filled & photos developed at the same time. In addition to medicines, they have a wide selection of beauty products, skin creams, perfumes, etc.

OTHER SUPPLIES You can pick up **clothing essentials** at the PEP store (*Mosi-oa-Tunya Rd, opposite Zambia National Commercial Bank*), or at Power Sales, a few doors down from the same bank, though you'll need to be selective. There are also plenty of shops selling a hotchpotch of stuff that includes assorted clothing, mostly from China. Nearly every shop sells a bit of everything so it can become rather a mission (or adventure) to find what you seek. For more fashionable wear try the clothing stores at the new Falls Park shopping centre or at the Sun Hotel, though these will be pricier. For shoes, try Bata, next to Autoworld by Barclays Bank, though both the selection and sizes are rather limited.

Despite its shortcomings on high fashion, Livingstone is a great place to find African wear – brightly coloured shirts, skirts and dresses, some complete with matching caps or headscarves – and garments can often be made to order with a few days' notice. *Chitenje*, the colourful lengths of traditional African cloth, can be found at most of the small Indian shops on the main road and on Kuta Way, one block down, parallel to the main road or at any of the local African markets. Alternatively, take a trip to the large, busy and colourful Maramba Market or – closer to the town centre – the Central or Zimbabwe Market where these vivid fabrics are on sale amid a multitude of stalls selling almost everything you can imagine. For the widest selection of ready-made clothing at reasonable prices, check out the Mukamba Boutique and Tailoring (*John Hunt Way, off Airport Rd: turn by Barclays Bank, go up one block and turn right*), who also have their own tailor.

Emma's Tailoring (*Mosi-oa-Tunya Rd*), on the right a block past 217, can tailor-make anything from clothing to tablecloths, quickly and affordably. Bring your own fabric (bought at a local market or an Indian shop in town) or choose one of hers.

For **dry cleaning or laundry,** try Sun International's warehouse (see above; ☏ *021 3320134,* f *021 3416927*). Clothing is returned within 24 hours and a same-day service is offered for items delivered by 10.00.

For **books** the newly opened Bookworld (*Falls Park Shopping Centre;* ☏ *021 3321414*) has the best stock in Livingstone and also sells stationery, games and the like. Otherwise try African Visions (*Mosi-oa-Tunya Rd*), near 217 area. They sell a good selection of new and second-hand books at reasonable prices. Jollyboys (see page 171) has a book-exchange system, as do many of the accommodations in town. Alternatively, several of the curio shops stock wildlife reference books and regional travel guides.

Current magazines may be harder to come by. Your best bet is at the new Spar at Falls Park shopping centre or Shoprite in town (though be warned, magazines are expensive). Be sure to check the issue date: magazines sold here tend to be several months old. Oddly the street vendors in front of the Capital Theatre often have more recent ones and at much lower prices, but this is very hit-or-miss.

Basic **camera supplies** can be found at the various chemists (see above), but a better bet is the Konica Film Centre on the main road or Kodak Express (*Liso House, next to Finance Bank;* ☏ *021 3320241*). Konica does one-hour photo processing, enlargements and passport photos, and stocks film, photo albums and related supplies. Also recommended is the convenient HK Photo Studio (*Mosi-oa-Tunya Rd*), next to Mo-Money, which sells Agfa film, and Kodak Express; both will process film in an hour.

For cassette tapes and DVDs of popular **music,** including many African selections, try the open-air market at the bottom of Kapondo Street (called 'Zimbabwe' or Central Market). They have a wide selection of cheap (probably bootlegged) cassette tapes (and DVDs and videos too). Follow your ears for blaring music and you'll find a kiosk selling tapes! Often goods will be brought direct to you from one of the many roving salesmen in town selling cassettes, DVDs and other sundries.

If you have **computer** trouble, Falcon Technologies (*Linda Rd, past Zig Zag;* ☏ *021 3322676;* m *097 747707*) offers repair and service and also sells new and used computers.

OTHER PRACTICALITIES

BANKS AND MONEY Livingstone has several major banks and various bureaux de change dotted throughout town. There are also freelance 'money-changers' around Eat Rite and at the border. Unless you are very savvy or desperate, avoid the money-changers. They always take advantage of unsuspecting (and even suspicious) tourists by short-changing them somehow.

You can also change money at many of the lodges and hotels. This is the least favourable exchange rate, but most convenient method. There's an ATM at Barclays Bank, but don't rely on it to have money when you want it.

The major banks are situated around the post office area, parallel to the main road. Most open Monday to Friday 08.00–14.00, but get there early if you want to avoid long queues.

$ **Barclays Bank** ☏ 021 332114/5, 3324196; f 021 3322317. Also has a small branch at Sun's resort complex.

$ **Zambia National Commercial Bank** ☏ 021 3321901, 3320171, 3320995; f 021 3320182

$ **Standard Chartered Bank** ☏ 021 3321743, 3321745; f 021 3321721

Of these, Zambia National Commercial Bank is our favourite with its spacious air-conditioned interior and more private exchange facilities. Barclays tends to be the most crowded with slow service, and money doled out in front of the watchful eyes of everyone else. There are several bureaux de change in Livingstone, many of them close to or opposite Barclays Bank (and one at the Falls Park shopping centre).

Falls Bureau de Change In the post office complex, next to Zamtel Telecom Centre; ☎ 021 3322088; ⏰ 09.00–13.00 & 14.00–17.00 Mon–Fri, 09.00–13.00 Sat.
Mo-Money Ground floor, Stanley Hse, on the main road by the Capital Theatre; ☎ 021 3323431;

⏰ 08.00–17.00 Mon–Fri, 09.00–13.00 Sat/Sun. Consistently has the best rates in town & does not charge commission. Accepts travellers' cheques or cash, & can even do cash advances on your Visa card.

COMMUNICATIONS

Internet Internet cafés have cropped up all around town, including the new one at Falls Park shopping centre. Others include Vuma service station (*Mosi-oa-Tunya Rd*), a fuel station with a small grocery shop between the town and the border; and Thunderbird Investments (see page 166). While rates are low and comparable, the standard of computers, speed and service varies widely, so it's best to enquire before you log on. For those with a laptop, Wonderbake is a WiFi hot zone, so a good place for a cappuccino while you check your emails.

Virtually all places of accommodation offer some kind of internet access though costs and speed vary from place to place Note, though, that high-speed service has yet to come to Livingstone.

Telephone and fax If you need to make phone calls or send/receive faxes, and can't do so where you are staying, then try one of the internet cafés or shops advertising telephone and fax service, such as PostNet (*Mosi-oa-Tunya Rd past the Capital Theatre*), or the post office itself. Alternatively, Zamtel's Public Telecommunications Centre (⏰ *08.00–13.00 & 14.00–17.30 Mon–Fri, 08.00–12.30 Sat, though hours can be erratic*) is conveniently next to the post office in a modular trailer. Phone calls from here within Livingstone are about US$0.20 per minute, but about US$1.20 per minute to elsewhere in Zambia. International calls to Europe, USA and Australia average about US$15 for three minutes. On the other side of the post office, adjacent to the postboxes, is a small office offering international phone and fax. They are open throughout the day, and tend to keep more reliable hours than Zamtel.

Post and courier You can't miss the Livingstone post office (☎ *021 3321400; ⏰ 08.00–17.00 Mon–Fri, 08.00–13.00 Sat*) in the centre of town in a sprawling complex of banks and shops, adjacent to the main road. The post office is also the agent for Western Union (but PostNet is not, despite the sign advertising as such).

FedEx Mosi-oa-Tunya Rd; ☎ 021 3322742. The agent for FedEx ships documents & parcels worldwide.

DHL Mosi-oa-Tunya Hse; ☎ 021 3320044. Located in the centre of town in the big high-rise building on the bottom floor.

MEDICAL EMERGENCIES Medical facilities are limited in Livingstone, and the local hospitals are not up to the standard of those in the West, but in the event of an emergency contact:

SES Speciality Emergency Services, cnr Likute Way & Obote Av; ☎ 021 3322330; emergency control centre ☎ 021 1273302–7; m 097 7740307–8, 095 5772132; e seslivingstone@zamnet.zm. The local

base is staffed with South African-trained paramedics (for details, see page 91). To find the office, turn left on to Obote Av; it is well signposted two blocks up on the left side.

For less serious medical assistance, Sun hotels have a mini-clinic with nurse for their own guests. Alternatively, try:

Dr Shafik's Hospital ✆ 021 3321130 (24 hrs);
📱 095 5863000, 096 6863000, 097 7863000
Health Point (Dr Shanks) Office ✆ 021 3322170;
📱 095 794888; e shanks@zamnet.zm

Southern Medical Centre ✆ 021 3323547, 323786 or
095 797577; e southmed@zamtel.zm

Should you need an optician, head for Falls Park shopping centre. For pharmacies, see page 185.

TRAVEL AGENTS For international airline tickets and fares, your best choice is Southend Travel (*Liso Hse;* ✆ *021 3320773, 320241, 322128;* e *southend@ zamnet.zm;* ⊕ *08.00–17.00 exc 12.30–14.00 Mon–Fri, 08.00–12.30 Sat*), next to Finance Bank along Mosi-oa-Tunya Road. They are agents for 20 different airlines and are able to advise on special air fares. They can book Nationwide, British Airways and SAA flights in and out of Livingstone and other regional or international destinations. Bear in mind when paying by credit card that you'll be charged 5% commission.

VEHICLE REPAIRS The two biggest workshops in town are Foley's Africa (*Industrial Rd;* ✆/f *021 3320888;* e *foleys@zamnet.zm*), near Bundu Adventures, catering for Land Rovers; and Bennett Engineering, also known as Harry's workshop (✆/f *021 3321611, 3322380;* e *bqes@zamnet.zm*), opposite the new Falls Park shopping centre, who service most of the tour-operator vehicles in town. Although both are generally very busy, they are your best bet for more serious problems and employ the most qualified mechanics.

For more basic repairs, contact Fallsway Motors (✆ *021 3321049*) at the corner of Nakatindi Road, or Channa's Motors (✆ *021 3320468*) on the main road just across the railway line. Their facilities are somewhat limited and service can be slow but they can often help get you moving again, barring major problems. For punctures and tyre repairs try the Total fuel station, on the right side of Mosi-oa-Tunya Road as you head up towards the centre of town, or Zambezi Tyre Centre (✆ *021 3324405;* f *021 3324406;* e *zambezityres@zamnet.zm*) on Industrial Road, who sell new tyres at good prices and offer a full range of tyre services from wheel balancing to retreads. If it's parts or vehicle accessories that you need, the most central place is Autoworld (✆ *021 3320264;* f *021 3320265;* e *autoworld@zamtel.zm*) next to Barclays Bank.

WHAT TO SEE AND DO

The falls area has been a major crossroads for travellers for over a hundred years. From the early missionaries and traders, to the backpackers, overland trucks and package tourists of the last few decades – virtually everyone passing through the region from overseas has stopped here. Recently this has created a thriving tourism industry and, apart from simply marvelling at one of the world's greatest waterfalls, there are now lots of ways to occupy yourself. Some are easily booked after you arrive; one or two are better pre-arranged.

The past decade has witnessed a huge shift in the area's atmosphere. Visitors used to be from southern Africa, with perhaps the odd intrepid backpacker and the fortunate few who could afford an upmarket safari. Now the sheer volume of visitors to the falls has increased massively. This increase, especially noticeable in the proportion of younger visitors, has fuelled the rise of more active, adventurous pursuits like white-water rafting, bungee jumping, river-boarding and other thrill-based pastimes.

A genteel cocktail at a luxury hotel is no longer the high point of a visit for most people. You are more likely to return home with vivid memories of the adrenalin rush of shooting rapids in a raft, or the buzz of accelerating head-first towards the Zambezi with only a piece of elastic to save you.

TOUR OPERATORS In a town where tourism is such big business, almost everyone – from hoteliers to car-hire companies to taxi firms – can handle bookings for individual activities. Those listed here are the specialists.

Many companies offer **guided sightseeing tours** around Livingstone, including visits to traditional villages, local markets, museums, the falls, game park and historical sites. If you are staying in one of the lodges, sightseeing tours for guests using their own guides and vehicles are generally included. Bushtracks, Wild Side Tours & Safaris and Bwaato Adventures are popular operators, although there are many others; see below. Of these, Wild Side is run by people who have lived in Livingstone for years, and who understand the place well; it can personalise tours to suit individual requirements. Bwaato Adventures, operating here for ten years, is also well positioned, while Bushtracks is larger, based at Sun International's activity centre and with set trips aimed primarily at Sun's clientele and incentive groups. In all cases, trips are professionally run with competent guides. Most tours can be either stand-alone or in combination with others.

Abseil Africa (Zambia) aka The Zambezi Swing Fawlty Towers; ☎ 021 3321188, +263 11 213835, 213837; e theswing@zamnet.zm; www.thezambeziswing.com. Gorge swinging, abseiling, highwiring and rap-jumping activities at their site atop the 5th gorge on the Zambian side, some 5km from the falls.

African Extreme/Vic Falls Bungi Mosi-oa-Tunya Rd; ☎ 021 3324156 (town), 3324231 (bridge), +263 11 407696; e reservations@shearwater.co.zw; www.shearwateradventures.com. Bungee jumping & bridge tours.

African Queen ☎ 021 3321513; m +263 11 417953; e reservations@livingstonesadventure.com www.theafricanqueen.co.za

Angle Zambia ☎/f 021 3327489; m 097 707829; e anglezam@microlink.zm; www.zambezifishing.com. Operates half-day, full day & multi-day fishing trips with experienced guides.

Batoka Sky Maramba Aerodrome, off Sichango Rd; ☎ 021 3320058; m +263 11 409578; e reservations@livingstonesadventures.co.zm; www.batokasky.com. Turn off Mosi-oa-Tunya Rd at the signpost by Tunya Lodge. Microlights & helicopters for scenic flights over the falls, gorges, game park & upper river.

Bundu Adventures 699 Industrial Rd, off Mosi-oa-Tunya Rd; ☎ 021 3324407; e zambezi@zamnet.zm; www.bundu-adventures.com. Near the railway crossing – look for the sign. Rafting, riverboarding & canoeing.

Bushbling! ☎ 021 3327458; e info@bushbling.com. Owner operated & highly reputable company with 15 years' local experience of advising on regional travel, product development & special assignments for upmarket clients, the media & travel industry.

Bushtracks Africa ☎ 021 3323232; e victoriafalls@bushtracksafrica.com; www.bushtracksafrica.com. Signposted from Mosi-oa-Tunya Rd, Bushtracks is located in a stand-alone complex down past the railway station, just where the railway line crosses the road. One of the best, most reliable tour operators in Livingstone, it's an effective one-stop shop for everything from game drives & river cruises to day trips to Botswana.

Bwaato Adventures New Fairmount Hotel; ☎ 021 3324106; e bwaato@zamnet.zm

Cholwe Adventures Mosi-oa-Tunya Rd, 217 area; ☎ 021 3321044; m 097 7586803; e cholweadv@zamtel.zm; www.cholweadventures.com. Newcomer operating rafting, canoeing & tours plus booking office.

Chundukwa Adventure Trails ☎ 021 3324006; e chundukwa@zamnet.zm

Gwembe Safaris Mosi-oa-Tunya Rd; ☎/f 021 3321733, 321648; e gwemsaf@zamtel.zm; www.gwembesafaris.com. Booking agents, tour operators, & owners of the Crocodile Park, situated 1km along the main rd towards the falls.

Hemingways 021 3320996; m 097 7866492, 7870232; e info@hemingwayszambia.com; www.hemingwayszambia.com. Speciality vehicle hire, day tours, safaris & transfers.

Jet Extreme 021 3321375; e jetx@zamnet.zm, jetextremereservations@zamnet.zm. New-Zealand-style jet-boat trips in the gorge.

Kayak-the-Zambezi, Zigzag; 095 5838408; e kayak@thezambezi.com, sventhunderlord@yahoo.com. For novice & experienced kayakers.

Livingstone's Adventure Group 021 3320058; e reservations@livingstonesadventure.com; www.livingstonesadventure.com. Another convenient one-stop shop for a variety of activities. The group includes Batoka Sky (helicopter & microlights), the *African Queen* & Victoria Falls River Safaris (river cruises), Livingstone Quad Bikes, Victoria Carriage Company (horse trails & carriage rides from Sun International) & Jet Extreme (jet boat trips in gorge).

Livingstone Quad Bike Company Maramba Aerodrome, off Sichango Rd; 021 3320058; m +263 11 409578; e reservations@livingstonesadventure.com; www.batokasky.com, www.livingstonesadventure.com. Quad-bike excursions.

Makora Quest 131 Mosi-oa-Tunya Rd; \/f 021 3320732; e quest@iconnect.zm; www.wildsidesafaris.com. One of Livingstone's top canoe operators, with extensive local knowledge & friendly service.

Nomad African Travel Zambia \/f 021 3327769; m 097 846164, 755429; e nomad@microlink.zm; www.nomadafricantravel.co.uk. Owner-operated tour operator & fully outfitted & professionally guided mobile safaris throughout southern Africa.

Raft Extreme 2 Maambo Way; 021 3324024, 323929; \/f 021 3322370; e grotto@zamnet.zm; www.raftextreme.com. Caters predominantly for white-water rafting groups, with bookings from individuals if there's space.

Safari Par Excellence (SafPar) Zambezi Waterfront & Activity Centre; 021 3320606; m 097 7434143; e zaminfo@safpar.com; www.safpar.com, www.safpar.net, www.zambezisafari.com. One of Livingstone's larger tourism enterprises, 'SafPar' is a one-stop shop for everything you need.

Thunderbird Investments Mosi-oa-Tunya Rd (across from 217); 021 3320331; e thunderbird@microlink.zm. Car & vehicle hire, taxis, transport, tours plus internet cafe & business centre.

Taonga Safaris Sichango Rd; \/f 021 3322508, 3324081; m 097 7795535; e taonga@zamnet.zm; www.thezambezi.com/taonga. On the riverbank next to the Boat Club (off Mosi-oa-Tunya Rd at the Tunya Lodge). Catering mainly to backpackers.

United Air Charters \/f 021 3323095; e uacbookings@microlink.zm; www.uaczam.com. Operates a fleet of helicopters for scenic & charter flights from its spectacular base on Baobab Ridge, to the east of Mosi-oa-Tunya Rd.

UTC 360s Mosi-oa-Tunya Rd next to Heritage Hse; 021 3324413; e utczam@zamnet.zm; www.utctravelplanner.com. Part of a larger group; guided tours & transfers.

Victoria Carriage Co (part of Livingstone's Adventure Group) 021 3320058; e reservations@livingstonesadventure.com; www.batokasky.com. Horse-drawn carriage trips on Sun International property and horse-back riding in the bush near the falls.

Victoria Falls River Safaris Contact via Livingstone's Adventure Group, above. Aluminium 'safari' boats with shade. Can go far beyond the reach of conventional craft.

Wild Side Tours & Safaris 131 Mosi-oa-Tunya Rd; \/f 021 3320732; e wild@iconnect.zm; www.wildsidesafaris.com. Located in a restored railway house in the 217 area; look for the big 'i' sign indicating tourist information. Owner operated, & one of Livingstone's long-time tour companies. Their tour of Livingstone & the surrounding area costs US$54 pp ¹/₂ day, inc entrance fees & refreshments, or US$110 full day, also inc lunch.

VICTORIA FALLS The falls are 1,688m wide and average just over 100m in height. Around 550 million litres (750 million at peak) cascade over the lip every minute, making this one of the world's greatest waterfalls.

Closer inspection shows that this immense curtain of water is interrupted by gaps, where small islands stand on the lip of the falls. These effectively split the falls into smaller waterfalls, which are known as (from west to east) the Devil's Cataract, the Main Falls, the Horseshoe Falls, the Rainbow Falls and the Eastern Cataract.

Around the falls is a genuinely important and interesting rainforest, with plant species (especially ferns) rarely found elsewhere in Zimbabwe or Zambia. These are sustained by the clouds of spray, which blanket the immediate vicinity of the

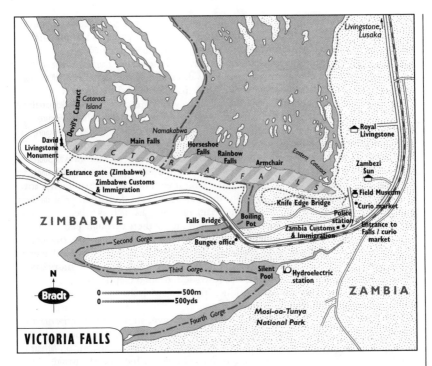

VICTORIA FALLS

falls. You'll also find various monkeys and baboons here, whilst the lush canopy shelters Livingstone's lourie amongst other birds.

The flow, and hence the spray, is greatest just after the end of the rainy season – around March or April, depending upon the rains. It then decreases gradually until about December, when the rains in western Zambia will start to replenish the river. During low water, a light raincoat (available for rent!) is very useful for wandering between the viewpoints on the Zimbabwean side, though it's not necessary in Zambia. However, in high water a raincoat is largely ineffective as the spray blows all around and soaks you in seconds. Anything that you want to keep dry must be wrapped in several layers of plastic or, even better, zip-lock plastic bags.

The falls never seem the same twice, so try to visit several times, under different light conditions. At sunrise, both Danger Point and Knife-edge Point are fascinating – position yourself carefully to see your shadow in the mists, with three concentric rainbows appearing as halos. (Photographers will find polarising filters invaluable in capturing the rainbows on film, as the light from the rainbows at any time of day is polarised.)

Moonlight is another fascinating time, when the falls take on an ethereal glow and the waters blend into one smooth mass which seems frozen over the rocks.

On the Zambian side (*entry US$10 pp; gate ⊕ 06.00–18.00 daily, & evenings at full moon*) viewing the falls could not be easier. If you are touring on your own a good starting point is the small Field Museum directly across from the falls entrance, which provides a good overview of Victoria Falls and the area's fascinating geology. Knowledgeable museum guides are on hand to answer questions and give tours, or you can explore at your leisure. The museum is packed full of informative exhibits and interesting photos on the area's rich archaeology, geology and history, complete with an excavation right in the middle. Cost is included in the falls entrance. One track leads upstream for a while. For photographers, this is best explored in the early morning (ideal for photos as the sun is still behind you and illuminates the falls) or in the late afternoon when you may catch a stunning sunset.

If you visit when the river is at its lowest, towards the end of the dry season, then the channels on the Zambian side may have dried up. While the falls will be less spectacular then, their fascinating geology, normally obscured by spray, is revealed. Every season brings a reason to visit the falls: low water presents a good opportunity to view the rocks, gorge and interesting geology. In recent years, the diversion of water to generate power has been curtailed so the flow of water is more constant with generally some water flowing over the edge on the Zambian side.

The main path leads along the cliff opposite the falls, then across the swaying knife-edge bridge, via scenic points, photo stops and a good vantage point from which to watch bungee jumpers. This finishes at the farthest west of the Zambian viewpoints.

A third path descends right down to the water's edge at the Boiling Pot, which is used as a raft launch-site during the main rafting season. It is a beautiful (but steep) hike down, first navigating big cement steps, then through palm-fringed forest and finally scrambling over boulders, but well worth the long, hot climb back as long as you have good footwear. Take a picnic and relax by the river if you've time (and if you notice a smell of urine, it's probably from the monkeys!).

Viewing the falls by moonlight is not restricted, though elephants wander about occasionally and it is best not to go alone. If you can visit during a full moon then watch for a lunar rainbow, an amazing sight.

While the falls can easily be explored on your own, most tour operators offer excellent guided tours of the falls (both Zimbabwe and Zambia sides) and the surrounding area, either stand-alone or in combination with historical, cultural, game-viewing and other sightseeing tours. These are highly informative with professional guides offering detailed explanations of the formation of the falls and gorges, the river, local history and flora and fauna. Tours cost around US$25–40 per person, including entrance fees.

From the Zimbabwean side, viewing the falls is more regulated. The easiest way to organise this is through a tour operator, who will arrange visas and transfers as well as entry fees (*US$20 pp, payable in cash; no change available*). Alternatively, make an afternoon of it and have tea at the Victoria Falls Hotel. Visiting in the afternoon, when the angle of the sun offers the best views, is ideal.

If you're planning to visit independently, allow at least half a day, and expect a fair delay at the border (⊕ *06.00–22.00*). The cost of a visa depends on nationality. As an indication, US citizens pay US$30 for a single-entry visa; UK citizens US$55. There is a small ticket booth and display at the entrance gate to the falls, which is a few hundred metres from the Zimbabwean border post. Tickets are valid for the whole day, so you can return for no extra cost during the same day.

Technically this area is within the Victoria Falls National Park – and you will find a map of the paths at the entrance. Start at the western end, by Livingstone's statue – inscribed with 'Explorer, Missionary and Liberator', and overlooking the Devil's Cataract.

Visiting the viewpoints in order, next is the Cataract View. If water levels are low, and the spray not too strong, after clambering down quite a steep stairway you will be greeted by views along the canyon of the falls. Climbing back up, wander from one viewpoint to the next, eastwards, and you will eventually reach the slippery-smooth rocks at Danger Point.

Few of these viewpoints have anything more than brushwood fences and low railings to guard the edges – so going close to the edge is not for those with vertigo. Viewing the falls by moonlight is possible by special arrangement.

LIVINGSTONE ISLAND (*Prices inc transfers & park fees. Breezer (full English b/fast) US$45; lunch US$90; afternoon tea US$70 (inc traditional high tea and a full bar with hors d'oeuvres)* Livingstone Island lies in the middle of the great waterfall, and is the island from which Dr Livingstone first viewed the falls. Trips are run exclusively by Tongabezi (see page 174) between July and March (subject to water levels), with guests transferred to the island from the Royal Livingstone launch site by boat. There you'll have the opportunity to take in the scene – gazing over the edge, perhaps taking a thrilling dip in the Devil's Pool right on the falls edge, and having a gourmet meal in an exclusive setting. Several trips are offered daily; choose either morning (called 'breezer'), gourmet lunch or afternoon tea and cocktails. When the water's at its lowest, around October and November, you can sometimes walk across the top of the falls, climbing over rocks, exploring pot-holes and crossing small streams along the way. Strictly speaking, it is not permitted for safety reasons and to keep people from trespassing on the island so this is not encouraged. More than likely, you will be turned back and prohibited from accessing the island. You also run the added risk of being stuck on top of the falls, should water levels unexpectedly rise. If you do venture onto the falls, be aware of the risks, proceed cautiously, stay along the falls' edge and respect the privacy of the island

RIVER CRUISES Floating on the Upper Zambezi with a glass in one hand, and a pair of binoculars in the other, is still a pleasant way to watch the sun go down, even if nowadays the river is full of booze-cruise boats operating round the clock (you can choose from breakfast, lunch, sunset or dinner cruises), and sometimes all congregating close together.

African Queen (*US$44 pp b/fast, 2hr lunch or sunset cruise, inc drinks & canapés*). On the Zambian side, surely the most elegant and leisurely way to experience the river is aboard the *African Queen*, an old-style double-decker riverboat complete with gleaming brass that cruises regally upriver from its dock on the aptly named Royal Mile (the name is derived directly from royalty, in fact, for it was from here that George VI and his entourage took a launch onto the river during their visit in 1947). In the rarified atmosphere on board, guests sip cocktails or soft drinks to the rhythmic accompaniment of xylophones, or marimba, sounding the vessel's imminent departure. As the boat makes its stately way upstream, you take a gentle look around the Zambezi's islands, surrounded by national parks on both sides of the river. You may well spot the odd hippo, crocodile or elephant – or even, if you're very lucky, a white rhino – not to mention numerous birds. Such luxury doesn't come cheap, but the price is inclusive of drinks and a substantial finger buffet and is good value. Lunches and dinners are also of a high standard, giving a memorable and unique dining experience.

Other boats (*Wild Side US$35 pp for sunset or coffee cruise inc drinks & snacks. Others US$20–40 pp*) On the Zambian side, smaller craft plying the same route are organised by Victoria Falls River Safaris, Safari Par Excellence, Bwaato Adventures and Taonga Safaris, the last three the most popular with backpackers, boasting all you can drink. These used to be strictly at sundown, and the drinks were free. Now, though, the booze-cruise boats are often less generous – with drinks bought from a bar on board. However, you can still take a gentle look around the Zambezi's islands, surrounded by national parks on both sides of the river. Away from the crowded waters near the falls, Wild Side Tours & Safaris offers a more serene alternative, 25km upstream. Here you can cruise in solitude, taking in the scenery, prolific birdlife and wildlife along the banks of the Zambezi National Park. Hippos, elephants and crocodiles are commonly seen as well as waterbuck, bushbuck and even buffalo. Victoria Falls River Safaris operate several propeller-free aluminium safari boats in and around the falls area.

FISHING EXCURSIONS (*US$98/110 half/full day inc lunch; multi-day trips upon request*)
Among the angling fraternity, the Zambezi River is synonymous with great fishing for prized tigerfish and Zambezi bream. If you dream of hooking a 'tiger' then a memorable day on the river with a knowledgeable guide leading you to the finest fishing spot can help make it come true. Angle Zambia (see page 189) with excellent local knowledge and friendly, personalised service is highly recommended. Owner-operated by Gerard and Viv Simpson, they run half- and full-day fishing trips in the Upper Zambezi waters, about 30km from Livingstone. Catering to both novice and experienced anglers as well as fly-fishermen, Angle Zambia is well outfitted, with three 6m aluminium boats complete with fish finders, sunshades and radio communications to their base. Trips are fully inclusive of fishing equipment, tackle, boat hire, fuel, transfers, qualified guide and refreshments. For those who prefer fishing from the banks of the river, this can also be organised. The company can also arrange multi-day fishing excursions to Mwandi (about 200km upriver) for world-class angling during the prime fishing season, which runs from June to September.

BIRDWATCHING Birdwatching isn't normally regarded as an adrenalin sport, but with the outstanding avifauna to be found in and around the falls, serious 'twitchers' (as keen birdwatchers are known) might disagree.

Even the casual visitor with little interest will often see fish eagles, Egyptian geese, lots of kingfishers, numerous different bee-eaters, ibis (including sacred), and various other storks, egrets and herons. Meanwhile, avid twitchers will be seeking the more elusive birds like Taita falcon, as they occur only rarely and the Batoka Gorge is certainly one of the best sites to look for them. Rock pratincoles have almost as restricted a distribution (just following the Zambezi), but can often be seen here balancing on boulders by the water's edge and hawking for insects, while African skimmers can be found nesting upon sandy shores of islands. Look in the riverine forest around the falls and you may spot a collared palm thrush rummaging around, and again these are really quite rare birds recorded in only a few areas.

In contrast, African finfoot occur throughout the subcontinent, but are always shy. They prefer slow water, overhung with leafy branches, and they find the upper sections of the Zambezi perfect, so are often seen there if you look when it's quiet.

Bob Stjernstedt, known locally as 'Bob the Birder' (**m** *097 7769333;* **e** *bob@ zamnet.zm; www.birdingwithbob.com*), is one of Zambia's leading ornithologists. He is based in Livingstone and leads guided birdwatching excursions in the area for US$50/100 per half/full day. Alternatively you can arrange a half-day trip with Cliff Sitwala (**m** *097 7747837*), or with a member of the Zambian Ornithological Society, for US$40 per person.

CULTURAL ATTRACTIONS

Museums Given its fascinating history, it is no surprise that Livingstone has several good museums. The main Livingstone Museum is the most important of these, and certainly one of the best in the country.

Museum tours (*1hr tours, inc entry fees & transfers, from US$15 pp with Bwaato Adventures, up to US$32 with Bushtracks*) can be organised to visit the Livingstone Museum or the Railway Museum, or both. Although you can readily visit on your own, an organised tour is an easy alternative, especially as part of a full day's sightseeing trip, with transfer included.

Livingstone Museum (*entry US$5/1 adult/child;* ⊕ *09.00–16.30 daily*) In a prime position on the crest of Mosi-oa-Tunya Road, in the middle of town, Livingstone's main museum has undergone extensive renovation. There are exhibits on the Stone Age, and features on Zambian culture, politics, history, animals and traditional village life in the area. There is also a unique collection of Livingstone's personal possessions and the museum often has special exhibits, of which the witchcraft one is especially interesting, if somewhat hair-raising. Sculpture and paintings by Zambian artists are also displayed and available for sale, as are local handicrafts and curios.

The staff are friendly and knowledgeable and guided tours are included. It is well worth a visit, if only to familiarise yourself with the area and culture. There is also an excellent large relief map depicting the falls and gorges, which puts everything into good perspective.

Railway Museum (*National Heritage Conservation Commission* ❯ *021 3323622;* e *nhccsowe@zamnet.zm*) This specialist museum is now undergoing renovations following a serious fire to restore its collection of beautifully preserved old steam locomotives and memorabilia, including a working 1922 10th Class 156 out of Glasgow, and displays on railway history – appropriate for a town where the railway was built in 1905.

Field Museum (*entry inc falls admission fee; see page 191*) Much smaller than the main museum in town, the Field Museum is directly across from the falls entrance and concentrates on the origin of the falls, and the development of early man here. Packed with informative displays and photos, this small museum gives an excellent overview of the area's geology, archaelogy and history, and there are even guides on hand to answer questions and give tours. Snacks and cold drinks are available in the shop next door.

Markets Livingstone has many colourful local markets, of which Maramba Market is the largest and the most fascinating. At the heart of Livingstone's community, it offers everything from fresh produce to second-hand clothes (called *salaula*), from hand-fashioned metal pots to live chickens, from *chitenges* (the traditional African cloth) to hand-crafted wood furniture and more. Several companies handle market tours (*Makora Quest US$15 pp (1hr); Bwaato Adventures City and Market Tour US$15 pp (2hrs); Bushtracks US$32 pp*).

Craft markets Just inside the Zambian border, next to the Field Museum, is an outstanding curio market. The carvers and traders come mostly from Mukuni village, though the goods come from as far as the Democratic Republic of Congo and Malawi. Mukuni Park, in the centre of town (see page 184), has a similar area of curio vendors. Both are excellent places to buy wood and stone carvings, handicrafts, chessboards, masks, drums, malachite bangles, baskets and the like. There are usually about 20 or 30 individual traders, laying their wares out separately. All compete with one another and vie for your business. The best buys are makenge baskets (these come exclusively from Zambia's Western Province), malachite and heavy wood carvings: hippos, elephants, rhinos, giraffes and smaller statues, often made out of excellent-quality, heavy wood. However, you should consider the ethics of encouraging any further exploitation of hardwoods. Note, too, that some wooden items, especially wooden salad bowls and tall giraffes, are prone to cracking once you get them home due to changes in climate and that very rarely are 'antiques' sold at craft markets anything other than fakes. Unless you have the expertise to tell the difference, it's better to buy such artefacts from a reputable shop in town.

The curio market is a place to bargain hard, and you can expect to hear all sorts of prefabricated stories as to why you should pay more. When you start to pay, you will realise how sophisticated the traders are about their currency conversions, reminding you to double-check any exchange rates. Traders will accept most currencies and sometimes credit cards.

For something rather less demanding, there's an ad-hoc craft and curio market in the car park at the Falls Park shopping centre every Friday, Saturday and Sunday.

Village visits (*Bwaato Adventures Paradise Island Village Tour US$70 (8 hrs) inc transfers, lunch & refreshments. Bushtracks Mukuni Village Tour US$32. Livingstone Quad Bike Company village & bush tour US$90/105/115 for 1¹/₂/2/3 hrs*) The Livingstone Quad Company (Batoka Sky) offers guided quad-bike excursions to outlying villages and the bush. If your heart is set on a more remote village off the beaten path and you have the time, Bwaato Adventures offer a day trip some 45km upriver to one of the rural villages along the Zambezi.

To the east of the falls is **Mukuni village**, a settlement of over 6,000 Leva people. An organised tour here will give you a glimpse of how local people live and work in a traditional setting along with informative explanations. You can visit local huts, view villagers at work, watch curio making and even sample traditional beer and food. However, Mukuni village, with its proximity to the falls and popularity with tour operators, relies heavily on the tourist trade, so tends towards a commercial, rather than authentic, feel, with often relentless though friendly pressure to buy curios made there.

Further afield is **Songwe village** (not to be confused with the lodge of the same name), about a 40-minute drive through the bush, and less commercial as it receives fewer tourists.

Simonga village (m *097 9374550;* ☉ *all day. Kw75,000 pp fully inc for overnight stay, exc transport; day visitors Kw15,000–40,000*) An alternative that's easily accessible for independent visitors, this traditional village some 15km from Livingstone has been welcoming day visitors since 2001, with three traditional huts added in 2005 as tourist accommodation. During a tour of the village, a guide will explain about daily life: culture, housing, agriculture, water supply and medical care. You can see the basic school, watch cultural performances and visit the traditional healer, as well as meet the head lady. For those staying overnight, traditional food is served at breakfast, lunch and dinner, and the village has its own water supply.

To get there from Livingstone, go to Mingongo station along the Kanzungula Road (by taxi Kw10,000), then hitchhike or take a minibus/taxi to the turn off for Simonga Basic School. The fare should be Kw5,000, though *mzungus* may be asked to pay double or more; stand firm! A taxi all the way from Livingstone will cost Kw30,000–40.000. In the village ask for Bernard or the head lady, Inonge.

Historical tour of Livingstone (*Bushtracks US$32 pp; UTC 2¹/₂hr city tour inc market & museum US$25 pp*) Livingstone, the capital of Northern Rhodesia from 1907 to 1935, has a fascinating history marked by many old historical buildings and accented by colourful characters, intriguing tales and a once-vibrant social life. A guided historical tour through town – on foot and by vehicle – will trace the town's history from frontier town to modern-day tourist capital, including the first hospital, school, library, churches, sports clubs, shopping districts, hotel and other historical sites.

Drumming (☎ *021 3321440;* m *097 7388214;* e *thedrummingco@zamcentive.com*) This is the opportunity to learn something about the history and cultural importance of drumming, and to have a go at playing the Djembe drum. Each session lasts an hour.

Crocodile Park (✆ *021 3321733, 3321648;* e *gwembesafaris@zamtel.zm.* *www.gwembesafaris.com; entry US$8;* ⊕ *all year*) Just to the south of Livingstone, the Crocodile Park offers the opportunity to see some huge crocs at close quarters – from behind the safety of a chain-link fence or from covered walkways – and to get some great photographs. Well-informed and friendly guides offer explanations about the behaviour and history of the animals, and feeding times (usually early afternoon) are posted at the entrance. The park has a valuable educational role, with visiting groups from local schools and the wider community learning about these dangerous creatures, and in many cases developing a new-found respect for them. Picnic tables are set in the landscaped grounds,

The adjacent 'reptile park' features some of Zambia's snakes, housed in glass cages. It, hopefully, will be your only chance to see Africa's most dangerous snakes – black mamba, cobra, puff adder – up close and personal; you can even hold the 'safe' snakes to get a feel for them. There is also an activity centre here where visitors can book any of a wide range of activities or go on one of Gwembe's game drives in the Mosi-oa-Tunya National Park (in which case you get free entrance to the Crocodile Park).

SPORTS AND SPAS

Golf The Livingstone Royal Golf and Country Club (✆/f *021 3323052;* m *099 374308;* e *info@livingstonegolf.com; www.livingstonegolf.com*), established in 1908, was once a popular social and sports club (complete with tennis and lawn bowling). It remains a national monument and is the second-oldest golf club in Zambia. To get to the club from the centre of town, turn onto Akapelwa Street, cross the railway line, turn left at the junction towards the central police station, and then immediately right. Follow the signs.

> ### THE LIVINGSTONE GOLF CLUB
>
> The end of June 2006 marked the official reopening of Livingstone Golf Club, one of the oldest clubs in Africa and a Zambian National Heritage Monument. For years, golf was limited to the Elephant Hills course in Zimbabwe, as Livingstone's golf course and facilities had fallen into a state of disrepair. But golf has now returned to Livingstone. The course and clubhouse have undergone a total renovation, breathing new life into a club that was once visited by royalty and was the site of many tournaments. The first nine holes of this par-72, 6,205m parkland-type golf course have been entirely re-landscaped, the fairways and greens replanted with Bermuda and Hybrid Bermuda grass, respectively. The entire property has been fenced, and landscaping work continues with improvements slated for the back nine. Players, visitors, members and non-members are all welcome to play a round of golf on the newly refurbished front nine holes, enjoy a meal in the beautiful Edwardian style clubhouse, or simply relax, drink in hand, on its sweeping veranda. The clubhouse itself was renovated with great care to preserve its teak woodwork and many historical features, and the result speaks for itself – a stunning colonial-style clubhouse with restaurant and bar, in a genteel setting in the heart of Livingstone. The golf club also houses an excellent **gym and fitness centre** with personal trainer in residence. Further renovations on the cards include refurbishing the back nine holes, renovating the old bowling green and building a swimming pool, tennis and squash courts. For the kids there are a trampoline, boules and a wooden climbing frame with swings.
>
> In Livingstone's heyday, the golf club was the epicentre of the city's social life and activities. By the looks of things it will soon be that again. Golf lessons and club hire (left- and right-handed) are available.

8

Massages and pampering When you are exhausted from all the sightseeing, shopping and other diversions, relief is only a phone call away. If your idea of the ultimate massage is in a billowing white tent on the banks of the Zambezi with spray from the falls and hippos as backdrop, then the Royal Livingstone Hotel is the place to go. Its Royal Salon (✆ *021 3321121–7, ext 2546;* ☉ *10.00–19.00 daily*) offers riverside massages (Swedish, aromatherapy, sportsman's, Zambian Ukuchina and more) in stylish tented gazebos, each with one side open to the river and two massage beds. A trained masseuse offers what has to be one of the world's most scenic ways to unwind, though such divine pampering isn't cheap: expect to pay upwards of US$65 per person for an hour. Also available within the salon itself are all the usual spa services: manicures, pedicures, facials, waxing, basic hair care and beauty products, all catering to foreign visitors and priced accordingly. Many of the lodges have trained massage therapists on staff or on call.

In the Falls Park mall, **Salon Namel** (✆ *021 3324272;* e *namelslodge@zamnet.zm*) offers hair and beauty care including massages, manicures, pedicures, facials, haircuts, etc. The salon is rather plain and uninspiring in design but the services are generally good and offer value for money.

THRILLS AND SPILLS The falls area is indisputably *the* adventure capital of southern Africa. There is an amazing and seemingly endless variety of ways to get your shot of adrenalin: white-water rafting, canoeing, bungee jumping, kayaking, abseiling, gorge swinging, riverboarding or simply a flight over the falls.

None comes cheaply. Most are in the US$50–150 range per activity, which adds up quickly. If you wish to do multiple activities, check out the many combination packages on offer. These can be slightly cheaper than booking individually. There are also choices of operator for most of these, so if you book locally, shop around to find something that suits you before you decide. Prices won't vary much, but you will find the true range of what's available. Whatever you plan, expect to sign an indemnity form before your activity starts.

On the Zambian side, construction has been under way on two gorge lifts, a funicular-style railway at Rapid 23 and a single cable car at Rapid 25, to bring clients out of the gorge after rafting trips, with the cost to be included in the activity price. The race is on to see which of these is operational first.

Flight of Angels Named after Livingstone's famous comment, 'Flight of Angels' describes any sightseeing trip over the falls by small aircraft, microlight or helicopter. This is a good way to get a feel for the geography of the area, and is surprisingly worthwhile if you really want to appreciate the falls. If you're arriving from Kasane, or leaving for there, consider combining a sightseeing flight and a flight transfer. Otherwise any of these trips can be readily booked by agents in the area, including:

Light aircraft (*US$123 pp; min 2 people*) If you prefer something more conventional, Livingstone Air Safaris offers scenic flights over the falls in a light aircraft, departing from Livingstone airport.

Microlight (*US$90 pp for 15 mins inc circuits over the falls & a flip over the game park; US$180 for 30 mins, inc safari flight upriver*) This is a totally different experience from a light aircraft: essentially sightseeing from a propeller-powered armchair 500m above the ground. It is only available on the Zambian side and is operated by Batoka Sky out of their Maramba Aerodrome. Microlights take only two people: one pilot, one passenger. Because the passenger sits next to the propeller, cameras cannot be carried for safety reasons. However, you can arrange to be photographed, or even pictured on video, above the falls from a camera fixed to the wing. This is the closest you can come to soaring like a bird over the falls.

The microlights are affected by the slightest turbulence, so when you book a flight in advance, it's best to specify early morning or late afternoon, when conditions are ideal. Transport between the Maramba Aerodrome (about a five-minute drive from the border) and Livingstone or Victoria Falls border is provided.

Helicopter (*Flights typically US$100/200 pp for 15/30 mins, inc transfers from either Livingstone or Victoria Falls*) This is the most expensive way to see the falls, but it is tremendous fun. United Air Charters takes passengers in four-, five- and six-seater helicopters from their aptly named Baobab Ridge just south of town. A 15-minute trip takes in the falls and the national park, or for 30 minutes you will fly over the gorges below the falls as well (you can even stop in the gorge for a one- or two-hour picnic, at extra cost). Alternatively, if you plan to raft, riverboard or ride a jet boat, you can get an exhilarating lift out of the gorge by helicopter – at extra cost of course, but including a scenic flight over the falls and Zambezi gorges. Batoka Sky, based at the Maramba Aerodrome, operate similar flights using a five-seat Squirrel helicopter. Both operators have helicopters designed to give all passengers a good view – though the front seats are on a first-come, first-served basis.

Bungee jumping (*US$90 per jump (no refund if you change your mind); tandem jump US$130. Minimum age 14, but under-18s require attendance of parent or guardian & their signature on the indemnity form. Min/max client weight 40/140kg (88/308lb)*) There's only one company organising bungee jumping: Vic Falls Bungi, an offshoot of the original pioneers from New Zealand, Kiwi Extreme. You jump from the middle of the main bridge between Zambia and Zimbabwe, where the Zambezi is 111m below you. It is among the highest commercial bungee jumps in the world, and not for the nervous. Alternatively, 'tandem' bungee jumps are possible for two people.

You can book in advance, through any of the agencies or directly with Vic Falls Bungi (see *African Extreme*, page 189), or simply turn up at the bridge and pay there. Hours are 9.00–17.00, though at high water they begin at 10.00 due to spray from the falls. Digital pictures (US$10) and videos (US$40) of your jump are available, and there is often a '2 for 1' promotion whereby clients who purchase video or merchandise to the value of US$40 qualify for a complimentary second jump, with the footage added to their tape at no extra cost.

Bridge walks (*US$45 pp, min 2 people*) There's no one better positioned to show you the ins and outs – no, make that ups and downs – of the Victoria Falls Bridge than the bungee folks, whose intimate bridge knowledge will not only fascinate you but have you clambering around and underneath the bridge like a monkey. Vic Falls Bungi now offers bridge tours in which, with safety harness on and accompanied by guide, you have the opportunity to explore its superstructure while hearing all about the bridge's construction and riveting history. While not as adrenalin-charged as bungee jumping, it's still bound to get your heart beating as you navigate your way around the bridge 111m above the Zambezi.

Abseiling, high-wiring and gorge swing (*US$115/95 pp for a full/half day, inc insurance, transfers & snacks. Gorge swing only: US$75/60 dbl/sgl. Flying fox or cable slide only: US$35. ⊕ from 08.00*) A very popular addition to the adventure menu is the Zambezi swing, a cable swing set across the gorge which, together with a 90m-high cable slide (flying fox), abseiling and rap jumps (abseiling forwards) down the side of the gorge, offers daring fun for all ages. These are currently offered only by Abseil Zambia at the top of the fifth gorge on the Zambian side.

The swing is a fixed 135m cable spanning the gorge. Participants are harnessed to ropes attached to the cable's sliding pulley and, after stepping off the cliff face, experience a heart-stopping 53m, three-second free-fall, followed by an exhilarating pendulum-like swing across the gorge, accelerating up to 140km/h (with a pull of roughly 2.5 times gravity) for some two minutes before being lowered to the ground. Described by participants as 'even more thrilling than bungee jumping', it's definitely not for the faint-hearted, though participants as young as eight and as old as 76 have braved it. It's even possible to try it out in tandem.

A slightly tamer alternative is the high wire or flying fox, set on another static cable stretched across the gorge. With harness and pulley, you leap off a platform and 'fly' (slide) across the gorge some 90m above the ground. It can be done in either a sitting or a flying position, and is suitable for children. For more thrills, there are abseiling (rappelling: lowering yourself down a cliff face with a rope while facing inwards) and rap-jumping (facing and jumping forwards), down a 45m cliff at the edge of the gorge. Except for the flying fox, be prepared to hike some 30 minutes out of the gorge after each go.

A full day's activity allows you to go up, down and over the gorge to your heart's content. Lunch, beer and cool drinks are included and sundowners are offered. Videos or floppy disks of your activities are available at extra cost. It's also possible to spend just a half day, or to do any activities on their own.

The site is 5km from the falls. If you're driving yourself, turn off the main road to the falls just before the Zambezi Sun, and follow the signposts.

Upper Zambezi canoeing (*Canoeing US$85/105 for half/full day, with b/fast and lunch on full day. Floating US$75*) Canoeing down the Upper Zambezi is a cool occupation on hot days, and the best way to explore the upper river, its islands and channels. Zimbabwe's Zambezi National Park stretches all along the western shore providing ample opportunity for game viewing, while lodges, farms, villages and bush dot the Zambian side as you head downstream to the upper reaches of the Mosi-oa-Tunya National Park. The silence of canoes makes them ideal for floating up to antelope drinking, elephants feeding or crocodiles basking. Birdlife is prolific – you may hear the cry of the African fish eagle or see pied kingfishers hover and dive. Hippos provide the excitement, and are treated with respect and given lots of space.

There is a variety of options available, from half- to full-day excursions, combo canoeing and game drives, and even overnight camping trips. You'll find any of them generally relaxing, although paddling becomes a bit more strenuous if it's windy. All canoe trips must be accompanied by a licensed river guide. Canoes range from two-seater open-decked kayaks to inflatable 'crocodiles'.

There are some sections of choppy water if you'd like a little more excitement, though it's possible to avoid most of these easily if you wish. Trips concentrating on these shouldn't be confused with the white-water rafting beneath the falls (see below).

For those who'd like the experience but don't want to paddle, canoe operators also run guided 'float' trips known as the Livingstone Drift on the Upper Zambezi. Participants can paddle when they feel like it or simply float downstream on a raft.

No prior canoeing experience is necessary, and once you are used to the water, the better guides will encourage you to concentrate on the wildlife. Lunch is typically served on an island. Trips on the Zambian side are run by Makora Quest, Bundu Adventures and Safari Par Excellence, all of whom also run float trips using rafts. SafPar offers an 'Elephant Encounter' trip combining a half-day canoeing safari, riverside brunch and an opportunity to interact with their elephants used for elephant-back safaris. Both offer a half-day's canoeing (or floating) followed by lunch and a drive in the game park. SafPar also operates overnight trips with the evening spent under the stars on an island opposite Thorntree Lodge, with a full camp set up.

White-water rafting The Zambezi below the falls is one of the world's most renowned stretches of white water. It was the venue for the 1995 World Rafting Championships, and rafting is now very big business here, with keen competition for tourist dollars. (About 50,000 people now go down the river every year, paying about US$90–140 each. You can do the sums.)

Experienced rafters grade rivers from I to VI, according to difficulty. Elsewhere in the world, a normal view of this scale would be:

- Class I   No rapids, flat water.
- Class II   Easy rapids, a float trip. No rafting experience required.
- Class III   Intermediate to advanced rapids. No rafting experience required.
- Class IV   Very difficult rapids. Prior rafting experience highly recommended. No children.
- Class V   For experts only. High chance of flips or swims. No children or beginners.
- Class VI   Impossible to run.

The rapids below the falls are mostly graded IV and V. This isn't surprising when you realise that all the water coming slowly down the Zambezi's 1.7km width is being squeezed through rocky gorges that are often just 50–60m wide.

Fortunately for the rafting companies, most of the rapids here may be very large, but the vast majority of them are not 'technical' to run. This means that they don't need skill to manoeuvre the boat while it is within the rapids, they just require the rafts to be positioned properly before entering each rapid. Hence, despite the grading of these rapids, they allow absolute beginners into virtually all of the rafts. That said, you should think very carefully about committing yourself if you have no experience. Boats do flip over, and the consequences can be severe. It's also important to ensure that your chosen operator will give a thorough safety briefing before departure, explaining what to do in the event of a capsize.

High or low water, and which side of the river? Rafting is offered from both sides of the river by a wide range of companies. Some, like SafPar, operate from both sides.

From July to January, when the water is low, full- or half-day trips leave from the Boiling Pot just below the falls: a spectacular start to the day. (Trips departing from Zimbabwe leave from Rapid 4 at this time of year.) This period, when the river's waves and troughs (or 'drops') are more pronounced, is probably the best time to experience the Zambezi's full glory.

In high-water months (February to July), only half-day trips are offered, starting below Rapid 9 on both sides of the river. Note that when the river is highest its rapids may seem less dramatic, but it is more dangerous, due to the strong whirlpools and undercurrents. If the water is too high, rafting is suspended until it recedes to a safer level.

The trips A typical rafting trip will start with a briefing, covering safety/health issues, giving the plan for the day and answering any questions. Once you reach the 'put-in' at the river, you will be given a short safety/practice session to familiarise yourself with the raft and techniques that will be used to run the rapids. Half-day trips will run about half of the rapids, but a full day is needed to get through all the rapids from 1 to 23. Lunch and cool drinks are included.

It's also possible to organise a multi-day trip of between one and five days with SafPar.

Note that the climb up and out of the gorge at the end can be steep and tiring, especially in hot weather. On the Zambian side, a new 'ecolift' based at Rapid 23 makes this a thing of the past – albeit at a price (though the cost of the lift is included in SafPar's rates). There's also a second 'cable-car' type of lift a little further on. Alternatively, most companies offer a heli–raft combo, whereby you can opt to fly out instead at additional cost. Beyond the obvious advantage of 'taking the easy way out', the heli flight is an exhilarating end to an exciting day, zipping you out of the gorge with a bird's-eye view of the rapids you've just run and the falls as well.

A trained river guide pilots every raft, but you need to decide whether you want to go in an oar boat or in a paddle boat. In an oar boat expect to cling on for dear life, and throw your weight around the raft on demand – but nothing more. Oar boats are generally easier and safer because you rely on the skills of the oarsmen to negotiate the rapids, and you can hang onto the raft at all times. Only occasionally will you have to 'highside' (throw your weight forward) when punching through a big wave.

In a paddle boat the participants provide the power by paddling, while a trained rafting guide positions the boat and yells out commands instructing you what to do. You'll have to listen, and also paddle like crazy through the rapids, remembering when and if you are supposed to be paddling. You can't just hang on! In paddle boats you are an active participant and thus are largely responsible for how successfully you run the rapids. The rafting guide calls commands and positions the boat, but then it's up to you. If your fellow paddlers are not up to it, then expect a difficult ride. Paddle boats have a higher tendency to flip and/or have 'swimmers' (someone thrown out of the boat).

Originally, only oar boats were run on the Zambezi. However nowadays paddle boats have become more popular as rafting companies compete to outdo each other in offering the most exciting rides. There is, of course, a very fine line between striving to be more exciting, and actually becoming more dangerous.

With either option, remember that people often fall out and rafts do capsize. Despite this, safety records are usually cited as excellent. Serious injuries are said to be uncommon and fatalities rare.

Rafting operators (*Half/full-day trips approx US$110/135–140 pp, inc transfers; extras may include gorge lift, meals or snacks, & cool drinks*) All rafting companies offer broadly similar experiences at prices that are invariably identical. To gain a competitive edge, some now offer freebies like dinner and sundowners in their prices, so it's well worth asking around and comparing what's included as this changes from time to time. For example, Raft Extreme and Safari Par Excellence have specials that include breakfast, lunch, sundowners and barbecue dinner in their rates. All offer videos and photos of your trip at additional cost.

Zambian operators include Bundu, Raft Extreme, Safari Par Excellence and newcomer Cholwe Adventures. The rapids are numbered from 1 to 23, starting from the Boiling Pot, so it's easy to make a rough comparison of the trips on offer.

In addition to day trips, there are four-day expeditions that go as far as the proposed Batoka Gorge Dam site, while seven-day expeditions reach the mouth of the Matetsi River. These offer more than the adrenalin of white water, and are the best way of seeing the remote Batoka Gorge, though trips are few and far between.

Riverboarding (*Riverboarding US$125 pp, riverboard & raft combo US$150 pp inc transfers, light b/fast, lunch & sundowner*) For a more up-close and personal encounter with the Zambezi rapids, adrenalin junkies can try their hand at riverboarding (also known as boogie-boarding) or combo riverboarding and rafting. After donning your fins, lifejacket and helmet, you and your foam board (the size of a small surfboard) will have an opportunity to 'surf' the big waves of the Zambezi, after being taught basic skills in a calmer section of the river. A raft accompanies each trip and takes you downstream to the best spots of the day. Here you can try your hand at finding the best 'standing waves' where you can stay still and surf as the water rushes beneath you. Experts can stand, but most will surf on their stomachs. It's thrilling for the fit who swim strongly, but not for the faint of heart. Trips are offered by both Bundu and Safari Par Excellence.

White-water kayaking (*SafPar: tandem kayaking US$135 pp full day, inc transfers, visas & lunch*) Yet another option for white-water enthusiasts is tandem kayaking in the gorge in Topolino Duo Kayaks. Trips are run by Bundu and Safari Par Excellence, in conjunction with their rafting trips for logistics and safety. A qualified kayaker-guide sits in the back, piloting and manoeuvring the kayak through rapids, while you sit in front and assist with paddle power. Kayaking experience is not necessary, but you must be a confident swimmer: kayaks, smaller and lighter than rafts, may capsize in bigger rapids, and although your guide will attempt to right it by executing an 'Eskimo roll', you (and your guide) may have to swim the rest of the rapid.

For experienced kayakers, Kayak-the-Zambezi (see page 190) offers one-day trips below the falls and fully outfitted multi-day expeditions by special arrangement.

Jet boats (*US$90 pp incl gondola lift*) Jet-Extreme, on the Zambian side, runs 30-minute jet-boat trips between Rapids 23 and 27 and operates its own gondola lift for easy access in and out. These promise a thrilling ride, zipping up and down rapids at breakneck speeds, screaming past gorge walls and spinning on flat water. Though criticised as noisy and damaging to the river's tranquil ambience, jet boats are nevertheless highly popular with thrill-seekers, and fun for all.

Horseriding (*Chundukwa Adventure Trails: 1¹/₂/2¹/₂hr ride US$35/45, half day without/with lunch US$65/70, full day with lunch & drinks US$90*) Riding along the Zambezi and through the bush is a wonderful way to experience nature up close. You can choose from rides as short as a couple of hours to half- and full-day trips with lunch along the river and/or through the bush in search of game. Operators offering horse-back safaris are Chundukwa Adventure Trails along the Upper Zambezi, and the Victoria Carriage Company in the area by the falls. Both offer guided trips for all levels in the bush: from novices to more experienced riders.

Would-be polocross players are invited to watch and, if experienced, join in with local teams playing at Chundukwa on Thursday and Sunday afternoons (from about April through September).

Elephant riding (*US$120 half day, plus US$10 park fees, inc transfers & either b/fast/ brunch or sundowners & snacks*) SafPar's Zambezi Elephant Trails, based at Thorntree River Lodge on the Zambezi River, offer the only elephant-back safaris in Zambia. Here you and your *nduna* (the elephant guide) will ride African elephants through the bush and along the river in the upper reaches of the Mosi-oa-Tunya National Park, where you may encounter wild elephant, buffalo, bushbuck or small game.

All the elephants were originally orphaned and raised on family farms, so are comfortable around people, and they are shown great respect and sensitivity. You will have a chance to feed them and interact with them close up, and to see the baby elephant born on site. This is also a chance to learn about elephant issues and conservation efforts in Africa. Advance booking is essential if you have your heart set on this very popular activity!

Quad bikes (*US$55 for 1½hrs at Batoka Land; village & bush tours US$90/105/115 for 1½/2/3hrs; inc refreshments & transfers. Other destinations & tailor-made trips also available*) Guided quad-bike (four-wheel motorbike) excursions are operated by the Livingstone Quad Bike company (see page 190), a joint venture between Batoka Sky and Voyagers. Options include the 'eco-trail' at 'Batoka Land' (starting at Maramba Aerodrome), consisting of 17ha in and around the unfenced portion of the national park, or venturing out into the bush to explore African villages and the landscape by the Zambezi gorges. This is a fun and leisurely way to explore the bush at your own pace, on your own all-terrain vehicle. No experience is required; quad bikes are easy to operate and participants are given an introduction and a chance to practise before heading out on the trail of their choice. All trips are accompanied by a qualified guide.

Segway tours (e *ernest@segway.co.za; general tour US$35, sundowner tour US$30, or US$45 inc walking tour of falls*) This latest introduction to Livingstone's activity circuit sees visitors gliding along laid-out trails on Sun International property to observe wildlife such as giraffe, baboons, zebra, impala and monkeys. No experience is necessary, since coaches are on hand to teach the basics of riding the two-wheeled, stand-on segway. Operated by Bushtracks.

Paintballing (*Zambezi Paintball;* m *097 9993999;* e *zambezipaintball@microlink.zm; US$55 pp*) It was probably only a matter of time before something as urbane as paintballing came to Livingstone, but it's proving popular, with sessions in the morning, midday and afternoon. Equipment is provided, & costs include mineral water & transfers from Livingstone and the Sun International complex.

SAFARIS AROUND THE FALLS AREA
Mosi-oa-Tunya National Park (*Park fee US$10 pp. Guided game drive US$45 pp inc park fees, transfers & refreshments. Bwaato Adventures game walk US$55 pp inc park fees, transfers & drinks; Livingstone Walking Safaris,* ℡ *021 3322267;* e *gecko@zamnet.zm, US$65; Frosia Tours,* m *097 7794870*) Much of the Zambian area around the falls is protected within the Mosi-oa-Tunya National Park, of which 66km² is fenced off. This recently enlarged sanctuary, locally known as 'the game park' is often referred to as MOT National Park. In a few hours' driving you'll probably see most of the common antelope, including some fine giraffe, as well as buffalo and zebra, though only one of its four white rhino had evaded poachers by the end of 2007. More positively, during 2008 they are expected to release roan and sable antelope, hartebeest, a second species of both giraffe and zebra, and further white rhino. Visitors can also visit the old cemetery at Old Drift, Livingstone's first settlement. You can drive yourself around easily, or go with one of the many operators who run trips (see pages 189–90). For the more adventurous, there are also walking safaris, led by licensed safari guides, which – beyond the excitement of tracking game on foot – are an excellent way to learn about the flora and fauna. The best time to go is early in the morning.

Other national parks On the Zimbabwean side of the river, a good section of land is protected within the Victoria Falls National Park. About 6km from Victoria Falls and extending about 40km upstream, Zambezi National Park also borders the river.

For excursions of four or five days, there are a number of superb game parks within easy reach. Some of the local operators (see pages 189–90) run trips from Livingstone, and for backpackers there are usually a few operators running buses or trucks to Windhoek or Maun. Like cut-down overland trips, these often stop at parks on the way. Options include Kafue National Park (see pages 413–36), and Botswana's Chobe National Park.

9

Lake Kariba and the Lower Zambezi

Zambia's border with Zimbabwe is defined by the course of the Zambezi as it slowly meanders towards the Indian Ocean. Below the Victoria Falls, it flows east, sometimes northeast, and today's biggest features of this river are artificial: Lake Kariba, between Zambia and Zimbabwe, and Lake Cabora Bassa, in Mozambique.

Zambia's attractions on Lake Kariba are limited to a few islands in the lake, accessed from Sinazongwe, and perhaps Siavonga, which is a pleasant place to relax. Of the two inhabited islands, Chete is large enough to be a credible wilderness destination with some good wildlife on it, while Chikanka offers access to the lake at a much lower cost, making it accessible for those on a mid-range budget, or even for more affluent backpackers.

Below the wall of Kariba Dam, the Zambezi continues through the hot, low-lying Lower Zambezi Valley and some of the best game viewing in the country. On both sides of the river – Zambian and Zimbabwean – are important national parks. This is also the place to canoe down one of the world's great rivers, whilst game spotting and avoiding the hippos. It should be on every visitor's list of things to do in Zambia.

FROM LIVINGSTONE TO LUSAKA (see also map *Southern Zambia*, page 158)

This main tar road is only 473km, but it seems longer. Despite its many sections that are faultlessly smooth, particularly as far as Mazabuka, there are some rough patches, so allow about six or seven hours for the journey if you're driving yourself, and stick to a safe 80km/h or so. Better still, stop along the way and explore, making Choma's museum top of your list. If you've more time, then detour to Sinazongwe and on to one of Kariba's islands.

Those brave few hitchhikers will find it one of the easiest roads in the country: lots of towns, regularly spaced, and plenty of traffic. The buses are frequent if you get stuck.

Here I've arranged a few brief comments on what you'll find if you're heading towards Lusaka from Livingstone, with suggestions for places to stay en route.

ZIMBA Zimba is the first town reached from Livingstone, after about 76km. It's about 397km to Lusaka and really only notable for having a large local market beside the main road. Aside from a church and a couple of small shops, there's little else to detain you here.

🏠 Where to stay

⅄ Mabula Farm Campsite m 097 7866517. About halfway between Livingstone & Zimba there's a campsite signposted to the east. This is 200m from the road, with has showers & toilets. BBQ packs are available, as are simple meals if you give the staff a little bit of notice. If you're driving north & need to stop, this makes for a more peaceful night than one spent in Livingstone. Other possible places to stay en route are listed under the nearest town. *US$10 pp.*

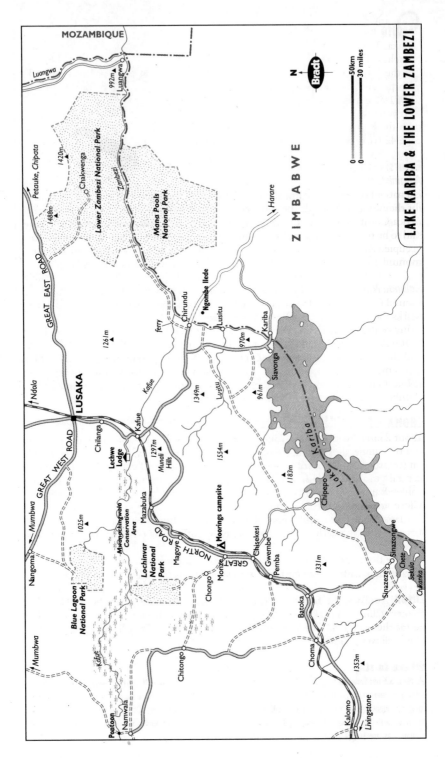

LAKE KARIBA & THE LOWER ZAMBEZI

KALOMO Kalomo is a small town about 126km from Livingstone and 347km from Lusaka. It has a general hospital that serves the whole district, a fuel station, branches of both Barclays and Finance banks, and Catholic and Anglican churches. On the Livingstone side of town you'll find Chris's Guesthouse (no connection with the author), and the main police station. In the centre is the Kalomo Hotel (↘ 021 3265231, 3265300).

If you want to drive into the southern section of Kafue, and have your own 4x4, then the Kalomo Hotel marks where you turn off the main road. See *Chapter 14*, page 429, for details of this route, which passes through the Dumdumwenze gate.

Excursions from Kalomo

Administrator's House Between the centre of Kalomo and its main suburb/township is a national monument, the Administrator's House. This was built around 1903–04 for the Administrator of Northwestern Rhodesia, as appointed by the British South Africa Company. Then Kalomo was the 'capital' of the territory, and the house is said to be the first non-traditional brick house built in Northern Rhodesia. It is now occupied and so not open to the public. As you pass though Kalomo there's a small monument by the roadside to record this history.

Kalundu Mound About 3km north of Kalomo, on the main road, is a slightly raised mound (a matter of just a few metres) of earth through which the road passes. This marks the site of an Iron-Age village, and the mound is the accumulated debris of many centuries of occupation.

It was excavated in the late 1950s and early 1960s when the road was being built, and the archaeologists estimated that it might have been occupied as early as the 4th century AD, although it was certainly full of people from about AD800–1300. (Note that the occupants during this latter period are sometimes referred to by Zambian archaeologists as following the 'Kalomo Tradition'.)

CHOMA Choma (⊕ 16°48.547'S; 026°59.302'E) is another small, friendly town, about 285km from Lusaka and 188km from Livingstone. The main road between the two, here called Livingstone Road, runs through the centre of the town, and on (or just off) it you'll find all the facilities of small-town life: shops, market, cafés, central post office, a couple of petrol stations, and branches of four of the major banks: Barclays, Standard Chartered, Zambia National Commercial and Finance. Close to Barclays, in the same building as the Savanna Café, is an internet café. Perhaps more surprisingly, there's a super little museum (see below). Choma's largest supermarket is a new Spar, which is proving popular in the town. .

North of the town, the occasional craft stall has been set up at the side of the road by the charcoal sellers, and you'll also see local fishermen touting their catch by waving it aggressively in the face of passing cars.

Where to stay There are half-a-dozen very ordinary hotels and so-called lodges on the main road in and near the town, a guesthouse in the suburbs and a couple of excellent spots on farms just outside of town (see also *Nkanga River Conservation Area*, below). These include:

⌂ **New Kalundu Motel** (40 rooms) Livingstone Rd; ↘ 021 3220655. Southwest of town, behind whitewashed walls, lies the New Kalundu (unsurprisingly, it used to be the Kalundu Motel). It's a typical small-town motel with space for cars beside the rooms. ⑤

⌂ **Kozo Lodge** (rondavels, camping) ↘ 021 3220377; e kozo@coppernet.zm. About 5km south of Choma, Kozo Lodge is signposted to the east of the road, across the railway. Simple rondavels sit on a spacious, well-maintained site, where it's also possible to camp. ⑤

🏠 **Riverside Lodge** (25 rooms) ☎ 021 3220131; 📱 097 7747807. Situated 2km to the west of the town, this lodge was opened in 2002. All but 2 rooms are en suite. $

🏠 **Gwembe Safari Lodge** (4 chalets, camping) ☎ 021 3220021, 3220169; f 021 3220119, 3220169; 📱 097 7803292, 7777719; e gwemsaf@zamtel.zm; www.gwembesafaris.com. About 3km southwest of Choma a sign points to Gwembe Safaris, which is 1.5km off the road on the west side. This is a working crocodile farm (transgressors beware) run by the Brooks family. Its en-suite brick chalets with thatched roofs are built around a quadrangle in landscaped gardens. Two of these sleep 4 people & have ceiling fans; the others are twins. All have solid wooden beds, built on the farm, also cane chairs, curtains, & carpets on the floor. Each of the rooms is decorated with local art & baskets made by the Tonga people. If you prefer to be outside, then there's also a campsite under lovely shady trees adjacent to the chalets.

There's an open-sided dining room, with reed mats that roll down to keep in some of the heat when it's cold. Sometimes the staff will put burning braziers inside to keep everyone warm or will light them on the patio outside, which makes a good place to relax.

Activities include ox-cart rides, walking & birdwatching on the 1,000-acre farm, with volleyball & swimming for the more energetic. Dinner is by prior arrangement only & a laundry service is available. $-$$, inc cont b/fast. Camping US$5 pp.

✕ Where to eat

✕ **Savanna Café & Take-Away** ☎ 097 7803292; ⏰ 08.00–17.00. Next to the bus stop on the main road in the centre of town, this is the place for a selection of simple home-cooked meals, from hotdogs & hamburgers to fish 'n' chips or steak, egg & chips. All can be taken away or eaten in clean, landscaped surroundings with secure parking. WiFi & internet available while you wait. $-$$

What to see and do Choma's popular small museum and crafts centre (CMCC, ☎ 021 3220394; 📱 097 9323929; e cmcc@coppernet.zm; chomamuseum.com; ⏰ 09.00–17.00 daily) is on the main road through town. In addition to a collection of regional artefacts, the centre focuses on contemporary crafts and – to a lesser extent – art, showcasing the work of rural craftspeople throughout the area, with a particular emphasis on basketry. Entry is currently free, but an admission fee is under consideration.

NKANGA RIVER CONSERVATION AREA About 5km before Choma, as you approach from Lusaka, there's a signpost on the road to Nkanga, 20km away. There you'll find a conservation area that's been set up covering a number of local farms. It now protects antelope including sable, eland, puku, hartebeest, wildebeest, kudu, tsessebe and many other species. The area is also one of Zambia's important bird areas (IBA), with a total of 439 species noted here, including Zambia's only endemic, Chaplin's barbet, which is perhaps most easily seen in the fig trees around Muckleneuk House.

As it's a conservation area that sustainably manages its populations of native game, some trophy hunting is also conducted, though this never interferes with the photographic visitors.

🏠 Where to stay

🦌 **Nkanga River Conservation Area** (2 cottages, camping) ☎ 021 3225592, 📱 097 7863873; e nansaibm@zamnet.zm. Within the area are en-suite cottages & a basic campsite on the riverbank, with cold showers, toilet & electric lights, as well as firewood & the facility for BBQs. Note that it can become cold down by the river, & do bring mosquito protection. Game drives are available (max 8 people; US$48/vehicle), as are guided walks for game & birdwatching (US$5 pp). Other activities include fishing for bream & barbel (US$12 per group), for which basic equipment is provided, & riding (experienced riders only) for US$12 pp per hour. In addition, Nkanga runs valuable educational bushcamps Apr–Oct for groups of 8–24 children aged 5–18, covering bush knowledge, skills & outdoor activities. Lodge US$60 pp (under 12s US$35), inc FB & laundry. Camping US$6 pp. ⏰ all year. Advance booking essential.

☖ **Masuku Lodge** (6 rondavels) ✆ 021 3225225;
e masuku@zamnet.zm, 760756@zm.celtelplus.com;
www.masukulodgezambia.com. Located on a farm in
the Nkanga River Conservation Area, about 25km from
Choma, Masuku is owned by ex-diplomat Bill Somerset
& his wife, & comes well recommended. Guests stay in
twin-bedded, thatched rondavels, & the lodge overlooks
a vlei which has been dammed to provide a lake.
Much of the farm's game, inc sable & zebra, can be
spotted in the immediate vicinity, where there are
some good walks; game drives can also be arranged.
US$85 pp B&B; US$95 DBB; US$105 FB. ⊕ all year.

BATOKA Little more than a market-lined road with a small post office, Batoka is
significant for visitors as the turn-off for Sinazongwe and Lake Kariba, which is
signposted to the east of the road. It's almost the midway point between
Livingstone (222km) and Lusaka (251km). This isn't a natural choice for
somewhere to stop, but if you're stuck, then camping is advertised at **Batoka
Lodge** to the west of the main road.

PEMBA Another small town, scarcely more than a dot on the map, Pemba is about
261km from Livingstone.

CHISEKESI The linear community of Chisekesi, 270km from Livingstone, boasts a
useful fuel station. Just to the north is the **Mayfair Guesthouse**.
      Chisekesi is the turn-off to Chipepo Harbour and some of the non-commercial
Kariba islands, at a distance of 92km. This is one of the settlement areas of the
Tonga people displaced when the dam was constructed (Siavonga/Lusitu is
another). As a form of compensation, ZESCO and the World Bank are involved
with restoring the 'bottom road' that connects Siavonga, Chipepo, Sinazongwe and
Siameja, all the way down to Sianzovo with its amethyst mines and market. (Stones
are sold illegally here by Senegalese traders known as the Masenesene.) Beyond
Sianzovo the road continues to Syagulula, where there's a women's basket-making
co-operative that is the source of some of the baskets sold at Choma Museum, and
on a further 15km to Devil's Gorge. At present, this is rough going, and you'll need
some large-scale maps of the area, but the scenery is rewarding. A similarly poor
road connects Sianzovo market back to Kalomo.

MONZE Monze (✪ 16°15.436'S; 027°28.588'E) is another small town with little of
note except a fuel station (a second is temporarily closed).

☖ **Where to stay**

⚑ **Moorings Campsite** (chalets, camping) ✆ 03
255049; m 097 7863241; e tsavory@zamnet.zm.
Clearly signposted to the east of the main road, about
11km north of Monze, this is probably the best place
to camp between Livingstone & Lusaka. Opened early
in 2003, the campsite is set in a grassy field on Thea
& Tom Savory's mixed 2,600ha farm, supplementing
their income from cattle, maize & soya. The site is
also well placed for Lochinvar National Park, about
2hrs' drive away. Tom is a keen birdwatcher, so do
ask him about the area's birding potential — keen
birders may spot Chaplin's barbet here.
      Campers at the Moorings can pull up alongside
one of a number of thatched rondavels that are
dotted about the field, each with electric light &
space for a large open fire, for which wood is
available. The ablution block is spotlessly clean &
visitors may use the small kitchen — although Thea
will do home-cooked meals on request. There's also
a large, airy bar area with plenty of chairs.
      Visitors to the campsite are welcome to look
around the farm. Thea originally came to Monze
from the Netherlands to work in the local hospital;
now she runs a medical clinic, primarily for the
farm's permanent workers & their families, for whom
treatment is free; other patients pay a small fee.
Education is of equal importance on the farm, which
effectively has its own primary school. Crucially,
secondary education, too, is partially funded by the
farm.
      Finally, there is the Malambo Women's Craft
Centre, whose primary purpose is to provide work

for the local women, who come to the centre to put together quilts, cushion covers & other items ready for sale at both Ababa House & the monthly Dutch Reformed bazaar in Lusaka (see pages 148 & 154). The centre is also home on Sat afternoons to adult education classes, with English lessons followed by a topic such as cookery or gardening. It all adds up to so much more than a campsite so it's well worth breaking your journey. *Camping US$5 pp; chalets US$30/45 sgl/dbl.* ⊕ *all year.*

Excursions from Monze

Fort Monze 16km to the west of the town is the site of Fort Monze, which was one of the first police posts established in Zambia by the colonial powers. (Access is now only possible in the dry season, and the track is in very poor condition. It's signposted from town.) This post was founded in 1898 by the British South Africa police, led by Major Harding, who was subsequently buried in the cemetery here. The post was demolished soon after, in 1903, by which time the colonial authorities had a much firmer grip on the country. Now all that's left is a rather neglected graveyard and a monument in the shape of a cross.

Lochinvar National Park Lochinvar National Park, northeast of Monze, has been designated by the WWF as a 'Wetland of International Importance' for its very special environment. It's about 48km from Monze, and if you have an equipped 4x4 and some time to explore, then it's well worth a visit. See pages 436–43 for details.

MAZABUKA This large, tree-lined town, 349km from Livingstone and 124km from Lusaka (✪ 15°51.489'S; 027°45.747'E), is at the centre of a very prosperous commercial-farming community. The huge Nakambala Sugar Estates dominate it, and you'll see their fields of mono-culture sugarcane lining the main road either side of town.

⌂ **Where to stay** The perhaps surprising number of simple guesthouses in Mazabuka reflects the importance of the sugar industry to the town's economy. There's little to choose between these and the rather basic motel to the north of town, but you could camp at the Cane Break.

⌂ **40 Winks** (6 rooms) ☎ 021 3230643. Comfortable but very simple. $
⌂ **Mazabuka Motel** (6 chalets) Livingstone Rd; ☎ 021 3230284. 3km north of town, this is a small & quite acceptable stopover, but not at all plush. $-$$
⌂ **Namusa Lodge** (7 rooms) Chachacha Rd; m 097 835392. One of the town's better offerings, with

clean rooms, some of them en suite. To get there, pass Shoprite on your left, then turn right into Chachacha Rd; Namusa is on the left – as are a couple of other guesthouses. $-$$
⋏ **Cane Break Guesthouse** About 3km south of the town, to the west of the road, this is a simple place where you could also stop for a drink or a snack. $, camping US$5.

Other practicalities As the provincial capital, Mazabuka is the most developed of the towns between Livingstone and Lusaka, with a major branch of Shoprite at the junction with the main road from Lusaka, and the good-sized Kontola hypermarket on the roundabout leading south from the town, both of which have their own fast-food outlets. In addition, there are numerous small shops, including a pharmacy.

The town has several 24-hour fuel stations, and branches of Barclays, ZNCB and Stanbic banks, the last with an ATM. There's an internet café, Zelogix, near Shoprite.

Around Mazabuka

Mwanachingwala Conservation Area (m 097 7808743, 7872688; *www.mca-kafueflats.org; entry Kw1,500 pp*) This relatively new conservation area on the Kafue Flats, some 25km north of Mazabuka, covers about 470km² beside the Kafue River, northeast of Lochinvar, and just south of the river. It has been made up of land contributed by the local community of Chief Mwanachingwala, and also some of the private commercial farms in the area, and is rich in birdlife. The area is also home to the Kafue lechwe and the shy sitatunga.

There are currently no facilities for visitors, but those who make the journey are welcome to walk, fish, or hire a mokoro to explore the area's hidden lagoons. Arrangements can also be made to meet Chief Mwanachingwala and to visit his village, or a large, semi-permanent fishing village.

For access, in the dry season only, you'll need a 4x4. Head south of Mazabuka towards Livingstone for around 5km, then turn right on Ghana Road, cross the Kaleya Stream, then after 3km or so take another right to Etebe School. A further 3–4km brings you to a turn off to Mamba Fishing Camp – you're then on the Kafue Flats.

In theory, information about the area is available at the municipal offices in Mazabuka, and this is where arrangements to visit the area should be made. (If you're heading south, turn left turn at the junction by Shoprite, and they're on the left.). However, there's no guarantee that the office will be staffed, so it's safer by far is to check the website for the latest details and to contact them by email before you leave for your trip.

MAZABUKA TO LUSAKA The final stretch of the journey between Livingstone and Lusaka covers a distance of 131km. North of Mazabuka, the road surface has deteriorated significantly, so take particular care on this stretch. The road passes through the Munali Hills, where – 56km north of Mazabuka – there's a sign to **Munali Hills historic site**, a stone cairn 1km along the Munali Pass road commemorating Livingstone's passage through the hill pass that separates the Lusaka high plateau from the Kafue Flats. (Munali, meaning 'you have been' or 'you have passed through', was the nickname given to Livingstone.) This area is also the site of the new **Albidon nickel mine**, an Australian venture on which construction started in 2007. Although it promises to bring new prosperity to the region over a ten-year period, it also – controversially – involves the displacement of scores of people from their land.

Further north, you come to the small town of Kafue, which is the turn-off to Chirundu and the Lower Zambezi, and Siavonga on Lake Kariba. Look out at the junction for roadside stalls selling baskets, from small decorative items to large linen baskets. For details of this road and the town, see *From Lusaka to Chirundu*, page 225.

LAKE KARIBA

Lake Kariba was created by the construction of a huge dam, started in November 1956 and completed in June 1959. It was the largest dam of its time – 579m wide at its crest, 128m high, 13–26m thick – and designed to provide copious hydro-electric power for both Zimbabwe and Zambia. It was a huge undertaking that turned some 280km of the river into around 5,200km² of lake. It has six 100,000kW generators on the Zimbabwean side, and five on the Zambian side – although the electricity generated here is promptly sold to Zimbabwe. The total construction cost was £78 million.

In human terms, construction of the dam immediately displaced thousands of BaTonga villagers, on both sides of the border, and took the lives of 86 workers in the process – around 18 of whom are entombed within the dam's million cubic metres of cement. It has opened up new industries relying on the lake, just as it closed off many possibilities for exploiting the existing rich game areas in that section of the Zambezi Valley.

Heather Chalcraft

According to legend, the name of Kariba should be *kariwa*, 'the trap', for long ago a lake behind the hills broke through and the violent torrent tore out the gorge; when the water subsided it left behind a massive stone slab, the *kariwa*, until it collapsed.

The real trapping of the river took place on 2 December 1958, when the peaceful course that the Zambezi had run for centuries was stopped in its stride. This was the day on which the gap in the wall was closed. Less than 100 years ago, the Kariba Gorge was considered an obstacle to river navigation, for in its 26km the river ran fast. In 1912, a district commissioner visiting from Southern Rhodesia (now Zimbabwe) reported on the potential dam site with a view to irrigation of the Zambezi Valley. Ten years later, it was suggested as a source of hydro-electric power but, as in 1912, there was no money available for this. By 1937 it was recognised that the potential of Zambia's copper mines could not be realised without cheap electrical power but it was only in 1951 that Kariba was recommended as a suitable site for the construction of a dam.

The project was dogged by controversy. A similar scheme had already been suggested on the Kafue River, but the experts backed Kariba as it was the bigger of the schemes. When the announcement was made in March 1955 that the dam was to be built at Kariba there was outrage north of the Zambezi where politicians called it the 'Great Betrayal'.

Finance for the dam, a total of £80 million, came from a variety of sources, including the World Bank, the Colonial Development Corporation, the British South Africa Company and the Rhodesian Federal Government. The closing date for tenders was 17 April 1956 and one tender arrived in Salisbury (now Harare) with only ten minutes to spare – the aircraft with the courier from Italy had been delayed due to a technical fault. Three months later, the main contract for the construction of the dam and south-bank power station was awarded to an Italian firm – Impresit South Africa – at a value of over £25 million. Another Italian-controlled firm, Rhodesia Power Lines, was awarded the contract for the transmission lines at a value of nearly £10 million. The British companies that had tendered for the job were outraged.

It inevitably drowned much wildlife, despite the efforts of Operation Noah to save and relocate some of the animals as the floodwaters rose. However, the lake is now home to rich fish and aquatic life, and several game reserves (and lodges) are thriving on its southern shores.

For the visitor, Zambia's side of the lake is less well developed than Zimbabwe's and lacks a national park, although with the demise of most of Zimbabwe's tourism, this is changing rapidly. Only on its islands, Chete and Chikanka, will you find much game. However, the fishing is very good and the small resorts of Siavonga and Sinazongwe make pleasant places to relax, or to base yourself for outings onto the lake.

There is a commercial ferry in operation between Kariba and Milbibezi, both on the Zimbabwe side; otherwise the only way to go on the lake is to hire your own boat, or to visit one of the islands (see pages 222 and 223–5).

HEALTH AND SAFETY AROUND THE LAKE

Bilharzia Bilharzia is found in Lake Kariba, but only in certain areas. Unfortunately, it isn't possible to pinpoint its whereabouts exactly; but shallow, weedy areas that suit the host snail are likely to harbour the parasites, and you're unlikely to contract bilharzia whilst in deep water in the middle of the lake.

See *Chapter 5*, pages 98–9, for more detailed comments on this disease. Local people who engage in watersports consider it an occupational hazard, and are

One of the earliest contracts awarded, to Costain, was for the construction of Kariba township where those involved in the building of the dam would live for the duration. Original estimates were that the township would take two years to complete, but this was cut down by a third. Work went on for 18 hours a day, seven days a week, with temperatures sitting at 43°C at 22.00 and 32°C at 05.00. Fitters took to carrying tools in buckets of water to prevent them becoming too hot. Houses, from foundations to door locks, were being completed at the rate of three every two days. A bank was built from start to finish in nine days.

The building of the dam was an outstanding engineering feat. A great river which could in the space of a few hours become a raging torrent had to be tamed; the site was remote with no roads leading to or from it; the gorge in which they had to work was narrow; and the temperatures and humidity were high. In November 1956, the first skip of concrete, two tons of it, was poured. This was only the first of nearly three million tons used in the wall – enough to pave a road from Zambia to Russia. On 22 June 1959 the last skip of concrete was released on the curve of the wall by the federal prime minister, Sir Roy Welensky – ten months ahead of schedule despite the floods of 1957 and 1958 when the Zambezi did its best to fight man's intentions.

Meanwhile virgin bush was being cleared to the north for the transmission lines – a job which was started in 1955 and was to take four years. The trees, which would be covered with water, were being pulled down and work was commencing on the south-bank power station. For those who worked at Kariba, they needed no references or testimonials – they only had to say 'I worked at Kariba' and the job was theirs. But there were human tragedies too – a number of people lost their lives during the construction of the dam; some are still buried within the wall. Eight of Chief Chipepo's people who were forcibly being moved to higher ground were killed during violent clashes with the police. And the human tragedies continue for those displaced people …

First published in The Lowdown, January 2004

regularly treated to expel the parasites from their bodies (those who can afford the treatment, that is).

Animal dangers The lake contains good populations of crocodiles, and also a few hippos. Both conspire to make bathing and swimming near the shore unsafe. However, it is generally considered safe to take quick dips in the middle of the lake – often tempting, given Lake Kariba's high temperatures and humidity. The crocodiles have apparently not yet learned how to catch water-skiers.

SIAVONGA
Approaching Siavonga The road to Siavonga (⊕ 16°32.371'S; 28°42.545'E) leaves the main Lusaka–Chirundu road (see page 225) a few kilometres west of the Chirundu Bridge over the Zambezi. From that turn-off, it is some 71km of rolling road (excellent tarmac) to North Bank Guesthouse in Siavonga, mostly through areas of subsistence farming. From Lusaka to Siavonga takes around 2½ hours, or longer while the Chirundu road is being resurfaced. The area is relatively densely populated, largely the result of 'forced migration' when the dam was built and entire villages, such as Lusitu (⊕ 16°08.050'S; 028°44.329'E), which now lies along this road, were relocated. You can expect animals wandering over the road, so drive slowly. While straight after the rains this makes an attractive drive, enhanced by some marvellous ancient baobabs, during a visit I made at the end of the dry

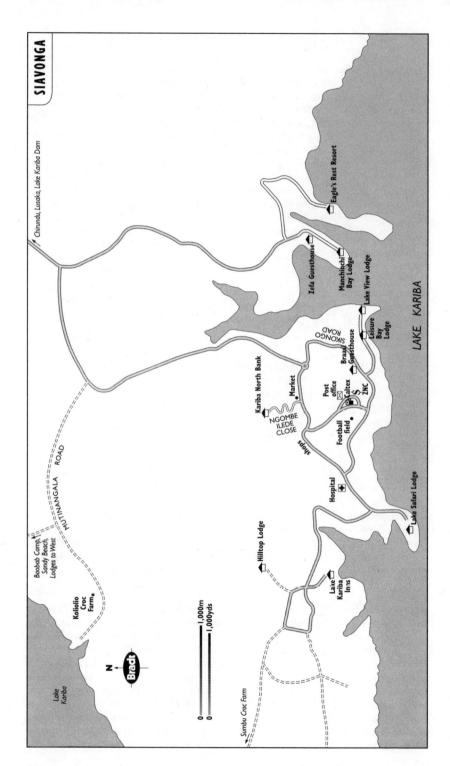

SIAVONGA

Chirundu, Lusaka, Lake Kariba Dam

Baobab Camp,
Sandy Beach,
Lodges to West

MUTINANGALA ROAD

Koliolio
Croc Farm

Lake
Kariba

N

Bradt

0 — 1,000m
0 — 1,000yds

Sumbu Croc Farm

Hilltop Lodge

Lake
Kariba Inns

Hospital

Football field

Lake Safari Lodge

Market

Kariba North Bank

NGOMBE ILEDE CLOSE

shops

Post office

Caltex

$ ZNC

Brazzi Guesthouse

SIKONGO ROAD

Leisure Bay Lodge

Lake View Lodge

Zefa Guesthouse

Manchinchi Bay Lodge

Eagle's Rest Resort

LAKE KARIBA

214

season, the problems of erosion and overgrazing seemed especially bad. Numerous gullies cut through the powdery red soil, there was little green grazing to be seen anywhere, and even the goats were looking thin. It is, though, a good route for roadside stalls – selling a range of baskets from small decorative ones to large linen baskets, as well as numerous pieces of quartz, for which you'll need to be prepared to bargain very hard.

About 15km after the turning off the main road, there's a track to the left (✤ 16°07.948'S; 28°44.290'E) leading to Ngombe Ilede, 'the cow that is lying down', some 13km away. Now designated a national monument, the flat, square, sacred stone lies in a stark landscape devoid of all but baobabs. More details can be found in D W Phillipson's book, *National Monuments of Zambia* (see *Appendix 3*, page 511).

Approaching Siavonga, the road winds its way around the hills in steep spirals, affording some superb views, before finally dropping down into the town, on the edge of Lake Kariba.

Like Kariba, its Zimbabwean neighbour over the dam, Siavonga has a strange layout as the result of being built on the upper sections of three or four hills – the lake's artificially created shore. What started out as a camp for the builders working on the dam in the 1950s eventually developed into a quiet holiday resort. There are a few things to do here, mainly focusing on the lake. The one thing that everyone should try is the local fresh fish (mainly *tilapia* bream) from the dam that is offered by all hotels and lodges.

Getting there and away Minibuses ply the route between here and Lusaka each day, costing Kw10,000 one way. Alternatively you could take a minibus between Lusaka and Chirundu, then hitch from the junction.

Getting around The small town is quite spread out, and the roads curve incessantly, sticking to the sides of the hills on which the town is built. Each of the hotels is tucked away in a different little cove or inlet, and to get from one to another usually involves several kilometres of up-and-down, winding roads. So while you could walk everywhere, you'll find it much easier with your own transport.

Where to stay Siavonga has a surprising amount of accommodation considering its size and relatively few attractions (though the lake itself is a powerful draw). The reason is its proximity to Lusaka – normally just 2¹/₂ hours' drive away – which makes it very convenient for conferences to be held here, the stock trade for almost all Siavonga's hotels. On a quiet night, you can find a good bed at a reasonable price. Because the town is used to the 'packaged' conference trade, check the rates for dinner, bed and breakfast, and full board – these are often good value, especially as there are no sparkling local restaurants to compete. Campers have less choice, but are well catered for at the refurbished Eagle's Rest, although those with their own transport could consider heading out to Sandy Beach. On a practical note, the fact that this is predominantly a business area means that most of the hotels accept credit cards – which is particularly useful as Siavonga's only bank has limited opening hours.

Lakeside

🏠 **Lake Safari Lodge** (54 rooms) ✆ 021 1511148, 1511024; f 021 1511029; e info@lake-safari.com; www.lake-safari.com, www.lakesafari.com. This pleasant hotel is perched on a headland slightly above the lake, with its rooms spread out between its main building & a slipway into the water. For the energetic, the lodge has a gym, an excellent swimming pool & good facilities for watersports: cabin cruisers, speedboats, 'banana' boats, and the kit for waterskiing, windsurfing & paragliding. There's also the larger *African Eagle* (see page 220). Inside, the bar is open most of the time, & popular with locals. Try playing on the 'winner stays on' pool table: an evening's fun for Kw2,000, if you're good with a cue. The kitchen serves good, inexpensive food — inc bream which the hotel farms itself — until late, & the presence of conference guests justifies a business centre with internet.

Rooms vary in size & quality, but all are en suite. Arguably the best are the simple rondavels which are clean, good value & have a great view. Of the rest, all with AC, twin rooms are larger, with DSTV & a ceiling fan, while those that are modernised don't really justify the extra cost, & have little in the way of a view. This is a relaxed, good-value choice for a few days by the lake. *Rondavel Kw180,000/230,000 sgl/dbl; room Kw190,000–250,000/270,000–350,000 sgl/dbl, all B&B. Lunch/dinner Kw60,000 pp.*

🏠 **Lake Kariba Inns** (41 rooms) ☏ 021 1511249, 1511290; m 097 796958; f 021 1511188; e info@karibainns.com; www.karibainns.com, or via Lusaka office ☏ 021 1253768; f 021 1252518; m 097 796958. With its pleasant gardens that afford good views, Lake Kariba Inns is currently the best & most expensive of Siavonga's options yet still good value for money. It's often full of convention participants, however, so it pays to book ahead. All rooms have en-suite shower, AC, & cable TV, while in executive rooms you can expect a small entrance hall, space for 2 children's beds if needed, & a veranda — some overlooking the lake. The food is good & the staff both efficient & attentive.

The main building has a large bar, buffet restaurant, & the requisite pool, as well as a gym & sauna. Guests may use all of these & the pedal boats free of charge, but all other water-based activities, including fishing (from Kw110,000 plus fuel & tackle for 1hr), waterskiing & boat trips, are extra. A steep set of stairs leads down to the water, many metres below, where the inn's boats — *Chipembere, Annelisa & Matusadona* (see page 216) — are usually moored. *Kw396,000–473,000/616,000–704,000 sgl/dbl, B&B, inc short boat cruise. Lunch/dinner Kw60,000 pp.*

🏠 **Manchinchi Bay Lodge** (30 rooms) ☏ 021 1511240; ☏/f 021 1511563. In its heyday, this was Siavonga's plushest place, with the best gardens in town thanks to its extensive manicured lawns, shrubby borders, & a main swimming pool with an adjacent shallow one for children. Since then, the hotel has gone to seed, & the pool is covered with algae, although a new owner has started by putting the gardens to rights. Let's hope that the trend continues. For now, the rooms all have en-suite

shower, AC, DSTV & a private veranda, some with a lake view, making this is a reasonable place to stay if you're pushed. *Kw230,000/290,000 sgl/dbl, B&B.*

🏠 **Leisure Bay Lodge** (20 rooms) ☏ 021 1511136, Lusaka office ☏ 021 1251734; e gardengroup@zamtel.zm; www.gardengroupzambia.com. Nestled in a small cove with sandy beach & thatched umbrellas, the lodge has a large patio restaurant & adjacent bar (with TV) which is often busy with locals — & is a good place to meet people. To the front, a recently built pool is a feature in itself, set in lawns right by the beach. Most of the small twin rooms overlook the lake, & all have AC & en-suite toilet & shower. They're simple but clean — nicer than those at their sister hotels in Lusaka — yet still manage to appear rather dingy. This is also the base for canoe trips run by Vundu Adventures (see page 221). *Kw180,000/250,000 sgl/dbl, B&B; dinner Kw36,000–50,000.*

🏠 **Eagle's Rest Resort** (12 chalets, camping) ☏ 021 1511168; f 021 1511526; e eagles@zamnet.zm; www.eaglesrestresort.com. Eagle's Rest is 10km from the Kariba Dam wall. To find it, turn left at the gate to Manchinchi Lodge, then follow the winding road for about 1km. The only place in Siavonga itself to be geared more to tourists than to conferences, it has recently changed hands & the improvements are marked. Its compact chalets are undergoing renovation, with completion due by end 2007. Each has a dbl bed, AC, fridge & en-suite shower & toilet, while outside is a sheltered area for preparing food, with a sink, & a BBQ stand overlooking the bay. The adjacent campsite is beautifully located & nicely maintained, with ablutions block & points for electricity & water. There's a modest restaurant/bar for b/fast, lunch & evening meals, but much nicer is the lively thatched beach bar, a recent & welcome addition. With its pool & beach volleyball the place is popular with families, who can also take part in canoeing trips, camping on islands, & houseboat cruises. *Chalet Kw175,000 pp B&B; camping Kw30,000 pp.*

🏠 **Zefa Guesthouse** (18 rooms) ☏ 021 1511480. Located on an inlet close to Manchinchi Bay & owned by a former minister of tourism, Mr Hampunda, this lodge is geared more to conference overspills than tourists. To get there, take the turn-off to Manchinchi Bay/Eagle's Rest, go past the Manchinchi turn-off & turn right just before reaching Eagle's Rest. Rooms, each with AC & DSTV, are a cut above most guesthouses in town, but none has a view of the lake. For this, you'll have to go to the restaurant, though even here don't hold your breath. *Kw220,000/250,000 sgl/dbl, B&B.*

In town

⌂ **Bhaasi Guesthouse** m 097 7960526. This simple guesthouse has both en-suite rooms & those sharing facilities. *Kw80–120,000 dbl; b/fast Kw20,000.*

⌂ **Hilltop Lodge** (9 rooms) ☎ 021 1511520. About 1km up a steep 4x4 track leading from Lake Kariba Inns, this new guesthouse has sweeping views across the lake from the bar and terrace. Rooms – the better ones en suite – are very simple, & sadly with no view. *Kw120,000–160,000/ 140,000–180,000 sgl/dbl B&B.*

⌂ **Kariba North Bank Guesthouse** (9 rooms) ☎ 021 1511197; f 021 1511425; e karno@ zamnet.zm. This pleasant guesthouse located high on a hill overlooking the town & lake was once for government staff only but is now open to the public; most of its clients are civil servants, business people & conference overspills. Mrs Mziba, the manager, keeps the place in good order. Rooms are very well appointed & spotlessly clean, each with a balcony, albeit with high walls so there is no view of the lake except from the suites. These, though, are huge, plush affairs with heavy drapes & heart-shaped beds – truly amazing! The kitchen's output is modest by comparison, offering typical government-guesthouse fare (chicken/beef/fish with rice/nshima/chips). *Standard Kw218,000/377,927 sgl/dbl, suite Kw282,282/477,191 sgl/dbl, all B&B; lunch/dinner Kw32,313–45,238.*

Other places in town are little more than adequate. They include **Chimutuzi Guesthouse** (☎ 021 1511381) which is near the football field and has a difficult/rocky access; and the government-run **Lake View Lodge** (☎ 021 1511102, 1511168) which is usable at a pinch.

West of town Sandy Beach Safari Lodge has operated in this area for several years, but in 2007 several new options were set to open along the coast. To reach these, take the turning to the west about 2km north of Siavonga (⊕ 16º24.290'S; 028º43.763'E). It's a very rough track, for which a high-clearance vehicle is essential, and a 4x4 in the rainy season.

▲ **Baobab Camp** The first campsite you come to, 14km from the turn off, Baobab Camp is owned by two sisters & was opening in 2007, though contact details & rates were not available at the time of research. It is marked by a sign stating 'Baobab Grocery' hung on a huge baobab tree just at its entrance.

⌂ **Sandy Beach Safari Lodge** (8 rooms) m 095 5446263, 095 5824444; e sandybeach@uunet.zm, herman@sandy-beach.net; www.sandy-beach.net (⊕ 16º29.240'S; 28º39.874'E) It's a somewhat Bohemian affair, this lodge, a motley collection of chalets set on a wide, red-sand beach with views south across the lake. German owner Herman & his nephew Alex share a decidedly laid-back approach. Come for the location, the tranquillity or perhaps to indulge in the multitude of activities (canoeing, windsurfing, sailing, hiking trails, abseiling & even diving are on offer, depending on your experience), but don't expect any frills. To find it, continue past Baobab Camp (above) for a further 2km, & it's signposted on the right. Chalets range from the basic to the simple, but all are adequate, with a fan & – in some cases – an en-suite shower; a family room was under construction in 2007. Camping is possible, too, with campers using a shower & toilet in one of the rooms, or visitors can arrange to camp on Banana Island across the lake. *Kw225,000/265,000 pp sharing/sgl FB, Kw195,000 per room, b/fast extra (Kw30,000); camping Kw30,000.*

⌂ **Fisherman's Cove** (13 rooms) ☎ 021 1210115, 1260055; f 021 1262110; m 097 803798; e cmuzariri@yahoo.com. At the western end of Sandy Beach, with mature trees for shade & a large pool fronting the beach, this new lodge was poised to open when visited in spring 2007. It appears to be aiming predominantly for the conference market, yet its location a good 40 mins' bumpy drive from Siavonga would suggest that the leisure market is the more likely. En-suite rooms are individually kitted out in a motley range of styles, with fans & mosquito nets. Some are larger or more modern in décor than others, or have a lake view, but all are the same price. There's a restaurant & a couple of bars, while activities centre on boating & fishing. *Kw360,000 dbl, DBB.*

⌂ **Butete Bay** (chalets, camping) m 097 7713752, 7791078: e 713752@zm.celtelplus.com. The small fishing camp in Siavonga's Gwena area is run by Iain & Trish Kennedy & overlooks a bay thick with

Heather Chalcraft

Kapenta (*Limnothrissa miodon*) fishing is an important commercial enterprise on Lake Kariba, giving a living to a significant number of people around the lake. It first came to the towns and cities of Zambia from Lake Tanganyika, although as early as 1860 the explorer Richard Burton had described the use of circular nets lowered from a canoe to catch fish attracted by the light of an *mbaula* (a wood-fired brazier). Today, kapenta rigs have enormous lights on the surface and are fitted with the same circular nets, although they are much larger, and the lights are lowered into the water. The lights attract the fish and, when there are sufficient numbers, the net is lifted to the surface with the catch.

The possibility of introducing kapenta into Lake Kariba was considered as early as 1956, although the first experimental attempts began in 1952. Under the supervision of Dr George Coulter, Senior Fisheries Officer in the then Northern Rhodesia, a brood of sardine fry of the genus *Limnothrissa* was netted near Mpulungu and placed into two galvanised-iron transport tanks. They all died within five hours. It was decided that this was probably due to mechanical injury, so a method was used whereby the fry were caught in a large polythene net and placed in polythene bags. This resulted in a greater survival rate, although mortality was still high. However, some individual fry had survived and were growing beyond the maximum transportation size. Thus a trial run to Kariba was attempted. On the morning of 25 February 1953, 350 fry were caught and transferred to polythene bags which were then stored in insulated metal containers. These were transported by road to Abercorn (now Mbala) Airport, by air to Kariba Airport and by road to the lakeshore.

At Kariba, 7½ hours after capture, 45% of the fry had survived. Half of these were introduced immediately to a lakeside storage dam where they all died within a few minutes, possibly because of a difference in water temperatures. The next day only 14 of the original 350 were still alive. These were placed in a keep-net in the lake where they lived and grew for more than three months until a storm wrecked the net and the fry escaped into the lake. Albeit accidentally, the first introduction of sardines to Lake Kariba had taken place.

But it was still not known whether they would find conditions suitable for breeding, nor which of the two species involved would be the better. Investigations were carried out and by September 1966 it was decided that *Limnothrissa miodon*, the larger, less specialised species, would be the one. *Limnothrissa miodon* was known to grow to 17cm in Lake Tanganyika and did not require such deep water for laying its eggs as the other species. Further experiments on the catching, handling, keeping and transportation of the sardines were also undertaken and a trial flight involving 12,000 sardine fry was made to Sinazongwe. About 50% of the fry survived.

the skeletal branches of drowned trees. It's popular with groups, who can cook for themselves (freezer space is available), or have their own food cooked by the staff; alternatively, meals can be provided. Each thatched chalet is built on a stone platform with simple dbl or twin beds, & a shower room at the rear; the front can be left open with views of the lake. Campers have their own cooking area, plus hot & cold showers. Outside there's a plunge pool for cooling off. Activities inc boat hire, fishing, bush walks and village visits. *US$40 pp self-catering, US$50 pp with brunch, US$65 pp FB; camping US$10 pp.*

🏠 **Lotri Bay Lodge** (chalets, rooms, camping) m 097 7600531, 7455422, 7889284. In a fine gorge location west of Butete Bay, this is another place with options for either self-catering or full catering. En-suite chalets accommodate up to 4 people in each, with a kitchen & gas stove. Rooms, too, can take up to 4, in bunk beds with shared facilities, while the campsite has space for 3 groups. If self-catering doesn't suit, there's a restaurant & bar serving home-cooked meals. Water enthusiasts can hire a catamaran or splash out on a 4-berth yacht, *Dadulmanzi*, complete with skipper.

Between July and November 1967, approximately 250,000 sardine fry were released into Lake Kariba from Lake Tanganyika, involving 26 airlifts. The following year, a second series of flights took place and over 120,000 sardines were released.

In Lake Tanganyika the fry were located in the shallows and herded with hoop-nets into a funnel and then into plastic containers. When sufficient numbers had been caught they were transported to Mbala and flown to the Fisheries Training Camp at Sinazongwe, where they were loaded into a twin-hulled boat and set free in the lake. Thereafter it was a matter of wait and see, but hopes of success were high. In 1969 fish of varying sizes were caught and identified as kapenta, suggesting that they had not only survived but also bred in their new environment. The Kariba kapenta grew much smaller than the Tanganyika ones, reaching sexual maturity before a length of 5cm and rarely growing beyond 6cm.

The first attempts to catch the kapenta were made using banana boats, lights and scoop, and lift nets. The catches were not spectacular but large numbers of fish could be seen under the lights, and by the end of the first year some had been caught 64km east of Sinazongwe.

Since the declaration of UDI (Ian Smith's Unilateral Declaration of Independence) in 1965, communication between the Zambian and Rhodesian (Zimbabwean) sides of Kariba had been virtually non-existent and Rhodesian biologists were unaware of the introduction of kapenta into Kariba. In June 1969 they found a strange fish inside the stomach of a tigerfish, caught in the Sanyati Basin, 210km west of Sinazongwe. On closer examination it was found to be a kapenta.

Commercial fishing of kapenta started on the Rhodesian side in 1976 and on the Zambian side in the early 1980s, after Zimbabwe's independence. At night one can see the flickering lights across the dark waters of Lake Kariba. These are the fishing rigs at work. Catches are seasonal as during the summer months the kapenta move inshore to breed in protected bays. Commercial catches rise again after March when the adults return to open waters. However, if the rain has been poor, there is less food for them, which means poor harvests for fisherfolk (and for the fish and birds which feed on them).

But it is not only on Lake Kariba that man, fish and birds benefit from this 'silver gold'. These hardy little fish are sucked into the turbines and spewed into the stilling pool below the dam. They survive, only to fall prey to the hundreds of tern and kingfishers that are waiting for their dazed emergence at the dam's tailrace. Survivors have even made the 220km journey through a river devoid of plankton and infested with predators, to establish new shoals in Lake Cahora Bassa in Mozambique.

First published in The Lowdown, *January 2004*

🏠 **Village Point** (4 chalets, camping) m 097 9523572, 9278676; e mail@jamiehope.com; www.chiboola-lodges.com, www.village-point.com. Designed & built by Jamie & Vanessa Hope, this upmarket lodge opened in 2007 & is definitely for the more hedonistic of bush lovers. Set in 20ha on a peninsula in Lotri Bay, it is 40km west of Siavonga, or 30 mins by speedboat. Tall chalets are perched above the lake with an open-fronted upper storey under thatch to make the most of the breeze — and the views. There's also a campsite, with tents available to hire. Dinner is served outside under the stars. To balance some excellent fishing, walking & birdwatching opportunities, the lodge offers village tours & will in time be adding a spa. *Kw300,000 pp FB, exc drinks. Camping Kw20,000 pp, or Kw40,000 with hired tent.*

Other practicalities Siavonga is quite a sleepy, relaxed place but it does have a post office, a few shops and a ZNCB bank (⊕ *08.15–14.30 Mon–Fri, 08.15–12.00 Sat*), albeit with no ATM. These, together with the civic centre (which includes a police station and a courtroom), form the 'town centre' which is perched on one of the hills, close to the only fuel station.

For shopping, a simple supermarket and a bakery stock the basics, while fresh produce can be found at one of the town's two markets.

What to see and do Most of the activities in Siavonga revolve around the lake: boating, fishing and watersports – note the comments on safety on pages 212–13.

Watersports For windsurfing, paragliding or waterskiing, try Lake Safari Lodge and Manchinchi Bay, which both have equipment.

Lake/sundowner cruises These cruises are offered by Eagle's Rest, Lake Kariba Inns and Lake Safari Lodge. The cost is about Kw130,000/hr.

Houseboats/fishing trips There are several options for hiring boats or pontoons (essentially floating platforms) in Siavonga (and one in Sinazongwe; see page 222). Rental prices for houseboats are around Kw1.3 million per day. Individual boats may be hired direct, as follows:

Bateleur (12 berth) Contact via Eagle's Rest (page 216). A relatively large boat offering sunset cruises, as well as day & overnight trips. Day trip Kw600,000 (up to 15 people); overnight Kw2,000,000 per night, plus Kw185,000 pp per day for catering.

Matusadona (6 berth) Contact via Lake Kariba Inns (page 216). A proper houseboat, on which overnight cruises can be arranged, the Matusadona has 2 private cabins with bunks & one dbl cabin. There's a kitchen, bar & shower/toilet on board, & a shaded upper deck you can sleep on to keep cool. A small crew will normally accompany you, inc a chef,

& a tender boat is brought along to allow forays to the shore. US$500 per night, inc fuel, tender & fishing tackle.

Chipembere Contact via Lake Kariba Inns (page 216). A much simpler affair, Chipembere is little more than a flat pontoon, about 5m x 7m in size, with an engine at the back & flush toilet on board. Accommodating up to 40 passengers, it runs trips to the dam wall & the islands. Kw530,000 to dam wall; Kw670,000 to inc islands.

African Eagle Contact via Lake Safari Lodge, page 215. This 2-storey pontoon boat is suitable for a day trip for up to 25 people. Kw750,000 pp, DBB.

Canoeing Canoe trips into the gorge – and on the Lower Zambezi – are organised by Vundu Adventures (↘ 021 1511136; m 095 5917313, 097 7485208; e bakasajulius@yahoo.com, vunduadventures@yahoo.co.uk), which is based at Leisure Bay Lodge (see page 216), but is an entirely independent operator. Most popular is the 22km day trip through the Kariba Gorge (US$100 pp inc food), but there are also various packages, including a five-night, six-day trip (US$650 pp, inc camping equipment, all meals, soft drinks, lifejackets, insurance & transfers).

Visiting the dam Whilst you're here, take a walk over the dam wall (despite the border controls on each side) and perhaps even up to the observation point on the Zimbabwean side. In theory, if you leave your ID at the Zambian border post you are allowed to drive the 2km down to the dam wall and enjoy an east/west view of lake and gorges, huge spillgates, and Zam and Zim's power stations. Cars are not allowed to stop on the wall, which is for pedestrians only, but there is a place to park. There's an excellent little craft shop at the observation point, well known for its Nyaminyami sticks on which the river guardian is represented as a snake with its head at the top of the stick. The local carvers have become adept at carving intricate, interlinked rings and cages containing balls out of just one piece of wood. They're not cheap, but make great souvenirs.

Note that both Zimbabwe and Zambia are acutely aware of the vulnerability of the dam to damage or terrorist attack. So don't appear 'suspicious', and always ask before taking photographs – it may be just a wall to you, but it's of vital importance to them. There used to be morning tours available of the underground hydro-electric power station, so ask at the dam if these are still running. Due to the ongoing political turmoil in Zimbabwe, a drive to Kariba is currently not recommended.

Kapenta rig tour Kapenta are small, sardine-like fish introduced on commercial grounds into Kariba in the 1960s (see box, pages 218–19). Since then, fishing for them has become an important new industry around the lake, in both Zimbabwe and Zambia. When dried, kapenta are tasty, high in protein, and very easy to transport: an ideal food in a country where poorer people often suffer from protein deficiency.

Look out over the lake at night and watch the fishing rigs use powerful spotlights to attract the fish into their deep nets. These are then brought back to shore in the early morning, sun-dried on open racks (easily smelled and seen), and packaged for sale. Short tours lasting a couple of hours in the early evening can be arranged to one of these rigs through the hotels in Siavonga, and you'll bring back fresh kapenta to eat.

Crocodile farms Siavonga boasts two private crocodile farms, both open to the public. At Kaliolio, located on the Mutinangala Road, the foreman most ably leads visitors around ('appreciation' appreciated). There's also Sumbu, situated past Lake Kariba Inns, but not signposted. Only the old/breeding crocs can be viewed here; the delicate youngsters are out of bounds (crocs are amazingly susceptible to disease). There's no guide around this place, though a worker might come running if he sees you.

SINAZONGWE Zambia's second small town on Lake Kariba is roughly equidistant between Livingstone and Siavonga. It is a typical small Zambian town, originally built as the fishing and administrative centre for the southern lakeshore area, and is used mainly as an outpost for kapenta fishing. Despite the town's location, its centre is actually up the hill away from the lake, with a couple of simple restaurants, a small hospital and the appropriately named Budget Guest House, while Sinazongwe post office is actually a couple of kilometres further inland, at Sinazeze.

When the lake was first flooded Sinazongwe was a much busier harbour, and even had the only lighthouse on the lake. Although its prosperity has faded somewhat, it is well placed to become the hub of operations for Zambian tourism to Lake Kariba, and its first campsite has now been developed into attractive self-catering chalets.

Getting there and away There's a good tar **road** from Batoka, signposted to Maamba Mines, on the main Lusaka–Livingstone road (30km northeast of Choma), to within 17km of Sinazongwe, and then the rest is a reasonable, all-weather gravel road. Hitching is certainly a possibility, and shouldn't be that difficult. Driving time to/from Lusaka is approximately four to five hours, or from Livingstone three to four hours.

By air, light aircraft charters from Livingstone would cost at least US$1,000 for a six-seater plane (five passengers), one way, or more if the aircraft is based in Lusaka. Sinazongwe lies almost directly beneath the flight-path between Livingstone and the Lower Zambezi National Park – between which there are occasional direct charter flights. Organising a seat on these would be tricky, so you must check with a knowledgeable tour operator.

Where to stay

⌂ Lake View (3 chalets) m 097 9493980; e siansowa@iwayafrica.com; www.gwembesafaris.com. This is a quiet, laid-back place to unwind, with just reed cormorants & lizards for company. Cream-painted chalets are simply furnished with 4 beds, a low table & chairs, & en-suite shower, with ceiling fans to help out the breeze coming off the lake. Each has a secluded, airy terrace that looks straight over the lake towards Chete Island. Lawns lead down to the reed-fringed lake shore, backed by large boulders that shelter a small sandy beach. There are braai facilities & an attractive eating area, with trestle tables, stone pots & cooling ceiling fans. There's also a boat-launching area. Lake View is about 1km from Sinazongwe and is clearly signposted. $$, *inc cont b/fast. FB available on request.*

⌂ Kariba Bush Club (2 houses, backpackers lodge, chalets, camping) Siansowa; m 097 9493980; e guesthouse@siansowa.com; www.siansowa.com. Worth considering for a quiet couple of days, this complex is right on the lake shore, over 60km from Sinazongwe. To get there, take the Maamba turn-off at Batoka, go past the Sinazongwe turn-off after Sinazese & continue for about 30km on the tar, following the green & blue sign (which is a total of 80km from Batoka). About 2km before Maamba, take the good dirt road to the left with another signpost. Follow this road (and the signposts) for about 30km until you reach a security gate; stay on this road until you get to the club.

The thatched **Clubhouse** stands among indigenous trees & caters for backpackers & low-budget travellers. All the buildings have been constructed in the traditional way — pole & dagga with thatched roofs. It has 2 dbl rooms, 2 dormitories that each sleeps 8, a 'honeymoon' chalet, & camping; further en-suite chalets are being added, along with an internet café & craft shop. All rooms have mosquito protection & fans. There are BBQ facilities & a self-catering kitchen; alternatively meals can be provided inc specialities such as crocodile stir fry & lake bream. There's a lounge with satellite TV, a swimming pool & a bar (open till late) with a spectacular 200° view of the lake. Laundry, luggage storage, & travel advice complete the package.

Baobab & Marula houses sleep 6 & 11 people respectively, so are ideal for families & groups of friends. Both are fully equipped & serviced. Marula has 2 units: the main house (3 bedrooms, bathroom & separate toilet, kitchen, lounge with DSTV, & verandas back & front), plus a 2-bedroom cottage with bathroom. Baobab has a kitchen, lounge, bathroom & 3 bedrooms — 2 twins & a dbl. There's a swimming pool which is partially shaded by some enormous trees, & the entire area is lawned to the lakeshore, making it cool during the hot months. Plans are in hand to build a bush lodge on one of the islands.

There are boat-launching facilities on site (US$10 inc orientation guide), but no fuel is available. There are also tours of a large crocodile farm (US$12 pp), bush walks on one of the islands (US$12 inc boat transfer), game viewing & sunset cruises (US$12–18 pp), fishing (US$35/50 pp ¹/₂/full day) & birdwatching (US$6 pp); fishing tackle can be hired at US$12/day.

The islands are either Maaze Island or Mashapi Island which are both privately owned and have been stocked with game. In addition to various antelope (eland, kudu, impala, waterbuck, sable, hartebeest & wildebeest), there are zebras, monkeys & baboons — & elephants have made their own way over. There are plans to add buffalo. *Marula House US$120–190; Baobab House US$85–120 per house per night, self-catering (higher rates are for w/ends & public holidays).Honeymoon chalet US$80. Clubhouse US$24 dbl/twin; dorm bed US$10 pp. Camping US$5 pp.*

Camping You can camp on the lakeshore at a site owned by the Houseboat Company (*www.houseboatcompany.com; US$4 pp*) or at Kariba Bush Club's Clubhouse (see above).

Houseboats Although most houseboats are hired from Siavonga, there is one company based in Sinazongwe that runs group trips on a large boat:

⌂ Houseboat Company \f 03 323496, m 097 7717116, 098 7545821; e zambianhouseboats@zamnet.zm; www.houseboatcompany.com. The houseboat accommodates up to 30 people in rooms with AC, & most with en-suite facilities. It operates out of Sinazongwe, with most trips lasting 48hrs. Most guests are self-catering (there's a cook on board, but bring your own food); alternatively, full catering services are available on request. *Group charter US$1,200 per day self-catering; for FB add US$35 pp per day.*

Tricia Hayne

It's not every day that a safari trip throws up an opportunity for sailing, but if you're bound for Chete Island, this is very much part of the experience. The three-sailed 30ft (10m) *Siamwiinga* (the name means 'trimaran' in the Chi-Tonga language) is the favoured means of transport of those at Chete, which means that most guests bound for the island will find themselves and their luggage bundled on board at the mooring on the mainland at Sinazongwe for the short crossing to the island.

With the prevailing wind blowing across the lake, it's a reach in both directions for the transfer, so the crossing involves no laborious tacking; should the wind be blowing in another direction, or if it's slightly rough, then the passage is made under motor. Then, the rhythmic throb of the engine can be heard for several hundred metres across the water.

For those keen on sailing, longer trips on the lake offer a really unusual experience. Navigating in these waters throws up some rare challenges, even when it's calm; when it's windy, expect to get wet, though in these temperatures that's no great hardship. It's a somewhat eerie passage at any time, as the boat is steered through the skeletal trees of drowned forests that break the usually calm surface, topped by the occasional lone fish eagle.

Here and there, kapenta rigs loom large; those twinkling night-time lights belie the ugly reality of the exposed life on board these rusting, twin-hulled pontoons. Life is tough for the fishermen, who spend up to three weeks on board, with precious little shelter from either the sun or the occasional storms that lash the lake.

Towards the shore, attractions take on a very different form. Here, where the occasional crocodile basks in the sun and hippos can be heard grunting in the distance, the sight of an elephant near the jetty as the old trimaran draws near to Chete Island seems nothing short of surreal. Don't miss it.

ISLANDS ON LAKE KARIBA Of the numerous islands on Lake Kariba, only two are inhabited, Chete and Chikanka, although another two, Zebra and Sekula, can be seen on game-viewing trips. Maaze Island and Mashapi Island can be visited from Kariba Bush Club (see above).

Chete Island Chete is the largest island on the lake, and after a quick glance at the map you'll realise that it's much nearer to the Zimbabwean mainland (150m) than it is to Zambia (15km). This is because the border is defined as the deepest part of the Zambezi's old river course, not a line through the middle of the lake. In fact, the island lies just offshore from Zimbabwe's Chete Safari Area – so it's no surprise to learn that it's become recognised under Zambia's national parks system as a private wildlife reserve and bird sanctuary. The island is owned by Westlake Investments.

Chete is in a remote southern part of the lake, isolated except for the occasional twinkle from the nocturnal fishing of kapenta rigs in the distance. The island's game isn't tame, nor as dense as you'll find in the Luangwa or the better areas of the Kafue, but there is a sense of solitude and wilderness such as only a wild island like this can give. Its closest point of contact is really Sinazongwe, 17km away across Lake Kariba.

Much of the bigger game migrates to and fro between Zimbabwe and the island. This is especially true of the elephant bulls, but typically there's a resident breeding herd of around 80–100 elephants on the island. A pride of lion frequents the island,

9

too, including a large male whose spore is often spotted following his strolls near the lodge in the early hours of the morning. Then there are perhaps half a dozen leopard, a herd of eland, and plenty of waterbuck, bushbuck, impala and some magnificent kudu. Not forgetting the many crocodile and hippo that surround the shores, and a wide variety of birds – to date, 378 species have been counted here and in the surrounding area. Vultures circle in the thermals over the high ground, and a solitary martial eagle may be spotted over the centre of the island, while lower down, numerous smaller birds come to the fore, including little bee-eaters and colourful blue waxbills.

Typically, a guided walk across the centre of the island will take around two hours. The landscape is very varied, similar in parts to Zimbabwe's Chizarira and Matusadonna national parks. Areas of dense cover, rugged interior woodlands and gorges contrast with lightly wooded clearings criss-crossed with game tracks; nearer the shore, the terrain opens up into expansive floodplains. There are no roads here, and with the exception of one small but very good lodge by the lake, the island is totally deserted.

Getting there Chete is not directly accessible by water from Zimbabwe, but transfers are run from Sinazongwe on the Zambian side by the owners of the island's safari lodge (see below). The relatively short trip across the lake is either by trimaran (see box) or motorboat, depending on the weather, and is included in the overnight cost for guests at the lodge. Sailing into the wind and the wilderness is the stuff of dreams in good weather, but take a waterproof jacket just in case. (There's always a tiny dry cabin if life on deck becomes too challenging!)

Where to stay

Chete Island Safari Lodge (8 chalets) m 097 9415594; e reservations@cheteisland.com; www.cheteisland.com. Started in 1998 by Rob Fynn – the founder of the excellent Fothergill & Chikwenya safari camps in Zimbabwe (on Lake Kariba & in Mana Pools, respectively) – this small camp is somewhat out on a limb from mainstream Zambian tourism. It's off the normal routes & so ignored by most operators, & omitted from their brochures. Perhaps that's fortunate, as it's a lovely quiet camp in an exclusive & remote island location.

Comfortable & well-equipped Meru-style tented chalets, each with a private patio, are widely spaced on either side of a central living area facing the shoreline, with views over a classic Kariba scene of skeletal trees & islands beyond. Inside each are twin or large dbl beds, with attractive use of local fabrics. Solid furniture is also locally made from wood & wrought iron, with good bedside lights & a ceiling fan. The bathroom, at the back, is built of stone, & fully covered to keep out the elements, while judicious use of reed fencing ensures that each chalet is both secure & private.

The lofty central lounge/dining area is beautifully designed with a thatched roof in which is set an upper platform looking out over the water. Comfy armchairs are set to one side, & a large square solid-wood dining table to the other, all with uninterrupted views across a wide expanse of green lawns to the lake. After 3 courses of good, home-cooked food, you'll often retire outside to sit around the fire, while during the day guests can relax around the lake-water pool. The atmosphere is one of comfort & tranquillity, rather than over-the-top luxury, with managers Paul & Sonja Clay going out of their way to make visitors feel welcome.

Activities include walking safaris (with armed game scout), boating safaris around the islands (using motorboats and/or two-person Canadian-style canoes), & fishing from an open pontoon for both tiger & bream; fly-fishing is also available. For those staying longer, there are trips to Sekula Island to see buffalo, or to Zebra Island, while those preferring to stay closer to the lodge could spend hours watching the varied birdlife. The lodge's 30ft sailing trimaran, usually used for transfers to & from the mainland, is also available for longer trips across the lake (see above); if you've any interest in sailing, it's a must. *US$295 pp, inc all meals, park entry fees, activities, laundry and full bar.* ⊕ *all year.*

Chikanka Island Chikanka Island is now strictly an archipelago of three islands due to a rise in the level of the lake since it was formed. It lies about 8km from the Zambian mainland, 10km west-southwest of Chete and 18km southwest of Sinazongwe. Covering 240ha (2.4km²), it is smaller than Chete, and is also privately owned. The islands are mostly wooded, with mopane trees, marulas and the occasional baobab contrasting with the stark skeletons of drowned trees in the surrounding lake. Rock figs display their intricate root system; wild purple morning glory entwines its way through the waterplants along the shoreline, and dwarf plated lizards flash their brilliant blue tails as they dart among the rocks.

Chikanka has some plains game, including kudu, zebra, impala and bushbuck, and elephants occasionally visit too. Not surprisingly, there are also hippos and crocodiles around the shores, so it's not sensible to swim. The channels between the islands boast a good variety of fish, including bream, tiger fish, Cornish jack and bottlenose.

Where to stay

Chikanka Island Camp (5 chalets) m 097 9493980; e siansowa@iwayafrica.com; www.gwembesafaris.com. Transfers to Chikanka Island are by boat from Kariba Bush Club at Siansowa (see page 222). A-frame chalets have been built on one of the islands, each in a peaceful & secluded spot on a low cliff, looking east over the lake towards Zimbabwe, so the view at dawn is truly memorable. Stone clad, with a Tonga-thatched roof, each chalet is gauzed to deter insects & is simply furnished with twin beds (plus mosquito nets) & en-suite shower & toilet. There is no electricity; lighting is battery powered. The large thatched dining area is fronted by a terrace that leads down to the lake, & a small paddling pool. Visitors can opt either for full board or – if part of a group – for self catering. US$70/90 pp sharing/sgl FB; self-catering group US$410 per night (8–10 people); US$470 (11–15 people). Transfers from US$53 (up to 3 people) to US$140 (9–15 people).

Sekula Island This uninhabited island is administered by ZAWA, but day trips are possible from Chete Island to see the island's herd of buffalo.

FROM LUSAKA TO CHIRUNDU

The tar road from Lusaka to Harare, via Chirundu, is an important commercial artery, so is usually kept in good repair. During 2007 and 2008, though, the entire road between Kafue and Chirundu is being upgraded, giving rise to significant hold-ups on this busy stretch as lumbering trucks negotiate the steep, sharp bends – and frequently break down. Work is being carried out in sections that may not tie up, so you can expect stretches of smooth, wide tar to be interspersed with little warning by gravel or the old pot-holed surface. With work not scheduled for completion until 2008, it's important to allow extra time for the journey and to take particular care. Even at the best of times, there are numerous accidents along this route.

Leaving Lusaka, you soon pass through the town of Kafue and, shortly before the busy turning to Livingstone, cross over the wide and slow Kafue River that is also heading to join the Zambezi. From here the road gradually, consistently and occasionally spectacularly, descends. It leaves the higher, cooler escarpment for the hot floor of the Zambezi Valley, before passing the turn-off to Siavonga and crossing the busy bridge at Chirundu into Zimbabwe.

Between Kafue and Chirundu, there are occasional craft stalls set up on the side of the road selling carved wooden animals, drums and other mementos. Just 1km north of the turn-off to Lechwe Lodge are found the famous giraffe carvers: wooden giraffes (and other animals) of all sizes line the roadside. If you're tempted to buy, and you're flying home, remember that these carvings have to be put in the plane's hold, so make sure they're very carefully packed.

KAFUE This straggling industrial town about 50km from Lusaka is dominated by the Nitrogen Chemicals factory to the north, and lies close to the Norwegian-built hydro-electric dam on the Kafue River (see box, *Kafue River floods*, page 439).

Kafue has a post office and a bus station, but more important for the visitor are its fuel stations: two in town, and a Total garage located towards Chirundu, just after the turn-off to Livingstone. The recent launch of the *Kafue Queen* (see opposite) could serve to put the place on the map.

Where to stay Outside town is the impressive Lechwe Lodge, while rather more mundane, and closer to town, is the River Motel. In the centre, there's a clutch of small guesthouses and a motel that predominantly serves the town's industries.

Highway Park Lodge (10 rooms) Great North Rd; m 097 872167. Opposite the BP garage to the north of town, right on the main road, this is a spacious if noisy site. Simple thatched en-suite chalets, each with 2 dbl beds, are set in grassy surrounds; the higher rate brings DSTV. A fast-food restaurant at the back serves all meals. $, b/fast extra.

Lwanginga Guesthouse (6 rooms) Great North Rd; m 097 584859. Just opened about 1km north of Kafue town, this simple local guesthouse is quieter than the Highway Park, & offers en-suite rooms with fans at very reasonable rates, some with DSTV. $, b/fast extra.

New Bayi Motel (20 rooms) Great North Rd; ☎ 02 312140, 360006; ☎/f 02 312332. Next to the Total garage in the centre of Kafue town, the motel was being completely renovated in 2007 when visited. En-suite rooms are formulaic with DSTV, fridge & desk. The refurbished nightclub, though, offers the potential for a very disturbed night. $, inc cont b/fast.

River Motel (48 rooms, 30 chalets, camping) Great North Rd; m 097 774613. This large motel about 5km south of Kafue is surprisingly good for a small-town hotel in Zambia. To get there, follow the main road through Kafue, heading south. The motel is on the main road, about 5km from the town, with a stone lion guarding each side of the big white gates. The motel's relative prosperity is largely explained by its 3 conference rooms.

Its rooms have a dbl bed with simple pine furniture: a bedside table, dressing table, desk & wardrobe. A few have AC & all have en-suite shower & toilet. Alternatively, the slightly decrepit chalets have a kitchenette for which cooking equipment can be supplied, as well as a small lounge with comfy chairs & DSTV, & a bathroom with shower & bath. Outside, a limited space is available for camping. Facilities include a small gym, 2 TV rooms, a good swimming pool & a cocktail bar called 'Surf & Turf'; there is also a boat launch on the river. The

restaurant, with its cheerful yellow runners on white tablecloths, serves buffet meals at Kw40,000. Staff are friendly, & the atmosphere pleasant & relaxed. If you need to stop, do so without fear! $. Camping Kw20,000 pp

Lechwe Lodge (6 rondavels) ☎ 021 1212578; m 095 704803; f 021 3230707; e students@ zamnet.zm; www.lechwelodge.com (⊕ LECHWE 15°44.818'S; 28°05.595'E). On a working farm just west of Kafue town, this immaculate small lodge owned by Di Flynn was started in 1990. It lies 13km from the junction with the main road. To get there, turn west off the main road just north of Kafue town, pass the Nitrogen Chemicals factory immediately on the left, & later African Textiles, & you come to a 90° bend to the right. Beyond here, take the next left turn – it's not terribly clear, but is just after a church – then stay on a gravel road for about 3.2km. Then take the left turn signposted to Kafue Fisheries & Lechwe Lodge, & follow this for a final 4km or so. Reservations are essential.

The lodge's rondavels are spread around almost manicured lawns & are very well kept. All are roomy with solid wooden furniture standing on expanses of cool polished floor. Two are family units, with 4 beds in 2 rooms; the others have twin beds or lovely wood-framed dbls. All the beds are covered with mosi nets & each rondavel has an en-suite shower & toilet. The food is good, fresh & plentiful, richly deserving the cliché 'wholesome farm fare' in its best possible sense.

Lechwe's 13km² farm varies from brachystegia & acacia woodlands through a 'termitaria' zone to open floodplains & the river itself. The game includes giraffe, eland, Lichtenstein's hartebeest, Kafue lechwe, oribi & sitatunga, as well as the more common antelope of the region. None of the large land predators is here, but serval are plentiful, apparently due to the prevalence of cane rats in the reeds. In & around the river you'll find Cape clawless & spotted-necked otters, hippos & crocodiles.

The lodge's activities are tailored to individual guests. Boat trips along the river are a super way to watch birds in the dry season – & tackle is always available if you prefer to fish. The birdlife is very good, with more than 444 species recorded. You should see wide ranges of waterfowl, kingfishers, herons, egrets & even a visiting osprey or flock of Caspian terns. Walks, with or without a guide, are easily arranged, as are short game drives for the less energetic (although you shouldn't expect guides of the calibre that you'd find in the best safari lodges). The 4 (6m-high) viewing platforms overlooking the Kafue are always good spots at which to stop & just watch. Experienced riders (you must be comfortable with a rising trot for 15–20 mins at a time) can ride out on the farm's own horses with a guide, who will take 2 guests out for as long as they wish; hard hats are provided & must be worn. Finally if you're interested in farming, then ask for a farm tour; it's fascinating. Pigsties are situated near to large fishponds. Their manure promotes the growth of infusoria, which feed the small organisms on which fish feed. Thus the farm produces commercial quantities of pork & bream (*Tilapia delonoticus*), in a very eco-friendly way.

Lechwe is a very gentle, civilised & relaxing place, perfect for your first (or last) few nights in the country. It's also excellent value & open all year. It's just a shame that, for most people, it is a little too far from Lusaka for 1 night. *US$163 pp, inc all activities, meals, drinks & laundry. Road transfers to/from Lusaka extra. Air transfers (15–20 mins) around US$250 per plane (max 5 people) one way.*

What to see and do With the launch of the colourful **Kafue Queen** (✆ *097 232949, 097 232949, 095 813984;* e *finot@zamnet.zm; Kw80,000 pp with cash bar; Kw135,000 pp all inc;* ⊕ *all year*) in late 2006, visitors have the opportunity to explore the gorges of the Kafue River from a two-storey shaded pontoon boat that can take up to 100 passengers. The brainchild of Ian Finaughty, the boat leaves its mooring just north of the bridge over the river, some 8km south of Kafue town, making its way downstream past a number of local villages and into the gorges. Aside from hippo and crocodile, wildlife along this stretch includes the Cape clawless otter, and the birding potential is excellent, with numerous species of kingfisher, as well as African fish eagles and black eagles. Each cruise lasts 2½–3 hours. On the practical side, there's a cash bar on board, and toilets, while braai packs (cooked to order) can be bought for Kw120,000 per person, with nshima and vegetable relish an additional Kw30,000. The bulk of the market is likely to be the local conference trade, but tourists, too, will find the trip of interest, though as yet there are no scheduled departures. For something a little more personal, **fishing** or **speedboat** trips can be arranged for Kw250,000 per person for up to half a day.

In addition to these, Ian has plans for two community projects, both of which he expects to go live during 2007. The first, on the southern (Mazabuka) side of the river, is the establishment of a small, **traditional village** – a homestead, not a show village – where visitors will be able to find out about local culture and see displays of dancing (Kw20,000 pp). To the north of the river, plans are in hand to establish a series of one-, three- and five-day guided **hiking trails**, the last taking participants within 20km of Lusaka. Participants would be expected to carry all their own equipment, so this isn't a walk in the park. Costs for one day/night will be Kw346,000 per person, plus Kw150,000 for each additional day.

Tours of the **Kafue Dam**, at the eastern end of the gorges, can occasionally be arranged with the Zambian electricity suppliers, ZESCO, which even has its own small lodge for both conference and individual visitors.

CHIRUNDU BORDER AREA A few kilometres before Chirundu, just after the turn-off to Siavonga and Kariba, keep a lookout for a roadside plaque indicating the Chirundu Forest Reserve – a small area around the road where the remnants of petrified trees can be seen strewn on the ground.

The border post at Chirundu always seems to be busy with a constant stream of trucks going through, or at least waiting to go through. There's a BP garage here –

though it hasn't had fuel for some years (the nearest supply is at Gwabi River Lodge). There's also an office for the Manica Freight Company, a post office and the rather dubious Nyambandwe Hotel, where some of the rooms are hired by the hour. It's a promising place to look for a lift if you are hitchhiking, but otherwise there is a slightly seedy, unsafe feel typical of a town where many people come and go, but few ever stay. On the plus side, there's a good mission hospital in the town.

The unsignposted road to Gwabi River Lodge and the Lower Zambezi branches east from the main road about 200–300m from the border. It's always clogged with parked trucks. To find it, take the road past the border-post's chainlink fence and the watchman, then turn left. After 4.5km you'll pass the sign for Zambezi Breezers, then a further 6.5km is the Gwabi turn-off before, after another 2km, the road descends to the Kafue River. The road from Chirundu has been improved considerably in recent years. To reach Chiawa or anywhere beyond, the river has to be crossed on the pontoon (⊕ 06.00–18.00; US$20 per foreign-registered vehicle each way).

🏠 Where to stay

🏠 **Zambezi Breezers** (6 chalets, 7 rooms, camping) m 097 9279468; 097 7628120; e ZambeziBreezers@ gmail.com; http://zambezibreezers.googlepages.com (⊕ 15°59.112'S; 028°52.833'E). Right on the banks of the Zambezi River, this new camp is about 6km from Chirundu. To get there, turn left just before the border and follow the dirt road for around 4.5km until you come to a white pillar indicating the camp. Turn right here, and follow the signs for a further 1.5km. If you're stuck in town, give them a ring and they'll arrange to pick you up.

Accommodation is in en-suite tented chalets, or in dbl rooms which share ablutions with those at the campsite. There's a bar & restaurant where the menu is limited at present, but will be extended in future. There is also a small swimming pool. Activities focus on boat hire & fishing trips. *US$30 per room, chalet US$60 pp, B&B; camping US$7.50 pp.*

🏠 **Gwabi River Lodge** (8 chalets, camping) ☎ 021 1515078; m 097 9650920; e gwabi@mwebafrica.com, jackieg@zamnet.zm; www.gwabiriverlodge.com. This well-known small lodge, self styled 'the gateway to the Lower Zambezi' has recently changed hands, & undergone a series of significant improvements. It is set in green lawns on the Kafue River about 12km from Chirundu, 3km up from its confluence with the Zambezi. You'll find everything has its price here, from a bag of drinking-water ice to use of the car park for non-residents (US$4 per night) — but these prices are generally reasonable.

The chalets are solidly built with stone floors, AC, mains electricity, en-suite showers/toilets & DSTV. Camping is alongside the river, on a well-lit site with ablution block, braai & electric points, & nightly entertainment provided by a percussion band of painted reed frogs. There's a great pool, overlooking the river (some distance below) with superb sunset views from the sundeck & terrace, next to which sensibly priced drinks are served in a cool thatched bar area. An à-la-carte menu includes sandwiches from US$4 & steaks at around US$15.

Various activities are possible, inc guided walks & boat cruises. If you want to fish, rods & tackle are available to hire; boats cost US$50 per ½ day plus the cost of fuel. You can also hire speedboats. The lodge is fenced & small game can be found on the property, while elephant & hippo can often be seen from the river. *US$44/50 pp sharing midweek/weekend, B&B. Camping US$8 pp.*

LOWER ZAMBEZI VALLEY

The Lower Zambezi Valley, from the Kariba Dam to the Mozambique border, has a formidable reputation for big game – leading UNESCO to designate part of the Zimbabwean side as a World Heritage Site. The Lower Zambezi National Park protects a large section of the Zambian side. Across the river, much of the Zimbabwean side is protected by either Mana Pools National Park or various safari areas. This makes for a very large area of the valley devoted to wildlife, and a terrific amount of the bigger game, notably elephants and buffalo, actually cross the river regularly.

However, take a look at a map of the Zambian bank and you'll realise that the land up to 55km east from the Kafue River (from Gwabi River Lodge) is not in the national park at all; the river defines the border with the Chiawa Game Management Area (GMA), which is owned by the operators within the area, obtained with permission from the chieftainess. Only to the east of the Chongwe River are you in the national park.

As you might expect, the game densities increase as you travel east, with the best game in the national park, and fewer animals on the privately owned land nearer to Chirundu. The situation is similar on the other bank of the river, in Zimbabwe, so if you want good game viewing then do get into the park if you can, or at least near to it.

GEOGRAPHY From Chirundu to the Mozambique border, the Zambezi descends 42m, from 371m to 329m above sea level, over a distance of over 150km. That very gentle gradient (about 1:3,500) explains why the Zambezi flows so slowly and spreads out across the wide valley, making such a gentle course for canoeing.

From the river, look either side of you into Zambia and Zimbabwe. In the distance you will spot the escarpment, if the heat haze doesn't obscure it. At around 1,200m high, it marks the confines of the Lower Zambezi Valley and the start of the higher, cooler territory beyond which is known as the 'highveld' in Zimbabwe.

The valley is a rift valley, similar to the Great Rift Valley of east Africa (though probably older), and it shares its genesis with the adjoining Luangwa Valley. The original sedimentary strata covering the whole area are part of the karoo system, sedimentary rocks laid down from about 300 to 175 million years ago. During this time, faulting occurred and volcanic material was injected into rifts in the existing sediments.

One of these faults, the wide Zambezi Valley, can still be seen. In geologically recent times, the Zambezi has meandered across the wide valley floor, eroding the mineral-rich rocks into volcanic soils and depositing silts which have helped to make the valley so rich in vegetation and hence wildlife. These meanders have also left old watercourses and oxbow pools, which add to the area's attraction for game.

So look again from one side of the valley to the other. What you see is not a huge river valley: it is a rift in the earth's crust through which a huge river happens to be flowing.

FLORA AND FAUNA Most of the park, made up of higher ground on the sides and top of the escarpment, is thick bush – where game viewing is difficult. This is broadleafed miombo woodland, dominated by brachystegia, *julbernardia*, *combretum* and *terminalia* species. Fortunately, there's little permanent water here, so during the dry season the game concentrates on the flat alluvial plain by the river.

Acacia species and mopane dominate the vegetation on the richer soils of the valley floor, complemented by typical riverine trees like leadwood (*Combretum imberbe*), ebony (*Diospyros mespiliformis*), and various figs (*ficus* species). Here the riverine landscape and vegetation are very distinctive: similar to the Luangwa Valley, but quite different from other parks in the subcontinent.

Perhaps it is the richness of the soils which allows the trees to grow so tall and strong, forming woodlands with carpets of grasses, and only limited thickets of shrubs to obscure the viewing of game. The acacia species include some superb specimens of the winterthorn, *Faidherbia albida* (which used to be known as *Acacia albida)*, and the flat-topped umbrella thorn, *Acacia tortilis*. Both of these produce seedpods which the game love, the former looking like apple-

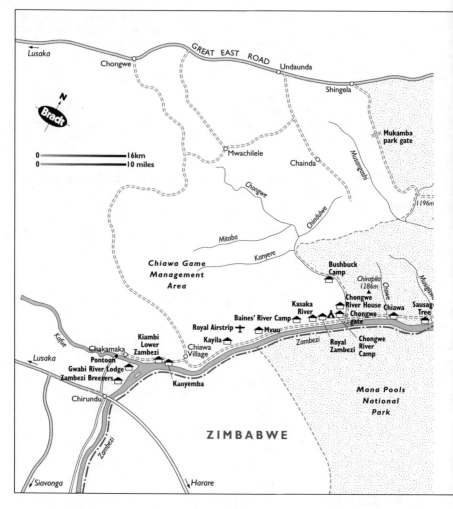

rings, the latter being tightly spiralled seedpods which are very nutritious (19% protein, 26% carbohydrate, 5% minerals). It all results in a beautiful, lush landscape that can support a lot of game, and is excellent for the ease of viewing which it allows.

MAMMALS The Lower Zambezi has all the big game that you'd expect, with the exceptions of rhino (due to poaching), giraffe and cheetah. Buffalo and elephant are very common, and can often be seen grazing on the islands in the middle of the river, or swimming between Zimbabwe and Zambia. It is normally safe to get quite close by drifting quietly past these giants as they graze.

The antelope in the valley are dominated by large herds of impala, but good populations of kudu, waterbuck, bushbuck, zebra and the odd duiker or grysbok also occur. Giraffe are notable for their absence – in fact, there's no record of them ever having lived here.

Lion, leopard and spotted hyena are the major predators. There have long been plans to reintroduce cheetah but these have not yet come to fruition. On my first

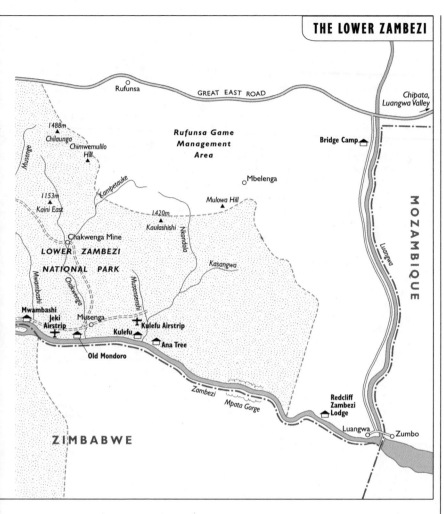

visit, back in 1995, lion were very visible, with one marvellous pride having in excess of 30 animals – and the game viewing has improved a lot since then. Many of the larger trees have branches that seem made-to-measure for leopards, which are sometimes seen on night drives, and increasingly during the day, too. There are also positive plans to reintroduce rhino into the park.

In the river, crocodile and hippo are always present, but look also for the large water monitor lizard, or *leguvaan*, and the entertaining Cape clawless otter, which both occur frequently though the latter are very seldom seen.

BIRDS Around 350 species of birds have been recorded in the valley. By the river you will find many varieties of water-loving birds like pied, giant, woodland, malachite and brown-hooded kingfishers, to name the more common of the species. Similarly, darters, cormorants, egrets and storks are common, and fish eagles are always to be found perching on high branches that overlook the river. Less common residents include ospreys, spoonbills and African skimmers, and it's rich in waders, both resident and migrant.

Once widely distributed throughout the Lower Zambezi Valley, and indeed Zambia as a whole, the African wild dog, *Lycaon pictus*, is now threatened on every side from loss of habitat, disease and human persecution. In the last 30 years, the population of this highly social species in the valley has fallen dramatically, to the point where its very existence is threatened. Now classified as 'endangered' by the international Union for the Conservation of Nature, it is found in viable populations in just six countries.

For a population of wild dog to be viable, it needs a huge area, around a million hectares, in which to live out its nomadic lifestyle. Restriction of this area curtails the animal's natural tendency to roam many hundreds of kilometres in search of a mate (see also page 493). Even within the national park, the dogs are under threat from predation by lion, and harassment by spotted hyena, that can seriously reduce their chances of successfully raising their cubs. Outside the park boundaries, in spite of legal protection, the dangers multiply, from poaching activities as they accidentally get caught in snares to road-traffic accidents and diseases transferred from domestic dogs.

It was against this background that African Wild Dog Conservation (AWDC) was set up to identify the threats to the wild dogs in the park and surrounding areas. After ten years working with African wild dog populations in the Lower Zambezi, Australian Dr Kellie Leigh, founder and trustee of AWDC has come up with recommendations that are currently being incorporated into a management plan for the national park. AWDC has recently expanded its research area to include both the South Luangwa National Park, and the GMAs connecting the park with the Lower Zambezi. South Luangwa National Park has an estimated health population of nearly 98 adult dogs. Within two packs that are being monitored, 11 pups survived the 2006 rainy season to become energetic yearlings, helping to raise the following year's litter of pups. Several single-sex dispersal groups are being monitored by satellite collars and on-the-ground field work, and it is hoped that the creation and support of a safe corridor between the two national parks will result in the natural restocking of the Lower Zambezi with African wild dog.

While Kellie has returned home to Australia, the project is now being co-ordinated by Dr Tasila Banda, a Zambian with a background in conservation ecology, and a small team of conservation scientists. For further information, or to make a donation to the group's work, see www.awdczambia.org.

POACHING The original inhabitants of the valley, the Senga people, were moved out of the area during the colonial era. Although the valley was declared a national park in 1983, poaching has long been an issue here – partly because the surrounding peoples had always hunted for food in the valley, so they were not happy to stop. Then in the mid-1980s commercial poaching for ivory and rhino horn completely wiped out the park's black rhino population, and threatened to do the same to the elephants.

Fortunately, the CITES ban on the world ivory trade did much to stop this; the elephant population in the park is now good, and the Lower Zambezi's game is generally in good shape. While poaching occurs occasionally, it is monitored very closely by game scouts stationed around the park.

CONSERVATION LOWER ZAMBEZI Many of the camps are involved with helping Conservation Lower Zambezi (CLZ), which is an initiative to support the work of the Zambian Wildlife Authority (ZAWA) in the valley, funded by donations from camps in the valley and concerned individuals. They help to back up and train the ZAWA scouts from a new school established for the purpose, mount aerial patrols and back research projects. They also organise conservation education programmes in the communities and from a new purpose-built centre. Visitors should understand that supporting these camps helps to stop the poaching – both by providing a livelihood for the rangers, and by keeping a presence of people in the park that makes it more difficult for poachers to operate.

GETTING THERE There are three ways of getting into this area: by road, by air and by boat – or any combination of these. Most visitors stay at one of the private camps as a base, and go for game-viewing drives, walks and trips on the river from there. Arriving by air is not only the fastest means of transport, but often the most economical as well. Planes land at one of several airstrips in the valley, including Royal Zambezi (✪ 15°43'S; 29°17'E), and Jeki (✪ 15°38'S; 29°36'E), Kayila and Kulefu, with the drive to and from the lodges being an activity in itself. A few lodges can arrange for transfers by road and river from Lusaka, though this tends to be very expensive.

More economical, for those with their own vehicle, is to drive to Gwabi River Lodge (see page 228) and arrange to be collected from there by boat; again, this is an experience that is an intrinsic part of a trip. Alternatively, the well equipped can drive themselves all the way (see below), but this is neither an easy nor a fast option.

Finally, there are popular canoe safaris (see pages 234–6) that run along the river, using simple temporary fly camps at night.

Visiting independently The last option is for the adventurous and well equipped – to drive in with their own vehicles, either staying at lodges or fully equipped with all their own supplies and camping gear.

The roads into the park need a 4x4 vehicle (ideally two, for safety's sake) but are not difficult driving in the dry season, though the going is very slow. Get detailed maps of the whole valley before you leave Lusaka, and pack a compass and GPS. It would be wise to get a permit before you arrive, from the National Parks office in Lusaka or Chilanga, though you can usually get one at the scout's camp at the entrance to the park itself. Permits cost US$30 per person per day, plus US$15 per day for the vehicle.

To find the right track, take the turning left off the main road as you enter Chirundu and follow the signs to Gwabi River Lodge. Where the sign points left, indicating that the lodge is 2km ahead, continue straight on to reach the pontoon which crosses the Kafue River into the Chiawa GMA (⏰ 06.00–18.00). Until recently the crossing was free of charge, but there is now a rather steep fee of US$20 per foreign-registered vehicle, each way. The village by the pontoon has a police post and a small, very basic grocery; don't raise your expectations. Then for the most part it's a simple case of sticking close to the river, and following the main track. Initially, you'll be driving alongside the fertile fields of the river valley where maize, paprika and beans are the staple crops, and past small villages where children variously wave shyly or shout 'Hello', while elsewhere the chant 'Sweets, sweets' echoes through the houses. The western entrance to the national park, Chongwe gate, lies about 67km from the pontoon. Once inside the national park itself, the terrain levels out into a broad plain that continues for several kilometres, inhabited only by plains animals and birds, before eventually dropping down into *albida* forest where shallow lagoons among the trees attract brightly coloured saddle-billed storks.

For those heading for the eastern side of the park, there's a little-known approach road accessed from the Great East Road, some 100km east of Lusaka. To find this, continue past Chengwe, then turn right shortly after Undaunda (✪ TOUNDA 15°14.188'S, 29°10.032'E). From here, follow the road to the

Mukanga gate (⊕ MUKANG 15°21.015'S, 29°17.135'E). Shortly after the gate there's another checkpoint marking the entrance to the Chakwenga Mine, which has recently been reopened. The road then drops over the escarpment, a steep descent culminating in a series of sandy riverbeds, and the main game-viewing area on the valley's floor in the Kulefu area. For many years this route wasn't an easy option at all, being little used and very overgrown, but with recent investment in the mine we have very credible reports that it has improved substantially. Nevertheless, you'll need to allow at least five hours from Lusaka to Kulefu, and a good 4x4 remains essential.

There are also reports of a 4x4 track starting from Leopards Hill in Lusaka, and currently being graded.

ACTIVITIES Most of the lodges along the river offer similar activities, concentrating primarily on drives, boat trips, walking safaris, canoeing and fishing, but each has its own individual atmosphere and areas of expertise, and some specialise.

Game drives Day and night drives, both in the Chiawa GMA and into the Lower Zambezi National Park (closed November to April/May), are high on the list of priorities for most visitors. They are offered by almost all camps, whether they're located inside or outside the park – though it's worth remembering that the further you are from the national park, the less game you're likely to see; game drives on the west of the GMA can be uneventful.

Walking safaris Walking safaris with a professional guide, and an armed scout, are also widely available, affording the opportunity to get closer to the wildlife on their terms. There are now strict exams, organised by the CLZ (see pages 232–3), for potential guides which match the quality and scope of those in the Luangwa Valley. I would never go walking with an unqualified guide. Most trips are two to four hours, and done as an activity from a lodge or camp.

Birdwatching Birdwatching is usually built into most walks, drives or boating trips if you're interested. With a range of habitats it's a great place for birdwatching at any time, but especially from September to March, when migrants from central Africa can be spotted in the area.

Fishing Fishing on the Zambezi – primarily for the tigerfish – is also offered by most outfits, and is at its best when the waters are clear, from around May–June until towards the end of the year. Catch and release is practised by all lodges/camps, both within the GMA and in the national park, where it is obligatory. Fishing is banned between December and February, but many of the lodges are hoping to be allowed to continue to fish on a catch-and-release basis during that period. Those fishing in the national park will need a permit, costing US$5 per person per day.

In recent years a deal has been struck with the local community to prevent over-fishing. In return for financial compensation for the community, it has been agreed that there will be no netting of fish either in the GMA or in the national park.

Canoeing Canoeing on the Zambezi is another firm favourite for the more adventurous. It's a terrific way to relax in the open air and see the river, whilst doing some gentle exercise and game viewing at the same time. Most operators use stable Canadian-style fibreglass canoes which are 5.7m long, and large enough for two people plus their camping equipment and personal belongings. Trips are usually limited to a maximum of five canoes led by a fully qualified canoe guide; while this means that the guide has control over the group, you could still occasionally find yourself closer to a pod of hippos than to your trusty guide.

Broadly there are two different ways to go canoeing. You can canoe as an activity from a lodge or camp, or you can canoe from A to B, sleeping on islands or at points on the bank along the way.

Canoeing guides In the 1990s the question asked about these canoeing trips was always 'Which section should we canoe?' Now the question is more usually 'How qualified is the guide?' Paddling for miles through areas with little game seems to have fallen out of fashion, and now more people are doing less mileage, but aiming to see a lot more game. They want to canoe inside the park, and they want a good guide. (Often this means more canoeing from camps, and fewer paddles from A to B.)

You should understand from the outset that canoeing on this river has a risk attached to it that no guide can ever take away. Even with the very best of guides, it's possible to get into dangerous, even life-threatening, situations with both hippos and crocs. People are killed and injured every year on this river. However, canoeing with, and listening to, a good guide who knows the river will give you the best chance of avoiding dangerous situations, and of escaping those which prove unavoidable.

Day or overnight trips: from a camp or lodge Most of the lodges/camps along the Lower Zambezi will offer options for you to go canoeing for your morning or afternoon activity, taking about three to four hours paddling at a time. Typically, you're driven upstream with the canoes, and you paddle back to the lodge.

This has several advantages. Firstly, there's no hurry, so the guide can build in time to stop and investigate the game en route; secondly, if you're at a good lodge then you're probably spending all of your time in a prime game area, within the park; thirdly, you're not committing yourself to more than three or four hours paddling; finally, you've got a comfortable bed lined up for the night back at camp. Occasionally lodges organise full-day or even overnight trips.

Longer trips: from point to point On these trips you put all your kit in the canoe, and paddle downstream for a number of days. Typically, you'll carry tents and food, and camp en route.

Physically, you will feel tired at the end of a day, but canoeing downriver is not excessively strenuous (unless you meet a strong headwind), and no previous experience is demanded. To some extent that feeling of exertion often leads to a feeling of achievement at the end of the trip, which increases with the length of the trip and the distance covered.

Canoe safaris were started on the Zimbabwean side in the early 1980s and were led by qualified canoe guides who had to pass National Parks examinations. In the early 1990s, with the emergence of the Lower Zambezi National Parks Wildlife Protection Programme, Zambia also started canoe safaris. As in Zimbabwe, these became enormously popular among more adventurous visitors.

Which section to canoe? Several different canoe safaris run through different sections of the Lower Zambezi River. The first, taking two nights/three days, covers the uppermost section of the river from Kariba to Chirundu, with the Kariba Gorge a highlight early on. The stretch from Chirundu to the mid-Mana Pools region of the Lower Zambezi River features larger numbers of game and birdlife due to the proximity of the national parks on both sides of the river, and takes four nights/three days. The final section, undoubtedly the wildest, runs through the entire length of the two national parks, passing through floodplains and the spectacular Mpata Gorge, and ending at the confluence of the Luangwa River some 163km downstream; for this, allow eight nights/nine days.

Costs include basic camping kit, food (and wine with the evening meal), guide, canoes, paddles etc. Transfers are extra.

Canoeing operators There really isn't the choice of trips, or operators, doing longer canoe trips here that there were in the early 1990s, but the major operator is:

Zambezi River Adventures aka River Horse Safaris
\ +263 613332; m +263 912 407661;
e zambezi@iwayafrica.com;
www.zambezicanoeing.com. A maximum of 5 canoes per expedition, with larger groups split up & coming together during the evenings. Trips range from 3 days/2 nights between Kariba & Chirundu, costing

US$345 pp, to the 9 days/8 nights Zambezi Explorer at US$895, both exc VAT, national park fees & transfers (though trips ending at the confluence of the Luangwa River inc the road transfer back to Lusaka. No children under 15 except with special permission.

Walking trails Most of the camps organise walking safaris as a normal part of their activities. However, Safari Par Excellence (see page 190) runs three-day small-group walking trips in the Lower Zambezi for a maximum of eight guests, who are accompanied by a professional guide and a national parks game scout, as well as by porters who carry such essentials as a packed lunch and refreshments. Visitors meet at Kayila Lodge, from where they are transferred by vehicle into the national park. Accommodation on the first two nights is in established campsites outside the national park with hot showers; the final night is spent at Mwambashi River Lodge (see page 241). Trips cost US$940 pp, and are run from June to October. Walks are also conducted in the GMA by Vintage Africa Safaris (*www.vintageafricasafaris.com*).

WHERE TO STAY There are several lodges in the valley and a few campsites as well. Almost all are good, although they have quite different styles of operating. For the most part, power is either solar generated or supplied by battery, so needs to be used sparingly. With advance booking and a 4x4, you can drive yourself into any of these, but most people arrange for a transfer by road or charter flight. Establishments to the west of the national park are in the Chiawa GMA. All visitors in the park will be asked to pay a levy of US$2 per person per day towards Conservation Lower Zambezi, an organisation committed to the protection of the wildlife and habitat of the national park (see pages 232–3) and the Chiawa GMA. Looking at the various establishments from west to east:

Outside the national park in the Chiawa GMA

⌂ **Kiambi Lower Zambezi** (3 chalets, 8 Meru tents, cottage, camping) m 097 876003, 097 186106, 096 655878; e kiambi@coppernet.zm; www.kiambi.co.za. Clearly signposted 12km from the Kafue pontoon, Kiambi Lower Zambezi is the first lodge that you come to en route to the national park; for those travelling by boat, it's just 5 minutes from the pontoon. Now privately owned, & with a slight change of name, it is set at the confluence of the Zambezi & Kafue rivers with views across to Kanyemba Island. Not surprisingly, with relatively easy

access & reasonable rates, the camp is particularly popular with w/enders & can get very busy.

The camp has several accommodation options. The original Meru tents are erected on wooden platforms, with a view over the river. Each has a thatched roof & a large veranda with chairs & table at the front. Inside are twin beds (with space for a further 2) & at the back, under a tented roof, is an en-suite shower, toilet & washbasin. New to the camp are en-suite 'luxury' chalets, complete with AC. There's also a self-catering cottage with 3 twin bedrooms, bathroom, lounge, fully equipped kitchen & a fireplace/braai area overlooking the river. Power is supplied by mains electricity. Finally, there's the campsite, with 8 pitches on a flat grassy area, & an ablution block with hot showers privately enclosed by reed & wooden walls. While each of the pitches has its own fireplace, the campsite offers a communal fireplace/braai area as well as an air-conditioned bar with snooker table & DSTV, & its own swimming pool.

High over the river, next to a young baobab tree, is the main camp's lounge/bar, with great river views from the terrace. Behind is a cool, thatched dining area surrounded by reed walls, although dinner is normally served around the fire. There's a small pool nearby.

Activities from camp include boat trips in flat-bottomed motorboats with canopies. These hold up to 12 people, plus a guide. Canoeing is also possible if booked in advance, from US$30 pp for a 3hr trip around Kanyemba Island to US$100 pp per day for a guided overnight safari downriver. Fishing is a prime attraction, with boats available from US$55 per half day, & a small amount of tackle on hand. Off the water, the camp is planning to commence game drives into the national park, though it's worth noting that the distances here are quite significant. *Chalet US$140 pp sharing, tent US$98 pp sharing, both FB, inc afternoon boat cruise; self-catering cottage US$140; camping US$10 pp (tent & bedding extra US$15 per night).*

🏠 **Kanyemba Lodge** (6 rondavels, 1 family unit) m 097 7755720; e info@kanyemba.com; www.kanyemba.com. One of the newer lodges in the valley, just 1km from Kiambi, Kanyemba was opened in 2002 by Zambian-born Italian Riccardo Garbaccio. From its bougainvillea-adorned entrance to the expanses of green lawns, it's clear that this place is aiming upmarket – with one eye firmly on the Italian traveller – & there's no doubt that foodies will appreciate the Italian-based cuisine.

Guests stay in cool, spacious stone-&-thatch rondavels, one of which is a honeymoon suite, or in the larger family unit with 3 en-suite rooms. Stone floors offset solid wooden furniture with dbl or twin beds & a walk-in wardrobe; each room has an en-suite bathroom, & a private wooden veranda facing the river. In similar style, the central restaurant/bar is comfortably furnished & decorated with batik wall-hangings, with a small library upstairs. To the front, a stone terrace is shaded by a wild mango tree, & chaises longues are set by a small pool near the river. The lodge is connected to mains electricity.

Activities include birdwatching, game walks on Kanyemba Island, canoeing, fishing (tackle is included), boating, village walks & sunset cruises. Game drives may be organised on request, but given the lodge's distance from the national park, it isn't in the best location to see game. Kanyemba are currently building a bushcamp on Kanyemba Island, the largest island on the Zambezi, which they have just purchased.

Unusually for this area, Kanyemba is open almost all year, closing only in Feb. *US$295/365 pp sharing/sgl FB, inc cordials, tea/coffee & activities (but not park entry fees). Transfers from Lusaka US$100 pp return (min 2).* ☺ *Mar–Jan.*

🏠 **Kayila Lodge** (8 chalets, tree house) Contact via Safari Par Excellence, page 190, or e kayila@safpar.com. Visitors to Kayila often delight in the dizzy heights of the tree house, set high up in a sausage tree with a bird's-eye view of the river below, & with its own bathroom at the bottom of the tree. There are also several chalets & a large, secluded honeymoon suite. This last, with its king-size bed & stone bath, is open to the river on one side, which lends a feeling of space.

The lodge's central thatched lounge/dining area is built with open sides, & set in a small group of baobabs on a low rise, with views of the river & surrounding escarpment. The inside of 1 of those great trees has been converted into a toilet, complete with washbasin, accessed by a small door in its trunk – quite a feature! Nearby is the lodge's swimming pool.

Activities include day & night game drives, game walks in the area around Kayila, village tours, sunset cruises, fishing (bring your own rods & tackle), canoeing & even hiking in the mountains on the edge of the escarpment. The lodge is located in the Chiawa GMA, some 45km from Chirundu and about an hour's drive from the national park. Visitors can fly in by charter plane to Kayila's airstrip (◉ 15°47'S; 29°12'E), 1km or so east of the lodge, or transfer by boat from Gwabi River Lodge. *US$140 pp inc all meals & 2 activities per day, but exc drinks and transfers.* ☺ *15 Mar–15 Jan.*

🏠 **Mvuu Lodge** (10 rooms, camping) ☎ +27 16 987 1837; m 083 277 3031, 628 7364; f +27 16 987 2655; e info@mvuulodge.com; www.mvuulodge.com. It's difficult to escape the hippos at Mvuu (the name means 'hippo'), a relaxed & welcoming lodge 18km west of the national park that has been completely rebuilt since a fire in 2002. Most visitors arrive by boat from Gwabi River Lodge.

Narrow, flower-lined paths wind through the grass, linking the central area to various styles of accommodation. Five chalets are for self-catering guests, with their own braai & fire, & all equipment provided; just bring your own food. A further 5 Meru-style tents each have a reed-screened bathroom (with shower or bath) & a wooden terrace looking across to the river; quilted bedcovers & wooden shelves indicate a thoughtful hand behind the décor. Lighting is provided by paraffin or battery lamps. There are 3 campsites: one in the centre of the site, a second right on the river, & the third secluded & shady; each has its own braai area, plus private shower & flush toilet. In addition, there's an open-air ablutions block with stone-&-reed walls & running hot water. The place is popular with overlanders & canoeing safari companies, with tents available for rent.

The large central area is open on three sides with a stone terrace & views over the river. Simply furnished with wooden dining table & chairs, it also has a small area with cane chairs. Carved hippos sit atop the posts & on the circular bar, & more hippos adorn the doors. There's a boma area by the river & a small plunge pool.

Activities include game drives, short walks, fishing (tackle may be hired), half-day canoeing safaris, & overnight hikes. There are also plans for lunch trips to the islands & perhaps to a waterfall in the mountains. *Luxury US$240 pp, sharing, inc FB, 2 game activities, sundowner cruise; budget US$200 inc meals, 1 game activity; self-catering US$100/150 per lodge (2/4 people); camping US$20 pp. 3-day canoe safari US$400 pp FB (min 2); game activities from US$30 pp; fishing/canoeing from US$75 pp (min 2). 40% sgl supplement. Bar, transfers, park fees & bed levy extra. Closed Jan.*

🏠 **Baines' River Camp** (6 chalets) ☎ +27 33 3242293; m +27 82 8064074; f +27 33 3429778; e info@bainesrivercamp.co.za; www.bainesrivercamp.co.za. Recently rebuilt from the earlier Kiubo Camp, Baines' is located just 16km west of the national park, & about 50km from the pontoon, although most guests arrive by plane at the nearby Royal or Kayila airstrips. The lodge is notable for being at a point on the riverbank where the Zambezi Escarpment comes very close to the river, which makes a lovely scenic backdrop.

Accommodation has been completely revamped, taking the camp seriously upmarket. Set amongst giant tamarind & jackalberry trees, colonial-style suites, each with a large, private veranda & chairs, face the river across to Mana Pools. Inside, king-size

or twin beds under a ceiling fan are enhanced by good-quality fabrics & natural hardwood; there is also a minibar & personal safe. All have luxurious bathrooms with bath & shower, & canvas roofs to shade them from the sun. A further 2 suites, to be completed in Oct 2007, will feature outdoor showers, cast-iron baths & private plunge pools.

In the new lodge area, to be completed by Mar 2008, redesigned public areas will include reception, dining, lounge, bar, wireless internet & conference facilities overlooking teak decks and a 15m pool.

As you would expect, the full range of activities is on offer here. In addition, there are opportunities for the enthusiast to participate in fly-fishing clinics, birding weeks & photographic workshops. *US$500 pp sharing, inc FB, drinks, minibar, activities, laundry, airstrip transfers, WiFi connectivity, exc park fees & govt taxes; 30% sgl supplement.* ☺ *Apr–Dec.*

🏠 **Kasaka River Lodge** (8 chalets, family house) ☎ 021 1268145; ☎/f 021 1260012; e kasaka@coppernet.zm; nyamsaf@coppernet.zm; www.kasakariverlodge.com. Opened in 2001, Kasaka is well situated 5km to the west of the national park. The cool entrance lodge leads through to well-tended lawns, where tented chalets on stone-clad platforms face a pool with umbrellas & chaises longues. Suspended wooden walkways lead over an ornamental pool past the dining area & beyond to a further 4 chalets 'on the wild side', which include a secluded honeymoon suite complete with Ottoman-style bed & its own open-air bath. If the other rooms are a bit on the small side, they're also well equipped. For families, there's an entirely separate 2–3-bedroom unit, the 'Hippo Pod', with its own viewing deck. A hexagonal living area with comfortable leather chairs is cut into the steep hillside with views across the river far below.

A change of ownership in 2006 brought a change of focus, with activities now taking centre stage. Aside from game drives (by day & night), river cruises & fishing trips, canoeing & fly fishing have been introduced, as have cultural visits; the lodge is actively involved with local schools. Those seeking privacy can indulge in bush picnics, private dinners or lunch on Nyamangwe Island, while families are unusually well catered for, with children's menus, games and an entire 'Bush Kids' programme. *US$350/380 pp sharing/sgl Apr, May; US$395/425 Jun–Nov, all inc FB, activities & drinks, exc park fees. Hippo Pod US$1,500 per night (max 6 people).* ☺ *Apr–Nov.*

🏠 **Royal Zambezi Lodge** (14 suites) ☎/f 021 1261265; e royalzambezihq@iwayafrica.com;

www.royalzambezilodge.com. Situated just 4km west of the national park, with a full 3km of river frontage, Royal Zambezi reopened in 2007 after a complete facelift. Luxurious tented suites with twin or dbl beds are elegantly furnished, their walls softened by all-round white mosquito netting. Each has en-suite facilities & is protected from the sun under a thatched roof. Wooden doors open on to a porch, where rocking chairs offer the perfect vantage point for watching the antics of vervet monkeys on well-watered green lawns against the broader picture of the river beyond. The night silence is broken by the grunting of hippos, sounding far closer than they really are.

The intimate Sausage Tree Bar, right on the river, is built around the trunk of a large sausage tree, *Kigelia africana*, with wooden decking & a newly built infinity pool alongside for cooling off. Meals are usually taken under the stars, near the river, although there's a small dining area as well, complete with formal white napiery. A recent addition is the Royal Bush Spa, offering a variety of beauty treatments.

While activities include drives into the park, canoeing, & short walking trips, the camp specialises in fishing, a firm favourite with the manager. To get here the camp offers a daily plane shuttle service from Lusaka to Royal Airstrip (US$85pp sgl). Alternatively you can drive yourself to Gwabi River Lodge, leave your vehicle there for US$4 per day, then transfer by boat for US$450 return; the boat trip takes about 1½hrs. *US$350 off peak, US$600 pp high season, all pp sharing, inc FB, drinks & all activities, but exc park entry fees.* ☺ *all year.*

Ⓧ Chiawa Community Campsite On the edge of the national park, right on the river, & quite close to Chongwe River Camp, this is a flat, sandy site with some shade. Its basic showers & toilets were being refurbished in 2007, but there are no other facilities at all, so visitors need to be entirely self-sufficient. It is primarily used by companies running organised canoeing trips. *US$10 pp, per night.*

🏠 Chongwe River Camp (8 chalets) ☎ 021 1286808; f 021 1286688; e info@chongwe.com; www.chongwe.com. Set right on the Chongwe River that marks the boundary between the GMA and the national park, at its confluence with the Zambezi, Chongwe has an enviable location, with a far greater concentration of game here than further west, but without the high charges levied by the park's authorities.

Most visitors arrive by private plane at Royal Airstrip, or by boat, but if you're driving yourself,

keep left at the forked entrance to the national park, then follow the signs along a sandy track.

Originally a campsite, the lodge now has Meru-style tented chalets widely spread along the river, each with twin pine beds, small shaded porch & an open-air bathroom. And to cool off, there's a swimming pool behind the chalets.

Central to the site is a large lounge & bar with a sandy terrace for dining, in the shade of an old winterthorn, *Faidherbia albida*, its pods beloved of the local elephant population. In fact, the whole place feels very much part of the bush, with elephants wandering around very close to the tents, a tame impala, Silky, who roams freely through the large camp, & good birding, explained in part by the proximity of the Lower Zambezi Escarpment. The atmosphere is informal & friendly, with knowledgeable & informative staff & good guiding, & the lodge is also popular with fishing groups. *US$600 pp sharing, inc FB, drinks, park permits & activities.* ☺ *Apr–mid-Nov.*

🏠 Albida Suite (2 chalets) Contact via Chongwe River Camp, above. This exclusive addition to Chongwe River Camp opened near the confluence with the Zambezi in 2007. Each of its en-suite octagonal tents has a private lounge/dining area & its own pool, making this ideal for families or groups of 4, but still able to provide privacy for 2 separate couples by prior agreement. Bathrooms, with a bath and double shower, are canvas covered but open to the bush, while pathways connect through the gardens. Guests can retain total privacy, or can join the main camp for meals and a drink if they prefer. *US$700 pp sharing, inc FB, drinks, park permits & activities.* ☺ *Apr–mid-Nov.*

🏠 Bushbuck Bushcamp (3 chalets) Contact via Chongwe River Camp, above. This fly-camp was set up in the bush for those who would like to include a night or two outside of Chongwe River Camp. It is set high above the river on the red cliffs, about a 30-minute drive upstream, with views of the Muchinga Escarpment. Each of the mulati tents has space for 2 beds, & a grass-walled bathroom with bucket showers. There's an interesting day trip to the Chongwe River Falls, about 2hrs' walk north of the camp.

Bushbuck is a classic small bushcamp – as most were 15 years ago – which concentrates its activities on walking safaris, although drives may be possible also; it's best used as a 1–2-night complement to Chongwe River Camp. Note that Chongwe is planning a similarly simple 'Island Camp', further west in the GMA, which is likely to have activities run in conjunction with one of the local communities. *US$600 pp sharing, inc FB, drinks, park permits & activities.* ⊕ *Jun–mid-Oct.*

⌂ **Chongwe River House** Contact via Robin Pope Safaris, page 261. At the end of a massive winterthorn grove, *Faidherbia albida*, this unique private retreat lies on the banks of the peaceful Chongwe River, with a spectacular view of the nearby mountainous escarpment. The entire house is built of ferro walls & wild wood, so its structure follows the natural lines of the branches used. There is not a straight line to be seen! The main room looks out over the deck & pool to the river & mountains beyond. Furniture in the sitting room has been carved from a sgl huge fallen winterthorn tree, as if it had come to rest across the room, while

embedded in the ceilings are pastel-coloured pebbles from the river. Each of the ground-floor bedrooms is entered through a tunnel, rather like walking through a cave; the curved entrance gives privacy without the need for doors. Downstairs bathrooms have water pouring out of the stone ceiling instead of the normal shower rose, & upstairs the showers are waterfalls. There are wooden 'taps', & the basins have been carved out of wood & white marble by the Zambian artist, Eddie Mumba. From the bedrooms, the sitting room & the deck you will have game in view, feeding & watering; even the unusual baths in the upstairs bedrooms afford a view across the bush, inc the huge elephants attracted by the house's winterthorn trees. *US$850 pp sharing Jun–Oct (Jun & Oct min 4, Jul–Sep min 6), US$650 pp sharing Apr–May & Nov (min 4).*

Within the Lower Zambezi National Park (park fees US$30 pp per day, plus US$15 per vehicle per day)

⌂ **Chiawa Camp** (9 tented chalets) G&G Safaris; ☏ 021 1261588; f 021 1262683; e info@ chiawa.com; www.chiawa.com. Chiawa is a small, friendly & highly efficient camp set beneath a grove of mahogany trees, about 8km (30 mins' drive) inside the national park. Being in the park, Chiawa is a seasonal camp used only during the dry season, so is mostly built of wood, canvas & reeds, giving it a pleasantly rustic air. Its rooms are well spaced, insect-proof, Meru-style tents on raised timber decks facing the river, with 12v lighting, 220v power for charging, & en-suite facilities – flush toilets & hot showers – at the back. Several have dbl beds, the rest twin. Three new 'superior' tents have king-size beds, with facilities that feature a bath, indoor & outdoor showers, & twin washbasins. Central to the camp is a lounge/bar area of dark wood construction, with a small library of books & magazines, while above is a second comfortable seating & viewing area. Meals are taken in the open air to the front, overlooking the river.

There are 2 ways of getting to the camp from Lusaka: by road transfer (3hrs) then motorboat (a further 2 hrs) which is fun but very expensive, or by flying (40 mins) into either Jeki or Royal Airstrip, each about 1hr's drive away. Private flights from elsewhere, inc the Luangwa, can also be organised.

A full range of activities is offered, from walking safaris & 4x4 trips (inc night drives), to motorboat & short canoe trips along the river; the team is notably flexible about arranging activities around their guests. Chiawa has also maintained a top

reputation for serious fishing trips for tigerfish (all catch & release), though only a few of its visitors just want to fish. For those choosing to while away a few hours in camp, there's a high viewing platform overlooking the river.

In 2006, out of about 200 game-viewing days, the camp had 230 separate sightings of leopard (about half in daylight hrs), 262 of lion, & 9 of wild dog; unusually, there were also 2 sightings of aardvark. This is a very good record, but typical of what a top private camp with good guides can achieve in Zambia.

On a broader front, as part of its commitment to the development of conservation education, Chiawa & its guests fund the education of 160 AIDS orphans in local village schools, & is a top contributor to the funding of anti-poaching, environmental education programmes & conservation in the area. Chiawa is run by a family team & has carved out a reputation as one of Zambia's top camps. 'Classic' *US$795/1,035 pp sharing/sgl (US$595 Apr–May),* 'superior' *US$895/1,165, all pp sharing sgl, inc FB, all activities, drinks, laundry & park fees.* ⊕ *15 Apr–15 Nov.*

⌂ **Sausage Tree** (7 tents) ☏ +260 1223697; f +260 1223689; e info@sausagetreecamp.com; www.sausagetreecamp.com. Sausage Tree is set in a beautiful position inside the Lower Zambezi National Park, & it is usually accessed by a short flight to either Royal or (closer) Jeki Airstrip. A possible alternative is to transfer by boat from Gwabi River Lodge, a trip of almost two hours. If you're planning to drive in, you'll need to warn them well in advance; this isn't an easy place to find.

Sausage Tree is privately owned & professionally staffed & run, with first-class food & attentive service. Its tents are large & unusual, being of an oval marquee design in cream canvas, with reed walls around the sides & tree-shaded bathrooms; each of the 2 honeymoon suites – a third is under construction – also has a bath. Solid teak furniture is used throughout, as are 1st-class ivory fabrics & linen sheets, & there's an emergency radio in each room. Each tent is the responsibility of an individual *muchinda* or butler, & power is supplied by generator.

The sense of an English summer wedding extends to the creamy-coloured canvas of the circular living & dining tents, both right by the river. Now lying in the shallows just in front is the sausage tree after which the camp was named; its branches are popular perches for various species of bee-eater. One of the camp's main assets is the proximity of a lovely backwater, the Chifungulu Channel, which runs parallel to the main river for about 14km & makes a great area for a gentle paddle. It's popular with the local hippo population, too, particularly Frank. *Chifungulu* is said to be the local name for *Combretum microphyllum,* the 'flame creeper' with blood-red flowers that grows up winterthorn trees here. Smith's book on the Luangwa's flora, see *Appendix 3,* page 512, observes that some local people used to grind up the roots of this creeper, mix them with dog turds, & then burn the mixture – using the ashes as a cure for lunacy. It's uncertain if anyone at the camp has ever tried this. Expect the full range of day & night drives, canoeing, walking, boating & fishing trips, while in the evening private dinners can be arranged. *US$795–995 pp sharing (US$565 Apr, May, Nov), honeymoon US$895 pp sharing, all inc FB, drinks, all activities & park fees, but exc flight transfers from Jeki at US$90 pp, one way.* ⊕ *Apr–15 Nov.*

⌂ **Mwambashi River Lodge** (8 tents) , ☎ +27 41 581 6437, +26 01 278 249; e francie@ lionroars.com, mwambashi@gmail.com. Mwambashi occupies a well-shaded site with large *albida* trees, typical of this riverine environment. Most visitors arrive by plane at Jeki Airstrip, with transfers costing US$300 from Lusaka, return.

Its large, walk-in tents are all built on wooden platforms with verandas overlooking the river. Each has a dbl or twin beds with mosquito-netted walls & large en-suite toilet, shower & washbasin at the back under a canvas roof. The central living/dining area is on a raised platform, with a thatched roof &

an open balcony, & a bar (& toilet) on the ground level beneath. Dominated by a large wooden table, this feels rather grand, although the effect is softened by batik wall-hangings & a small area with reference books & games. Close to the river, there's a plunge pool with its own deck.

Activities involve day & night game drives, walking safaris, canoeing & boat trips, & fishing. *US$575 pp–Nov, US$490 Apr–Jun, inc FB, activities & park entry fees.* ⊕ *Apr–mid Nov.*

⌂ **Old Mondoro** (4 chalets) Contact via Chiawa or Sausage Tree (both opposite). This remote bushcamp started life as the old Potato Bush Camp & is the only bushcamp in the Lower Zambezi National Park. Today, it is jointly owned & run by Chiawa Camp & Sausage Tree, & staffed independently by an experienced team. Although it is normally recommended that visitors coming to Old Mondoro (*mondoro* means 'lion' in the Shona language) should spend a little time first at either Chiawa or Sausage Tree, it can also work well as a stand-alone camp.

A canvas-roofed central area with timber decking overlooks the Zambezi, as do the chalets, each with its own wooden veranda. Chalets are set on temporary concrete platforms with reed walls that are low enough to give views onto the river; canvas sides can be rolled down for greater warmth or privacy. Simply furnished with comfortable teak beds (2 chalets have a dbl) & teak chairs, they have en-suite facilities with flush toilets, hot & cold water & bucket showers. Lighting comes from lanterns, but a generator – run only when guests are out of camp – supplies power for freezers & charging batteries. Dinner is taken outside at solid tables under the trees, alongside a sitting area, with a firepit by the river. The camp is surrounded by open woodland, with a focus on walking, day & night game drives, canoe trips & game viewing by boat. Note that no fishing trips are available here. This is very much a bushcamp experience, for those seeking an emphasis on guiding & wildlife rather than creature comforts, though the standard of food & service remains very high. *US$650/975 pp sharing/sgl, inc FB & all activities. Private safari (entire camp) US$4,550 per night.* ⊕ *May–Oct.*

⌂ **Zambezi Kulefu Camp** (7 chalets, max 12 guests) Contact Sanctuary Lodges & Camps, page 261. Taken over in 2007 by the exclusive Sanctuary Lodges & Camps group, the already-upmarket Kulefu lies deep within the national park, almost cut off from the main track by a small river. Most visitors are transferred by boat from the nearby Kulefu Airstrip.

Built alongside a channel of the Zambezi, the camp is being completely refurbished as this guide goes to press. The existing large brick-and-canvas chalets will remain, set on platforms either side of the camp's communal areas. Each will have 4-poster twin beds with mosquito nets & large ceiling fans, its own shaded veranda, & covered, en-suite facilities which inc twin washbasins, a shower & separate bath, & a toilet. Teak furnishing will be complemented by white muslin tent linings & tie-back curtains, adding a touch of luxury to the tented sides. Electric lighting is supplied by a generator.

The spacious lounge is linked to the open dining area on the riverbank, under *Faidherbia albida* & *Acacia robusta* trees, although meals are often served al fresco on one of the nearby islands. A spacious deck leading to a small pool at the water's edge makes an airy place to spend the afternoon, watching game & the river's birdlife.

Activities will remain very flexible, with the camp's relative location ensuring that game drives & boating are very private. Walking & fishing are also options. *US$595/775 pp sharing/sgl Jun–Oct, US$400 pp Apr–May, Nov, inc FB, most drinks, laundry, activities & park fees. No children under 12. ☺ Apr–16 Nov.*

🏠 **Ana Tree Lodge** (8 chalets) Eastern Safaris; ☏ 021 1287508; ☏/f 021 1223779;

e anatreelodge@zamnet.zm; www.anatreelodge.com (✪ 15°61.013'S; 029°76.990'E). Formerly Mushika Camp, Ana Tree Lodge is located within the Lower Zambezi NP, on the Mushika River a few kilometres east of Zambezi Kulefu & just 4km from a new airstrip; the lodge has its own 8-seater aircraft which can be used for transfers.

Opened in 2004, the lodge has tented chalets spread out along an old riverbank. Each stands on a tiled, concrete deck & inside has cane furniture & an en-suite shower, washbasin & toilet. The décor & style are a little dated, & the fabrics far from modern, but the tents are functional & comfortable. There's a large, thatched central dining room/lounge/bar, furnished in similar style, outside of which is an open firepit area, surrounded by paraffin lanterns, & a small plunge-pool. Activities include game viewing by boat or vehicle, canoeing, fishing & birdwatching. Ana Tree is seldom full, & often relatively quiet — it's certainly in a fairly quiet area of the park — so it might make an interesting possibility if the aesthetics of the camp's décor isn't on your list of priorities.

Note that for religious reasons the camp's owners have nothing to do with the running of the camp's bar — so this is usually run by the managers. Thus alcoholic drinks are always charged as an extra. *US$485/660 pp sharing/sgl, inc FB, activities, laundry, park fees & bed levy. ☺ Apr–Nov.*

East of the national park There are normally a few small camps operating to the east side of the national park & the Mpata Gorge. These are usually reached from the village of Luangwa (See *Chapter 10*, page 245), which itself is readily accessible by 2WD from the Great East Road. At present, the most reliable is:

🏠 **Redcliff Zambezi Lodge** (6 chalets) ☏ +27 12 653 2664; f +27 12 654 4015; e info@redcliff-lodge.com; www.redcliff-lodge.com. Tucked away in a game management area between the dramatic scenery of the Mpata Gorge & the village of Luangwa (often referred to as 'Luangwa boma') on the Mozambique border, is the South-African-owned Redcliff Zambezi. Access is either from Luangwa Boma Airstrip (✪ 15°38'S; 30°24'E), or by boat from the village; the trip takes about 30 mins. Luangwa can be reached fairly easily by road from the Great East Road (turn south on the west side of the bridge over the Luangwa), or by charter flight from Lusaka or Livingstone.

Accommodation is in en-suite tented chalets, with 2 or 4 beds, the latter layout designed for families. An 'entertainment area' encompasses the lounge, dining room & bar, its veranda overlooking the river. The lodge is said to be particularly popular for fishing, mostly on a catch-&-release basis. Visitors may also take day trips through the gorge by boat into the national park, or to see the vestiges of the slave-trade industry in the vicinity of Luangwa village. *US$300 pp sharing, FB, inc transfers from Luangwa village, laundry & fishing. ☺ all year.*

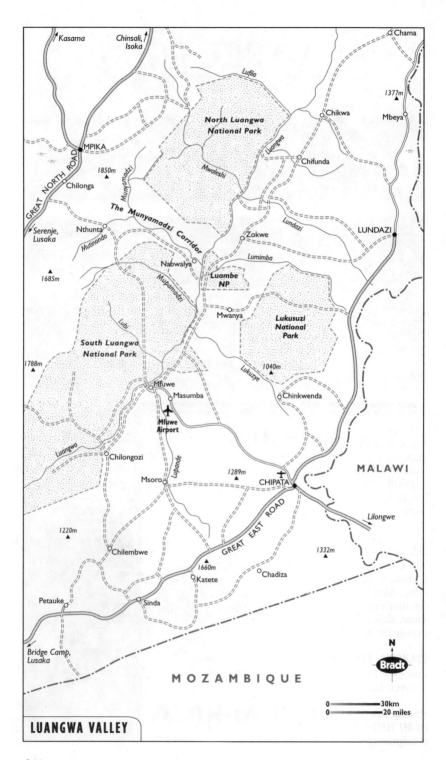

LUANGWA VALLEY

10

The Luangwa Valley

This lush rift valley, enclosed by steep escarpment walls, is one of the continent's finest areas for wildlife. Four national parks protect parts of the area: South Luangwa, North Luangwa, Luambe and Lukusuzi. Separating these are game management areas (GMAs), which also contain good populations of game. This entire valley is remote but, for the enthusiast, the wildlife is well worth the effort made to get here.

For most visitors, South Luangwa National Park (known locally as just 'the South Park') is by far the most practical park to visit in the valley. This is the largest of the parks, with superb wildlife and many excellent camps. Organising a trip to South Luangwa is not difficult, and its infrastructure is easily the best. However, it is still a very remote park, and so most visitors arrive on trips organised outside Zambia. A few arrive independently and, though this is possible, it does limit their accommodation and activity choices.

The more intrepid might organise a safari from the South Park into North Luangwa, which is even more remote and exclusive. Its wildlife is now flourishing, thanks to some intensive conservation efforts over the past decade, and the few safaris that do run concentrate on taking small groups for purely walking trips.

Luambe National Park is much smaller than either the South or the North parks, and there's one very promising new camp there that makes a perfect stopover if you're heading that way. The birdwatching is good, as with the other parks, though there is less game.

Finally, Lukusuzi National Park is something of an unknown quantity. Few people have even visited this park and there are currently no facilities or camps there.

THE GREAT EAST ROAD

The Great East Road leads from Lusaka to Chipata, the Luangwa's 'gateway'. That is about 570km of tar which is good in places, and pot-holed in others. It's a long drive. Alternatively, there are regular buses – though even leaving Lusaka early in the morning might not get you to Chipata by evening. There's relatively little en route, although just beyond Chipata is the little-visited town of Lundazi, notable mainly for its anachronistic castle.

LUANGWA RIVER AREA There's one **place to stay** on the west bank of the Luangwa River, close to the Great East Road. It's the obvious place to sleep between Lusaka and the Luangwa (or Malawi):

⌂ **Bridge Camp** (10 chalets, camping) Feira Rd;
m 097 7197456; f 021 1295546;
e bridgecamp@gawab.com; www.bridgecamp.com.

This budget camp, operating under Changa Changa Adventures, is 230km east of Lusaka; to find it, turn off the Great East Rd just before the Luangwa

Bridge, then continue for a further 3km, as indicated by the signpost. It offers a range of simple accommodation, from twin & 3-bunk chalets to family chalets with 4 beds. All are built of stone, with thatched roofs, windows of gauze (chicken-wire), & generator- or solar-powered electrics. Some are en suite; others share toilets & showers. There are also 2 separate tree-shaded campsites, with BBQ facilities & their own ablution blocks. The camp runs a bar & has a small pool (which was empty when I last visited), both open to all guests. It's also possible to organise meals on request. Activities include guided hiking & canoeing trips; overnight hike to the confluence of the Lunsemfwa & Zambezi, followed by canoeing back the following morning; & 4–7 nights' trekking in the Lunsemfwa Gorge. Overnight trips are self-catering, & you'll need your own equipment, though you can hire tents & sleeping bags. *Chalet Kw120,000/175,000 pp, sharing facilities/en suite; camping Kw25,000 pp. B/fast Kw20,000–40,000, lunch from Kw20,000, dinner Kw60,000–90,000. Hiking Kw25,000–50,000 ¹/₂/full day; self-paddle canoe (dry season only) Kw60,000–360,000 per canoe; overnight hike/canoe trip Kw600,000 per boat per day, max 4 people; Lunsemfwa Gorge trek Kw600,000 per group per day.*

PETAUKE Little more than a dot on the map, this small town nevertheless does have a campsite and a simple motel.

Where to stay

⌂ **Nyika Motel** ☎ 021 6371002, 6371153. This comes recommended as a clean & safe place to stay, & as serving a decent meal of chicken & rice if requested. $

KATETE This is another fairly nondescript town on the way to Chipata from Lusaka. Katete is home to a large mosque, a useful filling station, a Finance Bank, post office, and half a dozen grocery shops. There's also a Catholic church on the southern side of the road at the western end of town and the St Francis Mission Hospital. Perhaps of most interest to travellers, there are a couple of simple places to stay, including the Mphangwe Motel (☎ *021 6252311, 6252396*), and, on the north side of Katete a couple of kilometres from the centre, the Tikondane Guesthouse.

⌂ **Tikondane Guesthouse** ☎ 021 6252122; m 097 7382875; e tikocc@zamtel.zm; www.tikondane.org. Next to the hospital, this was set up to raise funds for the Tikondane Community Centre, which brings together a school, skills training & adult education programmes. Guests are welcome to get involved in the community, with opportunities to visit the hospital, join a workshop for drumming or dancing, learn the local language or help out in the centre. A structured programme of voluntary work means that those with as little as 2 weeks can contribute to the project. *US$11/14 sgl/dbl; dorm bed US$6–7.*

CHIPATA Chipata (⊕ CHIPAT 13°38.557'S; 32°38.796'E) is a relatively small but busy town that is more than just a gateway to South Luangwa; it is also a border town just 30km from Malawi. Known in colonial days as Fort Jameson, and now the capital of Eastern Province, Chipata stands in a valley, surrounded by quite a fertile area of subsistence farms with low bush-covered hills around. To the east of town is an attractive mosque.

Getting there and away

By air The easiest way to get to Chipata is by air. The town has a good all-weather asphalt airstrip. Zambian Airways (see page 67) has flights linking Chipata to Mfuwe and Lusaka on Monday, Wednesday and Friday. Flights leave Lusaka at 11.30, arriving in Chipata at 12.40, then continuing to Mfuwe at 13.00, to arrive at 13.30 – though schedules change regularly. During the safari season (June–October) it should be a reasonable cost to charter a plane from Mfuwe to Chipata.

By bus In additional to the slower local buses, there's a regular coach service between Chipata and Lusaka. It leaves Chipata at around 05.00 from opposite the Chipata

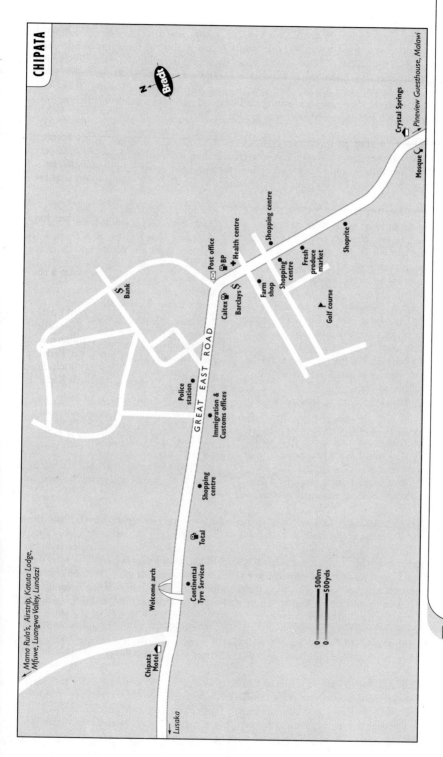

CHIPATA

The Luangwa Valley THE GREAT EAST ROAD

10

247

Farm Shop (south of the Caltex Garage), taking seven to eight hours to Lusaka; tickets cost around Kw95,000 one way. Chipata is also the terminus of one of the postbus routes out of Lusaka, with buses departing from Lusaka every Tuesday and Saturday at 07.00, arriving in Chipata at 14.00; the fare is K75,000 one way.

Local minibuses ply between Chipata and Mfuwe, costing Kw40,000 one way; alternatively, there are taxis available. The good news for travellers is that the road between Chipata and Mfuwe was graded in 2007.

Where to stay Most visitors continue to the Mfuwe area, down in the Luangwa Valley, if they can. However, if you arrive late then staying in Chipata is a wise move, and hitchhikers could easily end up here for a night or two due to lack of lifts. There are several places to lay your head, of which Mama Rula's is probably the best.

Chipata Motel Mfuwe Rd; ℡ 021 6221540. Just on the left on the way to Mfuwe, this is a very basic, run-down motel with twin & 'executive' rooms (the latter with TV), used mainly by low-budget local businesspeople. If you are hitchhiking then it is convenient: the bar will sell you fizzy drinks while you wait, & if traffic is scarce you can stay — though live music could disturb your sleep. $

Crystal Springs Hotel ℡ 021 6222006. Opposite the mosque, this hotel is a cut above the Chipata Motel (above), for just a few kwacha more. $

Dean's Hills View This English-owned place has been recommended recently by a reader; details would be welcome!

Katuta Lodge (20 rooms, camping) Mfuwe Rd. Located about 4km past Mama Rula's turn off, near the airport, the lodge is set in 20 acres of landscaped grounds. Clean, en-suite sgl or dbl rooms are all en suite, & local & Western food is available in the restaurant. $. *Camping US$5 pp.*

Mama Rula's (10 rooms, camping) m 097 7768021, 7790226; e mamarula@iwayafrica.com;

www.mamarulas.com. Probably the best place in Chipata, Mama Rula's is well signposted about 2km off the main Mfuwe road. It's run by Andrea, & 4x4 adventurers should note that she has close contacts with Luangwa Wilderness Lodge (see page 293). The campsite covers a large lawn under a canopy of marvellous red mahogany (*Khaya nyasica*) trees & the odd banana or papaya. The ablutions are clean & well-kept. There are also simple en-suite guest rooms, all slightly different, & an annexe with en-suite 'executive' rooms with twin beds. There's a dining room with a bar & DSTV for the use of guests, as well as a tree-shaded pool. With a week's notice, & a fee of US$20 to cover the taxi fare, they'll organise a visa waiver at the border; you'll need to supply full passport details. *Guesthouse Kw285,000–330,000, annexe Kw382,500, all DBB. Camping Kw25,000 pp. Special rates for overland trucks.*

Pineview Guesthouse ℡ 021 6221633. Another option to the southeast of town, with dbl rooms. $

Other practicalities On your right as you arrive by road from Lusaka, just after the welcome arch, there is a useful Total fuel station. The police station is about 1.5km after this on your left, after which there is a left turning that leads to the main township and market – from where all the local buses depart. The road then bends to the right, and shortly after that are the main post office, a couple of fuel stations and two banks, of which Barclays has an ATM (but note that it accepts only VISA cards, not MasterCard). There's a bureau de change in town, but rates aren't great. Further southeast, a large branch of Shoprite is set back from the right side of the road. This is the town's largest and best supermarket, although the market on the same side of the road is well worth a visit, with fresh and varied produce. There's a good health centre next to the BP fuel station by the traffic lights.

LUNDAZI About 180km north of Chipata, well off any obvious route for travellers, lies the small, friendly town of Lundazi. It's perched high above the eastern side of the Luangwa Valley, and close to a quiet border crossing to Malawi.

Lundazi has no large supermarkets, but plenty of small, local shops where you can buy most essentials. There are a lot of farming areas around, so fresh produce is available. It also has a few banks, a post office, a police station, an airstrip, assorted places of worship (Christian and Muslim), a mission station, a convent – and a fairy-tale Norman-style castle complete with a dungeon, turrets and battlements.

Getting there The easiest way to reach Lundazi is **from Chipata**. Then it's just 180km of (very pot-holed) tar, accessible in a sturdy 2WD if you've got the patience. This drive will take about five hours in a strong high-clearance 4x4, longer if you need to be gentle with your vehicle.

From the north reaching Lundazi from Isoka is trickier, requiring a high-clearance 4x4 and even more time and patience. Shortly after the left turning to Isoka on the Great North Road as you head northeast, you come to a turning to the right, signposted to the 'airport bar'. Take this turning, which will lead you through Ntendere and up into the mountains. After about 75km, there's a fork and you turn right, heading almost south to reach Muyombe 50km later. It's a rocky road on the escarpment with many gullies, but the scenery is beautiful. From Muyombe, continue south towards Nyika Plateau and the border with Malawi, dropping down from the mountains as you do so. After around 25km, just before the Malawi border, turn right (southwest) onto a dirt road. This is generally good, though sandy in parts. After shadowing the border for some 70km, there's a fork and Lundazi is signposted to the left, whilst Chama is about 35km away if you take the right turn. Lundazi is now about 110km south of you; making the whole journey a very full day's drive from Isoka.

From the Luangwa Valley there are two roads. Both are impassable during the rains, and even in the dry season require hours of hard 4x4 travel. The better of them leaves the main road on the east side of the valley about 20–25km north of Luambe National Park. It then climbs up the escarpment directly to Lundazi, about 130km away. It's a five-hour drive.

The second turns eastwards around the northern boundary of South Luangwa National Park and then cuts up the escarpment through Lukusuzi National Park. It then joins the Chipata–Lundazi road some 60km south of Lundazi (120km north of Chipata).

Where to stay There's only one place of choice (though it's pretty basic). If the castle's full then the town has several other small, basic resthouses, including the Tigone, where all the rooms are en suite.

Lundazi Castle Hotel (17 rooms) ☎ 021 6480251. Dick Hobson's excellent *Tales of Zambia* (see Appendix 3, page 510) tells of how the district commissioner in the late 1940s, Errol Button, needed to build a resthouse here. Tourism was then taking off & visitors needed to stop between Nyika Plateau & the Luangwa Valley (the same could be said today!). Button designed & had built a small castle in Norman style, with thick walls & narrow slits for archers, overlooking a lake. It has a dungeon, high turrets at each corner & battlements all around. It was christened 'Rumpelstiltskin' after a fairy-tale character favoured by his daughter, and cost a mere £500 at the time. The castle quickly became very popular, & was extended in 1952 to accommodate more visitors.

Now the castle remains a small, basic hotel, very cold in winter & often fully booked. All but 4 of the rooms share bathrooms, though running water is not always available. Simple traditional meals are served, normally a choice of meats with nshima. $

SOUTH LUANGWA NATIONAL PARK

(*Park fees US$35 pp, plus US$15 per vehicle, per day*) There are many contenders for the title of Africa's best game park. The Serengeti, Amboseli, Ngorongoro Crater, Etosha, Kruger, Moremi and Mana Pools would certainly be high on the list. South

10

Luangwa has a better claim than most. Some of these other areas will match its phenomenally high game densities. Many others – the lesser known of Africa's parks – will have equally few visitors. One or two also allow night drives, which open up a different, nocturnal world to view, allowing leopards to be commonly seen and even watched whilst hunting.

However, few have South Luangwa's high quality of guiding together with its remarkable wildlife spectacles, day and night, in the isolation of a true wilderness. These elements, perhaps, are how the contenders ought to be judged, and on these the South Luangwa Park comes out around the top of the list.

BACKGROUND INFORMATION

Note on prehistory Some of the earliest evidence of humans in south-central Africa is currently emerging from excavations in and around the South Luangwa National Park. Stone tools dating to at least two million years ago have been found, and all other periods of the Stone Age are represented in the park. There is also evidence emerging of early farmers in the valley, appearing by AD400. As yet there are no sites accessible to the public, but plans have been afoot for some years to build a museum Mfuwe, on the site of the old cultural centre at Nsendamila, to showcase the valley's rich prehistory.

History

With thanks to John Hudson OBE for his help in preparing this text

With the Zambezi established as a trade route by the 8th century, it seems reasonable to assume that small settlements were also appearing on the neighbouring Luangwa River, though it is harder to navigate and was, at that time, probably used mainly to reach the abundant game of the valley, rather than for any trading purposes. Records tell us that Zumbo, on the eastern banks of the Luangwa, was founded in 1546 by the Portuguese – their first settlement in what is now Zambia – and one can only surmise that Luangwa township itself, situated at the strategically important confluence of the Luangwa and Zambezi rivers, must have been founded at around that time too. Both these settlements were subsequently abandoned and resettled, until about 1763 when Zumbo was recorded as having 200 Portuguese families living within its boundaries.

In the 19th century the area was crossed by many European explorers who came to hunt, trade, bring the Gospel or simply to satisfy their curiosity. Around 1810–20, a trading post was opened at Malambo, some 100km north of Mfuwe. This was on the main trade route from Tete to Lake Mweru, which had first been established by Lacerda as early as 1798.

In his last book, *Kakuli*, Norman Carr quotes a Portuguese captain, Antonio Gamitto, as writing of the Luangwa in around 1832: 'Game of all kinds is very abundant at this season of drought; great numbers of wild animals collect here, leaving dry areas in search of water … we can only say that this district appears to be the richest in animal life of any we have seen.'

Later, in December 1866, when Livingstone crossed the Luangwa at Perekani (a place north of Tafika and south of Chibembe), he was just one of many Europeans exploring the continent. He commented: 'I will make this land better known to men that it may become one of their haunts. It is impossible to describe its luxuriance.'

In 1904 a Luangwa Game Park was declared on the eastern bank of the river. However, this was not maintained, hunting licences were given out to control allegedly marauding elephants, and the park came to mean little. Then on 27 May 1938 three parks were defined in the valley: the North Luangwa Game Reserve, the Lukusuzi Game Reserve and the South Luangwa Game Reserve – which

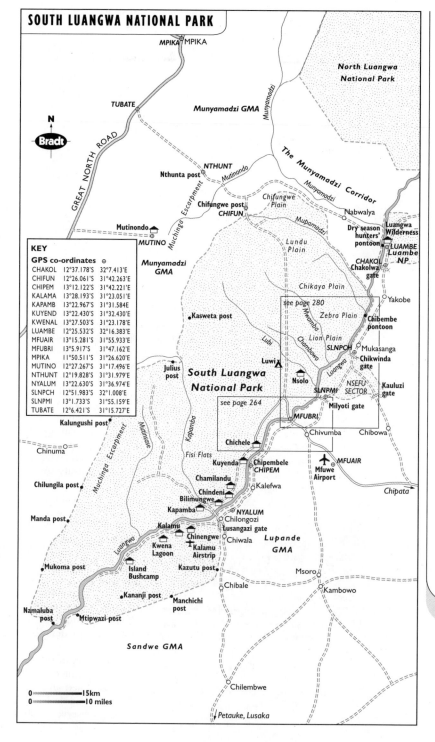

SOUTH LUANGWA NATIONAL PARK

MPIKA MPIKA

North Luangwa
National Park

TUBATE

Munyamadzi GMA

N

Bradt

The Munyamadzi Corridor

GREAT NORTH ROAD

NTHUNT

Nthunta post

Mutinondo

Chifungwe
Plain

Chifungwe post
CHIFUN

Munyamadzi

Nabwalya

Dry season
hunters'
pontoon

Luangwa
Wilderness

Mutinondo

MUTINO

Lundu
Plain

CHAKOL
Chakolwa
gate

LUAMBE
Luambe
NP

Munyamadzi
GMA

Chikaya Plain

see page 280

Zebra Plain

Yakobe

Kasweta post

Lion Plain

Chibembe
pontoon

KEY

GPS co-ordinates ⊕

CHAKOL	12°37.178'S	32°7.413'E
CHIFUN	12°26.061'S	31°42.263'E
CHIPEM	13°12.122'S	31°42.221'E
KALAMA	13°28.193'S	31°23.051'E
KAPAMB	13°22.967'S	31°31.584E
KUYEND	13°22.430'S	31°32.430'E
KWENAL	13°27.503'S	31°23.178'E
LUAMBE	12°25.532'S	32°16.383'E
MFUAIR	13°15.281'S	31°55.933'E
MFUBRI	13°5.917'S	31°47.162'E
MPIKA	11°50.511'S	31°26.620'E
MUTINO	12°27.267'S	31°17.496'E
NTHUNT	12°19.828'S	31°31.979'E
NYALUM	13°22.630'S	31°36.974'E
SLNPCH	12°51.983'S	32°1.008'E
SLNPMI	13°1.733'S	31°55.159'E
TUBATE	12°6.421'S	31°15.727'E

SLNPCH

Mukasanga

Chikwinda
gate

Julius
post

**South Luangwa
National Park**

Luwi

Nsolo

SLNPMI

NSEFU
SECTOR

Kauluzi
gate

see page 264

Milyoti gate

MFUBRI

Kalungushi post

Chivumba

Chibowa

Chinuma

Chichele

Kuyenda

Chipembele
CHIPEM

MFUAIR

Mfuwe
Airport

Chilungila post

Fisi Flats

Chamilandu

Kalefwa

Chipata

Chindeni

Bilimungwe

Manda post

Kapamba

NYALUM

Chilongozi

Lusangazi gate

Kalamu

Chinengwe

Chiwala

Lupande
GMA

Msoro

Kwena
Lagoon

Kalamu
Airstrip

Mukoma post

Island
Bushcamp

Kazutu post

Kambowo

Kananji post

Manchichi
post

Chibale

Namaluba
post

Mtipwazi post

Sandwe GMA

0 ——— 15km
0 ——— 10 miles

Chilembwe

Petauke, Lusaka

The success of safaris in the Luangwa Valley is due in no small measure to one man: Norman Carr. Originally a ranger within the newly formed reserves in the valley, Carr was quick to spot the potential of tourism as a lucrative source of income for the park. Although originally an advocate of hunting safaris, Carr soon recognised that there was an alternative – and one that didn't involve hunting down and killing the local fauna.

By 1950, Carr had persuaded Senior Chief Nsefu to establish a private reserve on the eastern bank of the Luangwa River. (Interestingly, a reliable local historian maintains that the colonial provincial commissioner was nervous about this. He feared that ultimately the local people would lose both their land and their access to collect salt at the pans in the centre of the Nsefu Sector. His concerns proved valid when, 20 years later, in 1971, the Nsefu Sector was combined into the national park.) In partnership with the chief, Norman founded Nsefu Camp in 1952. The camp's original site was close to the present-day Nsefu Camp (it's still visible on the Nsefu Luangwa Wafwa), though the camp was subsequently moved when the river changed its course.

In 1961, Carr moved on to set up his own wilderness safaris, based out of another camp, Kapani Camp. This had been established in 1960, when he was warden of the Luangwa Valley, and it was here that he stayed with Big Boy and Little Boy, the two lions that he famously kept as companions. Kapani Camp lay just north of the Nsefu Sector, some 60km upstream of the present-day Kapani Lodge, and close to today's Tafika. In 1961, he leased what was later known as Old Lion Camp, close to Kapani Camp but on the opposite (western) bank of the Luangwa River.

In those days the whole operation was basic, with Carr wading across the Luangwa every morning to fetch his clients from Old Lion Camp before taking them on a walking safari. Further camps were tried by the lower Kapamba River in 1963, and the Mwaleshi in the north of the reserve, but none was commercially viable. The venture to Mwaleshi, in North Luangwa, ended with the sad death of one of the guides, Peter Hankin, who was killed by a lioness.

Norman was more successful with his next venture. In 1965, he started to base walking safaris out of Chibembe Camp, just north of the Chibembe/Luangwa confluence. With this as a hub, he established a circuit of several small bushcamps, made of poles and grass, with his clients walking from camp to camp. Nine years later, in 1974, he built Chibembe Lodge nearby (as this was larger and built of permanent materials, it had to be sited outside the park, on the east bank). He then used this as his main base, and continued to use the old Chibembe Camp as one of its walking bushcamps. This *modus operandi* of a number of small, temporary walking bushcamps working like satellites for one more permanent lodge is still the model on which many of the valley's operations work today.

Norman's clientele in those early days came mainly from the UK, with a few from Southern Rhodesia, South Africa and America. The expense of travelling to and from Zambia ensured that such safaris were a very expensive, elite activity.

Two years after Chibembe Lodge, Mwamba Bushcamp was constructed on the East Mwamba River, close to present-day Crocodile Bushcamp. This was the first exclusive bushcamp, a place where clients could hire the whole six-bed camp and have their own vehicle and guide and do whatever they wanted, free from any other tourists. Other camps and lodges followed, including Chikoko and Kasansanya (1974). In 1977 Norman founded Chinzombo, which could be reached all year (Chibembe had always been inaccessible during the rains), then later came Kakuli, in 1984, and Kapani Lodge in 1986.

corresponded roughly to the present park, though without the Chifungwe Plain or the Nsefu Sector.

In the following year, Norman Carr and Bert Schultz were appointed as game rangers and villages within the reserves were moved outside its boundaries. Initially Norman Carr recommended that hunting safaris be started, but over the coming decade he realised that visitors would also come for what are now called 'photographic safaris'.

In 1949 the Senior Chief Nsefu, prompted by Norman Carr, established a private game reserve on the Luangwa's eastern bank, between the Mwasauke and Kauluzi rivers. A safari camp was started here which sent some of its income directly back to the local community. (Norman Carr was ahead of his time!) This soon moved to the site of the present-day Nsefu Camp. The chief's reserve became the Nsefu Sector, which was absorbed into the boundaries of the present park – along with the Chifungwe Plain, north of the Mupamadzi River – when new legislation turned all game reserves into national parks on 15 February 1972.

In the later years of his life, Norman Carr lived at Kapani Safari Lodge, having played a pivotal role in the history of the valley by pioneering commercial walking safaris, upon which South Luangwa has founded its reputation. He remained an important and highly outspoken figure to the end, and devoted much energy in his latter years to development projects designed to help the surrounding local communities to benefit from the park. He was especially involved with projects involving local schools, encouraging the next generation of Zambians to value their wildlife heritage.

His excellent example is increasingly being followed by many of the more forward-thinking safari operators. Increasing numbers of operators are taking their role in the community seriously, often by sponsoring schools and clinics in the surrounding countryside. Kawaza village (see page 282–3) is a highly visible tourism venture run by and for one of the local communities.

Geography The South Park now covers about 9,050km² of the Luangwa Valley's floor, which varies from about 500m to 800m above sea level. The western side of the park is bounded by the Muchinga Escarpment, and from there it generally slopes down to the eastern side of the park, where, except in the extreme south, it is bounded by the wide meanders of the Luangwa River.

Near the banks of the Luangwa the land is fairly flat, and mostly covered with mature woodlands. There are few dense shrubberies here, but many open areas where beautiful tall trees stand perhaps 10–20m apart, shading a mixture of small bushes and grassland. Occasionally there are wide, open grassland plains. The largest are Mtanda Plain in Nsefu, Lion Plain just opposite Nsefu, Chikaya Plain north of there, Ntanta around the Mupamadzi's confluence with the Luangwa, the huge Chifungwe Plain in the far north of the park, and the little-known Lundu Plain, south of the Mupumadzi River. These are not Serengeti-type plains with short grass: instead they usually boast tall species of grasses and often bushes. It is their lack of trees that makes them open.

Understandably, the highest density of animals (and hence camps) is around the Luangwa River. However, increasingly camps are being set up elsewhere in the park. The trio of bushcamps run by Norman Carr Safaris is located along the Lubi River, one of the Luangwa's smaller tributaries, while walking camps run by Robin Pope Safaris are dotted around the Mupamadzi River rather than the Luangwa.

The Luangwa River For the visitor, perhaps the most notable feature of the Luangwa Valley is the pristine river that runs through it. Take a close look at it: very few rivers of this size in Africa (or anywhere else!) have been so unaffected by man.

Nsefu Camp, started in 1950, was the valley's first camp for photographic visitors. From the first, one of Nsefu's founding principles was that the local indigenous people, the traditional owners of the wildlife, should benefit from the visitors. This mirrors the approach that most thinking on conservation and development has taken only in the last few years (in the jargon, this is now called 'community-based natural-resource management'!). Norman Carr was a conservationist far ahead of his time.

Not only did Norman start a number of these camps, he also started education projects in the valley, and worked alongside and helped to train many of those who are now the valley's most experienced guides. These include:

PHIL BERRY, who came to the Luangwa in 1963, and in 1973 joined the Zambian National Tourist Bureau to manage walking safaris, in competition with Norman's safari operations. Three years later they joined forces to start Chibembe. Phil is now the valley's most senior guide, and still leads some walks from his small bushcamp, Kuyenda. He's widely respected not only for his guiding, but also for his meticulous keeping of flora and fauna records, and work with Thornicroft's giraffe.

ROBIN POPE came into the valley in 1976, working with Phil and Norman at Chibembe and then Nsefu Camp. Tena Tena started around 1983 as one of Nsefu's walking bushcamps, then Robin took it over in 1986 – and branched off to start perhaps the valley's most successful safari operation, Robin Pope Safaris.

JOHN COPPINGER started as a guide at Nsefu in 1984, whilst Robin was manager. He managed Nsefu for a few years, and then became general manager of Wilderness Trails – which then ran Chibembe, Nsefu, Big Lagoon and a travel agency in Lusaka. Eventually he left there is 1994, to start his own operation, Remote Africa Safaris, based out of Tafika.

ISAAC ZULU originally studied as an agriculturalist, but was trained by Norman from 1974. He guided in the valley for many years, including at Chibembe in the late 1980s. Eventually he left the valley in 1989 and worked with Tongabezi in Livingstone for many years, until returning to the valley in 2001 with Chilongozi Safaris (now defunct). Currently he's again guiding with John at Remote Africa Safaris.

ABRAHAM BANDA was trained by Norman in 1989, having come straight from the Kapani School. (This was set up by Norman to offer local children the chance of a good education.) Eighteen years later, Abraham is one of the leaders of the new generation of Luangwa guides; he now manages the safari operation at Norman Carr Safaris, and is lodge manager for their main lodge, Kapani. In addition, he runs a very successful charity to support Yoseffe School, and a number of other community projects.

The way that the Luangwa Valley's safari business here has created opportunities for an increasing number of locally born people like Abraham, both in education and tourism, is part and parcel of why Norman started safaris in the Luangwa over 50 years ago. Perhaps Norman's greatest legacy is not the wealth of high-quality walking safaris here, but the impressively strong conservation and development ethics which underpin virtually all of the better, long-standing safari operations in the valley.

There are no dams on it, no commercial agriculture along its banks, and incredibly little pollution. Hence here you can still see the natural seasonal fluctuations of water levels and flooding which lead to the dynamic nature of a river in a really natural state. It's not only beautiful but also text-book geography.

Note how the river's twisting curves easily cut through the valley's fertile soil, leaving a sprinkling of crescent-shaped oxbow lakes in their wake. Every year new sandbanks arise as its original banks are cut back and the river's course changes with the floods. Just look at the number of riverside camps and lodges that, over the years, have either moved or gradually been swallowed up by river erosion.

Geology The Luangwa Valley is a rift valley, similar to the Great Rift Valley of east Africa, though probably older, and it shares its genesis with the adjoining Lower Zambezi Valley. The original sedimentary strata covering the whole area is part of the karoo system, sedimentary rocks laid down from 175 to 300 million years ago.

During this time, faulting occurred and volcanic material was injected into rifts in the existing sediments. One of these faults is the wide valley that the Luangwa now occupies. In geologically recent times, the Luangwa has meandered extensively across the wide valley floor, eroding the volcanic rocks and depositing mineral-rich silts. These meanders also left behind them old watercourses and oxbow pools. The most recent of these can still be seen, and they are an important feature of the landscape near the present river.

Flora and fauna

Vegetation To understand the Luangwa Valley's vegetation, the base of its productive ecosystem, consider the elements that combine to nurture its plants: the water, light, heat and nutrients. The rainfall in the valley is typically 800 to 1,100mm per annum – which is moderate, but easily sufficient for strong vegetation growth. Occupying a position between 12° and 14° south of the Equator, the valley lacks neither light nor heat. (Visit in October and you may feel that it has too much of both.)

However the key to its vegetation lies in the nutrients. The Luangwa's soils, being volcanic in origin, are rich in minerals, and the sediments laid down by the river are fine, making excellent soils. Thus with abundant water, light, heat and nutrient-rich soils, the valley's vegetation has thrived: it is both lush and diverse.

Unlike many parks, the 'bush' in the Luangwa is very variable, and as you drive or walk you'll pass through a patchwork of different vegetation zones. See *Flora and Fauna*, in *Chapter 3*, pages 32–6, for more detail, but the more obvious include some beautiful mature forests of 'cathedral mopane'. Just outside the national park on the way to the salt pans (south of Mfuwe) is one area where the mopane are particularly tall.

Along the Luangwa's tributaries, which are just rivers of sand for most of the year, you'll find lush riverine vegetation dominated by giant red mahogany trees, *Khaya anthotheca* (formerly known as *Khaya nyasica*) and *Adina microsephala*. Sometimes you'll also find Natal mahoganies, *Trichilia emetica*, and African ebony trees, *Diospyros mespiliformis*. There are several locations in the park where the latter form dense groves, casting a heavy shade on the sparse undergrowth. Look for such groves where the tributaries meet the Luangwa; there's one beside Mchenja Camp.

Elsewhere are large, open grassland plains. Chief amongst these are probably the plains in the Nsefu Sector. These surround some natural salt springs, which attract crowned cranes in their thousands.

Antelope and other herbivores With its rich vegetation, the Luangwa supports large numbers of a wide variety of animals. Each species has its own niche in the food chain, which avoids direct competition with any other species. Each herbivore has its favourite food plants, and even species that utilise the same food plants will feed on different parts of those plants. This efficient use of the available vegetation – refined over the last few millennia – makes the wildlife far more productive than any domestic stock would be if given the same land. It also leads to the high densities of game that the valley supports.

The game includes huge herds of buffalo, commonly hundreds of animals strong, and seemingly endless family groups of elephants; both are particularly spectacular if encountered whilst you are on foot. Despite Zambia's past poaching problems, South Luangwa's elephants are generally neither scarce nor excessively skittish in the presence of people. Just north of Mfuwe Lodge, you'll find an open plain with few trees, just the skeletal trunks of an old cathedral mopane forest. This has always been attributed to elephant damage from the 1970s, before ivory poaching became a problem, when there were around 56,000 elephants in the park (100,000 in the whole Luangwa Valley) – though very recent research suggests that soil changes and even heart rot disease may have contributed to the trees' demise.

The park's dominant antelope species are impala and puku. Whilst impala are dominant in much of southern Africa, puku are rare south of the Zambezi. They stand a maximum of 0.8m high at the shoulder and weigh in at up to about 75kg. Puku form small breeding groups which are exceedingly common in their favourite habitat – well-watered riverine areas. Groups are dominated by a territorial male adorned with the characteristic lyre-shaped horns. Impala do occur here but are not the most numerous antelope, as they are in the Zambezi Valley and throughout Zimbabwe.

Luangwa has a number of 'specialities' including the beautiful Thornicroft's giraffe, *Giraffa camelopardalis thornicroftii*. This rare subspecies differs from the much more common southern giraffe, found throughout southern Africa, in having a different (and more striking) colouration. When compared with the normal southern species of giraffe found in Kafue and south of the Zambezi, Thornicroft's have dark body patches and lighter neck patches; their colour patches don't normally extend below the knees, leaving their lower legs almost white; and their faces are light or white.

Fortunately, around the Mfuwe area there is a widespread traditional belief that people who eat giraffe meat will get spots like those of a giraffe. Hence giraffe are rarely hunted by the local people, and are even very common in the GMA to the east of the river, outside the national park.

Cookson's wildebeest, *Connochaetes taurinus cooksoni*, a subspecies of the blue wildebeest found throughout sub-Saharan Africa, are endemic to the valley. They are more common in more northerly areas of the valley, such as the North Luangwa, and Norman Carr's wildlife guide (see *Appendix 3*, page 512) maintains that they also seem to favour the east side of the river, rather than the west. That said, in South Luangwa you've also a fair chance of seeing them in the Nsefu Sector, and on Lion Plain, and particularly around Mwamba Bushcamp area. They differ from the blue wildebeest in having cleaner colours including slightly reddish bands, and being a little smaller and more compact.

Another special of the Luangwa Valley is Crawshay's zebra, *Equus burchelli crawshaii*, a subspecies of the more common Burchell's plains zebra, which is found in much of the subcontinent. Crawshay's zebra occur east of the Muchinga Escarpment – in the Luangwa Valley and on Nyika Plateau – and lack the brown shadow-stripe that Burchell's zebra usually have between their black stripes.

In contrast to these examples, it is the common waterbuck (*Kobus ellipsiprymnus*) that is found in the valley, rather than its rarer subspecies, the defassa waterbuck (*K. e. crawshayi*), which is found over most of the rest of Zambia. The defassa has a white circular patch on its rump, whereas the common waterbuck has the characteristic white 'toilet seat' ring.

Other antelope in the park include bushbuck, eland and kudu. The delicate oribi occur occasionally in the grassland areas (especially Chifungwe Plain), while grysbok are often encountered on night drives. Reedbuck and Lichtenstein's hartebeest also occur, but not usually near the river, whilst sable are occasionally seen in the hills near the escarpment. Like sable, roan antelope seem to be most frequently seen in the hills – often on the roads south of Chichele, although in the late dry season there are frequent sightings in the Chikoko area, on the fringes of Chifungwe Plain, and in the 'corridor' area between the North and South parks.

A special mention must go to the hippopotami (and crocodiles) found in the rivers, and especially in the Luangwa: their numbers are remarkable. Look over the main bridge crossing the Luangwa at Mfuwe – sometimes there are hundreds of hippo there. Towards the end of the dry season, when the rivers are at their lowest, is the best time to observe such dense congregations of hippo. Then these semi-aquatic mammals are forced into smaller and smaller pools, and you'll appreciate their sheer numbers. These congregations reach their peak in October and November when, for example, you'll find a concentration of 1,000 hippo in just 2km of river, in the Changwa Channel, north of Chibembe. This is probably easiest (and certainly most spectacular) to see by flying over it in a microlight from Tafika.

Predators The main predators in the Luangwa Valley are typical of sub-Saharan Africa: lion, leopard, spotted hyena and wild dog. During the day, the visitor is most likely to see lion, *Panthera leo*, which are the park's most common large predator. Their large prides are relatively easily spotted, and to witness one of their hunting trips makes a gripping spectacle.

South Luangwa seems to have made a name for itself amongst the safari community as an excellent park for leopard, *Panthera pardus*. This is largely because leopard hunt nocturnally, and South Luangwa is one of Africa's few national parks to allow operators to go on spotlit game drives at night. Estimates made whilst filming a BBC documentary about leopards in the park suggest an average leopard density of one animal per 2.5km² – roughly twice the density recorded in South Africa's Kruger National Park. So perhaps the reputation is justified. In my experience, night drives in Luangwa with experienced guides do consistently yield excellent sightings of these cats – at a frequency that is difficult to match elsewhere on the continent. In contrast to this, I'm not aware of any sightings of cheetah for over 20 years.

Wild dog are also uncommon, though their population seems to oscillate over a period of years. A study of wild dogs in Zambia by Kenneth Buk in 1995 (see *Appendix 3*, page 512) suggested that the Luangwa holds Zambia's second-largest wild dog population, even though this was badly depleted by an outbreak of anthrax in 1987. Since the late 1990s, wild dog have gradually been making more appearances. They're now regularly seen south of Mfuwe, near the Nkwali pontoon, especially from around February to May, and recent research shows that their numbers are building up (see box, *Wild dogs in the Lower Zambezi and South Luangwa*, page 232).

Birds The Luangwa boasts the rich tropical birdlife that you would expect of such a fertile valley. This includes species that prefer a dry habitat of plains and forests, and those that live close to water. It is difficult to mention more than a few of the Luangwa's 400 species, but several books listed in *Appendix 3* (pages 511–12) cover the region's birds. As the Luangwa is situated between southern and east Africa, keen birdwatchers may want to arrive with two field guides, each describing birds from one region, so that between them they will cover the full range of species encountered in the valley.

Better still, bring a good guide to southern Africa's birds, like Newman's guide, and buy Aspinwall and Beel's Zambian guide locally (see *Appendix 3*, which explains the logic of this). Alternatively, get hold of a single guide to the birds of sub-Saharan Africa or the more concise Collins Illustrated Checklist to the *Birds of Southern Africa*.

Species of note include flocks of crowned cranes occurring on the marshes of the Nsefu Sector; the colonies of iridescent carmine bee-eaters which nest in sandy riverbanks in September and October; the African skimmers found along the river; and the giant eagle owls which are sometimes picked out by the spotlight on night drives.

The best time for birds is the summer: the rainy season. The birds' food supply is then at its most abundant, and the summer migrants are around. Just drive into the park during the rains and it becomes immediately apparent that both the vegetation and the birdlife are running riot. Dry plains have sprouted thick, green vegetation mirrored all around in shallow water. Flocks of egrets, herons and storks wade through this, around feeding geese and ducks.

Many species breed here, including storks that often form impressive colonies. There are several sites of tall trees in the Nsefu Sector which, when surrounded by shallow water, regularly become breeding colonies. The most amazing of these has half a dozen huge trees filled with nests of yellow-billed storks in their spectacular pink breeding plumage. This is one of the Luangwa's most remarkable sights.

Conservation in the Luangwa

Hunting and poaching South Luangwa has always been Zambia's 'most favoured park'. Over the years it has been given a disproportionately large share of the resources allotted to all of the country's national parks. Many would argue that this has been to the detriment of the other parks, though it did enable it to fight the plague of commercial poaching, which hit the country in the 1980s, with some success. The poachers came for rhino horn – which is sold to make dagger-handles in the Middle East and Chinese medicines for the Far East – and, of course, for ivory.

Sadly the valley's thriving black rhino population was wiped out, as it almost certainly was throughout Zambia; the last confirmed sightings in the Luangwa were in 1987. (One or two sources suggest that a couple of individual animals may be left in the wild, but this is probably just wishful thinking.) However, the good news is that five black rhino re-introduced into a specially protected area within the North Luangwa National Park in 2003 were followed by a further ten in 2006. I was lucky enough to be there to watch as the first animals were each fitted with a radio transceiver, prior to their release. Although two of the rhino have died, two calves have since been born, and further relocations are planned for 2008. It's a tremendous achievement for conservation in the Luangwa, acknowledging a real volte-face in conservation in the valley.

Fortunately, the valley's elephant populations didn't fare as badly as the rhino; they were only reduced. In recent years, thanks in part to the CITES ban on the ivory trade, they have bounced back – and South Luangwa, especially, has very healthy, large herds of relaxed elephants.

Today there is minimal poaching in the park, as demonstrated by the size of the animal populations, and certainly no lack of game. Only in the nervous elephant populations of North Luangwa does one get any echo of the poaching problems of the past.

Chipembele (✆ 021 6246108; e info@chipembele.org; www.chipembele.org; ⊕ CHIPEM 13°12.122's; 31°42.221'E) came about through the determination of Steve & Anna Tolan, who retired from the British police force in 1998 to invest in their dream of educating children in conservation matters. With a passion for African wildlife born of years of travelling and reading, they set about building an education centre, which was finally opened on the eastern bank of the Luangwa River, about 16km southwest of Mfuwe, in 2001.

The centre's work focuses on teaching through active involvement and fun. Children come for the day from schools all over the area, spending time en route spotting game that many of them may never have seen before. There's also a large interpretive room complete with displays and exhibits that tourists are welcome to visit by prior arrangement.

From this central project, Anna has branched out into school improvement projects and working with a number of women's groups, while Steve has taken on anti-poaching work and forestry protection. Rehabilitation of orphaned and injured animals is a further aspect of their work, together with an active involvement in the South Luangwa Conservation Society.

South Luangwa Conservation Society (e slcs@iwayafrica.com; www.slcs-zambia.org) Formed in 2003 in order to support the Zambia Wildlife Authority and Community Resource Boards, the South Luangwa Conservation Society pulled together the work initially undertaken by the honorary rangers and volunteers in the valley. Now with its own premises just outside the national park, it continues to focus on the original aspect of its work, funded by a combination of membership fees and donations. The society directly supports 35 members of staff, most of whom are village scouts with salaries, accommodation, rations, equipment, incentives and ongoing training.

In addition, the society is actively involved in education programmes with the local community. An ongoing anti-snaring programme helps to make both adults and children aware of the impact of poaching and snaring on the wildlife and on the local environment, while a darting programme helps to rescue animals that have been snared by poachers. From another angle, the introduction of chilli fences (see page 318) is helping farmers whose crops are threatened by wildlife.

Conservation and development in Lupande GMA South Luangwa has always been protected from poaching in a way that Zambia's other parks were not. This wasn't always 100% effective, but it was a lot better than elsewhere. Several years ago a project was started in sections of the Lupande GMA, which is immediately adjacent to the national park, to distribute direct cash benefits from the park to the local people.

This has worked very well beside the river (ie: alongside the park), where the animals are plentiful and the hunting income has been very good. Certainly one of the local chiefs has a very nice brick-built palace with satellite television and an impressive new twin-cab Land Cruiser parked in front.

However, further from the park the hunting isn't so good, and the fees have certainly been less. Locals comment that the influx of people into the Mfuwe Bridge area over the last decade has been very noticeable. Even I can see that there are now far more people around that when I first visited in 1995.

Much of the cause of this may be simply the employment prospects generated directly (and indirectly), by the lodges. However, this influx means that the GMA's revenues are being effectively divided among more people. It also puts more strain on the area's agriculture, to increase cultivated land in the area. The danger is that with more people and more cultivation, there will inevitably be a reduction in the GMA's game densities.

This is another Gordian knot for those working on conservation and development in the area to tackle. See *Conservation* in *Chapter 3*, pages 36–40, for a more general discussion of these issues.

GETTING ORGANISED

Local safari operators When choosing a camp or local operator, it's important that you pick a good and reliable one. You're in such a remote area that you can't afford to have problems. One safeguard is to seek advice from a good, independent overseas tour operator. For all except the budget camps, you should find that booking your trip with a good overseas tour operator will be cheaper than booking it directly with the camps.

Perhaps also check out Expert Africa's website, www.expertafrica.com (even if you're not arranging a trip with them), as I will be posting updates there for all to see. Many of the smaller one-or-two-camp operations are excellent. Meanwhile, here are the contact details and selected snippets of background information on a few of the higher-profile safari operators, in alphabetical order:

Bushcamp Company ⟍/f 021 6246041; e info@bushcampcompany.com; www.bushcampcompany.com. The Bushcamp Company was formed in 2000 from 2 very old bushcamps (Chamilandu & Kuyenda), both originally owned by Chinzombo, & 2 new ones (Bilimungwe & Chindeni), which were originally owned by Mfuwe Lodge. A 5th camp, Kapamba, was added in 2005. The company is run by Andy Hogg & Andrea Bizzaro. Andy worked with Chinzombo for years, & has helped to make this a very good, reliable operation.

Bushcamp Company is the most long-standing serious operator to the south side of South Luangwa, & has carved out a niche by offering small, high-quality bushcamps. Each camp is different, & although all emphasise their walking safaris, all also offer night drives. Guiding standards are high, as you would expect of the better camps in the valley; one of their guides, Manda Chisanga, won the prestigious *Wanderlust* 'Guide of the Year' award in 2006. Note that it's possible to walk from Chamilandu to Chindeni to Bilimungwe to Kapamba.

Land & Lake Safaris ⟍ +265 1757120, 1754303; ⟍/f +265 1754560; e reservations@landlake.net; www.landlake.net. This Malawi-based safari operator is opening a second camp in the valley in 2007, geared respectively towards the budget and mid-range markets. They also operate safaris throughout the park, inc the North Luangwa, some using the It's Wild! camps.

Norman Carr Safaris ⟍ 021 6245015; f 021 6245025; e kapani@normancarrsafaris.com;

www.normancarrsafaris.com. Norman Carr himself lived at Kapani until his death in 1997, and his family is still involved with the company. Operations encompass Kapani Safari Lodge & 4 bushcamps used for walking trips — Nsolo, Luwi, Kakuli & Mchenja — & all are now run by a very capable team. If you want to walk between different bushcamps, going from one to the next every few days, then the walk down the dry Luwi River is difficult to beat. All are excellent camps & Norman Carr Safaris rightly retains one of the best reputations of any company in the valley. It is currently the only company to organise regular river safaris in the park (see page 282).

Remote Africa Safaris ⟍ +264 61 240561; f +264 61 240561; e tafika@remoteafrica.com; www.remoteafrica.com. Founded by John & Carol Coppinger, Remote Africa Safaris is a small but high-quality operator with truly innovative ideas. They run 4 excellent camps: Tafika in South Luangwa, plus the 2 Chikoko Trails walking camps (Chikoko & Crocodile), & Mwaleshi in the North Park; all were undergoing some refurbishment in 2007. John used to run Wilderness Trails in the valley, & is regarded as one of the most experienced guides in the region. His guides also include Ernst Jacobs & Stephen Banda, who are experts on the area in their own right.

John is one of the very few people to have canoed the length of the Mwaleshi & Luangwa rivers and was the first to run river safaris in the valley (though he no longer does these). He also pilots the valley's only microlight aircraft, which is based at

Tafika. Remote Africa is another of the valley's very best operators.

Robin Pope Safaris ❯ 021 6246090–2; f 021 6246094; e info@robinpopesafaris.net; www.robinpopesafaris.net, www.robinpopecamps.com. Robin Pope was raised in Zambia, trained by Norman Carr, & is another of the top wildlife guides in the valley. His English wife, Jo, was the first woman to qualify as a walking guide in the valley – but it is her efficiency with the marketing & business side of the operation that make her legendary. Together with a very good team they run what is probably the valley's most complex set of camps & trips, inc Tena Tena, Nkwali, Nsefu, & a range of different walking safaris (inc some true mobiles & the valley's first true bushcamping). RPS is an excellent & highly reliable company.

Sanctuary Lodges & Camps ❯ +27 (0)11 438 4650; e southernafrica@sanctuarylodges.com; www.sanctuarylodges.com. Since the late 1990s, several of Zambia's top lodges have been run by Star of Africa. In 2007, however, most of their properties were taken over by Sanctuary Lodges & Camps, which is closely associated with Abercrombie

& Kent & owns a number of small, luxury properties in both Botswana & east Africa. Two of these camps, Chichele Presidential Lodge & the neighbouring Puku Ridge Camp, are in the South Luangwa; the others are Zambezi Kulefu Camp in the Lower Zambezi, Lechwe Plains Tented Camp in Lochinvar (to be reopened in 2009), & Sussi & Chuma in Livingstone.

Shenton Safaris ❯ (May–Oct only) 021 6245190, 6245064; e info@kaingo.com; www.kaingo.com. Established by Derek Shenton, Shenton Safaris runs Kaingo Camp & Mwambwa, both classic, small camps in a good game area with a strong focus on good guiding & game viewing. Derek was joined a few years ago by Juliet, whose influence has led to a steady rise in standards of service & comfort. Notable are the value they place on using game hides, of which they have up to 8 available at anyone time, and – almost unique in the valley – a willingness to organise 3 activities a day, which makes them particularly attractive to keen photographers. The family also owns Forest Inn, near Serenje (see page 297).

Wilderness Safaris See page 417.

Orientation If you're arriving on an organised trip, then you can relax. A vehicle will be waiting to take you to camp, and there's no need to think ahead. However, if you are driving or hitching here, then you may be aiming for a dot on the map marked 'Mfuwe'. Forget it. Mfuwe is more of an area than a place, although there is a BP fuel station (albeit with an erratic and expensive supply of diesel and/or petrol) here, and some very basic shops. In spirit, the centre of Mfuwe is probably the airport and Moondog Café (see page 262). This is the terminus from which most of the valley's visitors arrive and depart – and so it is a hub frequented by vehicles from the valley's camps.

About 25km northwest of this is the main Mfuwe Bridge (⊕ MFUBRI 13°5.917'S; 31°47.162'E) over the Luangwa River. This lies at the heart of the park's all-weather road network, and many visitors entering the national park pass this way. Between the airport and the bridge is a stretch of road where you will pass the occasional farm stalls selling vegetables, a BP fuel station, a school, some small shops, a church and a clinic – but don't look for a small town here, as there isn't one – yet.

However, do look for **Tribal Textiles** (e gillie@zamnet.zm) on the right, marked by large, painted pillars. Better still, ask to stop here for half an hour before you leave. This was started to create local employment. You'll find perhaps Zambia's best hand-painted textiles, a guide to explain how they're made and to take you round the factory, and a large, well laid-out shop with very reasonable prices (credit cards accepted). Don't miss it.

As you approach the bridge, there's a left turn to Kapani, Nkwali and the lodges and camps on the southern side of Mfuwe, then a little further on the left is the road down to Flatdogs.

GETTING THERE

By air During the main safari season, from June to the end of October, Mfuwe is one of the easiest places in Zambia to reach by air. Currently it is regularly serviced

In early November 2002, two German visitors borrowed a relative's brand-new 4x4 to explore the South Luangwa. The car was a small, low-slung 4x4 saloon, one of the latest models and very much state-of-the-art. It had on-board computers to control much of the vehicle, from the engine to the suspension.

Coming from Mpika, they entered the Luangwa Valley by the tricky 'corridor' road, successfully reaching the remote Chifungwe game scouts' camp. They planned to take the road known locally as the '05', which passes near the old site of Zebra Pans Bushcamp, before eventually reaching a crossroads near Nsolo Bushcamp, and then the heart of the Mfuwe area. It's a dead straight road (with a bearing of about 5°), mostly through thick bush. It's used very little, and was sure to be very quiet then as all the valley's bushcamps close at the end of October.

All went smoothly until they were crossing the Mupamadzi River, about 3km after the scouts' camp. Halfway across, they got stuck. Then the driver realised that he hadn't locked his hubs (some 4x4 vehicles require one to physically turn a switch on the wheels), so he got out in the river and turned the hubs. Surprisingly, they managed to drive to the other side.

All seemed well and the pair continued south, but 25km further along the road, the car died. Water had got into the wiring; the car's computer had shut down and with it the engine. If the car had broken down in the river, the two men would have been only 3km from the scouts' camp. Now they were 28km away. As is normally wise, they decided to wait with their car for a passing vehicle to summon help. Unfortunately, 24 hours later, not one vehicle had passed by. The '05' is one of many bush roads in Africa which may see only a handful of vehicles per year; just because it's marked on the maps, it is a mistake to assume that it's used frequently!

The men were starting to feel desperate. They had told nobody local what their plans were; nobody was expecting them anywhere. Nobody would raise an alarm. The only food they had with them was some fruit juice, water, butter and cheese. Their water was running out fast, so they decided to walk to find help – southwards towards Mfuwe. After 25km, the elder of the two men, sore and tired from his exertions, decided that he could

by Zambian Airways. Expect a one-way trip between Lusaka and Mfuwe to cost around US$220 per person; double that for a return.

Mfuwe Airport Mfuwe Airport (✛ MFUAIR 13°15.281'S; 31°55.933'E) is an international airport, with customs and immigration, but it feels like a small, local one. There's one terminal building, and if you're on one of the smaller flights in and out of the valley, then you're likely to have the pilot coming to find you.

Inside the terminal are toilets, a few small shops and a very small bank. There's also the It's Wild! Community Shop (see box, page 290). Just outside you'll find the labelled parking spaces where 4x4s from the lodges wait for their pre-booked incoming passengers. A few yards away are two gems, well worth investigating:

🍴 **Moondog Café** ☏ 021 6245068; ☼ all year, normally 08.00–17.00. Apart from the airport, & the camps, this is the one essential place to know about. Situated beside the airport, & run by Fil & Tony Hide, it's a relaxed place to have a drink as you arrive, or before you leave, or even a tasty snack or bite to eat. It's also got a useful noticeboard, pigeonholes for all the Luangwa camps, a bookshop with a good selection of natural history guides & a fair bit of local wit. (Ask about 'Coppinger's Corner', amongst other local legends.) However, in an emergency, Moondog is also a valuable communications hub – for its radio & phone links to the valley's camps. So if you have problems near the airport, then sit down, order a drink & ask nicely for their help.

walk no further. They agreed that he should stop there, whilst the younger, fitter man would continue.

Then their fortunes turned: it rained. The older man, who had been sitting in temperatures of 43°C during the day, took off his clothes and lay on the ground to soak up the water. At 16.00 the next day, he was discovered by a scout patrol, sitting by the side of the road. He was naked and approaching delirium; the scouts estimated that he was about three to four hours from death.

Meanwhile, the younger man had continued walking through the night, but lost the main road whilst avoiding a small herd of elephants. Miraculously, in the morning he stumbled across Nsolo Bushcamp. Being November, everything had just closed down for the rains, but a rummage through the bins uncovered tin cans, while the dry river nearby yielded water where the elephants had dug up the bed with their tusks. Boiling the water in the cans on an open fire, the man felt better. The next morning, the scout patrol who had found his friend followed his tracks to Nsolo, and found him there. He was relatively well, although concerned by the two lionesses who had been watching him closely.

Both men were very lucky and now safe – but what of the car? It took nine hours to tow it northwards and back across the river. Then it rained for two days, and the river flooded – making the road impassable. Anyone who knows the area would have told them that November was a crazy time to drive across that river.

Meanwhile, a mechanic flew up to attempt repairs. Plugging his laptop into the car, he restarted its computer and had it working in minutes. Apparently it just needed resetting! Later the men learnt that it would have been possible to shut down the computer entirely.

There are many lessons to draw from this, but the big picture is clear. Unless you're an experienced old Africa hand with a good network of local contacts, unless you take good advice, and drive a vehicle that you know, then driving yourself around the more remote corners of Zambia is asking for trouble. Just because I indicate GPS positions and bush tracks in this book does not mean that these routes are suitable for drivers who aren't experienced in remote African travel.

The menu has a variety of meals & snacks from US$2 upwards, with a full meal at around US$8. Tequila is served all day, without an eyebrow being raised, & the menu includes home-made pasta, pizzas, nachos, tacos, quesadillas & chilli, burgers, toasted sandwiches, meat pies & samosas.

Magenge Crafts ✆ 021 6245064; f 021 6245025; e magenge@zamnet.zm; ◷ late-Mar–early-Jan; closed only during the height of the rains. Next to the Moondog Café, outside the main airport building, is a small & stylish shop selling craftwork. The crafts include textiles, baskets, wirework, wooden carvings, elephant-dung greetings cards (much nicer than they sound!), papier-mâché animal heads, embroidered T-shirts & various artefacts – many of which make super souvenirs. Virtually all are locally made, providing a valuable income for the people who produce them. Look out especially for items by Mango Tree Crafts, a community project recently initiated by Gillie Lightfoot (Tribal Textiles), using local materials to make mobiles, table mats, wooden animals &, using old snares collected by national parks, wire flowers & animals. Magenge is one of the valley's few outlets for such crafts, & is run with these development aims in mind. (Magenge is the local name for termites – noted for the impact of their co-operative schemes despite their small size.)

By road Driving from Chipata is long and tedious, but not usually difficult in the dry season provided that your vehicle has a good suspension. Rumours that the road is soon to be upgraded will come as a welcome relief. Coming from the north, or Mpika, is a totally different story: it requires a small expedition of at least two well-equipped 4x4 vehicles, driven by experienced bush drivers with a high degree of self-reliance.

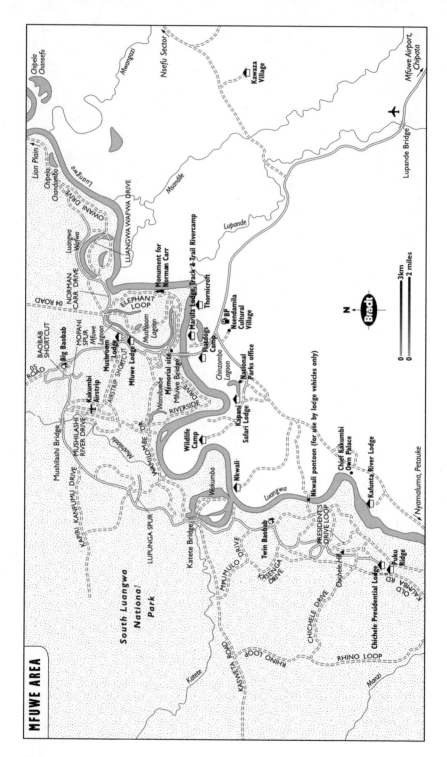

MFUWE AREA

South Luangwa National Park

Chipela Chansefu

Mwangazi

Nsefu Sector

Kawaza Village

Mfuwe Airport, Chipata

Lupande Bridge

Lion Plain

Chipela Chandombo

OWANI DRIVE

Luangwa Wafwa

LUANGWA WAFWA DRIVE

NORMAN CARR DRIVE

04 ROAD

Msandile

Lupande

Monument for Norman Carr

Maridi Lodge Track 2 Trail Rivercamp

Thornicroft

ELEPHANT LOOP

Mushroom Lagoon

BAOBAB SHORTCUT

Big Baobab

MOPANI SPUR

Mfuwe Lagoon

Mushroom Lodge

Mfuwe Lodge

Memorial site

Wamilombe

Mfuwe Bridge

Mfuwe Drive

RIVERSIDE

Nsendamila Cultural Village

BP

Raildogs Camp

Chinzombo Lagoon

National Parks office

05 ROAD

Kakumbi Airstrip

AIRSTRIP SHORTCUT

Kakumbi Airstrip

Mushilashi Bridge

MUSHILASHI RIVER DRIVE

Mushilashi

NAMILOMBE DR

Wildlife Camp

Kapani Safari Lodge

KAPIRI KANJUMU DRIVE

LUPUNGA SPUR

Nkwali

Wikumba

Luangwa

Nkwali pontoon (for use by lodge vehicles only)

Chief Kakumbi Own Palace

Kafunta River Lodge

Nyamaluma, Petauke

Katete Bridge

MPUMULO DRIVE

Twin Baobab

KASENGA DRIVE

PRESIDENT'S DRIVE LOOP

Puku Ridge

Katete

KASNETA ROAD

RHINO LOOP

CHICHELE DRIVE

Chichele Hill

Chichele Presidential Lodge

OLD KALUMBA RD

RHINO LOOP

Manzi

N

Bradt

0   3km
0   2 miles

264

From Chipata Approaching from Chipata is by far the easiest way to reach the park if you are driving. As you enter Chipata from Lusaka, you pass under a 'Welcome to Chipata' arch spanning the road (the independence memorial archway). Instead of going under this, turn left before it. The turn-off to Mfuwe is marked, and the route is fairly obvious, even without the waypoints points noted here.

This road winds down from the high escarpment and into the valley. The views are spectacular, and you will pass many local villages on the way. Keep the windows open and you will feel both the temperature and the humidity rise as you descend.

After around 45km you will pass over the first hill (◈ HILL1 13°18.498'S; 32°1.490'E), and then about 20km later, you'll reach the Chisengu turn-off (◈ TUSLNP 13°18.131'S; 32°13.234'E) where the right-hand road becomes a rough track leading to the Kauluzi and Chikwinda gates. (This is part of an old district road which used to connect Chipata and Lundazi, though sections of it further north have not been passable for more than ten years, so it's unlikely to be reopened.)

For Mfuwe keep left; the road leads to Jumbe after about 16km, before forking left again over a bridge. After this there's a short stretch of tar over Mpata Hill (◈ HILL2 13°26.728'S; 32°20.489'E); if you're driving in the wet season, you'll appreciate the need for this tar. Some 15km further on, after passing a small Catholic church, the road forks again. Keep left. Shortly there's a tarmac T-junction. Turn left for 3–4km to reach Mfuwe Airport (◈ MFUAIR 13°15.281'S; 31°55.933'E), or right for Mfuwe Bridge (◈ MFUBRI 13°5.917'S; 31°47.162'E) and the park. From Chipata by this route it's about 95km to Mfuwe Airport, or about 115km to the main bridge into the park, over the Luangwa River.

From Petauke Fully-equipped 4x4 vehicles coming from Lusaka might be tempted to take an earlier turn off the Great East Road, and approach the south side of the park, via a turn-off from Petauke. I haven't driven this road; it's very rarely used and is much slower and more difficult than the Chipata road (above), though also more scenic and interesting. It's about 150km to the park's southern gate at Chilongozi, then a further 40km to Mfuwe, during which time you're unlikely to see any other vehicles.

For those who have the back-up and want to try this, some old directions and GPS waypoints (with special thanks to Ed, Claire and Flatdogs) are as follows: turn off the Great East Road to Petauke (◈ PETAUK 14°17.730'S; 31°20.253'E) next to the BP filling station (last fuel-up before Mfuwe). It's 4km until you pass the police station, on the right. Then turn left and then continue up the hill, taking a left fork after about 200m (◈ PETS01 14°14.982'S; 31°20.280'E). Head for Ukwimi which is about 50km of ungraded track, following this route:

◈ PETS02 13°56.842'S; 31°36.867'E	◈ PETS08 13°37.398'S; 31°34.609'E
◈ PETS03 13°50.448'S; 31°35.188'E	◈ PETS09 13°34.183'S; 31°34.183'E
◈ PETS04 13°48.282'S; 31°34.699'E	◈ PETS10 13°31.152'S; 31°34.360'E
◈ PETS05 13°47.971'S; 31°34.555'E	◈ PETS11 13°25.981'S; 31°33.354'E
◈ PETS06 13°46.096'S; 31°35.789'E	◈ PETS12 13°26.011'S; 31°33.593'E
◈ PETS07 13°38.386'S; 31°34.774'E	◈ PETS13 13°22.746'S; 31°36.775'E

This brings you to the Chilongozi area and the Nyamaluma pontoon (◈ NYALUM 13°22.630'S; 31°36.974'E – if it's still running). Cross this to reach Bilimungwe, Chendeni and the camps on the west of the Luangwa River. The easiest way to the Mfuwe from here is probably not across the pontoon into the park, although you can go that way; better to continue roughly northeast, shadowing the east bank of the Luangwa, and you'll eventually emerge into Mfuwe just east of the bridge.

If you're aiming for Kalamu Lodge, then at Ukwimi village, a boom gate crosses the road; and you should turn immediately left after this. You will pass Chief Malama's village, and continue until you reach Lusangazi village. Here you turn left, crossing the Lusangazi River – which is only possible in the dry season, from about June to October. (The road to your right here is the road to Mfuwe.) You have now entered the South Luangwa National Park, and it is a further 20km to Kalamu Lodge.

From Mpika via the Corridor Road and '05' Driving south from Mpika, down into the Luangwa Valley between the North and South parks, and then crossing the Mupamadzi into South Luangwa, is possible only in the dry season – but it's probably the trickiest of the ways to get here. See the section on getting to Luambe National Park, entitled *From Mpika via the Corridor Road,* on page 292, for the start of the route. After turning east from the Great North Road (⊕ TUBATE 12°6.421'S; 31°15.727'E) about 40km south of Mpika, you pass Nthunta Scout Camp (⊕ NTHUNA 12°19.828'S; 31°31.979'E) and then drop over the escarpment and eventually reach the Mutinondo River. About 8.8km after crossing this, there's a left turning which leads to Nabwalya village and the Luangwa River (though the pontoon across the river is no longer operational).

However, if you continue straight on and don't turn left to Nabwalya, then after a further 7.3km you will reach the Chifungwe game scouts camp (⊕ CHIFUNG 12°26.061'S; 31°42.263'E), just before the Mupamadzi River. This is the boundary to South Luangwa National Park, reached about 73km from the Great North Road. Crossing the Mupamadzi (which should only be attempted when low) is tricky, but then it's a simple, if long, journey to head due south.

About 3.4km after the Mupamadzi crossing you reach a junction: to the left is a small road to the private Mupamadzi Walking Area, to the right is the '05' road (see also box, pages 262–3) which is very little used but will take you right across the heart of the park, skirting the western side of Zebra Pans. About 55km after the Mupamadzi, you will reach the Luwi River (⊕ 05LUWI 12°56.381'S; 31°45.468'E) near Nsolo Bushcamp (just deep sand), and then some 10km after that you join the network of all-weather roads in the Mfuwe area, just north of the 'Big Baobab' and Mfuwe Lodge (see map of the Mfuwe area on page 264).

From Luambe See pages 291–2 for details of this route in reverse, and backtrack.

Hitchhiking With plenty of water and stamina, getting to Mfuwe from Chipata is possible. Start hitching early at the turn-off, or outside the Chipata Motel. (You can always sleep there if necessary.) Don't accept local lifts going just a few kilometres, there's no point – better to wait for a vehicle going at least to Mfuwe Airport. Some of the camps have trucks doing supply runs to Chipata, there are occasional tourists (though fewer with space to spare) and there is a small amount of local traffic. I took five hours just to get a lift from here one October morning, so expect a long wait.

That said, with an increasing population in Mfuwe there are now small minibuses which ply between Chipata and Mfuwe. These cost under U$10 per person one way, but usually won't leave until full. Small groups of travellers may be able to hire a vehicle for a reasonable rate; make sure you agree on the airport as the drop-off location.

GETTING AROUND

In your own vehicle South Luangwa's network of roads is not as extensive as you might expect. A few all-weather roads (mostly graded gravel) have been built in the park around the Mfuwe area – accessible over the main bridge into the park. These are the only roads that can be relied upon during the wet season.

Elsewhere, the park has seasonally passable roads that are (optimistically) marked on some of the maps. Such tracks follow both banks of the Luangwa, north and south of Mfuwe, and a few penetrate westwards into the park. In the areas near camps, there are numerous 'loop' roads, which leave these main tracks and return to them. These are just side roads for game viewing, and trying to be precise about their position is pointless – they are usually made simply by the passage of a few vehicles, and will disappear again very swiftly once the vehicles stop.

Note that if you are driving your own vehicle around the park then you are limited to being in the park from dawn to dusk. You are not allowed to stay in and drive around after dark, as only the local safari companies have licences to conduct night drives. (Note also that the Nkwali pontoon marked on many maps opens 1 June to 31 October and is not for use by private vehicles.)

Without a vehicle If you do not have a vehicle of your own, then you should organise your camps or lodges before you arrive. If you haven't done so before you arrive, then you may be limited to the Wildlife Camp or Flatdogs. If your budget is higher, then you might consider stopping at Moondog Café (by the airport) and asking them to radio a few of the more upmarket camps to see if any have space left. This is unusual, and don't expect bargains (you won't find any), but it is a real waste to get all the way here and then not make the most of the park. So if you can, splash out on the best place that you can afford.

Maps Two different maps of the South Luangwa National Park are available in Lusaka. One showing South Luangwa and Luambe national parks was compiled for the national tourist board, and is useful in giving the general scheme of the area's roads. Otherwise the information on its reverse side is fairly dated, and so not very valuable.

A second very different map concentrates on just the South Luangwa National Park. This was produced in 1989 using aid donations and shows the landscape and vegetation in considerable scientific detail; it's a scholarly work. Its reverse side details the various land systems in the area: the different combinations of land form, rock, soil and vegetation in the park. This is a fascinating map which has some of the camps marked, but only a few of the existing roads.

In the unlikely event that you need to navigate yourself at all, get both of these and consider also buying more detailed Ordnance Survey-style maps available from the surveyor general's office in Lusaka. Such detailed maps (preferably together with a GPS and good local guide) would be essential for visits to Luambe or Lukusuzi.

WHERE TO STAY

Upmarket camps and lodges Most of South Luangwa's camps aim at upmarket visitors from overseas. Given the park's remote location, this is not surprising. They incur great difficulties (and costs) in communicating, organising supplies and actually getting their clients into the valley. Then remember that most of them can operate for only six months of the year, after which they pack up, returning to rebuild their camps after every rainy season. Thus, they do have some plausible reasons to be costly.

The rates at these camps generally include your meals and activities from around US$400–700 per person per day. Most will also include your bar bill and park fees in this.

Most offer a special 'safari rate', typically about 5–10% cheaper than the normal rate, if you stay in camps run by just one operator for seven nights or more. This can be very convenient and is certainly recommended. It will provide a welcome continuity whilst you visit totally different camps. Such combinations include Kapani and its bushcamps; Nkwali, Tena Tena and Nsefu; Tafika and its bushcamps, including Mwaleshi; Mfuwe Lodge and the camps of the Bushcamp Company.

A few offer discounts if you are a resident of Zambia, especially in the quieter parts of the season. At busier times (including July–October), they are likely to be full and such deals are usually 'unavailable'. Then the best deals are usually available from overseas operators (see pages 45–8) – whose volumes of business give them access to significant discounts.

Note that although many of the camps cost around a similar level, their atmospheres and styles differ greatly – so choose carefully. For the sake of completeness, I've included here a few camps whose names are well known, but have now closed. And no mention of the South Luangwa would be complete without a word for the old Chinzombo, which stood just south of Kapani. It had a respected history as one of the valley's first safari camps, but was closed in the early 2000s as the very ground on which it stood was being eroded (about 3–5m of riverbank would disappear per year into the floodwaters) – and now there is nothing left.

The valley's camps, in alphabetical order, include:

Big Lagoon Camp Planned in the same mould as Lion Camp (see page 273), but long disused, Big Lagoon Camp is an old safari site on the north side of the Luangwa Valley.

⌂ **Bilimungwe Bushcamp** (4 twin-bed chalets) Contact via Bushcamp Company, page 260 (⊕ BILIMU 13°23.295'S; 31°34.198'E). Some 46km (as the eagle flies) southeast of Mfuwe, Bilimungwe stands about 100m from the Luangwa, slightly upstream of its confluence with the Kapamba River. *Bilimungwe* means 'chameleon' in the local Kamanga tongue; hence the exquisitely carved chameleon in the central bar/dining area, which has been beautifully designed as a thatched roof suspended between the trunks & branches of some tall old trees (mostly Natal mahoganies, *Trichilia emetica*, & winterthorns, *Faidherbia albida*). Underneath is a platform of wooden decking with a bar one end & tables at the other. Overlooking a permanent waterhole, it's a fascinating design whose open sides are permeated by a cool breeze in the heat.

Accommodation is in very comfortable chalets, which overlook a vlei. These have tall thatched roofs, & walls made of cane & reeds at the bottom, & mosquito gauze at the top. Each has 2 dbl beds with separate mosquito nets, an en-suite shower, toilet & 2 washbasins. There's usually just one guide in camp, running activities on a consensus basis. These will include game drives & walking safaris, as well as night drives, which are normally part of the programme.

Transfers here from Mfuwe take about 3hrs, & the drive down is mainly through miombo woodlands. A stay at Bilimungwe is usually combined with staying at other Bushcamp Company camps, lasting at least a week. US$$540/730 Jun–Oct, US$360/485 Nov–Dec, all pp sharing/sgl, inc FB, bar, laundry, park fees, airport & inter-camp transfers, & activities. ⊕ Jun–Dec.

⌂ **Chamilandu Bushcamp** (3 chalets) Contact via Bushcamp Company, page 260 (⊕ CHAMIL 13°19.023'S; 31°38.526'E). About 2hrs' drive southwest of Mfuwe, Chamilandu was originally set up in 1988 as a bushcamp for walking safaris. Rebuilt on a new site in 1999, again on the banks of the Luangwa River but with the Nchindeni Hills in the background, which look beautiful in the late afternoon sun, it was totally refurbished & upgraded. Set on high wooden decks, the chalets are made of thatch & reeds, & have open-air showers, dbl washbasins & flush toilets. The twin or queen-size dbl beds are all wrought iron & have mosquito nets & small solar-powered reading lights.

A hide overlooking 1 of 7 oxbow lagoons that surround the camp makes a great spot to sit & watch game. Game drives are offered as an alternative to the usual walks. It is easily possible to do a walking trip between Chamilandu, Chindeni & Bilimungwe — walking between them with your luggage taken ahead for you — as they're only about 10km apart. US$540/730 pp sharing/sgl, inc FB, bar, activities, park fees, & airport & inter-camp transfers. Min 2 guests in camp at any time. ⊕ Jun–Oct.

Chibembe Lodge Closed. In the northwest of the park, Chibembe was a large & busy lodge with a long history. There was a hunting camp recorded here as long ago as 1932, & later it became the centre of operations for Wilderness Trails, an old Zambian company closely connected with the Luangwa. In 1998 it was sold to Chilongozi, who went bust. The site is now unused, but it's such a good area that you may hear the name resurrected at any time ...

Chibembe also had 5 small satellite bushcamps, all situated in a private walking area within the park to the west of the camp: Mumbulu, Kasansanya. Changwa, Nakalyo & Nyakabvumo. They're in a superb walking area, so don't be surprised if you do hear of them being used again. (Just make sure you're booking with a very reliable operator who won't go bust!)

🏠 **Chichele Presidential Lodge** (10 rooms) Contact via Sanctuary Lodges & Camps, page 261. (⊕ CHICHE 13°10.008'S; 31°42.605'E). About 15km southwest of Mfuwe Lodge, Chichele was another large & decaying lodge, once owned by the parastatal 'National Hotels', which was put out to private management. It opened in September 2001, standing in a hilly area where the Luangwa River starts to come much closer to the escarpment. Around it are a variety of environments inc miombo woodland & mopane glades, on soil that varies from patches of gravel/sand to patches of black-cotton soil. The lodge itself is high up, atop a hill named President Hill, as Chichele was the president's private lodge in the Luangwa during KK's reign. It's got a great view!

Both Chichele & its sister camp, Puku Ridge, were completely rebuilt by Star of Africa, then in 2007 moved into the Sanctuary Lodges & Camps' stable. Each of Chichele's elegant rooms boasts verandas, minibars, AC, hair dryers & tea/coffee-making facilities, & a mosquito net that's part of the bed's canopy, while en-suite facilities comprise a glass-fronted shower room, bath & twin washbasins. There was an obligation to keep many of Chichele's present buildings for their alleged historical value, so the design has had to take these into account, & the place retains a colonial feel. The communal areas are huge, inc a large dining area with candelabra, ceiling fans & even a cappuccino maker, while outside is a relaxing pool and a 360° view of the surrounding area.

Activities major on game drives (with night drives considered to be a must), although walks are also available. Small groups or conferences can also be accommodated, in combination with the nearby Puku Ridge. *US$595/775 Jun–Oct pp sharing/sgl,US$380 Nov–May, all inc FB & game activities.* ⊕ *all year.*

⚓ **Chikoko Trails** (2 camps, each with 3 chalets) Contact via Remote Africa Safaris, page 260. These 2 bushcamps operate slightly upstream of their parent camp, Tafika, on the opposite bank of the Luangwa. This is around the spot where David Livingstone crossed the Luangwa in 1866, & little seems to have changed since then; it's still a beautiful corner of the valley with excellent game densities.

Being in a wilderness area, there are no roads to these camps & all the luggage & supplies are carried by porters. From Tafika this means a brief drive along the river, followed by a quick crossing by canoe & then a short walk. There are two small bushcamps here: **Chikoko & Crocodile**.

Chikoko Walking Camp is only about 10 mins' walk from the Luangwa, beside the small, seasonal Chikoko Channel. The simple grass-walled chalets are raised about 3m off the ground, & topped by a canvas shade to keep off the sun & any rain. This also gives the nervous an added sense of security, & provides a good vantage point for spotting wildlife. Private flush toilets & showers (hot on request) are downstairs.

Crocodile Walking Camp is further from the river, about a 40-min walk, & stands in a great location on an old river bank, overlooking a large & usually dry oxbow lagoon. The 3 dbl chalets have en-suite flush toilet & showers (hot on request), open to the air.

At both you'll find a very busy but relaxed air, solar lighting & efficient refrigeration. But to focus on the camps themselves is to miss the point; Remote Africa's guides are amongst the valley's most experienced — so though simple, these are amongst the valley's very best bushcamps. *US$400/600 pp sharing/sgl, inc FB, bar, activities & park fees.* ⊕ *Jun–Oct.*

⚓ **Chindeni Bushcamp** (4 tents) Contact via Bushcamp Company, page 260 (⊕ CHINDE 13°22.056'S; 31°36.426'E). About 7km further upstream than Bilimungwe, Chindeni is about 3hrs' drive south of Mfuwe. It stands on the banks of a large, permanent oxbow lagoon, which stretches away from it on both sides. The main river is about 1km away, & in the near distance rise the Nchindeni Hills, overlooking the park's eastern boundary.

Chindeni's tents are each tucked into the vegetation beside the lagoon, & raised up on hardwood decks. Each has a shaded veranda with chairs at the front, & an en-suite (hot & cold) shower, flush toilet & pair of washbasins at the back. These are very well furnished for such a small camp, with large writing desks & deck chairs, big wooden wardrobes, twin or dbl beds & great attention to detail. (The room at the left-hand end is my favourite; it's got an enormous balcony with its own hammock.) The central dining room/bar area is also on wooden decking, between the 4 tents, & underneath ebony & tamarind trees.

It's usual to spend a few days here as well as time at Bilimungwe. Chindeni is primarily a walking camp, though night drives are always available. Wild dog regularly frequent the area & are often seen from the company's camps. *US$540/730 pp sharing/sgl, inc FB, bar, laundry, activities, park fees, & airport & inter-camp transfers.* ⊕ *Jun–Oct.*

⌂ **Chinengwe** (4 Meru tents) Wilderness Safaris, page 417. Another new bushcamp under the Wilderness umbrella, Chinengwe is scheduled to open in 2008, with all its rooms overlooking the Luangwa River. Guests will be able to walk the 5km trail between Kalamu & Chinengwe camps, & other activities will include game drives.

⌂ **Gwala & Zungulila Walking Camps** (4 chalets) Contact via Bushcamp Company, page 260 (⊕ 13°20.850'S; 31°30.877'E). Situated in an untouched section of the park, the remote Gwala & Zungulila walking camps offer the opportunity to explore an unspoilt section of wilderness on foot. The route travelled is the Hippo Pools trail, which runs along the Kapamba River through some of the most untamed sections of the bush. All game activities are limited to walking & no night drives are available. Despite their remote location, Gwala & Zungulila boast all the comforts of home, including en-suite facilities & sweeping views of game from private verandas. *Rates not available at time of going to press; contact the Bushcamp Company.* ⊕ *Jun–Oct.*

⌂ **Island Bushcamp** (5 chalets) Contact via Kafunta River Lodge (see below). About 2hrs' drive south of Kafunta, Island Bushcamp was opened in 2002. It stands on the banks of the Luangwa River, in the far south of the park, where the river no longer forms the border of the national park but rather runs though it. Guests are normally driven from Kafunta. Its chalets are built on raised platforms with open views to the river; all have twin beds, private hot showers & flush toilets. The camp is mainly a base for walking safaris, & limited game drives are possible. *US$350/440 pp sharing/sgl, inc FB, drinks, activities & park fees.* ⊕ *Jun–Oct.*

⌂ **Kafunta River Lodge** (10 chalets) ☎/f 021 6246046; e kafunta@luangwa.com; www.luangwa.com (⊕ KAFUNT 13°9.785'S; 31°44.360'E). Kafunta is about 9km from the main road between Mfuwe Airport & the bridge. To get there take a left turn before the bridge, signposted

to Kafunta, Kapani & other lodges. Then around where the tar ends (just before Kapani) you'll see a left turn signposted to Kafunta. Believe it or not, this is the main road that runs southwest outside the park & follows the river downstream. There are 3 left turns: one to the Wildlife Camp, one to Nkwali Camp, & the third to Kafunta. It's well signposted all the way.

Kafunta stands on a spacious site beside the river & was built from scratch in 1998 by a team inc Ron & Anke Cowan, who now own & run the camp. Its central dining/bar area under a huge thatched roof is very impressive – built around a wild mango tree. Dinner is often served by candlelight on an open-air deck to the front, with views over the floodplains. Beside the bar is a small swimming pool, & nearby is a natural hot tub supplied by water from a local hot spring.

Kafunta's rooms are, as yet, unique in the Luangwa: thatched wooden chalets built about a metre off the ground on stilts. Each has an en-suite bathroom, with a shower (hot & cold), washbasin & flush toilet. Two $^3/_4$ beds lie under a large, walk-in mosquito net. All the rooms have minibar/fridges, coffee makers & ceiling fans – powered by mains electricity. Their windows are gauzed & each chalet has a veranda overlooking the river. All are comfortable, spacious & airy, though their steps made me feel somewhat separated from the land around.

Activities from Kafunta centre around 4x4 game drives (day & night) & walking safaris. Kafunta is only about 1.5km from the Nkwali pontoon, or 9km from the Mfuwe Bridge. *US$375/465 Jul–Oct, US$260/315 Nov, Dec, Apr, May, US$220/275 Jan–Mar, all pp sharing/sgl, inc FB, activities, & park fees; drinks extra except Jul–Oct.* ⊕ *all year.*

⌂ **Kaingo Camp** (6 chalets) Contact via Shenton Safaris, page 261 (⊕ KAINGO 12°55.370'S; 31°55.441'E). Where the seasonal Mwamba River meets the main Luangwa River, the small camp of Kaingo looks over the water towards the Nsefu Sector from beneath an old grove of mahogany & ebony trees. The open-sided sitting room cum dining area is a large thatched *chitenge*, with an amazing bar made from an old leadwood tree trunk. Outside, a deck extends over the river – perfect for relaxing & game viewing. Four of Kaingo's chalets are brick with a thatched roof. Inside each are twin beds with mosquito nets, a lockable box for valuables, a couple of solar lights & an en-suite shower/toilet. Each has a solid, stable-style door which opens onto the bank overlooking the main river. A little further upstream are 2 riverside honeymoon suites. These have en-suite bathrooms (hot & cold water) & skylights that have been cut from the roof above the king-size beds, to give a view of the stars as you drift off to sleep. Outside, on the riverbank, is a luxurious bath. (Riverbank bathtubs are also a feature of 2 of the other chalets.)

Close to Kaingo, the camp has 3 hides: the 'elephant' & 'hippo' hides, & the seasonal 'carmine bee-eater' hide. These are fairly rare in the Luangwa, & have been variously occupied for long periods by film-makers from both the BBC & *National Geographic*. If you're too active for a late morning snooze, or are keen on photography, this is the place to come & keep watch; it's even possible to spend a night in the elephant hide – an amazing experience. In fact, photographers are particularly well catered for, with such extras as camera dust covers & bean bags available, & convertible vehicles that can allow for each guest to have an outside seat.

Derek Shenton, who owns & runs the operation with his wife Jules, is quiet & unassuming, which has perhaps helped the lodge to attain a solid, established & yet very calm air. It's been open since 1993 & its main guides, Patrick Njobvu & Ian Salisbury, both have almost 20 years' experience of guiding in this part of the world. The usual walking safaris & day & night drives are offered, plus picnics in the bush & hide trips; many guests take in 3 activities a day. Those staying 7 nights or more with Shenton Safaris can pre-arrange an overnight camping trip with Derek Shenton, walking out from Kaingo in the afternoon, camping in the bush overnight & walking into Mwamba Bush Camp the next morning. Note that the Shenton family also run Forest Inn, near Mkushi (see page 297). *US$595 pp sharing Aug–Sep, US$545 May–Jul & Oct, all pp sharing, inc FB, drinks & activities.* ⊕ *20 May–31 Oct.*

🏠 **Kakuli Bushcamp** (5 chalets) Contact via Norman Carr Safaris, page 260. A camp was first started here in 1984 by Norman Carr, overlooking a wide bend in the Luangwa. In the 1990s it was owned & run by Savannah Trails, but as of 1996, it came under the umbrella of Norman Carr Safaris. *Kakuli* is the local word for an old buffalo bull which has left the main herd, & by association was also Norman Carr's nickname amongst the local people before he died.

Kakuli Bushcamp is linked to Nsolo camp (10km away) & Luwi camp (20km away) by the seasonal Luwi River, which makes 3-day walks between these 3 sister camps a very interesting option. The

bushcamp was redesigned in 1998 & its reed chalets replaced with large, walk-in tents equipped with simple solar lights. These have an open-roofed, enclosed area at the back, with a toilet, shower & washbasin under the stars. Inside each is a dbl or twin beds, whilst the veranda at the front, with its canvas chairs & a table, is shaded by a high thatched roof.

The dining-room/bar area is small, simple & comfortable: a thatched, reed-walled structure with one open side, a sprinkling of cushioned chairs & a good bookshelf. The camp seldom takes more than 6 guests, & it concentrates firmly on walking, though night drives are possible in the area. A stay here is usually combined with the main Kapani Lodge & sister-bushcamps, Luwi, Nsolo & Mchenja. *US$500/550 pp sharing/sgl, inc FB, activities, drinks & park fees.* ⊕ *Jun–Oct.*

🏠 **Kalamu Lodge** (4 Meru tents) Contact via Wilderness Safaris, page 417. Built in the same concession as the old Luamfwa Lodge, Kalamu was opened in 2007, overlooking the Luangwa River & just 5km from its own airstrip (⊕ **KALAMA** 13°28.193'S; 31°23.051'E). Each of its neatly pegged tents has comfy twin beds with a walk-in mosquito net, & en-suite shower & toilet. The traditional feel of the tents is offset by glazed wooden doors, looking over the river, where tree-shaded wooden decking makes a good vantage point for watching wildlife. The camp's dining & bar area lie under a canopy of trees, with a nearby plunge pool. Activities consist of guided walks (which from 2008 will inc a 5km trail to Chinengwe) & game drives. *US$510/635 pp sharing/sgl, inc FB, local drinks, activities, laundry, taxes & park fees.* ⊕ *May–Nov.*

🏠 **Kapamba Bushcamp** (4 chalets) Contact via Bushcamp Company, page 260 (⊕ **KAPAMB** 13°22.967'S; 31°31.584'E). The newest of the Bushcamp Company's camps is quite different from the rest. Unencumbered by a 4th wall, each of Kapamba's en-suite chalets (with dbl or twin beds) is open fronted, with sweeping views of the Kapamba River – which is shallow enough to paddle through barefoot or even to sit in during the dry season. Wrought-iron gates span the front of each chalet, offering protection from unwanted visitors & creating a spider-web effect against the African sky. Inside each en-suite bathroom are twin showers above a bath the size of a small plunge pool (a happy accident, resulting from a specification given in centimetres, which the builders assumed was in inches!).

Activities continue the theme, with the camp's guide accompanying guests as they wade through the shallow waters of the river on the way to a sundowner or intimate dinner. As with Bushcamp's other camps, game drives are offered during the day as an alternative to walking, & night drives are usually on the menu. *US$540/730 Jun–Oct, US$360/485 Nov–Dec, all pp sharing/sgl, inc FB, bar, laundry, activities, park fees, & airport & inter-camp transfers.* ⊕ *Jun–Dec.*

🏠 **Kapani Safari Lodge** (10 rooms) Contact via Norman Carr Safaris, page 260 (✪ KAPANI 13°7.237'S; 31°46.057'E). To get to Kapani turn left just before the Mfuwe Bridge; it's well signposted on the right about 3km after that junction. The lodge overlooks a beautiful old lagoon, within Lupande GMA, just south of the main Luangwa River — thus ensuring that changes in the river's course won't wash away its bank.

Founded by the late Norman Carr, the present camp was built as recently as 1986 (& completely refurbished in 2004), though its quality accommodation still feels reliably solid. The large brick rooms have thatched roofs, heavy wooden furniture & cool floor tiles. Mains electricity powers efficient (& quiet) ceiling fans, sensibly placed within the walk-in mosquito nets surrounding the beds. The rooms are big, & each includes a separate sitting area with large, mosquito-netted windows overlooking a lagoon, & its own small drinks fridge. They are amongst the most spacious & comfortable of the valley's smaller camps.

Central to Kapani is its lounge & bar area, containing a bookshelf of local interest surrounded by pictures of the area in former times, inc some of Norman & his children when young. (A few of Norman's extended family are still involved with the safari operation.) There's a dining room under thatch by the lagoon & a wooden deck over the water, which is often used as a b/fast venue. The food here is consistently good. Rates include good house wines, as is the norm for most camps in the valley, but Kapani also has a modest wine cellar with a selection of fine vintage wines available at extra cost.

Activities involve game drives into the park, or occasional walks if requested. The guiding is well up to the valley's high standards; Kapani is notable for having several excellent & long-serving Zambian guides from the local community who were originally trained by Norman Carr. It also acts as base camp for 4 small, satellite walking camps: Luwi, Nsolo, Kakuli & Mchenja. Together the 5 make a fine combination: usually staying at Kapani for the first few nights (and possibly also for the last night) &

then a combination of the walking camps. *US$500/550 Jun–Oct, US$375 Nov–May, all pp sharing/sgl, inc FB, activities, drinks & park fees.* ⊕ *all year.*

🏠 **Kuyenda** (4 rondavels) Contact via Bushcamp Company, page 260 (✪ KUYEND 13°22.430'S; 31°32.430'E) About 75 mins' drive south of Mfuwe, this small, very traditional bushcamp (max 6 visitors) concentrates on walking safaris with the occasional drive. It overlooks the Manzi River, a sand-river tributary of the main Luangwa.

Much of the guiding here is done by Phil Berry — the valley's most experienced guide with a legendary reputation for his knowledge of the area's wildlife. Though Phil no longer leads all the walks, he still spends most of the season at the camp guiding many of the walks & sharing his extensive knowledge of the bush. In the evening, the conversation over dinner can be particularly interesting & convivial, especially when Phil & his partner, Babette, are in camp. The round chalets, made of thatch & reeds, have en-suite toilets & showers under the sky (hot water for showers is heated & brought on request). Kuyenda's chalets have twin queen-size beds, or a king-size dbl, veiled by mosquito netting, & atmospheric paraffin lanterns.

Though walking is the main focus here, drives are also possible — & night drives are always a feature of your time here. Returning to the camp when it's dark is a great pleasure as the whole camp is lit by romantic hurricane lamps which look magical as you approach across a wide sand river. *US$540/730 pp sharing/sgl, inc FB, bar, activities, park fees, & airport & inter-camp transfers.* ⊕ *Jun–Oct. Min 2 guests needed for camp to be open.*

🏠 **Kwena Lagoon Camp** (9 rooms) Contact via Wilderness Safaris, page 417 (✪ KWENAL 13°27.503'S; 31°23.178'E). Overlooking a huge permanent lagoon, Kwena is the latest of the Wilderness Camps in Zambia, accepting its first visitors in July 2008. Built on the site of the old Luamfwa Camp, it's in the south of the park, overlooking the Luangwa River from a superb site. Most clients will fly in to the nearby airstrip, but for experienced drivers with a 4x4 it can be approached in the dry season only, using the back roads from Petauke (see route on pages 265–6). In addition to twin-bedded en-suite rooms, there will be 2 family suites, each with 2 bedrooms with their own bathroom. *U$510/635 pp sharing/sgl, inc FB, local drinks, activities, laundry, taxes & park fees.* ⊕ *May–Nov.*

🏠 **Lion Camp** (9 chalets) e info@lioncamp.com; www.lioncamp.com (✪ LIONCA 12°53.089'S, 31°58.032'E). Situated inside the park & to the north of the Mfuwe area, Lion Camp stands on an old site on the edge of an oxbow lagoon, overlooking an open plain. Having completely fallen into disuse, it was rebuilt some 6 years ago, & for 2007 was fully renovated once again to a high standard of comfort. Each chalet is built on its own wooden platform & is linked to the others & the main area by a raised wooden boardwalk. They're solid, spacious structures with canvas walls, thatched roofs, & private decks fronted by the lagoon. Style oozes from the interior, with polished wood floors & a 4-poster king-size dbl or twin beds, each with walk-in mosquito nets. There's also a stand fan, a large wardrobe & an en-suite shower & toilet, not to mention a separate day bed for afternoon relaxation. 220V inverter power is available in each chalet.

At the heart of the camp, a central boma with a fireplace is encircled by thatched seating areas, a library & curio shop, & a central bar, while beyond is a lower viewing deck & a serene infinity swimming pool to unwind after a long day.

Activities revolve around game drives & walking safaris with experienced guides. *From US$450/550 pp sharing/sgl, inc FB, activities, local drinks & park fees.* ⊕ *May–Oct.*

🏕 **Luangwa Bushcamping** See *Fly-camping*, page 281, for details.

🏠 **Luangwa River Lodge** (5 chalets) ☎ 021 6246031; e luangwariverlodge@iwayafrica.com; www.luangwariverlodge.com (✪ LUARLO 13°04.459'S; 31°48.636'E). In a riverside setting 10km north of Mfuwe, and bordering the South Park, Luangwa River Lodge is both stylish & supremely accessible. Chalets, built of ochre-painted brick under thatch, sit seamlessly within their surroundings, blending the simplicity of angled corners & smoothed curves with natural woods & palms, & neutral furnishings, right down to the showers & sunken baths.

The theme continues into the open-plan lounge & dining area, where even the food has a designer feel. If all that's not sufficiently refreshing, then there's always a cooling dip in the infinity pool or a holistic massage. For the more active, options centre on walking safaris & game drives, plus boat trips when the water level in the river is sufficiently high. The relative accessibility of the lodge also makes cultural trips possible, inc visits to Chipembele Wildlife Education Centre (see page 259), & various craft & village projects. *US$600 pp Jun–Oct,*

US$400 pp Nov–Jan, Apr–May, inc FB, activities & airport transfers. ⊕ *Apr–early Jan.*

🏠 **Luangwa Safari House** Contact via Robin Pope Safaris, page 261. Built in 2005 on the Nkwali property (see below), this large & traditional-looking house is constructed around 25 weathered leadwood trees. From the front entrance, a huge door opens into the spacious main room, some 12m high, with comfy sofas, large marble dining table & views through the open front across a tiled terrace. Wooden staircases lead to 4 bedrooms, overlooking a lagoon; all are en suite & individually styled to reflect different materials: copper in one; sand-blasted aluminium in another. To the side of the terrace is a plunge pool, & a long walkway leads to a wooden deck around a group of huge ebony trees in the middle of the lagoon. Here, there is a large leather sofa, a hanging chair & dining table & chairs for al fresco meals. The nearby waterhole attracts families of elephant that come to bathe. *US$700/pp sharing Jun–Oct (min 4 people in Jun & Oct, min 6 Jul–Sep) US$550/pp sharing Nov–May (min 4). No children under 7.* ⊕ *all year.*

🏠 **Luwi Bushcamp** (4 chalets) Contact via Norman Carr Safaris, page 260. A further 10km up the Luwi River from its sister camp, Nsolo, Luwi is an equally rustic camp set under a group of tall shady trees (*Vitex, Breonadia & Khaya nyusica*), looking out over a small plain. The chalets, which can be twin or dbl, are similarly of reed & thatch, with grass matting covering their earth floors, mosquito nets, storm lanterns, solar lights & a small veranda. All have en-suite facilities, with their toilet, shower & washbasin under the stars.

A very short walk leads to a large, permanent lagoon at a bend in the river (usually frequented by a pod of about 60 hippos). This is purely a camp for walking: either for day walks based here, or for walks linking with Nsolo, Kakuli & Mchenja bushcamps. It's not a camp for game drives & seldom takes more than 7 guests. Time at Luwi is often combined with its sister-bushcamps &/or a few nights at Kapani. *US$500/550 pp sharing/sgl, inc FB, activities, drinks & park fees.* ⊕ *Jun–Oct.*

🏠 **Mchenja Camp** (5 chalets) Contact via Norman Carr Safaris, page 260. Mchenja has long been owned by Savannah Trails, but for the last few years has been ably run under the umbrella of Norman Carr Safaris. It stands in one of the very best locations of any camp in the valley, beside the Luangwa River in deep shade at the end of a serenely beautiful grove of African ebony trees, *Diospyros mespiliformis* (which, incidentally, are known as *muchenja* in the local dialect of ChiNyanja).

Accommodation consists of raised thatched wooden chalets. These are Swiss-style A-frame in design, each with a large open veranda at the front, & en-suite (hot) showers & flush toilet at the back, in an open-air bathroom. Inside is a dbl or twin beds, each with their own mosquito net & solar-powered lights. Though originally these rooms weren't large, the addition of the veranda & the outside bathroom has made a huge difference, & it's now a delightful little bushcamp.

About 30km from Mfuwe, Mchenja stands opposite the Nsefu Sector, between Nsefu Camp & Tena Tena. It makes a good last stop at the end of a walking safari, being an easy 10km walk (3–4hrs) from either Nsolo or Kakuli. *US$650 pp sharing, inc FB, activities, drinks & park fees.* ① *Jun–Oct, & 20 Jan–end Mar for river safaris.*

⌂ **Mfuwe Lodge** (18 chalets) Contact via Bushcamp Company, page 260 (✪ MFUWEL 13°4.725'S; 31°47.441'E). Mfuwe Lodge stands in a prime location at the heart of the South Luangwa National Park, where the game is prolific & relaxed. It overlooks the picturesque Mfuwe Lagoon in the centre of the park's all-weather road network.

In the 1980s & early '90s the lodge degenerated, until it was bought by the Bizzaro family, owners of a successful lodge in neighbouring Malawi, Club Makokola. They demolished & rebuilt it, starting from scratch: a huge project. Completed in 1998, this has made Mfuwe Lodge one of the grandest safari lodges in Zambia. It is relatively big by standards of the Luangwa's tiny camps, accommodating up to 36 guests.

Mfuwe has beautiful timber-&-thatch chalets, many of which are split level. Each overlooks the lagoon & has dbl or twin beds, encased in a walk-in mosquito net & cooled by a fan; plus a writing desk, minibar/fridge, tea/coffee maker, comfy chairs & rugs. The wide expanse of polished wooden flooring (dotted with rugs) opens, through sets of dbl doors, onto a broad veranda. In the bathroom there's a separate toilet, a sunken bath/shower with a view, & dual washbasins. Each chalet is beautifully designed, down to the individual fabrics & pottery.

Mfuwe's dining/bar area shelters under a vast thatched roof, surrounded by the now familiar wooden decking. The food is good & the bar well stocked. Morning & afternoon/night drives are in Land Rovers with 3 rows of seats. Walks are also possible, though keen walkers would be best to combine their stay here with time at one or more

bushcamps — & favourites for this would be some of those run by the Bushcamp Company, whose office is based here. There's no doubt that this lodge is a tremendously impressive place, & a match for many of Africa's more grand establishments. If luxury is your top priority, look no further. *US$265/360 pp sharing/sgl Jan–May & Nov–Dec; US$425/575 pp sharing/sgl Jun–Oct.* ① *all year.*

⌂ **Mushroom Lodge & Presidential House** (12 chalets) \ 021 6246117, 6246116; m 097 7467436, 097 9816599; f 021 6245 063; e info@ mushroomlodge.com; www.mushroomlodge.com. The historic Mushroom Lodge overlooking Mfuwe Lagoon was built in the early 1970s for President Kaunda and his guests, and remained in use until the fall of UNIP in 1991. In the ensuing years, the house fell into disrepair, but it has now been redeveloped as a safari lodge. To get there, take the main park gate and follow the road for about 2km, before turning to the right.

Guests are accommodated in en-suite dbl or twin chalets, painted a deep red & shaded under thatch. Each has its own lounge area with wicker furniture, a minibar & wireless broadband, & outside is a private veranda fronted by the lagoon. Children are particularly welcome, with special meals & games laid on for them, & a babysitting service available. Central to the lodge are a restaurant & bar area with an extensive veranda & a swimming pool, while nearby is an open-sided *nsaka* where massages are offered.

In addition to game drives and walks, guests can take part in tours to Mfuwe & the surrounding villages, while for relaxation between excursions there's a pool,.*Chalet US$400/490; US$210/275 both pp sharing/sgl, inc FB, 2 game drives & airport transfers; exc park fees, drinks.*

⌂ **Mwamba Bushcamp** (3 chalets) Contact via Shenton Safaris, page 261 (✪ MWAMBA 12°52.973'S; 31°55.940'E). About 6km north of Kaingo, or a morning's walk away, lies Kaingo's satellite bushcamp, Mwamba, at the confluence of the East Mwamba & main Mwamba rivers. The approach to the camp is lovely as the rivers are usually dry & sandy, & the banks open & green. There's an area of mopane forest nearby, as well as ebony groves & grasslands. The reed-&-thatch chalets are themselves shaded within a grove of ebonies (*Diospyros mespiliformis*), where there are some particularly beautiful trees, & have wide gauze panels on the roof, enabling guests to enjoy the sky & stars without leaving their beds. Each has a large en-suite bathroom, open to the stars, with a hot bucket shower & flush toilet.

Activities include walking & driving safaris, & hide trips. The camp has 3 hides, 2 in the camp, & a 3rd just outside; all are focused on waterholes, which regularly attract a pride of lion. It's one of South Luangwa's best areas for Cookson's wildebeest, & eland are also sometimes sighted around here. *US$595 pp sharing Aug–Sep, US$545 May–Jul & Oct, all pp sharing, inc FB, drinks & activities.* ⊕ *Jun–Oct.*

🏠 **Nkwali** (6 rooms, Robin's House, Luangwa Safari House) Contact via Robin Pope Safaris, page 261 (⊕ NKWALI 13°6.989'S; 31°44.414'E). Nkwali is the main base for Robin Pope Safaris. It overlooks the Luangwa & the park beyond from the Lupande GMA which encompasses some beautiful tall acacia & ebony woodlands, a favourite haunt for giraffe & elephant. As you turn left just before the main bridge at Mfuwe, Nkwali is well signposted. Take the road for about 5km, then turn left just before the end of the tarmac. Take this for about 2km, then turn right for a further 4km.

Each of Nkwali's comfortable, airy rooms has a thatched roof resting on wicker-work, creamy-white walls, & a dbl or twin beds surrounded by a large walk-in mosquito net. At the back of each chalet the en-suite shower is open to the sky, while the toilet & 2 basins are under cover. All the chalets have views over the river & are on mains power, with a back-up generator.

The camp feels rustic, but very stylishly so. Its bar is spectacularly built around an ebony tree, & there's a small waterhole behind the dining room that often attracts game very close to the camp. The food is predictably good. It's usual to combine time here with time at Tena Tena &/or Nsefu camps, further north.

The private, 5-bed Robin's House stands on the riverbank, under a grove of large ebony trees near the main camp's swimming pool. Inside, the house has been stylishly decorated, with traditional African touches. It has a central sitting room & 2 large bedrooms (one dbl & one trpl), each with its own bathroom. Large windows give great views across the river. The house has a private guide, hostess & chef, so it's ideal for families &/or those seeking more privacy. There is also the brand-new Luangwa Safari House (see below).

Most trips from Nkwali will be drives into the park, which is accessed either by boat across the river, or over the conveniently close Nkwali pontoon. Walks are led into both the park & in the surrounding GMA; often you'll just cross the river by boat & walk from there. The camp has permission

to run walking safaris throughout the year. *US$480/645 Jun & Oct, US$550/800 Jul–Sep, US$390 sharing/sgl Nov–May , all pp sharing/sgl, inc FB, drinks, activities & park fees. Robin's House US$600 pp (min 3 adults) Jun–Oct, US$450 Nov–May.* ⊕ *all year.*

🏠 **Nsefu Camp** (6 rondavels) Contact via Robin Pope Safaris, page 261 (⊕ NSEFU 12°56.236'S; 31°55.289'E). Nsefu is superbly situated on the Luangwa River, in the middle of the Nsefu Sector. It was first opened in 1951 by Norman Carr – making it Zambia's oldest safari camp – & moved to its present location in 1953. Then the camp consisted of raised brick rondavels that were entered via a few steps.

In recent years these deteriorated until, in late '98, the camp was bought by Robin Pope Safaris, who completely rebuilt & refurbished it. (Robin himself had guided there for many years before starting up his own company, so had always been closely connected with Nsefu.) Now it is once again one of the best camps in the valley.

Nsefu's original row of round rondavels has been retained, but each now has a shady wooden veranda at the front. Inside are twin beds surrounded by a walk-in mosquito net. Soft colours & quality fabrics are used throughout. Large windows look out over the river, stylishly curtained. At the back, each rondavel has had an en-suite shower & toilet added – complete with old-style bath taps (but efficient hot water) – which is partially open to the outside.

The camp has been furnished with taste & elegance, in the style of the 1950s – complete with wind-up gramophone & traditional silver service. The whole effect is impressive &, despite the camp's creature comforts, it has retained an old, solid feel of history.

Nsefu's thatched bar stands beside a huge termite mound, overlooking a small lagoon & a sweeping bend in the river. In a separate dining area, under thatch, the food is very good, & the atmosphere relaxed – although the tables are often laid beside the riverbank, or elsewhere under the skies. A stay here is often combined with Nkwali, Tena Tena, or one of Robin Pope's walking safaris. *US$550/715 Jun & Oct, US$650/900 Jul–Sep, all pp sharing/sgl, inc FB, bar, activities & park fees.* ⊕ *Jun–Oct.*

🏠 **Nsolo Bushcamp** (4 chalets) Contact via Norman Carr Safaris, page 260. The 2007 Nsolo is a brand-new & upgraded camp, following a fire the previous season. Set on a sweeping bend of the seasonal Luwi River, with a permanent waterhole to the front, it focuses on a central *chitenje* in the shade of mahogany & sausage trees. This is an airy thatched room with a separate open-air seating area & a good library — inc the *Nsolo Journals*, written by Craig & Janelle Doria when they managed the camp in the 1990s. Meals are normally taken here, but on special occasions the table is laid in the sand river, lit by the soft glow of hurricane lamps.

The large chalets were designed by Shadrack (Shaddy) Nkhoma, who has managed & guided here for 10 years. Built simply on wooden decks with reed walls & high thatched roofs, each has either twin beds or a dbl under a walk-in mosquito net. En-suite bathrooms are open to the stars with a flush toilet & shower with a view. A dbl door (rather than the old canvas curtain) opens onto a tree- or thatch-shaded private deck, with comfortable chairs & a great view over the river. Solar lights are used in the evenings.

The camp was named for the nsolo or honeyguide bird, *Indicator indicator*. It lies 9–10km inside the park from the main Luangwa River, directly west of the Nsefu Sector in a sandy area dominated by mopane trees. Though short game drives during the day & evening are possible, walking is the major attraction. On my first visit to Nsolo the ranger accompanying our walks was Rice Time, a sprightly Zambian hunter who strode through the bush with speed & confidence — despite being over 70 years of age. Sadly he died in 2006, but there is a memorial for him in camp, & his stories are still told & retold.

A stay here is usually combined with the main Kapani Lodge & its sister-bushcamps. It is 10km east to Luwi, & about the same to either Kakuli or Mchenja, so a few days spent walking down the sand river between the camps makes a great trip. *US$500–550 pp sharing, inc FB, activities, drinks & park fees.* ⏲ *Jun–Oct.*

🏠 **Puku Ridge Tented Camp** (7 tents) Contact via Sanctuary Lodges & Camps, page 261. Barely a kilometre from its sister-lodge, Chichele, Puku Ridge opened in July 2003, & has since been taken over by Sanctuary Lodges & Camps. It stands on the side of a rocky outcrop, overlooking a lovely floodplain on the south side of South Luangwa. Like Chichele, this gives it a view from a height that few of Luangwa's camps can match.

Each of Puku Ridge's walk-in safari tents has a private veranda outside, whilst inside are a king-size or twin beds, surrounded by a walk-in mosquito net with a ceiling fan above the bed. There's also a private bathroom with twin

washbasins & flush toilet, plus indoor & outdoor showers & a bath — demonstrating a relatively high level of luxury by Luangwa standards. Morning tea or coffee are delivered to the tents by your room steward.

Activities inc walks & day or night game drives. *US$525/685 pp sharing/sgl Jun–Oct, US$350 pp Apr–May, Nov–Dec, all inc FB, most drinks, laundry, activities & park fees. No children under 12.* ⏲ *Apr–Dec.*

🏠 **Tafika** (6 chalets) Contact via Remote Africa Safaris, page 260 (⊕ TAFIKA 15°51.250'S; 31°59.811'E). Tafika stands on the bank of the Luangwa, overlooking the national park, & is perhaps the smallest of the valley's main camps. It was founded by John & Carol Coppinger, who managed Chibembe for years until they branched off on their own to start Tafika around 1995. John's years of experience in the valley are augmented by the experience of several other top guides working here, inc Bryan Jackson, Isaac Zulu, Ernst Jacobs & Stephen Banda; thus Tafika's guiding is amongst the best in the valley.

Four of the reed-&-thatch chalets have 2 dbl beds in each, surrounded by separate walk-in mosquito nets. The family chalet, built around the trunk of a stunning sausage tree, *Kigelia africana*, has 2 rooms, while a new honeymoon chalet was added in 2006, with a king-size bed, dbl showers & a private hammock. All have en-suite facilities, inc a flush toilet, washbasin, & excellent shower that is open to the skies. Lighting is by solar-powered storm lanterns. The bar/dining area has comfortable chairs & large, circular dining tables, though dinner is a relaxed affair, often eaten together outside. Tafika is not luxurious in any conventional sense, though it is very high quality: the food is superb, the atmosphere friendly & unpretentious, & the guiding truly expert.

Game activities include day & night drives, as well as walking safaris. John (who had a commercial pilot's licence at one stage) keeps a microlight aircraft nearby, which can take a passenger. If he's in camp, as is usually the case, flights can be arranged for about US$95 per 15 mins — let them know in advance if possible. So if you stay here, don't miss seeing the park from an eagle's point of view. Back on land, it's also possible to do a mountain-bike safari.

During the dry season, Tafika acts as the hub for Chikoko Trails (see page 269), which use 2 walking bushcamps, Chikoko & Crocodile, just over the river in a wilderness area of the park, & also

with Mwaleshi Camp's walking safaris in North Luangwa National Park (see page 291).
US$460/660 pp sharing/sgl 15 May–30 Jun & Nov; US$535/735 pp sharing/sgl Jul & Oct; US$650/850 pp sharing/sgl Aug–Sep. ⊕ 15 May–Nov.

🏠 **Tena Tena** (5 tents) Contact via Robin Pope Safaris, page 261. Tena Tena overlooks the Luangwa River at the southern end of the Nsefu Sector of the park, about 20km northeast of the bridge at Mfuwe. Tena Tena is not only a widely recognised name in safari circles, it's also one of the park's best camps. Accommodation is in large canopy-&-thatch structures – each set on a solid base with twin or dbl beds, & an en-suite shower & toilet at the rear. These tents are large, comfortable & insect-proof. They're all spaced well apart & set into quite thick vegetation, allowing one side of the tent to open up almost completely during the day to give a full view of a game-productive waterhole only metres away. There is an unobtrusive sgl strand of electric wire surrounding the camp, to discourage elephants from wandering through.

Tena has a dining area & also a separate, well-stocked bar (with small library) under the shade of a spreading Natal mahogany tree. It's lit by a generator in the evening, which is usually switched off as the last person goes to bed. Tena's been built on a lovely sweeping bend in the river, & there's a comfortable seating area set on the bank so that you can relax & watch the river's wildlife just on the edge of camp.

Tena's activities concentrate on morning & afternoon walks, & game drives (inc night drives). The guiding, like everything else at Tena, is first-class – it ranks with the best in Africa. A stay here is often combined with Nkwali, Nsefu (camp or bush camping), or one of Robin Pope's walking safaris.
US$550/715 Jun & Oct, US$650/900 Jul–Sep, all pp sharing/sgl, inc FB, bar, activities & park fees. Open Jun–Oct.

Zebra Pans Bushcamp Currently closed. Zebra Pans was the location for a small bushcamp, deep in the north of the park. It's 30km from the Luangwa or Mupamadzi rivers, near the '05' track from Mfuwe to the Chifungwe Game Scouts Camp on the edge of the Kabvumbu Pans. It was run by Robin Pope Safaris, but closed in 1998 because of its high density of tsetse flies (which are thankfully not a problem in most areas of the Luangwa Valley) & inaccessibility. The camp was in a landscape of low undulating miombo woodland, one of very few which were not near a river – so it offered a contrast to the flora & fauna more usually associated with the Luangwa. In the area there are good numbers of uncommon species like hartebeest, roan, reedbuck & eland. As the areas around the Luangwa River become more popular, it's likely that more esoteric bushcamps like this will eventually be reopened, so watch this space ...

🏠 **Zungulila Walking Camp** (4 chalets) Contact via the Bushcamp Company, page 260 (⊕ 13°20.114'S; 31°29.547'E). For details, see Gwala Walking Camp, above.

BUDGET AND MID-RANGE CAMPS South Luangwa National Park is not an ideal safari destination for the impecunious backpacker. Hitchhiking into the park from Chipata is difficult (flying is the best way to arrive 'independently'), and there are no touts selling cheap safaris. There are a few budget camps as well as a lot of smaller, more exclusive ones (with all-inclusive rates). The latter don't cater well for unexpected visitors; they're best booked in advance.

If you want to be independent, then really the only way to arrive is in your own fully equipped 4x4 – as then you can see the park for yourself. Note, though, that self-drive vehicles may not be driven in the national park when it's dark; only registered guides can conduct night drives. Make sure that you bring supplies of food (fresh vegetables and limited tinned foods can be bought locally), and the best maps that you can buy in Lusaka.

I've seen the park several ways over the years – I've hitchhiked here and camped, I've driven myself around, and I've flown in with advanced bookings at lodges and small bushcamps. I think that much of the Luangwa's magic is about being guided by some of Africa's best guides – in a vehicle, or especially on foot. These guys know this area, and its flora and fauna, like the back of their hands. So although driving yourself around is fun, it's a pale shadow of the experience that you get at one of the better small lodges.

Most budget travellers who come to the Luangwa arrive in overland trucks. These travel between Malawi and Zimbabwe, stopping here and in Lusaka. They usually stay, together with a few backpackers and independent travellers, at one of Luangwa's less expensive camps:

⌂ **Flatdogs Camp** (8 chalets, 4 safari tents, treehouse, camping) ⏎ 021 6246038; e info@ flatdogscamp.com; www.flatdogscamp.com (⊕ FLATDO 13°6.298'S; 31°46.546'E). 'Flatdog' is a local nickname for the crocodile, so when a campsite was opened at the location of the old crocodile camp near the main Mfuwe Bridge in 1992, the choice of name was no surprise. Gradually the camp grew until Flatdogs had outgrown its original site. In 2000, its maverick owner-manager, Jake da Motta, moved it to about 100ha of land beside the river, just to the left of the main Mfuwe Bridge. It's a lovely spot, with plenty of shade from winterthorn, *Faidherbia albida*, & mahogany, *Trichelia emetica*. A lot of game wanders through the area, inc a good population of giraffe, attracted by the acacia trees. When the camp was sold in 2006, the other directors stayed on & the atmosphere remains unchanged.

Flatdogs today is an extensive & imaginatively designed camp. It includes a 'Dog & Gat' (*sic*) bar; a games room with satellite TV & wireless internet; a swimming pool; a shop for crafts, bush clothes & toiletries; & an à-la-carte restaurant serving meals (inc vegetarian food) throughout the day. This is certainly the social hub of the valley – especially during its entertaining Fri night gatherings. That said, facilities are well spaced out, so you can get as much privacy as you want.

The campsite is split, one section for overland trucks & another for backpackers & those with their own vehicles. Both areas have BBQs & washing-up stands, & an ablution block with 8 hot showers & flush toilets. Water is from boreholes; there are lights & mains electric points; firewood & laundry services are available. Tour leaders get free use of simple thatched cottages or tree platforms when available.

Thatched, 2-storey chalets, built with groups & families in mind, have a communal kitchenette/dining area (self-catering equipment provided) & en-suite bathroom; downstairs is a dbl room with fan & a wraparound veranda, while upstairs is a twin room with a view of the river. In addition, there is a family chalet, with 2 sgl beds on a mezzanine floor with viewing deck, 1 room with 3 sgl beds, & 1 with a dbl & sgl, as well as a separate kitchen with oven, hot plates, kettle & dishes. All beds have mosquito nets. New for 2006 was the Jackalberry treehouse, with 2 en-suite bedrooms & a sitting room on a tree platform overlooking a small dambo, while in 2007 en-suite safari tents were added, permanently pitched on the riverbank.

Activities organised by the camp include day & night drives in the park, walking safaris, & all-day drive/walks. Flatdogs' 4x4 vehicles are often full, & carry more people per vehicle than those of the smaller safari camps. The camp offers a very different experience from that offered by the upmarket camps – & charges different prices too. *Chalets US$40 pp room only, or US$200 pp inc FB & activities. Camping US$7.50 pp. Game drive US$35 per drive. Walking safari US$40 per walk, exc park entry fees.* ⊕ *all year.*

⌂ **Marula Lodge** (13 rooms) Contact Land & Lake Safaris (see page 260), or ⏎ +265 6246034, 6245073. In a classic position just upstream from the main Mfuwe Bridge, Marula is reached by turning right towards the croc farm (and the old Flatdogs site), just before entering the park over the bridge. Despite its beautiful position, this camp is not well known, perhaps because it caters mainly for local visitors from the surrounding Zambian provinces & Malawi.

Marula's chalets are dotted over well-kept lawns & built like conventional rooms. With high ceilings & concrete floors, all are en suite with a ceiling fan, 10 with twin beds, the others with 2 twin-bedded rooms sharing a shower & toilet; mosquito nets are provided. Each room has small, louvred windows that instil a slight feeling of claustrophobia.

The camp's focal point is a large dining/bar area situated under an impressive winterthorn tree. There is a dbl-storey building with 1 twin room & 1 family room downstairs; the upper storey is generally used as a dormitory for large school groups. Mains electricity is backed up by a generator.

Guests at Marula can supply their own food (fridges & freezers are available), which they can cook themselves or with the help of one of the camp's chefs. Alternatively, the camp can provide meals. Game drives & walks are available, & there's a pool near the river. This is a very simple camp, used mostly by local groups & businesspeople, as well as those on budget safaris from Malawi. *US$120/135 pp sharing/sgl, inc FB & 2 game activities/days; US$35/50 pp sharing/sgl self catering. Game drive US$25 pp. Park fees extra.* ⊕ *all year.*

⋏ **Mwanya Bushcamp** (3 chalets) ⏎ 021 1226082; m 095 5958642; www.itswild.org (⊕ MWANYA 12°45.348'S; 32°04.555'E). Mwanya sits on elevated ground about 100km from Mfuwe, surrounded by floodplain & the old channel of the Luangwa River, where a lagoon attracts animals almost into camp. Opposite is the island of Chilufya, within a ½hr walk, characterised by smaller lagoons & open plains, so ideal for game viewing. There is also easy access to the national park, subject to park entry fees. For further details, see *It's Wild!* box, page 290. *US$35 pp self-catering, US$70 pp FB. Camping US$10 pp; with cook & kitchen facilities US$15 pp. Guiding US$5 pp ½ day.* ⊕ *May–Sep.*

🏠 **Thornicroft** (10 rooms) Contact via Land & Lake Safaris, page 260, or m 097 8163603; e thornicroft@landlake.net. Opening in October 2007, this new lodge 1km downstream of the confluence of the Luangwa and the Lupande rivers aims to appeal both to the local market and to international visitors. Chalets built of stone, wood & canvas look over the Luangwa River from their own verandas. Each is en suite, with beds inside a walk-in mosquito net. At the heart of the lodge is the restaurant, bar & lounge area, where tea & coffee is available throughout the day. There's also a swimming pool for cooling off during the hot summer months. Game drives are undertaken in open safari vehicles, & game walks are available in the dry season. *US$145/175 pp sharing/sgl, inc FB & 2 game drives/day & airport transfers. Park fees extra.* ⊕ *all year.*

🏠 **Track & Trail Rivercamp** (4 chalets, 4 tents, camping) ☏ 021 6246020; m 097 7600556; e info@trackandtrailrivercamp.com; www.trackandtrailrivercamp.com (✪ 13°09.979'S; 31°79.261'E). This Dutch-owned camp, opened in 2006, is just 5 mins' drive from the park entrance, overlooking the river. Thatched, en-suite chalets are of a split-level design, with a private veranda, electricity & mosquito nets, & accommodating up to 4 people. At the shady campsite, individual pitches have water, electricity & BBQ facilities, with all sharing a central shelter & separate ablution block. Sharing the ablutions are 4 tents, each sleeping 2 people. BBQ packs are sold, with fresh fruit & vegetables available at the local market, or campers can eat in the main camp. There's an above-ground pool to keep cool, & aromatherapy or hot-stone therapy massages to ensure complete relaxation.

In addition to guided safaris on foot & in an open game vehicle, this is a good place to pick up photography tips from owner-photographer Peter Geraerdts. Village visits are possible, as are trips further afield. *US$85/90/95 pp sharing FB Nov–Apr/May & Jun–Oct; US$210/215/245 inc FB,* activities, park entry fees, airport transfers, laundry; sgl supplement 20%. Camping US$7.50/10 pp Nov–May & Jun–Oct.

🏠 **Wildlife Camp** (9 chalets, 5 safari tents, 4 bushcamp tents, camping) Contact via Lupande Safaris; ☏ 021 6245026, 6246026; e info@wildlifezambia.com; www.wildlifecamp-zambia.com (✪ WILDLI 13°6.320'S; 31°45.133'E). Coming from Mfuwe Airport, turn left just before the main Mfuwe Bridge, following the signs to Kapani, Nkwali, the Wildlife Camp & others. Past the entrance to Kapani, about 4km beyond the main road, the road forks; take a left & drive a further 1km to the camp. Wildlife is a popular, buzzing camp that's large by Luangwa standards. It's owned & run by the helpful Patsy & Herman Miles.

Each of the chalets (with 2–4 beds) & twin-bedded safari tents is en suite; all are clean & pleasant, but not luxurious. If you have your own kit & prefer to camp, there's a campsite set well apart on the river in a large grove of mopane trees, though it's probably not wise to sleep outside without a closed tent. In addition to an ablution block, the campsite has thatched shelters, & its own pool & bar.

Self-catering is an option, & facilities include the use of basic kitchen equipment both for the chalets & at the campsite. Bear in mind, though, that you'll need to bring your own food — there are no corner shops around here! — so this is really for those with their own fully stocked & equipped vehicles, or for very intrepid (& strong) backpackers. Note that there are monkeys in camp, so don't leave food lying around. Those self-catering can arrange for staff to cook for you at US$10 per tent/chalet per day, but this must be booked at least 24hrs in advance.

The camp is run in association with the Wildlife & Environmental Conservation Society of Zambia (WECSZ, see pages 51–2). Sixty per cent of accommodation fees goes straight to the Chipata branch of the WECSZ, to be used for their conservation/development projects. So if you can afford to have a chalet rather than camp, you'll know that much of your extra money is going to a good cause.

The bar/restaurant area (inc a small curio shop) is often busy & always relaxed. It overlooks the main Luangwa River & serves both à-la-carte meals & snacks. The camp runs activities inc exceedingly popular day & night game drives, & walking safaris both on WECSZ land & in the park; the bushcamp makes a great overnight walking safari option. If you have your own vehicle then you can drive

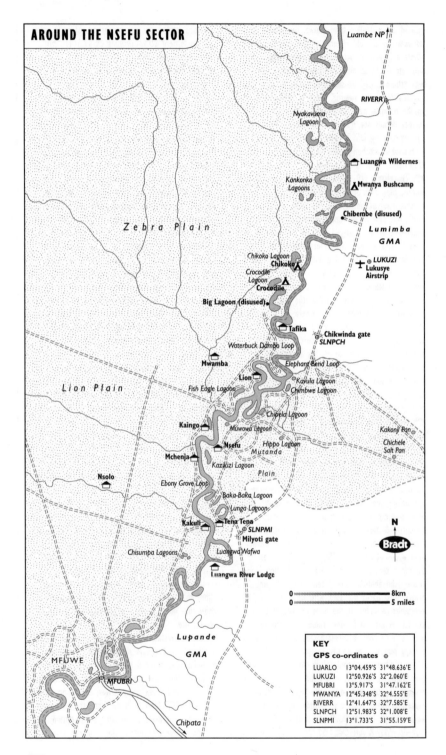

AROUND THE NSEFU SECTOR

Luambe NP

RIVERR

Nyakavuma
Lagoon

Luangwa Wildernes

Mwanya Bushcamp

Chibembe (disused)

Kankonko
Lagoons

Lumimba
GMA

Zebra Plain

LUKUZI
Lukusye
Airstrip

Chikoko Lagoon
Chikoko
Crocodile
Lagoon
Crocodile

Big Lagoon (disused)

Tafika

Chikwinda gate
SLNPCH

Waterbuck Dambo Loop

Mwamba

Elephant Bend Loop

Lion Plain

Lion

Kavula Lagoon
Chimbwe Lagoon

Fish Eagle Lagoon

Chipela Lagoon

Kaingo

Muwowo Lagoon

Kakonji Pan

Nsefu

Hippo Lagoon
Mutanda

Chichele
Salt Pan

Mchenja

Kazikizi Lagoon

Plain

Nsolo

Ebony Grove Loop

Baka-Baka Lagoon

Lunga Lagoon

N

Kakuli

Tena Tena
SLNPMI
Milyoti gate

Chisumpa Lagoons

Luangwa Wafwa

Luangwa River Lodge

0 ————————— 8km
0 ————————— 5 miles

Lupande
GMA

MFUWE

KEY
GPS co-ordinates ⊕

LUARLO	13°04.459'S	31°48.636'E
LUKUZI	12°50.926'S	32°2.060'E
MFUBRI	13°5.917'S	31°47.162'E
MWANYA	12°45.348'S	32°4.555'E
RIVERR	12°41.647'S	32°7.585'E
SLNPCH	12°51.983'S	32°1.008'E
SLNPMI	13°1.733'S	31°55.159'E

MFUBRI

Chipata

yourself into the park during the day, though only licensed guides are allowed to conduct night drives.

The camp makes a good base if you have your own vehicle, & visitors can arrange to be collected from Mfuwe Airport. *Chalet US$50/70 Jul–Oct, US$40/50 Nov–Jun, pp sharing/sgl room only; US$180/230 Jul–Oct, US$150/180 Nov–Jun, pp sharing/sgl inc FB, activities, airport transfers, exc*

drinks, park fees. Overnight walking safari & bushcamp US$180pp all inc. Safari tent US$35/45 Jul–Oct, US$25/30 Nov–Jun. Camping pp US$10 Jul–Oct, US$7.50 Nov–Jun. Airport transfer US$20 pp (min 2). Game drive US$40 pp (min 3); walk (Jun–Nov only) US$40–50 pp (min 3); village tour US$20–25 pp. Park fees extra. Discount for WECSZ members. ⊕ all year.

OTHER TYPES OF TRIPS/ACCOMMODATION

Mobile safaris There's a lot of hype about mobile walking safaris. Perhaps images of Livingstone or Stanley striding through deepest Africa with an entourage of trusty porters and guides are to blame. I don't know. But these days, let's be honest, it is somewhat different. The term 'mobile safari' is overused.

It used to mean that you set off with all your kit on the backs of porters and camped where you stopped. Think, for a moment, of the consequences of this. You'll realise that it resulted in either very basic camping stops with few facilities, or more comfortable camps requiring a safari of enormous cost. It also required total freedom to camp where you liked, which is now limited and controlled by the National Parks Board for very good reasons.

Although the term 'mobile safari' is often abused, there is one operation in the Luangwa that comes close to running a proper mobile operation:

Robin Pope's Mobile Safaris Contact Robin Pope Safaris, page 261. Between late June & late Sep, RPS organises 12 mobile walking safaris along the Mupamadzi River, in the far north of the park. The trip itself lasts 6 days & 5 nights; participants also spend at least 2 nights prior to the trip at Nkwali, & 3 at the end at either Tena Tena or Nsefu – though a few more days either side would be ideal.

The walks are about 10km per day & a truly mobile camp is used, moved by the back-up vehicle to meet you. The camp has comfortable walk-in tents (each with twin beds), shared hot & cold showers, shared long-drop toilets, & a staff of 8 or 9. Typically they'll use 3 different sites for the 5 nights, & the choice depends on the game & the walkers' interests.

These trips are organised on fixed dates each year, & take a max of 6 people. They are always oversubscribed, & sometimes booked up a year or two in advance. There's usually a premium charged for walks that Robin leads himself.

The real attraction of these trips is, firstly, that they are just walking in a wilderness area. There's no driving, & you are away from everything but the bush. Secondly, you're in a small group that stays together with just one guide. You get to know each other & have a lot of time with one of the valley's best guides. They're very relaxing. (As there is no sgl supplement whilst walking, these trips are popular amongst sgl people.) *US$680 pp per night (sharing or sgl) whilst at the walking camps (US$800 if the walk is led by Robin Pope himself), plus costs at Nkwali & Tena Tena.*

Fly-camping In Africa, the term 'fly-camp' usually means a simple campsite with a campfire and a small, very simple tent. This is obviously a far cry from the luxurious en-suite tents of most modern safari camps – but camping like this out in the bush, with nothing around you apart from the darkness, does have a real appeal for many cosseted travellers. They're ideal for the thrill of no-frills camping in the bush; there's certainly no better way to get close to the wildlife at night.

Lodges have operated fly-camps in some areas of Africa for years – most notably the Selous Game Reserve in southern Tanzania – but they're still new to the Luangwa. The main company offering them is Robin Pope Safaris, which terms them 'bushcamps', and offers them either individually, or as part of a set departure that combines Nkwali, Palmgrove and Luangwa Bushcamping, and Nsefu, each for two nights.

🏠 **Luangwa Bushcamping** Contact Robin Pope Safaris, page 261. If you're staying at Tena Tena and/or Nsefu camps, then it's possible to have 2 nights bush camping within your itinerary. The bushcamps consist of small, 'walk-in' tents; there's a bucket shower under a tree, & a long-drop toilet. These are walking trips which average around 8–10km per day. You'll walk with your guide, & an armed scout, & when you arrive at the camp in a remote corner of the bush, there will also be a cook & camp assistant there. US$550 Jun & Oct; US$650 Jul–Sep, all pp sharing per night (no sgl supplement); min 2 people, max 4 (unless booked by a group, when max 6). Available Jun–Oct.

🏠 **Palmgrove Bushcamping** Contact Robin Pope Safaris, page 261. This area is up the Mushilashi River, one of the seasonal tributaries of the Luangwa, where there is a huge palmgrove, the nesting site of the white-back vultures. The bushcamp is set up on demand for a couple of nights on an island in the middle of the dry river bed. Walking is along ridges overlooking the valley & valleys of the sand river; there's not much game, but it doesn't get wilder than this. US$550 Jun & Oct, US$650 Jul–Sep, all pp sharing (no sgl supplement); min 2 people, max 4 (unless booked by a group, when max 6). Available Jun–Oct.

River safaris River safaris are only possible around February to April, depending on the water level in the Luangwa River; then this is the only way to get around most of the park. See *When to go*, in *Chapter 4*, page 42, for more comment on the wet season – but from that you'll realise that the rain is usually in short, sharp, late afternoon bursts. The rest of the day is often sunny – for photographers the clarity and quality of the light is extraordinary. So if you've been on safari quite a bit, but only seen the Luangwa (or southern Africa) in the dry season, you should aim to make a trip during the rains. The place comes alive with animals and plants you just don't see in the dry season, and the birdlife is phenomenal. You won't see the density of animals that you'll find in October, but you will have some amazing sights – like the Nsefu stork colony in full flow.

Only one operation, Norman Carr Safaris (see page 260), currently runs river trips during the rainy season, although Robin Pope Safaris also do boat trips. Norman Carr Safaris' package, their Rivers and Rainbows Safari, starts with four nights at either Kapani or Nkwali, followed by a transfer to Mchenja Camp for a further three nights (*US$2,700 pp sharing, inc FB, bar, laundry, activities, local transfers & park fees*).

For ten months of the year most of the river's tributaries are sand rivers, but for just a few months they fill with water. Often they are lined by tall old hardwood trees. In a few areas the trees open out onto wide, shallow floodplains, usually dotted with egrets, waders or geese, while in the middle are several nesting colonies for storks and herons, of which the most well known are those in the Nsefu Sector of the park. These rely on a high water level, and the birds won't nest unless the area is flooded. (This is probably a protection mechanism against nest raiders who would be deterred by the water at the foot of the trees.) The main one of these is a huge colony for yellow-billed storks. These take on a beautiful, delicate pink hue when breeding and collectively make for an amazing sight.

Cultural tourism Though wildlife is often the main draw of the Luangwa Valley, increasing numbers of visitors are enjoying meeting the local people and learning more of their traditional lifestyles. Cultural tourism is gradually taking off. Currently this has two main points of focus:

🏠 **Kawaza Village** (9 huts) Contact via Robin Pope Safaris, page 261. Born of an initiative suggested to local villagers by Robin Pope Safaris, this venture was jointly developed between the company & the village. Now Kawaza is an efficient & viable small business for the village which involves visitors staying either for an afternoon, or (much better) overnight in the village. Here they can spend time with people from this Kunda community & learn more of their daily ways of living, traditions & culture.

It started as an effort to end the villagers' feeling of exclusion. Some of the communities around

Mfuwe felt that a lot of overseas visitors arrive & leave, but without ever having any meaningful form of social contact with them. They also wished to get involved in tourism, to raise funds for the local school & to support vulnerable members of their community (orphans & the elderly). Kawaza is a real village & visitors are encouraged to participate in its normal everyday life – to help the women cook *nshima* & relish, to visit the local traditional healer, to tend the crops, or visit the local school, church or clinic. Villagers will tailor-make an agenda to suit your interests & time.

Eventually, after many discussions, the villagers built a handful of rondavels just for visitors. These are small, clean huts of traditional design with thatched roofs. Then, with help from Jo Pope, a Danish aid fund & others, the village bought a few utensils for visitors. Advance payment for a booking by a group of Scandinavian visitors helped them to buy items like mattresses & mosquito nets.

Now there are 9 huts for visitors, some with beds raised off the ground & mattresses, others without. All have spotlessly clean sheets & mosquito nets. There are several separate long-drop toilets & rondavels for bathing (using a large tin bath & a scoop for the water). The food is grown locally & prepared in the village – including tasty cassava eaten for breakfast, with coffee, tea & milk.

A committee of villagers runs the scheme & David Mwewa, the headmaster of the adjacent school, is secretary of the project. He explained to me that the village's objectives are 'to provide an authentic Zambian experience and raise money for the community'. For the visitor, this means that the village's earnings from their stay help the village, while Kawaza offers a fascinating & genuinely moving insight into another culture.

Activities are really just taking part in whatever is going on when you are there, & whatever you are interested in. That might mean going into the bush to the village's plots of arable land, collecting local plants & herbs, preparing the food, or even going to help teach a class at the school. Depending on the time of year, you will even be allowed to see some (though not all) of the initiation ceremonies for the young people. Men attend only the men's ceremonies & women only the women's, as you'd expect.

Of special interest, usually arranged on request, would be a visit to a traditional healer, or a local clinic, or a meeting with the area's senior chief Nsefu – the paramount chief of the 6 local chiefs. In the evening, the community's elders tell traditional stories or sing songs around the campfire.

The effects of this on the community are gradually showing. Some of the villagers are learning more English in order to communicate better with visitors. David commented, 'When the visitors first came the villagers could not imagine dancing together with a white person or eating together. But when guests come to the village they are instructed to join in all the activities ... when they see the villagers putting up a roof they join them ... it's fantastic. The visitors like it that way.'

Further, the school is benefiting very directly, as a proportion of the money paid automatically goes straight into school funds. The school's 5-year plan now includes building more staff housing & making sports facilities for the children, as well as getting solar lighting units & buying a few radio-cassette machines.

If you've never really tried to put yourself in a totally different culture, then you must spend a night here. It'll make you think about your own culture as much as Kawaza's, & you'll remember it long after you've forgotten the animals. *Guests staying at most camps in the Luangwa can add a night at Kawaza to their itinerary (min US$40 per night). Robin Pope Safaris charge US$130 pp per night, of which US$80 is paid directly into Kawaza's school fund, & the rest goes to the village. Backpackers & other independent travellers can either book by advising RPS, who will pass the message to the village, or simply arrive at Kawaza – although it's always best to give a few days' notice if possible. Day visits US$15 pp, & you can arrive without notice.*

Nsendamila Cultural Village Very close to the hub of the Mfuwe area, Nsendamila village has been closed for several years, but reports suggest that there are moves in hand to put the project back on track. Should that happen, it is easily found by turning left towards Kapani & Nkwali just before the Mfuwe Bridge. Then it is off the road, shortly on the left. The village was originally built by the local communities, with the backing of various charities & NGOs, its traditional rondavels laid out to demonstrate a local village's way of life. There are plans to build a new cultural & heritage centre, where a local drama group will perform for visitors. The centre will also house prehistoric artefacts from the Luangwa Valley, many of them unearthed during a series of archaeological digs conducted by students from Liverpool University. The village is also the site of Uyoba Community School, built and sponsored by the SLCS, at which visitors are welcome.

NORTH LUANGWA NATIONAL PARK

(Park fees US$20 pp, plus US$15 per vehicle per day, plus bed levy US$10 pp per night)
North Luangwa National Park (known usually as 'the North Park') covers about
4,636km² of the Luangwa Valley; it's half the size of the South Luangwa National
Park (aka the 'South Park'). It shares the same origin as the South Park, being part
of the same rift valley, and its eastern boundary is also the Luangwa River. It has
the same geology, soil types and vegetation as South Luangwa, and so its landscapes
are very similar.

However, unlike the South Park, which is basically bounded by the steep
Muchinga Escarpment to the west, the North Park takes in a lot of this within its
protection. About 24% of North Luangwa lies within the escarpment, compared
with about 5% of South Luangwa. This means that North Luangwa has a more
diverse range of habitats, which is especially interesting for birdwatchers, although
there are also mammals found on the hill which aren't normally seen on the valley
floor.

From a conservation point of view, it also means that much of the catchment
area of North Luangwa's main rivers falls within the boundaries of the park –
giving the park authorities more control of its rivers and habitats.

For visitors to the wilderness camps, perhaps the park's most important natural
feature is the Mwaleshi River – which is unlike the Luangwa or any of its
tributaries in the South Park (except, possibly, stretches of the Mupamadzi). It's a
permanent river that flows even in the heat of the dry season, when it's generally
very clear and shallow.

THE PARK'S ZONES For the visitor, it's important to understand that North
Luangwa is now 'zoned'. Most of the southern side of the park is strictly reserved
as a wilderness area. It has very few roads and is currently used only by three small
camps, which concentrate on walking safaris. The only way to visit this is to
arrange your trip with one of these operators, and stay in one of these tiny camps.
If you're not staying at a camp, then you cannot even pass through this area; you'll
find clear signs and even booms across the tracks.

However, north of this is a 'zone' was opened to wider access in 2002. Now
it's possible for experienced travellers to bring fully equipped vehicles into the
park, and drive through from east to west, or vice versa. These are strictly
restricted to the more northerly zone of the park, which has one main track
across it and several side-tracks. This is a new way to see parts of this remote
park, whilst getting between Luambe National Park and the Great North Road. It
also opens up the possibility of an interesting (if challenging) circular drive
around eastern Zambia.

HISTORY

Before the mid-1980s Without the conservation efforts and funds that were
devoted to South Luangwa, the country's premier game park, the North Luangwa
National Park has until recently been a 'poor relation'. Poachers hunting rhino and
elephant met less resistance there, and local people crossed its boundaries freely in
search of food. The impact on the game was inevitable.

North Luangwa remained a wilderness area for many years, officially accessible
only to the Game Department, until 1984 when Major John Harvey and his wife
Lorna (daughter of Sir Stewart Gore-Browne, of Shiwa Ng'andu) started to run
walking safaris here. They were the first safari operators here and their son, Mark
Harvey, runs one of the three camps currently in the North Park (*Buffalo Camp*,
pages 289–90).

The Owens's ideal In 1986 a couple of American zoologists – Mark and Delia Owens – visited the park in search of an African wilderness in which to base their animal research, and returned in October '87 to base themselves here. They came from a project in Botswana's Central Kalahari Game Reserve, with an uncompromising reputation for defending the wildlife against powerful vested interests. They also had behind them an international best-selling book about their experiences – *The Cry of the Kalahari*. This had brought conservation issues in Botswana to a popular audience, which earned them considerable financial backing for high-profile conservation efforts, including the vital support of the Frankfurt Zoological Society.

Their presence here was to have a profound impact upon the park. In the early 1980s, elephant poaching was estimated at about 1,000 animals per year. Their second best-seller, the highly readable *Survivor's Song* (called *The Eye of the Elephant* in the US; see *Appendix 3*, page 511), relates their struggles to protect this park from the poachers, and their efforts to find alternatives for the local people so that they would support the anti-poaching work.

Read it before you arrive, but don't be alarmed: the place is much safer now. Also be aware that their book has been written to sell. It's an exciting yarn, but does describe events as if they were a personal campaign. It doesn't mention any real contribution to education, development or anti-poaching from anyone apart from Mark and Delia. Others involved with the park have long maintained that this was not a true picture, and that the Owens's book simply ignored the 'bigger picture' of all the efforts which were going on at the time. Whatever the truth, it's worth reading.

With the dedication of the Owens, and the vital financial assistance that they could attract, poaching has been virtually eliminated. The park's game scouts were paid well and properly housed, and became the most zealous and effective in the country. Local education and development programmes were initiated in villages around the park, aiming to raise awareness of conservation and to provide alternatives for people who relied upon poaching for food.

However, Mark and Delia left Zambia in a hurry in 1996. This followed an alleged incident in which forceful anti-poaching actions went too far. It was precipitated by a documentary screened in the US by the ABC television network, *Deadly Game: The Mark and Delia Owens Story*, in which an alleged poacher appeared to be executed. Mark and Delia have never returned to Zambia.

PRESENT SITUATION Perhaps the real, lasting legacy of Mark and Delia is that they introduced the Frankfurt Zoological Society to North Luangwa. The FZS's constant financial support over more than 20 years has done an amazing amount to safeguard this terrific park. Thanks to them, and other important donors, the privately financed North Luangwa Conservation Project continues to support the park and its authorities.

The NLCP's input has concentrated on support for the law enforcement effort, through training and the supply of essential field equipment, rations, vehicles and the building of houses for the field staff. Thus the park's scouts continue to be keen, well trained and well motivated. They also help to conduct regular aerial surveys of large mammals, records of which stretch all the way back to the late 1980s, and to maintain and gradually expand the road network – as well as other aspects of the park's management and conservation.

Various programmes continue to support the communities around the park. These vary from a conservation education programme, with material that is specific to this area, to work on land-use plans – to get the nearby communities to think critically about their future and how they can generate income, whilst safeguarding some of their natural resources for the future.

The rhino Meanwhile, the game goes from strength to strength. In 2003 five black rhino were introduced into a large fenced-off intensive protection zone, at the heart of the park, with a further ten added in 2006 and more to be added in 2008. Despite the death of two of the animals, two baby rhinos were born in the sanctuary, a measure of the project's success, and a big step towards the aim to establish 20 animals within the now extended sanctuary area.

These are now probably the only black rhino in the country; their presence is a strong sign of how secure the North Luangwa is, and that the park expects to enjoy the long-term support of the FZS. It's worth noting that while there are 4x4 tracks through the protection zone, no-one is allowed to stop within the fenced area. Other animals, however, can get under or over the fencing; it is only the rhino that are kept within the zone.

The future for North Luangwa seems bright – and perhaps Zambia's positive experience of having a national park run with the strong support of a donor-funded private organisation has helped it to look to the future in places like Liuwa Plain, where an analogous project is just in its infancy.

FLORA AND FAUNA In general, the flora and fauna of the North Park are the same as those found in South Luangwa (see pages 255–8). However, the inclusion of the escarpment in the park certainly brings a new dimension to the flora here. An excellent example is the road from Mano down from the escarpment, which is about 12km long. This brings you from the two-storey woodlands of the upper and plateau escarpment, with a lightly closed canopy of semi-evergreen trees 15–20m high, and down through the miombo woodlands on the hills to vegetation more typical of the valley as most people know it.

Often there are bird species here that aren't usually found on the valley floor, and sometimes sable antelope, bushpig or blue monkeys. In the dry season, look also for signs of elephant, which often move into the mountains.

On the valley floor, the ecosystems of the two parks, and the native game species found therein, often seem virtually identical. The North Park has some east African bird species that don't occur further south – like the chestnut-mantled sparrow weaver, the white-winged starling and especially the yellow-throated longclaw – but the differences in species are minor.

However, several differences are apparent. You're more likely to see Cookson's wildebeest, *Connochaetes taurinus cooksoni*, one of the valley's endemic subspecies. The population seems much larger in the north of the valley than in the south. However, you won't find any giraffes here, as they don't seem to occur much north of the Mupamadzi River. (Phil Berry has reliable records of a few sightings here until about the mid-'80s. John Coppinger comments that in his years operating to the North Park since 1990, he's only ever received a report of one giraffe … and that was probably lost!)

Eland, the largest of the antelope, are more common here, and hartebeest are also seen more often than in the South Park. Given their long lifespan, and slow regeneration after poaching, elephant are scarce and skittish in the North Park. This is changing, and the population is growing, but it'll take a long time before they are as numerous, or as relaxed, as they are around Mfuwe.

Lion and buffalo seem to be numerous in the north, with buffalo herds even larger than those in the South Park, and some very strong prides of lion. Hyena are also common, and those in the North Park seem to hunt more than those in the South, and have developed a tactic of chasing puku into the Mwaleshi River in order to catch them. Those in the South Park tend perhaps to do a little more scavenging, and less hunting. Then, of course, there are the reintroduced black rhino – see above.

GETTING THERE Prior to 2002, the only way for visitors to see North Luangwa was to come to one of the few camps for walking safaris within the park. That's still the way that most people visit, and certainly the way to get the most out of the park. Typically a three- to five-night stay at one of the walking camps is perfect. Most visitors (and there are only a total of a few hundred in the average year) combine a walking trip here with some time in the South Park, and fly between the two. For the cognoscenti, it's one of Africa's top safari destinations

By air Transfers to and from North Luangwa are normally organised as part of your safari package, on small four- to six-seater light aircraft. A short hop here by light aircraft from Lukuzi or Mfuwe (both in South Luangwa) takes about 10–20 minutes and costs in the region of US$150–170 per person (for a minimum of two people).

Driving The very adventurous and experienced may now plan to drive themselves through the newly opened north side of the park. Although the road is currently being upgraded, and should be finished in 2008, it's a very remote and wild area, so you'll need two fully equipped 4x4 vehicles, the expertise to use them, and a high degree of self-sufficiency. Read *Lessons in bush travel* box, on pages 262–3, before you even consider this! Then directions are as follows:

From Mpika via Mano gate The turning to North Luangwa from the Great North Road (✪ TUNLNP 11°26.378'S; 31°44.307'E) is well signposted just over 60km northeast of Mpika, and 28km south of the turning to Shiwa Ng'andu. There are a few buildings at the junction, a place called Luanya, and the altitude here is 1,556m. This isn't a difficult track, and there is talk of grading it during 2008, further improving access; follow it for about 32km until another sign points left (✪ TUNLN2 11°35.698'S; 31°55.229'E). It's then a further 11km to the Mano gate, by which time you've descended about 390m from the Great North Road. Although Mano is outside of the park, it acts as entrance gate to the park (✪ NLNPMA 11°36.509'S; 32°0.766'E), where you sign in, pay your park fees and find out about the latest park news.

Here there are maps available from the scout post to chart the route that you are allowed to take across the park. They can also tell you where you're allowed to camp. The obvious first stop, not more than 1km further down the road, is the Natangwe Community Campsite (see page 288).

From Luambe National Park Approaching North Luangwa from Luambe, you'll be travelling on the east side of the Luangwa River – very much a continuation of the road from South Luangwa to Luambe. (See pages 291–2 for directions.)

Starting at Chipuka Scout Camp (✪ CHIPUK 12°26.923'S; 32°12.516'E), which marks the northern edge of Luambe National Park, you'll be driving north through some very rural country with a scattering of remote villages. About 9km after the scout camp you need to take a very sharp left turn (✪ TULUA1 12°25.313'S; 32°16.547'E).

Some 17km or so after that turn, you'll reach the very basic Zokwe Scout Camp (✪ ZOKWE 12°17.965'S; 32°19.782'E), which is followed by a lovely stretch of fairly undisturbed cathedral mopane woodland. Around 30km after Zokwe, there's a junction in the track (✪ TULUAM 12°7.664'S; 32°29.487'E) at Chiweza village school. Turn left here, and continue for another 2.9km until there's a right turn onto another track at ✪ 12°07.778'S; 32°27.922'E.

Straight on would lead you into the South gate of the North Luangwa, ultimately to a crossing of the Luangwa near the Kanunshya scout post

(✤ KANUNS 12°4.797'S; 32°21.612'E). This entry to the park is only for the wilderness zone, and for use by the operators that work there.

Hence take a right turn at ✤ CHAD-T and continue north and slightly east for about 31.2km until you reach the chief's palace at ✤ CHIEFP 11°52.585'S; 32°34.358'E. There you ignore the road which carries on straight towards Chama, and instead take a sharp left turn, almost doubling back, to head slightly south of west. After about 4.5km you pass a place called Old Luelo Camp (✤ OLDLUO 11°52.308'S; 32°32.026'E), and then about 12km later, as you're approaching the Luangwa River, take a right turn (✤ TUPONT 11°53.566'S; 32°26.223'E) along the track that shadows the river. After almost 8km you'll reach the pontoon across the Luangwa (✤ LUPONT 11°51.227'S; 32°26.238'E) into the North Park. Note that the pontoon is normally operated from 1 June until the end of October, but it's always wise to check in advance.

This is usually monitored by the park's very sharp scouts. In case of vehicle problems they can arrange for help, but a substantial vehicle recovery fee will be payable.

WHERE TO STAY
Northern zone
Outside the park If you're self-sufficient and driving yourself through the northern zone of the park, there are two simple community camps here, one to the west, by the Mano gate, the second close to the Luangwa pontoon in the east of the park. Alternatively, you can camp at the community campsite in the GMA to the north of the park, or at Luangwa Wilderness Lodge (see page 293) in Luambe National Park.

Ⓐ **Natangwe Community Campsite** e moses@fzs.org; natwangw@yahoo.com. Opened in 2002 with the help of the North Luangwa Conservation Project, Natangwe is run by the local Mukungule community, & all the proceeds are put into a fund that will, eventually, benefit that community. The campsite is set in beautiful thick mushitu forest, just 1km or so inside the Mano gate (✤ NLNPMA 11°36.509'S; 32°0.766'E) on the banks of the Mwaleshi River. Its private camping pitches were being upgraded in 2007, with flush toilets & hot-water showers. There are fireplaces for BBQs, & a central shelter, but you need to have all your own supplies; nothing is available apart from water & firewood.

If you stay for a while you can walk along the river from here, arrange a visit to one of the local villages, & perhaps do a little birding or fishing. Look out for Ross's turaco & the uncommon green twinspot. Natangwe is the best place to camp on the western boundary of the park for those who plan to drive east the following morning. US$10 pp. Guided birdwatching US$5 pp/2hrs. ⊕ all year.

Ⓐ **Chifunda Community Bushcamp** (3 chalets) ☏ 021 1226082; m 095 5958642; www.itswild.org. The middle of 3 community bushcamps set up in the area, Chifunda is near the Luangwa pontoon on the eastern side of the park, overlooking the river & the national park. The camp is surrounded by tall, shady trees, & offers a diversity of habitats within easy walking distance. For further details, see *It's Wild!* box, page 290. US$35 pp self-catering; US$70 pp FB. Camping US$10 pp; with cook & kitchen facilities US$15 pp. Guiding US$5 pp ¹/₂ day. ⊕ May–Sep.

Ⓐ **Chikwa Bushcamp** (3 chalets, camping) ☏ 021 1226082; m 095 5958642; www.itswild.org. Chikwa lies 200km from Mfuwe, in a GMA to the north of North Luangwa park. Chalets are tucked beneath spreading tree canopies overlooking the Luangwa River. Surrounded by old-growth forests, the camp is at a point in the river where it is possible to walk across & explore the lagoons on the opposite side. For further details, see *It's Wild!* box, page 290. US$35 pp self-catering; US$70 pp FB. Camping US$10 pp; with cook & kitchen facilities US$15 pp. Guiding US$5 pp ¹/₂ day. ⊕ May–Sep.

Southern wilderness area Being very remote, and only accessible for part of the year, the park's southern zone – the walking wilderness area – is a difficult place for a safari company to operate. Hence for many years there have been only two or

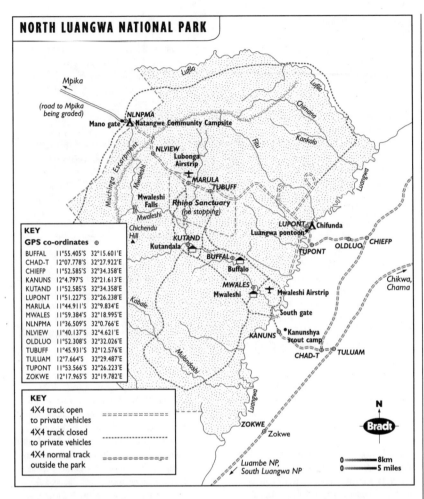

KEY

GPS co-ordinates ⊕

BUFFAL	11°55.405'S	32°15.601'E
CHAD-T	12°07.778'S	32°27.922'E
CHIEFP	11°52.585'S	32°34.358'E
KANUNS	12°4.797'S	32°21.613'E
KUTAND	11°52.585'S	32°34.358'E
LUPONT	11°51.227'S	32°26.238'E
MARULA	11°44.911'S	32°9.834'E
MWALES	11°59.384'S	32°18.995'E
NLNPMA	11°36.509'S	32°0.766'E
NLVIEW	11°40.137'S	32°4.621'E
OLDLUO	11°52.308'S	32°32.026'E
TUBUFF	11°45.931'S	32°12.576'E
TULUAM	12°7.664'S	32°29.487'E
TUPONT	11°53.566'S	32°26.223'E
ZOKWE	12°17.965'S	32°19.782'E

KEY

4X4 track open to private vehicles	===========
4X4 track closed to private vehicles	-----------
4X4 normal track outside the park	===========

N

Bradt

| 0 | 8km |
| 0 | 5 miles |

three camps here, all of which concentrate on walking rather than driving. North Luangwa offers an experience that is even more remote and isolated than the rest of the valley, and you can guarantee that you won't be disturbed by anyone else whilst walking here.

All three of the park's bushcamps stand on the banks of the Mwaleshi, and it's one of the few sources of water for the game, which consequently gravitates to it. It is shallow enough to be easily crossed on foot, allowing you to follow game back and forth across the river. This isn't usually an option beside the main Luangwa, but is easy here. Certainly in the heat of October I relished the cool of paddling across it and even the chance to just sit down in the middle with a drink at sundown. Having such a convenient, cool stream next to camp does make a big difference to both your comfort in the heat and your game viewing.

🏠 **Buffalo Camp** (6 chalets) m 097 7749002;
e (no attachments): gameman@zamnet.zm; in case
of problems, contact via Shiwa Ng'andu,
e kapishya@shiwasafaris.com; www.shiwasafaris.com

(⊕ BUFFAL 11°55.405'S; 32°15.601'E). Situated at a
bend in the Mwaleshi River, surrounded by plains
areas, this small camp is set under some welcome
shade. All the chalets have been recently rebuilt, with

289

A collaborative effort between the Wildlife Conservation Society of Zambia and the local community has resulted in three bushcamps along a 250km stretch of the Luangwa River: Chifunda (page 288), Chikwa (page 288) and Mwanya (page 278). Marketed with the help of Community Markets for Conservation (COMACO; ☏ 021 1226082; www.itswild.org), this is truly a local initiative, employing local people – some of them ex-poachers – and with profits shared between individual villages in the area.

Each bushcamp is located in a game management area outside the national park, and has a qualified manager with trained staff, and a 24-hour security guard on the surrounding fence. Accommodation is in simple reed-&-thatch chalets, each with twin (or double) beds, open-air toilet and shower, and solar lighting. Guests can cater for themselves, or opt for meals to be provided; each bushcamp has a fully equipped and staffed kitchen.

Activities concentrate on guided walks, led by local guides with an armed escort. While game densities cannot compare to those inside the park, most of the species of the Luangwa Valley are to be seen in the vicinity of each bushcamp. Visitors can also visit a traditional Zambian village to find out more about local traditions.

Under another COMACO initiative, the tangle of snare wire that has been handed in by poachers in exchange for training in organic farming methods is finally being put to good use – as jewellery. Designer Misozi Kadewele has come up with a series of designs for necklaces, bracelets and earrings based on strands of wire combined with colourful natural beads. Catchily labelled 'Snarewear', the results are on sale at the It's Wild! shop at Mfuwe Airport.

en-suite flush toilets & hot showers. They're traditional in style: square, thatched buildings built of mud bricks, & all fronting the river. Hammocks are available for relaxing during the heat of the day.

Buffalo is good value & more offbeat than the other 2 camps in the park; having a laid-back attitude to your time here is a prerequisite to enjoying it! Predominantly a walking camp, it's owned & managed by Mark Harvey, brother of Charlie Harvey at Shiwa Ng'andu; he's a very experienced, knowledgeable & entertaining guide who was born & brought up at Shiwa & speaks a number of the local languages fluently – though note that he isn't always in camp as he also runs Kapishya Hot Springs at Shiwa.

If you're driving yourself through the park, & want to stop for a night or two, cooking for yourself, it's worth checking if that's an option: Mark will accept self-catering guests at US$100 (exc park fees/bed levy & activities) if no others are booked in. US$300 pp, FB, exc drinks & park fees/bed levy (US$25 pp per day). ⊕ mid-Jun–31 Oct.

⌂ **Kutandala Camp** (4 chalets) e rod@ kutandala.com; www.kutandala.com (✪ KUTAND 11°53.325'E, 32°110.237'S). Kutandala Camp was

started in Jun 2001 on the south bank of the Mwaleshi River by Rod Tether & his (now) wife, Guz. Rod knows the park exceptionally well, having first guided in the Luangwa Valley in 1989; for several years he ran mobile trips to the North Park, & after that guided from Tafika & Mwaleshi. Guz's speciality is conjuring faultless cuisine from minute grass huts with open fires – remarkable stuff! The food & hospitality are excellent, with b/fast & dinner stylishly served under the sky.

Together Rod & Guz spend about 5 months of every year here, in one of the valley's smallest bushcamps. Each of the simple chalets is built of grass & poles, with an en-suite flush toilet & a hot shower under the stars. Each also has a wide veranda overlooking the Mwaleshi River. The camp has a small library of books near the bar.

But the main point of Kutandala is to explore the park with Rod on foot. It's strictly a walking camp & most visitors stay here for 4–5 nights. The camp takes 6 people max at any one time – a good number for a walk!

Note that Kutandala is often included on trips marketed by Robin Pope Safaris. The only easy way to get here is with a flight transfer; Kutandala is about 50 mins' drive from Mwaleshi Airstrip.

US$485/585 pp sharing/sgl, inc FB, drinks, laundry, all activities & park fees. ⊕ 7 Jun–7 Nov.

🏠 **Mwaleshi Camp** (4 chalets) Contact via Remote Africa Safaris, page 260 (⊕ MWALES 11°59.384'S; 32°18.995'E). John Coppinger originally set up Mwaleshi Camp for Wilderness Trails in 1989, then retained control of it when he set up his own operation, Remote Africa Safaris. Most people fly between North & South Luangwa national parks; & it's a very short hop from the Lukuzi Airstrip, near Tafika. However you arrive, a min stay of about 4 nights is sensible.

Mwaleshi is a delightfully simple bushcamp consisting of just 4 chalets made out of reeds & grasses, set on the southern bank of a scenic stretch of the Mwaleshi River. Each chalet has a bathroom en suite, under the stars, with a flush toilet & simple hot shower. There's a small, thatched dining & bar area, also overlooking the river. There's a permanent manager/guide on site, one of the experienced team from Remote Africa Safaris – so it's a top-class operation & one of my favourite bushcamps in Africa. Walking really is the activity here (very convenient, given the amount you'll be tempted to eat of their excellent food), & the first time you get on a vehicle from camp may well be when you're leaving. US$450 pp, inc FB, bar, activities & park fees. ⊕ mid-Jun–31 Oct.

LUAMBE NATIONAL PARK

(*Entrance US$5 pp, plus US$15 per vehicle per day*)
This small park, just 330km², is situated between North and South Luangwa national parks and can be reached only between about May and October. The first serious rains turn the area's powdery black-cotton soil into an impassable quagmire – impossible even for the best 4x4. Even in the dry season the roads are bad, albeit passable, as the black-cotton soil then seems to set into bumps.

GETTING THERE Although there is an airstrip (Waka Waka) nearby, many of the park's visitors are adventurous 4x4ers passing through, heading to or from the North Park.

By air If you are not driving, then you'll probably need to charter a six-seater plane (pilot plus five passengers) from Mfuwe, which would cost around US$260 for the one-way trip. Transfers are regularly done by Luangwa Wilderness Lodge as well as by other lodges in Mfuwe for around US$200 per vehicle.

Driving Do read *Lessons in bush travel*, pages 262–3, before you attempt to get to this remote corner by yourself! When you've taken heed of this, the directions are as follows.

From South Luangwa Approaching Luambe or North Luangwa from the South Park, you'll be travelling on the east side of the river. From Mfuwe, head north through the Nsefu Sector, and finally exit the park from Chikwinda gate (⊕ SLNPCH 12°51.983'S; 32°1.008'E). It is then about three hours' drive to Luambe, and perhaps eight to the edge of North Luangwa.

On this road, especially near the start, there are a number of small tributaries of the Luangwa to cross. Between about mid-June and the end of October these will usually be fairly easy; outside of that they can be very tricky. About 26km after Chikwinda gate, one of the more notable of these is the Lukusuzi River (⊕ RIVERR 12°41.647'S; 32°7.585'E). I know from experience that this is easier to cross going south–north than north–south, as the southern bank stopped me for about five hours on one muddy night in early June. Fortunately, virtually the whole of the nearby village soon appeared – many helped to push and manoeuvre, while some just came for the entertainment. I hope it was better than TV for the villagers, as their unstinting help certainly saved us from a wet and uncomfortable night in the river.

The turning east to the Lukusuzi National Park is (at least in theory) on the south bank of this river, although in practice very, very few people ever venture that way.

About 10km after that you'll pass the Chakolwa Scout Camp (⊕ CHAKOL 12°37.178'S; 32°7.413'E), the entry into Luambe National Park. The road around here was particularly bad when I last travelled this way shortly after the rainy season; leaving second gear was a novelty.

Some 20km later (⊕ TULUA2 12°28.869'S; 32°9.486'E) you'll pass a left turning to Luangwa Wilderness Lodge (see opposite for details), which is about 3km away. The road through Luambe is primarily thick black-cotton soil; it's often hard and bumpy when dry, and impassable when wet.

Continuing north, barely 10km later you'll reach Chipuka Scout Camp (⊕ CHIPUK 12°26.923'S; 32°12.516'E), which marks the northern edge of Luambe National Park.

From North Luangwa See pages 287–8 for the route from Luambe to North Luangwa, and back-track along that.

From Lundazi There's a 4x4 route from Lundazi to Luambe that is passable in the dry season only. It's a scenic drive of 140km or so, but not to be rushed, particularly when going down the escarpment.

From Mpika via the Corridor Road There is in theory a very difficult route into the Luangwa Valley which leaves the Great North Road south of Mpika, but it's rarely passable nowadays. Even in a good year it's viable only in the dry season – and even then only when the river is very low, in September or October; the 'Corridor pontoon' across the Luangwa River has not been operational for several years, and there are no plans to reinstate it.

The 'Corridor' is the area between the North and South parks, usually used by professional trophy hunters (hunting on a sustainable basis). They have a few simple camps there, they make the roads and they used to ensure that the pontoon across the Luangwa was working. So if there's no hunting in any given year, then many of the tracks through here will be impassable.

That said, in a normal year you can turn east from the Great North Road about 40km south of Mpika, at ⊕ TUBATE 12°6.421'S; 31°15.727'E – on the track that passes the old Bateleur Farm after 26km. The next landmark is Nthunta Scout Camp (⊕ NTHUNT 12°19.828'S; 31°31.979'E). About 46km from the main road you reach the Nthunta Escarpment, with its breathtaking view over the whole Luangwa Valley.

The road is very rough as it descends down the escarpment, but after about 11km (it feels longer) you will reach the Mutinondo River. Cross this, and after 8km there's a turning to the left which takes you to Nabwalya village, in the middle of the Munyamadzi Game Management Area. Unfortunately, this is the point at which the route comes unstuck. In the dry season, the hunters used to keep a pontoon across the Luangwa, just south of here (near Nyampala Hunting Camp), which linked up with the track between Luambe and the South Park. So unless the river is very low – and it's absolutely essential to check this before you even consider embarking upon this route – you cannot get through.

If you were to carry straight on, instead of turning towards Nabwalya, you would be heading directly over the Mupamadzi River into the South Park. For those directions, see the section on getting to South Luangwa, *From Mpika via the Corridor Road and '05'*, on page 266.

High on the Nthunta Escarpment, near the Nthunta scout post, stands a small memorial to Mary Gough. Memories of the origins of this are hazy, but it's said that she was a woman who went (against all advice) to camp alone and unprotected for a long time on the Chifungwe Plain in the 1970s. Some remains of her body and clothing were found, from which it was deduced that she had been eaten by lions – and hence she was buried here.

I'm told that a few years later, during the height of Zimbabwe's war for independence, her son from Rhodesia (now Zimbabwe) came here to revisit the memorial. Local sources allege that he was a spy, who fed back information to the Rhodesian armed forces – resulting in the bombing of several bridges along the Great North Road. However, it seems he was never caught or charged with this – so the truth is uncertain.

Perhaps a reader could confirm or refute this rough history for sure, so that I can expand on the facts and stories around this memorial in another edition!

FLORA AND FAUNA Luambe is mostly riverine forest, and stretches of mopane woodland; some of this is beautiful, tall cathedral mopane with lots of space between the trees and very little undergrowth. There are also areas of miombo woodland and grasslands.

Luambe is a small park in the middle of a large GMA, where controlled hunting is allowed. Thus, although the ecosystem is virtually identical to that of the North and South Luangwa parks, game densities are lower, though they have recovered significantly since the arrival of the lodge and the German NGO Luangwa Wilderness, and – as a bonus – the park is less crowded than its larger neighbours. On my last trip through here in June, I saw a sprinkling of small antelope – especially around the lodge and near the river: bushbuck, kudu, and waterbuck are common, and both the shy oribi and the endemic Cookson´s wildebeest are occasionally seen. There are also reports of regular sightings of leopard and other cats. So it would be well worth investigating further, and you could expect good birdwatching in this very isolated corner of the Luangwa Valley.

WHERE TO STAY

Luangwa Wilderness Lodge (5 tents, family chalet, camping) Contact via Outback-Sambia, Germany (e info@luangwawilderness.com) or Kamili Safaris, UK (see page 47). Lodge e daktari@iwayafrica.com; www.luangwawilderness.com (⊕ LUAMBE 12°25.532'S; 32°16.383'E). This improbably remote lodge is just 3km from the main road, & well worth staying at, especially if you're driving between the South & North parks. It is linked to Luangwa Wilderness, a German NGO that is committed to maintain and further develop the park, so every visitor plays a role in local conservation work.

The lodge has been built rather beautifully, under the cool & dense shading of thick riverine vegetation. Very comfortable tents, each built on a platform looking over the river, have good firm twin beds & en-suite bathroom (with flush toilet & hot & cold shower). The lodge also has a shaded dining area with a bar, & comfy chairs for relaxing. The camp is powered entirely by solar power, & the tents have battery-powered lights for night-time. Adjacent is a similarly well-kept campsite; with enough advanced notice, campers can arrange to eat at the lodge (b/fast US$10) & join game drives (US$60 sgl, or US$40pp for more than one).

Whilst few overseas visitors will fly over the camps in the South Park to get here, Luangwa Wilderness does have a nearby airstrip, & remains a surprisingly good little lodge which will be an essential stop on the very long road from Mfuwe to North Luangwa. Increasingly, it is also seen as a destination in its own right. *US$290/360 pp sharing/sgl, inc FB, laundry & activities, exc drinks & park fees; US$200/245 pp sharing/sgl, FB. Camping US$10 pp, inc hot shower & firewood, but exc park fees.* ⊕ *Jun–Oct.*

This remote park is on the eastern side of the Luangwa Valley, slightly higher in altitude than the other parks in the valley. There are no facilities here at all – just a game scouts' camp near the gate, and an exceedingly poor track leading through the park. Equally, it is uncertain how much wildlife has survived the poaching, though it is thought that the dominant predator here is the spotted hyena, rather than the lion. The vegetation is mostly miombo woodland, dotted with grassland. Visiting the park requires a major expedition.

GETTING THERE There is a track that turns east from the South Luangwa–Luambe track, and then continues through Lukusuzi National Park until it reaches the Great East Road. This track east to the Lukusuzi National Park starts (at least in theory) on the south bank of the Lukusuzi River (✷ RIVERR 12°41.647'S; 32°7.585'E). See page 292 for more directions, and don't expect this turning to be very clear or well marked.

This track is bound to be impassable during the rains. The easiest approach to the park would be to take the Great East Road to Chipata, then turn north towards Lundazi. About 110km beyond Chipata there is a track on the left to Lukusuzi. There is a game scouts' camp at the park's entrance, so stop and ask them for advice about the park before you go any further. I haven't driven on either of these routes myself.

11

Bangweulu Area

The spectacular Bangweulu Wetlands are, after the rains, a fascinating water-wilderness similar in size to Botswana's Okavango Delta. A huge wetland area with its own endemic species of antelope, it is also a breeding place for one of Africa's strangest and rarest birds: the shoebill.

Nearby Kasanka National Park is a jewel of a reserve, proving beyond doubt that small can be beautiful, while the manor house and estate at Shiwa Ng'andu are a must for anyone seeking an insight into Zambia's colonial history. Meanwhile Mutinondo is a relatively new area, ripe for modern adventurers to explore. Apart from these four main attractions there are numerous fascinating stops around here – from waterfalls to caves and old colonial monuments – in this area where David Livingstone, literally, left his heart.

If you want to explore Zambia beyond the obvious trio of great game parks (Luangwa, Lower Zambezi and Kafue) then this is perhaps the first area that you should visit. The region is perfect for adventurous self-driving visitors with fully equipped 4x4s, but most of the main highlights here can also be visited on fly-in trips using light aircraft for transport.

THE GREAT NORTH ROAD

Access to much of the region is via the Great North Road out of Lusaka. For the most part this is a good tar road, almost pot-hole-free as far as Serenje, though beyond here watch out for the occasional lapse in maintenance.

From the turn-off at Kapiri Mposhi, the road passes Mkushi and Serenje, then on to Mpika further north. None of these towns is a really attractive destination for most visitors, but all can be useful bases for the area's real draws: Kasanka, Bangweulu, Mutinondo and Shiwa Ng'andu.

MKUSHI Some 92km from Kapiri Mposhi, Mkushi (✦ MKUSHI 13°38.633'S; 29°23.976'E) is 1km off the Great North Road on the north side of the railway. Far from being just another stop on the TAZARA line, it's a thriving little town, the centre for a prosperous farming area, with a number of large commercial farms in the vicinity keeping cattle and cultivating cash crops. As you'd expect in a small town this size, there are plenty of shops, fuel, a post office, three banks and a police post.

Getting there In addition to the TAZARA trains, which stop here, several buses heading north stop in Mkushi, including the postbus between Lusaka and Kasama.

Where to stay and eat In Mkushi itself a handful of small hotels vie for attention, of which the best is the Motel Mariana; others include the **ATB Lodge** near the Total garage, and **Shalom Lodge**. Just outside the town, one in each direction, are

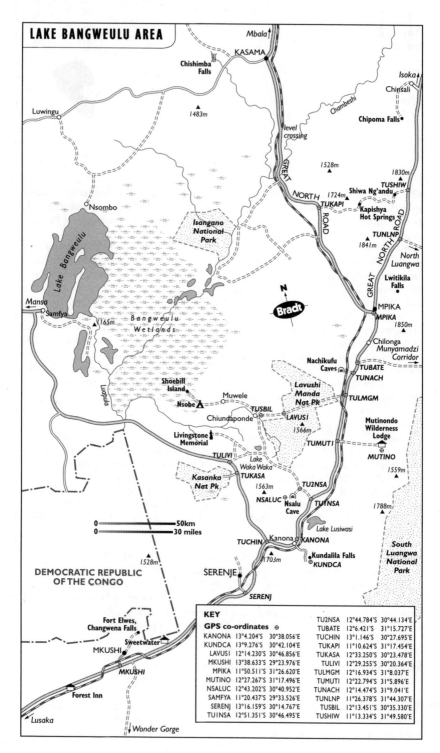

LAKE BANGWEULU AREA

Mbala↑
KASAMA
Chishimba Falls
Isoka↑
Chinsali
Luwingu
▲1483m
Chambeshi
level crossing
Chipoma Falls●
Nsombo
Isangano National Park
▲1528m
▲1724m
▲1830m
Shiwa Ng'andu
TUSHIW
NORTH
TUKAPI
Kapishya Hot Springs
GREAT
TUNLNP
▲1841m
North Luangwa
Lake Bangweulu
Lwitikila Falls
ROAD
Mansa
Samfya
▲1165m
Bangweulu Wetlands
MPIKA
MPIKA
▲1850m
Chilonga Munyamadzi Corridor
Luapula
Nachikufu Caves
TUBATE
TUNACH
Lavushi Manda Nat Pk
Shoebill Island
Nsobe
Muwele
TUSBIL
LAVUSI
▲1566m
TULMGM
Mutinondo Wilderness Lodge
MUTINO
Chiundaponde
Livingstone Memorial
TUMUTI
TULIVI
Lake Waka Waka
▲1559m
TUKASA
Kasanka Nat Pk
▲1563m
TU2NSA
NSALUC
Nsalu Cave
TU1NSA
▲1788m
Lake Lusiwasi
South Luangwa National Park
0 ──── 50km
0 ──── 30 miles
DEMOCRATIC REPUBLIC OF THE CONGO
▲1528m
TUCHIN
Kanona
KANONA
Kundalila Falls
KUNDCA
▲1703m
SERENJE
SERENJ
Fort Elwes, Changwena Falls
Sweetwater
MKUSHI
MKUSHI
Forest Inn
↙Lusaka
↓Wonder Gorge

KEY

GPS co-ordinates ⊕

KANONA	13°4.204'S	30°38.056'E	
KUNDCA	13°9.276'S	30°42.104'E	
LAVUSI	12°14.230'S	30°46.856'E	
MKUSHI	13°38.633'S	29°23.976'E	
MPIKA	11°50.511'S	31°26.620'E	
MUTINO	12°27.267'S	31°17.496'E	
NSALUC	12°43.202'S	30°40.952'E	
SAMFYA	11°20.437'S	29°33.526'E	
SERENJ	13°16.159'S	30°14.767'E	
TU1NSA	12°51.351'S	30°46.495'E	

TU2NSA	12°44.784'S	30°44.134'E
TUBATE	12°6.421'S	31°15.727'E
TUCHIN	13°1.146'S	30°27.695'E
TUKAPI	11°10.624'S	31°17.454'E
TUKASA	12°33.250'S	30°23.478'E
TULIVI	12°29.255'S	30°20.364'E
TULMGM	12°16.934'S	31°8.037'E
TUMUTI	12°22.794'S	31°5.896'E
TUNACH	12°14.474'S	31°9.041'E
TUNLNP	11°26.378'S	31°44.307'E
TUSBIL	12°13.451'S	30°35.330'E
TUSHIW	11°13.334'S	31°49.580'E

two small guesthouses, both with campsites, of which **Forest Inn** is particularly geared to the needs of passing travellers.

🏠 **Motel Mariana** (5 rooms, 10 chalets) m 097 7925810. On the left as you enter Mkushi from the main road, the Mariana was built in 2004. Its neat thatched chalets surrounded by well-tended lawns have the air of a model village. Twin rooms each have a TV & en-suite shower, while the chalets, with dbl beds, also have a fridges. There's a simple bar & restaurant, where fish, steak or chicken from Kw20,000 are served every evening. $

🏠 **Forest Inn** (11 chalets, camping) Great North Rd; ☏ 021 5353003; f 021 5362003; e forestinn@iwayafrica.com; www.forestinn-zambia.com. About 62km from Kapiri Mposhi, or 30km west of Mkushi, Forest Inn is to the south of the main road, & is clearly signposted. The 4hr drive from Lusaka makes it a convenient place to stop for lunch or overnight for those heading towards Kasanka, Mutinondo or Shiwa N'gandu.

The inn's thatch-on-brick chalets have simple wooden furniture & electric lights, as well as en-suite toilets & hot showers or baths. They are secure, clean & functional rather than opulent, but set in large grounds, with cultivated plants & trees, cut grass, & even an old steam engine. In one area, the campsite has its own well-lit shelter with BBQ facilities, & a good ablution block. The gate is kept closed, but there's a gatekeeper & guard on 24hr duty.

Fresh farm produce is available in the restaurant, which is a good place to stop for b/fast (Kw15,000) or lunch (mains Kw40,000). Entertainment in the form of a pool table & darts is in the bar, while the lounge area comes complete with a TV & a real fire for cooler winter evenings. Signposted trails afford the opportunity for short woodland walks, with birding highlights including Boehm's flycatcher & chestnut mantled sparrow weaver. $$. *Camping Kw25,000 pp.*

🏠 **Sweetwater Guesthouse** (6 rooms, camping) Great North Rd; ☏/f 021 5351124; m 097 7226124; e sweetwtr@chengelo.sch.zm. On a working farm beside the Mkushi River, this small guesthouse is signposted to the left about 32km east of Mkushi or, approaching from the north, about 81km from the turn-off to Serenje, just after you cross the Mkushi River. It's about 1km up the hill from the main road.

Sweetwater's twin rooms are built in a concrete block, overlooking the plains & benefiting from a cool breeze, They have mains electricity & en-suite showers & toilets, but it's all pretty basic. Campers have a grassy area set slightly below the rooms, & are given a room key to use the shower. Meals, based on local vegetables & beef, are available in a separate dining area (mains Kw25,000). When last visited, this felt rather neglected, but there are some interesting walks (with good birding) in the local area. $$. *Camping Kw15,000 pp; b/fast Kw16,000.*

Excursions from Mkushi There are two interesting sites to the north of Mkushi, and one to the south, though you'll need a self-sufficient 4x4 to reach any of them. If heading north, note the proximity of the sites to the border with DRC (ex Zaire), and check the security situation locally before you go. Make sure that you don't inadvertently drive too far, which would be surprisingly easy to do. Explaining an illegal entry into DRC might not be fun.

Finally, if you are staying here, you're also within reach of Nsalu Cave and the Kundalila Falls, covered under *Around Kasanka and Bangweulu* on pages 321 and 320.

Changwena Falls This is a very pretty waterfall, near to Fort Elwes and Mount Mumpu. It's about two hours north of Mkushi, accessible using a bush track road through a forest reserve. These tracks are highly seasonal, so do ask for local directions from Mkushi before you set off. Camping is allowed.

The falls themselves are where a small stream leaves its dambo and cascades through a series of three rock pools. The rocks around are a very attractive copper colour, helping to make this remote spot very beautiful. From here you can climb Mumpu and easily visit Fort Elwes (see below).

Fort Elwes Almost on the border with the DRC, Fort Elwes lies about 40km northeast of Mkushi at an altitude of 1,600m. The tracks to get there are in poor condition; ask local directions before you embark upon this trip.

The fort was built around 1896–97 by Europeans who came to seek gold in the area west of the Luangwa Valley. They feared reprisals from the local Ngoni people, if (as planned) the British attacked them near Chipata and the Ngoni were forced west.

It's an impressive structure, with superb views of the hills in the surrounding area. Four huge drystone walls, some 2m thick and 3m high, form a rectangular structure, which originally had a single entrance under one of them. Today it's disintegrating, but a few remnants of the original wooden structures still survive. The *National Monuments of Zambia* booklet (see *Appendix 3*, page 511) attributes the building to Frank Smitheman.

Lunsemfwa Wonder Gorge This is a spectacular and steep gorge marking where the Mkushi River meets the Lunsemfwa, as both cut through deep (300m) gorges into the sedimentary rocks of the Muchinga Escarpment. It is east of Kabwe, and about 130km south of Mkushi, further south than what is known as Old Mkushi.

The best vantage point is Bell Point. It was apparently named after a Miss Grace Bell, a friend of the first European to see the gorge, who visited in 1913. The easiest approach is from the south. Bell Point is technically a national monument but entry is free and there are places you can camp. It's in a very rural, remote area so you'll need a reliable and sturdy 4x4, good maps of the area, and someone to come and look for you if you get stuck.

To get there from the south, drive to Kabwe and turn right just before you cross the railway on the town's southern side. Follow this road parallel to the railway, cross a railway sidetrack, then swing left and cross a bigger railway crossing. On the other side are two roads; take the dirt track on the right signposted 'Mulungushi Boat Club 55km'. There's a good campsite at the club. Otherwise, continue beyond that turn across the Mulungushi, following the power lines northeast to Kampumba and on to Lunsemfwa. Crossing the bridge over the Lunsemfwa, take the RD204 to Old Mkushi.

The turn for Bell Point, a good track on the right that seems to head back the way you came, lies around 20km from Lunsemfwa. Bell Point itself is 35km away from this turning. After 1km there's a fork: take the right track. Ignore all turn-offs for 21km then, following an area of farmland, take a left onto a less used track. The last village on the route lies at 22km, after which the scenery grows ever more beautiful despite the presence of a car wreck at 32km (a casualty, so it is said, of the Rhodesian war). At Bell Point (✪ 14°38.500'S; 29°08.600'E) you can either scramble down to the bottom to keep exploring the gorge, or get to a vantage point and sit and enjoy. The latter is recommended.

SERENJE Northeast of Mkushi, the town of Serenje is about 3km north of the main Great North Road (turn-off ✪ SERENJ 13°16.159'S; 30°14.767'E). To get there, turn at the fuel station (which used to be a BP station, until the company disowned it!). In addition to a TAZARA station, the town has a (noisy and busy) bus station, with daily buses to Lusaka (Kw50,000 one way) and Kashikishi on Lake Mweru. There is also a Total fuel station, a branch of the Finance Bank (⊕ *08.15–14.30 Mon–Fri*), a Catholic mission, a teacher training college, a post office, a police station and a small hospital.

Getting there There are regular buses through Serenje, linking Lusaka with northern Zambia, and the Lusaka–Kasama postbus also stops here three times a week in both directions. Of note is the Time Bus that leaves for Lusaka from the Café de la Restaurant in Serenje every weekday at 07.00.

Where to stay and eat Of Serenje's selection of guesthouses, one – the Mapontela – shines out above the others; it's also the best restaurant in town. For the rest, there's a better than average **Government Resthouse** (☎ *021 5382070*) as you enter the town, the **Ibolelo Valley View Inn**, near the market and bus station, and the **Malcolm Moffatt College Guesthouse,** which is at the college, 2km from the centre of town beyond the market. The **Sige Siga Resthouse** at the turn-off from the main road rents more rooms by the hour than by the night and is best avoided. For simpler meals, you could try **Café de la Restaurant** on the main street, open for lunch and dinner, or perhaps the 'Human Filling Station' that's **Yussuf Restaurant**, with branches both in town and at the crossroads.

Mapontela Inn (8 rooms) m 097 7227522, 9587262. Serenje's best place to stay, if rather pricy, is on the right as you enter the town, just past the police station. It's a small warren of a place, run by a delightful Zambian family headed up by a charming matriarch, Anna Mulenga, & her husband Steve Luker, a retired builder who came to Zambia with the Peace Corps. With its smart green-painted exterior, umbrella-shaded restaurant veranda & spotlessly clean rooms it makes a welcome contrast to the norm.

Most of the rooms, each with dbl bed, bath or shower, TV, fan & mosquito net, are brick built & lead off a courtyard; the older 2 are slightly smaller (& cheaper) but just as well maintained. Some rooms have 3 beds, making them more economical.

There's a pleasant separate restaurant, serving a range of meals from omelette & chips to nshima & steak (**$–$$**). $–$$. *B/fast extra Kw15,000 approx.*

Excursions from Serenje There are various other waterfalls in the area, including the narrow but spectacular cascades of **Mulembo Falls** (⊕ MULEMB 13°13.067'S, 30°25.809'E), reached by turning off at Kalwa Farm sign, 12km northeast of the Serenje turn-off. From there drive 4km, until just before the self-catering guesthouse, then turn left and immediately right. It's then just over 5km to a rounded, domed rock, and a further 6.2km to the falls themselves. The right track leads to the falls, whilst straight on will take you to the river.

Another place that would be interesting to reach is Danger Hill – where there is apparently a monument and a waterfall on the Lwitikila River. However, I've not been able to find reliable directions to these, and haven't visited them myself.

MPIKA Though no bigger than Mkushi or Serenje, Mpika (⊕ MPIKA 11°50.511'S; 31°26.620'E) is a busy crossroads of a place which seems to have an importance outweighing its size. Here the Great North Road forks: one branch goes to Kasama, Mbala, and Mpulungu on Lake Tanganyika; the other heads directly for the Tanzanian border at Nakonde. It is about a day's travel from Lusaka, Mpulungu or the Tanzanian border, which perhaps explains why one often ends up stopping here overnight.

Getting there Getting to Mpika is easy. with a choice of public transport if you are not driving.

By bus Daily local bus services link Mpika with Lusaka, Mbala and (to a lesser extent) northeast to Isoka and Nakonde. Buses run by Germins stop next to the BP garage on the main road through town; others, including Juldan Motors, operate from the opposite side of the road. Sometimes, the same buses will pick you up if you wave them down on the side of the road, but not always. The town is also serviced by the thrice-weekly postbus between Lusaka and Kasama.

Buses to Nakonde leave daily between around 22.00 and 01.00, with tickets costing Kw50,000–55,000. To Lusaka they depart at around 20.00, costing Kw75,000–80,000.

By train Mpika is one of the stops between Kapiri Mposhi and Dar es Salaam, in Tanzania, on the TAZARA railway. Tickets between Mpika and Kapiri Mposhi cost Kw50,000, Kw30,300–35,000 for second and Kw25,500 for third.

The TAZARA station is about 5–6km out of town, almost on the road to Kasama, and private pick-up trucks operate shuttle runs between there and the central boma in Mpika, fitting as many people onto the vehicles as they can carry. If you arrive by train in the early hours of the morning then your options are to get one of these shuttles quickly, or to sleep rough on the station until daybreak and then try to get one. At times like this, the station is crowded but fairly clean and safe.

Hitchhiking With clear roads and a reasonable amount of traffic, hitching is a very practical form of transport to and from Mpika. There is probably more traffic going towards Mbala than towards Nakonde, but if you're heading to Lusaka you can hitch around the BP station where both roads join.

If you're going towards Kasama and Mbala, then hitch on the turn-off by the BP station. Alternatively, and especially if it is late in the day, walk a further 2–3km down that tarred turn-off road, until you reach a smart, fenced compound on your right. This is known as the DDSP compound – it houses offices for various aid and semi-governmental groups, small businesses, and a nice resthouse (see below). You may pick up a lift from one of its workers, who travel widely in the district. You'll certainly see them come and go in a variety of plush 4x4s, and if the worst happens and no lift appears then you can wander across the road and sleep comfortably.

Where to stay and eat

DDSP Compound 021 4370118. Traditionally the best place to stay in Mpika, this resthouse is set alongside numerous offices that include the MLGH (Ministry of Local Government & Housing) & the Development Organisation for People's Empowerment – more usually known as DOPE. (It's also known as the MLGH or MAFF compound.) For directions, see under *Hitchhiking* above. There are both communal & en-suite rooms, as well as self-contained houses sleeping 4 people. Meals are available with advance notice in the simple restaurant with its own bar. $

Malashi Executive Guesthouse (4 rooms) Great North Rd; m 097 7412964. A few hundred metres closer to town than the Mazingo, & on the same side of the main road, this is small & basic, but friendly, with 2 en-suite rooms & 2 with shared facilities. $

Mazingo Motel (20 rooms, camping) Great North Rd; m 096 6804010 (⊕ 11°48.570'S; 31°27.091'E). Almost 3km north of Mpika on the way to Isoka, to the west of the road, this new motel with its apricot & blue painted chalets is in a secure, quiet compound with pleasant gardens. Well-

maintained rooms with solid wood furniture come in 3 types, all with en-suite bath or shower, kettle & TV. Campers can use the parking area, & are given the key to one of the rooms. Lunch & dinner is from an à-la-carte menu. $, *exc b/fast* (Kw12,000).

Musakanya Resthouse (28 rooms) There's nothing special about the Musakanya, except perhaps that it's central & relatively cheap. 8 rooms are en suite. $

Melodies Lodge (11 rooms) Great North Rd; m 097 7352218. On the main road through town, Melodies was new to Mpika in 2006, with simple but clean rooms (5 en suite), & secure parking. There's an on-site restaurant (*mains* Kw15,000) & bar, so it could be noisy at weekends. $

CIMS Restaurant This clean, modern place opposite Melodies Lodge feels more US diner than Zambian restaurant, but the meals combine the traditional with the more cosmopolitan. If you fancy being adventurous, try *ifishimu* – caterpillar. There's a selection of bread, cakes, pies & dairy produce too, making it a good place to put together a packed lunch.

Other practicalities Mpika has a couple of fuel stations, right next to each other on the Great North Road close to the turn-off to Kasama. For supplies, there's a central PEP store, and GM Trading is worth a glance. There's also the Kalolo Bakery, a busy little market, and a good butcher where the meat comes from the Shiwa N'gandu estate.

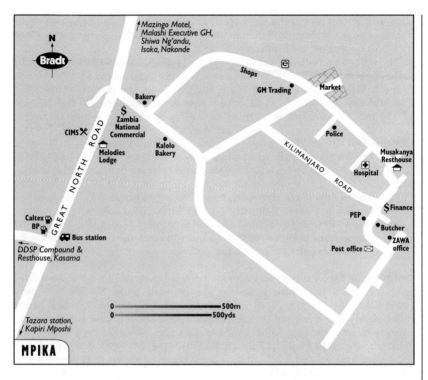

If you need to change any money there are two options: the Finance Bank near PEP, and a branch of the ZNCB just off the main road. And for communications, in addition to a post office, there's an internet café, near the market.

Excursions from Mpika There are a few interesting caves and waterfalls around Mpika, whilst both Mutinondo and Shiwa Ng'andu (see pages 302–5 and 305–11) are worthy of large sections of this chapter on their own. To go anywhere away from the main roads you'll really need a self-contained 4x4, even in the dry season.

Nachikufu Cave (*Entry US$3/2 per adult/child; camping US$10 pp*) This cave complex contains excellent San/Bushman rock paintings. When excavated in the 1940s it was estimated to have been occupied intermittently for about the last 15,000 years. This is no surprise when one considers that all the essentials for survival are here: a regular supply of water from a nearby stream, shelter provided by the cave, firewood in abundance, grass for bedding and a good supply of game and vegetable food sources from the local environment.

It's worth a brief detour because of its geometric rock art and striking setting. Nachikufu Cave is also the 'type' site of the Zambian Late Stone Age, which is known to archaeologists as the 'Nachikufan Industry' (25,000–2,000 years ago). A small display of artefacts is kept within the cave entrance and access is only with an official guide who is stationed on site.

Both the rock shelter and the cave look north over a wide plateau, and are formed from a ridge of quartzite rock – perfect for stone tools. There's also a perennial stream about 500m away from the cave. The paintings inside are fairly simple: various figures silhouetted in black, including a couple of elephants, a beautifully drawn antelope, and human figures, some of whom are depicted with

11

bows and arrows and one with a spear. It has to be said, however, that these paintings are not brilliant, and though the cave is delightful, it's debatable whether it's worth turning off the road just to see it.

The signposted turning (✪ TUNACH 12°14.474'S; 31°9.041'E) to Nachikufu is about 55km southwest of Mpika, about 5km northeast of the Lavushi Manda turn-off. This turning leads you north and west from the main road, over the TAZARA railway, and reaches the cave within about a kilometre at ✪ NACAVE 12°13.939'S; 31°8.693'E. It is easily within walking distance of the main tar road.

Chipoma Falls About 20km south of Chinsali, the Lubu River drops 40m over a distance of 500m at this large set of rapids and cascades (✪ CHIPOM 10°44.998'S, 32°00.284'E). It's a lovely spot for exploring, and there are basic camping facilities here.

To reach the falls from Mpika, head for Chinsali and Isoka and then turn left about 24km before you reach the turn-off for Chinsali (that's about 57km past the turning to Shiwa Ng'andu). Follow this road for around 6km, taking left turns at all the forks and junctions encountered, until you reach the caretaker's house by the falls. There's an entrance fee of a few dollars.

Lwitikila Falls Take the road to Chinsali and Isoka from Mpika for about 15km, until you see a right turn signed to the Lwitikila Girls' Secondary School (✪ TOLWIT 11°43.600'S; 31°28.572'E). Continue along this track, which bends round slowly to the left and then goes uphill, until you see some houses on the right. In front of the first house a smaller track goes off to the right – this leads directly to the small Lwitikila Falls (✪ LWITIK 11°43.810'S, 31°29.674'E). It is a good place for a dip and lunch, though don't expect to have it all to yourself as it lies in a local community area.

AROUND MPIKA

MUTINONDO WILDERNESS AREA Mutinondo Wilderness is a private 100km² reserve, run by Mike and Lari Merrett. It encompasses a pristine area of verdant miombo woodland near the edge of the Luangwa escarpment, complete with huge granite whalebacks, crystal-clear rivers, stunning waterfalls, pristine woodlands and some small wetland areas. There are great plants and birds, which all make for a lovely ambience.

It's a lovely bit of Africa to explore on foot or on horseback, as well as being terrific value; ideally you should spend at least three nights here. While Mutinondo is quite off the beaten track (if there is a beaten track in this part of Zambia?!), access has recently been improved with the opening of an airstrip.

History Although this area has been occupied for centuries, as witnessed by the Iron-Age workings about 6km from the lodge, Mutinondo was first really put on the visitors' map in 1994, when Mike and Lari started looking for a place suitable for both conservation and tourism. By 1999 they had finally sorted out all the legalities with the local authorities and chief, and had a direct access road to their lodge site. Throughout the process, they seem to have made every effort to develop the area sensitively, with minimum impact and maximum use of renewable natural resources, such as solar and wind power.

Flora and fauna Some of this area's smaller flora and fauna has been meticulously catalogued – including over 300 different plants and trees, dozens of butterflies and a good range of the varied birdlife.

Flora The main vegetation here is classic miombo woodland, which is in pristine condition with plenty of *Brachystegia* and *Julbernadia* species. This is interspersed with numerous lush, herby dambos, many of which drain into permanent rivers and streams on the reserve. This water, together with the shade of the established woodland, makes the atmosphere relatively moist – which helps to promote such lush plant growth. Beside the rivers, you'll also find thin strips of riverine forest, and occasional patches of moist evergreen forest (*mushitu*).

Judging by the thick lichens on the rocks and 'old man's beard' (*Usnea*) hanging from the trees, the air is very clean, and looking into the night sky you'll be hard pressed to spot any light pollution at all.

Visiting recently, I found a huge cycad in the woodland, as well as various flowering plants. There is an impressive array of flowering proteas and a great range of orchids – many of the latter have been carefully relocated around the chalets after they were rescued from the trees felled to build the lodge's access road. At the end of winter, in mid-September, it's a magical place to witness the 'miombo flush', when the fresh new leaves bring a hint of red to the trees. If you're visiting during the rains, keep a look out for specimens of *Termitomyces titanicus,* which is the world's largest edible mushroom. The largest that Mike and Lari have found so far had a diameter of about 85cm but they grow up to a metre in diameter. The local people have known about these for centuries; but it seems that they were first described to science as late as 1980.

Fauna Mutinondo is a good spot for birding and is one of Zambia's 'important bird areas', according to Birdlife International. There's a bird list available to visitors (also see the lodge's website) which currently stands at 315 species, and is constantly growing. Obvious 'specials' include Anchieta's barbets, long-toed flufftails, bar-winged weavers, half-collared kingfishers and Ross's turaco.

While Mutinondo is not primarily a game destination, if you spend enough time here you'll find a variety of mammals, from duikers and klipspringer to sitatunga. As the area remains protected, it's likely that larger antelope species like roan and sable, which are already in the area, will become more numerous with time. Of much more interest really are the plants, flowers, trees, mushrooms and smaller wildlife, which also help to make walking here a real pleasure.

Getting there The Mutinondo turn-off on the Great North Road (⊕ TUMUTI 12°22.794'S; 31°5.896'E) is a few hundred metres south of Kalonje railway station on the TAZARA railway. It's about 12km southwest of the turning to Lavushi Manda, and 77km southwest of Mpika, or 364km northeast of Kapiri Mposhi. From the signboard to the lodge it's a further 25km along this level track to the camp (which is accessible by 2WD year-round).

With advance notice, it is possible to arrive at Kalonje by train, and arrange for the team at the lodge to collect you.

A new airstrip was opened in 2007 just over 1km from the lodge (⊕ MUTAIR 12°26.998'S; 31°16.954'E), making access to Mutinondo much easier for those on a fly-in trip. It has a 900m runway, and is suitable only for single-engine aircraft.

⌂ **Where to stay and eat** For individual visitors there are three options: the lodge, the nearby campsite and the new self-catering camp, Kankonde. All are open year round, and share the same contact details. Activities available are detailed below. Note that special arrangements can be made for scientific, educational and school groups, which are warmly welcomed.

🏠 **Mutinondo Wilderness Lodge** (4 chalets) m 097 9862545; e 2mwl@bushmail.net; www.mutinondozambia.com (✪ MUTINO 12°27.267'S; 31°17.496'E). The lodge is a lovely spot to stay — though quite idiosyncratic in its way, with both the chalets & the bar & dining areas carefully built around the rocks, each some distance from the other. Every effort has been made to source the building materials locally, & to use local skills & labour in the lodge's construction. The bricks, stone & thatch used were all manufactured, quarried or harvested locally, & all the woodwork, including the furniture, was constructed by a father-&-son carpentry team from the village of Salamo. As you'd expect, most of the staff are from the surrounding villages.

Each of the chalets is large & individually designed: solid, but not luxurious; a 5th is under construction. One has a particularly spectacular balcony, while all have great views over the wilderness. The 'spacious' chalets are effectively suites, with 2 'rooms' & 3 beds, whilst the 'standard' ones are smaller — although still very roomy. In each chalet you'll find a wardrobe; some also have a fireplace, for when it gets cold. And given the altitude of about 1,400m, it can get very cold! In all but one of the chalets you can expect an en-suite shower with a washbasin & separate toilet. This last, arguably the most spectacular, is the large stone 'Mulombwa', which has a separate bathroom with a home-built bath as well as a shower & a 'loo with a view'. Water is heated by individual solar heaters & wood-burning boilers.

The lodge has a shop whose offerings include jewellery that is designed, & often made, by Lari from locally cut stones, silver & beads, as well as village crafts, local art & photography. Ask nicely for a demonstration of stone-cutting & jewellery-making! *Standard Kw288,000/480,000 sgl/dbl, spacious Kw336,000/600,000 sgl/dbl, inc FB & activities. Extra bed Kw192,000 pp.*

⛺ **Mutinondo Wilderness Camping** (4 camping sites). The campsite here is lovely, with raven-proof cupboards for storing items, good hot showers & clean long-drop toilets. Note that there are a limited number of pitches so you should consider booking in advance if possible. The campsite is adjacent to the lodge; campers are welcome in the bar &, with advance notice, to dine here (*evening meal Kw67,000*). Firewood is available at no extra charge. *Kw40,000 (own tent), Kw192,000/336,000 sgl/dbl tent, inc bedding & meals.*

⛺ **Kankonde Camp** (1 chalet, camping) (✪ KANKON 12°30'S; 31°19'E). Some 11km from the main lodge & camp, on a bank of the Mutinondo River, Kankonde offers the independent traveller a further degree of freedom. Its open-air grass chalet has 2 twin beds, & there's ample room for pitching tents. These share a long-drop loo with a view, a bucket shower (with staff to carry hot water), though further ablutions will be added when a 2nd chalet is built. An *nsaka* rounds off the amenities. Firewood is supplied, & water for bathing & drinking is sourced from the Mutinondo and is safe to drink or can be boiled if preferred. Otherwise you'll need to bring your own, along with all bedding, food, crockery, cutlery, etc, though a few basic ingredients are sold in the shop at the lodge. Visitors usually check in at the lodge first to collect a map & other information before heading for Kankonde. *Camping Kw40,000 pp, chalet Kw50,000 pp.*

What to see and do Although Mike and Lari love to guide visitors around when they are able to, Mutinondo best suits those who feel comfortable exploring. It's a magical place for 'old Africa hands' who want to go off for hours on their own. It's less ideal for those who are new to the bush, although those with some degree of independence can hire one of the lodge's team to guide them around (Kw48,000 per day), and still have a great time. It's not the perfect place if you need your hand held all of the time, or if you're reluctant to abandon your vehicle, as there are relatively few motorable tracks (although, apparently, there is one track which extends 25km to the escarpment). For lodge guests, activities are included in the rates; campers and those staying at Kankonde pay extra, as below.

Walking There's a good network of trails, and the country is hilly without being particularly strenuous. The huge granite whalebacks are great for scrambling up, giving you access to superb views of the surrounding country and, in the east, to the Luangwa escarpment and beyond. It would be very easy to spend three or four days exploring the tracks and whalebacks alone. Trail maps are available at the lodge; I'd also suggest that you take a GPS.

Dedicated and totally self-contained hikers who want something more challenging can arrange longer hikes here, including bush-camping stops. These might encompass the adjacent community-based conservation area, some of the magnificent escarpment waterfalls, or possibly even a long walk down into the Luangwa Valley.

On the water There's a network of very clear rivers and waterfalls, with no crocodiles, hippos or bilharzia. (Though *always* double-check the safety of such a comment locally before you swim, rather than trust any guidebook, even this one!) These have been restocked with indigenous fish: red-breasted, three-spot and green-headed bream – so fishing is possible, albeit on a strict catch-and-release policy.

There are two canoes stationed above one of the waterfalls, beside an idyllic section of quiet, tree-lined river. The more adventurous might take advantage of the inflatable tubes, also available, to just float down river. The cost to campers for canoe hire is Kw24,000 per ½ day.

On horseback Mutinondo has a stable with a number of horses, suitable for all levels of expertise; even complete beginners can arrange to be led by a guide. The horses are surefooted animals, ridden without shoes, and free to roam during the day. It's a very pleasant area for a short walk or a longer hack, with plenty of options. Hard hats are available, adjustable to fit. If you're camping or self catering, riding costs Kw48,000 per hour.

SHIWA NG'ANDU
Background
The early days Shiwa Ng'andu was the inspiration of Stewart Gore-Browne. Born in England in 1883, Gore-Browne first came to Africa in 1902, at the tail end of the Boer War, and later returned in 1911 as a member of the Anglo-Belgian Congo Boundary Commission. On his way back to England, in 1914, one of his carriers guided him north towards Tanzania, passing beside Shiwa Ng'andu, the 'Lake of the Royal Crocodiles'. He intended to settle in Northern Rhodesia, so he negotiated with the local chief to buy the land around the lake – and then, after World War I, he returned to establish himself by the lake. He borrowed money from his beloved Aunt Ethel, and began to build Shiwa.

Gore-Browne was uncomfortable with the colonial attitude towards the African people. He was determined to establish a utopian state, and in his hands Shiwa grew into a vast enterprise with schools and a hospital run with benevolent paternalism. By 1925, Shiwa Ng'andu was employing 1,800 local people.

Gore-Browne passed on skills to them, and together they built neat workers' cottages with tile roofs, as well as bridges and workshops and finally a magnificent manor house, set atop a hill overlooking the lake. Anything that could not be made locally was transported on the heads and backs of porters, along the arduous route from the nearest town, Ndola. At that time it took three weeks to reach Shiwa from Ndola: 70 miles on foot or horseback to the Luapula River, followed by a boat through the Bangweulu Wetlands, and a further ten-day walk from the Chambeshi River to Shiwa.

The heavy English-style furniture was made out of local wood; the large gilt-framed portraits and paintings, silver ornaments, and an entire library of books came from England. Everything came together to create an English country mansion in the heart of Africa – a testament to the determination with which Gore-Browne pursued his vision.

In 1927, when he was 44, Gore-Browne met and married Lorna Goldman, the 'ravishing' 18-year-old daughter of his first love, Lorna Bosworth-Smith. She came to Shiwa, threw herself into her husband's projects, and the estate and its inhabitants prospered. Gore-Browne built a distillery for the essential oils that he hoped to make into a profitable local industry. (Given Shiwa's remote location, the estate's produce had to be easily transportable: a non-perishable, valuable commodity of low bulk.) He had several failures, trying roses, geraniums, eucalyptus, peppermint and lemon grass with no success. Eventually, he succeeded with citrus fruit, which flourished and brought a good income into the estate ... until a *tristezia* virus killed off the fruit trees. This hit the estate hard, forcing Gore-Browne to turn to more conventional, less profitable, agriculture.

Regrettably, the stresses of the estate and Gore-Browne's constant travelling took a toll on his marriage; it resulted in his separation from Lorna, who had found it difficult spending such a great deal of time alone at Shiwa with their two daughters, Lorna and Angela. Lady Lorna returned to live in London in 1945. She came back to Shiwa once, in 1958, and then never again. Even in England she would rarely speak of Shiwa; in December 2001 she died, aged 93.

By this time, Gore-Browne had become a rare, political figure in Northern Rhodesia: an aristocratic Englishman, with excellent connections in London, who commanded respect both in the colonial administration and from the African people. He had been elected to Northern Rhodesia's Legislative Council as early as 1935, and was the first member of it to argue that real concessions were needed to African demands for more autonomy. He was impatient with the rule of the Colonial Office, and resented the loss of huge amounts of revenue through taxation paid to Britain, and 'royalties' paid to the British South Africa Company.

He was knighted by George VI and became mentor to Zambia's first president, Kenneth Kaunda, who, in 1966, appointed him the first ever Grand Officer of the Companion of the Order of Freedom, the highest honour ever bestowed on a white man in Zambia. He died, an octogenarian, in 1967, and today I believe that he remains the only white man in Africa to have been given a full state funeral. He is buried on a hill overlooking the lake at Shiwa – an honour only bestowed on the Bemba chiefs. In the words of Kaunda, 'He was born an Englishman and died a Zambian. Perhaps if Africa had more like him, the transition from colonial rule to independence would have been less traumatic.'

A highly readable and very successful historical account of the life and times of Stewart Gore-Browne and Shiwa Ng'andu, *The Africa House*, was first published in 1999 (see *Appendix 3*, page 510), although note that reservations have been expressed by the family about the historical accuracy of the book.

After Sir Stewart On Sir Stewart's death, the estate at Shiwa passed to his daughter Lorna and her husband, John Harvey, who lived in the house with their four children, Penny, Charlie, Mark and David. However, with the very poor agricultural soils, both the farm estate and the manor house proved difficult to run and maintain. In 1967 the Harveys bought a dairy farm near Lusaka, where both John and Lorna were murdered in 1992. On their deaths, the estate passed to three of Gore-Browne's grandchildren. Initially David took over its management, and by 1995 there were moves to turn the manor house into a museum. Finally, in 2000, Charlie Harvey, Sir Stewart Gore-Browne's grandson, bought the estate from his siblings and now runs it with his wife, Jo, and their two children, Tom and Emma.

Shiwa reinvented Until 2000, Shiwa typified an old English-style country estate that was gradually slipping back into the African bush. In 2001, Charlie and Jo sold their property and literally 'picked up' their entire farming and business just north of Lusaka and translocated it 750km north to Shiwa. Together they brought endless farm equipment, 800 cattle, 600 sheep, 500 assorted wild game animals, eight horses, five cats and five dogs. It was a massive undertaking: for the cattle it was a three-day train ride, followed by a ten-day trek through the bush. With them came two large buses carrying the families – women and children – of the 34 men who had elected to follow the Harveys north.

Soon the house became a hum of activity, with builders and renovators raising much dust and gradually restoring Shiwa's past glory. When I visited Shiwa in 2003, some eight years after I'd first been there, the transformation was startling and impressive. The stranglehold of a slow, tropical decay had been arrested by sheer determination – and the whole feeling of the place had changed. Now it's a thriving family estate, combining a strong sense of history with a vibrant present and a solid future.

Before 2001, Shiwa's only real story – and the only reason to visit – was its history: Gore-Browne and the estate's past glories. Shiwa had been reduced to a curious anachronism in the African bush. By contrast, Shiwa's history is now just that: history. A visit here today will look at the past, but also explore the present: Shiwa's people, its animals and its environment – and how these are developing and changing. At one point during a stay here I saw a young carpenter making one of the internal windows over the courtyard. He was doing a good job, clearly deep in concentration. I asked him if he had also made some of the freshly painted windows on the outside of the house. 'No,' he replied, without pausing, 'my grandfather made those.'

So by all means come to Shiwa to wonder at its past, and the story of Sir Stewart; but expect to leave enthralled by the present – and intrigued by the apparently seamless continuity between the two.

Shiwa today

The manor house As you approach from the main road, the rectangular cottages built for farm workers come into view first, their whitewashed walls and tiled roofs saying more of England than of Africa. Then a red-brick gatehouse appears, its design of Italian influence. An old clock tower rises above its tiled roof, and through its main arch is a long straight avenue, bordered by eucalyptus, leading to the stately manor house.

Climbing up, the avenue leads through typically English gardens – designed on several levels with bougainvillea, frangipani, jacaranda and neatly arranged cypresses. These gardens have been restored with beautiful flowers and well-maintained lawns, though their maintenance represents a continuing battle with bushpigs and the increasing herds of antelope.

Above the front door is a small carving of a black rhino's head, a reminder that Gore-Browne had earned the local nickname of Chipembele, black rhino. At the centre of the manor is the square tiled Tuscan courtyard, surrounded by arches, overlooking windows and a red tiled roof. Climbing one of the cold, stone-slab staircases brings you into an English manor house, lined with old paintings and its wooden floors covered with old rugs.

Much of the old heavy wooden furniture remains here, including the sturdy chests; together with muskets and all manner of memorabilia, including pictures of old relatives and regiments. Two frames with certificates face each other. One is from King George VI, granting 'our trusty and well-beloved Stewart Gore-Browne, esq' the degree, title, honour and dignity of Knight Bachelor. Opposite, President Kaunda appoints 'my trusted, well-beloved Sir Stewart Gore-Browne' as a Grand Officer of the Companion of the Order of Freedom, second division; it is dated 1966.

The library remains the manor's heart, with three huge walls of books, floor to ceiling, which tell of Gore-Browne's interests – Froeude's *History of England* in at least a dozen volumes, *Policy and Arms* by Colonel Repington and *The Genesis of War*

11

by the Right Honourable H H Asquith. His wife was very keen on poetry: there is a classic collection of works by Byron, Shelley, Coleridge, Eliot and others. Gore-Browne left behind a wealth of diaries and personal papers, and much work is in progress cataloguing and archiving these. Central to the room is a grand fireplace, surmounted by the Latin inscription: *Ille terrarum mihi super omnes anculus ridet* – 'This corner of the earth, above all others, smiles on me'.

It's now possible to stay in the manor house; see *Where to stay*, below, for details.

Shiwa estate The working estate extends to include a farm, a well-stocked game-ranch, a lake, stables and all the support necessary for almost total self-sufficiency – directly employing a permanent staff of around 80, with another 120 or so working on a casual basis. It covers just over 100km² of land, and encompasses the domestic livestock, including about 5,500 laying hens, 1,200 cattle, 900 sheep, 20 pigs and 12 Sennea goats, imported from the USA, whose milk is used to raise orphaned children; there's also a small dairy herd to provide milk for the house. Seven years after the move, the game farm has expanded considerably, with over 1,500 head of assorted game, and these are being continuously augmented to improve the bloodlines of the existing herds, and increase the numbers; Shiwa boasts one of the largest closed breeding herds of pure-bred Boran cattle in Zambia (originally imported from Kenya), and has its own butchery in Mpika. Pasture crops are grown largely to feed the livestock but the workers and their wives are encouraged to cultivate vegetable gardens and blocks of maize for their own consumption and for sale on and to the farm.

Gore-Brown's hospital has been brought back to life, thanks in part to grants from the British and German embassies – whilst smaller grants from diplomatic and private sources have enabled it to complete a very good maternity ward. The two government schools are now thriving once more, supplemented by tuition in IT from visiting British students.

Getting there Shiwa Ng'andu is reasonably well signposted off the main road to Isoka and Nakonde; the turn-off (✪ TUSHIW 11°13.334'S; 31°49.580'E) is about 87km northeast of Mpika. The manor house (✪ SHIWAH 11°11.924'S; 31°44.289'E) is about 13km from this turn-off. The road then continues westwards to Kapishya Hot Springs and onto the Mpika–Kasama road.

Alternatively Shiwa can be reached directly from the Mpika–Kasama road; again turn off about 87km from Mpika (✪ TUKAPI 11°10.624'S; 31°17.454'E). It's then a little over 30km to Kapishya, and about half of that again to the manor house.

Where to stay There are two very different places to stay on the estate:.

⌂ **Shiwa Ng'andu Manor House** (5 rooms) ☎/f 021 4370134; e shiwa@shiwangandu.com; gameman@zamnet.zm; www.shiwangandu.com. Charlie & Jo Harvey accept paying house guests, & make engaging & energetic hosts. Their guest rooms, hung with paintings from the Shiwa collection, retain many original features, inc fireplaces in which fires are lit every night in winter. Traditional hardwood furniture is complemented by new 4-poster bedsteads made on the estate, while en-suite bathrooms add a touch of modernity – but only a touch; some have huge old metal baths rather than modern showers, & an aura of Edwardian style prevails. Meals are very simple farm fare, much of it sourced on the farm, but served with style in the grand setting of a formal dining room. It's very much like staying in an English stately home in Africa – which you'll realise isn't a contradiction in terms when you visit.

Jo & Charlie are very generous with the time that they give to their guests – but there is also a house manager on hand, & a professional guide to take you around the estate. Days are very full, with plenty of activities – you can choose what you would like to do from a wide range of possibilities (pretty much as below).

Most people come to Zambia on safari, then wonder about adding on Shiwa as an afterthought. That's sad, as I found my last stay here to be among the most interesting & engaging few days that I've spent anywhere in Zambia – a view backed up by the visitors that I've sent here since. If you do come, then allow at least 3 or 4 nights; any fewer would be far too frustrating for you! US$400 pp, fully inclusive. ⊕ all year.

🏠 **Kapishya Hot Springs** (6 chalets, camping) m 097 7939277; e 2mark@bushmail.net, kapishya@shiwasafaris.com; www.shiwasafaris.com (⊕ 11°10.263'S; 31°36.057'E). Kapishya is run by Mark Harvey, Sir Stewart's second grandson, a mine of local information & a top local guide. The camp lies on the Manshya River & has been considerably upgraded in recent years, with flourishing gardens where individual plants are carefully labelled & a rustic bar/dining area.

The thatched brick chalets are simple but comfortable, each sleeping 4, & with its own porch & brick floors covered with reed mats. Mosquito-netted windows & en-suite facilities that include flush toilets & large showers are standard. One of the chalets is dbl-storey, with a particularly good

view of the river from the top & its own firepit. Right by the river, the grassy campsite has soft earth that's easy on tent pegs, good hot showers (fed from a new water tank) & clean flushing toilets, as well as a dining shelter & BBQ areas. All visitors can order meals, ideally with advance notice, or can cater for themselves (chalet guests can use the camp's kitchen). To spice up the self-catering option, homemade jams & chutneys are for sale.

Kapishya Springs themselves are a great attraction, as is the birding on the property (Ross's turaco is a relatively common visitor) but guests here can also take part in most of the activities on the Shiwa estate; US$20 pp will cover a game drive or a lake trip. Alternatively, there are some lovely waterfalls nearby to explore yourself – see *Excursions from Shiwa* below.

Kapishya combines well with a visit to Buffalo Camp (see pages 289–90), in North Luangwa National Park, also run by Mark. With lots of advance notice, it's sometimes possible to pre-arrange vehicle transfers between here & Buffalo Camp. US$70/100/150 pp self-catering/DBB/FB. US$10 pp camping. Dinner Kw100,000. ⊕ all year.

What to see and do Shiwa's a great place for a surprising variety of activities, so there's no question of being bored. For those staying at the manor house, these are generally included; for guests at Kapishya they're optional extras. Always bear in mind that numbers of visitors here are fairly small, so where I refer to a 'tour' you should generally visualise half a dozen visitors or fewer! Here are just a few of Shiwa's highlights.

Kapishya Hot Springs About 20km from Shiwa Ng'andu, the hot springs in the Manshya River at Kapishya were always a favourite spot of Gore-Browne's and a great place to unwind. Within a shallow part of the cool rocky river, surrounded by *combretum* bushes and gently curving raffia palms (*Raphia farinifera*) is an inviting pool of hot spring water. It makes a great site for bathing.

Those not staying overnight on the Shiwa estate can visit for the day for Kw20,000 per person, or US$5.

Boating and rafting There are several activities possible on the water. It's lovely to take a slow boat trip around the edges of the lake, looking out for wildlife, from birds and otters to crocodiles, and it's also possible to do this by traditional *mokoro* (dugout canoe). During the fishing season, you can bring a rod and reel.

Alternatively, take a full-day trip around the lake, and then from there down the Manshya River. This goes over some small (Grade 2) rapids and back to Kapishya Camp – and is a particularly good option for birdwatchers (though do remember to protect any belongings in waterproof containers in case they should be thrown out).

Nature walks and drives Much of Shiwa estate is now a game area, so early morning walks or game drives can be very much a feature of staying here. It's a particularly good place for spotting the elusive blue duiker, whilst the more common game includes puku, kudu, defassa waterbuck, Kafue lechwe, Lichtenstein hartebeest, common duiker, oribi, zebra, bushbuck, reedbuck, impala, yellow baboon, vervet monkey, grysbok and wildebeest.

The lechwe and the wildebeest are of a different subspecies than you'll find elsewhere in this part of northern Zambia; they're unlike those in the Luangwa and Bangweulu areas. With patience, sitatunga can usually be spotted from the hide, whilst bushpig, wild cat, civet, genet and clawless otters are around but often less visible. As in many of Zambia's isolated kopjes, there's a resident population of fairly elusive klipspringers.

One of the estate's natural highlights occurs in November, at the start of the rains, when thousands of straw-coloured fruit-bats return to Shiwa to roost. For details of a similar spectacle at Kasanka, see page 315.

Guided walks The Shiwa estate, and the area around it, is a lovely place for scenic walks, with a number of stunning hills and sites of interest. It's as easy to have a good hour's walk alone as it is to stay out for the day with a local guide, perhaps wandering beside the river and getting as far as the Chusa Falls – which are 10km downstream from Kapishya Springs.

Another notable spot is Nachipala Bareback Hill – a large granite whaleback which affords stunning panoramic vistas and a magnificent view of the lake. This is an energetic three-hour walk from the manor house, and on the top a small cairn marks the spot where, on his last journey in 1867, Dr David Livingstone took compass bearings in his final attempt to find the source of the Nile.

Birdwatching Shiwa has been identified as a priority site for conservation and is listed as one of 31 'important bird areas' in Zambia (see *Appendix 3*, page 512). You can stroll around the estate and game ranch with or without a guide (there aren't usually any lion, buffalo or elephant here, so this is fairly safe), and some of the walks lead through beautiful raffia palm forests.

In total, over 373 species of birds have been seen on the estate. Birding highlights include palm-nut vultures, bat hawks, Ross's turacos, white-cheeked bee-eaters, white-tailed and blue flycatchers, Stanley's bustards, African finfoot, black-rumped buttonquail, long-toed flufftail, greater snipe, grass owls, black-chinned quail finch and a veritable kaleidoscope of different sunbirds. Down by the water, the swamps, rivers and lakes offer a haven for a variety of waterbirds, including pygmy geese; cormorants; yellow-billed, knob-nosed and white-faced teal; giant and lesser egrets; blue, grey, night and goliath herons; Fulleborn and rosy-breasted longclaws; malachite, half-collared, giant and pied kingfishers; golden-rumped tinkerbird; splendid starlings; black-bellied seed cracker; Bocage's robin; bar-throated apalis; and white-headed saw-wing. Fish eagles and even ospreys may be spotted, as well as transient flocks of pelicans and flamingoes.

Horseriding Horseriding here is generally for experienced riders only, with good hard hats available. Many of the horses are polo ponies, which are exceptionally well trained and respond exceedingly well to instructions. Particularly attractive is the hour or so's ride up to the 'View of Angels' – an oft-photographed spot where there is a spectacular view of the lake from the family graves of Sir Stewart Gore-Browne and his daughter and son-in-law, Lorna and John Harvey.

Around the estate If you've time to spare then take a slow wander around the estate, and perhaps down to the lake, ideally with a guide. You will find an exceedingly positive atmosphere, with the local people very welcoming and friendly, and usually happy to talk about what they are doing.

The farm itself is run on commercial lines, but methods are far from the intensive farming beloved of the West. The environment is a key factor, and nothing is left to waste. This is no place for shiny new gadgets; spending an hour or so watching the sort of machinery usually confined to a museum being coaxed into life can be fascinating in itself. There are numerous community initiatives going on, too, from fish-farming to bee-keeping and bio-gas projects – as well as a variety of projects within the estate's hospital and school.

Tours of the manor house Guided tours of the manor house are by prior arrangement only. If you're staying at the manor house then this is merely a case of asking Jo and Charlie to show you around; it's delightfully informal and totally fascinating.

If you're staying at Kapishya, or just dropping in for the day, the only way to see some of the interior of the house is to book on to a daily 'tour' (*Mon–Sat 09.00–11.00, Sun 10.00–11.00; the fee of US$20 pp goes towards the community fund*). Within the house the tour is limited to the lower floors; the upper floors are strictly for the family and their guests. (Remember that this is a family home first, and a small exclusive guesthouse second, and you'll realise that neither the family, nor their guests, will want a steady stream of visitors looking through the manor house.) Also included are a game drive and a historical guided tour of the estate.

Shiwa's archives Putting Gore-Browne's extensive collection of diaries, letters and papers into an ordered archive has been a long-term project for Jo, and is still not complete. Guests interested in the manor house can have some access to this, on request; it's fascinating to read some of Gore-Browne's old diaries even if you're not an amateur historian. Then there's the enormous library, and Gore-Browne's collection of early records!

Historical tours on the estate Jo is a trained archaeologist, and has been in the forefront of excavating some of the older sites on the estate – already uncovering the kilns that were built to make the bricks and the tiles for the manor house, and the locations of an old summerhouse.

There are a number of other spots of historical interest, including the old hospital, the essential oils distillery, the traction engine and the graveyard – and any can easily be integrated into a historical tour of the estate.

Excursions from Shiwa Shiwa is really a destination in itself, and isn't often used as a base for excursions, although Kapishya makes quite a good base for visiting a few local waterfalls, detailed below. If you ask the team at the springs, they could probably arrange for a guide to go with you to make locating them easier.

Chusa Falls Chusa Falls (✦ CHUSAF 11°09.353'S; 31°33.093'E) are the closest to Kapishya, making a good day trip. On foot, they're a distance of 7km away, or 10km by road. The falls are quite clearly a short series of three steps, each being several metres high.

Senkele Falls These falls (✦ SENKEL 11°06.150'S; 31°21.922'E) are a 15m drop on the Mansha River. The turn-off to them from the Mpika–Kasama Road is at ✦ TUSENK 11°11.712'S; 31°18.903'E, about 3.5km north of the turning to Kapishya and Shiwa. From there the track turns north and continues for 10km. Continue north where the road forks, then after about 2km of high grass, stop at the deserted house; the falls are 100m from here. This might be a lovely place to bush-camp.

Namundela Falls Finally, the stunning double Namundela Falls (✛ 11°06.760'S; 31°27.606'E) are about two hours' drive from Kapishya, followed by a 90-minute walk to the falls along the Mansha River. To get to them, head 28km west from Kapishya, turning north at Chilombo School (✛ CHILOM 11°13.525'S; 31°24.624'E). Follow this track about 13km north and slightly east to the Anderson Farm (✛ ANDERS 11°07.861'S; 31°26.542'E), and then further to the Kapololwe Homestead, marking the start of the walk along the river.

KASANKA NATIONAL PARK

(Park fees US$10 pp, US$15 per vehicle, per day) This small park is the first privately managed national park in Zambia. It is run by a charity, the Kasanka Trust, and the proceeds from tourism go directly into conservation and development in the park and surrounding communities. It is only 420km² in area, but encompasses a wide variety of vegetation zones from dry evergreen forests to various types of moist forest and permanent papyrus swamps. The park and its camps are so well kept that it is a delightful place to spend a relaxing few days, and keen birdwatchers will find many more pressing reasons to visit.

HISTORY Kasanka was made a national park in 1972, but it was poorly maintained and poaching was rife until the late 1980s. Then an initiative was started by David Lloyd, a former district officer, and Gareth Williams, a local commercial farmer. With the approval of the National Parks and Wildlife Department and the local community, they started to put private money into revitalising the park.

In 1990 the National Parks Department signed a management contract with the Kasanka Trust, giving the latter the right to manage the park and develop it for tourism in partnership with the local community. The Trust, which is linked to a registered charity based in the UK (e *uktrust@kasanka.com*), has trailblazed a model for the successful private management of a Zambian national park. It has been fortunate in gaining financial backing from various donors, but now relies almost entirely on tourism income to fund its activities.

The Kasanka Trust aims to manage the area's natural resources for the benefit of both the wildlife and the local people, and so it closely supports and consults with a locally elected community resource board.

GEOGRAPHY Kasanka is on the southern fringes of the Bangweulu Swamps, and just 30km from the border with DRC. It is almost completely flat and, lying at an altitude of about 1,200m, it gets a high rainfall during the wet season (about 1,200mm) which results in a lush cover of vegetation.

Although there are several small rivers flowing through the park, the evenness of the land has resulted in an extensive marsh area known as the Kapabi Swamp. There are also eight lakes in the park, though seven of these are really just small permanently flooded dambos.

FLORA AND FAUNA

Flora The park's natural flora is dominated by miombo woodland, in which brachystegia species figure heavily. The local people use fire as part of their cultivation and hunting/gathering activities, which can spread into areas of the park, so some of this is less tall than it might be – perhaps reaching only 5m rather

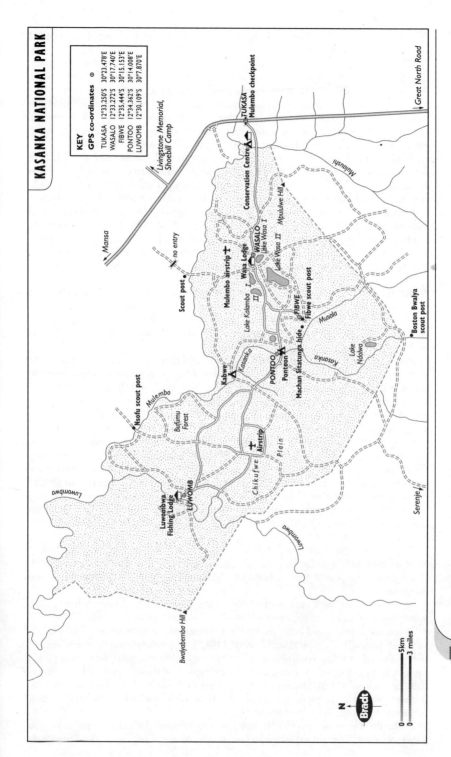

KASANKA NATIONAL PARK

KEY

GPS co-ordinates ⊕

TUKASA	12°33.250'S	30°23.478'E
WASALO	12°33.272'S	30°17.740'E
FIBWE	12°35.444'S	30°15.153'E
PONTOO	12°34.362'S	30°14.008'E
LUWOMB	12°30.109'S	30°7.870'E

than its normal 20m. The park operates a programme of limited, controlled burning to reduce the damage caused by hotter fires later in the dry season.

There are also sections of much taller dry evergreen forest, where the tallest trees have an interlocking canopy, and the *mateshi* undergrowth is dense and woody. A good area for this is near the Kasanka River around the Katwa guard post.

Elsewhere you will find evergreen swamp forest, with some superb tall specimens of waterberry (*Syzygium cordatum*) and mululu, or red mahogany, trees (*Khaya nyasica*). One of the guides here told me a story of a biologist asking a local Chewa person the name of this tree, and getting the reply 'Khaya', which means 'I don't know'.

Around the Fibwe guard post is one such area of forest, and the Machan Sitatunga Hide (see page 318) is perched in a huge mululu tree. Similar species also occur in the areas of riparian forest found by Kasanka's small rivers. One notable tree is the wild loquat (*Oxyanthus speciosus*), whose fruit is a major draw for bats.

Interspersed in these forested areas are seasonally flooded grasslands and swamps. The latter include large areas of permanent papyrus beds and *phragmites* reeds, often with very little open water to be seen. The wild date palm, *Phoenix reclinata*, is one of the most common species of tree found here. Keep a lookout, too, for the large tree-proteas that bloom spectacularly around May and June.

Mammals Poaching in the 1970s and '80s drastically reduced the numbers of animals in the park. However, this seems to have had few long-term effects on the species now present. Many of these move into and out of the park quite freely and, as they gradually learn that the park is a safe haven, they are staying longer or becoming resident, and appear to be less shy.

Puku are the most common antelope here, and they are found in a particularly high density along the Kasanka River. Other relatively common residents include bushbuck, reedbuck, defassa waterbuck, Sharp's grysbok and the common duiker. Lichtenstein's hartebeest, sable and roan occur in good numbers, while oribi, zebra and buffalo are more scarce. Elephants move through the park, but a recent count suggested that a population of about 75 were probably resident here.

Of particular interest are the shy sitatunga antelope, which can almost always be seen in the very early morning from the Machan Sitatunga Hide (see below), near Fibwe guard post. This offers one of the subcontinent's best opportunities for viewing these beautiful creatures in an undisturbed state – far superior to simply getting a fleeting glance of the back of one as it flees from the speedboat in which you are travelling, as with so many sitatunga sightings in places like the Okavango Delta. On occasion, 70 different animals have been spotted in a morning from here. It's excellent.

The smaller carnivores are well represented in Kasanka, with caracal, jackal, civet, genet and Cape clawless otter all regularly recorded. Others, including lion, leopard, serval, spotted hyena, honey badgers and the African wildcat, are more rarely seen.

Mongooses are well represented: the water (or marsh), slender, white-tailed, banded, dwarf and large grey mongoose are all found here.

In the lakes, rivers and swamps, hippo and crocodiles are common. The slender-snouted crocodile, a typical resident of DRC's tropical rainforest rivers, occurs here – though it is less common than the 'normal' Nile crocodile. Given the park's proximity to DRC, other species, which are typical of those equatorial rainforests (but rare for southern Africa), can be spotted in Kasanka. For example, the blue monkey is often sighted, occurring together with the area's more common primates: baboons and vervet monkeys.

Probably the most spectacular sight occurs around the start of the rains (in November and December) when an enormous colony of straw-coloured fruit-bats

One of Kasanka's highlights is the magnificent tree-hide, perched high in a red mahogany tree overlooking the Kapabi Swamp. Most come here to spot sitatunga, but if you climb up on a late November afternoon, around the time the rains are beginning, then you'll also witness one of Africa's strangest wildlife spectacles. Between about 18.15 and 18.45, some five million straw-coloured fruit-bats will take to the air above you. These large, fruit-eating bats have wingspans up to about a metre. They start by circling overhead like a vast, slow whirlwind. Gradually, individuals and groups break off and spread out over the forest in search of wild fruits. For an amazing 20–30 minutes the sky is filled, as far as you can see, with squadron upon squadron of bats, heading off into the twilight.

'They come to roost in the evergreen swamp forest, near the Musola River,' Edmund said, gazing down through the canopy. 'It's very unusual vegetation for Zambia – only found near rivers. Tremendously fragile and easily destroyed,' he added. 'During the day the bats occupy just a small area. They hang off the Mushitu trees in such numbers that they pull off the branches, leaving just the woody skeletons to hang on to. This lets light on to the forest floor which, together with the inordinate amount of fertiliser that they drop, promotes very rich undergrowth. Imagine, five million bats, weighing about 700g each ... that's 3,500 tons of animals.' Edmund had clearly done his arithmetic before. 'The equivalent of a thousand elephants, hanging around in perhaps one hectare of forest, suspended from the trees,' he grinned.

Visiting this colony isn't for the faint-hearted though, even during the day. Large crocodiles wander under the trees, far from the nearest water, scavenging for dead bats – along with vultures, gymnogenes and a host of other predators. All of which provided further reasons why that high tree-hide was such a wonderful place to be.

Edited from an article by the author that first appeared in Travel Africa, *and reproduced by kind permission.*

roosts in the *mushitu* forest. Each night they pour out of their resting-place just after sunset, filling the sky as they fly in search of food. The bats have wingspans of up to 1m, making a grand spectacle that is best observed from the area of the Machan Sitatunga Hide.

Birds Kasanka has lush vegetation with a wide range of habitats including three large rivers, five natural lakes, a papyrus swamp (Kapabi) and real moist evergreen swamp forest. In this small area over 430 bird species had been identified by mid-2007, including many 'specials', and the number continues to rise – so it's a very good place for quiet, undisturbed birdwatching.

The rivers, lakes and wetland areas have excellent populations of ibis, storks, herons, kingfishers and bee-eaters as well as many waterfowl. Water rails, greater and lesser jacanas, white-backed ducks and pygmy geese are common. The larger birds include wattled cranes and saddle-billed storks; around Lake Ndolwa there have even been two sightings of the rare shoebill, which breeds in the Bangweulu Swamps to the north. Reed cormorants and African darters are easily spotted on the more open stretches of water.

Many species common in east or central Africa occur here, on the edges of their ranges (South African bird books just won't be enough!), like the grey apalis, olive sunbird, red and blue sunbird (Anchieta's), green lourie, Boehm's flycatcher, Boehm's bee-eater, Sousa's shrike, black-backed barbet, Anchieta's tchagra, and both Schalow's and Ross's turacos (the latter also known as Lady Ross's lourie).

Meanwhile, a quiet drift in a canoe down the Luwombwa River should produce sightings of finfoot, giant and half-collared kingfishers, narina trogons and yellow-throated leaflove, to name but a few.

The park was the site for a recent study of hornbill species by a team organised jointly by the universities of Manchester (UK) and Lusaka.

The more common raptors in the area are the bateleur, martial, crowned, Ayre's, African hawk and steppe eagles, plus the snake eagles (black-breasted, western-banded and brown) and the chanting goshawks (pale and dark). Kasanka's fish eagles are often seen and crowned eagles breed here. There are also several pairs of Pel's fishing owls.

GETTING THERE The entrance to Kasanka, on its eastern border, is marked with a large sign. Coming from Kapiri Mposhi, do refuel in Serenje, as there is no fuel available in the park. Then 36km northeast of Serenje, take the main left turning signposted to Samfya and Mansa. This used to be referred to as the 'Chinese road' because, like TAZARA, a Chinese company built it. After about 55km (the milestones on the left of the road are no longer readable!) turn left, where you will find the the Mulembo scout post and the entrance gate to the park (✪ TUKASA 12°33.250'S; 30°23.478'E). You may need to register and pay an entrance fee here, but if the post is unmanned then just proceed to Wasa Lodge, bearing left at the fork after 1km or so (turning right here takes you to the new information centre). For those flying in, the park has two good 1,200m airstrips for light aircraft – and they're very aviation-friendly.

WHERE TO STAY The Kasanka Trust (*PO Box 850073, Serenje; satellite* ❧ *+873 762 067957;* f *+873 762 067959;* e *wasa@kasanka.com; www.kasanka.com*) runs all the camps in the park. Although Kasanka can often accommodate 'drop-in' visitors who have their own food, booking in advance is always a good idea. All visitors pay park fees on top of accommodation, except those staying at the conservation centre, which is just outside the park boundary.

⌂ **Wasa Lodge** (8 rondavels) ✪ WASALO 12°33.272'S; 30°17.740'E. About 20 mins' drive from the main road, in a delightful spot on the shore of Lake Wasa, is the park's main camp. Wherever you are going in the park, you should report here first. Wasa's thatched rondavels, have undergone fairly major upgrades in recent years. Now, there's a variety of accommodation, with dbl, twin & family rooms available. All have en-suite flush toilets & hot bucket showers, & the large, new ones are very comfortable. At night the camp is lit by atmospheric lanterns & small solar-powered lights.

Wasa is well staffed & equipped, & staying here can work in 2 different ways. If you're driving in, then you can bring your own supplies & the camp's staff will cook them for you. They will also prepare hot water for showers, & are generally around for any reasonable help that you might need. A bar is always available. Alternatively, if you are flying into Kasanka, or don't have your own food, catering can be arranged for you.

Similarly, with your own vehicle you can drive yourself around the park or take a local guide to accompany you. However, if you're flying in then you will need the use of one of the camp's 4x4s & guides, which should be pre-arranged. *Kw200,000 pp self-catering, exc park fees; US$310/420 pp sharing/sgl, inc FB, activities (best pre-arranged), laundry, & park fees.* ⊕ *all year.*

⌂ **Luwombwa Fishing Lodge** (5 chalets) ✪ LUWOMB 12°30.109'S; 30°7.870'E. This very pleasant & peaceful lodge sits on the bank of the Luwombwa River in the western half of the park. Accommodation consists of 3 A-frame thatch-on-brick chalets, 2 of which have twin beds upstairs as well as a sgl & dbl downstairs, while the 3rd has 1 floor only, containing a dbl & sgl bed. All have an en-suite toilet, washbasin & shower. There are also 2 older, much simpler chalets with separate facilities. All feel a lot roomier than the older chalets at Wasa, so it's worth coming over the Luwombwa for at least a night or 2 if you're staying in the park for any time.

The camp's simple bar & dining area is made of reeds & thatch, & it is dominated by a huge & quite magnificent mpundu (or mobola) plum (*Parinari curatellifolia*). This has edible fruits, around Oct–Jan, which are variously described as 'sought-after', 'pleasant-tasting' & 'disgusting'.

The camp works on a similar basis to Wasa – you bring your supplies & the camp's staff will look after you, or you make arrangements for meals & drinks with the camp in advance. To reach Luwombwa before dark, make sure that you get to Wasa before 17.00, or it will be too late to continue on here. Motor boats (5 seats) with guides are available for hire here, as are canoes (3 seats). *Kw200,000 pp self-catering, exc park fees; US$310/420 pp sharing/sgl, inc FB, activities (best pre-arranged), laundry, & park fees. ⊕ all year – but high-clearance 4x4 required to reach it.*

Å Pontoon Campsite Set under a beautiful stand of red mahogany (mululu) trees (*Khaya nyasica*) near the main Kasanka River crossing (which is a pontoon as I write, but may soon be a bridge!).

There are simple bucket showers & long-drop toilets as well as 2 cooking shelters. Staff are on hand to supply firewood, draw water, prepare hot showers, & give basic guidance to visitors. The site can accommodate groups of up to about 15 people. *Kw30,000 pp.*

Å Kabwe Campsite Overlooks the Kasanka River plain. It's a smaller site, for around 6 people at most, with just 1 toilet & 1 shower. Due to the sensitivity of its location, it is not always available & must be booked in advance. *Kw30,000 pp. No children (so as not to disturb the wildlife).*

⌂ Conservation Centre (4 rooms, dormitory, camping) Accommodation at the conservation centre, 1km from the park gates, is designed primarily for students or long-term researchers. Rooms are set up in pairs, sharing a shower & toilet, & there's a dormitory for larger groups. It's also possible to camp. Some meals can be provided from the on-site kitchen or visitors can cook for themselves. *Room Kw150,000 pp, camping Kw30,000 pp. No park fees applicable.*

Fly-camping Guided walking safaris led by expert, armed game scouts last three to five days and offer a real bush experience. This is the chance to see the many different vegetation types, insects, birds and animals, and to discuss the bush, the project, and anything else at leisure! They usually also include some time canoeing. The fly camps are simple, but supplies are delivered ahead by vehicle so you don't need to carry a heavy pack. Note that experienced **backpackers** who arrive fully equipped with food and supplies, and who are prepared to carry all their own kit, can often arrange to go for an extended walking trip with an accompanying scout at a much lower cost. (*US$310/420 pp sharing/sgl, inc FB, activities & equipment. ⊕ May–Dec, though you may have rain in Nov–Dec.*)

WHAT TO SEE AND DO During the dry season Kasanka's roads are generally good, and accessible with a high-clearance 2WD. There is a manually operated pontoon (✪ PONTOO 12°34.362'S; 30°14.008'E) for crossing the Kasanka River in the centre of the park, with staff stationed nearby who can assist. (There are plans to build a bridge here eventually.)

Activities organised by the Kasanka Trust include escorted walks, game drives (including night drives), canoeing, motorboat trips and fishing (bream and tigerfish). I can highly recommend the excellent canoe trips from Luwombwa.

Anglers should head for Luwombwa Fishing Lodge (get a permit in advance from Wasa Lodge), as the best waters for fishing are normally those of the Luwombwa River. The main species found here are vundu catfish and large-mouth, small-mouth and yellow-belly bream. The camp's cooks will prepare your catch for dinner, if you wish, but note that there are strict rules that allow only large fish to be removed for eating.

There's also the chance to see some of the workings of Kasanka's community-based conservation projects, and meet their participants. One such project was initiated in the Kafinda area in 1997, aiming to raise awareness of the importance of conservation, and to provide alternatives to poaching for the community. Requested in advance, it is often possible for visitors to see some aspects of this project.

One of the greatest problems facing the successful operation of a national park is managing the conflict between conservation and community. Kasanka is no exception: with a small elephant population in an unfenced park, and a considerable number of arable farms in the vicinity, problems are almost inevitable. Villagers understandably object to elephants trampling their valuable maize and cassava crops, but keeping the animals at bay is rarely straightforward.

In 2000, two researchers in Zimbabwe came up with a simple idea: chilli fences. The aim was to create a barrier that would repel the elephants without resorting to costly and often ineffective barricades or electric fencing. In 1997, Guy Parker and Loki Osborn in Zimbabwe set up the Chilli Pepper Development Project, based on the premise that elephants have a strong aversion to the smell of chillies. Using cheap, easily available materials, they created a fence made of wooden posts linked by sisal rope and hung with strips of mutton cloth that had been doused in used engine oil and chillies. Their results were impressive.

Taking their research as a base, Victoria Paterson, a research student from Glasgow University, spent much of 2007 at Kasanka studying the potential of chilli fences for the villages around the national park. With a focus across five sites, she set up a series of fences, with control experiments to check the efficacy of the combination of materials, and worked with local farmers to explain the methods. Despite considerable resistance, some of the farmers have taken the suggestions on board, with very positive results for their crops. The next stage is to ascertain how long the protective fences will work, assuming that eventually the elephants will overcome their dislike of the chillies. One method of reinforcing the fences is to create a buffer zone between the precious maize crop and the elephant's forest habitat, by growing a secondary crop around it. The European potato, for example, doesn't find favour with elephants, so sowing this between the forest and the maize may be sufficient to persuade the elephant to look elsewhere rather than wading through a field of unappealing fare.

While persuading people to try out new ideas can be an uphill struggle in itself, it's important that putting these ideas into practice should be affordable. With this in mind, villagers have been encouraged to use fibre for rope, and to grow chillies as one of their crops. Here, water is a huge factor, but if the chillies are grown alongside another, profitable crop that requires irrigation, such as rape, then a successful outcome is more likely.

Now, though, the elephants – thwarted of their free meal – have taken to heading for village grain stores, and so the cycle continues.

Alternatively driving yourself around is easy, though it's a shame to go by yourself when good guides are available and their community relies on their income. A few places within the park are worth specific mention.

Machan Sitatunga Hide A magnificent mululu or red mahogany tree (*Khaya nyasica*), near to the Fibwe Guard post (✛ FIBWE 12°35.444'S; 30°15.153'E), can be climbed, using a basic ladder, to reach a platform almost 18m above the ground. The views over a section of the Kapabi Swamp are excellent, and if you reach this in the early morning and climb quietly then your chances of seeing sitatunga are excellent.

However, more leisurely risers should take heart: I have seen a number of sitatunga from here as late as midday. In short, this is probably the best place for seeing sitatunga in the wild anywhere in Africa – and so certainly one of the best tree-hides on the continent!

Meanwhile, when you're not searching for sitatunga, it's also a particularly productive birding spot with specials such as Ross's and Schalow's turaco, Boehm's bee-eater, black-backed barbet, Anchieta's chagra, speckled mousebirds and various sunbirds often visible in the nearby forest.

Lake Ndolwa Although shoebills have been spotted here at a quiet place on the southern side of the park, there have been just two recorded sightings; they're very, very rare. A small bench on an old termite mound affords good views over the lake, which has a resident population of sitatunga and some excellent birdlife.

Chinyangale Plain This lies between the Kasanka River crossing and the Fibwe Hide. A game-viewing road winds through the open plain with palm clumps and plentiful puku. Another road runs along the western side of the Kasanka, going downstream from the crossing. There are often large herds of puku here, and you'll frequently spot bushbuck and warthog.

Chikufwe Plain The Chikufwe Plain (✪ CHIFUN 12°33.066'S; 30°09.645'E) is a large open area of seasonally flooded grassland, which is a favourite place to spot sable, hartebeest and reedbuck. There is a good grass airstrip here, and a loop road around the southern side of the plain.

Conservation centre A new visitor centre was opened in July 2007 to showcase the park's work in conservation and to act as an interpretation centre, with posters, displays, information and videos of the annual bat migration. There is also a limited amount of accommodation designed primarily for students or groups. The centre is 1km from the park gates, but has been built just outside the boundary in the surrounding GMA, so visitors here do not have to pay park fees.

FURTHER INFORMATION If possible, get hold of a copy of *Kasanka – A Visitor's Guide to the Kasanka National Park* before you arrive. It is a delightful and generally comprehensive little guidebook which covers the park in detail (see *Appendix 3*, page 510). You'll also find much useful information on www.kasanka.com.

AROUND KASANKA AND BANGWEULU

There are several sites of interest in the area around Kasanka and Bangweulu, though you'll need a self-contained 4x4 to reach any of them, and local help for some.

LIVINGSTONE MEMORIAL A plain stone monument, under a simple cross, marks the place where David Livingstone's heart was buried in 1873, in the village of Chitambo. (The village has since moved, but Livingstone's heart – and the monument – remain.) After his death, from dysentery and malaria, his followers removed his heart and internal organs, and buried them under a *mupundu* tree that once stood where the monument is now.

In an amazing tribute, his two closest followers, Susi and Chuma, then salted and dried his body before disguising it in a tree and carrying it over 1,000 miles to Bagamoyo (on Tanzania's coast). The journey took them about nine months. From there they took the body by ship to London, where Livingstone was finally buried with full honours in Westminster Abbey on 18 April 1874.

Twenty-five years later, in 1899, the Royal Geographical Society in London sent out a small expedition to cut down the *mupundu* tree and bring a section of its trunk, which had been engraved with the names of Livingstone and three of his party, to London, where it remains to this day.

The present Chief Chitambo, Freddy Chisenga, is the great grandson of the chief who received Livingstone. If you are lucky, and willing to pay him for his time and energy, then he will guide you from his home in Cholilo village to the memorial at Chipundu.

Getting there The monument is clearly marked (if sometimes vaguely positioned) on most maps. The easiest route is to turn north off the Great North Road at ⊕ TUCHIN 13°1.146'S; 30°27.695'E towards Mansa and Samfya. After some 65km, or 10km beyond the sign for Kasanka National Park, turn right in Cholilo onto a dirt road. There is a signpost and sometimes a small market at this turning (⊕ TULIVI 12°29.255'S; 30°20.364'E), which is 27km from the memorial.

Follow the main track here for 1km, turning left at Musangashi School (there's a sign to the chief's palace). After 500m, bear right to avoid the chief's palace, or left if you want to visit the chief. Then continue straight on, passing Mupopolo Health Centre, for about a further 25km, till you get to a clinic on the left. Here you should sign the visitors' book and will sometimes be asked to pay a small entry fee. The memorial (⊕ LIVMEM 12°17.970'S; 30°17.580'E) is signposted a little way beyond the clinic, to the left, just before Chipundu School. There are toilets on site.

On your return, it's best to avoid forking left along the old road which is marked on many maps, as this takes a very long time to get back to the tarmac road. It is, however, a useful short cut if you're heading towards Lake Waka Waka or the Bangweulu Wetlands.

KUNDALILA (NKUNDALILA) FALLS (⊕ KUNDAC 13°09.260'S; 30°42.119'E. *Entry US$3 pp; camping US$10 pp*) Kundalila, which means 'cooing dove', is one of Zambia's most beautiful waterfalls. Set in an area of scenic meadows and forests on the edge of the Muchinga Escarpment, the clear stream drops 67m into a crystal pool below; it makes a great place for a picnic among the granite boulders. Look out for blue monkeys that are said to inhabit the forests here, and some cheeky white-necked ravens.

At the bottom of the parking area, there is an old bridge across the Kaombe River. The path then splits and the right branch leads you to the top of the gorge – with no safety fences. The left takes you on a longer walk to the bottom, where there's a beautiful pool for swimming, if you can bear the water's chill. Take a close look at a good topographical map and you'll realise that you're in one of Zambia's highest areas, at an altitude of around 1,500m, so it's frequently cool, windy and pleasantly devoid of mosquitoes.

Campers can pitch in the parking area, where there are basic long-drop toilets but no other facilities, although a new shelter was under construction in 2007. Those with children should be exceedingly careful as there are no fences here, and many of the paths around the falls lead straight to very steep drops at the edge.

Ilse Mwanza reports that the caretaker should also be able to take you to the nearby Kaudina Falls, and possibly also direct you to the Chilindi Chipususha Falls, on the Musumpu River.

Getting there About 65km beyond Serenje, turn southeast off the Great North Road at the small settlement of Kanona (⊕ KANONA 13°4.204'S; 30°38.056'E), where a good dirt track is clearly signposted 'National Monument Kundalila Falls, 14km'. (If you were to take another right turn off this track almost immediately, you would reach the local ZAWA offices.)

Soon you'll cross the railway, then 6km further on there's a Kingdom Hall of Jehovah's Witnesses on the left, before finally reaching the falls. Generally you'll sign in with the caretaker, and pay your entry fee, either at the top of the track, or in the parking/camping area at the new shelter.

NSALU CAVE (*Entry US$3*) This huge semicircular cave, cut into Nsalu Hill, stands about 50m above the level of the surrounding plateau, and contains some excellent San/Bushmen rock paintings. Sadly a few years back the caves were vandalised, but since then the graffiti have been fading much faster than the paintings, so once again most of the paintings can still be seen. It may be possible to camp here, in which case you can expect to pay US$10 per person, plus entry fees.

Archaeological investigations have demonstrated occupation for at least 20,000 years, firstly by Middle and Late Stone-Age people, and later by Iron-Age settlers. The oldest paintings are in yellow and include parallel lines, circles and loops. Later drawings were executed in rust-coloured paint, and even later ones in red and white paints used together. The last paints applied appear as grey-white pigments and have been applied rather clumsily. They contain animal fats and are thought to have been the work of Iron-Age settlers within the last 2,000 years.

When you've finished looking at the paintings, the view from the cave's mouth over the surrounding countryside is great – and if you've lots of energy then a scramble to the top gives an even better view.

Getting there Head north on the Great North Road and take a left turn (✛ TU1NSA 12°51.351'S; 30°46.495'E) at the signpost for Nsalu Cave. This is between Serenje and Mpika, about 30km northeast of Kanona (where you turn to Kundalila Falls) and 15km north of Chitambo Mission Hospital.

Follow this road north for about 14km and then turn left at the rather marvellous sign to 'National Nonument' (✛ TU2NSA 12°44.784'S; 30°44.134'E). After a further 8km this track ends and the cave (✛ NSALUC 12°43.202'S; 30°40.952'E) is visible about halfway up the hill, on which a walking trail is marked. In theory there's a caretaker around to look after the cave, and he may charge a small entry fee – though often there's nobody around. The cave is about half an hour's drive from the main road.

If you continue north on this road, past the 'National Nonument' sign, then you're heading to Lake Waka Waka, Chiundaponde and the Bangweulu Wetlands.

LAKE WAKA WAKA If you're looking for some relatively untouched bush and a quiet setting, where you're very unlikely to encounter anyone else, then this lake is a lovely tranquil spot. It's good for walking, makes a convenient camping stop on the way to Bangweulu Wetlands, and provides a pleasant lunch spot if you're not staying. The views from the surrounding hilltops are panoramic, and I'm reliably informed that the lake is safe to swim in, with no bilharzia, hippos or crocodiles – though I haven't done this myself. There are few settlements around here, and hence a scattering of game is present, including sitatunga and roan antelope, though both are skittish and scarce.

Getting there However you approach, you're really going to need a high-clearance 4x4 once you leave the main tarred roads – and even then you'll find travelling in the rainy season is a challenge.

From the west From the Great North Road, take the road north towards Mansa and Samfya for about 65km, turning right 10km after the sign to Kasanka National Park. (See the directions to the Livingstone Memorial, opposite.) About 1km from the tarmac, keep straight ahead at the Cholilo Basic School, rather than turning left to the Chief's Palace and Livingstone Memorial. Continue past Musangashi

School for about 30km, before turning left (⊕ TUWAKA 12°31.524'S; 30°36.366'E) at a sign for Lake Waka Waka. Note that you'll need a high-clearance vehicle for this track at any time of year; it doesn't get much traffic.

From the south There's a wonderful track from the Great North Road to Lake Waka Waka, but the more northerly sections of this are seldom used. Somewhat inexplicably, the whole track was graded in 2004, so with little traffic it is now one of the country's better bush tracks. But don't be lulled into taking half measures; you'll still need a high-clearance vehicle all year round, and a 4x4 during the rainy season.

Start by turning north at the signpost for Nsalu Cave (⊕ TU1NSA 12°51.351'S; 30°46.495'E), 30km northeast of Kanona. After 14km you'll pass the left turning to Nsalu Cave (⊕ TU2NSA 12°44.784'S; 30°44.134'E), but you continue heading north-northwest. This track basically follows a watershed, with the Lukulu to the east, which drains into Bangweulu, and tributaries of the Kasanka to the west, which drain into the park. Thus with no rivers crossing it, it should be passable even during the rains. When I journeyed in late May, this road was particularly beautiful, though I don't think that more than half a dozen cars had been through since the previous December. The grass was high, the miombo woodlands apparently untouched, and there were very few villages.

About 22km north of the Nsalu turning, the track bumps over a very rocky hill (⊕ WAKHIL 12°36.573'S; 30°39.333'E), and becomes quite indistinct in places. Carry on, and aim for the junction of this track with the 'main' track from Kasanka to Chiundaponde, at ⊕ TUWAKA 12°31.524'S; 30°36.366'E. This is barely a kilometre from the lake.

Where to stay Sadly the little camp that was doing so well here has burned down, but there are hopes that it will be re-opened in time. If it is, you can expect to pay US$5 per person to camp, sharing long-drop toilets and bucket showers using water from the lake. You'll need to be totally self-sufficient and to bring all your own food.

CHIUNDAPONDE Chiundaponde is a typical small Zambian village that lies at the heart of the area covered by this chapter. The inhabitants are mainly small-scale farmers from the Bisa tribe. In the fields around the village they grow cassava, finger millet, sorghum, maize and groundnuts as their staple crops. Finger millet and sorghum are also used to make beer for selling; groundnuts are grown as a cash crop. Some also keep goats and chickens, either for subsistence or to sell, and you'll often have to avoid these as they wander across the road in front of your vehicle. Chiundaponde isn't really a destination for most visitors, but you will go through it if you're visiting the Bangweulu Wetlands, and so it's useful to be able to navigate to/from here.

For directions from Chiundaponde to the Bangweulu Wetlands, see page 330.

Getting there and away
From the south or west Follow the directions (see above, *From the west* and *From the south*) from the Great North Road to the turning for Lake Waka Waka (⊕ TUWAKA 12°31.524'S; 30°36.366'E). From there, head on the track leading north – which bounces gently though miombo woodlands and, increasingly, small farming settlements. By 17km beyond the lake, you'll pass through a small village with a school where, like anywhere else here, you'll probably be the object of much curiosity and interest – if only from the local children. Although you'll be in third gear and the track is sandy in places, this isn't difficult driving.

After about 23km you'll cross a large dambo (✤ DAMBO 12°21.947'S; 30°36.321'E), where the track follows a short causeway. A further 9km on and there's another large dambo to cross (✤ DAMBO2 12°17.384'S; 30°35.407'E), and around 3km later there may be a sign to the new Nakapalayo village (see below) where you can stay. Some 6km after the second dambo, you reach Chiundaponde (✤ CHSCHL 12°14.724'S; 30°34.741'E), where amongst other buildings you'll find a large school.

From the east Approaching from Mpika, leave the Great North Road about 65km from Mpika, and follow the directions given below to get across Lavushi Manda National Park. In the dry season it takes about three hours to reach Chiundaponde from the turn-off. In the wet season, the Lavushi Manda road is so bad that you should consider an alternative route – perhaps even going all the way to Kasanka, and approaching from the west.

🏠 **Where to stay** Although many people will press on to reach Shoebill Camp, there's one option near Chiundaponde that's worth considering:

🏠 **Nakapalayo Village** (6 local-style chalets, camping) Contact via Kasanka (see page 316) (✤ NAKAPA 12°16.542'S; 30°34.565'E). This new tourism project, started in early 2004, is about 3–4km south of Chiundaponde, & is signposted from the main track between Chiundaponde & Waka Waka. The village has built extra chalets in the traditional style: neat, rectangular structures made out of traditional mud bricks with smooth, small, arrow-shaped open windows, & twin or dbl beds with mattresses & mosquito nets. They share very clean long-drop toilets, & bathrooms that are simply reed shelters with showers – buckets on a high shelf from which you scoop water over yourself.

Nakapalayo's people have been trained by members of the Kawaza village community, in South Luangwa, and offer a variety of activities. Most visitors will take a wander around the village with one of the local guides to see, learn & try everyday activities like drawing water, pounding cassava or cultivating the fields. However, there are also opportunities to visit the village headman, or local chief, to learn about the culture & history of the Bisa people; to visit Chiundaponde School, the rural health centre or one of the local churches; to meet the village's traditional healer to learn about the medicinal uses of the area's flora; & to enjoy dancing & storytelling around the fire. If you're staying, then the villagers will also prepare tasty traditional meals for you. This project is still relatively new, but I've had a glowing report from one visitor, who described the people as 'just the most lovely lot in the world'. Nakapalyo is worth supporting if you're passing through the area. *US$45 pp in chalet, or US$15 pp camping, to inc activities & traditional food. Day visit US$10 pp, inc lunch & activities. US$5 pp camping only.*

LAVUSHI MANDA NATIONAL PARK This park is potentially interesting for its hilly and very pleasant landscape, though sadly it has lost some of its animals to poachers over the last few decades. Lavushi Manda's rocky, undulating land would make parts of it difficult to farm, so, until tourism to Zambia is substantially bigger, there is little incentive for anyone to try to rejuvenate its fortunes by restocking it with game. That said, it's likely that for 2008 the Kasanka Trust, working as part of a donor-funded development project, will start to implement some anti-poaching and road-building plans. Watch this large space …

Geography Lavushi Manda is over three times the size of Kasanka, and covers 1,500km² including the Lavushi Hills. It is easily reached from the Great North Road, is almost equidistant from Serenje and Mpika, and the landscape is attractive and undulating. To the north the land slopes away, and the park's streams all drain into the Lulimala, Lukulu or Lumbatwa rivers and thence ultimately into the Bangweulu Basin.

Miombo woodland covers most of the park, with some areas of riparian forest nearer the larger streams and many grassy dambos. Though this is attractive and the scouts report that there are still populations of game left, the area has only one accessible road.

Getting there and around The one east–west road through the park can be dreadful. Driving in the dry season is a challenge with big muddy gullies and areas where the road has just been washed away; when last crossing the park in June, I averaged about 15km/h. In the wet season, I'd expect this to be exceedingly time-consuming at best, and totally impassable at worst.

From the east The turning to Lavushi Manda from the main Mpika–Serenje road (✪ TULMGM 12°16.934'S; 31°8.037'E) is about 141km northeast of the Chinese road (the turning to Mansa and Kasanka) and about 60km from Mpika. There is currently a large and very old signboard here pointing the way to Lavushi Manda and Bangweulu Swamps – but it looks as if it will disintegrate at any moment.

This road goes across the TAZARA railway line, and 12km later enters the park via a scout post and checkpoint (✪ MUFUBU 12°16.240'S; 31°2.627'E). After another 20km or so you'll reach a good, solid concrete bridge over the lovely Lukulu River (✪ LUKULU 12°14.480'S; 30°52.227'E).

From the west There is only one good track which heads east from Chiundaponde, passing the turn-off to Bangweulu. A little over 20km later you'll enter Lavushi Manda at the Lutimwe scout post (✪ LAVUS1 12°14.230'S; 30°46.856'E) – which is just above a crossing of the Lutimwe River. This is a little over 10km from the good bridge over the Lukulu River (✪ LUKULU 12°14.480'S; 30°52.227'E) mentioned above.

Where to stay/What to see and do As yet there are no camps or campsites in Lavushi Manda, and doubt over whether camping is even allowed, although the possibility of a small campsite is under consideration. For the present, if you want to camp, then drop by the regional NPWS office in Mpika and enquire there. If the answer is yes, you'll need all your food, water and equipment. If you are planning on venturing off the main road, then you'd probably want to arrange for one of the scouts from the gate to accompany you.

Driving through the park makes an interesting diversion; it is a convenient route into the Bangweulu Game Management Area. Although few regard it as a destination in itself, it might make a good area for exploration if you are a very dedicated hiker. Talk to the team at Kasanka if you're curious about the latest situation here.

LAKE BANGWEULU AND THE WETLANDS

This area is often described, in clichéd terms, as one of Africa's last great wilderness areas. That might be overstating its case a little, but it is certainly a very large and very wild area, which very few people really know and understand.

Under the Ramsar Convention of 1991, it was designated as a Wetland of International Importance, and since then the WWF has been involved in trying to help the local communities in the GMA to manage it sustainably as their own natural resource; the area covered by the Ramsar protection was enlarged in 2007 to cover the whole swamps. In addition, the United Nations Development Programme (UNDP) has been looking at the potential for reclassifying the area, and as a result the chiefs have agreed to make the entire area into a community partnership park where all illegal fishing will be stopped and the area intensively managed like a national park. As a first step to implementing this decision, all the fishing weirs in the park were to be levelled, with the expectation that fishing would be drastically reduced.

Though most visitors' image of a wilderness area is an unpopulated, barren tract of land, this GMA area does have small villages. It remains home to many local people, who still hunt and fish here, as their ancestors had done for centuries. The old way of conserving an area by displacing the people and proclaiming a national park clearly hasn't worked in much of Zambia: witness the minimal game left in many of the lesser-known parks. This more enlightened approach of leaving the people on the land, and encouraging them to develop through sustainable management of their natural resources, is a more modern way to attempt to preserve as much of the wildlife as possible.

Despite this approach, the area has a growing population of poor, rural people. Many rely, at least partially, on hunting and fishing for their survival. Locals involved with conservation express strong fears for the wildlife's future if no national park is declared here. They comment that it is changing fast, and the wildlife scouts do little to prevent or stop illegal hunting. They doubt that the area's wildlife will live long enough to see a sustainable solution to the problem of co-existence. This would be a shame, as then Zambia will have lost one of its most precious ecosystems, and the local people will have lost a great resource for their future.

GEOGRAPHY The low-lying basin containing Lake Bangweulu and its wetlands receives one of the highest rainfalls in the country – over 1,400mm per annum. On the northwestern edge of the basin is Lake Bangweulu itself, about 50km long and up to 25km wide. This is probably the largest body of water within Zambia's borders, and an excellent spot for watching the local fishermen but, apart from the lake's remarkable white, sandy beaches, is of little interest to most visitors. It is easily reached at Samfya, a small town on the main road from Serenje to Mansa. See also *Chapter 12*, pages 357–8, for comments on Samfya and the surrounding area.

The more fascinating areas here are the vast wetlands to the southeast of the lake, which cover an area two to three times the size of the lake, and the seasonally flooded grasslands to the south of those wetlands.

The wetlands and grasslands are areas with few roads and lots of wildlife. It's one of the few regions of Zambia where the local communities are beginning to use the wildlife in their GMAs as a really sustainable source of income. There is little development here, just a small, tented lodge and a simple community-run camp for visitors who arrive on their own. The area still has many residents who continue to fish and eke out a living directly from the environment, but gradually the community development schemes are beginning to tap into tourism as a way to fund sustainable development.

FLORA AND FAUNA With access to the wetlands, the birdlife can be amazing and the animals impressive. However, choose the time of year for your visit very carefully: the type of fauna to be seen, and the activities required to see it, will vary hugely with the season.

Animals The speciality here is the black lechwe, an attractive dark race of the lechwe that is virtually endemic to the Bangweulu area. The only other places where it has been recorded are the swamps beside Lake Mweru, where its status is now exceedingly questionable, and the Nashinga Swamps near Chinsali, where it has been reintroduced. It is much darker than the red lechwe found throughout

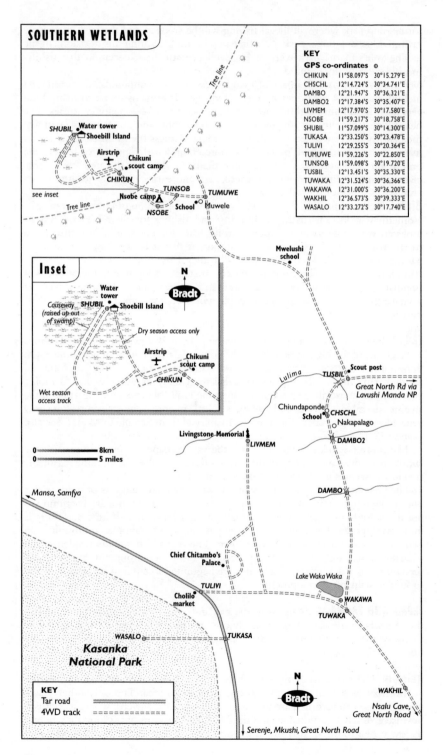

SOUTHERN WETLANDS

KEY

GPS co-ordinates ⊕

CHIKUN	11°58.097'S	30°15.279'E
CHSCHL	12°14.724'S	30°34.741'E
DAMBO	12°21.947'S	30°36.321'E
DAMBO2	12°17.384'S	30°35.407'E
LIVMEM	12°17.970'S	30°17.580'E
NSOBE	11°59.217'S	30°18.758'E
SHUBIL	11°57.099'S	30°14.300'E
TUKASA	12°33.250'S	30°23.478'E
TULIVI	12°29.255'S	30°20.364'E
TUMUWE	11°59.226'S	30°22.850'E
TUNSOB	11°59.098'S	30°19.720'E
TUSBIL	12°13.451'S	30°35.330'E
TUWAKA	12°31.524'S	30°36.366'E
WAKAWA	12°31.000'S	30°36.200'E
WAKHIL	12°36.573'S	30°39.333'E
WASALO	12°33.272'S	30°17.740'E

southern Africa, or the race known as the Kafue lechwe which occur in the Lochinvar area. I think it's by far the most attractive of the three.

The current population in this area is estimated at 115,000 animals, and herds measured in their thousands are common on the dry floodplains around the wetlands. As well as these huge herds of black lechwe you'll find other animals including sitatunga, tsessebe, reedbuck, common duiker and oribi. Zebra are doing very well; about nine were released here at first, translocated from a game farm near Lusaka, and they have now bred up to a healthy herd which is often visible on the plains. Elephant and buffalo are frequently seen; predators are uncommon but hyena, leopard and jackal are sometimes observed. Often seen at dusk or dawn, or on a night drive, side-striped jackal are very common. White-tailed mongooses, civets and genets are also frequent nocturnal sightings.

Birds The Bangweulu area's big attraction is the unusual and rare shoebill (sometimes known as the whale-headed stork). This massive grey bird, whose looks are often compared to a dodo's, is now reckoned to be more closely related to the pelican family than the stork. The shoebill's main stronghold is in the swamps of the Sudd, in southern Sudan, although they are also found in Uganda's Murchison Falls National Park and several other parks in central Africa. The population of shoebills in Bangweulu is reckoned to be as high as 500, making this a vital refuge for this very threatened species. They do not migrate, and so are particularly sensitive to disturbance. They breed in the papyrus here, in May–June, and nowhere else in southern Africa – so visitors should be careful not to disturb them when they are sitting on their nests.

Aside from the elusive shoebill, the birdlife after the rains is amazing. The commoner birds here include the little, cattle, black and great white egrets; black-headed, purple, squacco and grey herons; sacred, glossy and hadeda ibis; knob-billed, yellow-billed, fulvous and white-faced whistling ducks; open-billed storks, pygmy geese, pratincoles and grey-headed gulls. The plovers are well represented, with blacksmith, wattled, three-banded, crowned, Caspian and long-toed varieties – and recently there's also been an influx of spurwing plovers.

Migrants that stop here while the floodwaters are high include flamingos, whilst pelicans and spoonbills are normally resident. Meanwhile Bangweulu is a very important reserve for wattled cranes, which occur in large flocks and are readily seen. (There are greater numbers here than almost anywhere else, with the possible exception of the Kafue Flats.) The wetlands' shallow waters are ideal for smaller waders, like sandpipers, godwits and avocets. Other smaller birds worthy of particular note include the swamp flycatcher, lesser jacana, white-cheeked bee-eater (aka blue-breasted in east African literature) and Fülleborn's and rosy-breasted longclaws (which is the local name for the birds known as pink-throated further south). There are plenty of raptors around, with fish eagles, marsh harriers and bateleur eagles particularly common. On the flat grass plains around the wetlands, Denham's bustards are frequently seen striding around.

The whole area is a remarkable place for birding, and well worth the effort required to get here.

WHEN TO GO There are many reasons to come to Bangweulu – only one of which is the birding. So choose your season carefully.

January and February are the heart of the rainy season, when the waters are rising. It's the worst time of year for the small, biting lechwe flies and other insects, so insect repellent is vital. Arriving with a head-net, covering your face and neck below your hat, would not be going too far.

11

With thanks to Stephanie Debere

The huge, rare and prehistoric-looking shoebill is found only in a few inaccessible spots between southern Sudan and northern Zambia – making it Africa's most sought-after species for birdwatchers.

Shoebills stand up to 1.4m tall, with a strong likeness to the dodo. They have always been named for their ungainly beaks, which resemble a wooden shoe, and older literature refers to them as whale-headed storks, whilst Arab traders knew them as 'abu markub', which means father of the shoe. Their scientific name, *Balaeniceps rex*, means 'king whalehead'.

Shoebills can look rather sinister when viewed head-on, with their massive beaks and a frowning glare, but in profile they appear charmingly dolphin-like with a mouth that apparently smiles, and huge eyelashes. Despite this beguiling look, their mandibles are razor sharp; their upper bill ends in a curved hook that's used to pierce and hold their slippery prey. Their plumage is bluish slate-grey, with a slightly darker head which sports a small tuft of feathers that can be raised to form a crest. Their legs are long and dark, and their toes lack any webbing.

Shoebills inhabit a precise ecological niche: they specialise in feeding on large fish that live in poorly oxygenated waters of swamps and wetlands – particularly lungfish. They are usually seen standing motionless beside slow, deep-water channels, particularly in areas where fish concentrate – like the narrow channels where spreading waters spill out onto seasonally flooded areas. They remain still for hours, waiting for fish to surface for air, when they ambush with a swift and powerful strike. They will prey on species other than lungfish, and are also said to take amphibians, water-snakes, monitor lizards, terrapins, rats, young waterfowl and, some sources report, even young crocodiles.

Although they prefer to hunt in fairly open areas, where it's easy for them to take off if disturbed, they nest in large, flat nests found in denser vegetation – often papyrus. Between one and three eggs are laid, though only one chick usually survives. It takes about four and a half months for this silvery-grey chick to fledge and become independent, then a further three or four years until it first breeds.

Taxonomists have long debated if the shoebill is a member of the stork, the heron or the pelican family, as various characteristics suggest one or another. However, DNA studies now conclude that shoebills are closely related to pelicans, but in a family of their own.

Given their restricted and remote habit, shoebills are incredibly difficult to study and consequently relatively little is known about them. Estimates of the total world population seem to be around the 10,000–15,000 mark. We know that their main stronghold is in the Sudd, in southern Sudan, and that they are also found in Murchison Falls National Park in Uganda, the Moyowosi-Kigosi Swamp in western Tanzania, Manovo-Gounda-Saint Floris National Park in the Central African Republic, and, allegedly, in Akagera National Park in Rwanda (though nobody on the ground in Rwanda seems to know about them!).

We also know that they are, sadly, occasionally sold for meat by local people and for profit by foreign collectors – as shoebills are one of the most expensive birds in the trade. So if you are fortunate enough to see them, try to keep your distance and minimise any disturbance.

This is a great time for birding, as many of the residents will be in breeding plumage, and there will be lots of migrants around – although shoebills usually arrive only at the end of February. The lechwe are in the swamps at this time, whilst other mammals have retreated to the woodlands on the margins of the water.

Water levels peak in **March**, though the rains draw to a close only around April. From **April to May** the water levels start slowly to recede and travelling begins to get easier by the end of May. This is the best time to go for shoebills, which are often seen within sight of Shoebill Camp, along with countless other wading and water-loving species. Like many of these birds, visitors to Bangweulu will often spend a lot of time wading if they're keen to see shoebills at close range!

Towards the end of this period and into **June and July**, the waters pull back from the flat, seasonally flooded plains around the wetlands, exposing large areas of fertile, open grasslands – like the Chimbwi Plain. These attract huge herds of black lechwe along with tsessebe and other herbivores from the woodland margins. It's a great time for game drives, with night drives often yielding genets, side-striped jackals, civets and various mongooses. In the wetlands, the water has receded further and the shoebills have moved closer to the lake – so seeing them involves longer mokoro (dugout canoe) journeys from Shoebill Camp. That said, in early June I managed half a dozen sightings in one long day – and even later in July you are still almost guaranteed to see a shoebill if you apply enough effort. Though days are warm, the nights are very cold – with temperatures dropping to almost freezing.

In **August and September** the floodplains and outer reaches of the wetlands become even drier; Shoebill Camp is no longer an island, and most wildlife viewing is done on foot or by 4x4. The shoebills have retreated deep into the permanent swamps, and it takes a lot of determination (and a mini-expedition) to get close to them. The Lukulu River is the focus of much wildlife, whilst concentrations of storks and other birds form 'fishing parties' in the remnants of drying pools where fish and snails are stranded.

By **October** the land is parched and dusty everywhere except deep in the heart of the wetlands, far from Shoebill Camp. In **November and December** the first rains bring some relief, as well as a flush of new grass on the plains, which attracts massive herds of black lechwe back from the wetlands, and tsessebe in more moderate numbers from the woodlands.

GETTING THERE Getting to Bangweulu isn't always easy. You'll need to do one of the following:

- Organise a special 'mobile' trip here with an experienced safari company. (I know of none that regularly runs trips here – although the Kasanka team will sometimes organise 4x4 transfers to/from Bangweulu.)
- Fly into here, and then continue by flying out. This is how most people visit; although not cheap it is the easiest way to organise, and the most relaxing way to visit.
- Drive in here with your own fully equipped 4x4. This isn't easy or quick, but it can be fun if you've an adventurous streak and can be self-sufficient.

Organised trips There's only one company working on the ground in this area – and that's the Kasanka Trust (see page 316 for contact details, and www.kasanka.com for an informative website). They run Kasanka National Park and (having bought it a few years ago) Shoebill Camp. You can book a trip with them directly or, more usually, arrange it through the tour operator (see pages 46–8) who is organising the rest of your trip in Zambia for about the same price as booking direct.

Fly-in trips These must be pre-arranged. You can fly in to Shoebill Camp, as there is an airstrip (called Chimbwe) at Chikuni, just 3km from Shoebill. You'll be transferred to the camp from there, and your activities will be arranged for you. There is currently no 'schedule' for these flight transfers, and so they are relatively costly for one person because you need to hire the whole plane. Consequently, the price becomes more economic for two or three passengers. Flying in will give you a view of the wetlands and surrounding plains that you can't get from the ground – it's fascinating!

Driving yourself From around November to April, driving yourself on any of these routes can be very challenging – not to say wet, muddy and very slow. If you don't know what you're doing, you're likely to get stranded. By contrast, in the dry season it is fine, although note that there are very few vehicles on some of these tracks, and you always need a fully equipped 4x4 – with your own food and supplies

From Chiundaponde to Chikuni If you're approaching from Waka Waka, then to reach Bangweulu just continue straight through Chiundaponde, heading roughly north. After leaving the village, you'll find the track bends slowly round to the right before crossing a small bridge. Barely 500m after this bridge is a left turn (✪ TUSBIL 12°13.451'S; 30°35.330'E) onto a track which is small and easy to miss; this leads northwest to Bangweulu. This turning is about 4km east of Chiundaponde, and a fraction under two hours' drive from Waka Waka.

Barely 100m north of the turning is a scout post – and it's always worth checking with the scouts here for the latest news and directions. (There's a fairly reliable radio here that's in close touch with Chikuni and, in case of problems, could even reach Kasanka.) Follow the track northwest, and after about 19km you'll pass Mwelushi Middle Basic School. In another 20km you'll reach Muwele village (✪ TUMUWE 11°59.226'S; 30°22.850'E) where the track splits; the left fork leads in a more westerly direction towards Chikuni. At times this track resembles more of a footpath than a road, but don't give up!

About 6km after the village, the road forks (✪ TUNSOB 11°59.098'S; 30°19.720'E), with the left turn going to Nsobe Camp. If you continue straight on, without turning to Nsobe, you will soon emerge from low scrub into a plain of open grass, stretching for as far as you can see. (Look around you – that dark reddish colour on the horizon may just be thousands of black lechwe!) Here you'll see the start of a long causeway leading to Chikuni; this is in poor condition, and generally not used. In recent years it has been better, in the dry season, to follow the vehicle tracks which run parallel to the causeway. In the wet season you really need experienced, up-to-date local advice – which, when levels are low, will generally be to splash through the water on existing tracks. During periods when water levels are very high, Chikuni has been inaccessible by vehicle.

However you are proceeding across the plains, about 8km after the turning to Nsobe, you reach the small scout post of Chikuni (✪ CHIKUN 11°58.097'S; 30°15.279'E). Chikuni literally stands out as it's on top of a small rise in the plains, marked very clearly by a tall eucalyptus tree. This is one of the few trees within sight on the plains; there is another at Kaleha, about 8km east along the Lukulu River.

If you're going to Shoebill Camp then you need to have pre-arranged your stay, and Chikuni is often the rendezvous point where you leave your vehicle, and continue by mokoro; in any case, you should stop, check with the scouts, and sign the register. The scouts here have a radio to contact Shoebill Camp (as well as the ZAWA scout post on the road from Chiundaponde). Somewhere beyond Chikuni, depending on water levels, the wetlands begin.

From Chikuni to Shoebill You should pre-book your time at Shoebill Camp, so take advice from the Kasanka team about how to get from Chikuni to Shoebill at the time of year when you are going. If the water's high (typically January to June) then you may need to leave your vehicle at Chikuni and reach the camp by mokoro.

Later in the year you should be able to drive, in which case you sign in with the scouts at Chikuni and then pass straight through. Follow the direction of the airstrip for part of its length, and then hit out at 30° to your right, where you should find the tracks of other vehicles to the Shoebill Island causeway. If in doubt, try scanning the flat horizon for Shoebill's distinctive rectangular water tower amongst a patch of small trees.

Facing the camp, you will need to bear slightly to the left in order to join the beginning of the causeway (or later on, depending on the water levels). However, the route varies a lot with the particular season, and so it's vital that you get directions from the team at Kasanka, or the scouts at Chikuni, before you try to drive here.

Where to stay There are two main camps in the Bangweulu area, Shoebill and Nsobe, but the latter is now entirely dedicated to hunting, and is no longer a suitable place for photographic guests. If you're on an organised trip, or flying in, then you'll be staying at Shoebill.

If you're driving yourself in a self-contained 4x4 with all your supplies (there is no other sensible way!) then you could possibly stop at Nakapalayo village on the way to Bangweulu (the campsite at Muwele village is no longer recommended except in an emergency). However, note that Shoebill Camp is further into the wetlands than the other camps – so most trips end up there at some stage!

Shoebill Island Camp (5 Meru-style tents, 4 chalets) Contact via Kasanka (see page 316) (⊕ SHUBIL 11°57.099'S; 30°14.300'E). Shoebill Camp stands on a small, permanent island which lies only 2.5km northwest of Chikuni, as the stork flies. During the rains & for a few months afterwards, this is within the wetlands, surrounded by channels & lagoons. Later in the year, it's left high & dry & accessible by 4x4 from Chikuni.

Facilities are simple in this old-style safari camp. The original walk-in Meru-style tents each have a private bucket shower (hot water supplied on request) just behind it, & a private flush toilet a few metres further away. Added to these there are now 4 rather larger reed-&-thatch chalets, also with private flush toilets. Alternatively, it is sometimes possible to camp.

The camp's other buildings are also built with thatched roofs on grass walls, including a bar/dining area & a breakfast room-cum-lookout point. During your stay, do make the effort to see the camp's

best view over the swamps – by climbing the water tower.

Activities from here depend on the time of year; if there isn't enough water to travel through the swamps by canoe, the usual form of water transport, then the guides will take you walking over the floating reed bed in search of shoebills & other wildlife. Alternatively, drives will take you to the drier areas of the plains & into the surrounding woodlands.

Shoebill Camp isn't luxurious by modern safari standards, but it is gradually being upgraded & becoming more comfortable. It remains by far the best option in this area, where the environment, flora & fauna are fascinating, & the activities can be excellent. This is a great destination for the adventurous who are keen on their wildlife, but it really needs to be booked in advance. *Kw200,000 pp self-catering; US$340/460 pp sharing/sgl, inc FB, activities (best pre-arranged), laundry, & park fees; camping US$10 pp; boating & guides extra. ⊕ all year when accessible – usually Mar–Jan.*

WHAT TO SEE AND DO Driving, walking (often wading!), boating and canoeing are the activities here, all of which must be done with guides. While the black lechwe are spectacular, the birdlife is Bangweulu's main attraction, and the ungainly shoebill is a particular favourite among visitors.

As you might expect from an area which is seasonally flooded, and whose name translates as 'where the water meets the sky', Bangweulu is a largely trackless wilderness. It is easy to get lost if you simply head into it by yourself, and indiscriminate driving does much damage to both the soil structure and the ground-nesting birds. It is strongly recommended on safety and conservation grounds that 4x4 owners use one of the camps as a base for their explorations; and you should take local advice about where to go and how to minimise your environmental impact.

ISANGANO NATIONAL PARK

East of Lake Bangweulu, Isangano National Park covers 840km² of flat, well-watered grassland. The western side of the park forms part of the Bangweulu Wetlands, which are seasonally flooded.

While the park's ecosystem was originally the same as that of the Bangweulu GMAs, it is reliably reported that the game in Isangano has totally disappeared because of settlement, agriculture and the consequent subsistence hunting. There is no internal road network within the park at all, though there is quite a high density of subsistence farmers settled within its boundaries. With this in mind, it's very doubtful that Isangano will ever become a national park in anything but name. Visitors are advised to look toward the Bangweulu area if they want to visit this type of region. At least there is some infrastructure, and the local communities in the area will derive benefit from your visit.

12

Northern Zambia

To explore northern Zambia properly, and to visit the national parks here, requires some determination, or at least advance planning. All of the area's three main national parks have suffered from neglect over the years. However one, Sumbu, is hanging on with a couple of small lodges that could lead to a promising future. This large reserve is bounded by GMAs and Lake Tanganyika, and promises fishing and diving as well as more traditional safari pursuits.

Tanganyika is one of the largest lakes in east Africa's Great Rift Valley, and has a rich aquatic life found nowhere else. Even outside the park small lodges have sprung up for casual visitors – the snorkelling and fishing are good and it's a pleasant place to relax.

The north's other two parks, Mweru Wantipa and Lusenga Plain, may take more to get them back on the map, as neither has organised facilities for visitors, or good roads within it. Years of poaching have reduced the populations of game animals within them, and what animals are left remain shy and understandably wary of humankind. Outside of the national parks, this part of northern Zambia is a fascinating area, and there are numerous sights and waterfalls at which to stop and wonder.

Finally, a word about Nyika, a high plateau that straddles the Malawi border and provides the Luangwa with many of its tributaries. There are national parks on both sides of the border. Nyika Plateau National Park, on the Zambian side, is unlike anywhere else in the country: high mountains clothed in rolling heathlands and often draped with mist. It's a great walking destination, a cool respite after the heat of the Luangwa Valley and home to numerous endemic species. However, it's easiest to access from the east, from Malawi, and so it's often forgotten when talking of Zambian national parks.

GETTING ORGANISED

Most tour operators based in Zambia specialise in wildlife safaris, but one is dedicated to northern Zambia:

Thorn Tree Safaris ℡ 021 4221615; m 097 7436267, 096 6436267; e claire@ thorntreesafaris.com, thorntreesafaris@yahoo.com; www.thorntreesafaris.com. Run by Claire Powell, daughter of the owners of Thorn Tree Guesthouse, the mobile-safari operation of the same name covers the whole country but specialises in the north. All trips are tailor made, & can combine diving & dhow safaris on Lake Tanganyika with more conventional wildlife safaris.

THE GREAT NORTH ROAD TO MPULUNGU

The Great North Road stretches from Lusaka through Kapiri Mposhi to Mpika. Here it divides, with one fork going through Kasama and on to Mbala and

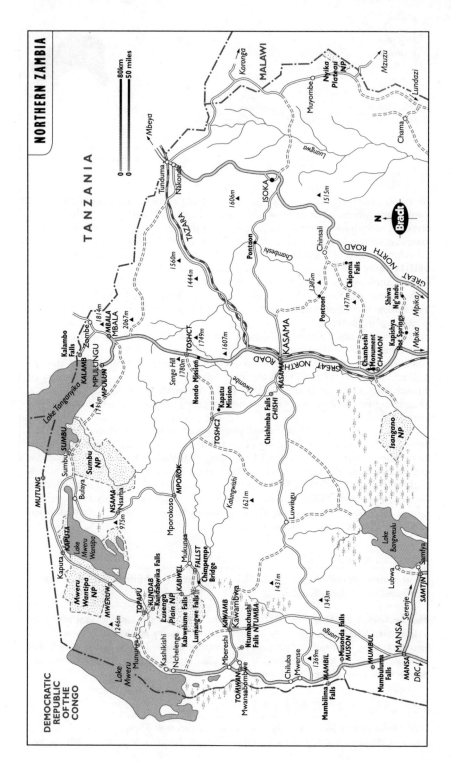

NORTHERN ZAMBIA

Mpulungu – about 1,150km. This is the region's main artery, and is tarred all the way but is in a variable state of repair. Broadly, the road from Lusaka to Kasama is in pretty good condition, but from here the pot-holes increase, made considerably worse by the heavy rains of 2007, and several stretches require considerable care; don't even think of exceeding 80km/h along here. The final stretch, between Mbala and Mpulungu, is particularly bad.

If you are driving between Lusaka and Lake Tanganyika, then one of the small lodges near Mkushi, and perhaps one of Kasama's guesthouses, could provide essential respites from long hours of pot-hole dodging on the main road.

KASAMA Kasama is centrally located, about 860km from Lusaka. Visitors to northern Zambia will invariably end up spending some time here, even if only to refuel and buy a few soft drinks. It is a busy little town, the regional capital, with lots going on. As it acts as a supply centre for much of the north of the country, there are some well-stocked stores, and a relatively large amount of traffic coming into, and leaving, town.

Getting there

By air There have been no scheduled flights to Kasama since 2005, so those wishing to fly in the vicinity are reliant on charter flights. The regional specialist is Sky Trails (see page 67).

By train The TAZARA station is about 7km south of town, on the right as you enter from Mpika. This is your last chance to disembark at a major town before the railroad turns east, away from Lake Tanganyika, towards the border at Tunduma.

The express train from Kapiri Mposhi to Dar es Salaam passes through Kasama on Wednesday and Saturday at about 03.19, returning at 22.07 on Tuesday and Friday. A return ticket to Dar costs about Kw70,000 in third class, rising to Kw120,000 in first class. For details, see pages 381–2.

By bus Kasama is an important regional hub for buses between Lusaka and the north, linking the town with Mbala and Mpulungu on Lake Tanganyika. Confusingly, each bus company has its own terminus, though the most reliable – Germin and Juldan Motors – are both based on Golf Road.

GPS REFERENCES FOR NORTHERN ZAMBIA

CHAMON	10°54.634'S; 31°05.344'E	MPULUN	08°45.907'S; 31 °06.368'E
CHIMBR	09°33.082'S; 29°26.937'E	MUMBUL	10°55.801'S; 28°44.178'E
CHISHI	10°06.465'S; 30°55.100'E	MUSON	10°42.856'S; 28°48.858'E
FALLST	09°32.239'S; 29°27.874'E	MUTUNG	08°33.839'S; 30°12.405'E
KABWEL	09°31.432'S; 29°21.267'E	MWANSA	09°49.25'S; 028°45.35'E
KALAMB	08°35.831'S; 31°14.397'E	MWERUP	08°53.572'S; 29°28.878'E
KAPUTA	08°28.503'S; 29°39.990'E	NSAMA	08°53.448'S; 29°56.896'E
KASAMA	10 °12.440'S; 31°11.290'E	NTUMBA	09°51.167'S; 28°56.652'E
KAWAMB	09°47.605'S; 29°04.675'E	SAMFYA	11°20.437'S; 29°33.526'E
KUNDAB	9°13.058'S; 29°18.258'E	SAMTJN	11°21.126'S; 29°29.453'E
MAMBIL	10°33.791'S; 28°48.858'E	SUMBU	08°31.221'S; 30°28.629'E
MANSA	11°12.076'S; 28°53.451'E	TOKAPU	09°07.531'S; 29°412.996'E
MBALA	08°50.694'S; 31°22.325'E	TOMWAN	09°49.317'S; 28°45.474'E
MBERES	09°44.078'S; 28°47.350'E	TOSHCT	09°27.486'S; 31°13.136'E
MPOROK	09°21.831'S; 30°07.432'E	TOSHC2	09°40.270'S; 30°41.620'E

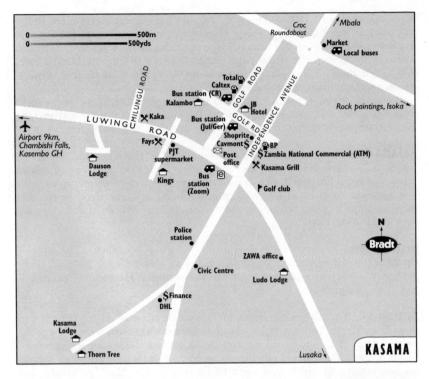

In a recently introduced service between Kasama and the capital, buses leave Lusaka at 16.00, arriving in Kasama at 02.00; the return bus departs from Kasama at 22.00, arriving in Lusaka early in the morning. Fares are Kw110,000 one way. Heading north, coaches depart from Kasama at about 14.00, arriving in Mpulungu at around 17.00 each afternoon.

There is also a postbus to Kasama from Lusaka, arriving in the town every Monday, Wednesday and Friday at 17.00.

For those heading west to Luwingu, the bus station is on the Luwingu Road towards the airport.

Going east is usually fairly straightforward, and the road to Nakonde is pretty good, but it's worth checking the state of the roads at the end of the rainy season. If any of the pontoons are out of action, there's usually a sign on the way out of town saying so. An alternative option is to take the TAZARA train to Nakonde, at the border, then go south by bus.

Hitchhiking Kasama is a good place for hitching. If you want to go north, to Mbala or Mpulungu, walk out beyond the roundabout with the crocodile statue, near the market, and start hitching there.

If you're heading south towards Mpika then you need to walk out past the TAZARA station, or perhaps a little further, hitching as you walk. There are some memorable speed humps on this road, which should slow down even the most ardent of speed-kings to a crawl.

Heading west or east is more difficult, as there is much less traffic. However, a traveller going in either direction is something of a rarity, so novelty value will encourage potential lifts. That said, most drivers will not have a clue where you're heading for.

Where to stay and eat

There's no shortage of places to stay in Kasama, which boasts over 30 guesthouses. Of these, a few stand out, with Thorn Tree and Kasembo particularly recommended.

In town

🏠 **Dauson Lodge** (7 rooms) Luwingu Rd; m 097 7760900. Just off the Luwingu Rd to the airport, & a 5-min walk from the crossroads, this is a quiet, pleasant lodge. Its en-suite rooms, each with a dbl bed, fan, mosi net, TV & fridge, are spotlessly clean, & for TV addicts there's a large lounge with a big screen. Meals are available to residents, with the house special (*chicken or beef stew at Kw18,000*). $ *inc cont b/fast.*

🏠 **JB Hotel** (30 rooms) Golf Rd; ☎ 04 221452; m 097 7844149. With its central location opposite the town's fuel stations, JB is a pleasant hotel set in unexpectedly attractive gardens, with an outside bar & shaded gazebos. Inside, the rooms, 20 of them en suite, lead off rather institutional corridors but all are clean & cool, with tiled floors, as well as TVs, mosi nets & fridges. Meals are served in the restaurant (*lunch & dinner* $). $ *inc cont b/fast.*

🏠 **Kasama Lodge** (11 rooms) Zambia Rd; ☎/f 04 221039, 222825. Opposite Thorn Tree Guesthouse, & professionally run by the Hostels Board of Management, this small hotel has an airy location overlooking the escarpment. En-suite rooms are clean & modern, each with TV, kettle, mosi net & fan, & some ($$$) with a sofa & fridge too. There's a bar & restaurant (*b/fast Kw25,000, lunch/dinner Kw40,000*), and at the back is a pleasant courtyard. $$

🏠 **King's Guesthouse** (12 rooms) 2 Mulilansolo Cres; m 097 7513255. Tucked away behind gates off Luwingu Rd, King's seems to be larger inside than would seem possible. Rooms & chalets are dotted around the mature gardens, some with a veranda & chairs, & all en suite. Thatched sunshades shelter groups of tables & chairs among the trees, interspersed with life-size models of kudu, hippo & other animals. Inside there's a central lounge with a seriously ornate TV, & a dining area (*where lunch or dinner cost* $$). $ *inc cont b/fast.*

🏠 **Ludo Lodge** (9 rooms) Mpika Rd; m 097 7450745. On the right of the road to Lusaka, just past the golf club and next to the ZAWA offices,

Ludo Lodge is well managed & very clean. En-suite rooms are nicely appointed with pine furniture & tiled floors, as well as a TV, fan & fridge. Meals are served in the restaurant (*b/fast Kw25,000; lunch or dinner* $$). $ *inc cont b/fast.*

🏠 **Thorn Tree Guesthouse** (6 rooms) Zambia Rd; ☎/f 04 221615; e kansato@zamnet.zm. Hazel & Ewart Powell came to this area of Zambia to teach in 1969 & stayed on to combine teaching with running a guesthouse. Consequently they've a fund of knowledge on the local area & its people, & can help you get the best out of the region.

You'll find Thorn Tree about 1km southwest of town, on the edge of an escarpment with a great view; it's a 2-min drive or 10-min walk. To get there, turn left at the main crossroads as you enter Kasama from Lusaka, & continue for about 300m. Pass the government offices on the left, & a park on the right, then take the right-hand fork & carry on for a further 650m; the guesthouse is on the left.

Rooms are divided between the main house, which has 2 dbl bedrooms, one en suite & the 2nd with a private bathroom, & a purpose-built block whose en-suite rooms overlook the garden. All have mosquito nets, fans & TV, & all share a lounge, bar & dining area (*dinner* $$$). Hazel will arrange good, family-style meals to suit you, with most of the ingredients produced here on the farm – from oranges & limes to eggs, coffee & tea, & even the jams or peanut butter at b/fast.

You can arrange for Ewart to collect you from the airport, station or buses. Similarly, if you want to play tennis or golf, or swim, or if you need transport to a local attraction such as Chishimba Falls, they can help. For trips farther afield, Claire Powell runs a small safari company, Thorn Tree Safaris (see page 333) with a particular focus on the Northern Province. Closer to home, Thorn Tree also has a small plunge pool in the grounds. It's a very homely place, suitable for children, where you can easily feel part of the family. $

Out of town

🏠 **Kasembo Guesthouse** (9 rooms) Luwingu Rd; ☎ 04 221369 (office hours only); e bshone@zamnet.zm (✪ KASEMB 10°13.714'S; 31°07.506'E). Some 8km west of Kasama, Kasembo Guesthouse is

on the farm of the same name. To get there, take Luwingu Rd east for about 750m beyond the airport, then turn left turn down a farm road (✪ TOKASE 10°13.239'S; 31°07.665'E), signposted to

Kasembo Farms, & follow the signs to the guesthouse; it's about 1km from the turn-off.

Kasembo Farms was founded 50 years ago & is now owned & run by the Missionaries of Marianhill. It stretches for about 1,000 acres, & keeps around 175 Friesian cows (40 are milked), 150 pigs, 150 sheep, 2,000 hens for egg laying, & a few thousand chickens for the pot. The priests say that they leave things as natural as possible. 'Our vegetable garden has never seen a grain of fertiliser in its existence,' commented one. With most of the basic ingredients grown on the farm, it's no surprise that meals are a highlight here.

Accommodation for visitors (of any creed) consists of large rooms grouped in pairs around a grassy central area, shaded by indigenous trees, & near a good pool. Each pair of rooms shares a toilet & separate shower, while each room has locally made pine furniture with a dbl or twin beds, mosquito nets, a fan, fridge & TV. Just one has its own bathroom & separate lounge. It's a cool, tranquil spot, completely without hassle.

The missionaries make a point of ensuring that the service is attentive & discussions with them can give you an interesting insight into the area. Several types of local beer & a few spirits are on offer during meals (b/fast $; lunch/dinner $$). If you arrive in town & want to stay then ask at the Kasembo Farms shop, behind PEP Stores & near the Caltex fuel station. $, b/fast extra.

Bushcamping If you just want a quiet place in the bush to camp 'rough' around Kasama, then one very experienced old Zambian hand recommended the old (defunct) Kalungwishi State Ranch to me, about two hours' drive from town. He comments that it's a fantastic place to explore and is enormous with very few local people about and lots of nice habitat for birds, including good miombo woodlands and large dambos.

To get there take the Luwingu Road, then turn north before you reach Luwingu (about 20km). Drive past Chitoshi and aim for the headwaters of the Kalungwishi River. (You'll need a good map of the area!) Pass the trig-point tower (from which there is a good view, if you climb it) and take a left into the old ranch. There are two entrance roads to Kalungwishi, and at least one still has a sign.

The reality is that you can camp safely pretty well anywhere in this region – just be sure to ask if you are near a village.

✖ Where to eat
For a bite to eat there are lots of small cafés, including Fays on Luwingu Road. For something a bit more substantial, head for the **Kasama Grill** on Independence Avenue, close to the crossroads.

If you are driving towards Mbala, you won't go hungry on the road, since 107km north of Kasama you come to a collection of roadside stalls near Senga Hill (✪ SENGA 09°21.968'S; 31°14.496'E). These sell all manner of fast food, including chicken and chips, fritters, and delicious potato samosas that almost justify a stop in their own right.

Other practicalities Shoprite has come to Kasama, and with it a vast array of foodstuffs and commodities are now obtainable that were very difficult to find previously.

Should you need information on the national parks, there's a ZAWA office in town, next to Ludo Lodge on the Lusaka road.

Excursions around Kasama
Rock paintings (*Entry US$3 pp*) There are over 700 cave paintings outside Kasama, most of them to the east of the town, making this one of the richest areas for rock art anywhere in Africa. While a few of the images are representational, the tradition here is of enigmatic geometric designs that defy easy interpretation. The art is generally considered to be the work of the Twa people, around 2,000 years old, but has variously been dated to late Stone-Age peoples.

The paintings are spread over a wide area across six recognised sites: Sumina, Mulundu and Changa are to the south of the road; Mwela and Muankole to the north; while Luimbo lies in the opposite direction, just beyond the airport on the left. To reach the main sites, take the road towards Isoka, east of Kasama, for about 6km until you see a sign indicating that this is a national monument. Sign in at the kiosk with the caretaker, and he will lead you around the paintings (and would appreciate a tip at the end).

While it's possible to spend hours here, for most casual visitors just a few paintings will suffice to give an idea of the style and scale of the work. Highlights include the Lion at Sumina, and a series of three paintings on the Mwela site (⊕ MWELA 10°12.250'S; 31°13.958'E). An excellent book on the paintings, *Zambia's Ancient Rock Art: The Paintings of Kasama*, is available in Lusaka; for details, see *Appendix 3*, page 510.

Chishimba Falls (*Entry US$3 pp, US$3 per vehicle; camping US$10 pp*) The Luombe River at Chishimba is harnessed partially to run an unobtrusive hydro-electric station, but the water that is left makes for a super series of waterfalls: one artificial and the other two natural. The first, Mutumuna, has a drop of about 20m where it descends onto a rocky riverbed, and it's probably the prettiest of the three. In the centre, protected by a weir, is Kevala, more of a series of rapids than falls, with a large pool created by the weir. The third, Chishimba itself, is a short walk downstream. Here, water spouts over steep cliffs into a deep, rocky canyon that is, according to legend, inhabited by spirits. If you walk right down to the bottom you can stand behind the curtain of water with the rock face at your back and the water in front of you.

Close to the central weir are a sheltered picnic place and a campsite with long-drop toilets. Walkways have been constructed between the falls, with thatched viewing shelters at strategic points, but note that at Chishimba Falls in particular there is a sheer drop that is not fenced, so it is important to take extra care, especially if you are travelling with children. The helpful caretaker is usually happy to act as a guide.

To get to Chishimba (⊕ CHISHI 10°06.465'S; 30°55.100'E), head west out of Kasama on the tarred Luwingu Road towards the airport. Continue along here for 25km, to the end of the tar, then turn right onto the wide gravel road to Mporokoso. Follow this for about 11km to a clear signpost to the falls (⊕ TOCHIS 10°06.176'S; 30°55.694'E), where you turn left, then right again after about 200m, and continue for a further 500m to a parking area.

Chambeshi Monument At the north end of the bridge over the Chambeshi River, about 85km south of Kasama, is a monument beside the road (⊕ CHAMON 10°54.634'S; 31°05.344'E). It marks the place where General von Lettow-Vorbeck, Commander of the German forces in East Africa during World War I, surrendered to Hector Croad, the British District Commissioner, on 14 November 1918.

Von Lettow-Vorbeck and his forces had marched south from German East Africa (now Tanzania). They didn't realise that the war in Europe had been over for three days until told by Croad. Upon hearing the news from the British the Germans agreed to march back to Abercorn (now called Mbala) and there hand over their prisoners to the British. It seems as if it was all very civilised.

Part of the monument is a breech-loading field gun, made in 1890, which was the type that the German forces used during World War I.

MBALA The small town of Mbala lies just off the road from Kasama to Mpulungu. From here, the road to Mpulungu descends into the merciless heat of the rift valley – so enjoy the relative cool whilst you can.

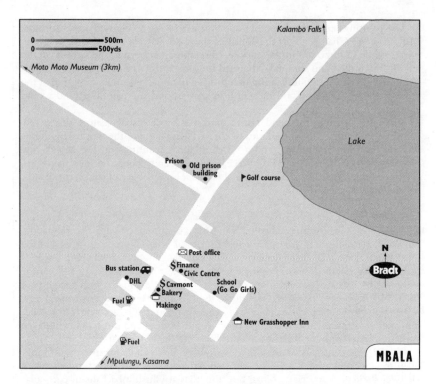

Known as Abercorn when the country was under British rule, Mbala was where the German General von Lettow-Vorbeck handed over his prisoners to the British at the end of World War 1 (see above). Today, it is a quiet backwater notable for the Moto Moto Museum, which is one of the country's best museums. It is also the access point by road for Kalambo Falls (see opposite).

Mbala has a couple of fuel stations, two banks, a post office and even a small prison (the old prison building is now a historic monument). You can buy most things in the shops, including a decent selection of fresh fruit and vegetables from Tafisa Trading, opposite the bus station.

Getting there and away Regular long-distance buses ply the route between Lusaka and Mpulungu, stopping at the bus station on Mbala's main street. Typically, southbound buses leave Mbala at around 04.30 each morning. The one-way fare to Lusaka is Kw110,000; to Kasama Kw35,000.

There are also buses to Kitwe run by both Germins and Zoom, between them covering every day except Monday, and leaving Mbala between midnight and 01.30.

Where to stay In theory, Mbala has a selection of places to stay, but the New Grasshopper Inn is the only place that is worthy of recommendation.

New Grasshopper Inn (24 rooms) m 097 7869441. In a relatively peaceful location, but within walking distance of the centre, the New Grasshopper is a friendly & reasonably secure place to stop for the night. Substantial meals such as chicken with

nshima or potatoes ($) are on offer in the simple restaurant, while next door is a cavernous bar that could become rowdy at weekends. $, b/fast extra.

Makungo Guesthouse (12 rooms) Formerly the Abercorn Arms, the Makungu (on the right of the main road, just after the BP station) has seen better days – and is best avoided. Not only are facilities very basic indeed, but I have had a report that it is not safe. Note that the telephone number also covers for the 'bar and bottle stall' ... so at least you're assured of a drink. $, b/fast extra.

⌂ **Christy Inn** (15 rooms) m 097 7869271. Despite early promise, the Christy has rapidly sunk into a state of disrepair. It's about 2km outside town, too, so there's little to draw the visitor. $, b/fast extra.

What to see and do

Moto Moto Museum (⊕ 09.00–16.45 daily exc Christmas & New Year; entry US$3 pp) (✦ MOTOMO 08°49.265'S; 31°21.416'E) Opened in 1974, the museum is perhaps the best place in the country for Bemba history and artefacts. To get there, head north through Mbala, then turn left off the main road towards Kalambo Falls by the old prison. Continue along this road for about 3km, following the signposts; it's clearly signposted.

At its heart is an extensive and well-presented collection of tools, craft instruments, and exhibits connected to traditional ceremonies and witchcraft, originally assembled by Father Corbeil, a missionary stationed at the nearby Kayambi Mission. The museum takes its name from Corbeil's nickname, Bwana Moto: he was renowned for calling for *moto* (KiSwahili for 'fire'). A large-scale reconstruction of a local village serves to put the various artefacts into context, while explanations of the traditional roles of a husband and wife, for example, add fascinating depth.

KALAMBO FALLS (⊕ 06.00–18.00 daily, entry US$3 pp, US$3 per vehicle, camping US$10 pp) (✦ KALAMB 08°35.831'S; 31°14.397'E) For a short distance the Kalambo River marks the boundary between Zambia and Tanzania. At the Kalambo Falls, it plunges over the side of the Great Rift Valley in one vertical drop of about 221m. This is the second-highest waterfall in Africa (after South Africa's Tugela Falls), about double the height of the Victoria Falls, and about the 12th-highest in the world.

The falls may have the impressive statistics, but the real appeal lies in the drama of the setting. On either side of the falls, sheer rock walls frame the river valley far below: Zambia to the south, Tanzania to the north. A large colony of marabou storks breed in the cliffs during the dry season. The falls themselves are at their most spectacular towards the end of the wet season, in February or March, though are worth visiting in any month.

You can camp here, with stunning views to the west across the rift valley. There's a caretaker on site all day, but aside from a small shelter, facilities are limited to a couple of long-drop toilets.

Archaeology Though few visitors realise it, the Kalambo Falls are also one of the most important archaeological sites in southern Africa. Just above the falls, by the side of the river, is a site that appears to have been occupied throughout much of the Stone Age and early Iron Age. The earliest tools and other remains discovered there may be over 300,000 years old, including evidence for the use of fire.

It seems that the earlier sites of occupation were regularly flooded by the river. Each time this occurred, a fine layer of sand was deposited, thus preserving each layer of remains, tools and artefacts in a neat chronological sequence. Much later, the river cut into these original layers of sand and revealed the full sequence of human occupation to modern archaeologists.

For years Kalambo provided the earliest evidence of fire in sub-Saharan Africa – charred logs, ash and charcoal have been discovered amongst the lowest levels of remains. This was a tremendously important step for Stone-Age humans as it enabled them to keep warm and cook food, as well as to use fire to scare off aggressive animals. Burning areas of grass may even have helped man to hunt. However, more recent excavations of older sites in Africa have discovered evidence of the use of fire before the time when we believe that the site at Kalambo was occupied.

The site is also noted for evidence of much later settlement, from the early Iron Age. Archaeologists even speak of a 'Kalambo tradition' of pottery, for which they can find evidence in various sites in northern Zambia. It seems that the early Iron-Age farmers may have gradually displaced indigenous hunter-gatherers from about the 4th century AD: no further Stone-Age remains are found after that date. However, oral history from northern Zambia, along with the extensive rock art around Kasama, speaks of a recent survival of hunter-gatherers alongside farming peoples.

Getting there

By boat-taxi The mouth of the Kalambo River is around 17km from Mpulungu, so adventurous backpackers can take a boat upstream to near the base of the falls, then return the following day. From the lake it is a fairly strenuous but enjoyable 2½-hour walk to the top of the falls, where camping is allowed. You will need to bring all your own food and equipment.

There's a regular boat service along this route (see page 347), on Monday, Wednesday and Friday, taking two hours in each direction. Boats leave the village of Chipwa very early in the morning, returning from Mpulungu the same day at around midday; one-way tickets should be Kw4,000, but a *mzungu* (white person) can expect to pay nearer Kw15,000. Since the times are very approximate, you could end up walking into the falls after dark, so it may be better to negotiate a private trip with one of the fishermen in Mpulungu.

A better option by far is to bring all your provisions and stay at one of the lodges nearer the falls – Mishembe Bay or (if either is open) Kalambo or Isanga Bay. Then you can make a day trip to the falls, perhaps even walking there.

Alternatively, small boats that ply between Mpulungu and Kasanga, in Tanzania, may drop you off one day, and pick you up on the next.

Driving The falls are about 38km from Mbala, along a good track that has been recently graded. In the dry season it's perfectly possible to get through with a 2WD vehicle. Head north out of Mbala on the tar road towards Zombe and the Tanzanian border. Just past the golf club and lake to the right, the tar comes to an end. Beyond the bridge, take the left fork and continue to a clear signpost (✪ TOKALA 08°45.543'S; 31°06.884'E); turn left here – it's about 6km from Mbala. The road goes through villages and woodland, passing the very poor track to Isanga Bay Lodge (✪ TOIBL 08°41.634'S; 31°17.969'E) to the left. After 29km, you'll come to a fork (✪ 08°36.619'S; 31°14.133'E); bear right and follow the road as it descends steeply to the entrance to the falls.

Because of Kalambo's border position, policing it has been difficult in the past, and vehicles left unattended have been likely targets for theft. While this is still a potential hazard, there is a caretaker on site in daylight hours, so the threat is now considerably less.

LAKE TANGANYIKA AND ENVIRONS

LAKE TANGANYIKA Lake Tanganyika is one of a series of geologically old lakes that have filled areas of the main East African Rift Valley. Look at a map of Africa and you will see many of these in a 'string' down the continent: lakes Malawi, Tanganyika, Kivu, Edward and Albert are some of the larger ones. Zambia just has a small tip of Tanganyika within its borders, but it is of importance to the country.

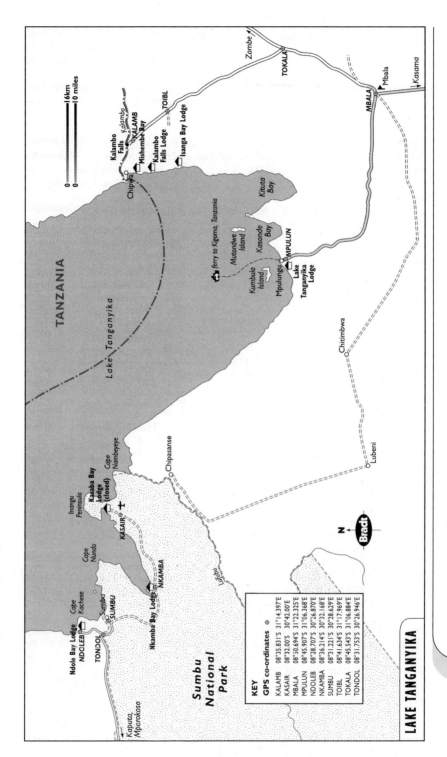

LAKE TANGANYIKA

12

KEY
GPS co-ordinates ⊕

KALAMB	08°35.831'S 31°14.397'E
KASAIR	08°32.00'S 30°42.00'E
MBALA	08°50.694'S 31°22.325'E
MPULUN	08°45.907'S 31°06.368'E
NDOLEB	08°28.707'S 30°26.870'E
NKAMBA	08°36.214'S 30°32.168'E
SUMBU	08°31.221'S 30°28.629'E
TOIBL	08°41.634'S 31°17.969'E
TOKALA	08°45.543'S 31°06.884'E
TONDOL	08°31.753'S 30°26.946'E

Access to Lake Tanganyika grants Zambia a real port with transport links to a whole side of Tanzania and (during peaceable times) direct access to Burundi. It also makes this one corner of Zambia totally different from the rest of the country, with a mix of peoples and a 'tropical central Africa' feel.

There are some well-established lakeside lodges, those to the east within striking distance of Kalambo Falls, and two in the vicinity of the little-known but viable Sumbu National Park.

Geography Lake Tanganyika is the deepest of the Rift Valley Lakes of central/east Africa, with a maximum depth of about 1,470m, and the second-deepest lake in the world. It has an area of around 34,000km² and is estimated to be about 10–15 million years old. The surface layers of water are a tropical 24–28°C and support virtually all of the known life in the lake.

Well below these, where it is too deep for the sun's light to reach, are separate, colder waters. Below about 200m, these are deprived of oxygen and hardly mix with the upper layers. They are currently the subject of much scientific study.

The lake has a variety of habitats around its 3,000km or so of shoreline, ranging from flat sands to marshy areas and boulder-strewn shores.

Flora and fauna

Flora The geology of the rocks around the lake has led to the water being unusually hard (between 7° and 11° dH), alkaline (average 8.4 pH) and rich in minerals for a freshwater lake. It is not an ideal environment for normal aquatic plants, so these are generally found near the entry of rivers into the lake but not elsewhere. Various species of algae have adapted to fill this ecological niche, and extensive 'lawns' of grass-like algae cover many of the lake's submerged rocks.

Animals The water's excellent clarity, the lack of cover and the rocky shores do not encourage either hippo or crocodiles, though both are more common around the relatively undisturbed shores of Sumbu National Park. They are also seen regularly near the mouths of rivers, and their presence must always be considered before you swim. The lake is a reliable source of water for the game, which often come to drink during the dry season.

Birds The birdlife on the shoreline is generally good, and the species found here also tend to represent many more of the typical east African birds than can be found elsewhere in Zambia. The area's more unusual residents include purple-throated cuckoo-shrikes, white-headed saw-wings, stout cisticolas, and Oustalet's white-bellied sunbird.

Fish Lake Tanganyika and the other lakes in the rift valley continue to fascinate both zoologists and aquarists as they have evolved their own endemic species of fish. So far, well over 450 have been identified in Tanganyika, of which over 252 species are in the Zambian part of the lake (and of those, 82 have been identified as endemic in a report by the Ramsar Convention, under which much of Lake Tanganyika and the surrounding area is protected). Most of the lake's fish species are from the *Cichlidae* family – or cichlids (pronounced sick-lids), as they are known. Many of these are small, colourful fish that live close to the surface and the shoreline. Here they inhabit crevices in the rocks and other natural cavities, avoiding the attention of larger, predatory fishes that patrol the deeper, more open, waters.

The lake is the most southerly home of both the goliath tigerfish and an endemic species of perch from the *Lates* family, the silver or Tanganyika perch, *Lates angustrifrons*. Three smaller species of perch are to be found in these waters too, including the smallest, the buka, which along with kapenta is the target of commercial fishermen. It's also an excellent place for the nkupi, which are the largest cichlids in the world. There are also freshwater jellyfish which, interestingly, don't sting, and – very occasionally – a freshwater coelacanth is sighted.

Reptiles Two reptiles are endemic to the lake: the fish-eating Tanganyika water-snake, *Lycodonomorphus bicolor*, and the venomous Tanganyika water cobra, *Boulengerina annulata*.

What to see and do in and around the lake Most of the lodges around the lake can organise a range of watersports and fishing, though it's as well to be aware that if these involve a boat trip, costs will reflect the high cost of fuel. For additional activities around Sumbu, see pages 355–6.

Swimming, snorkelling and diving Tanganyika is a marvellous lake in which to go snorkelling, or even scuba diving, as the numerous fish are beautifully coloured and there is seldom any need to dive deeply. Visibility depends on the state of the water, but can be as high as 10–20m in places. Halfway between Sumbu and Mpulungu is a series of cliffs and drop-offs that are of particular interest to divers, while other popular diving spots include the area around Katete.

If you plan on any watersports, you must consider the **safety** issues. Both crocodiles and hippos are common in parts of the lake, but can be very localised. There is also the venomous if non-aggressive Tanganyika water cobra, which grows up to 2m. While it usually avoids swimmers as terrestrial snakes avoid walkers, you should still watch out for it. There is some doubt about the existence of bilharzia in the lake but you should be aware of the possibility (and see pages 98–9 for general guidelines). If you are considering taking a swim, ask advice from the locals about the precise place that you have in mind. They may not be infallible, but will give you a good idea of where is likely to be safe, and where is not.

Fishing Lake Tanganyika (and especially the Sumbu area) has a first-class reputation in freshwater angling circles, because of the variety of fish that can be caught on rod and line. It is not unusual for visitors to catch a dozen different species in a single visit. The greatest appeal comes from the nkupi, the goliath tigerfish and the Nile perch, the last of which can reach an impressive 80kg in weight.

Northern Zambia **LAKE TANGANYIKA AND ENVIRONS**

12

The best time for fishing is between November and March. Each March sees the annual fishing competition held at Sumbu off the point near Nkamba Bay Lodge. Fly-fishing is becoming increasingly popular, particularly for nkupi and the perch species. Some of the tropical cichlids will also rise to a smaller fly.

There is considerable concern about the sustainability of commercial fishing on the lake, with the spotlight falling on both over-fishing and the impact of global warming on the breeding habits of the fish. Although fishing with nets is illegal within national park waters, the ban is regularly flouted by local fishermen. Nevertheless, commercial fishing is of significant importance, primarily for two species: the buka and the much smaller kapenta.

MPULUNGU Sitting in the heat of the rift valley, about 38km from Mbala, Mpulungu is Zambia's largest port. It's a busy place and visited by many travellers, most of whom are Africans but with the odd backpacker mixed in too. The atmosphere is very international, a mix of various southern, central and east African influences all stirred together by the ferries which circle the lake from port to port.

There is a strong local fishing community and a small but thriving business community, complete with a small contingent of white Africans, expats and even aid workers. So though Mpulungu might seem like the end of the earth when you get off a bus in the pitch-black evening, it isn't.

Getting there and away
By bus Mpulungu is at the most northerly end of the main bus route from Lusaka, via Kabwe, Kapiri Mposhi, Mkushi, Serenje, Mpika and Kasama and Mbala. Buses from Mbala tend to arrive around 07.00, and those heading south leave in the small hours. The fare to Lusaka is Kw120,000. There are several operators on the route, of which the best is considered to be Juldan Motors. The 'terminus' is on the main road, beside the market – you cannot fail to go through it.

There are also buses to Kitwe every day except Monday, departing around midnight.

Driving Mpulungu is the final town on the Great North Road out of Lusaka. The descent from Mbala affords some great views of the lake, but the surface is very uneven and pitted with huge pot-holes, so allow plenty of time.

Hitchhiking Hitching here from Mbala in the afternoon is very easy, with lots of lifts. However, getting out in the morning is virtually impossible. Everybody who has a little space in their vehicle goes to the bus terminus near the market and fills up with paying passengers, so few are interested in a stray hitchhiker walking away from the bus station. So, if you want to get out of Mpulungu, go with the crowd and hang around the main market area, quizzing any likely buses or vehicles. Because of the steep, twisting road out of the valley, heavy or under-powered vehicles can be painfully slow, so get a lighter, more powerful lift if you can.

By ferry Only one of the large international Tanganyika passenger ferries on Lake Tanganyika, the MV *Liemba*, is still operational. It calls at Mpulungu once a week, arriving on a Friday morning at around 07.00 and leaving the same afternoon at around 13.00; actual times very much depend on the cargo.

From Mpulungu the ferry sails over the Tanzanian border to Kasanga, then to Kigoma in the north of Tanzania, with countless places in between. The journey takes up to two days, arriving in Kigoma on Sunday at around 13.00, and departing on Wednesday at about 16.00. Due to the security situation in Burundi, the ferry does not currently dock there.

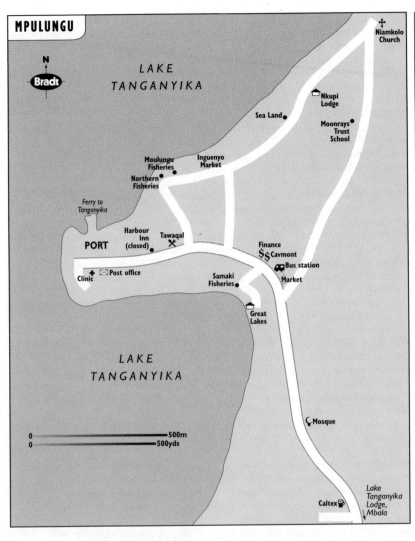

Ferry tickets fall into three classes. In first-class cabins, at US$50 per person, there are two bunks with a basin, while second-class cabins (*US$40 pp*) have four. Third-class passengers pay US$35 each, but take pot luck of seating around the ship. It is also possible to take a car or bike on the ferry. Tickets must be bought on the ship, so your best option is to arrange for them to be purchased in advance; for this, contact Charity at Nkupi Lodge (see page 348). Both food and water are available on board.

By boat-taxi If you need a short trip out to one of the **lodges** on the lake then hire a boat-taxi from the beach-side market, next to Andreas Fisheries. You will need to make sure that the driver knows the lodge that you want, and exactly where it is, and you may want to bargain over the rate a little. Alternatively, if time is on your side, you can use one of the regular boat-taxis that go up the lakeside to the Kalambo River (a 2½-hour walk from Kalambo Falls) on Monday, Wednesday and

Friday, stopping at several villages and taking around two hours in each direction. Boats leave the falls area very early in the morning, returning from Mpulungu the same day some time after midday; one-way tickets should be Kw4,000, but a *muzungu* can expect to pay nearer Kw15,000.

Visitors to **Sumbu** (see page 350) usually depart from Samaki Fishing. To get there turn left down the gravel road opposite the bus station, which is about 1km after the Caltex garage. Boats arrive from Sumbu in the morning every Monday, Wednesday and Friday, returning in the afternoon.

No matter where you are heading, it's essential that you have a crystal-clear deal over the price for the trip, including you and all your baggage, before you set off from Mpulungu – as disagreements on arrival (or worse still, on the lake) are bad news for you and the person running the boat.

Getting organised To organise accommodation, or anything else in the area, there are two excellent options. The first is to contact Mrs Beryl Neilson, who runs Mpulungu's Caltex fuel station (*PO Box 71, Mpulungu;* ℡ *021 4455185;* f *021 4455112*). Coming from Mbala, you pass this on your left about 1km before you reach the market. Mrs Neilson has radio contact with most of the lodges, and acts as a de facto agent for them in town. She'll usually be able to advise what is open, how much it is, and how to get there; she also runs her own boat.

Alternatively, speak to Claire Powell at Thorn Tree Safaris (see page 333). The company maintains a dhow on the lake at Mpulungu, and can organise transfers for up to 15 people, as well as accommodation and trips around the area.

Where to stay If you are backpacking through, or have arrived late in the day, staying in Mpulungu itself for a night or two is probably your best option. Effectively this gives you the choice of the established backpackers' favourite, Nkupi Lodge, or the newly opened Great Lakes. If both are full, you could try **Chamuluzi Guesthouse** opposite the market, or the **district resthouse**, but these wouldn't be top of my list.

For those wishing to stay longer the choice is considerably widened by several lakeside lodges, almost all of which are accessible only by boat.

Nkupi Lodge (9 rooms, camping) ℡ 04 455166; m 097 7456742; 095 5455166, 097 9693971. This relaxed backpackers' retreat has become something of a legend with overlanders, largely because of a total lack of competition & its laid-back owner, Denish. To find it, follow the tar road past the main bus/market area almost to the port, then turn right & follow the coast road until you find Nkupi Lodge on the right. While there are more direct roads leading from the market, it's a confusing area, & this is the clearest route.

Now managed by the very helpful & knowledgeable Charity, the lodge has several large rondavels with stone floors, mesh windows, mosi nets & a fan — on mains electricity. The campsite, & all but one of the rooms (a simple but spacious en-

suite dbl), share clean hot showers & toilets. Beer is available, as is scrupulously boiled water, while food, featuring African & Indian dishes, must be ordered a couple of hours in advance (*mains around Kw20,000*).

Charity can organise all sorts of activities, from Kalambo Falls to paddle-boat trips to one of the islands, to include a picnic & swimming. Just ask her! *Chalet Kw50,000 pp sharing facilities, Kw160,000 per chalet en suite; camping Kw25,000 pp (own tent), Kw35,000 pp in room without bedding.*

Great Lakes (4 chalets) m 097 7351002. This newcomer to the market, owned & run by Salim, is in a central location opposite the mosque. Accommodation consists of thatched en-suite chalets. With a restaurant scheduled to open in 2007, it's one to watch. $$

Lakeside lodges

Lake Tanganyika Lodge (5 chalets, camping) Contact via Thorn Tree Safaris (page 333). Reached

by a short boat-taxi ride, this basic self-catering lodge is right beside the lake, about 5km west of

Mpulungu on a lovely pebble beach. Technically you can reach it along a poor 4x4 track, but it's not currently advisable, though vehicular access is likely to be improved during 2007. To find it, turn west off the main tar road from Mbala about 6km before Mpulungu town centre, immediately after the police checkpoint. Alternatively, charter a boat from the market, costing around Kw25,000 per person, & taking an hour or so.

Both chalets & thatched shelters under which you can camp share toilets & showers, & a fully equipped self-catering kitchen; all visitors need to bring their own food & drink. While standards have slipped recently, there were plans in 2007 to renovate & upgrade the place, adding a deck & braai areas along the lake shore. There's plenty of scope for swimming (blissful) in the lake around the area of the lodge, & the friendly management team will help you arrange boats for fishing, snorkelling, diving, trips to Kalambo Falls & similar excursions. *Chalet US$20 pp, camping US$5 pp.*

Kasakalawe Lodge Although this lodge almost adjacent to Lake Tanganyika Lodge was closed at the time of research, its future was uncertain. However, as it's quite possible that it will have reopened by the time you read this, do ask around.

🏠 **Isanga Bay Lodge** (3 chalets) ☎ 021 1223608; m 097 7393868, 096 6646991; f 021 1235333; e info@isangabay.com; www.isangabay.com; or contact Thorn Tree Safaris (page 333). To the west of Mpulungu, about halfway to the Tanzanian border & within hiking distance of Kalambo Falls, Isanga Bay Lodge is usually reached by boat from Mpulungu; there is safe parking in the town. In theory you could drive in from the Kalambo Falls road north of Mbala (a map is available by email or from Beryl Neilson at the Caltex garage), but in 2007 the 26km track was so bad that it couldn't be recommended, even in a 4x4.

Thatched 4-person wooden chalets built on stilts stand on a beautiful white sandy beach, surrounded by coconut palms & indigenous vegetation. Each has a dbl bed & 2 sgls, all draped with mosquito nets, plus an en-suite shower & toilet, & a veranda overlooking the lake. The nearby campsite has communal ablution facilities. Meals are served in a central thatched *insaka*, where there's also a bar — but guests may also bring in their own drinks at no extra charge.

Activities include good snorkelling among the rocks, hikes to Kalambo Falls, canoeing, fishing, bird walks & even waterskiing. *Chalets US$90 pp FB;*

camping US$10 pp. Transfer from Mpulungu US$95 per boat.

🏠 **Kalambo Falls Lodge** (7 chalets) m 097 7703403. Run by Toby Veall, & often referred to as Toby's Lodge, this was Zambia's first upmarket lodge on the lake. It originally started as a base for catching aquarium fish for export, then the first curious aquarists arrived for trips. Now the lodge has twin-bed or 3-bed thatch-on-stone chalets, each with a private veranda, mosquito nets, solar-powered lighting & its own shower & flush toilet. Meals are taken in a lofty central area, built of stone & designed to remain cool. Activities focus on fishing, snorkelling & diving: underwater visibility in the vicinity is excellent. It remains an ideal spot for aquarists, who can visit the fish house, where a variety of cichlids are kept & bred. Walks to Kalambo Falls (about 2¹/₂hrs away) are also popular. The lodge is 16km from Mpulungu, close to the Kalambo River, & is reached by a short boat transfer or water-taxi. *Around US$175 pp FB.*

🏠 **Mishembe Bay – Luke's Place** (3 chalets, camping) Contact via Thorn Tree Safaris, page 333. Owned & run by Luke Powell, whose parents own Thorn Tree Guesthouse in Kasama, this occupies the last bay on the Zambian side of the shore. It's real Robinson Crusoe stuff — just a pure white sandy beach sheltered in its own bay. Mishembe is usually accessed by water-taxi from Mpulungu taking 1–3hrs (Mon, Wed & Fri, 3hrs), or in 30 mins by private boat (US$100 return for up to 15 people). Hidden among the trees on wooden platforms overlooking the lake are simple reed-&-thatch chalets. These are completely open sided, with roll-down canvas walls for protection against the rain, & walk-in mosquito nets around the twin or dbl beds; each has an en-suite shower & flush toilet. Meals are served under a large fig tree. Under the palm trees, amongst the baboons, monkeys & birds, there's space for campers, who should bring all their own food & equipment. It's a magical place, totally isolated & very good value.

The bay is ideally situated for walks up to Kalambo Falls, which is about 2¹/₂hrs each way, & there is very good snorkelling right in the bay — the visibility is up to 20m, depending on the wind. On a more personal level, Mishembe has strong links with the local community, supporting schools in nearby Chipwa, taking visitors to attend church services in the village, & inviting local choirs to sing at the lodge. *US$100 pp FB; camping US$25 pp.* ⊕ *all year.*

What to see Just a few kilometres east of Mpulungu, beside the lake, you may see a tall, rectangular turret rising above the shoreline as you head to Kalambo Falls or one of the lodges in a water-taxi. This isn't a fort, but the remains of one of Zambia's oldest churches, **Niamkolo Church**. It was originally built by the London Missionary Society around 1893–96, but abandoned in 1902 because of health problems suffered by the missionaries. The original buildings were burned, but in 1962 the walls were restored to their former height and cemented into place. Now they're all there is to see. At 80cm thick in places, they may last for another century yet.

SUMBU NATIONAL PARK

(*Park fees US$10 pp per day; vehicle US$15 per day; fishing US$5 pp per day*) Sumbu National Park covers about 2,020km², and borders on Lake Tanganyika. It also covers a small part of the lake, which means that those boating in these waters are subject to park entry fees, as well as those on land. To the north- and southwest, the park is adjoined by the 360,000ha Kaputa GMA, while between this and the park to the west is the smaller Tondwa GMA, which is leased out to a small professional hunting operator. These two act as a very effective buffer for the park, keeping the local subsistence hunters/poachers out and giving the game numbers a chance to increase. Combined with the presence of two (and potentially three) lodges in this area, this has made Sumbu's future look very promising indeed.

On another promising note, Sumbu is one of several parks in Zambia that have been designated as being 'viable game parks' under a study funded by the EU.

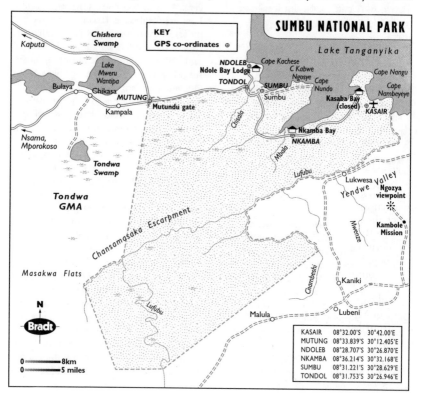

Plans are afoot to change the way the parks are run, and EU money is set to help the less developed parks to become self-sustaining. Eventually, each of Zambia's parks should have greater autonomy, which will allow them to use their own funds for community development schemes as well as anti-poaching operations. This is vital if the wildlife of parks like Sumbu is to recover and tourism is to become a worthwhile source of revenue.

FLORA AND FAUNA Sumbu protects populations of elephant, and a range of antelope including blue-and yellow-backed duiker, roan, sable, bushbuck, waterbuck, sitatunga, the occasional zebra and a large number of puku; there are also reports of eland in the hills. Buffalo herds range up to about 400 individuals, and move around between Sumbu and the neighbouring GMA. The park's main natural predators are lion and leopard, though numbers are uncertain. Although poachers continue to kill occasionally, the animal populations are increasing.

A study in the 1990s concluded that there were still wild dogs in the park and its surrounding GMAs, though there has been no follow-up, and their continued long-term survival was in doubt. I don't know of reports of wild dog since then.

Although Sumbu cannot yet boast huge herds of the larger antelope, elephant or buffalo, there is sufficient game to make a trip to the park worthwhile. Its vegetation and environment are, on the whole, in pristine condition and offer a real Zambian wilderness experience.

The birding is good, with 295 species recorded in the park and the adjacent Tondwa GMA. A number of east African species occur here that you won't find in the rest of southern Africa. Look out especially for the bare-faced go-away bird, common on the open floodplain areas; also a waxbill known as the red-cheeked cordon bleu, occasional ospreys, palmnut vultures and red-faced crombecs. Pel's fishing owl and bat hawks also occur, though not more commonly than elsewhere.

In the lake itself, there are plenty of hippos and a very healthy population of crocodile – some are sufficiently large to dissuade you from even thinking of dipping your toe in the water. For details of fish and reptiles in the lake, see pages 344–5.

GETTING THERE Access has long been the main problem for visitors to the Lake Tanganyika area, and getting to Sumbu is an added challenge. It's difficult, or time-consuming, or very expensive.

By air There is a fully tarred 1,500m airstrip (⊕ KASAIR 08°32.00'S; 30°42.00'E) at the currently closed Kasaba Bay Lodge, which is used by all the lodges for visitors arriving by air. Limited amounts of AV-Gas are usually available, but there are no customs or immigration facilities. Both Ndole Bay and Nkamba Bay lodges collect their passengers from the airstrip by boat, taking about 30 minutes to Nkamba Bay, or 40 minutes to Ndole Bay.

Unfortunately there are no longer any scheduled flights, so the only way to reach here by air is on a chartered aircraft. It's over 500km from Mfuwe or about 800km from Lusaka, so this is an expensive option.

By road Sumbu National Park can be approached relatively easily in a 4x4 via Kaputa or Mporokoso, though neither is a fast option. There is also a very difficult track from Mbala as far as the Lufubu River, which defines the park's eastern boundary – but it's not for the faint-hearted or ill-equipped.

From Mporokoso For most drivers, the most direct approach to the park is from Mporokoso (⊕ MPOROK 09°21.831'S; 30°07.432'E; see pages 366–7). Initially, the road heads more or less north through the village of Munyele and on towards Nsama (⊕ NSAMA 08°53.448'S; 29°56.896'E), close to the eastern shores of Lake Mweru Wantipa. This section is poorly maintained, so allow plenty of time, although the introduction of a number of metal bridges has improved access. **Nsama** itself has a few shops, a secondary school and a Catholic church, indicating its importance in the area.

Beyond Nsama, the road turns east towards Lake Tanganyika and the surface improves considerably. Keen birdwatchers should note that just north of Nsama there's a patch of miombo woodland where the relatively uncommon white-winged starling is easily spotted. There are numerous small villages lining the road, but nowhere of note. Despite mention of Bulaya on several maps, don't expect a town here: it's nothing more than a dot on the map.

About 135km from Mporokoso, and 39km before Sumbu, you'll reach the Mutundu gate (⊕ MUTUNG 08°33.839'S; 30°12.405'E), a game checkpoint that marks the beginning of the national park. This is also where the road from Kaputa (the area's administrative centre) joins the road from Mporokoso to Sumbu.

From here the road runs along the northwestern edge of the park towards Sumbu town (see page 356), with sweeping views over the bay as it descends from the plateau. Some 31km after the Mutondo gate, there's a left turn to Ndole Bay Lodge (⊕ TONDOL 08°31.753'S; 30°26.946'E). To reach the national park gate, continue along the increasingly poor main road for a further 8km or so to the turn-off to Sumbu Town. This also marks the entrance to the national park, at Sumbu gate, and is where you'll have to pay park fees. The road then continues to Nkamba Bay and Kasaba Bay lodges, both of which are within the national park.

From Nchelenge via Kaputa For the first stretch of this route, see *The road to Mweru Wantipa and Kaputa*, page 356.

Beyond Kaputa, the road widens, passing through numerous villages as it crosses the narrow strip between Lake Mweru Wantipa and the DRC border. The lake itself remains out of sight, although fishing nets laid out to dry indicate its proximity to the road. As the road descends, the land around becomes increasingly marshy, with papyrus beds and reeds, and pools dotted with purple water lilies. It's a haven for waterbirds, with reed cormorants, pied and malachite kingfishers, and African jacanas all easy to spot. Eventually, some 83km from Kaputa, you'll emerge onto the Mporokoso–Sumbu road (see above) at the Mutundu gate (⊕ MUTUNG 08°33.839'S; 30°12.405'E), marked on some maps as Kampela, where you turn left for Sumbu.

Note that the dirt road from Mununga to Nsama (⊕ 08°53.448'S; 29°56.896'E) along the southern side of Lake Mweru Wantipa is very bad and becoming impassable.

Cross-country from Mbala Strictly for adventurers, there is a very poor track (on some maps it's a veritable highway, confirming that the cartographers have never been here!) from Mbala into Sumbu National Park, as far as the Lufubu River. While some maps show the road right through to Ndole Bay Lodge, the bridge over the river has been out of commission for some time. The good news, though, is that in 2007 there were strong rumours that the World Bank was involved in plans to rebuild the bridge. If this happens, it will reinstate a superb link between the two sides of Lake Tanganyika, an attractive option in the dry season for experienced drivers with a strong sense of adventure. Note that the presence of the Lufubu River, which marks the park's southeastern boundary, helps to ensure that this track is totally fictional during or just after the rains. Be aware, too, that the road is allegedly used regularly by poachers.

Even in the height of the dry season, you're going to need a 4x4 with lots of spare wheels, a winch and a lot of patience. According to Gerard at Ndole Bay, 'the countryside is wonderful and the drop from the escarpment into the Yendwe Valley is breathtakingly beautiful – but it is no short cut. The track is about 90km long, but it takes at least six hours in a good vehicle.'

To find the start of the track, look for a left turn about 5km west of the Mbala T-junction on the road towards Mpulungu; there may be a sign to the Lufubu River.

By boat Though they're a long way away, the lodges in Sumbu are easily and commonly reached by boat from Mpulungu, where both use the harbour facilities of Samaki Fishing (see page 348). You need to arrange transfers in advance with one of the lodges.

Each lodge has different speeds and sizes of boat available, at different costs. A 'banana boat' (a long, thin chug-chug motorboat) will take about six hours to Sumbu, whilst a speedboat will arrive in around two hours. If you arrive with your own vehicle, or even towing your own boat, you can usually park your vehicle and trailer/boat safely at Samaki while you go to Sumbu. A launching ramp is available, and there's usually no charge for this, though you must ask permission from Samaki's staff and security guards. They're usually very helpful, and it's strongly recommended that you tip them for this very useful service.

Transport boats If you don't have a transfer organised, then transport boats do ply up and down, but they're very crowded. Ask around at Samaki in Mpulungu, or on the beach by the Congolese boat in Sumbu town, be prepared for a long wait (sometimes days) and expect to pay about Kw50,000–60,000 for the trip, which takes between ten and 18 hours, depending on the number of stops. Alternatively, you could negotiate to hire the whole boat for around US$100 plus about 75 litres of fuel (currently US$150), but make it quite clear that you wish to go direct to your destination, or you could still find yourself stopping everywhere; ask by the water taxis at Mpulungu's main market, or on the beach in Sumbu. Remember that the lake can be rough (and thus you could get wet), and that you'll need to take all food and water for the journey with you.

GETTING AROUND THE PARK With the growth of the privatised lodges in the area, the network of roads in the park has been extended and improved vastly in the last few years. Kasaba Bay Lodge has put in good roads around the Inangu Peninsula, Nkamba Bay Lodge has improved the roads in the Nkamba Valley, and Ndole Bay Lodge has helped to develop those around the Chisala River, putting in various game-drive loops. Plans are even afoot to develop further roads within the Nundu headland area. However, note that many of these areas cannot be accessed during the rains, and you'll need a 4x4 at any time.

Boat trips in national park waters can be organised through one of the lodges (see below).

WHERE TO STAY Despite the difficulty of access, Sumbu's future for tourism is looking bright, with two lodges, Nkamba Bay and Ndole Bay, currently operational. Kasaba Bay, however, was not open when visited in 2007.

All three lodges have a chequered history. Originally, both those in the park were run by the government, but by the early 1990s both were in terminal decline: expensive yet poorly maintained. Eventually they were put up for tender in late 1995 and snapped up by private operators, although later fortunes have been mixed. Ndole Bay Lodge was originally privately owned, but was taken by the government in 1989, only to be closed in the early 1990s when its trade disappeared. Now it has reverted to its previous owners and is once again thriving.

Both Nkamba Bay and Kasaba Bay lodges lie on the lake shore inside the national park boundary, with the former now catering for the seriously well-heeled visitor. Ndole Bay, by contrast, is situated on the beach just outside the park's northwestern boundary, and looks to a more casual market.

🏠 **Ndole Bay Lodge** (12 chalets, camping) ⦅ 021 2711150; f 021 2711390; m 096 6780196; e ndolebay@coppernet.zm; www.ndolebaylodge.com (⊕ NDOLEB 08°28.707'S; 30°26.870'E). Owned by Gerard & Barbara Zytkow, & now run by their son, Craig, Ndole Bay Lodge stands beside Lake Tanganyika in Cameron Bay, just northwest of the national park boundary. The location gives it a little more autonomy, allowing, for example, operation of a small campsite & the opportunity to swim or fish from the private beach in front of the lodge, which is considered to be perfectly safe.

Visitors usually arrive by boat, but those who drive in should take the well-signposted left turning as they approach Sumbu, about 5km before the town (⊕ TONDOL 08°31.753'S; 30°26.946'E). The lodge is 7km down a sometimes rocky track, for which you'll need a high-clearance vehicle at all times.

Both the chalets and the main central building are set back from the beach, well spaced among mature gardens on a gentle slope. The main area links the dining room with the bar under a grand thatched roof, all surrounded by a low stone wall. It's a practical design — cool and airy. Under a thatched shelter, hammocks swing in the breeze, while closer to the water is a second lounge area, with open sides & a wooden sundeck; just the place to relax after a cooling dip in the lake or the small pool. It's a lovely wild spot &, despite many creature comforts such as solar-powered electricity, still feels deep within the African bush.

The chalets are built of stone with thatched roofs, & most are en suite. They're large & comfortable, without being luxurious, some with space for extra beds if required. Set to one side along the beach, the campsite is shaded by beautiful spreading winterthorn trees, *Faidherbia albida*, that line the white-sand beach. There is running water & BBQ stands, & a new ablution block is in hand for 2007. Campers can book into the lodge for meals, & can use its facilities, provided they do not disturb other guests. Craig is also considering converting a house in the grounds to provide self-catering accommodation.

Craig is a qualified PADI instructor, & during 2007 was starting up a diving school here, the first on the lake. Other activities include angling, game drives, nature walks, birding trips, lake cruises & waterskiing. You can hire various types of boats (US$7–25/hr, or US$40–80/day plus fuel), as well as snorkelling equipment & basic fishing tackle. Further afield, it's possible to visit some local hot springs, a traditional village & perhaps a village healer, a kapenta fishing rig (a night trip to watch local fishermen catching fish using bright lights) or even Kalambo Falls. And on a practical note, there's a shop in hand for essential toiletries, local crafts & curios & fishing lures. There's plenty to do, but don't come expecting to be organised; this is a laid-back spot that is very much in tune with its location. *En suite US$115/100 sgl/pp sharing; shared US$95/80, sgl/pp sharing, inc FB, guided walks, village visits & sunset paddle; self-catering US$65/50 sgl/pp sharing. Camping US$10 pp.* ☺ *all year.*

🏠 **Nkamba Bay Lodge** (9 rooms) e nkambabaylodge@microlink.zm; www.nkambabaylodge.com, or contact via Voyagers, page 153 (⊕ NKAMBA 08°36.214'S; 30°32.168'E). Nkamba Bay reopened for business in 2006, firmly positioning itself upmarket. The lodge is located on a low rise above the lake shore some 20km from the Sumbu Park gate; there's a signpost indicating the turn-off. You'll need a 4x4 for this road, but most guests (& all in the rainy season) are transferred by boat, either from the airstrip at Kasaba Bay or from Mpulungu (2–4hrs).

Accommodation consists of 4 spacious rooms built in a block around a couple of old fig trees overlooking the lake, & a further 5 chalets set further back with partial lake views. All have been stylishly renovated to be modern but comfortable, combining crisp white linen softened by fabrics & paintwork in more earthy tones. Each room has a king-size bed hung with walk-in mosquito nets on a minimalist concrete plinth, smart en-suite shower, & a wooden veranda that — in the lake-view rooms — is partially enclosed, a useful extra during the rains. Note that some rooms are quite high up, so are not suitable for children.

At the lodge's heart is a large, airy bar/dining area, hung with huge wooden masks & outsize baskets. To one side, squashy sofas & low mukwa tables are fronted by a small (but deep) pool —

parents beware – and the lake beyond. Set to one side, the 'conference room' has become a cosy place to relax, with tea & coffee on tap, & a small library. Power is supplied by a generator. There are also plans for a curio shop.

Activities comprise walks from the lodge or into the rainforest, game drives, beach dinners, boat trips, canoeing & fishing, for which tackle is available to hire. This is no place to swim, though – as attested by a quick glance at the crocodiles basking in the waters off the beach. It is possible to arrange a trip to local landmarks such as the waterfalls on the Lufubu River or a nearby beach, as well as to Chieftainess Chomba's village. *US$420 pp FB, inc drinks (exc bottled wine), airstrip transfers, & land-based activities. Boats US$100/day plus US$3 per litre of fuel. Park fees extra.* ⊕ *all year.*

Kasaba Bay Lodge Although this lodge is currently occupied by ZAWA staff, and closed to the public, local reports indicate that it could reopen before long, so brief details have been left in case that should happen.

Kasaba Bay Lodge was built overlooking the lake as one of the 'presidential lodges' for Kenneth Kaunda & is the nearest of Sumbu's three lodges to Mpulungu. En-suite chalets are spacious, brick structures with thatched roofs & polished stone floors. The main lodge has a deck overlooking the lake, & space to eat inside or out (under a large tree). Historians will note that it was here that Mozambique's president Samora Machel met regional leaders before he caught his fatal flight in 1986 from the lodge's airstrip.

WHAT TO SEE AND DO Each of the lodges can organise a range of activities both on and off the water, but there are one or two local highlights that are worth singling out, detailed below. See also *Swimming, diving and snorkelling* (page 345) and *Fishing* (page 345). Further afield, it's possible to organise excursions to Mpulungu (see page 346) or Kalambo Falls (see page 341).

Balancing rocks One spot well worth an excursion is the balancing rocks (one large rock balancing on three small ones) that stand near Kasaba Bay Lodge on the Nundo Head Peninsula – it's a favourite trail destination shrouded in local mystery. Each year around early June, a pre-fishing ceremony is held here to mark the beginning of the five-month period in which local fishermen can fish within a small area of the waters of the national park.

Game viewing and birding As the lodges extend their influence and the numbers of animals increases, game viewing is increasingly drawing visitors up here. Apart from the ubiquitous puku, most antelope species are still re-establishing their populations; so although you won't see huge herds, you should see some good game here. The lodges have all worked to increase the road network for game drives, and the animals themselves are becoming much more relaxed as a result. Fortunately, with a large area and only a few lodges the roads are very quiet and other vehicles are a pleasant rarity. The birdwatching here has always been excellent: look out for Pel's fishing owl, palmnut vultures and numerous east African migrants.

Guided walks Close to Nkamba Bay Lodge is a small area of rainforest within the national park that is a favourite spot for guided walks. Trips usually involve a boat transfer, then a three to four-hour walk from the beach, and are accompanied by an armed ZAWA scout.

The rainforest section covers only about 300m² and is centred on an underground stream that bubbles up out of the ground and has water most of the year. Mature woodland species such as sausage trees, *Kigelia africana*, and Natal mahogany, *Trichilia emetica*, grow alongside plants that include the flame creeper, *Gloriosa superba*. Before entering the forest, the trail leads past a dense reed bed where sitatunga are frequently seen. The area surrounding the reed beds is also rich in puku and is a regular route for elephant, while the forest itself is regularly traversed by a pod of hippos on their way to the plains behind it. The park's lion frequent the area, too, and can often be heard from Nkamba Bay lodge. Among the birds species that are likely to be encountered are Pel's fishing owl, African broadbill, Angolan pitta and Narina trogon; crowned cranes are often seen on the plain, and during the rainy season the reed beds are the haunt of the black coucal.

There's also a small **waterfall** about an hour's walk from the beach to the east of Sumbu town, on the Chisala River.

Sumbu town On the edge of Sumbu National Park, about 8km east of the Ndole Bay turn off, Sumbu town has grown considerably over the last few years and now has an estimated 20,000 residents. With this sort of population, there's talk of upgrading the status of the town, and eventually tarring the road through to Kaputa. For now, though, it doesn't even have electricity (although there have been plans for several years to connect it to the grid). Nevertheless, while the town isn't nearly as cosmopolitan as Mpulungu (!) it can be fairly lively.

Most of the employed population either work for various government bodies – the national parks, police, immigration or council – or are involved in commercial fishing on the lake, mostly for kapenta. In the town square, a short walk from the harbour, small shops and bars surround the water pump, alongside a popular pool table. It's possible to buy most things, including fresh fruit and milk, if you ask around, and simple meals such as nshima and chicken are to be had for around Kw10,000–15,000. In the corner nearest the well, there's a small bar selling cool drinks, where the owner was building a simple guesthouse in 2007. To be called **Kampusa**, its rooms will cost around Kw20,000 a night.

An open-air market for vegetables, dried fish and second-hand clothing spills from the square down to the harbour. There is also a government-run clinic, with a medical officer available (but seldom any drugs), and a ZAWA post. Fuel – both petrol and diesel – is sometimes available in drums; just ask around in the square.

One curiosity at Sumbu is a Congolese naval vessel which is beached just by the harbour, a relic of the war with the DRC; photographers, though, should note that this is one subject to avoid.

THE ROAD TO MWERU WANTIPA AND KAPUTA

The western side of this region, skirting the shores of Lake Bangweulu to Samfya then continuing up the Luapula River north to Lake Mweru, is known to only a handful of visitors, but offers plenty of rewards. The river is a draw in itself, as are the waterfalls that characterise much of this area, while the journey is enlivened by countless small villages, their square, brick houses topped with a mop of loose thatch and often decorated in striking geometric patterns.

If you're coming northeastward on the Great North Road from Kapiri Mposhi, it's wise to refuel at Serenje (see map, page 296). Then, after a further 36km, take the main left turning signposted to Samfya and Mansa (and Kasanka National Park). This is the artery that runs over some 580km of very good tar to Nchelenge, in the far northwest corner of the country.

The section of road up to the T-junction just west of Samfya used to be referred to as the 'Chinese Road' because it was built, like the TAZARA railway, by the Chinese. After about 55km on this road you'll pass the entrance to Kasanka National Park (see page 312), then 10km later the right turn to the Livingstone Memorial (see page 319) and Bangweulu. Continuing north, the road crosses the impressive 3km-long Luapula Bridge, on the border with the DRC. During and after the rainy season, from around December to July, the river overflows onto the surrounding plain, which is dotted with miniature islands topped with palm trees. In the flooded fields, water lilies flower and water birds brighten the landscape. Permanent villages are augmented by temporary fishing camps, their inhabitants making the most of the months of plenty, and along the roadside fishermen tout their catch of bream or kasepa for sale.

Beyond the Luapula Bridge, watch out for the occasional pot-hole, although generally the road remains very good. About 350km from the Great North Road turn-off, or 115km from the Luapula Bridge, you'll reach a T-junction (⊕ SAMTJN 11°21.126'S; 29°29.453'E). Turn right here and a further 9km will bring you to the small town of Samfya.

SAMFYA With its location beside the powder-fine, white-sand beaches of Lake Bangweulu, Samfya seems to have the potential for a top resort. However, on closer inspection it's less tempting than it looks: accommodation could do with a serious shake up, strong winds blowing off the lake can be decidedly disruptive, and for the most part the lake is full of crocodiles, so this is really more of a stopover than a destination in its own right. (While people do bathe in the clear waters by the hotels, local advice is mixed; think carefully before wading in.)

On a more practical note, the town has a rather unpromising-looking fuel station, as well as a Finance Bank (⊕ *08.15–14.30 Mon–Fri, 08.15–11.00 Sat*), a post office, a small market and a range of basic shops.

Getting there Four **buses** a day run between Lusaka and Kashikishi via Kabwe, Kapiri Mposhi, Serenje, Samfya, Mansa and Nchelenge. Those heading north stop at the market in Samfya at around 08.00, but

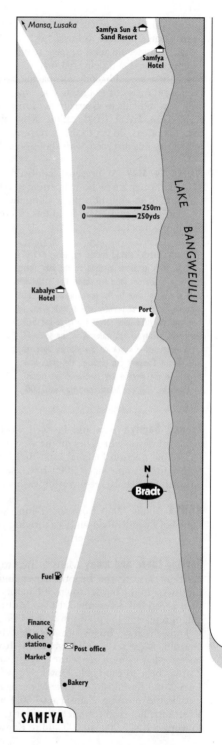

12

southbound buses must be boarded at the T-junction 9km west of town, at a similar time. The fare to Lusaka is Kw80,000; to Mansa Kw25,000–30,000.

Lake Bangweulu used to have regular **postboats** on it, similar to the postbuses, which collected and delivered mail to the island communities on the lake. Like the buses, these would happily take paying passengers, but in recent years the service has been contracted out to private concerns, and information is patchy. Even in Samfya itself it is difficult to ascertain any form of timetable, but the boat seems to depart every Thursday at 10.00, calling at Mbabala Island, Chisi Island and Muchinshi amongst others. To get to the port, turn left at the crossroads as you enter the town and follow this dirt road, with shops on either side, for about 300m to the end.

Where to stay At present, Samfya's accommodation leaves something to be desired, though a new hotel opening in 2007 may redress the balance, and there are rumours of another new place along the lake to the south of the town. At present, in addition to two lakeside hotels, there are several very basic guesthouses, all much of a muchness.

Samfya Beach Hotel (7 rooms, camping) m 097 7371136. With its prime location on the lake shore, & a huge beachfront *lapa* for shade, this established hotel at the entrance to the town should be a little goldmine, but lack of maintenance & high prices tell their own story. En-suite rooms are large but basic, albeit with plenty of hot water, & in the so-called bar & restaurant a knock on the kitchen door reaps little reward. Campers can pitch on the grass near the lake, & are given a key to one of the rooms for ablutions. $$, exc b/fast; camping Kw50,000 per tent.

Samfya Sun & Sand Resort (13 rooms, camping) m 095 5881540; e samfyasun@yahoo.com. Nearing completion when visited in summer 2007, this new hotel stands on a narrow strip of land facing the lake, right next to the Samfya Beach. Three of the rooms will be en suite; the remainder will share a toilet & shower. Separate buildings will house the restaurant & the Sun Bar. $$

Kabalye Guesthouse (4 rooms) On the right of the main road into town, this is one of several very basic guesthouses in Samfya, with little to choose between them. On the plus side, they're all pretty cheap. $

Around Samfya It would be well worth exploring the road north of Samfya towards Lubwe, which lies on the western side of the lake. Lubwe itself is home to a Catholic mission hospital built in 1926 and now run by the Sisters of Mercy. Active fundraising since 2000 has resulted in significant improvements at the hospital; for details, see www.lubwe-hospital.org.uk.

MANSA About 72km from the T-junction, or 81km from Samfya, Mansa is the capital of Luapula Region. It's a thriving provincial town, with tree-lined roads and an appealing air of prosperity.

Getting there and away Mansa's links to the rest of the region are enhanced by its position close to the Luapula River and the DRC border. A tarred road leads southwest to the border town of Chembe, where there's a pontoon over the river, then a road link across the DRC to Mufulira in the Copperbelt. There is currently talk of replacing the pontoon with a bridge.

Long-distance **buses** are operated by Zamsaf, Sierra, Juldan Motors and Germin. Most leave from Mulenshi Road in the centre of town, though each operator has its own departure and arrival point; the most obvious is that used by Zamsaf next to the Civic Hotel. From here, regular buses connect Mansa with Lusaka and Kashikishi on Lake Mweru, as well as to Kawambwa. Buses to Lusaka leave in the morning, Zamsaf at 07.00, Juldan Motors and Germins at 08.30, taking about nine hours to complete the journey. Fares to Lusaka are Kw95,000 one way; to Samfya Kw25,000–30,000 and to Kawambwa Kw35,000.

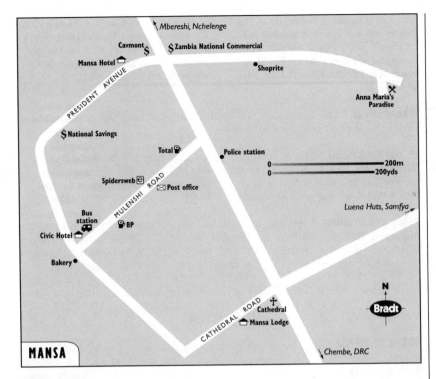

🏠 Where to stay

🏠 **Luena Huts Lodge** (7 rooms) ☎ 021 2821090 (✪ 11°12.279'S; 28°54.700'E). This newcomer to Mansa, opened in early 2007, is to the east of town on the north side of the road. Individual rondavels sit in a row behind a secure gate, each with a neat garden plant-lined path – including tomatoes. A TV, fan, nets, fridge & dbl bed are standard; some share facilities, while others are en suite. Away from these, a two-storey bar attracts a cool breeze & is very popular at w/ends (closing time Mon–Thu 22.00, Fri–Sun 24.00), so the place could be noisy. Between the two there's a simple restaurant, serving meals all day, every day (lunch & dinner at Kw17,000). Facilities don't stop there though – there are plans for a pool, a gym & sauna, & even a car wash. $, b/fast extra Kw30,000.

🏠 **Chukwuma Guesthouse** (20 rooms) ☎ 021 2821560, 2821531; m 097 7432610. This pleasant guesthouse is just north of town; to find it, head north from Shoprite, go over the bridge, then turn right. Simple en-suite rooms built in a low block are fronted by a formal grassed area. Meals are available to residents. $

🏠 **Mansa Lodge** (17 rooms) Cathedral Rd; ☎/f 021 2821414. (✪ 11°12.132'S; 28°53.357'E). Just down the road from the main Catholic church, this is run by the nationwide Hostels Board of Management. It's functional, very clean & efficient, if slightly soulless, with en-suite rooms in various categories, each with a bath & DSTV; executive rooms also have a fridge. All meals are available ($$). $

🏠 **Civic Hotel** (16 rooms) Mulenshi Rd; ☎/f 021 2821930; m 097 9291918. Signs are good for this new hotel, opened at the end of 2006 in one of Mansa's oldest buildings. The exterior may be unprepossessing, but inside, solid wood & stone floors give a sense of permanence. Rooms are off a long corridor, rather institutional in appearance but well maintained with en-suite showers, tea-/coffee-making facilities, a fan, mosquito nets & DSTV. The first-floor restaurant & bar, for guests only, overlook the road from a long veranda. Meals are served throughout the day from an à-la-carte menu. Unlikely facilities in a hotel of this size include a hairdresser, barber, 2 shops & an internet café (Kw500/minute). Staff are friendly & helpful, & the management is excellent. $, inc cont b/fast. Full b/fast extra Kw20,000.

🏠 **Mansa Hotel** (30 rooms) President Av; ☎ 021 2821606–7; f 021 2821171. The well-established

12

Mansa Hotel is immediately next to Cavmont Bank & down the road from Shoprite. Its brick-built rooms are arranged round a series of courtyards. Simply furnished but very clean & pleasant, each has an en-suite toilet & bath, as well as TV, fridge, ceiling fan & mosi nets.

The hotel also has a couple of well-stocked bars, & a restaurant serving b/fast (Kw25,000), lunch & dinner (Kw25,000–35,000). It's a cut above the average of Zambia's town hotels, professionally run with helpful staff. $$, inc cont b/fast.

✖ Where to eat
All the hotels have reasonable restaurants, but if you're in town head straight for the best restaurant for miles:

🏠 **Anna Maria's Paradise** President Av; ✆ 021 1821890; m 097 7453919. Italy's loss was Zambia's gain when Anna Maria moved to Mansa in the 1990s. A shady & welcoming retreat, her restaurant is a pleasant place for a lazy lunch that could range from pasta or pizza to chicken, excellent steaks, or the best bream & chips in the region. $–$$

Other practicalities As you might expect in a town of this standing, it has two all-important fuel stations (the last reliable source of fuel for several hundred kilometres if you're going north) and three banks, of which the Zambian Commercial Bank has an ATM. The range of shops includes a branch of Shoprite (⊕ 08.00–19.00 Mon–Fri, 08.00–17.00 Sat, 09.00–13.00 Sun); if you're heading north and self catering, this is the last chance to stock up on anything other than the basics. There's also an internet café, Spiderweb (⊕ 08.00–20.00 daily, Kw500/minute) – and a second in the Civic Hotel.

NORTH OF MANSA Some 9km north of Mansa the road splits. The left turn leads to Mwense, Mbereshi and Nchelenge, while the road straight ahead is for Kawambwa. Both appear beautifully tarred, but don't be fooled; after the first 25km or so the Kawambwa road deteriorates rapidly into a bad dirt road, which is well worth avoiding, while the road to Nchelenge is pretty good tar for most of the way. Thus, if you're heading towards Kawambwa, take the road towards Nchelenge via Mwense, then turn right at Mbereshi for Kawambwa. It's both easier and quicker.

The Nchelenge road follows the verdant valley of the Luapula River as it flows north into Lake Mweru, forming the border with the DRC and widening all the way to the lake. A succession of villages lines the road, which crosses several rivers, all flowing west towards the Luapula from Zambia's higher ground in the east. It's an easy but interesting drive, particularly after the rainy season when the flooded plains attract temporary fishing camps, as further south. The route is further enhanced by views across the river to the DRC and the lure of several attractive waterfalls (see below), many of which offer a good spot for a picnic or to camp.

There are two fuel stations along this stretch, one at Mwense, 111km north of Mansa, the second 18km further north in the village of Chiluba, but neither is reliable, so do fill up in Mansa.

The Luapula waterfalls Along this route are numerous lovely waterfalls, many virtually unmarked, including the following:

Mumbuluma Falls (⊕ MUMBUL 10°55.801'S; 28°44.178'E) About 32km north of Mansa (167km from Mbereshi) there's a signposted turning to the left (⊕ TOMUMB 10°55.536'S; 28°47.945'E). After about 8.4km of rather bad track you'll reach the falls The water goes over a two-stage drop, about 30m across. There are attractive rapids in between and a deep pool at the bottom – but no facilities at all though there is a village nearby and camping is possible, with a good spot about 100m east of the falls.

Thomas Morrow

During the last week of July, the people of the lower Luapula Valley in northern Zambia gather in the village of Mwansabombwe to celebrate their Lunda traditions and their paramount chief, Mwata Kazembe. For days prior to the main event, bars serve bottled beer, much of it imported from the DRC, to quench the thirst of guests who have arrived in the hot, dusty village; women from different village sections deliver pots of millet beer to Mwata Kazembe's palace; and the youth organise special sports competitions and cultural events. Towards the weekend when the main festivities are to take place, provincial, and on occasion national, political and military dignitaries dressed in their suits and ties arrive. On Saturday afternoon, following the performance of certain rituals in the morning, chiefs, headmen, state dignitaries and the villagers crowd together in a stadium on the outskirts of Mwansabombwe. A dignitary delivers a speech that highlights the importance of culture and tradition for progress, development and national well-being. Listening to the national leadership's calls for the preservation of these traditions, the chiefs and headmen appear in the traditional Lunda garb of long imikonso skirts (singular, umukonso), leather inshipo belts and ututasa crowns (singular, akatasa). After the speeches, on the instruction of Mwata Kazembe, selected aristocrats and members of the royal family dance. The day's events culminate in Mwata Kazembe performing the Lunda dance of conquest, the Mutomboko.

For further information, see www.mutomboko.org.

Musonda Falls (✪ TOMUSO 10°42.2952'S; 28°48.784'E) About 60km north of Mansa (141km south of Mbereshi) you cross the Mwense Bridge over the Luongo River. There is a reasonable set of scattered cascades (✪ MUSON 10°42.856'S; 28°48.858'E) near here, but you first need to get permission to view them from the nearby hydro-electric power station; stop at the bridge and ask ZESCO security. This can be time-consuming, and there's not much to be seen as the river disappears into the power station.

Mambilima Falls About 90km north of Mansa (111km from Mbereshi) there's a set of lovely rapids (✪ MAMBIL 10°33.791'S; 28°48.858'E) on the Luapula River, about 12km from the main road and 4km south of the Mambalimba Mission. Turn off west, as indicated by a signpost, and gaze over at the DRC on the other side of the river. These used to be called the Johnstone Falls and are scattered over a 5km stretch of the river. They make a very pleasant spot to stop for lunch and a footpath leads to the river for close-ups of some of the larger rapids.

MWANSABOMBWE The village of Mwansabombwe (✪ MWANSA 9°49.25'S; 028°45.35'E), just to the east of the main road (✪ TOMWAN 09°49.317'S; 28°45.474'E) and 13km south of Mbereshi, is the focus of the colourful Mutomboko Ceremony – the Dance of Victory – that takes place every year on the last Saturday of July (see box, above), starting at 08.00. Visitors are welcome to watch, but photographers will need a pass costing Kw120,000 for the day. A statue at the entrance to the village commemorates the event.

If you're heading east to Kawambwa, don't be tempted to take a 'short cut' before Mbereshi by turning off the road at Mwansabombwe; this may look promising at first, but quickly disappears into a series of tracks that aren't the easiest to follow; stick to the main road unless you've time to explore!

MBERESHI The importance of Mbereshi (✪ MBERES 09°44.078'S; 28°47.350'E) to the visitor is threefold. It has a fuel station, though the supply at Kawambwa is rather more reliable. It is also the junction where you turn off for Kawambwa, Lumangwe Falls and Mporokoso. And finally, just after you turn onto this road, there's a **church** to the left on the hill that is one of Zambia's earliest. It was built in the early 1900s by the London Missionary Society, which was responsible for several other buildings in the vicinity, the rest of which are now in varying states of disrepair.

There are some serious speed humps at each end of the village; if you're driving yourself, be warned.

NCHELENGE This small town near the shores of Lake Mweru is the base for an occasional ferry service out to the two populated islands in the lake: Kilwa and Isokwe. In addition to a post office and small market, there is fuel available, albeit not necessarily reliable.

Getting there and away Buses heading north from Lusaka via Samfya and Mansa stop in Nchelenge, continuing on to Kashikishi which marks the end of the tar road.

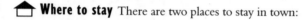 **Where to stay** There are two places to stay in town:

🏠 **Lake Mweru Water Transport Guest House** ☏ 021 2972064. Rooms at this waterfront guesthouse are clean with en-suite facilities, and meals are available. This is also the place to organise boat trips out to Isokwe and Kilwa, though you'll need your own tackle if you want to fish. $

🏠 **Nchelenge Resthouse** ☏ 021 2972010, 2972045. This slightly less attractive alternative is nearby and is run by the council. $

What to see and do The area by Lake Mweru will seem just like a continuous series of lakeside fishing villages. The fishing is (apparently) excellent, but there's also an abundance of crocodiles.

Birdwatchers might like to take a detour, using the track to the shore next to Chabilikila Primary School, which is just south of Nchelenge. This will lead you to some areas of papyrus near the mouth of the Luapula – a promising spot for finding swamp-dwelling species.

BEYOND KASHIKISHI TO MWERU WANTIPA NATIONAL PARK Some 3km beyond Nchelenge, at Kashikishi, the tar road comes to an end and the road deteriorates dramatically, so if you're aiming to get to Kaputa, allow plenty of time. Continue north along the edge of Lake Mweru for a scenic 30km or so, towards the village of Mununga then follow the road as it veers away from the lake until you reach the Kalungwishi River.

At the village of Mununga, turn right, then after around 30km go left (✪ TOKAPU 09°07.531'S; 29°412.996'E) towards Kaputa. There are often market traders at the junction, so it's a good place to pick up whatever produce is in season. The stretch of road from this junction through Mweru Wantipa National Park to Kaputa is stony but reasonably level; it was regraded in 2007 and is far better than many would have you believe, though you'll still need to drive with care. After 44km you'll come to a barrier, which marks the entrance to the national park (✪ MWERUP 054 08°53.572'S; 29°28.878'E). From here, continue straight through the national park and across the top of Lake Mweru Wantipa to Kaputa (see opposite).

Mweru Wantipa National Park This is another large tract (3,134km²) of Zambia that was once a thriving national park, renowned for large elephant and crocodile populations. Now poaching has much reduced these, though reports suggest that some big game still lives here, and claims are made that sitatunga can be found among the dense papyrus beds on the lake shore. Sadly, though, to the casual observer the park appears to be singularly devoid of life; even the birds seem to have deserted the place.

That said, the whole area, including the lake, was designated a Ramsar site in 2007, at the same time as three other wetland areas in Zambia. Ramsar reports that the diversity of habitats along the lake, featuring riverine forest, wetlands and miombo woodland, attracts numerous waterbirds, including the wattled crane, black stork and Goliath's heron.

The road to Kaputa goes straight through the park, on the western side of Lake Mweru Wantipa, a sedimentary and highly seasonal lake which itself forms part of the national park. Along this road, you'll come to a ZAWA scout post (✪ MWSCOP 08°47.807'S; 29°30.519'E). If you anticipate camping here, or even exploring away from the road, then ask if one of the scouts can accompany you.

KAPUTA Despite being the district capital, Kaputa (✪ KAPUTA 08°28.503'S; 29°39.990'E) is a rather unattractive place, its main street strewn with rubbish, and with the dejected air of a border town. There's a branch of the National Savings and Credit Bank in town, an internet café, a few shops and a market where you can pick up basic foodstuffs. The presence of a few simple guesthouses (all $), including **JMC Roadside Guesthouse** (m 097 7278551) by the barrier as well as **Chelewa Chalets** and **Twalifwaya Twalanaka**, is unlikely to deter most visitors from pressing on towards Lake Tanganyika (see pages 342–6).

FROM MBERESHI TO KASAMA

THE ROAD TO MPOROKOSO Turning east at Mbereshi, towards Mporokoso, you turn off the tar and onto a reasonable gravel road. Note that the pontoon across the Kalungwishi River at Chimpembe, about 86km from Mporokoso, has now been replaced by a solidly constructed bridge.

Places of interest along and around this road include:

Ntumbachushi Falls (*Entry US$3 pp, vehicle US$3 per day, camping US$10 pp*) These falls (✪ NTUMBA 09°51.167'S; 28°56.652'E) are very clearly signposted about 23km east of Mbereshi and 18km west of Kawambwa, and 20km from the valley turn-off (✪ 09°50.666'S; 28°56.450'E). They are just 1.2km south of the road along a good track, and surrounded by some beautiful thick *mishitu* forest.

The main falls drop about 40m into a dark pool, with a second cataract alongside. Don't swim in the main pool, as there are strong currents and undertows that can pull you under the falls themselves. However, both the pool at the foot of the second cataract and the gentle rapids above the first falls offer perfect places for a cooling dip or a proper swim. Clear footpaths lead from the car park in both directions.

Despite the derelict bungalows at the back of the car park, this is an idyllic spot to camp, though facilities are limited to a single long-drop toilet. You can pitch either by the car park or – more secluded but away from the toilet – above the falls. It is also an ideal base from which to visit other waterfalls in the area.

In the rainy season, there is a further set of falls, the **Witch Doctor's Falls** a short walk away, so called because there used to be *ng'anga* shrines at its base, one containing millet, the other a model canoe carved from bone. If you'd like to visit, ask the extremely helpful caretaker, Joseph Kangwa, to guide you there, and remember to offer him a tip.

Kawambwa Rather smaller than most maps of Zambia might suggest, Kawambwa is a pleasant backwater 18.6km from Ntumbachushi Falls, with little to detain the visitor. It is, though, widely known for the large Kawambwa Tea Estate, east of the town, which was privatised in 1996. Production has slowed considerably in the last few years, giving added poignancy to a road sign proclaiming that Kawambwa will be 'poverty free by 2030'.

There's a reasonably reliable fuel station at the junction with the Mbereshi road, and a small market in town, as well as a range of shops and a branch of the Zambia National Commercial Bank.

A regular bus service operates every day except Monday between Lusaka and Kawambwa via Mansa, stopping next to the fuel station. Fares to Lusaka are Kw100,000 one way; to Mansa Kw35,000.

If you're driving straight through the town from Mbereshi, you'll come to a T-junction; to stay on track, turn left here (right takes you into Kawambwa), then almost immediately right (at ⊕ KAWAMB 038 09°47.605'S; 29°04.675'E). After a further 24km you'll come to the end of the tar, just by the tea estate.

 Where to stay There are a few guesthouses in Kawambwa, of which the central St Mary's is fairly typical:

⌂ **St Mary's Guesthouse** (13 rooms) m 097 9648749. A simple establishment with mosquito nets over the beds. Most rooms share bathroom facilities. $

Lusenga Plain National Park Lusenga Plain was originally designated as a park to protect a large open plain, fringed by swamp and dry evergreen forest and surrounded by ridges of hills, but without enough support it is now a park in name only. Poaching has reduced the game considerably and, with no internal roads in the park, there are few reasons to visit.

On its northeastern side the park is bordered by the Kalungwishi River, which passes over three beautiful waterfalls: Lumangwe, Kabwelume and Kundabwika.

Getting there The park is usually approached from the Kawambwa–Mporokoso road, and you should be very well equipped for any attempt to reach it. Some visitors have had success in reaching the park by getting a game scout as a guide from the National Parks and Wildlife Office in Kawambwa. Otherwise the park is hard to enter.

Falls on and around the Kalungwishi River The Kalungwishi River forms the boundary between the Luapula and Northern regions of Zambia, and also the eastern boundary of Lusenga Plain National Park. Along the river are three major waterfalls in relatively close succession: Lumangwe, Kabwelume and Kundabwika. While Lumangwe is the most straightforward to reach, and well worth the visit, the greater draw is Kabwelume, 5km further on and a must for anyone in the vicinity. Getting to Kundabwika is altogether more demanding.

In addition to the falls themselves, there are miles of pleasant walking upstream, so consider staying overnight to give time to explore the other falls further downstream.

Pressure for electricity in Zambia is likely to impact on the river, with plans in hand for a hydro-electric power station between Lumangwe and Kandabwika falls.

Where to stay You can camp at Lumangwe or Kundabwika Falls, or stay at a nearby cottage:

Cascade Cottage (6 beds) There are two ways to reach the cottage. One is off the road to Lumangwe Falls from the main road. The second — & easiest — is to take the turning signposted on the left of the road, about 300m from the Chimpempe bridge on the Kawambwa–Mporokoso road, indicating 'Cascade Cottage Tourist Accommodation'; just follow the tracks for about 2km.

The cottage is simply furnished, with 4 beds & 2 sofa-beds (which can be joined to make a dbl) & a flush toilet. Otherwise you will need to bring everything with you, including bedding; there are no showers, & no electricity, though running water is powered ingeniously by a paddle-wheel driven by the Kalungwishi River.

There is a small cascade, Chimpempe Falls, in the river nearby. More impressive are the main Lumangwe Falls 5km away, & Kabwelume Falls (10km). A caretaker usually looks after the cottage & will guide you around if you want to walk to Kabwelume (for which he appreciates a tip).

The cottage is owned by an Australian couple, Ron & Lyn Ringrose, who now live mostly in Lusaka (☏ 021 1772052). They came to Zambia on an aid project in 1992, & were offered the land near the waterfalls by the local chief, in return for their help for the local community. Despite being due back in Australia in 1995, they've stayed in Zambia ever since. Kw30,000 pp.

Lumangwe Falls (*Entry US$3 pp, vehicle US$3 per day, camping US$10 pp*) To reach these, turn left off the Kawambwa–Mporokoso road about 2km east of the Chimpempe bridge (✤ CHIMBR 09°33.082'S; 29°26.937'E), which crosses the Kalungwishi River some 65km from Kawambwa and 86km from Mporokoso. There's a clear signpost to Lumangwe and Kabwelume Falls on the north side of the road, on the outside of a bend (✤ FALLST 09°32.239'S; 29°27.874'E). The track is narrow, level and fairly straight, continuing for about 10km to a fork (✤ LUMAFK 09°32.466'S; 29°23.296"E). Bear left here; the falls are just 300m away, manned by a caretaker.

Lumangwe is a solid white-and-green wall of water, 100m across and 30m high. It's perhaps the most spectacular of the waterfalls in this region and bears comparison to Victoria Falls. The noise is deafening and the air is filled with fine mist. There are two viewing points, one overlooking the main falls from the front, and a second – much drier! – from the top of the falls where you can see how a large island splits the river's flow. The energetic might want to climb to the bottom of the falls in order to reach the bottom of the rainbow that's seen on most days. There are no pots of gold here though, and the climb comes with a warning – instead of steps – so you'll be making your way down (and then up) a rope using the cliff side for balance.

You can camp at the falls in safety; long-drop toilets and a rubbish point are provided.

Kabwelume Falls (✤ KABWEL 09°31.432'S; 29°21.267'E) These falls are 5km downstream from Lumangwe, which makes a pleasant walk for two or three hours through the forest. Ask for precise directions at Lumangwe. Alternatively you can drive yourself, provided that you have a good 4x4: the track is very poor in parts and it's slow going. Simply return to the fork close to Lumangwe Falls, then turn left and continue for 5km or so to a small parking area.

Unlike that around many of the area's waterfalls, the vegetation at Kabwelume has been left to grow wild, enhancing the approach to the fall – provided that you come prepared (this is no place for flip-flops!). The increasingly overgrown path takes you across the river on stepping stones (probably inaccessible in the rainy season), then through thick vegetation dotted with bright flowers and alive with butterflies, and finally down a steep, slippery slope. You'll emerge after 300m or so to see a most magnificent waterfall – a curving curtain of water 20m high and 75m across. Below is a deep pool, which itself flows over a second fall of 20m. On the left are two cataracts falling the whole 40m; on the right water pours down the cliff face. Look about you and this makes 180° of water – with the cataract, the main waterfall and the waterspout. It's a truly beautiful sight, worth savouring.

Kundabwika Falls (⊕ KUNDAB 9°13.058'S; 29°18.258'E) These are the last major falls on the Kalungwishi before it flows into Lake Mweru. Despite that, they are accessed from a different road, which may be impassable after rain; ask for advice locally, perhaps from Joseph at Ntumbachushi.

There are two routes to the falls, both requiring a 4x4. The normal route is from the Kawambwa–Mporokoso road. About 21km east of the Chimpempe Bridge (⊕ KUNDTO 09°27.945'S; 29°36.447'E), or 63km west of Mporokoso, turn northwest onto a narrow, very poor track; it's just west of a road barrier and signposted to Chikwanda Basic School; some maps mark this as a place called Mukunsa. Continue along this track, which is deeply rutted and pot-holed, for about 50km. It passes through villages for about 30km, then descends into less populous woodlands. It's very slow going so allow around two hours to the turn-off. The turning towards the falls (⊕ TOKUND 09°11.397'S; 29°19.890'E), is into woodland, and almost invisible when the grass is high, so ask one of the villagers to point it out. From here, there's a straightforward 5km track that leads to the river.

Approaching from the opposite direction, drive 65km north of Nchelenge to the village of Mununga, on the banks of Lake Mweru. From there it's 35km to the falls on a reasonable dirt road, turning south at ⊕ TOKUND, as above.

The woodland track brings you out by a series of gentle rapids, known as the upper falls. An expanse of open grassland offers plenty of room to camp, with no villages nearby, and just the occasional fisherman for company. To reach the main falls, a further 1km downstream, involves clambering over boulders along the riverbank.

Kundabwika itself is a geometrical waterfall, a 25m-wide rectangular block of green-and-white water. It's not possible to get very close to the falls, but there are good long-distance views from the top of the rock outcrop.

As you approach the falls, about 3km from the road and to the left of the woodland track, there's a rocky outcrop where rock paintings can clearly be seen. You can explore yourself or, if you have time, ask if one of the villagers can take you to see them.

Mumbuluma Falls II These falls (⊕ MUMBII 09°13.024'S; 29°20.681'E) lie 3km from the Kundabwika Falls turn-off, between Nyausa and Lumpa villages. Just before Nyausa School and past Kakoma Stream there's a 1km winding path to the falls. To be honest, it's little more than a rapid (they're also known as Mwesa Rapids) but it's quite scenic, with views of the Lusenga Plain National Park.

Yangumwila Falls There is said to be another set of falls, Yangumwila, on the Itabu River. From Lumangwe Falls, head towards Mporokoso. The falls lie a three-hour walk away from Chiwala Primary School. Ask around for details.

MPOROKOSO Mporokoso (⊕ MPOROK 09°21.831'S; 30°07.402'E) is a useful small town in the heart of northern Zambia. It lies at a T-junction on the Kawambwa–Kasama road, and is also the main access point for Sumbu National Park (see pages 351–2 for directions to the park). The centre is to the west of the T-junction, along a wide, tree-lined avenue. Here you'll find a branch of the National Savings and Credit Bank, a police station, post office, shops and a small market – in short, a normal Zambian town.

The town's recent history is very much tied up with that of refugees from the war in the DRC. In early 1999, a number of refugees and loyalist Congolese troops fled across the border to Zambia, crossing around Kaputa and Sumbu. They were looked after by the UNHCR, the Red Cross, Oxfam and other agencies at Mwange Camp, about 60km outside Mporokoso, on the way to Kawambwa. Many of the aid agencies retain a presence here, and there's also a fairly large government hospital (with doctors but generally poor medicines and equipment), serving a large area of the country.

Getting there and away Most people coming to Mporokoso will be on the main Kawambwa–Kasama road. However, if you're approaching from Mpulungu or Mbala, there is a road that avoids Kasama, although it's over 70km long, and rough going (you'll need a 4x4) even in the dry season – so it's hardly a 'short cut'. To find it, head towards Kasama from Mbala. About 74km from Mbala you'll see a turning to the right (✪ TOSHCT 09°27.486'S; 31°13.136'E). This joins up with the Kasama–Mporokoso road at ✪ TOSHC2 09°40.270'S; 30°41.628'E, about 8km northwest of Kapatu Mission (81km southeast of Mporokoso).

For those heading to Luwingu, there's also a way to avoid Kasama. To find it, follow the road southeast to Kasama for around 55km to a right turning. Take this road, continuing southwest until it joins the Kasama–Luwingu road. It's not in superb condition, but is just passable in a normal car during the dry season, though you would certainly need a 4x4 when it's wet.

 Where to stay If you wish to break your journey here, there are a few very simple guesthouses, including:

⌂ **Holiday Rest House** (13 rooms) Right next to the T-junction, this is a very simple but acceptable guesthouse. Rooms are all en suite, albeit with peeling paint on the baths. No meals are available. $, exc b/fast.

⌂ **Cheers Guesthouse** (9 rooms) m 097 9534051 More central but rather less salubrious, Cheers has 3 en-suite rooms, with rates the same as those at the Holiday Rest House. $, exc b/fast.

Waterfall excursions from Mporokoso
Kapuma Falls These small but delightful falls (✪ KAPUM 09°23.235'S; 30°05.675'E), cascading over scattered wall-like rocks, make a pleasant half-day trip from town and are a great picnic spot. Around 7km southwest of Mporokoso, past the district hospital, turn left just before the Agricultural Training Centre, from where it's around 2km to the falls. The road ends on a private farm, so if somebody is home do ask permission to see the falls.

Pule Falls Also known as Chipulwe Falls, these (✪ PULEF 09°30.573'S; 30°17.001'E) lie just off the road to the (other) Luangwa River. Take the dirt road southeast of Mporokoso for 24km, turning off east after the Luangwa bridge onto a motorable path for 1km. There's a 500m footpath through cassava fields and banana plantations to these scenic, but not very deep, falls (about 15m drop). They're worth the two-hour trip from Mporokoso.

Mumbuluma Falls III These falls (✪ MUMIII 09°33.211'S; 29°44.736'E) are surprisingly impressive; surprising, as neither they nor the river that spawns them, the other Luangwa, are well known. They offer good places for camping, too, with no villages nearby. To reach them, head 33km west out of Mporokoso to Angelo village (✪ ANGELO 9°26.771'S; 29°49.511'E) where you should turn and head south for 14km, then west for 4km. From here there's a footpath to the falls across the clearing.

12

Lupupa Falls These (✪ LUPUPA 9°16.441'S; 29°46.910'E) make for a pleasant outing when combined with Mumbuluma Falls III, possibly by having lunch at the former and camping at the latter. To reach them, head west out of Mporokoso on the 28km fair dirt road to Njalamimba. From here, head on 10km to Chandalala, then take the 3km motorable footpath before finally crossing the bridge on foot. The main attractions are the views from the falls down the gorge along the Mukubwe, over the hills and into the pool itself.

MPOROKOSO TO KASAMA Perhaps surprisingly for what might appear to be a fairly important artery, the 196km road between Mporokoso and Kasama is for the most part very poorly maintained, so it's not a journey to rush; you should allow around four hours, without stops. There are few villages along this stretch, either, so little to alleviate the monotony of consecutive pot-holes and deep ruts.

After 106km you'll come to the Kapatu Mission (✪ KAPATU 09°43.148'S; 30°43.845'E) on the left of the road, where there are also a few shops. A further 54km brings you to the turn-off to Chishimba Falls (see page 339), shortly after crossing the picturesque Luombe River. The falls are close to the road and it's well worth stopping here for an hour or two. From the falls, it's just 11km to the tar road, then at last a smooth final 25km to the centre of Kasama (see pages 335–8).

NYIKA PLATEAU NATIONAL PARK

(*Park fees on Malawian side US$5 pp per day, plus US$2 per vehicle*) Nyika Plateau is a marvellous area for hiking, and has some unusual wildlife. It lies mostly in Malawi, with just a slim Zambian national park hugging the border, and is best approached from the Malawian side. For this reason, below is a description of the plateau as a whole, and how to see it, including directions within Malawi.

GEOGRAPHY Nyika Plateau National Park is a tiny Zambian national park of only 80km². However, it adjoins Malawi's Nyika National Park, which is the country's largest national park. This was established in 1965 and extended to its present size of 3,134km² in 1978. At the heart of both parks lies the gently undulating Nyika Plateau, which averages over 2,000m in altitude.

In addition to the main plateau, the Malawian National Park also protects part of the eastern slopes of the Nyika range, where grassland and forest are replaced by thick miombo woodland.

FLORA AND FAUNA
Flora Nyika is notable for its wonderful montane scenery, and as being an ideal hiking destination. The lower slopes harbour miombo woodland, which is replaced by more open grassland at the higher altitudes. Of particular interest to botanists are the roughly 200 orchid species recorded in the park, of which 11 species are endemic to Nyika.

Mammals Nyika protects a rich diversity of mammals – almost 100 species have been recorded – including an endemic race of Burchell's zebra, *Equus burchelli crawshaii*, and a very high density of leopard.

Game viewing is good all year round, and the open nature of the plateau ensures excellent visibility. In the area around Chelinda, the main camp, visitors are practically guaranteed to see roan antelope, scrub hare, zebra, reedbuck, bushbuck and eland. Your chances of seeing leopard around Chelinda are good.

The lower slopes of miombo woodland support good populations of buffalo and

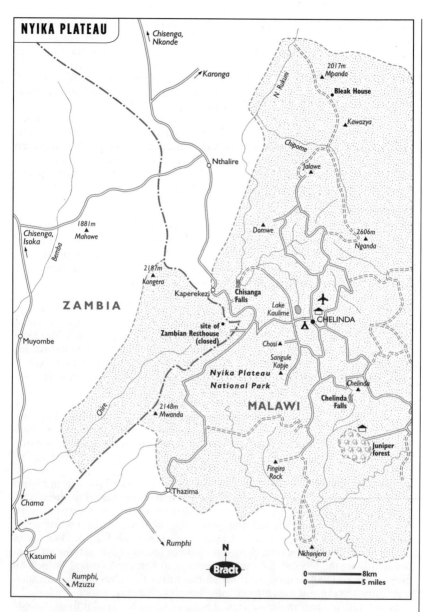

NYIKA PLATEAU

Chisenga,
Nkonde

Karonga

2017m
Mpanda

Bleak House

Kawozya

Chipome

N. Rukuni

Jalawe

Nthalire

Chisenga,
Isoka

1881m
Mahowe

Bemba

Domwe

2606m
Nganda

2187m
Kongera

Kaperekezi

Chisanga
Falls

Lake
Kaulime

CHELINDA

ZAMBIA

Muyombe

site of
Zambian Resthouse
(closed)

Chosi

Sangule
Kopje

Chelinda

Nyika Plateau
National Park

Chelinda
Falls

Chire

2148m
Mwanda

MALAWI

Juniper
forest

Fingira
Rock

Thazima

Chama

Rumphi

N

Nkhonjera

Katumbi

Rumphi,
Mzuzu

Bradt

0 ———— 8km
0 ———— 5 miles

elephant, though these animals only rarely move up to the grassland of the plateau. Lion and cheetah are also infrequent visitors to the plateau.

Birds With well over 400 species recorded, Nyika supports a great diversity of birdlife. However, this figure is rather deceptive as many of the species included on the checklist are found only in the inaccessible miombo woodland of the lower slopes, and are thus unlikely to be seen by visitors who stick to the plateau.

The grassland around Chelinda Camp is inhabited by several tantalising birds. Foremost are the wattled crane, Denham's bustard and the exquisite scarlet-tufted malachite sunbird (distinguished from the commoner malachite sunbird by its much longer tail). More rewarding than the grassland for general birding are the forests, particularly the large Chowo Forest near the Zambian resthouse, where localised species such as Sharpe's akalat, bar-tailed trogon, olive-flanked robin, white-breasted alethe and a variety of other robins and bulbuls may be seen.

Four birds found at Nyika (yellow mountain warbler, churring cisticola, crackling cloud cisticola and mountain marsh widow) have been recorded nowhere else in Malawi, while the Nyika races of red-winged francolin, rufous-naped lark, greater double-collared sunbird and Baglafecht weaver are all endemic to the plateau. There are also three butterfly species endemic to the plateau, and one species each of chameleon, frog and toad which are found nowhere else.

The rivers and dams on the Nyika Plateau are stocked with rainbow trout, and are thus popular with anglers.

GETTING THERE AND AWAY

By air By far the easiest way to Nyika is by air. The Nyika Safari Company offers charter flights between Mzuzu and Chelinda (*US$150 pp one way, min 2*). If you've picked a clear day with few clouds the views from the aircraft are stunning, and you can clearly see the foothills, the patches of natural forest, the plantations in Linnaean symmetry and the open expanses of rolling heathland.

Driving Coming from Malawi, Chelinda Camp lies roughly 100km from Rumphi, and is reached along recently regraded roads which shouldn't present any problem in the dry season but which may require a 4x4 vehicle after heavy rain. The route is clearly signposted: from Rumphi you need to follow the S85 westwards for roughly 50km, then turn right onto the S10 to Chitipa. Thazima entrance gate is 8km along the S10. About 30km past the entrance gate, a signposted turn-off to the right leads to Chelinda, a further 16km away.

The best place to stock up on food before you reach Nyika is Mzuzu, and the last place where you can be sure of fuel is Rumphi. The drive between Lilongwe and Nyika cannot be done in a day during the rains, and it's a very long (nine-hour) slog even in the dry season, so it may be worth considering an overnight stop in Mzuzu or Rumphi.

By bus/hitchhiking The Nyika Safari Company offers road transfers from Mzuzu (*US$112 pp, min 2*). For budget travellers, it's more complicated as there is no through public transport. In the dry season, there is a twice-weekly bus between Rumphi and Chitipa which will drop you at the last turn-off, from where you'll either have to walk the last 30km to Chelinda (it's reasonably flat!) or else hope to hitch a lift. In the rainy season, there is no bus but you can easily get a *matola* from Rumphi along the S85 (ask for a vehicle heading to Katumbi), then walk the 8km from where you will be dropped at the entrance gate. Provided you have a tent, it is permitted to camp at the entrance gate, though facilities are basic.

If you want to hitch all the way, you'd be wiser trying to get a lift from Rumphi through to Chelinda, to be sure of not getting stuck halfway. The best days to hitch are Fridays and Saturdays, which is when Malawian residents tend to head to the park (but also when accommodation is most likely to be fully booked – not a problem, of course, if you have a tent).

An alternative option for backpackers is to do a two-day hike to Chelinda from Rumphi, then to traverse the Nyika across to Livingstonia over two or three days.

WHERE TO STAY The only viable place to stay in the area is at Chelinda, which offers the choice of the original camp, an upmarket lodge or a campsite. It is run by the Nyika Safari Company (☎ +265 1 330180; e reservations@nyika.com; www.nyika.com).

The resthouse that used to be on the Zambian side of the plateau has fallen into disuse – so forget staying there.

🏠 **Chelinda Lodge** (8 cabins) An upmarket stone lodge on the edge of the forest. Luxurious en-suite log cabins command stunning views across the montane grasslands of the plateau. *US$310 pp, inc FB & game drives.*

🏠 **Chelinda Camp** (6 rooms, 4 chalets, camping) Overlooking a beautiful small dam, and encircled by extensive pine plantations, Chelinda Camp is a little lower down than the lodge. Its bar is open to all & will serve anyone staying around Chelinda, which means that it's normally very quiet.

Dbl rooms, each having an en-suite bathroom with toilet & bath, are simple & solid, with a huge fireplace that comes into its own in winter – roaring log fires are exactly what you need.

Alongside the rooms are private chalets, each sleeping up to 4 people. These have a large lounge, a bathroom with toilet & shower, 2 dbl bedrooms, & a fully equipped kitchen. There's a resident chef who will prepare your food for you if you wish, but you must bring it all with you. Realistically, this is only an option if you are driving up here: the nearest shop is 4hrs away in Rumphi.

About 2km from the main camp is a campsite, in a lovely spot in the forest with sweeping views over undulating grassland. Its large, clean ablutions block has hot showers. Campers should be careful to keep food well out of reach of the resident hyenas – which have even been known to gnaw on car tyres! If you wish to eat in the main camp then you can, provided that you book in advance (*US$5–10 for b/fast, US$10 for lunch & US$15 for dinner*). Note that there are no permanent tents here; you must bring your own.

A stable of 25–30 horses is kept here, with both short & long rides available – see *Horseback trails, page 373. Room US$150 pp sharing FB; chalet US$120 per chalet. Camping US$5.*

WHAT TO SEE AND DO Nyika National Park has many very scenic spots, archaeological sites and an extensive network of roads and trails. There are many different hiking and driving options. While visitors are free to walk where they please by day (and to explore the park by road if they have private transport), all guided activities and night drives must be organised through the Nyika Safari Company (☎ +265 1 330180; e reservations@nyika.com; www.nyika.com).

The following synopsis of major attractions serves as a taster only.

Walks around Chelinda Plenty of roads radiate from Chelinda Camp, and it would be quite possible to spend four or five days in the area without repeating a walk. The marshy area immediately downstream of Chelinda Dam (which lies right in front of the camp) is a good place to see bushbuck and a variety of birds, and the dam itself attracts nocturnal predators such as hyena and leopard. A good short walk for visitors with limited time is to the **two dams** near Chelinda. The road here follows a dambo (a seasonal or perennial marsh) and the area offers good game viewing, as well as frequent sightings of wattled crane. The round trip covers 8km and takes two hours.

Another good short walk (about an hour) is from behind Chalet Four to the Kasaramba turn-off and then left along Forest Drive through the pine plantation back to Chalet Four. At dusk, there is a fair chance of seeing leopards along this walk, and daytime sightings are not uncommon.

A longer walk takes you to **Lake Kaulime**, which lies 8km west of Chelinda. This is the only natural lake on the plateau and is traditionally said to be the home of a serpent which acts as the guardian to Nyika's animals. More certain attractions than legendary serpents are migratory waterfowl (in summer) and large mammals, particularly roan antelope and zebra, coming to drink. It is also a very attractive spot, circled by indigenous trees.

Night drives Spotlit night drives out of Chelinda offer the best opportunity to see nocturnal predators. Leopard and serval are often seen on the fringes of Chelinda Forest, while spotted hyena and side-striped jackal are common in grassy areas. When we last visited, we were lucky enough to see a pair of honey badgers crossing the road – a first for both of us. Especially in winter, the plateau gets really cold at night, and you should take all your warm clothing with you in the vehicle.

Walks and drives further afield Many of the more interesting points in Nyika are too far from Chelinda to be reached on a day walk, though they are accessible to visitors with vehicles.

Jalawe Rock is about 1km on foot from a car park 34km north of Chelinda. The views here are spectacular, stretching over a close range of mountains to Lake Malawi's mountainous Tanzanian shore. With binoculars, it is often possible to see buffaloes and elephants in the miombo woodland of the Mpanda Ridge below. A variety of raptors, as well as klipspringer, are frequently seen around the rock, and the surrounding vegetation includes many proteas.

Nganda Peak is, at 2,605m, the highest peak on the plateau. It lies about 30km northeast of Chelinda, and can be reached by following the Jalawe Rock road for about 25km then turning left on to a 4km-long motorable track. It's a 1.5km walk from the end of the track to the peak.

Kasaramba Viewpoint lies 43km southeast of Chelinda. You can drive to within 1.5km of the viewpoint and then walk the final stretch. When it isn't covered in mist, the views to the lake are excellent, and you can also see remnants of the terraced slopes built by the early Livingstonia missionaries. The most extensive rainforest in Nyika lies on the slopes below Kasaramba, and visitors frequently see the localised crowned eagle and mountain buzzard in flight. From Kasaramba, a 3km road leads to the top of the pretty 30m-high Nchenachena Falls.

Further along the road to Kasaramba, also 43km from Chelinda, is a large juniper forest, the most southerly stand of *Juniperus procera* in Africa. A short trail offers the opportunity of sighting forest animals such as leopard, elephant shrew, red duiker, bushpig and a variety of forest birds. The forest can also be explored from the firebreaks that surround it.

Zovo Chipola Forest, near the old Zambian resthouse, is of special interest to birdwatchers, and also harbours several mammal species, the most commonly seen of which are bushbuck, blue monkey and elephant shrew. An unmarked trail runs through the forest, which is best visited with a local guide, at least if you hope to pick up the calls of such elusive forest birds as the bar-tailed trogon.

Chowo Forest lies nearer to the old Zambian Resthouse in the Zambian part of the park. Larger than Zovo Chipola Forest, it used to be popular with people staying at the Zambian Resthouse, but it is now somewhat off the beaten track.

Fingira Rock is a large granite dome lying 22km south of Chelinda. On the eastern side of the rock, a cave 11m deep and 18m long was used as a shelter by humans around 3,000 years ago – excavations in 1965 unearthed a complete human skeleton and a large number of stone tools. Several schematic rock paintings can be seen on the walls of the cave. A motorable track runs to the base of the rock, 500m from the cave. The miombo woodland around Thazima entrance gate is rich in birds and noted for unusual species.

Mountain bikes There are mountain bikes for hire at US$5 per hour, or US$25 for the whole day.

Horseback trails A stable of around 25–30 horses is kept at Chelinda, with animals suitable for both novice and experienced riders. Visitors can do anything from a short morning's ride to a ten-night luxury riding trail. Shorter rides (*US$20/hr, US$100/day*) can be arranged at minimal notice, and are an excellent way of getting around, and getting closer to the game. Eland in particular allow horses to approach far more closely than they would a vehicle or pedestrian, as do the wary Nyika elephants. Longer riding safaris (*US$320 pp per night, all inc, except park fees & drinks*), using mobile tented camps, can be arranged given as much notice as possible.

Fishing The rivers and dams on the Nyika Plateau are stocked with rainbow trout, and are thus popular with anglers. The dams are closed to anglers from April to September, but the rivers are open throughout the year. Fishing permits must be arranged through the Nyika Safari Company. Licences cost US$4 per day and rods can be hired for US$5 per half day.

Wilderness trails Six wilderness trails have been designated within Nyika National Park, ranging from one to five nights in duration. Visitors wishing to use these trails must supply their own camping equipment and food, and are required to hike in the company of a national park guide. Most of the trails cost US$30 pp for the first night and an additional US$20 per night thereafter for the first two people. Additional people are charged US$5 per person per night. The Livingstone Trail commands a one-off payment of US$50 extra, above this. Porters can be arranged for a small extra charge. All the trails must be booked in advance through the Nyika Safari Company.
   Of particular interest are:

Livingstonia Trail (*US$80 for one or two people; US$10 pp for each additional person*) The most popular of Nyika's wilderness trails leads from Chelinda all the way to Livingstonia on the Rift Valley escarpment east of the national park. This three-day, two-night guided hike is recommended only in the dry season. Hiking the route in reverse is not permitted, as a guide and park fees cannot be organised at Livingstonia, though this may become possible in future.

Jalawe and Chipome River Trail Of particular interest for wildlife viewing is this four-night trail, which passes through the miombo woodland in the northern part of the park. It offers the opportunity to see elephant, buffalo, greater kudu and a variety of other mammals that are generally absent from the plateau.

NOTE ON GUIDEBOOKS If you have the opportunity, buy a copy of Sigrid Anna Johnson's book, *A Visitor's Guide to Nyika National Park, Malawi*. It is often available at the park reception at Chelinda, and is an excellent guide to the plateau. See *Appendix 3*, page 511, for more details. A small booklet containing a detailed map of the Chelinda area is also sold at the park reception for a nominal charge.
   The above description of Nyika Plateau has been edited from an original section in the excellent *Malawi: The Bradt Travel Guide* by Philip Briggs. If you plan an extended visit to Malawi, then get hold of a copy of this before you travel – it's the standard reference on travel in Malawi.

top **Elephant calf**
Loxodonta africana (CM)
page 500

centre **Herd of buffalo** (AZ)

right **Buffalo**
Syncerus caffer (CM)
page 502

opposite page:

above   **Lion** *Panthera leo* (MB) page 491

below   **Leopard** *Panthera pardus* (MB) page 491

this page:

above   **Cheetah** *Acynonix jubatus* (AZ) page 492

right   **African wild dog** *Lycaon pictus* (HA) page 493

below   **Spotted hyena** *Crocuta crocuta* (MB) page 493

above left **Burchell's zebra**
Equus burchelli (CM)
page 502

above centre **Black lechwe**
Kobus leche smithemani (CM)
page 499

above right **Oribi**
Ourebia ourebi (CM)
page 500

left **Puku**
Kobus vardoni (CM)
page 499

below left **Roan antelope**
Hippotragus equinus (CM)
page 496

above left **Greater kudu**
Tragelaphus strepsiceros (AZ)
page 497

above right **Blue wildebeest**
Connochaetes taurinus (CM)
page 496

centre **Waterbuck**
Kobus ellipsiprymnus (MB)
page 496

below left **Lichtenstein's hartebeest**
Alcelaphus lichtensteini (AZ)
page 496

below right **Bushbuck**
Tragelaphus scriptus (CM)
page 498

top left	**African fish eagle** (MB)
top right	**Little bee-eater** (AZ)
above left	**Giant kingfisher** (CM)
above right	**Carmine bee-eater** (MA)
left	**Yellow-billed stork** (CM)
below	**Pelicans** (CM)

top left   **Crowned crane** (CM)

top centre   **Wattled crane** (AZ)

top left   **Shoebill** (HA) page 327

right   **White-fronted bee-eaters** (HA)

below right   **African darter** (AZ)

below centre   **Three-banded courser** (AZ)

below left   **Giant eagle owl** (AZ)

top   **Warthogs,** (CM) page 503
above left   **Bird snake** (MB)
above right   **Genet** *Genetta genetta* (MB) page 503
below left   **Crocodile** *Crocodylus niloticus* (CM)
below right   **Porcupine** *Hystrix africaeaustralis* (MB) page 505

13

The Copperbelt

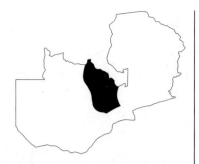

The Copperbelt is Zambia's industrial base, a prosperous area around Ndola, Kitwe and Chingola dotted with mines: the area's production of copper and cobalt is of global importance. The population density here is high, and the environmental impact of so many people can clearly be seen. Despite this, the centres of the Copperbelt's cities are pleasant and not the sprawling industrial wastes that might be expected.

For the normal visitor, these areas have very few attractions and so this chapter is deliberately concise. For simplicity's sake, this text also covers three of the main towns around the Copperbelt – Kabwe and Kapiri Mposhi to the south, and Solwezi to the west – even though these are outside the confines of the Copperbelt province.

The region tends to attract a higher level of rainfall than Lusaka, so bear this in mind if you are planning to travel in the rainy season. Note, too, that land in the Copperbelt is at a higher altitude than that further south – Ndola, for example, is 1,296m above sea level, and Solwezi higher still. As a result, it's generally cooler here than in the capital, so do remember to bring warmer clothes, especially for the evenings.

THE HISTORY OF THE COPPER

Zambia's rich copper deposits have been exploited since around the 6th or 7th century AD. There is evidence that the early Iron-Age inhabitants of Zambia mined, smelted and even traded copper with their neighbours – bracelets and bangles have been found at several sites.

However, large-scale exploitation of these reserves waited until the 20th century. Around the turn of the century, the old sites where native Africans had mined copper for centuries, like Bwana Mkubwa southeast of Ndola, were being examined by European and American prospectors. The demand for metals was stimulated from 1914 to 1918 by World War I, and small mines opened up to satisfy this need. They worked well, but these small-scale productions were only viable whilst the price of the raw materials remained high. Copper, zinc, lead and vanadium were among the most important of the minerals being mined.

Given Zambia's location, and the high costs of transporting any produce out of this land-locked country, it made economic sense to process the mineral ores there, and then export the pure metal ingots. However, this would require considerable investment and large-scale operations.

After the war, demand for copper continued to increase, fuelled by the expansion in the worldwide electrical and automotive industries. Large-scale mining became a more feasible option. In 1922 the British South Africa Company, who claimed to have bought all of the country's mining concessions in various tribal agreements, started to allocate large prospecting areas for foreign companies.

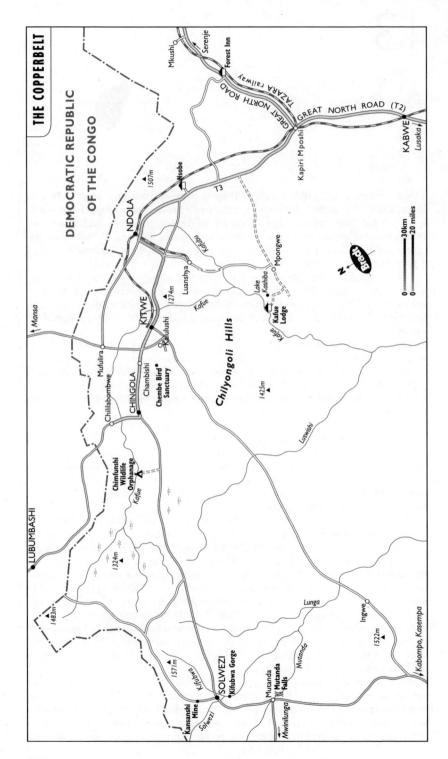

THE COPPERBELT

Steven Lewis

The Central African Copperbelt spans the border of northwestern Zambia and southern DRC and represents one of the largest copper provinces in the world. Known deposits falling within the Zambian Copperbelt contain approximately 88 million tonnes of copper, worth around US$650,000,000,000 at 2007 metal prices.

Archaeological evidence for copper mining in Zambia dates as far back as the fourth century when malachite was mined and smelted into cross-shaped ingots known as *nsanshi*, which were used for trading. Large-scale copper production, however, didn't start until around the turn of the last century when early European explorers were shown the out-cropping copper deposits near present-day Ndola, Kitwe and Solwezi. As a result, commercial mines were opened shortly after the Cape-to-Cairo railway line reached Ndola from the south, and mining has continued to the present day.

However, the full story of the Zambian Copperbelt began around 877 million years ago, when the oldest rocks of the so-called Katangan Supergroup were deposited in a series of basins that now form the heart of the Copperbelt. The earliest rocks of this group are made up of conglomerates and sandstones that were deposited by rivers and deltas in a series of narrow troughs during the early stages of the evolution of the basins. As the basins developed and deepened, the character of the rocks changed in response to the changing depositional conditions, resulting in dolomite-dominated rocks that were deposited on platforms under fairly shallow water. In response to further basin deepening a later group of rocks, comprising a transition from dolomite, through a mixed series of dolomites and siltstones to a dominant siltstone were deposited, indicating an accumulation of material in a deep-water environment. At this point, a major change in the geological environment occurred, indicated by the presence of a thick unit of debris flows known as the 'Grand Conglomerate', with overlying siltstones. The Grand Conglomerate is a remarkable unit that can be traced for hundreds of kilometres and probably reflects the breaking up of the Rodinian Supercontinent around 740 million years ago.

The origin of the copper deposits contained in these rocks has long been debated by geologists studying the Copperbelt. Early theories leaned towards a 'syngenetic' origin, suggesting that the copper was deposited at the same time as the rocks in which it occurs. More recent research favours a longer, multi-stage 'diagenetic' origin, in which the copper was introduced into the rocks via major fault systems over a very long period of perhaps 300 million years or more, long after the rocks were deposited.

Exploration skills from overseas flowed into the country, locating several large deposits of copper – well beneath the levels of the existing mining operations.

By the early 1930s, four large new mines were coming on stream: Nkana, Nchanga, Roan Antelope and Mufulira. These were to change Northern Rhodesia's economy permanently. Despite a collapse of the prices for copper in 1931, the value of the country's exports increased by 400% between 1930 and 1933 – leaving copper accounting for 90% of the country's exports by value. Thus began the mining industry which in 2004 accounted for about 17% of Zambia's GDP and 90% of Zambia's export earnings.

During 2001, the price of copper plummeted once again, leaving much of the Copperbelt's newly privatised industry in the doldrums. Since then, however, there has been a complete turnaround, with the price of copper rising by over 300% in the three years to 2007, when it hit around US$6,000 a tonne. Suddenly there's something of a goldrush mentality in the region, with prospectors from across the world in search of the 'green rock' way beyond the traditional confines of the Copperbelt itself. Among several investors in the region, First Quantum originally came to recycle waste from the Bwana Mkubwa mine near Ndola, but is now well ensconced in Kansanshi Mine at Solwezi, while 100km to the west of Solwezi, the huge Lumwana Mine is set to open in 2008. According to one industry source, it is estimated that by 2009, Zambian mines should be producing over a million tonnes of copper each year.

LUSAKA TO KAPIRI MPOSHI

The Great North Road out of Lusaka, the T2, rapidly slips off the city's dirty industrial belt for open bush and mile after mile of farmland, planted with everything from soya beans to maize and coffee. It's a good, tarred road, increasingly undulating beyond Kabwe, with the only problem likely to come from slow-moving haulage trucks transporting goods to or from the region's mines.

At intervals along the roadside, local produce is offered for sale. Look out for honey in large plastic containers to the north of Kabwe, and various small markets that you'll pass en route.

WHERE TO STAY If you're heading in this direction, but looking for somewhere to stay reasonably close to Lusaka, there are several options before the town of Kabwe. The best of these are listed below, from south to north.

⌂ **Protea Hotel Lusaka Safari Lodge** (40 rooms) Great North Rd; ☎ 021 1212843–6; f 021 1212853; e chisamba@zamnet.zm; www.proteahotels.com. Set in a private game reserve 45km north of Lusaka. For details, see pages 140–1.
⌂ **Fringilla Lodge** (46 rooms, 5 chalets, 2 flats, 2 houses, camping) Great North Rd, Chisamba; ☎/f 021 1213885, 1214364; f 021 1213638; e fringill@zamnet.zm; www.fringillalodge.com. Situated about 51km north of Lusaka towards Kabwe (look out for the sign on the east side of the road), Fringilla is part of a large, working farm that has expanded to include a butchery (which also makes processed meats), a dairy, a clinic & even a post office; the bank that was on site is now 500m up the road on the opposite side.
Gone is the erstwhile small B&B, its place taken by a rather ramshackle selection of accommodation that's capitalising primarily on the lucrative conference trade. A restaurant, lounge & kitchen occupy the old farm building, around which is a lawn & children's playground. The various rooms are arranged beyond this; all have en-suite facilities (some with just a low partition) & are simple but well kept, with ceiling fans, nets & the obligatory TV. Well back from the main house is a small shady campsite & basic ablution block, shared by 2-bed chalets. Meals are served from an à-la-carte menu, while at weekends there's always a braai. Horseriding

is possible free of charge to diners (but note that no hats are provided) & there are pleasant walks around the farm. Despite the slight air of disorganisation, the staff are helpful & friendly. $$–$$$; camping Kw25,000 pp. B/fast extra.
⌂ **Chaplin's Barbet** (8 rooms) ☎/f 021 1213762; m 096 848267; e arulussa@gmail.com. The small grassy camp at Chaplin's Barbet was opened for the eclipse in 2002, & continues to attract visitors. It's situated on an organic farm 73km north of Lusaka, about 1km off the Great North Rd to the west, & was named for Zambia's only truly endemic bird. If you're driving here in the wet season, be very careful – the approach road is flat but its cottonsoil base is deceptively slippery. With their red earthy tones, the square brick chalets under thatch are unpretentious but pleasant, each having a stone floor, twin beds with mosquito nets, & en-suite shower; plans are in hand to improve the lighting. As the name suggests, this is a good birding area; visitors are also welcome to look round the farm, which produces essential oils for aromatherapy. $$.
⌂ **Ibis Gardens** (37 rooms) Great North Rd; ☎ 021 1213764, 1213766; f 021 1214736; e ibis@zamnet.zm. Some 74km from Lusaka, Ibis is set in 18ha grounds down a 1km tarred drive to the east of the Great North Rd. With its painted chalets neatly arranged across flat, well-kept lawns, interspersed here & there with banana & guava

trees, the place has a rather suburban feel. The impression persists inside each of the rooms, with their white walls & simple but modern furnishings. If it's quite corporate, it's also very clean & pleasant. AC/heater, safe, fridge & tea-/coffee-making facilities come as standard, as does a huge en-suite shower. Larger houses have 2 or 3 bedrooms, a lounge & a kitchenette. During the week this is very much a business venue, with internet café, restaurant & bar, but at weekends it morphs into family mode, with pizzas & braais on offer, & sports facilities that include tennis, volleyball, basketball, a gym & a large, free-form pool complete with its own island. A further 23 rooms were under construction in 2007, with a campsite mooted for the future. *from* $$

KABWE This small town (✪ KABWE 14°26.655'S; 28°26.717'E) is situated little more than 60km south of Kapiri Mposhi and about 142km north of Lusaka. It was built on the old colonial model of a central business area with a perpendicular road-grid, surrounded by pretty, spacious suburbs and with 'satellite' townships containing lots of high-density housing for poorer people. These divisions have now melted a little, but the centre still has pleasantly wide streets lined with a variety of shops – although most of these have seen better days.

History Kabwe, when under colonial rule, was known as Broken Hill. In 1921 an almost complete human skull was unearthed here during mining operations, at a depth of about 20m. Together with a few other human bones nearby, it's estimated to be over 200,000 years old, making these the oldest human remains known from southern central Africa. Originally classified as *Homo rhodesiensis* by scientists, the remains are now generally attributed to *Homo heidelbergensis*, a large-brained species that was the common ancestor to *Homo sapiens* in Africa and the Neanderthals in Europe. However, to most people this human is best known as 'Broken Hill Man'.

In more recent times, the town's economy has been closely linked with mining, most recently for zinc and lead (with very high-quality silver as a by-product). The mine, which was only about 2km south of the centre, was closed in 1994. However, fortunes could be about to revive with the announcement in spring 2007 that a South African company, Silver Lining Ventures, plans to move in. Initially they will be processing copper ore from the DRC, but they then propose to restart zinc- and lead-mining operations. The town is also widely known for the large Mulungushi Textiles factory, from where cotton from all over the country is brought together then exported to China.

Getting there and away Regular long-distance buses connect Kabwe with both the Copperbelt and northern Zambia each day, as do postbuses on both the Lusaka–Ndola and Lusaka–Kasama routes. The Lusaka bus terminal is on Freedom Way, close to Tuskers Hotel; other buses use the area near the Kobil fuel station on Independence Avenue.

🏠 **Where to stay** Most visitors to Kabwe are in transit, and accommodation is limited to one decent hotel in the centre of town, plus a few simple guesthouses that include **Travel Lodge Executive, Broken Hill Lodge** and **Zambezi Source Lodge** (✎ *021 5223286;* m *097 7762978*). To the south, about 1km beyond the railway, there's the **VK Garden Motel** or, 200m further on, **Kabwe Green Inn Motel**.

🏠 **Tuskers Hotel** (35 rooms) Buntungwa St; ✎ 021 5222076–7; f 021 5222076; e tuskers@ zamnet.zm. On the southern side of town, on the corner of Freedom Way, this is Kabwe's main hotel. It's not an exciting place to stay, & survives mainly on the trade in local conferences, but the staff are helpful, & it's better than it looks at first glance. En-suite rooms are clean & a decent size, with all that you'd expect from a mid-range hotel, inc a safe & fridge. There's a standard hotel restaurant (serving

13

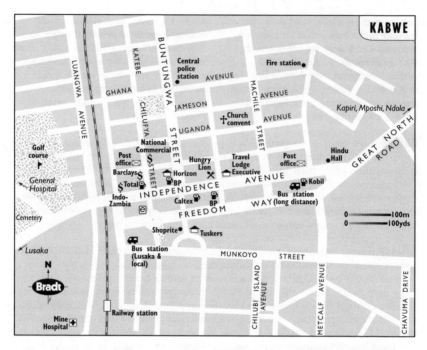

very good pizzas, we understand), as well as grills from the BBQ, & a pool in a pleasant courtyard. $$
Hotel Horizon (18 rooms) Cnr Independence Av & Buntungwa St; m 095 5 822049, 097 7822049.

The Horizon is pretty grotty; indeed, one local described it as plain 'bad'. Although it's a lot cheaper than Tuskers, we'd recommend paying the extra, unless every cent counts. $

✗ **Where to eat** Don't expect anything fancy in the food stakes, though the pizzas at Tuskers are said to be good. There are fast-food outlets near the fuel stations on Independence Avenue, though, so if you're passing through and in need of a quick break, it's a perfectly reasonable place to stop for a bite to eat.

Out of town, the offerings are more promising. To the north, about 5km along the tar road, **Tony's Stop** is a useful snack bar with a pleasant garden where you can sit with a drink and a fritter. Altogether in another league – and with a deli as well – is:

✗ **Maplehurst Restaurant & Deli** Great North Rd;
☏ 021 5222770; m 096 6768837, 097 7949165;
⊕ 06.00–19.30 daily. Some 10km south of town, the well-recommended Maplehurst serves meals from breakfast to burgers & sandwiches & even full-scale

grills. There's a shady garden or you can eat in the restaurant, where there's also a small bar. Maplehurst stocks a good range of frozen meat, pizzas & ready meals, plus various cheeses & honey – ideal if you're heading out on a self-catering trip. $$

Other practicalities The main shop in town is the large Shoprite supermarket, just off Freedom Way (which is parallel to, and one block south of, Independence Avenue), or you could try the large market, to the south of town near the railway line. For motorists, there are a number of fuel stations on Independence Avenue, and should you be in need of spares, try Autoworld, just south of the Kobil fuel station.

Excursions from Kabwe About 130km east of Kabwe is Lunsemfwa Wonder Gorge, a spectacular gorge 300m deep where the Mkushi River meets the

Lunsemfwa, and both cut into the rocks of the Muchinga Escarpment. It's in a remote and isolated position, but see page 298, for directions on how to reach it.

KAPIRI MPOSHI Kapiri Mposhi's main claim to fame is that it stands at one end of the TAZARA railway. There is a constant flow of people, buses and trucks through town which makes it lively, if slightly aggressive, but not safe. Kapiri is a town which visitors often pass through, but where they seldom linger. Expect people around at all times of the day and night, and be on your guard against opportunist thieves.

Kapiri's crossroads location ensures that there's no shortage of fuel stations along the main road. Total is by the market, with Caltex just to the north of the railway station. Most prominent of all is the conspicuous new 24-hour Continental Oil that sits right at the junction where the Great North Road splits from the road to the Copperbelt. As well as selling fuel, it's something of a practical one-stop shop, with toilets, a fast-food outlet and a basic shop, as well as plans for an ATM and bureau de change, a car-spares shop and an internet café. Here, as elsewhere in Kapiri, you'll come across people selling cheap pirate DVDs, CDs and cassette tapes, which are put together in Tanzania and brought in over the border. In 2007, a branch of Barclays Bank was under construction in the town.

To the east of town you'll notice a small, rather incongruous-looking hill that gives the town its name: *kapiri* means 'mountain'. The town is the home of the glassworks KGP, which uses stone mined from the hill, and as you head north towards the Copperbelt you'll see traders selling glasses and mugs alongside the road.

Getting there and away Kapiri Mposhi is a linear town, but with its location just south of the junction where the Great North Road splits from the road to Ndola, it is effectively a major crossroads for those travelling northwards from Lusaka, with excellent links to the rest of the country. Drivers should watch out for the large speed humps at both ends of the town on the main road.

By bus Kapiri Mposhi is easily reached by minibus, long-distance coach or postbus, as it stands on the main routes between Lusaka and both northern Zambia and the Copperbelt. There are very frequent arrivals and departures, especially to/from Lusaka and the Copperbelt; a ticket between here and Lusaka costs around Kw40,000–45,000. The bus terminus is in the centre of town, on the left if you're travelling north, behind a variety of market stalls. The town is on the postbus route between Lusaka and Ndola.

By TAZARA train If you continue along the road going north, it will soon cross a railway line. Turn right just before this and follow the road for about 1km to reach the bustling and quite imposing TAZARA terminus.

If you did not buy one at the TAZARA office in Lusaka (see page 125), this is the place to buy your ticket to Dar es Salaam, 1,860km from Kapiri, or north within Zambia to Kasama or Nakonde on the border. The station becomes exceedingly busy around train departure times, and foreigners will encounter considerable hassle. To avoid this, arrive well before the train is due to depart and take great care of your belongings. If you need to buy a ticket, then allow at least an extra hour.

TAZARA services have an excellent reputation for time-keeping, which is almost unrivalled in Africa. Nowadays, only express trains cover the route, leaving Kapiri Mposhi at 16.00 on Tuesday and Friday, and arriving in Dar es Salaam at 12.35 on Thursday and Sunday. The return express leaves Dar on the same days at

13

TAZARA TRAIN PRICES (IN KWACHA) FROM KAPIRI MPOSHI			
To	**1st class**	**2nd class (sleeper)**	**3rd class**
Mkushi	14,000	11,000	9,000
Mpika	50,000	35,000	25,500
Kasama	60,000	50,000	40,000
Border (Nakonde/Tunduma)	680,000	60,000	50,000
Dar es Salaam	180,000	150,000	110,000

15.50, arriving back in Kapiri Mposhi on Thursday and Sunday at 09.26. Trains stop at several stations en route, including Mkushi, Serenje, Mpika, Kasama and Nakonde in Zambia.

Tickets are available in first, second and third classes. Both first- and second-class compartments are sleepers (although there are second-class seaters, too), accommodating four and six passengers respectively; in third class, it's seating only. Food is available on the trains, as is bottled water.

Remember to check in advance with the Tanzanian High Commission (see page 151) if you'll need a visa to enter Tanzania. Travellers to Zambia can usually get their visa on the train, but again, do check your status first. (For details of visas, see pages 54–5.)

Hitchhiking Hitching to or from Kapiri Mposhi is fairly easy. Your best bet is to walk out of town for a kilometre or so until you find space. Alternatively ask around the truckers in town for a lift. If you are going north, then get a short lift or a taxi to take you the 2km or so to the Continental Oil fuel station where the road to Ndola splits from the Great North Road, which continues on up to Mpika and beyond. This is an excellent hitching spot. (But do remember that hitching in Zambia is not a free ride; you will be expected to contribute to the cost of the journey.)

WHERE TO STAY AND EAT There are a few run-down hotels here, including the **Kapiri Lodge**, **Chanika Lodge**, the **Unity Motel** and – probably the best of a rather dodgy bunch – **Eros Lodge**, all on the main road. These and others like them are basic and noisy, with rooms rented by the hour as well as the night. Kapiri is not a town to stay in unless you have to.

Relatively little fresh food seems to be available at the market, although street sellers will confront you with seasonal produce, which at the end of the rainy season will include tomatoes, peanuts and sweet potatoes. There are, though, lots of take-aways. If you are driving your best bet is the brand-new fuel station 3km north of town, where fast-food offerings include some good take-away chicken.

NDOLA

About 325km north of Lusaka, Ndola is the provincial capital of the Copperbelt, but slightly smaller than its neighbour, Kitwe. Considering its strong industrial base, it is a pleasant city with broad, leafy streets and little to indicate its industrial base. With the recent boost in the price of copper, the town has witnessed a parallel resurgence in prosperity, with several new guesthouses and restaurants in evidence.

In keeping with this general air of optimism, the town's football stadium is being rebuilt as a training ground for the 2010 World Cup, to be held in South Africa.

KWACHA ROAD

MACHA

MWATIANWA

BOUNDARY

↑ *Gecko Gallery*

CHIPULUKUSU

• North Rise Shopping Precinct

TANZANIA AVENUE

NORTH RISE

The Hill

LOWENTHAL

VITANDA

• Technical College

• Kansenshi Shopping Precinct

FITENTE

CHINTU

MULOBEZI

• Brewery

KANSENSHI

♜ Kaps Villa

KABINGA

KABELENGA

LEWANIKA

DR DAMIE

SHINDE

ARUSHA

PRESIDENT STREET

Paterson

Railway station

Chez Ntemba

Royal

Voyagers

MAINA

LUANGWA

♜ Michelangelo

BROADWAY

BP

Bus station (north)

Savoy
Autoworld
Caltex

Power station

Palmwood, Setanga, Kitwe, Luanshya

Catholic cathedral ✟

Anglican cathedral

Central Hospital ✚

CHIMWEMWE

Copperbelt Museum

Hong Kong

Ndola Boating Club

NKANDABWE

BLANTYRE

High Court

Barclays $

Total

Zambia $$ Stanbic
Danny's

MOFFAT

New Ambassador Hotel

DEPOT

Swimming pool

INDEPENDENCE WAY

BUTEKO

Indo-Zambia $

S SOKO

Stanbic

DAG HAMMARSKJOELD

HILL CREST

Lowenthal Theatre

Civic Centre

KANONGESHA

KAUNDA

Police station

Shoprite

CHIMWEMWE

CHISOKON

• Fire station

Stanbic $

KANINI

Squash Club

NKANA ROAD

• Rugby Club

Hilltop Hospital ✚

BP

Plaza Cinema

Bus terminal (south)

PRESIDENT AVENUE

MATELO

MAKOLI

Slave Tree

Kafubu

ITAWA

Ꞃ Caltex

N

Bradt

♟ Ndola Golf Club

Kafubu

RIVER

KABUSHI

MASALA

Chabanga Lodge

✈ Total

DRIVE

Strawberry Coffee Bar

AIRPORT ROAD

0 ———— 500m
0 ———— 500yds

Musa Kasonka Stadium ✦

KABWE ROAD

Ꞃ Caltex

✈ Airport

Mukuba Hotel, Showgrounds, Kabwe, Lusaka ↓

NDOLA

The Copperbelt NDOLA

13

383

Aside from mining, Ndola benefits from an unusually pure water supply, which explains why it is home to the large Mosi brewery.

GETTING THERE AND AROUND

By air Ndola's airport is on the southern side of the centre of town, clearly signposted off to the right as you enter town from the south. It is well served by several airlines, including Zambian Airways and Proflight/Copper Air, with several flights per day to Lusaka. There are also direct flights to Johannesburg with Zambian Airways and SAA.

The open-air café at the airport is one of the more pleasant places to while away time awaiting a flight. Inside, you'll find all you'd expect from a small-town airport: a bank, bureau de change and ATM (though this may not be the most reliable of machines), a curio shop, car-rental office, internet access, and offices for all the local airlines.

Copper Air Airport ☎ 021 2611796; m 097 7207957; e proflight@iconnect.zm; www.copperair.net. The Copperbelt arm of Proflight, Copper Air has scheduled daily flights between Lusaka & Ndola, & on Mon, Wed, Thu & Fri to Solwezi.

Interair ☎ 021 2618083, 2618087; airport ☎ 021 2612056; www.interair.co.za. Flights to Johannesburg Mon, Wed, Fri.

SAAirlink ☎ 021 2612206; f 021 2612207; www.saairlink.co.za. One flight a day, exc Sat, to Johannesburg.

Zambian Airways ☎ 021 2621466, 2613002, 2611485; m 097 7793947; www.zambianairways.com. Regular flights to Lusaka daily. One flight a day to Johannesburg, exc Sat.

By bus Ndola's main bus terminus is at the southern end of Chimwemwe Road, less than 1km south of the Savoy Hotel – though coaches to Lusaka start from around the Broadway Cinema or Buteko Avenue. There are very frequent links to the other towns of the Copperbelt (Ndola to Kitwe costs Kw10,000 by minibus), and also Lusaka (Kw55,000–60,000). To reach northern Zambia (accessed via the road through Mkushi and Serenje) first get a southbound (probably Lusaka) bus and change at Kapiri Mposhi.

A postbus service operates between Lusaka and Ndola daily except Sunday, stopping en route in Kabwe and Kapiri. Buses arrive in Ndola at 11.00 and 17.00, with a one-way fare of Kw40,000.

By train There are regular departures from Kitwe to Livingstone via Ndola, stopping at all stations, but these are too slow to be of use to many travellers. See page 390 for the timetable from Kitwe.

Hitchhiking Ndola is quite a big town, meaning that good hitch spots are a long walk from the centre – so consider getting a taxi for a few kilometres.

If you want to get to northern Zambia, via Mansa, then resist the temptation to 'cut the corner' by crossing into and out of DRC – it's far too dangerous.

Car hire

Avis Airport ☎/f 021 2620741; m 097 7800756; www.avisworld.com

Voyagers Arusha St; ☎ 021 2620990, 2620314; f 021 2620312; airport ☎ 021 2617062, 2620604; f 021 2620605; e carrental@voyagers.com.zm; www.voyagerszambia.com

WHERE TO STAY There is a small choice of hotels in Ndola, and a growing number of guesthouses, but all aim at visiting businesspeople and prices are correspondingly high. For most visitors, the better guesthouses are generally a more appealing option than the town's hotels.

Hotels

⌂ **Savoy Hotel** (146 rooms) 12 Buteko Av; ✆ 021 2611097–8; f 021 2614001; e savoy@zamnet.zm. The Savoy has long tried to maintain its image as the most lavish hotel in Ndola, priding itself on its casino & 'suspended swimming pool situated on the mezzanine floor' (open to non-residents for Kw10,000). It stands just off Maina Soko Road, near the eastern end of Broadway, with a secure car park. Its rooms, renovated in 2007, are relatively small & functional, but are comfortable, with DSTV, & both bath & shower en suite. In the restaurant, lunch & dinner are available (Kw65,000 pp). $$$

⌂ **Mukuba Hotel** (52 rooms) ✆ 021 2651000–4; f 021 2651007, 2651012; e mukhotel@microlink.zm; www.mukubahotel.com. The rather more attractive Mukuba is inconveniently located about 6km south of town, adjacent to the grounds used for the annual Trade Fair. To get there head south towards Kabwe, then take a right into the industrial area, onto Arkwright Rd, then Crompton Rd. A good-size floor rug softens the corporate effect in the rooms, each of which has AC, tea/coffee maker, phone, DSTV & a fridge. The hotel is built around a central courtyard where peacocks strut around the fishponds, while beyond roams a small resident herd of impala. There's a bar & restaurant, & an internet room. If you want the amenities of a hotel, & can live with the 10-min drive from the centre of town, this is better value than the Savoy. $$$

⌂ **Royal Hotel** (52 rooms) Cnr Vitanda St & Kabelenga Av; ✆ 021 2621840; f 021 2621850; e royhotel@zamnet.zm. Under the same management as the Edinburgh Hotel in Kitwe, & at the heart of Ndola's business district, the Royal is quite an old hotel, having opened in the mid-1940s. (Back then it had several different names, including the Coppersmith Arms & the Naaznina Hotel &, more recently, the Travellers' Lodge.) Its rooms are old-fashioned but adequate, each with en-suite facilities, as well as satellite TV, direct-dial phone, minibar/fridge & tea/coffee machine. Downstairs there's a restaurant, a bar & secure parking. $$

⌂ **New Ambassador** (30 rooms) President Av; ✆ 021 2617071. The New Ambassador is fairly near the Plaza Cinema, with en-suite rooms or cheaper rooms with shared facilities, all of which are more basic than those at either the Savoy or the Mukuba. $

⌂ **Baluba Motel** (38 rooms) Kitwe Rd; ✆ 021 2515009; f 021 2612080. Some 24km west of town, this former contractors' camp is a stereotypical Zambian motel: think lino tiles, block-built rooms, metal-framed windows & the obligatory TV. But rooms are clean enough, & fine if you just want somewhere to stop on the long drive through the Copperbelt. $–$$, inc cont b/fast.

Guesthouses

⌂ **Michelangelo** (11 rooms) 126 Broadway; ✆ 021 2620325; m 096 6780036; f 021 2620326; e vgstyle@zamnet.zm. The Italianate Michelangelo, with its columns, cool tiles & courtyard pool, is currently Ndola's best guesthouse. The theme continues in the rooms arranged round the pool, where warm terracotta colours are offset by limed furniture & good, soft lighting. Each is dominated by a large bed with all-round mosquito net, but there's still room for a desk with internet point, TV & hairdryer, & an en-suite bath & shower. The restaurant is warm & inviting, & the bar is popular in the evenings as well. $$$. Credit cards accepted over US$15.

⌂ **Palmwood Guesthouse** (6 rooms) 4753 Mukuni Rd; ✆ 021 2680725; f 021 2680187; e palmquest@zamtel.zm. Italian resident Previtera Pasqualina, known to everyone as Lina, has opened her home to guests, who can expect a very personal welcome. As befits a family house, each of the rooms is different, but they're all attractively finished with en-suite facilities, fridge, coffee maker, TV, fan & mosquito nets. Lina's lovely garden is an attraction in its own right, overlooked by a covered patio where b/fast is served (& other meals on request), & with its own pool. These, together with a BBQ/pizza area & bar, a large living room with TV, & secure parking, create something of a home from home. $$$

⌂ **Setanga Lodge** (14 rooms) 578H Freedom Way; ✆/f 021 2680002; e setanga@zamtel.zm. The attractive Setanga is a cut above most of Ndola's guesthouses, with a large lounge for guests' use & a pool dominating the garden. Bedrooms, some en suite & other sharing facilities, have well-chosen fabrics with pine & wrought-iron furniture; each has a dbl bed, TV & fan. $$ inc cont b/fast.

⌂ **Chabanga Lodge** (18 rooms) Nakatindi Rd; ✆ 021 2622353; m 095 5888195; f 021 2611218; e chabanagalodge@zamtel.zm. Down a narrow road off the approach road to the airport, Chabanga Lodge opened its doors in 2005, though the rather yappy dogs may be off-putting to some. The warm apricot wash of the walls & toning fabrics give a modern feel to the large, light rooms, offset by wrought-iron furniture & tiled floors. Each has a dbl bed & is equipped with AC, mosquito nets, DSTV, kettle, phone & fridge. In the public rooms, ornate formality contrasts with a decidedly simple dining area, where evening meals are available on request (around Kw40,000). $$

🏠 **Kaps Villa** (6 rooms) 2 Mulobwezi; ☎ 021 2615765; m 097 7117747; e vkaps@yahoo.com. Mutale Kapoka brings a lively but professional approach to the management of her father's new guesthouse. All rooms are en suite with TV, with larger ones having a kitchenette (and a higher price & only a cont b/fast). There's a small covered dining area with TV & bar (with dinner from Kw25,000). It's an affordable & pleasant alternative to Ndola's more upmarket offerings. $$

🏠 **Garden Park Lodge** (9 rondavels) ☎ 021 2622553; m 097 7466715. Situated on the left of the Kabwe Rd to the south of town, Garden Park is a no-frills place furnished in true bric-à-brac style. It's cheap enough, so could be an option if funds are tight, though the noisy bar is a potential irritant. $, inc cont b/fast.

Around Ndola

🏠 **Nsobe Game Camp** (10 tents, 4 chalets, camping) ☎ 021 2610113; m 096 6950327; e nsobe@coppernet.zm, miengwe@coppernet.zm; www.nsobegamecamp.com. Some 9km from the Great North Road along a track that's accessible by 2WD in the dry season only, the turn-off for Nsobe Game Camp is about 63km south of Ndola, or 65km north of Kapiri Mposhi. Set on a 1,500ha game farm in predominantly miombo woodland, with 3 dams (manmade lakes), the camp has 15 species of antelope, inc black lechwe, sable, eland & the rare sitatunga, as well as over 320 species of birds. The atmosphere is one of upmarket camping – & indeed there is a campsite at one end of the site, right on the lake with braais & hot-water showers, but no power. En-suite safari tents on raised wooden platforms have no frills, but everything you need, inc a wooden veranda, some overlooking the lake, while 2 more substantial family chalets can each sleep 4. Nearby, the bar (with TV) & separate restaurant are especially popular at weekends, when Nsobe is a favourite with visitors from the Copperbelt. A couple of fully equipped thatched chalets, sleeping 6 or 8 people in twin bedrooms, are built by a separate dam 5–10 mins' walk away. Food – much of it farm produce, inc fresh orange juice, fish, venison & pork (& their own sausages) – is good and plentiful. And those committed to self-catering won't miss out: there's a shop that sells farm produce.

This is a working farm, with around 1,000 pigs, bream-stocked fishponds, and a citrus orchard; the proximity of fish and pigs is managed in a way similar to that at Lechwe Lodge (see page 226). A farm visit is just one of many activities on offer; others include fishing, walks, & game drives in your own vehicle or theirs (this is no place for serious guiding, but there's a useful bird checklist & an identification sheet for the antelope). Day visitors can use braai sites, picnic tables & benches set near the water's edge. On the water itself, there's canoeing (lifejackets provided) or even swimming – the dams are said to be croc free. Others can just chill in the grounds, or take advantage of the jacuzzi or sauna. Tent Kw325,000/250,000 sgl/pp sharing, DBB; chalet Kw750,000–1,000,000 6–8 people; camping Kw25,000 pp. Day entry Kw25,000. Game drive Kw25,000 pp (min 4); self game drive Kw10,000; canoe Kw5,000/hr. No credit cards.

🏠 **Mukuyu Camp** (5 chalets) Contact via Nsobe, above. Set some 10 mins' drive from Nsobe Game Lodge, & very secluded, Mukuyu (meaning 'fig tree') is a private camp that sleeps a max of 10. With its thatched central dining/seating area lit by candles, it is more upmarket than Nsobe, relaxing & comfortable without being luxurious. Everything here is made on the premises, using locally sourced elephant grass for the walls & thatch, wood from the farm, & handmade clay bricks, while simple baskets adorn the walls. Square, thatched rooms have a small veranda overlooking a waterhole, & at the back is an open-air shower in a semi-open bathroom (1 has a sunken stone bath, too). With its own staff & kitchen, the camp is entirely self-contained, a perfect hideaway in the bush. In case the setting palls, there's a tiny plunge pool & night drives are on offer. US$180 pp FB; min 4, one group only.

🏠 **Lowden Lodge** (13 rooms) m 096 6701150, 6904291, 6907154; e lowden@coppernet.zm. Almost equidistant between Ndola & Kitwe, & about 1km off the main road in the direction of Luanshya, this small guesthouse with dbl, twin & sgl rooms is attractively set in well-kept gardens. Those in search of exercise will welcome the large pool, exercise room & jogging track, while others may find the sauna, bar & TV lounge more to their taste. Dinner, inc home-grown produce, is available to guests.

$$$

🏠 **Kafue Lodge** (8 rooms) Book via Voyagers, page 388 (⊕ 13°22.127'S; 27°58.166'E). Some 2hrs' drive, or 92km, from Ndola, Kafue Lodge is popular with Copperbelt residents for a w/end break. Although it is just 32km from Mpongwe, a huge farming area northwest of Kapiri Mposhi, it is most easily accessed from the north.

To get there, head towards Kitwe, then turn off to Luanshya after about 20km; continue through Luanshya & Mpongwe then, after a further 7km, turn right onto a dirt road & follow this for some 20km, bearing left after 1km; once you get to the airfield, turn left, continuing for a final 5km. The lodge is on a 20km² game farm on the banks of the Kafue River, stocked with 10 species of antelope, inc sable & kudu, & with excellent birding opportunities: Bob Stjernstedt, the Zambian birding expert, advises that it's a particularly good location at which to see Pel's fishing owl.

Relatively simple rooms have been built in pairs, 2 to a chalet. Each is en suite, with wrought-iron furnishings, twin beds, sliding windows, & rugs laid on the cement floor. Outside, to one side of the shared veranda, is a sink, crockery, cutlery & a tiny fridge (you'd need a coolbox & ice if you're self-catering), while on the other is a BBQ area. If self-catering doesn't appeal, there's a bar & restaurant, with produce from the lodge's organic vegetable garden on the menu.

Walks & game-viewing tracks meander through tall miombo woodland & dambos, characteristic of this part of Zambia, & offering good birding. It's also a popular spot for fishing, or for a cruise along the river, while close by is Lake Kashiba. *From US$65 pp sharing, self-catering. Lunch US$30 pp (need to pre-book).*

✗ **WHERE TO EAT** There are plenty of take-aways and fast-food joints around town, including the ubiquitous Hungry Lion near the police station on Blantyre Road, and the rather more interesting Paterson's Bakery on President Avenue North. For more substantial meals, either at lunch or in the evening, the choices are widening, and are no longer limited to the main **hotels**, although the Mukuba's restaurant is perfectly adequate. At lunchtime, the **boat club** overlooking the river is a dark but cool place for lunch (there's a gym and sauna here, too), while **Gecko Gallery** (see page 388) is a relaxing spot for tea and cake in the afternoon.

✗ **Danny's** President Av; ☎ 021 2621828; ⊕ 12.00–14.30, 19.00–22.30 daily. With its predominantly Indian menu (but with more than a hint of other cuisines thrown in), Danny's is one of the best places to eat in town. **$$**

✗ **Hong Kong Restaurant** President Av N; m 097 7752589; ⊕ 12.00–14.30, 18.30–22.00 daily. A super Chinese restaurant – the spring rolls & sweet-and-sour dishes come highly recommended. **$$–$$$**

✗ **Michelangelo** 126 Broadway; ☎ 021 2620325; ⊕ 08.00–14.00 & 19.00–22.30 Mon–Sat; Sun dinner for residents only. As you might expect, the menu at Michelangelo is dominated by Italian fare, boasting freshly made ricotta cheese, & listing a big range of pizzas (**$$**) & pastas (**$$$**). At lunchtimes, the emphasis is on salads, stuffed pitta bread & omelettes.

☕ **Strawberry Coffee Bar** Dag Hammarskjoeld; ⊕ 08.00–20.00 Tue–Sun. An unlikely find next to the Total garage, close to the airport, this is the place to seek out if you're craving a decent coffee or tea, or smoothies & shakes. The menu consists of mezze, pancakes, stuffed pittas & quiches, & salads, though at around Kw22,000 a throw, it's on the pricy side.

NIGHTLIFE Most of Ndola's residents spend the evening at one of the town's restaurants or clubs, with the bar at the boat club a favourite, and Michelangelo's a pleasant haunt after dinner. What the town's nightlife lacks in sophistication, it makes up for in sheer numbers. In addition to Circles, near Broadway, and Pink Panther (best before 21.00), there's Cactus, rather like an Irish pub near the Fairgrounds, and no fewer than five East Wing clubs – labelled simply East Wing 1, East Wing 2, etc, and not to be recommended. And for more hard-core drinking, places such as Chez Ntemba are popular with locals.

SHOPPING Ndola isn't somewhere that you'd seek out for a shopping spree, but it does have all the basics, including a branch of Shoprite on Chisokone Avenue. For something original, make your way out to **Gecko Gallery**, about 7km out of town at Cherry Farm (*Misundu Rd;* ✆ *021 2616045;* m *096 6780260;* e *sbrown@ microlink.zm;* ⊕ *14.30–17.00 Wed–Fri, 09.00–12.30 Sat*). Here, Shelagh Brown showcases an eclectic mix of original Zambian artwork, photography (photographer Stephen Robinson lives nearby), pottery, sculpture, jewellery and textiles – and lures visitors with tea and cakes on her peaceful veranda. She also sells skincare products and is herself a body alignment therapist. To find the farm, head north past the brewery and follow the road across two railway crossings; after another 1km, before the roadblock, turn right towards Cherry Farm down the main track for almost 2km. Ongoing roadworks mean that the way wasn't entirely clear at the time of research, so it may be wise to phone ahead.

For those planning a trip further afield, Ndola has its own Lands Office opposite the Lowenthal Theatre (*Independence Way;* ✆ *021 2620276*) where Ordnance Survey type **maps** similar to those at Mulungushi House in Lusaka are on sale.

OTHER PRACTICALITIES

Communications Internet cafés are located both next to and opposite the Savoy Hotel on Buteko Avenue, and opposite the Bank of Zambia on Broadway. Expect to pay around Kw200 a minute, with a minimum charge of Kw1,500.

Health Ndola's Hilltop Hospital (✆ *021 2611051/2;* m *097 7757272*) is on Independence Avenue. Alternatively, you could try the Miramar Medical Centre (*54/55 Ndibu Dr, Kansenji;* ✆ *021 2680077*). There are several pharmacies in town.

Travel agents If you're in town and need help with local arrangements then contact one of the following:

Voyagers Arusha St; ✆ 021 2621333–6; f 021 2621331; e headoffice@voyagers.com.zm; www.voyagerszambia.com. Ndola is the heartland of the generally highly regarded Voyagers, who have their head office in town. It's worth noting that they can collect travellers from the Kasumbalesa/Mokambo border post.
Steve Blagus 32b President Av; ✆ 021 2610993–4; ✆/f 021 2614402

WHAT TO SEE AND DO Most activities in the town centre around the local sports clubs: cricket, rugby, golf (with an 18-hole course) and sailing. There's also a recently refurbished swimming pool on Nkandabwe Avenue (*entry Kw10,000*). with a separate garden bar.

For the first-time visitor a walk to the top of the low, grassy **hill**, in a residential area just north of the centre, gives a good sense of location, with an excellent view across to the DRC – and the cement factories. In town itself, the oft-overlooked **Copperbelt Museum** (*Buteko Av, entry Kw3,000*) hosts small exhibitions on the geology and cultural history of the Copperbelt, with a rather unusual look at toys in the form of intricate wire models of mining machinery and the like, made by local children. Downstairs is a shop selling a range of baskets and other curios. All this is set to change, however, if the museum gets the go ahead to move to new premises on Independence Avenue, between the High Court and the Civic Centre. With the move will come a new name, the Museum of Science and Technology; for now, though, the museum is of only passing interest.

Not far from the museum, the old **Slave Tree** on Makoli Avenue is of historical importance, though behind its locked gates it seems rather neglected. The tree is a very old pod mahogany, *Afzelia quanzensis* (known locally as a *mupapa*), on which two species of figs are parasitic. In 1880 the Swahili slave-traders frequented this area and built a stockade, using the shade of the tree as a meeting place. It was also

The death of UN Secretary-General Dag Hammarskjoeld in a plane crash on 17 September 1961 shocked the world, not least because the circumstances of the crash were steeped in controversy. Sixteen people died when the DC6 travelling en route from Congo to Ndola crashed into a tree on farmland just outside the town. Whether the crash was a result of pilot error, or whether the plane was shot down by mercenaries fighting on the side of the Congolese against the United Nations, has never been ascertained, although no evidence was ever found of foul play, or indeed of any mechanical failure. Attempts to find out the cause of the crash were hampered by looters who were at the scene before the arrival of the rescue services.

Mr Hammarskjoeld was elected to the post of secretary-general in 1953, and takes the credit for introducing the idea of establishing a United Nations' peace-keeping force. At the time of his death, he had been taking part in talks in Leopoldville (now Kinshasa) to try to resolve the conflict, which by 1961 had been dragging on for a number of years. The talks ended in deadlock, and the delegates were travelling to neutral territory under cover of darkness, although stories of decoy planes and other spy-story antics are much exaggerated.

The memorial's curator, M K Nasilele, has written a (somewhat controversial) account of the incident in *Crashed Hopes Revived*, published privately in 2006 and available at the site. To give the memorial a more lasting significance, Mr Nasilele was also involved in the establishment in 2002 of the nearby Dag Hammarskjoeld Memorial School.

a place where slaves were bought and sold between the various traders. The slave trade was abolished in Zambia in the early 1900s, as the British established a colonial administration. Ndola was founded in 1904 and now just a representation of the tree features on its coat of arms, while a plaque at the foot of the tree reads:

This plate has been placed on this mupapa tree to commemorate the passing of the days when, under its shade, the last of the Swahili traders, who warred upon and enslaved the people of the surrounding country, used to celebrate their victories and share out their spoils.

A second slave tree, Chichele Mofu Tree, is to be seen in the centre of the dual carriageway to Kitwe, about 11km from Ndola.

A couple of kilometres closer to Ndola, and clearly signposted to the north of the road, the **Dag Hammarskjoeld Memorial** (*entry US$3*) commemorates the United Nations secretary-general who was killed here in 1961 (see box above). Designated a national monument, and a World Heritage Site, it lies along a 5km track through farmland, lined in part with tall pine trees from the secretary-general's native Sweden. In addition to a stone cairn on the site, there is a memorial garden and a visitors' centre displaying information about Mr Hammarskjoeld and his role in the UN, and documenting the circumstances leading up to the crash. Outside, pine trees at the memorial are laid out in the shape of a plane.

EXCURSIONS FROM NDOLA Relatively near Ndola are two lodges which are destinations in their own right, and are often visited on long weekends from Lusaka or the Copperbelt: Nsobe Game Camp (see page 386) and Kafue Lodge (see page 387).

Sunken lakes The landscape around Ndola and Kitwe features a series of water-filled limestone sinkholes which manifest themselves as lakes. Of these, two are particularly popular – and each tends to be known as simply 'the sunken lake'. The first, **Lake Chilengwa**, is about 16km southeast of Ndola, where fishing and boating make for a popular day trip.

Considerably further afield is the better-known **Lake Kashiba** (*entry Kw5,000 pp*), also known as the 'sacred lake', a reflection of its status in traditional beliefs. Go for a picnic, to swim or simply just to explore. It's located 70km south of Ndola, to the southwest of Mpongwe, and near Kafue Lodge (see page 387).

KITWE

Situated a few kilometres southwest of the large Nkana Mine, Kitwe is 59km from Ndola, the two towns linked by a very good dual carriageway. The extensive pine forests lining the north side of the road extend as far as the border with the DRC, and were planted by President Kaunda as part of a timber export initiative. Kitwe is Zambia's second-largest town and relies for its prosperity on copper mining, whose presence is all too visible in the extensive slag heaps on the edge of town.

Like most of the Copperbelt towns, Kitwe was in the doldrums for several years with a steady decline in amenities, activities and general infrastructure. However, in the last few years it has seen a resurgence in prosperity following privatisation of the mines and a rapid rise in the value of copper on the world market. Today, it's a thriving town with plenty of amenities.

GETTING THERE AND AWAY

By bus Getting to or from Kitwe is easiest by bus. Kitwe's main bus terminus is in Martindale (shown on some maps as the 'second class trading area') next to the main town centre. Here you'll find many departures for Ndola (from Kw10,000), plus daily minibus connections to Chingola (Kw8,500), Solwezi and Lusaka (Kw50,000). There are also regular buses to the Luapula area and northern provinces, although buses on these long-distance routes will hang around until they fill, even if this takes a day or two.

By air The town's Southdowns Airport, about 25km to the west on the Kalulushi and then Kalengwa roads, sees twice-weekly flights from Lusaka via Ndola on Tuesday and Thursday, operated by Copper Air (part of Proflight). The region's main airport is at Ndola.

By train Kitwe is the end of the line from Livingstone that passes through Ndola and Lusaka. The service is painfully slow, with trains leaving Kitwe at 08.00 on Monday, Wednesday and Friday, arriving in Lusaka at 23.00 the same day, then leaving Lusaka the following morning to finally arrive in Livingstone the next day at 20.00 on Wednesday, Friday and Sunday. Take the bus!

Hitchhiking Like Ndola, Kitwe is a large town, so good hitch spots are a long walk from the centre. It is best to get a taxi for a few kilometres.

WHERE TO STAY

In Kitwe There was a time (when the first edition of this book was written) when there was little choice of accommodation in Kitwe, and that which existed was poor value. However, that's all changed as small guesthouses seem to have sprung up everywhere, leaving the large old hotels like the Edinburgh with little choice but to reform radically or go out of business. Increased pressure on rooms in the town has seen many of the guesthouses expand, not always for the best.

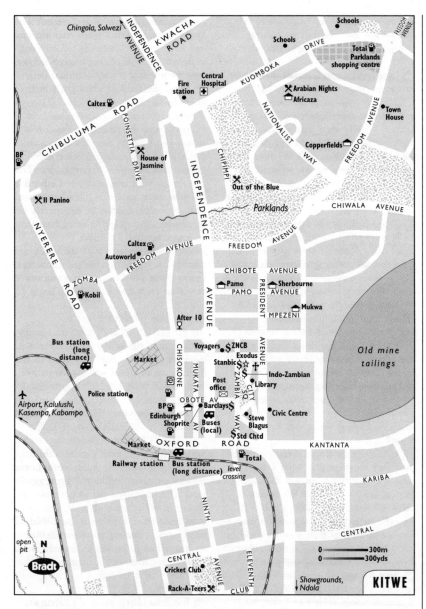

The current choices (which mostly accept Visa and MasterCard credit cards), in alphabetical order, are:

🏠 Africaza Guesthouse, aka Arabian Nights

(8 rooms) 11 Mushitu Cl, Parklands; ✆ 01 221097; e dcole@zamnet.zm. The new name for Arabian Nights may take a while to stick, but it reflects a considerable upgrade in guest accommodation. The guesthouse is centred on one of the town's best

restaurants (see below), but its rooms — albeit varied in style — are no longer an afterthought. The best of them, in the main house, are large & stylish, if slightly busy, with all mod cons that inc AC, phone & fridge, balanced by cane furniture, African-themed pictures & elephant-print fabrics. Those built in a separate block are slightly less cohesive in style, but have more modern shower rooms to compensate — and a slightly higher price tag. $$-$$$

🏠 **Copperfields Executive Guesthouse** (8 rooms) 48 Freedom Av, Parklands; 📞 021 2230709/10; f 2231027; e copperfields@microlink.zm; www.copperfields.co.zm. Copperfields is a 2-storey Tuscan-style building whose rooms are all a good standard. En-suite shower & toilet, DSTV, direct-dial phone, tea/coffee machine, safe & WiFi access are common to all, while a mosquito net around each dbl bed manages to be a design feature. The airy veranda restaurant is now for guests only, offering a set menu with 2 choices each night (Kw60,000–80,000 pp), then guests can adjourn to the TV lounge or bar. Laundry can be turned around rapidly & there's a facility for room service if you don't feel that social. As Copperfields is used a lot by visiting businesspeople during the week, it usually offers special weekend rates. $$$

🏠 **Edinburgh Hotel** (76 rooms) Obote Av; 📞 021 2222444; f 021 2225036; e edinburgh@ microlink.zm. Kitwe's main hotel is in traditional mould, rather dark & very old-fashioned, despite a recent change of ownership. Situated just west of the business district, it's centrally located close to the main railway & bus stations. Within the hotel, on its ground floor, are some useful service agencies — like a travel agent, & an internet café. Just behind the hotel is the Edinburgh Arcade, which has a variety of small shops.

The Edinburgh has a range of rooms at different prices. There are various suites, luxury & deluxe rooms, & a whole floor of somewhat dilapidated 'standard' rooms — all of which have en-suite facilities, AC, kettles, fridges, phones & satellite TVs. The Highlander Restaurant — complete with dance floor — is the focus for meals, & there are several bars, a casino, a swimming pool & secure parking. Room $$-$$$, suite $$$-$$$$

🏠 **House of Jasmine** (34 rooms) Jasmin Cl, Parklands; 📞 021 2215124, 2210134; f 2211142; e jasmin@microlink.zm. To reach Jasmine from Independence Av, turn left at the roundabout by the fire station into Chibuluma Rd, then take the first left into Poinsettia Dr, & Jasmin Cl is the second on the left. This is another site that has undergone considerable expansion, resulting in lots of nooks & crannies, & some of the rooms spilling over across the road. If the communal areas feel a bit random in design, the en-suite rooms are all compact, modern & clean, with DSTV, phones & AC or fans.

Accommodation ranges from sgl brick rondavels to 'family units' with 4 beds & 3 twin rooms within its main house. Outside is a swimming pool, overlooked by the restaurant & bar. Parking is outside the gate, under the supervision of a nightwatchman. $$$

🏠 **Mukwa Guest House** (19 rooms) 26–28 Mpezeni Av (off President Av); 📞 021 2224266; f 2224266; e mukwakit@zamnet.zm; www.mukwalodge.co.zm. Mukwa (the name of a colourful local wood) is an old colonial-style building surrounded by attractive gardens & with a swimming pool. Each of the spacious rooms has satellite TV, direct-dial phone, WiFi access, a fridge, complimentary fruit basket & a facility for making tea & coffee. The lounge, with its Africa-centric décor, is notable for the absence of a TV, so makes a pleasant spot to read a book, but the greatest attraction is the smart Indian/continental restaurant, which also hosts a lunchtime café, the Courtyard (see below for both). A separate annexe with 4 rooms is just 5 mins' walk away, & will shortly have its own kitchen serving meals. $$$

🏠 **Pamo Lodge** (10 rooms) 2 Pamo Av; 📞/f 021 2222769. One of the town's less expensive offerings, Pamo Lodge makes a feature of mix 'n' match furniture & décor that's heavy on the florals & frills. Rooms are clean, if dark, with en-suite shower or bath, & fan, fridge, DSTV & kettle. $$, inc cont b/fast.

🏠 **Sherbourne Guest House** (23 rooms, plus annexe) 20 Pamo Av; 📞 021 2222168, 2230548, 2230549; f 021 2226477, 2229580; e sherbo@coppernet.zm. Significant extension in recent years, inc a new conference room, means that the Sherbourne is now quite cramped, though it still has an annexe with 4 rooms at 14 Mpezeni Av. Rooms each have twin or dbl beds, as well as satellite TV, minibar/fridge & phone (though those in the annexe cannot make outgoing calls). A swimming pool & playground are set in established gardens with tables on the lawn & a separate restaurant. Lunch & dinner are available to all comers, inc a Sun buffet & hog roast (Kw55,000 pp). $$$

🏠 **Town House Lodge** (8 rooms) 65A Mabvuto Ct, Freedom Av; 📞/f 021 2221855; e townhouselodge@coppernet.zm. Opened in 2000, & now busy with renovations, the Town House is friendly & relaxed. While the corridors feel rather old-fashioned, rooms are modern & nicely appointed, with flashes of bright blue or touches of brown to enliven an otherwise neutral décor; the honeymoon suite, though, goes heavy on the leopard print. Each room has en-suite shower or bath, as well as AC,

DSTV, minibar/fridge, safe, & kettle for tea & coffee. Guests can relax on a sunny veranda or in the TV lounge, & there's a small dining room, too. $$$

⌂ **Plot 35 Guest Lodge** 35 Ndola Highway; ☏ 021 2239071. To the south of town, near the

Around Kitwe

⌂ **Shamabinga Retreat** (7 rooms) 174 Wolfram Av, Itimpi; m 097 7486354, 7852782; e cshiaka@yahoo.com. Shamabinga lies 15km from Kitwe on the Chingola road, in an area which in colonial days was developed as a sort of market garden to feed the towns of the Copperbelt. To get there, follow the main road for about 12km, then take a right turn towards Itimpi. Turn left at the roundabout, then right at the T junction; Wolfram Av is the first turning on the left. It was recently reopened, taking advantage of the upturn in the local economy. Owned & run by the delightful Constance Shiaka, it's a large old colonial house fronted by an attractive, English-style courtyard garden & lawns where Constance plans to build an outside bar. Accommodation, in the throes of being upgraded, is either in the main house, where there's also a cool, dark, comfortable lounge with satellite TV & separate dining room, or in one of 3 adjacent chalets. Each of the chalets has 2 en-suite rooms, some with a shared lounge, dining room & kitchenette. All are comfortably furnished & feature local Zambian curios & crafts. $$

Showgrounds, you can't miss this functional red-painted building, geared to exhibition visitors. It's about as inspiring as its name suggests, but it's quite adequate. All rooms are en suite with dbl bed, tiled floors, & TV, & some have AC. $$, inc cont b/fast.

⌂ **Riverane Guesthouse** (4 chalets) ☏ 021 2239131; m 097 7842093; e riverane@zamnet.zm. Tucked away on a bend in the Kafue River, 25km from Kitwe, Nicky & Craig Wright's large cattle farm is a tranquil spot to while away a weekend, especially for families or groups. Large A-frame chalets with a pole frame have corrugated roofing reaching to ground level. Each has solid wooden furniture, a dbl bed, cement floor with rush mats, gauze windows & a toilet/shower behind a low wooden wall. Guests are provided with bedding, & a basket of plates, mugs, cutlery, etc, but otherwise you're on your own. Power comes from 12v strip lights run off a vehicle battery. The chalets are set in isolation some way from the farmhouse, so privacy is guaranteed. For entertainment, there's a 3km walking trail (when the river is low) & a fishing raft; crocodiles preclude walking at high water, or fishing from the riverbank. More unexpectedly, there's also a Bengal tiger in an enclosure – rescued from Kitwe Zoo when it closed. Directions are provided at the time of booking (which is essential); you'll need a high-clearance vehicle. Kw250,000 per chalet.

✗ **WHERE TO EAT** Like Ndola, Kitwe has plenty of take-aways, with reliably hygienic standards – if not haute cuisine. The most notable include the **Hungry Lion** (opposite the main post office in the centre of town) for hamburgers and pies, and **After 10** (in Martindale – the 'second-class trading area') for snacks, sandwiches, pizzas, curries, Chinese and even Arabian dishes. The latter, predictably given its name, stays open late.

For a good evening meal you need to look more carefully. Try the following (and note that in addition to the restaurants listed here, both the House of Jasmine and Sherbourne guesthouses and the Edinburgh Hotel will accept non-residents for meals).

✗ **Arabian Nights** 11 Mushitu Cl, Parklands; ☏ 021 2221097; ⊕ daily. Sister restaurant to the one in Lusaka's Arcades, Arabian Nights specialises in Indian & Pakistani cuisine with a sprinkling of other dishes & a few special vegetarian options. With its new location in Parklands comes a classy package: the restaurant is sited both indoors & on a covered veranda, next to a series of fish pools with a fountain. It's dark & atmospheric, & has an excellent reputation – this is a place where you could justify dressing up. $$$$$

⌑ **Courtyard Café** 26–28 Mpezeni Av; ☏ 021 2224266; ⊕ 09.00–15.00. The lunchtime café at Mukwa Guest House is run entirely independently of the restaurant, albeit using the same premises. The café, though, spills over into a delightful shaded courtyard adjacent to the restaurant, surrounded by attractive plants. $$$

✗ **Danny's** 8117 Freetown Rd, Ontario Shopping Centre; ⊕ 12.30–14.30 & 19.00–22.30. A branch of the very good Indian restaurant that's based in Ndola. $$$

✗ **Dawat** Independence Av; ☎ 021 2228281; ⏰ 09.00–22.00 Tue–Sun. A newcomer to Kitwe, Dawat is another good Indian restaurant, also serving steaks & fish. **$$$**

🍴 **Il Panino** 3044 Lilongwe Rd; ☎ 021 2212329; ⏰ 08.00–16.00 Mon–Fri. An unexpected find in the industrial area of Kitwe, just off Nyerere Rd, this is a cool, modern place for b/fast or light meals, inc pancakes & salads. There's a delicatessen on site, too, so you can top up on supplies at the same time. **$$**

✗ **Mona Lisa** Parklands; ☎ 021 2229677; m 096 6785077, 097 7769258. Restaurant ⏰ 10.00–22.00; bar till late. One of 3 restaurants of the same name in the Copperbelt (the others are in Chingola & Mufulira), this is the place for pizzas, as well as pasta, steaks & grills. It's a popular watering hole, too, with a live violinist on Fri evenings, & DJ on Wed, Fri & Sat. **$$$–$$$$**

✗ **Mukwa Restaurant** 26–28 Mpezeni Av (off President Av); ☎ 021 2224266; ⏰ 19.00–21.00. Part of the guesthouse of the same name, Mukwa is an elegantly stylish restaurant serving a good variety of Indian food in the evenings only, as well as more usual continental fare. At lunchtime, it morphs into the Courtyard Café (see above). **$$$**

✗ **Out of the Blue** Old Greek Club Premises, Bridge Walk; m 097 7874913; ⏰ 10.00–late. To find this large, lively place, head north on Independence Av, take the first right after the bridge, follow the bend, then take the first right again. Despite the location behind the Greek church, there's no link with Greece – except perhaps the late-night music (live at weekends) & drinking. A standard, albeit expensive, menu is served in an open, café-style setting, with a pool table at the back & a large bar. **$$$$$**

🍴 **Prive Café** Parklands; ⏰ 08.00–20.00 Mon–Thu, 08.00–late Fri–Sun. A simple place for a salad or light meal. **$$**

NIGHTLIFE As you might expect, many of the local restaurants are popular watering holes in the evenings, with Mona Lisa offering live music on Friday, and a DJ on Wednesday, Friday and Saturday. There are several nightclubs in town – though do take local advice as the current 'in' places change regularly. The most popular are probably Circles (*Parklands*) and Club Zero (*Kwacha East township; turn right at traffic lights for Buchi on Independence Av, and it's about 3km down the road*), but you could also try Exodus or Hangover. All have pool tables, dance floors and disco music, tending to stick to rhumba and rhythm and blues. Expect to pay around US$5–10 admission.

The clubs are frequented almost exclusively by black Zambians, and they open until very late. Normally they have a very lively and friendly atmosphere, so overseas visitors should have no problems. If/when trouble develops, the owners of the clubs are generally quite good at sorting it out. You should, of course, take the standard precautions that apply in any such busy places, to avoid the attention of thieves and pickpockets – by dressing down and not carrying valuables.

SHOPPING While there's everything you need in Kitwe, the town doesn't as yet have anything in the form of a modern shopping centre, though there are rumours of a large new complex to be built soon. For now, Shoprite has a branch just off Zambia Way, near the Edinburgh Hotel, and there's a small supermarket at Parklands. More interesting perhaps is the main market, which runs alongside the railway, close to the Edinburgh Hotel. Adjacent to this, near the long-distance bus station, and right at the end of Obote Avenue past the Edinburgh Hotel, is the large Chisokone Curio Market. Alternatively, you could take a look at Medusa Crafts in Parklands. For books, it may be worth checking out Kickstart Bookshop in Parklands (☎ *021 2222594; e kickstart@microlink.zm*).

OTHER PRACTICALITIES

Car spares and repairs Toyota have a franchise at the Caltex garage (*Chingola Rd;* ☎ *021 2217571, 2217335*), and Ford spares can be obtained from the Vehicle Centre. More generally, car spares can be obtained either from Autoworld (*off Freedom Way;* ☎ *021 2221960*) or from Daniel's Motor Spares (☎ *021 2223927*).

Communications There are various **internet cafés** around town, including one on the ground floor of the Edinburgh Hotel and another, Sundiland, on the City Square. One of the best is Botech (*Ontario Shopping Centre, Freetown Rd; ⊕ 08.00–20.00*) with decent computers, and costing Kw150 a minute. The main **post office** is just off Zambia Way, opposite Shoprite and Barclays Bank.

Health If you fall ill in or near Kitwe, contact the Wusakili Mine Hospital (⤷ *021 2224144*). To find it, take a left at the first set of traffic lights as you enter Kitwe from Ndola, and go past the mine. There are several pharmacies in the town.

For situations that are more serious, and may require immediate evacuation, contact **Speciality Emergency Services** (*SES; Lilongwe Rd;* ⤷ *021 2211182;* m *097 7770306–7, 096 6782692;* e *seskitwe@zamnet.zm*), and see page 91 for details.

Money and banking Most of the large banks have branches in the centre of town, around the junction of Oxford Road and Zambia Way. There are also plenty of bureaux de change, including one by the Edinburgh Hotel.

Travel agents and car hire

Steve Blagus Mutuka Av, City Square; ⤷ 021 2229908, 021 2230725

Voyagers Enoschomba Rd; ⤷ 021 2225056, 2229102–3; f 021 2224834; e kitwe@voyagers.com.zm; www.voyagerszambia.com

WHAT TO SEE AND DO In itself, Kitwe has few intrinsic attractions; as in Ndola, activities tend to centre around the local sports clubs. That said, the town is sufficiently close to Ndola for the two to share local attractions (see pages 388–90). Nearer Kitwe itself, there are a number of places of interest, including the **crocodile ponds** at Chililabombwe – the last town to the north before the border with the DRC. It is also possible to visit a women's **weaving project** at Chililabombwe (m *097 7863626*), part of a church group. Understated cotton throws and table mats in natural colours are available for sale at very competitive prices; you can expect to pay around US$20 for a cream throw.

Chembe Bird Sanctuary (*Entry Kw5,000 pp*) This woodland reserve, owned by the WECSZ (see pages 51–2) and about half-an-hour's drive to the west of Kitwe, is just off the road between Kalulushi and Kasempa. Centred on a small lake, it's a haven for birders, with over 300 of Zambia's listed birds recorded here; *chembe* is the local name for the African fish eagle, a regular visitor. Line fishing is permitted on the lake, where spotted-neck otters may be seen, but this is no place to swim: crocodiles are plentiful. Rather safer is the 7km Chinkamba Drive around the lake, offering a two-hour walk or short drive: it's navigable by 2WD in the dry season. There's a picnic and camping site, with charcoal available from the warden.

In the same direction is **Mindolo Dam**, home of Kitwe Boat Club (where you can get drinks and snacks) and a good spot for picnics, boating and quadbikes.

CHINGOLA

Chingola lies at the western end of the Copperbelt, about 50km west of Kitwe on a good road with just the occasional pot-hole. Beyond here you either head west towards Solwezi and Mwinilunga, or proceed north towards Lubumbashi in the DRC. The town is dominated by the huge KCM open-pit mines – the largest in Zambia – that dominate the landscape on the eastern side of the town. Signs of renewed prosperity are everywhere, with investment attracted from all over the world, including China and India.

GETTING THERE AND AROUND Chingola is well served by buses to and from other towns in the Copperbelt and as far as Lusaka. For details see under *Kitwe*, page 390. A one-way fare to Solwezi is Kw25,000 by minibus, or around Kw35,000 by larger bus.

If you're driving yourself, note that several of the town's side streets are blocked at one end, making the concept of 'driving round the block' somewhat challenging! Note, too, that development of the KCM mine to the north of town has resulted in changes in the road layout from that shown on many maps. If you're driving yourself, note that the road between Kitwe and Chingola is considered to be extremely dangerous in terms of potential accidents.

WHERE TO STAY The recent boom in copper prices has had a dramatic effect on Chingola's accommodation options, attracting the South Africa Protea Hotels group to invest in the town. While some visitors choose to stay overnight at the Chimfunshi Wildlife Orphanage (see pages 398–401), others will opt to base themselves in Chingola, either at the new Protea or at one of the guesthouses, and visit the orphanage as a day trip.

Protea Hotel Chingola (40 rooms) Kabundi Rd; \ 021 2312810; f 021 2313510; e proteachingola@zamtel.zm; reservations@proteahotels.com; www.proteahotel.com/chingola. Opened in 2002, the Protea came like a breath of fresh air to Chingola. It's an L-shaped building, all blues & terracottas, set in an open position just outside town, fronted by trees & a large parking area. From its cool blue reception area it is modern, light & very well kept, with plenty of solid wood furnishings. Rooms have en-suite bath & separate shower, AC, armchair, kettle, TV, desk & WiFi access. They are set out in 2 wings either side of an apex formed by a pool & terrace, & backed by a smart but comfortable restaurant. Here, from 06.00 to 22.00, à-la-carte menus offer everything from light meals to pastas to grills. Round the front of the building, near the conference rooms, are a business centre with internet that's open office hours only, & a modern steel-&-chrome bar with upstairs lounge that can be heaving at weekends. $$$$

Hibiscus (5 rooms) 33 Katutwa Rd; \/f 021 2313635; m 096 6781045. The British-owned Hibiscus is close to the entrance to town, if you're coming from Kitwe. Turn left before the roundabout onto Kapele, then follow Katutwa round the bend; Hibiscus is on the left, set in attractive gardens with a small pool. The atmosphere is redolent of a family home, with a range of furniture in individual rooms, each of which has twin or dbl beds, a fan & mosquito nets & either private or en-suite bathroom. Guests have a lounge, kitchen & dining room for their own use, with lunch (*Kw25,000*) or dinner (*Kw42,000*) served on request. $$

Mica's Guesthouse (12 rooms) 59 5th St; \/f 021 2313653; m 096 6905146. Close to the hospital in the south of town, Mica's has spotlessly clean dbl & family rooms, each with TV, fan, mosi net, & en-suite bath or shower & toilet. There's a bar in the entrance, & meals can be provided on request. $$

Rosewood Guesthouse (12 rooms) 51 Kitwe Rd; \/f 021 2313114; m 096 6786131; e rosewood@zamnet.zm. Quite close to the main road, Rosewood suffers a bit from traffic noise, but there are pluses. Each en-suite room is dominated by a huge low bed, & adorned by occasional touches such as a carved cupboard door or colourful fabrics. 3 sgl rooms are in a separate cottage at the back. Most guests are long-stay visitors, attracted by the homely feel of the place. $$$

The Willows Guesthouse (7 rooms) 57 President Av; m 096 6906544, 6786140; e tandara@zamnet.zm. Just off the main roundabout at the entrance to town from Kitwe, this is another Zambian-owned guesthouse, but this time rather institutional in design, with little embellishment. That said, twin-bed rooms, off a long corridor, are clean, with en-suite shower & toilet, as well as TV, fan, kettle & safe. There's a well-appointed sitting/dining room, & an attractive garden where a braai area is formed between paths of railway sleepers that reflect the owner's work on the railways. $$ DBB

Nchanga Hotel (31 rooms) Kabundi Rd; m 095 5829115. The old-fashioned Nchanga in the centre of town was being renovated in 2007, but in a place when the only telephone number is the manager's personal mobile, don't hold your breath. Prices will go up when work is complete, but for now it's cheap, at least, & has a decent beer garden. $

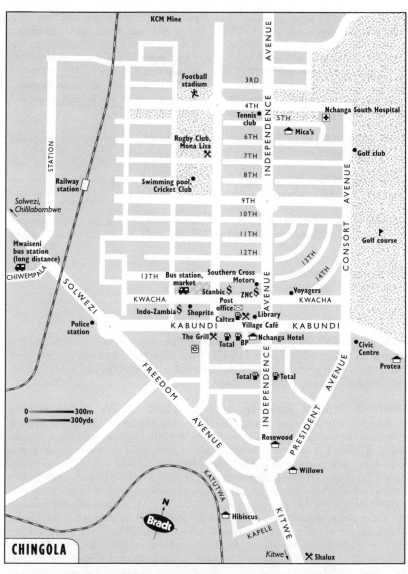

CHINGOLA

X **WHERE TO EAT AND DRINK** Until recently, Chingola wasn't well endowed with places to eat, but things are slowly changing. The restaurant at the **Protea** (see above) is popular for both formal and poolside dining, and there are now several other options. If you just fancy something sweet, try the **Village Café** (*Kabundi Rd; m 096 6786141*) near the library; despite the name, it's not a café, but does sell home-made cakes (as well as being a delicatessen & craft shop).

X **Golf Club** ◦ 021 2313765; ⊕ 10.00–16.00 daily. A good place to come for coffee & cake or the buffet lunch, the restaurant at the golf club is also open for b/fast.

X **The Grill** ◦ 021 2310079; m 096 6903411; ⊕ 10.00–21.00 Mon–Sat. The open-plan kitchen adds to the informality of this busy hungry-man's diner, where steaks cost Kw45,000–69,500 for the full blow-out. Less-hungry patrons can opt for burgers, pizzas & a range of light meals. $$$$

✕ **Mona Lisa** ☎ 021 2314762; m 097 7745336. Restaurant ⏲ 10.00–22.00 daily; bar till later. Sister to the restaurant of the same name in Kitwe, Chingola's Mona Lisa was moving to new premises by the Rugby Club in 2007. The restaurant's huge pizza oven was going too, so the popularity of its pizzas should remain undimmed. Other options include pasta, steaks & grills. There's a 3rd branch in Mufulira, next to a small motel. *Pizza/pasta* $$$$, *grills* $$$$$

✕ **Shalux** Kitwe Rd; ☎ 021 2311345; m 096 6908124; ⏲ all day Mon, Tue, Thu–Sat. Chingola's best Indian restaurant is to the south of town, & also serves steaks & fish. $$$

OTHER PRACTICALITIES Chingola's best shop for supplies is Shoprite. Otherwise there are plenty of small shops catering to everyday needs.

Car spares and repairs Spares for Mercedes, Mitsubishi & Chrysler vehicles can be obtained from Southern Cross Motors (☎ 021 2311651).

Health The place to head for in case of a medical emergency is the well-staffed and well-equipped Nchanga South Hospital (*4th St; ☎ 021 2351018*), which is run by the mine.

Travel agents and car hire

Voyagers 14th St; ☎ 021 2311642, 2311722, 2312195; f 021 2312552; e chingola@voyagers.com.zm; www.voyagerszambia.com

WHAT TO SEE AND DO Chimfunshi Wildlife Orphanage (see below) is the greatest draw in an area whose attractions are otherwise linked into the town's sports clubs. There is also Hippo Pool, a designated national monument and a favoured picnic spot, a few kilometres outside the town.

Chimfunshi Wildlife Orphanage (*PO Box 11190 Chingola; ☎ 021 2311293; e 2chimps@bushmail.net; www.chimfunshi.org.za*) Probably the most popular excursion from Chingola is to Chimfunshi Wildlife Orphanage. This refuge for some of Africa's great apes is very much a working wildlife sanctuary. Although tourists are welcome to watch the chimps being fed and at play, it is not specifically geared to visitors. It's well off the main Zambian tourist trail and, aside from a number of dedicated supporters, is virtually unknown outside the country.

Chimfunshi started off as a normal 10,000-acre cattle farm beside the banks of the Kafue River, close to the border with the DRC (formerly Zaire). It was run by Sheila Siddle and her husband, David, who died in 2006. Over the years, the Siddles established a reputation for rescuing wild animals in need. Then, in October 1983, Sheila's son-in-law brought her an orphaned chimpanzee, named Pal, who had been confiscated from Zairean poachers. Pal was sick and malnourished, and had been physically abused, yet against the odds Sheila eventually nursed him back to health.

It had been known for some time that Zambia was a conduit for the illegal export of chimps from Zaire, but as the authorities had nowhere practicable to release any confiscated animals, they had not been over-zealous in trying to stop the trade. Gradually they confiscated more chimps; and, by mid-1988, the Siddles had 19 chimps at Chimfunshi. At first, all were kept in cages, but taken out for regular forest walks. Then, as sending rehabilitated chimps back to Zaire wasn't a safe option, the Siddles decided to build a large enclosure at Chimfunshi. With minimal backing, they built a 4m-high wall around seven acres of their own forest land, and gradually introduced a group of chimps into the area. Unexpectedly,

Chimpanzees are not generally thought to be indigenous to Zambia. Currently the southernmost population of wild chimps is thought to live in a remote (and relatively little-documented) corner of the Rukwa Region of Tanzania – around the Loasi River Forest Reserve on the eastern shore of Lake Tanganyika.

Chimpanzee distribution in the wild is limited by suitable habitat, and especially by the distribution of suitable vegetation and the wild fruit on which they live. Although there are remaining populations in woodland areas, most occur in moister, thicker forests – where the availability of wild fruits is higher. The relatively open, dry miombo woodlands in northern Zambia wouldn't be a typical habitat, although in some areas chimps do inhabit more arid woodland areas.

Sheila Siddle maintains that chimps could have once lived in Zambia. She cites oral evidence, reported from older local people in Mbala, just south of Lake Tanganyika, who refer to a species of animal which is now extinct in the area as *socamuntu*, meaning 'like a man' in the Bemba language.

these chimps eventually melded into a coherent family-type group, which was clearly a great success. By this time orphaned chimps were being sent here from many corners of the globe, so in 1991 a second enclosure was constructed to accommodate another group of chimps, this time covering 14 acres and using a solar-powered electric fence.

A few years later, the Siddles acquired an adjacent 13,500-acre farm, and made over the land to the Chimfunshi Wildlife Orphanage Trust, ensuring that the chimps would have a permanent home – something that is particularly important for animals whose lifespan in captivity mirrors that of humans. The northern boundary of the farm is the Kafue River, which butts onto 2,500 acres of dense forest, with large grassy areas of river floodplain and several small tributaries of the Kafue River. There is also a particularly beautiful patch of tropical forest, which follows a narrow gorge. Generous donations enabled the construction of two large 500ha enclosures with plenty of mature musambya, *Chrysophyllum magalismontanum*, trees, followed by two smaller enclosures of 200ha each. Each of these has a concrete 'feeding centre' – essentially a building with a door onto the open enclosure, and bars for windows, and the larger two have a rooftop observation area.

In 2000, Sheila and David were jointly awarded the MBE for their work with the chimps, and travelled to London where their medals were presented at Buckingham Palace by the Queen.

Chimfunshi today By 2007 there were 119 chimps on the property. Sheila's insistence that each of the females should be allowed to have one baby means that several chimps have been born on the farm, but from 2007 all other animals were to be fitted with contraceptive implants. The larger enclosures housed 47 and 23 chimps respectively, while a further 15 were in the first of the 200ha areas, and the fourth enclosure was waiting for a new family to move in. A herd of impala grazes the land between the two large enclosures.

The chimps spend almost all of their time outside, coming inside only at feeding times, which means that they are close enough to be inspected by the keepers for any health problems.

Each of the 'family' groups is made up of animals that have been gradually introduced to each other until they become a cohesive unit, and only then can they be allowed into one of the large enclosures together. Those whose social groups are as yet incomplete live in a variety of pens and large cages near the house, with space at the back where they are free to roam for part of the day, when the keepers are around. Inevitably, there are a few chimps for whom socialising is a step too far, or who have escaped once too often, and these problem animals remain caged for safety's sake. It's not pretty, but the animals are well cared for, and the cages are almost certainly better than where the animals were before coming here; active fundraising is taking place to help improve their lot.

In addition to the chimps, Chimfunshi also rehabilitates various other orphaned animals. At any one time, you're likely to find a menagerie of furry, feathered and warm-blooded beings here, all either being nursed back to health, or being kept on after recovering. A typical story is that of Billy, the hippo, who joined the family in 1992. At ten days old, she was discovered on the bank of the Kafue, next to the body of her dead mother. She was adopted by Sheila, who kept her in the house when small. Now, at well over 1,500kg, she's fully grown, yet she still comes to the house each morning for her bottles of milk and wanders around the campsite and the farm with nonchalant disregard for her bulk – and anything that gets in the way of it. (Do remember, though, that she's still a wild animal, and treat her with respect.)

During 2006–07, Sheila arranged for one of her staff to study in England for an MSc in primate behaviour. As a result, it is hoped that the orphanage will in future be able to attract unaccompanied research students to conduct further studies here.

The orphanage is supported by a trust. If you would like to help, contact the Friends of Chimfunshi (e *adoption@mweb.co.za or PO Box 3555, Kempton Park 1620, South Africa; www.chimfunshi.org.za*). And to find out more, get hold of a copy of Sheila's book, *In My Family Tree* (see *Appendix 3*, page 511).

Getting there It takes about an hour and a quarter to drive to Chimfunshi from Chingola. Take the tar road towards Solwezi for about 42km until you come to a sign pointing right (✪ TUCHIM 12°28.476'S; 27°29.150'E) to the orphanage. If you're coming from Solwezi, it's around 118km to this signpost. From the turn-off it's a further 18km along a reasonably good farm track to the orphanage (✪ CHIMFU 12°21.460'S; 27°33.242'E), taking about 40 minutes to drive in the dry season. There are no buses to the orphanage itself, but plenty of transport plies the route between Solwezi and Chingola, so it would be easy to be dropped at the turning, although hitching (or walking) along the access road could take some time.

Where to stay Chimfunshi was not designed with the tourist in mind, so forget all ideas of upmarket lodge-style accommodation. Potentially, those wishing to stay at the sanctuary have the choice of simple, dormitory-style rooms or a riverside campsite. Either way, you'll need to come with all your own food; meals are not provided. On a practical note, it's important to be aware that there is no phone at the farm and communication can be very poor. Telephone calls are taken at an office in Chingola, almost next to the Nchanga Hotel above the BP garage (⊕ *08.00–16.00 Mon–Fri*), and emails are sent via bushmail, so if you're planning to stay, you need to allow plenty of time to set up your visit.

Education centre This modern centre, built with a US$250,000 grant from the Norwegian Embassy, is about 12km from the main farmhouse & incorporates accommodation for 20–30 people. The centre is used mainly for school classes, youth groups & undergraduate students from overseas, but when it is empty, private visitors are welcome to use the facilities. The buildings are simple modern prefabs, with small dormitory-style rooms, some with 7 beds, others with 2; bedding & towels are provided. All are clean, & are set around an open courtyard, with a large braai area, communal kitchens, & separate buildings with hot showers & long-drop toilets. Water is supplied from the site's own borehole. A cheerful classroom features posters showing the chimp 'family' groups, complete with individual portraits, while outside, each of the trees is labelled with both its Bemba & scientific names. US$20 pp.

Å Campsite Set on a gently sloping bank of grass leading down to the river, the campsite is close to the house owned by Sheila's daughter, Sylvia. Campers share old but hot showers & long-drop toilets, & it's usually possible to borrow a few pots & pans if you need them. Those without their own tent can make use of the (very basic) caravan that's parked at the educational centre. *Camping US$8 pp; Kw100,000 deposit for caravan.*

What to see and do Some visitors prefer to spend a few days here, taking advantage of the freedom to explore the farm's extensive walks and excellent birding (over 350 species have been recorded), and affording the time to watch the chimps at leisure. Most, though, come for just a half day, or perhaps bring a picnic and spend the day here.

The chimps are divided between the two main enclosures, and a variety of large cages and smaller enclosures near the farmhouse. These, the educational centre and the campsite are a considerable distance apart, making some form of vehicle very useful; you can walk between places, but it takes a while! Visitors can drive themselves, or you can arrange to be collected from the educational centre or campsite to go to the farmhouse, where the bush walks and feeding of the baby chimps takes place.

The chimps follow a straightforward routine, which makes it relatively easy to plan a day out. Feeding times are at 07.00, when the babies are fed their milk in bottles, and balls of nshima are shared out among the older animals. At 11.30, it's time for fruit and vegetables, and more milk for the whole group, with a final offering of milk at 14.00. (Milk provides the chimps with their protein requirement, substituting for the meat which would form a small part of their diet in the wild.) Outside of feeding time, when one of the keepers will explain something of the chimps' behaviour and routine, there are two options. Individual visitors are welcome to explore the enclosures themselves, observing the animals at tree level from the roof of the feeding centres, which makes for some excellent photographic opportunities. Those seeking more hands-on involvement can opt for a morning bush walk with some of the younger chimps, in the company of one of the keepers. If the idea of a baby chimp jumping into your arms or riding piggyback across the bush to a natural playground appeals, then don't think twice. Just remember that this is no place for smart clothes, and remove any jewellery or other items before the chimps do it for you.

(*Visiting enclosures and feeding time US$15 pp. Chimp walk US$30 for 1¹/₂hrs.*)

SOLWEZI

There has been a history of copper mining from the Kansanshi Hills north of Solwezi for hundreds of years, but commercial mining started only in the 20th century. Today, the Kansanshi Mine is a thriving business owned by First Quantum. Riding on the back of the mine's success, Solwezi has evolved from a small village to a busy little town in just 40 years. . There is even talk of moving the town's centre east towards the road to Kansanshi Mine. The opening in 2008 of the huge Lumwana Copper Mine, some 100km to the west, is bound to have a major impact on the town's infrastructure, not least because the road to the mine is currently in a poor state of repair, so visitors are advised to stay in Solwezi.

As it stands, Solwezi itself isn't a pretty town, or an attraction for most people, but it is useful for supplies if you're coming from Lusaka and heading west, or driving into Kafue from the north.

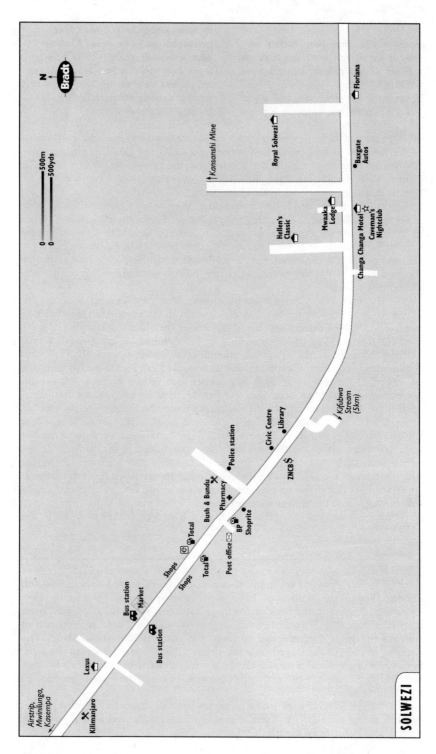

SOLWEZI

Airstrip,
Mwinilunga,
Kasempa

Kilimanjaro

Lexus

Bus station

Bus station

Market

Shops

Shops

Total

Total

Post office

BP

Shoprite

Bush & Bundu

Pharmacy

Police station

Civic Centre

Library

ZNCB$

Kifubwa
Stream
(5km)

Hellen's
Classic

Mwaaka
Lodge

Changa Changa Motel

Caveman's
Nightclub

Royal Solwezi

Baxgate
Autos

Floriana

Kansanshi Mine

N

Bradt

500m
500yds

0

0

GETTING THERE AND AWAY The main tarred road leading from Chingola runs right through Solwezi (✪ SOLWEZ 12°10.931'S; 26°23.960'E). It's a distance of 180km, and is in reasonable condition, but there are sufficient pot-holes to catch out the unwary. To the east, however, the tar road towards Kasempa is considerably less well maintained.

By bus Regular buses link Solwezi with Chingola, Kitwe and Lusaka, with departures from Solwezi at around 06.00 and 14.00. The one-way fare to Chingola is Kw25,000 by minibus, or around Kw35,000 by larger bus; the fare to Kitwe on a bus running to a timetable is Kw45,000, and to Lusaka Kw80,000. The bus station is on both sides of the main road, next to and opposite the market, at the western end of town.

By air Solwezi's airstrip is west of the town. Copper Air (part of Proflight) operates several flights a week on Monday, Wednesday, Thursday and Friday between here and Ndola, with four of them starting in/continuing to Lusaka. With so much industrial development in the area it can only be a matter of time before this is upgraded to take international flights.

WHERE TO STAY Like so many of Zambia's northern towns, Solwezi has benefited from the resurgence in the mining industry. Now, in addition to several larger, old-style motels, and an ever-increasing variety of small guesthouses, there are one or two entirely different places to stay, from the upmarket Royal Solwezi to the simple but well-run Floriana. Of the rest, most are reasonable – and reasonably accessible from the main tar road through town.

Royal Solwezi (48 rooms) 147 Old Chingola Rd; ☎ 08 821620; m 096 6271422; e reservations@solwezi.com; www.solwezi.com. At last, a hotel that dares to be a little different! Opened early in 2007, the Royal Solwezi is set on a low hill on the eastern edge of town, about 0.5km from the main road. Good views to the east make this a prime spot, & there's enough space to make it the envy of many a hotelier. Rooms are huge – sgls have a dbl bed; dbls have 2 of them – & redolent of a minimalist African safari lodge, with ultra-modern bathroom fittings, a TV & safe as standard. Bright splashes of colour & trendy photos documenting the hotel's phases of construction enliven tinted cement floors & bed plinths, & solid mukwa-wood desks. The rooms are built in 2-storey blocks, 2 each side of the cavernous central reception/bar/dining area. Patio doors from each lead onto a balcony or straight out to wide lawns stretching across to the pool & a sports bar with plasma TV screens – sufficiently far away for noise not to be an issue. Towards the bottom of the plot, 10 fully furnished 2-bedroom villas are available for long-stay visitors who prefer to be self-catering.

It's an exciting new employment opportunity for the town, & the managers have bravely taken on almost exclusively local staff, 80% of whom have not worked before, while the rest have been employed only by the mines. Service is attentive &, though it's inevitably unpolished as yet, the will is there. Already the veranda is established as an attractive place for a drink; once the menus are taken in hand, the business centre open & wireless internet access available throughout, this could set the standard for the whole region. $$$$; key deposit Kw50,000.

Floriana Lodge Trust (31 rooms) ☎ 08 821130; f 08 821765. At the entrance to the town from Chingola, this much-expanded lodge is named after an Italian nun & missionary who spent much of her life working in Zambia before tragically being shot dead by bandits. The Floriana is one of Solwezi's better guesthouses. Its en-suite rooms, each with a TV, phone, fan, fridge & tea/coffee facilities, have been built in blocks around 3 sides of a grassy, tree-shaded area, where thatched gazebos offer plenty of shade (& shelter) for a cool drink. Rates include a full English breakfast served in their restaurant, in which they also conjure up Chinese, Indian, English & Zambian dishes, with the local dish of Solwezi beans, *kingovwa* sweet potatoes, honey & mushroom – all sourced locally – a speciality that's available on request. $$

Hellen's Classic Lodge (5 rooms) m 097 7706995 (✪ HELLEN 12°11.165'S; 26°25.074'E)

Hellen's is just one of several guesthouses of a similar standard in Solwezi. A good, clear signpost directs you the short distance north from the main road. It's actually owned & run by Hellen's father, a vet by profession. In the house, 4 rooms share a separate toilet & shower, while a 5th outside is en suite & 3 more are under construction. Ask nicely & the owner will let you use the well-equipped kitchen to prepare dinner, though meals are available. It's somewhat lacking in maintenance but is clean, with a comfortable TV lounge/dining area, & parking under the eye of a nightwatchman. $, b/fast extra; lunch/dinner $$.

🏠 **Lexus Motel** (11 rooms) ☎ 08 821521. Easy to spot on the main road, the Lexus is an old-style motel where mismatched furnishings are the order of the day. It's clean & friendly enough, though noise from the bar could disturb an otherwise cheap night's sleep. $

🏠 **Mwaaka Lodge** (20 rooms) ☎ 08 821248. Right next to the main road, opposite the Changa Changa Motel (which isn't one we'd recommend), this little guesthouse, with its slightly jaunty, crazy-paving & stone look, seems to promise more than it delivers. Outside, a thatched bar & separate restaurant bode well, & there's secure parking, but the bedrooms are typical of guesthouse bedrooms anywhere, & could do with a bit of care. A TV, fridge & en-suite bath or shower come as standard, while the more expensive also have a sofa. $$, inc cont b/fast.

There are three further places to watch out for in an area where things are changing fast. Right in town, opposite the entrance to the Royal Solwezi, a small self-catering lodge was being built in 2007. To the north of town, on the road north towards the Kansanshi Mine, a new Indian-owned guesthouse is set to open with plans to run canoeing trips on the nearby river. Finally, in the other direction, near Mutanda, there is talk of a new tourist-orientated lodge, the Royal Mutanda River Lodge. No details were available of these at the time of research.

✕ **WHERE TO EAT AND DRINK** The Royal Solwezi is already a relaxing place for a drink or two and, once the restaurant has settled down, it's likely to be *the* place in town to eat, but there are alternatives. The Floriana, too, is worth trying. In addition, a couple of smaller establishments stand out from the crowd:

✕ **Bush & Bundu** ☎ 08 821216; ⊕ 09.00–22.00 daily. Opposite the police station, just back from the road near the civic centre, this lively restaurant, bar & take-away is an unexpected find. The outside terrace flanked by dugout canoes & with roll-up canvas walls leads into a good bar area. Standard fare of toasted sandwiches, burgers, pizzas & grills. $–$$

✕ **Kilimanjaro** ▥ 095 5925646; ⊕ 06.00–22.00 daily. Towards the western end of town, the Kilimanjaro has an attractive garden setting, with individual thatched rondavels & an indoor bar/restaurant. The menu is huge, offering everything from pasta & grills to Indian, Chinese & Zambian specials. $$

If you're after just a drink, PawPaws Pool Bar is a pleasant place for a beer, whereas by local standards, the **Caveman's Nightclub**, with its mirrored walls, is expensive.

OTHER PRACTICALITIES Solwezi is basically a linear town, with most shops and offices concentrated along the tarred road. That said, work on a new shopping centre along the road to Kansenshi Mine was scheduled to start in 2007, with another to follow. At present, of greatest practical use to most visitors is the branch of **Shoprite** supermarket, which has a prominent place on the main through road. It's by far the best shop in the region, and a good place to stock up, especially if you're heading south or west.

There are several fuel stations, including two large Total stations; this is generally a reliable place to refuel, and you should certainly fill up completely if you're heading west or south from here. There are several large branches of banks, including Zambian National Commercial Bank (beside the World Food Programme depot) and Stanbic, both of which have ATMs.

For vehicle problems, it may be worth a visit to Baxgate Auto Services on the main road.

In an emergency, there's a 24-hour Medical Centre (✆ *08 821225*). For other medical issues, the best place to go is Hilltop Hospital (m *097 7567892*), just off the main road through town.

COMMUNICATIONS Mobile phone coverage is good in Solwezi. The main **post office** is just off the main road near Shoprite, behind the BP garage. There are **internet** centres both on the main road and on the access road to Kansanshi.

WHAT TO SEE AND DO Solwezi may not be a tourist Mecca but there are still one or two places that offer an interesting diversion if you're passing through. For those visiting Kansanshi Mine, there is also an unexpected bonus. Since the approach road to the mine is largely privately owned, it is surrounded by security fences, which in turn keep out poachers. As a result, you can expect to see herds of impala along here, which comes as something of a surprise in an area not noted for its wildlife.

Kifubwa Stream Rock Shelter (*Entrance US$3 pp;* ⊕ *09.00–18.00 daily*) Quite close to the centre of Solwezi, where the Kifubwa Stream runs through a narrow gorge, there's a series of enigmatic engravings under an overhanging rock, dating to the late Stone Age. Although these had been known to local people for many years, they were first brought to wider attention in 1928. Subsequent archaeological surveys uncovered evidence of both quartz tools and charcoal fires, giving a clear indication of the site's provenance. Unfortunately, the engravings themselves have suffered at the hands of vandals, but it's an attractive spot, and worth a short visit.

To get there, turn off the main road to the south, towards the Teachers' College; it's signposted 'National Monument'. After about 3km, you'll come to the college; continue for a further 3km or so to a boom across the road. Stop here to pay the entrance fee, then you can either walk or drive the last couple of hundred metres down towards the river. Here, well-marked trails lead to the engravings, and interpretive signboards explain how they were discovered.

Mutanda River About 36km from town is the Mutanda River, where there's a series of attractive rapids, the Mutanda Falls. To get there, follow the tar road west out of town, go past the airport, and continue almost to the river. Just before this, take a left turning off the road and follow this track for about 1km.

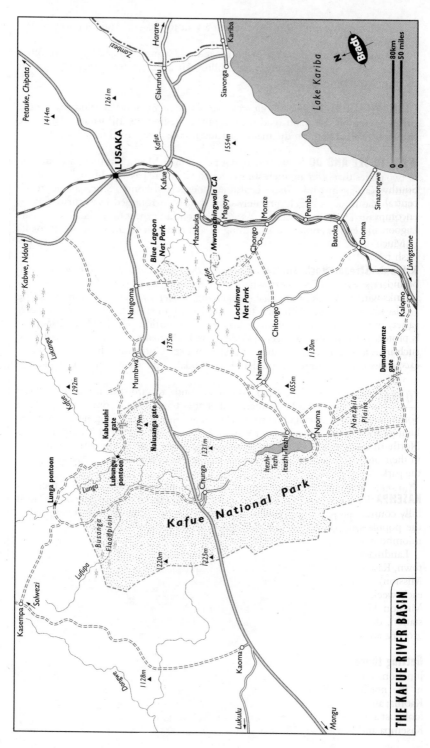

THE KAFUE RIVER BASIN

14

The Kafue River Basin

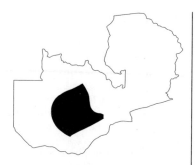

Southwest of the Copperbelt, the Kafue River Basin covers a large swathe of central Zambia stretching almost from the DRC to the west of Lusaka. It encompasses large areas of very sparsely populated bush as well as the Kafue, Blue Lagoon and Lochinvar national parks.

Much of this region of Zambia is difficult to visit, consisting of endless seasonal bush tracks which link occasional farming settlements. At its heart lies the huge Kafue National Park, which has some superb game-viewing areas within its boundaries. The best of these, the Busanga Plains, takes time to reach, but at times it ranks with the subcontinent's most impressive game areas.

Elsewhere, there are seasonal floodplains that sustain game and attract a rich variety of birdlife – like the Lukanga Swamps and the Kafue Flats. Part of the latter is protected by two small national parks – Blue Lagoon and Lochinvar – but most such areas remain outside the parks. The Kafue River Basin is a wild area, with some excellent game and endless possibilities for exploring, but very little development.

TOWNS AROUND KAFUE NATIONAL PARK

Southern Kafue is relatively near to Livingstone, and the towns along the Livingstone–Lusaka road are covered in *From Livingstone to Lusaka*, on pages 205–12. Northern Kafue has three useful towns around it which aren't usually destinations in their own right, but may be useful jumping-off points for the northern side of the park: Kasempa in the north, Mumbwa to the east, and Kaoma in the west.

KASEMPA Kasempa is a pleasant town with lots of space, in the midst of rolling, hilly country. There are many villages in the surrounding bush, although overall the population density doesn't feel very high as most of the area seems to be miombo woodland.

Landmarks include the tall microwave communication tower in the centre of town, Kasempa Boys' Boarding School (the equivalent girls' school is by Mukinge Mission), a post office, a small bank, with a second visiting on Tuesday and Friday each week (though neither accepts travellers' cheques), and the major Mukinge Mission Hospital (see below). Although there's a fuel station next to the bus station, don't rely on it; supplies are haphazard. Shops, including a very small grocery, are basic.

Getting there and away Kasempa has three roads running into it, meeting at a T-junction. The stem of the T (to the north) is an excellent, tarred road from Solwezi in the north. That meets a reasonably good gravel road heading southwest to Kaoma; and a variable bush track heading southeast towards Mumbwa. These both look just as good as each other when they leave town. There's a direct bus between Kasempa and Lusaka, via Solwezi, costing Kw120,000 one way.

From Solwezi Taking the good tar road southwest from Solwezi, you pass the airport then the road continues in a more southerly direction towards Kasempa, passing close to the Mutanda Falls. After some 140km, the M11 road joins you from the west (✛ TUKALU 13°3.302'S; 25°59.199'E), signposted left to Kalulushi, then a few kilometres further on there's another junction (✛ TUKASE 13°6.226'S; 25°52.252'E). The road straight on, heading west, is the good, gravel M8 to Kabompo. The left turn, signposted to Kasempa on the D181, continues on tar. The tar continues for the remaining 43km to Kasempa (✛ KASEMP 13°27.404'S; 25°49.779'E), and through the town as far as Mukinge Mission.

From Kaoma I haven't driven along this road, but am told it's a reasonable gravel road which is passable at any time of year.

To Kabanga scout post, Kafue National Park and Lunga pontoon See *Driving from Kasempa to Mumbwa*, below, for detailed directions to the park's northeast gate at Kabanga scout post and the Lunga pontoon.

 Where to stay and eat There are a few simple guesthouses in town:

🏠 **Tamara's Guesthouse** ☎ 021 8251027; m 097 7267974. The best of the bunch – & owned by the inspector general of police, so security shouldn't be an issue. Some rooms are en suite, with TV. Meals are available. $–$$

🏠 **Miracle Guest House** m 097 8513359. Self-catering rooms only. $
🏠 **TTG Guest House** At Kw5,000 per room, this makes 'budget' seem overpriced – but it's very basic! $

Kasempa boasts three Zambian-style restaurants, all simple but pleasant enough.

Mukinge Hospital Mukinge Mission started around 1925 when the Rev C S Foster came to this area as an evangelical missionary. His son, Bob, was born here, studied medicine in Toronto, and then returned to found a mission hospital in 1950 – even supervising its construction. Mukinge is still supported by the Evangelical Church in Zambia, as well as by the government.

The hospital has about 200 beds, and cares for about 150–160 in-patients per day (including around four births a day) as well as 160–180 outpatients. Patients may travel on foot or bike for five days to reach the hospital. The seven in-patient wards include one for malnutrition and another for isolation. There are also two operating theatres, a laboratory, a range of X-ray equipment, a physiotherapy department, a training school for nurses and a pharmacy with basic drug supplies. So, in short, it's the best hospital for a very long way.

Driving from Kasempa to Mumbwa
From Kasempa to the Lunga pontoon The road from Kasempa to the Lunga pontoon, or to Kafue National Park's Kabanga scout post, is basically very pleasant, with a few small rural settlements and a lot of open areas. It's generally easy driving, although there are lots of turnings on which to get lost, and a few nasty traps of deep sand.

Turning east at the main T-junction at Kasempa, you cross a bridge over the Lufupa River after 1.5km, then about 2.7km from the centre you pass the distinctive pyramidal steeple of a 'United Church of Zambia' church. A few kilometres later, about 4.4km from the centre, there's a turn on the right to the Mukinge Mission, and the road turns east-southeast – and becomes a good bush track.

About 11.2km from Kasempa the road forks; a left turn heads off east, but the right turn continues southeast towards the Lunga pontoon. It splits again at 21.3km; take the right fork going south-southeast. Similarly about 2km later

A few waypoints for this route, in sequence north to south, include:

✪ KALU01	13°29.949'S; 25°54.551'E	
✪ KALU02	13°33.530'S; 26°00.004'E	
✪ KALU03	13°37.362'S; 25°58.893'E	
✪ KALU04	13°45.647'S; 26°05.735'E	
✪ KALU05	13°55.201'S; 26°11.387'E	
✪ TUKABA	13°57.930'S; 26°11.858'E	(turning to Kabanga scout post)
✪ FERRYL	13°58.984'S; 26°20.784'E	(pontoon over the Lunga River)

there's another split and the road to Lunga pontoon is right; here it heads southwest for a while. Then about 48.2km from Kasempa there's another split; keep right for the pontoon.

About 78.6km from Kasempa the road forks (✪ TUKABA 13°57.929'S; 26°11.858'E): the left track heads east to the pontoon, whilst the right leads west of south for about 20km to the Kabanga scout post, on the northern border of Kafue National Park.

Staying on the road to the pontoon, you should ignore a clear left turn at 89.3km, which is an access road for a mine. A few kilometres later on the smaller track you pass Jifumpa Middle Basic School, and then within a kilometre there's a four-way junction. Again ignore the track off left. Going straight on leads, in 3km, to the pontoon across the Lunga (✪ FERRYL 13°58.984'S; 26°20.784'E).

Alternatively, a right turn leads you shortly to ✪ TULUNG 13°58.626'S; 26°20.076'E, the start of a very bumpy (black-cotton soil) track that shadows the east bank of the Lunga River for around 25km to Lunga River Lodge, on the boundary of the park. A continuation then heads northwest to the Kabanga scout post (✪ KABANG 14°5.808'S; 26°7.036'E).

Note that for the southern parts of this route, from around Tukaba, you are within a GMA, so are not free to camp – or indeed to do anything other than simply pass through.

From the Lunga pontoon to Mumbwa via the Lubungu pontoon Crossing the Lunga pontoon it is then about a 70km drive to Lubungu pontoon (✪ LUBUNG 14°33.750'S; 26°27.250'E), along a route which skirts the eastern boundary of the national park. Beware: this central section of the track between Kasempa and Mumbwa has historically been in exceedingly poor condition. See *From the Lubungu pontoon to the Lunga pontoon* on page 421 for directions along it.

Further south of there, from the Lubungu pontoon to Mumbwa, is currently a remarkably good gravel road. See *Driving from Mumbwa to the Lubungu pontoon* on page 410 for directions in reverse on this section.

MUMBWA I'm probably being very unfair to this thriving little town, but for some reason I always feel ill at ease here. However, it has a fairly reliable Total fuel station (✪ TOTALM 14°59.451'S; 27°03.642'E), the only one for miles around, so can be a very useful refuelling stop. That said, it would be wise to phone ahead (✆ *021 1800218*) to check that fuel is available. There's a branch of the National Credit and Savings Bank (⊕ *Mon–Fri, 08.30–14.30*); if you need to change US dollars into kwacha when it's closed, ask at one of the shops (the chemist on the left at the end may be able to help). Other facilities include a 'medi-test' laboratory, a large mosque with a dominant minaret, and endless small local shops.

Getting there

By bus On the far side of the shops, in the township, is the local bus station, where buses between Mongu and Lusaka travelling in both directions stop. It's a relatively busy route, with arrivals and departures at all times of day, though the highest frequency is the middle of the day, when buses that left from Lusaka or Mongu in the morning will pass through the town.

Driving from Lusaka About three hours' drive from Lusaka (148km), on the Great West Road towards Mongu, a large modern factory looms next to the road, and orderly warehouses stand behind well-watered lawns. This is perhaps the country's biggest cotton ginnery. A few kilometres further west is a turning off the road to the north, which leads – after about 4km of Zambia's most pot-holed tar – to the thriving township of Mumbwa.

Where to stay If you need to stop overnight in Mumbwa, there a couple of choices:

🏠 **Hacienda Hotel** This old hotel has been recently revamped, with good service & pleasant staff. Rooms are en suite with spotless tiled floors & dbl or twin beds. You can get a decent meal of beef stew or chicken curry & rice for Kw15–25,000, with Zambian dishes at Kw10,000, & there's even ice-cream –

albeit slightly melted.. The clean, tiled foyer has a TV & bar. $$ (cont b/fast)
🏠 **Mumbwa Motel** On the right as you drive into town, this has small round bungalows with sloping roofs. For amenities it boasts a cocktail bar, a restaurant & a public phone. $

Driving from Mumbwa to the Lubungu pontoon

Once you leave the tarred Great West Road, a high-clearance vehicle is essential throughout the year, with 4x4 a must in the rainy season. If you're heading round the eastern side of the park for Hippo Lodge or McBrides' Camp, or trying the adventurous eastern route towards Kasempa, read on. However, if you're driving to Lunga (which very few people do) then the route through the park, although longer than this one, is probably better (see page 420). You'll certainly see a few more vehicles (handy if you have problems) and a lot more game.

The road from Mumbwa to the Lubungu pontoon has been graded in recent years, and isn't in bad condition; it'll take about two hours (but do check locally to see if anything's changed recently). The pontoon itself is operational in the dry season from Monday to Saturday, 06.00–18.00; the crossing takes 15 minutes.

Via Kabulushi gate To drive along the park's eastern side, the easiest route is to strike north at Mumbwa. For this, turn north into Mumbwa township, then left at the first roundabout by the Total garage (✪ TOTALM 14°59.457'S; 27°03.617'E). At the top of the next rise, about 1.1km later, take a right turn onto the Kasempa road, a reasonable gravel road that goes to Lubungu pontoon. About 33km from the Total garage, there's a split in the road (✪ TUKAIN 14°45.599'S; 26°54.376'E).

Bear left at this fork for the Lubungu pontoon. (The right track leads to Kaindu, and eventually to a point just south of the Lunga pontoon, but it's very little used.) After 7km, at the Chitunda Open Air Reform School, keep right, then a further 22km brings you to Kabulushi gate (✪ KABULU 14°40.727'S; 26°39.338'E), where you may need to pay park fees (although fees for McBrides' are payable at the camp, not here).

Almost 20km after the gate, or nearly 86km from Mumbwa, the road bends around to the right, towards the Lubungu pontoon. A turning (✪ TUHIPP 14°37.866'S; 26°29.659'E) bears off from the main road towards the old Hippo

Mine, signposted to Hippo Camp and McBrides' Camp. Take this track, away from the graded gravel road and on to a bush track.

In the **dry season**, there's an alternative route to McBrides' from ⊕ TUHIPP. Instead of turning right here for the pontoon, continue straight on for 5km, then turn left at a second yellow sign to the camp; McBrides' is 14.5km from this point, bearing left at both forks encountered en route.

At other times of the year, and for Hippo Camp, ignore both the small barrier gate here, and yet another gate (⊕ MINEGT 14°39.169'S; 26°25.025'E) 5km further on (erected by the Zoo Copper Mining Company) and drive through. You'll soon pass the whitewashed buildings of the old Hippo Mine. This started in 1911, and gets its name from the fact that in the early days one of the workers was killed by a hippo, and buried here. It was the first commercial copper mine in Zambia, and closed only in 1971.

Finally about 97km from Mumbwa you'll drive onto the airstrip (⊕ AIRHIP 14°40.191'S; 26°23.417'E). This is where the tracks to Hippo and McBrides' separate; it's barely 2km to Hippo Camp and less than 3km to McBrides' Camp. Had you ignored the turning (⊕ TUHIPP 14°37.890'S; 26°29.658'E) to Hippo, and followed the main road right, you'd reach the Lubungu pontoon (⊕ LUBUNG 14°33.750'S; 26°27.250'E) in about 10km.

The pontoon is normally operational Monday to Saturday, 06.00–18.00; the crossing takes 15 minutes, and is free, but a tip of something like Kw5,000 each is always a good idea. The team that run the pontoon are often to be found in the buildings beside the road, a few hundred metres from the pontoon, so you may want to stop there first. (You may even want to make an arrangement with them for a later time if you're returning.) If the Lubungu's waters are very low, then the pontoon will not be in operation and you will have to ford the river a few kilometres upstream – but you will need a local person to guide you to this.

Via Nalusanga gate There is one other possible route here, though I've not heard of anyone using it for some time. It is suitable only for two or more 4x4s and is an old cut line track that skirts the eastern boundary of Kafue National Park. This starts from Kafue's Nalusanga gate (⊕ NALUSA 14°58.258'S; 26°42.718'E), which is about 37km west of Mumbwa on the Great West Road. From here there is a bush track which heads about 33km north (and slightly west) directly to the park's Kabulushi gate (⊕ KABULU 14°40.727'S; 26°39.338'E), on the road to the Lubungu pontoon.

Given that the direct road from Mumbwa to the Kabulushi gate has recently been graded, as described in the section above, it's likely that this cut road has fallen into almost total disuse, so ask at either scout post before you attempt it.

Driving from the Lubungu pontoon to the Lunga pontoon See Northern Kafue's *Route direction for 4x4s* section, page 421, for directions along this route.

KAOMA Kaoma is a small district town about 3km from the Great West Road between Kafue and Mongu, and about 76km west of Kafue National Park. Though not close to Kafue, it's on the edge of the Western Province, so is very much a gateway to the area. It has a post office, a Finance Bank, several guesthouses, numerous shops (of which the best stocked is Cheap & Best along the main road) and local eateries, and two vital fuel stations: vital to anyone travelling west, that is.

Whichever way you're travelling, it's wise to fill your fuel tank (and spare fuel drums) here. If you have spare space in your vehicle, then you'll find no shortage of people wanting to share the journey. Given the shortage of transport, and the

14

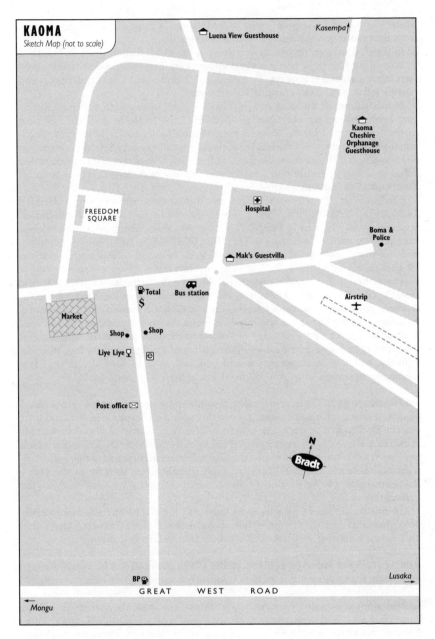

KAOMA
Sketch Map (not to scale)

Luena View Guesthouse

Kasempa

Kaoma
Cheshire
Orphanage
Guesthouse

FREEDOM
SQUARE

Hospital

Boma &
Police

Mak's Guestvilla

Total

Bus station

Airstrip

$

Market

Shop

Shop

Liye Liye

Post office

N

Bradt

BP

GREAT WEST ROAD

Lusaka

Mongu

insight that hitchhikers can give to visitors, don't appear rude to the locals by refusing a lift.

GETTING THERE AND AWAY

By bus All the buses stop at the bus station behind the Total filling station in the centre of town. Buses to/from Lusaka take about 5½ hours; those to/from Mongu take about 2 hours.

Driving

From Kaoma to Lukulu If you're heading west to Lukulu, take the tar road towards Mongu for about 25km, then there's a gravel road on the right, signposted as 195km to Lukulu. After 16km on this road it forks: keep to the right. Later there's a sign heralding a turn to the right, to the M8, which leads to the Watopa pontoon (◈ FERRY4 14°2.338'S; 23°37.744'E).

Lining this road are small villages, each consisting of thatched huts built in varying sizes. Ox-carts are also a frequent sight, straight out of a biblical scene.

From Kaoma to Kasempa Turning off the Great West Road at Kaoma, there's a reasonable gravel road that heads north and then northeast to Kasempa.

Where to stay and eat There's a choice of small local guesthouses in Kaoma, of which the best is at the Kaoma Cheshire Orphanage. Other guesthouses are **Luena View Guesthouse**, on the north edge of town, and **Mak's Guestvilla**, opposite the bus station. Both have fairly clean rooms and may be able to arrange simple meals. Mak's also has a bar.

⌂ **Kaoma Cheshire Orphanage Guesthouse** (6 rooms, 6 rondavels) m 097 7221782. With a beautiful view of the Luena valley, the guesthouse has decent, clean rooms in 2 semi-detached houses (one with a living room & DSTV, the other with a dining room) or in individual rondavels. There are mosquito nets in each room. Guests share communal hot showers & a kitchen where you can prepare your own food. Alternatively, simple meals can be provided with sufficient notice. By staying here you support the orphanage in raising funds for Zambia's ever-increasing number of AIDS orphans. *Kw20,000 pp*

Tom Kok reports that the three best places for a drink and a chat are all along the main shopping street: **Maseka** (which has an outside terrace, where you can meet plenty of local people), **Liye Liye** and **Luvu**. **C&C** near the Zamtel mast serves good nshima, chips or rice, with beef, chicken or occasionally fish and a drink (**$**), and is a pleasant place to spend an evening. More and more bars have satellite television.

What to do Local artist Kozhi Kawina has painted several murals that are well worth a visit. You can find them on the walls of the district hospital, the doctor's residence and the Cheshire orphanage. If you contact him direct (m *097 9314215*) Kawina can also take you to see his work at his studio in the nearby village of Chilombo, a nice walk of some 3km. In addition to his painting, the artist leads a cultural drum and dance troupe that has established quite a reputation in Zambia.

KAFUE NATIONAL PARK

(Park fees US$15 pp per day; US$15 per vehicle per day, camping US$5 pp per day)
Kafue is a huge national park, two and a half times the size of South Luangwa. Sadly, in the 1980s and early '90s, few resources were devoted to its upkeep and anti-poaching efforts were left to a couple of dedicated souls from the few safari lodges that remained in the park.

Now the situation is better. Although some of the camps mentioned are not fully operational, those that are bring a steady trickle of visitors into the park – which help add weight (and finance) to the ongoing effort to build the park back up to its former glory. Even the park's elephants are visibly recovering (both in number and in terms of losing some of their shyness), although it will be a while before they return to their former strength. It is very heartening to see that the rest of the game is thriving, and occurring in a volume and variety that belies the existence of any problems here.

14

Few of the camps here are as plush or well-oiled as the corresponding camps in the Luangwa, but in Kafue's best areas the game is at least as good. In particular, game viewing on and around the Busanga Plains can be stunning, so don't visit without at least a side trip into this remarkable area.

GEOGRAPHY, FLORA AND FAUNA

Geography Established in 1924, the Kafue National Park covers some 22,400km^2 (about the size of Wales, or Massachusetts) of very varied terrain and is one of the world's largest parks. Naturally, its geography varies considerably. Throughout the park, the permanent Kafue River follows a well-defined course, and widens in a few places where barriers of harder rocks near the surface force it into shallow, rocky rapids – Kafwala and the area beside KaingU Safari Lodge being the obvious examples. Bordering the eastern side of southern Kafue is Lake Itezhi-Tezhi – a large, manmade lake that was created in 1977. The primary function of its dam is to regulate the water levels experienced by the Kafue Gorge Hydro-electric Dam, further downstream, although it also generates some electricity.

The map clearly shows that the tarred Great West Road between Lusaka and Mongu bisects the park. This road provides the easiest route into the park, and also a convenient split that allows me to refer to 'northern' and 'southern' Kafue as simply meaning the areas to the north and the south of the road. These have slightly different habitats and species, and also very different access routes. As far as casual visitors are concerned, they could almost be two separate parks.

Surrounding the whole are no fewer than eight game management areas (GMAs), which provide a valuable buffer zone for the park's wildlife.

Flora Most of Kafue is an undulating mosaic of miombo woodlands and dambos, within which you'll find smaller patches of munga woodland, and bands of riparian forest and thickets along the larger rivers.

In the extreme northwest of the park are the permanently wet **Busanga Swamps**, surrounded by adjacent floodplains and now a designated Ramsar site. These are dotted with raised 'tree islands', notable for some mammoth specimens of sycamore figs, *Ficus sycomorus*, amongst other vegetation. These floodplains are ringed by a 'termitaria zone' of grasslands.

Northern Kafue receives slightly more rain than the south, resulting in richer, taller vegetation. In many areas such woodland is dominated by the large-leafed munondo tree, *Julbernardia paniculata*, though you'll also find 'Prince of Wales feathers', *Brachystegia boehmii*, and the odd mobola plum, *Parinari curatellifolia*.

Southern Kafue is dominated by areas of Kalahari sand, and also has a slightly lower rainfall than the north. Large stretches of Kalahari woodland are the norm here, typified by silver-leaf terminalia, *Terminalia sericea*, poison-pod albizia, *Albizia versicolor*, and *Combretum* species. Within this there are a few patches of mature teak forest – the Ngoma Forest being one of the most spectacular examples – whilst further south, on patches of alluvial clay, are some beautiful groves of cathedral mopane, *Colophospermum mopane*.

In the far south of the park, the Nanzhila Plains are a fascinating area. Wide expanses of grassland are dotted with islands of vegetation and large termitaria – often with baobabs, *Adansonia digitata*, or jackalberry trees, *Diospyros mespiliformis*, growing out of them.

Fauna Covering such a large area, with a variety of habitats, Kafue is rich in wildlife and many of its species seem to exhibit strong local variations in their distribution. This is a reflection of the wide variety of habitats in such a large park.

Antelope Kafue has a superb range of antelope, but you will have to travel throughout the park if you wish to see them all.

The **Busanga Swamps**, in the far north of the park, are permanently flooded and home to the secretive sitatunga, which is uniquely adapted to swamp life. These powerful swimmers will bound off with a series of leaps and plunges when disturbed, aided by their enlarged hooves which have evolved for walking around on floating papyrus islands. They will then stand motionless until the danger passes, or even submerge themselves leaving just their nostrils above the water for breathing.

The **Busanga Plains**, a little further south, is a much larger area that is seasonally inundated. This only starts to dry out around June (it's totally impassable by vehicle until then), when it's possible to visit and see large herds of red lechwe and puku, with smaller groups of zebra and blue wildebeest. Oribi are found throughout the park, but are particularly common here, and you also have a good chance of seeing roan and the beautiful sable antelope.

Across the rest of the northern half of the park, there's a good range of mixed bush environments, and here kudu, bushbuck, eland, reedbuck, common duiker, grysbok and defassa waterbuck (a subspecies without the distinctive white ring on the rump) are all frequently seen. Even within this there are local differences; the Kafwala area, for example, is notable for good numbers of Lichtenstein's hartebeest and sable. Numerically, puku dominate most of the northern side of the park, though they gradually cede to impala as you move further south.

On the south side of Kafue, the game has been more patchy. Generally it thrives in areas around lodges, which provide some sanctuary from poaching, but away from these it can be scarce. However, the success of anti-poaching measures and the presence of three lodges in the GMA on the eastern side of the river are certainly having an impact, and the game is improving as a result. The area around Puku Pan and KaingU Safari Lodge is particularly rich in impala and bushbuck, and the game is fairly relaxed.

The area from Itezhi-Tezhi south to Ngoma has Kafue's densest elephant population, with some groups also frequenting the Chunga area. In just a day around the Ngoma area and Riverside Drive, where the game was relaxed and fairly prolific, we found not only a number of elephant herds, but also a large herd of over 100 buffalo, plenty of impala and puku, family groups of Lichtenstein's hartebeest and waterbuck, and numerous bushbuck, warthog and baboons.

South of Ngoma, the picture is improving too. When I first visited in the early 2000s, the game was sparse indeed, and skittish. It was interesting that the only really good sightings that we had of large animals were around the Chelenje Pools Loop (what was navigable of it) and the old Nanzhila restcamp (now reopened as Nanzhila Plains Safari Camp) – so once again the animals were congregating in areas associated with visitors. Now we're getting credible reports that numbers are increasing, with species ranging from blue wildebeest and eland to roan and sable antelope, as well as waterbuck, kudu and impala.

Large predators Lion are relatively widespread all over the park, but the larger males are increasingly uncommon, with inevitable consequences for numbers as a whole. On the Busanga Plains, prides stalk through nervous herds of puku and lechwe nightly, using the natural drainage ditches for cover with deadly efficiency.

Leopard remain very common throughout the main forested areas of park, though they are seldom seen on the open plains. They are most easily observed on night drives, and continue with their activities completely unperturbed by the presence of a spotlight trained upon them. They seem to be particularly frequently seen in the area around Lufupa – though this is probably due to the success of Lufupa Tented Camp's guides in locating these elusive cats. This is a particularly good place for seeing leopard in the wild.

Spotted hyena are seen regularly, though not often, throughout the park. They appear to occur in smaller numbers than either lions or leopards. Cheetah are not common anywhere, but they're most frequently seen in the north of the park, where they seem to be thriving. Sightings have definitely increased since the late 1990s, with plenty of first-class reports of very relaxed cats here. It's certainly the best place in Zambia to look for cheetah.

Occasional sightings of wild dog occur all over the park (though fewer around the road on the east side), which is one of Zambia's best strongholds for them. The park's huge size suits their wide-ranging nomadic habits and I have had a number of reports of them being seen on the north side of the park in the last few years. Areas around the Busanga Plains seem a particular favourite. They remain uncommon in any locale, but a possibility all over the park.

Other large animals Elephants occur throughout Kafue, though overall their numbers are still recovering from intensive poaching during the 1970s, and their density varies hugely within the park. Just south of Lake Itezhi-Tezhi, around Chunga and, especially, Ngoma, there are large herds and a thriving population – though they're not always relaxed, so drivers there need to be very wary of getting too close to them. South of Ngoma, the situation was much gloomier, although anti-poaching measures have resulted in a resurgence in the elephant population.

On the north side of the park elephant densities are lower than around Ngoma, but they have improved a lot. When I first visited Lufupa in 1995, a few elephants spotted a kilometre from the lodge were a reason for excitement, causing us to leave dinner and jump into a vehicle. Now family groups are commonly seen in the Lufupa and Lunga areas, and are a lot less skittish than they used to be.

Buffalo, common in the 1970s and '80s, are rarely seen nowadays, though herds do frequent the Busanga Plains. Sadly, black rhino are thought to be extinct throughout the park, after sustained poaching decades ago.

The Kafue River and its larger tributaries like the Lunga are fascinating tropical rivers – full of life – and infested with hippo and crocodile, which occur in numbers to rival the teeming waters of the Luangwa. Vervet monkeys and yellow (*not* chacma) baboons are common almost everywhere, and you'll usually find porcupines, mongooses, civets and a wide variety of small mammals on night drives. One other curious but interesting fact: there seem to be more pangolins than aardvarks in North Kafue, which is a very unusual situation indeed!

Birds The birding in Kafue is very good. There have been about 495 species recorded here, suggesting that the park has probably the richest birdlife of any of Zambian park. This reflects Kafue's wide range of habitats, because in addition to extensive miombo woodlands (quite a Zambian speciality!), Kafue has plenty of rivers, extensive wetlands and seasonal floodplains in the north.

The wetlands and floodplains have the full range of herons, storks and ibises, plus crowned and wattled cranes, Denham's (or Stanley's) and kori bustards, secretary birds, and geese (spur-winged and Egyptian) by the thousand.

In the long, verdant stretches of riverine vegetation you're likely to spot Ross's turaco, Narina trogons, MacClounie's (black-backed) barbet, olive woodpecker, brown-headed apalis and the yellow-throated leaflove. Pel's fishing owl is also found here, with Bob Stjernstedt noting that there are pairs around Ntemwa, and African finfoot frequent the shady fringes of the slower rivers, swimming under the overhanging trees with part of their body submerged.

Kafue's extensive miombo woodlands have endemics such as pale-billed hornbill, miombo pied barbet, grey tit, miombo rock thrush, Sousa's shrike, chestnut-mantled sparrow-weaver, spotted creeper, and three species of eremomela. In the south, on the Nanzhila Plains, the black-cheeked lovebird – endemic to southern Zambia – is relatively common.

Hunting and poaching During the 1980s and early '90s there were few efforts or government resources devoted to protecting Kafue, and poaching was rife. This ensured the extermination of black rhino, and a sharp reduction in elephant numbers at the hands of organised commercial poachers. Fortunately the park is massive, surrounded by GMAs, and not easily accessible. So although the smaller game was hunted for meat, this was not generally on a large enough scale to threaten their populations. Nor did it adversely affect the environment.

Organised commercial poaching is now relatively rare, and the remaining incidence of smaller-scale poaching by locals (for food) is being tackled by a number of initiatives. The ZAWA team protecting the park has become much more active in recent years, having received a lot of training and more resources (notably aid from Danish and Norwegian agencies).

Some of these initiatives concentrate on increasing the physical policing of the park, the most obvious being the Kantipo anti-poaching patrols, which have been partially funded by some of the lodges. Others try to tackle the underlying reason for this poaching, and attempt to offer practical alternatives for the local people of the surrounding areas that are more attractive than shooting the game. For example, one such project allows local people in neighbouring areas to come into the park to collect natural honey. Both types of initiatives work with the help and support of some of the more enlightened local safari operators.

GETTING THERE AND GETTING AROUND To get to Kafue, and to get around once there, you have three choices. Firstly, you can fly in and stay at one of the better camps or lodges – and the team from the camp will walk, drive and boat you around their area of the park. Secondly, you can drive yourself into and around the park. Thirdly, you can arrange for a company from outside to drive you in here, and drive you around.

By air or scheduled transfer This is certainly the most relaxing way to get to the park, especially if your time is relatively limited, or you like the idea of a holiday here rather than an expedition. However, it limits your choice of lodge to one, or perhaps two, of the better ones. Lunga and possibly KaingU spring to mind. There are various airstrips dotted around the park and some are in good repair. There are no scheduled flights into the park, but Lunga River Lodge does run an extensive programme of charter flights between the lodge, Lusaka and Livingstone – and several charter companies in Lusaka will fly you out on request.

Although not by air, the regular road transfers which connect Lusaka with Lufupa Tented Camp (and hence Shumba) run to a reliable schedule, and so I'd think of them in this bracket also – albeit that the driving takes five to seven hours instead of 40 minutes!

Until recently, lodges and camps in the Kafue National Park were for the most part individually owned and run, but by 2007 this was starting to change, with one company in particular moving into the area:

Wilderness Safaris ☎ 021 1618008–10; f 021 1840024; e zambia@wilderness.co.zm; www.wilderness-safaris.com. Although well established in Namibia & South Africa, Wilderness have only recently set up an operation in Zambia, headed up by 2 experienced operators, Dave &

14

Linda Bennett. Most of their camps are in the Kafue National Park, but they also have a small presence in the South Luangwa, with their first, refurbished camp opening in 2007, followed by a second brand-new operation in 2008. Wilderness deals only with agents, so reservations for their lodges should be made through a tour operator (see pages 46–8).

By 4x4 If you want to drive here, then think of it as an expedition. You will need two good 4x4 vehicles and all your provisions as camping is usually possible, but proper facilities or places to re-supply are few and far between. If you have problems, you must be able to solve them yourself, as you can expect little help. Although there are many camps listed in the sections below, only a handful would be capable to offering any help in an emergency.

However, if you come well equipped then the park is wonderful. Many of the camps will be happy to help you with advice on the area and, if they have them to spare, will usually sell you a bed and a cold beer. If you do come, then you can be assured of seeing very few other vehicles during your stay in this stunning area.

Note that camping in the north of the park is quite regulated – making the south a better bet for self-driving in many ways; camping is certainly more relaxed in the south.

Arrive with the best maps of the place you can find, and use them in conjunction with those in this book. Do bring a GPS; you will need one. Remember that many of the tracks in Southern Kafue have started to grow over with lack of use, so rediscovering them is all part of the adventure.

Mobile operators in Kafue A couple of safari operators run trips into Kafue without having a permanent base there. Some do this with permission from the National Parks Board, others without. Some work well, though without a long-term presence in the park, they clearly don't know the ground as well as the established camps. Further, if they encounter serious difficulties, they seldom have the logistical support to solve their own problems. (There are tales of one inexperienced company that recently came up into the Busanga Plains too early, and ended up with its vehicle stuck in mud for two days.)

Perhaps more importantly, most of the established camps work hard to maintain the park's roads and minimise poaching. Few, if any, of the mobile operators contribute to this vital work.

As Kafue starts to receive a few more visitors, the Busanga Plains (especially) is becoming better known and the focus for more attention from many small mobile operators. If you want to get the very best from it, and also to support operators who work to preserve the area, then I recommend that you support the area's permanent operators.

NORTHERN KAFUE The northern section of the park is a slightly undulating plateau, veined by rivers – the Lufupa, the Lunga, the Ntemwa, the Mukombo, the Mukunashi, and the Lubuji – which are all tributaries of the main Kafue, whose basin extends to the border with DRC. The main Kafue River is already mature by the time it reaches this park, though it has over 400km further to flow before discharging into the Zambezi.

Thus in the park its permanent waters are wide, deep and slow-flowing, to the obvious pleasure of large numbers of hippo and crocodile. Tall, shady hardwoods overhang its gently curving banks, and the occasional islands in the stream are favourite feeding places for elephant and buffalo. In short, it is a typically beautiful large African river.

Occasionally it changes, as at Kafwala. Here, there is a stretch of gentle rapids for about 7km. The river is up to about 1,000m wide and dotted with numerous

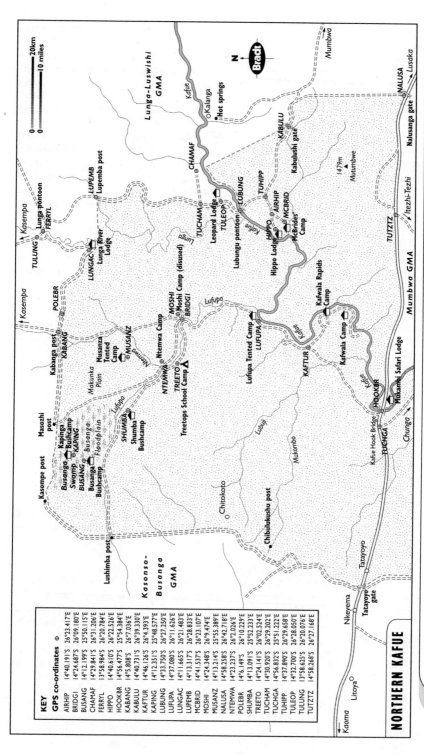

NORTHERN KAFUE

KEY

GPS co-ordinates ⊕

AIRHIP	14°40.191'S 26°23.417'E
BRIDGI	14°24.687'S 26°09.180'E
BUSANG	14°12.199'S 25°50.115'E
CHAMAF	14°29.841'S 26°31.206'E
FERRYL	13°58.984'S 26°20.784'E
HIPPO	14°40.610'S 26°22.526'E
HOOKBR	14°56.477'S 26°54.384'E
KABANG	14°5.808'S 26°7.036'E
KABULU	14°40.731'S 26°39.330'E
KAFTUR	14°46.126'S 26°4.393'E
KAPING	14°12.351'S 25°48.577'E
LUBUNG	14°33.750'S 26°27.250'E
LUFUPA	14°11.665'S 26°11.626'E
LUNGAC	14°37.080'S 26°21.483'E
LUPEMB	14°13.317'S 26°28.833'E
MCBRID	14°41.537'S 26°23.107'E
MOSHI	14°24.348'S 26°9.474'E
MUSANZ	14°13.214'S 25°55.389'E
NALUSA	14°58.258'S 26°42.718'E
NTEMWA	14°23.237'S 26°2.026'E
POLEBR	14°6.149'S 26°10.229'E
SHUMBA	14°13.091'S 25°52.233'E
TREETO	14°24.141'S 26°02.524'E
TUCHAM	14°30.920'S 26°29.202'E
TUCHGA	14°56.832'S 25°51.222'E
TUHIPP	14°37.890'S 26°29.658'E
TULEOP	14°32.700'S 26°28.050'E
TULUNG	13°58.625'S 26°20.076'E
TUTZTZ	14°58.268'S 26°27.168'E

islands, all supporting dense riverine vegetation – making a particularly good spot for birdwatching.

Most of the park's northern section, between the rivers, is a mosaic of miombo and mopane woodlands, with occasional open grassy pans known as dambos. The edges of the main rivers are lined with tall hardwood trees. Raintrees (*Lonchocarpus capassa*); knobthorns (*Acacia nigrescens*); jackalberries (*Diospyros mespiliformis*); leadwoods (*Combretum imberbe*); and especially sausage trees (*Kigelia africana*), are all very common.

The Kafue's tributaries are smaller, but the larger of these are still wide and permanent. The Lufupa is probably the most important. It enters the park from the Kasonso-Busanga GMA in the north, and immediately feeds into a permanent wetland in the far north of the park: the Busanga Swamps. In the wet season these waters flood out over a much larger area, across the whole Busanga Plains, before finally draining back into the river, which then continues its journey on the south side of the plains.

The swamp and seasonal floodplain together cover about 750km², and are a superb area for game. The seasonal floodwaters on the plains are shallow, but enough to sustain a healthy growth of grasses throughout the year on the mineral-rich black-cotton soil. These open plains are dotted with numerous small 'islands' of wild date palms, *Phoenix reclinata*, and wild fig trees (various *Ficus* species).

The area is perfect for huge herds of water-loving lechwe and puku, which are joined by large numbers of zebra, wildebeest and other plains grazers, as the waters recede at the end of the wet season. However, the Busanga Plains are very remote, and normally impossible to reach by vehicle until about June/July. Hence, until recently, few people (even in the safari business) had heard about them, let alone visited them, and so this remarkable area continues to go largely unrecognised.

Route directions for 4x4s You really need a high-clearance 4x4 for any of these routes. You'll have problems on all of them during the rains, although the Lunga–Lubungu road, or anything close to the Busanga Plains, is likely to be impassable between about November and July.

Driving from Kasempa in the north For directions to the Kabanga scout post (⊕ KABANG 14°5.808'S; 26°7.036'E), which is effectively the only park entrance gate to serve the northeast corner of the park, see the detailed directions earlier in this chapter under *Driving from Kasempa to Mumbwa*, page 408. Kabanga is the easiest way to enter the park from the north, and from there a track proceeds southwards into the park keeping on the east bank of the Ntemwa River until around the (old) site of Moshi Camp (⊕ MOSHI 14°24.348'S; 26°9.474'E).

From the Lusaka–Mongu road From Lusaka, Mumbwa has the last fuel station before you reach the park. If you are driving into the north of the park, then you're probably heading in the direction of either Kafwala or Lufupa. In this case the route is very easy: simply turn north off the main road at the scout gate beside the Kafue's west bank, just beyond the Hook Bridge (⊕ HOOKBR 14°56.477'S; 25°54.384'E).

From here the track (⊕ KAFTUR 14°46.126'S; 26°4.393'E) heads northeast through the heart of the park for about 44km, where a right turn leads east to Kafwala Camp. Continuing roughly northeast for about a further 26km will lead you to Lufupa (⊕ LUFUPA 14°37.080'S; 26°11.626'E). In the dry season it's basically a good track, fine for a 2WD with high clearance, though designed more for game viewing than speed. In the wet it is impassable due to the toffee-like consistency of the black-cotton soil.

Apart from possibly the river, this track is the main artery through northern Kafue, and will take you on to Moshi, where the road splits. The right fork heads to the Kabanga scout post (✛ KABANG 14°5.808'S; 26°7.036'E), whilst the left passes Ntemwa and continues to the Busanga Plains.

From the Lusaka–Mongu road to the Lubungu pontoon See *Driving from Mumbwa to the Lubungu pontoon*, page 410, for more details of this route on the northeast side of the park.

From the Lubungu pontoon to the Lunga pontoon Although the road between the pontoons over at Lubungu and Lunga is barely 70km long, it is certainly one of the slowest and most unpleasant tracks in the country. It's a drive that's known for reducing the hardest of 'Bushmen' to tears of frustration! One very experienced old hand commented: 'I always called this one the "road of death" because I have spent many days broken down and ... well ... just broken on it.' It's impassable during the rains, and exceedingly slow-going when dry.

Starting at the Lubungu pontoon (✛ LUBUNG 14°33.750'S; 26°27.250'E), it's about 2.5km north to the right turning (✛ TULEOP 14°32.700'S; 26°28.050'E) to Leopard Lodge. About 6.5km beyond that is another turning (✛ TUCHAM 14°29.367'S; 26°28.583'E) on the right which leads to Chamafumba Camp (currently closed). Both of these are on the north bank of the river, upstream from the pontoon.

From this second turning, it's fractionally over 30km to the Lupemba scout post, and a crossing (✛ LUPEMB 14°13.317'S; 26°28.833'E) of the Lupemba River. A further 15km on there's another small bridge over another river at ✛ SBRIDG 14°05.983'S; 26°25.267'E – and then there's a final 16km stretch before you finally reach the Lunga pontoon (✛ FERRYL 13°58.984'S; 26°20.784'E), north of which the track is in much better shape as far as Kasempa.

The 70km which I've so swiftly described above is unlikely to take you less than eight hours, and you'd be exceedingly foolish to try it with fewer than two very sturdy vehicles. See *Driving from Kasempa to Mumbwa*, page 408, for more details of the track north of the Lunga pontoon.

🏠 **Where to stay** Though the range of camps listed here appears to be long, most non-Zambian visitors are probably best to choose between a combination of Lufupa and Shumba (and the new Kafwala Rapids Camp), or alternatively a combination of Lunga's River Lodge and one of the Busanga camps. (That said, Hippo Camp might soon become a plausible option for those feeling more offbeat!) All of these camps have been here for years and are closely involved with the park and its conservation. They are very reliable, and will deliver a consistent experience – and yet they are totally different. Read on.

Centre of the park and north

🏠 **Lufupa Tented Camp** (15 tents) Contact via Wilderness Safaris, page 417 (✛ LUFUPA 14°37.080'S; 26°11.626'E). With a change of ownership in 2006 comes an entirely new camp at Lufupa. Overlooking the confluence of the Lufupa and Kafue rivers, it's a relatively large camp & is the centre of activity in the northern Kafue. Access is easy, taking about 5–7hrs from Lusaka, inc a break for a packed lunch. If you're driving yourself, enter the park at the Nalusanga gate, continue straight on until you cross the Kafue River at the Hook Bridge (✛ HOOKBR 14°56.477'S; 25°54.384'E), then take an almost immediate turn north from the tar road, past a game scouts' checkpoint. Follow that track about 44km northeast, ignore the right turn to Kafwala (✛ KAFTUR 14°46.126'S; 26°4.393'E) & continue for about 26km more to Lufupa.

Accommodation is in 12 simple, brand-new twin-bed tents that face the Kafue River, each with en-suite hot & cold shower, toilet & washbasin; 3 family tents will be added in 2008.

The camp prides itself generally on a no-frills approach, so you won't be waited on hand & foot; it's just not that kind of place. However, there's always someone to help when you need it. The dining room serves buffet-style meals &, whilst there is little choice, the food is good (& any food restrictions will be well catered for). There's a good, comfortable bar, & you can always help yourself to tea & coffee. The atmosphere is friendly, casual & very unpretentious.

The lodge is large enough to run several activities at once. Most are by 4x4 & boat (an afternoon boat trip up either the Lufupa or the Kafue river is excellent), though walks can be organised on request. The guides are highly adept at locating local wildlife, & especially the area's leopards, which helps to make exciting night drives one of the lodge's chief attractions. Watching a leopard stalk by night is unforgettable, & Lufupa offers visitors one of the best chances in Africa of spotting these cats. *US$400/525 pp sharing/sgl, inc FB, activities, local drinks & park fees. Flights from Lusaka can be arranged at additional cost.* ⊕ *May–early Jan.*

Å Lufupa Campsite (camping) Contact via Wilderness Safaris, page 417. For those with a 4x4 vehicle Lufupa has an entirely separate campsite, with wood & charcoal available & a slipway for launching boats. The site has its own bar area, dining room & pool; visitors to this site may not use the facilities at the tented camp. *US$7 pp.* ⊕ *May–early Jan.*

⌂ Kafwala Camp (2 chalets, 2 rondavels) m 097 7771347; e kafwala@zamtel.zm, ashworth@zamnet.zm; www.wcsz.org.zm; or book through WECSZ in Lusaka (see page 51). This camp is built on the bank of the Kafue River in a stunning location, about 700m below the start of the Kafwala Rapids, northeast of the main bridge over the Kafue. Simply enter the park by turning north from the tar road on the western side of the main bridge, past the game scouts' checkpoint. Follow that dirt road about 44km northeast, then take the right turn which leads to Kafwala.

Access to the camp is restricted to members of the WECSZ, & it must be booked in advance. If you're thinking of staying here then join the society in Lusaka: it does a lot of good & needs more support. Accommodation is in simple 3-bed chalets, joined by a walkway that has 2 more beds, or dbl rondavels, one of which is larger than the other. Toilets, shower & bathroom are communal, as are the lounge & BBQ area. Deep freezes, fridges, lamps, crockery, cutlery & bedding are all provided – but

you must bring all your own food & drink, as well as a decent torch. The camp's staff will cook for you, so don't forget to bring flour & yeast if you'd like some fresh bread. If you bring light fishing tackle then the cook will fillet & prepare your catch for dinner. The staff will also service the rooms, do the washing, & help with anything else that is reasonable. (You should tip them at the end of your stay.) *Rondavel US$35–42.50; chalet US$37.50–47.50.* ⊕ *all year.*

⌂ Kafwala Rapids Camp (3 rondavels) Wilderness Safaris, page 417. Very near to the WECSZ camp, this is in a stunning location, about 1½hrs' drive from its parent lodge, Lufupa. Lots of wild date palms line the banks of the river, lending a lush, tropical air to the place.

The camp is let to only one client at a time, so is ideal for a group of friends or an extended family. Large, self-catering rondavels with en-suite facilities come fully equipped & have their own chef & general worker. You will need to take all your own food, drinks & equipment, ideally in a 4x4 – though a 2WD will do in the dry season; there are no fridge/freezer facilities or lighting. There is, though, a dining-room/bar area, overlooking the rapids. Note that the hippos & crocs in this area have not read the textbooks, & seem to be living happily in & around the fast-running water of the rapids – so don't be tempted to take a cooling dip, however inviting the gently bubbling water looks. Kafwala Rapids is a good spot to either start or end your visit to the northern Kafue. *US$30 pp.* ⊕ *Jun–3 Jan.*

⌂ Moshi Camp East of Ntemwa (see box), Moshi (⊕ MOSHI 14°24.348'S; 26°9.474'E) is on the east side of the most southerly pole bridge across the Lufupa River. Like Ntemwa, it had been derelict for several years before Star of Africa put up a basic camp here for the solar eclipse in 2001, but it's a difficult area in which to operate unless your guides know it very well, & eventually they closed the camp. It's possible that it might reopen, but I wouldn't hold my breath on it.

⌂ Shumba Bushcamp (6 rooms) Contact via Wilderness, page 417 (⊕ SHUMBA 14°13.091'S; 25°52.233'E). Rebuilt from scratch in 2007 as a Wilderness Premier Camp, Shumba is set on a picturesque 'island' of large fig trees, in the middle of the plains about 75km (2½hrs' drive) north of Lufupa, & some 15–20 mins' drive south of the base of the permanent swamps. The camp faces east, so catches the sunrise, making its deck the perfect spot for a light b/fast. With a strongly angular

Two projects in the park underline the importance of ensuring that local children have the opportunity to explore their own heritage.

Wilderness Safaris has recently taken over **Ntemwa Camp** as the focus of its charitable 'Children in the Wilderness' project, a scheme set up in partnership with actor Paul Newman. Local children, many with serious problems, visit the camp with both counsellors and teachers from the USA, and Wilderness staff, as part of an ongoing programme to oversee their development. With a series of follow-up assessments every six months, many of these youngsters have seen their lives transformed, and some have even gone on to work for Wilderness themselves. The camp lies 105km north of the main bridge over the Kafue (◈ NTEMWA 14°23.237'S; 26°2.026'E) in a secluded location on open savanna just south of the Busanga Plains.

A second camp, **Treetops Conservation School Camp** (◈ TREETO 14°24.141'S; 26°02.524'E), was very run-down, but has been renovated by a group of schools in Lusaka, including Baobab School. It accepts small groups of school children for short stays to learn more about the park, its flora & fauna. Educating Zambia's next generation about the country's remaining wildlife is vital if it is to be conserved throughout the next century, so initiatives like these are essential to the park's future.

design & cool brown & aqua décor, there are no soft edges here. Rectangular chalets, each topped with a mop of thatch, are linked by wooden walkways some 3m off the ground, making this a relatively safe spot for children (usually over 8 only). In fact its height makes for some interesting wildlife possibilities: in 2007, a lion kill right under the buildings made riveting viewing for the guests.

The living area is all squares, with glazed doors overlooking the plains (& affording both safety & protection from the winds). In the central area, glass patio doors effectively form 2 walls. Guests can eat either as a group at the long dining table, or at individual tables, as preferred.

Activities revolve around driving, with night drives a highlight, & Shumba's guides are also expert at locating the Busanga Plain's resident prides of lions. US$770/895 pp sharing/sgl, inc FB, activities, local drinks & park fees. No children under 8. ☉ May–5 Jan.

⌂ **Musanza Tented Camp** (4 rooms) Wilderness Safaris, page 417 (◈ MUSANZ 14°13.214'S; 25°55.389'E) Another new camp in the Wilderness portfolio, Musanza is near Kapinga, and can be booked only as part of a Wilderness 'Exploration' trip – normally a package that comprises 3 different Wilderness camps in Kafue. No nightly rate available.

⌂ **Busanga Bushcamp** (4 tents) Contact via Wilderness Safaris, page 417 (◈ BUSANG

14°12.199'S; 25°50.115'E). This is a small camp situated on the Busanga Plains about 3hrs' drive (or 20 mins by helicopter) from Lunga. Accommodation is in walk-in tents, each with twin beds, en-suite shower (hot & cold water) & flush toilet, & a veranda. These are dotted around a small fig-tree island in the middle of the flat, open plains.

The trees also shade a simple but comfortable central dining area that blends into the bush. With meals often prepared over an open fire, & served al fresco by paraffin lanterns, this is a close-to-nature experience, with plenty of super game around you. Day & sundowner drives are the primary focus, & walking is possible, though several days' prior notice are usually needed in order to organise a game scout to escort the walk. US$470/610 pp sharing/sgl, inc FB, drinks, activities, laundry, taxes & park fees. ☉ Jun–end Nov.

⌂ **Kapinga Bushcamp** (4 rooms) Wilderness Safaris, page 417 (◈ KAPING 14°12.351'S; 25°48.577'E). Just 15 mins' drive from Busanga Bushcamp, Kapinga is one of Wilderness's premier camps, its rooms identical in layout to Shumba. Here, though, the design is softer, with the angularity of Shumba replaced by a circular theme. In the circular central area, under canvas, warm red cushions add to the intimacy, while in an adjoining tent, guests dine at the round dining table, set with silver & glass & with all the air of a smart dinner party. On the deck, chairs are set out around the campfire. (Of

The Kafue River Basin **KAFUE NATIONAL PARK**

14

note is the guest loo with a view — & a hand-carved toilet seat!) And the (inevitably circular) plunge pool looks across the plains, almost as an infinity pool. Walkways between the central hub & the rooms are at ground level, so this isn't a place for the nervous or those with young children. Each of these rooms has both open-air & inside shower, dual basin & all overlook the plains. U$770/895 pp sharing/sgl, inc FB, local drinks, activities, laundry, taxes & park fees. ⊕ Jun–30 Nov.

⌂ **Lunga River Lodge** (6 chalets) Contact via Wilderness Safaris, page 417 (⊕ LUNGA S14°11.398'S; 26°21.286'E). Standing on the bank of the Lunga River, overlooking Kafue from its northern boundary, Lunga was taken over by Wilderness in 2006 from its original owner. Much of the foliage fronting the river has been cleared to give a more open view. The lodge's spacious & comfortable thatch-on-brick chalets all have a king-size bed (or twins, with the option of 2 trpls), with a walk-in canopy of mosquito netting, bedside tables & electric lanterns (12v, powered by solar cells & a back-up generator), a dressing table, mirror & separate wardrobe. The bathroom has a large & efficient shower, flush toilet & washbasin with a mirror. Everything is tastefully made, mostly using solid local woods, & the whole chalet oozes quality. However, perhaps the best part is to be found in 2 rooms where the wooden deck outside cantilevers over the river, enclosing a sunken bath. It's perfect for soaking by moonlight.

At the centre of camp, beside the well-stocked bar, a sundeck extends over the river, & across the lodge's central lawn is a small swimming pool. Although there's a central, thatched dining area, dinner is normally served by candlelight on the deck or in the new boma, high on a large termite hill. Wilderness have retained the experienced lodge staff, mostly from local villages, & service is very good.

Activities include walking safaris, day & night 4x4 trips, & river excursions by motorboat: the Lunga is a great river for birding. Guiding standards are high, with an experienced team of Zambian guides augmented by visiting guides who normally stay for a season or 2.

Lunga isn't a place that anyone normally drives to (except this author, on several slightly insane occasions); guests usually arrive by light aircraft with Sefofane, then it's best to stay about a week in the area, spending a few nights at the lodge (often inc your first or last nights, as the lodge is very close to its own airstrip), & some time in Busanga Plains at the new Busanga Bushcamp, Shumba or Kapinga. Wilderness bases a helicopter at Lunga to transfer guests to Busanga in a fraction of the time it takes to drive. Note that there's a slight reduction in the costs if you spend 7 nights or more at a combination of Lunga & the Busanga camps.

Despite the formidable logistics of such a remote location, Lunga is one of Kafue's top lodges, & when combined with one of the bushcamps on the Busanga Plains, it offers a high-quality wildlife experience. US$555/680 pp sharing/sgl, inc FB, local drinks, activities, laundry, taxes & park fees. ⊕ Jun–end Nov.

The Lubungu pontoon area

⌂ **Hippo Lodge** (4 houses, 2 tents) \/f 021 1295398; m 097 7788910; e hippolodge@zamnet.zm; www.hippolodge.com (⊕ HIPPO 14°40.610'S; 26°22.526'E). On the site of the old Lubungu Camp, which closed in 1992, this was mainly used privately until about 2002, when its owners started to renovate it. The camp is now run by one of its owners, the capable Bruce Whitfield, who ran Lufupa Lodge (barely 20km west of here) for many years in the late 1990s.

The camp's more impressive rooms are the stone-built 'houses', all with fine river views. Each of these is different; all are quirky! There's a stone & thatch dbl room, built to an A-frame design, & one of slightly more conventional layout, with both dbl & twin rooms. All are individually designed & solidly built from largely local, natural materials, with large unconventional baths & en-suite showers & toilets. The largest, Stony House, is a self-contained family house, complete with its own kitchen &, if requested, a chef. This can sleep 2 in a dbl room, 2 in a twin room downstairs, & a further 2 in an upstairs section; all share a large bathroom. Hippo also has 2 walk-in safari tents covered with a thatched shade roof, each with a stone-built, open-air, en-suite bathroom at the back, with flush toilet, washbasin & hot shower. Inside are twin beds, each with a mosquito net. Recently a spacious thatched open-air pub has been added which overlooks the swimming pool.

Bruce is a good guide who knows Northern Kafue well, & can organise a number of activities. A network of game-viewing roads has been graded in the area &, whilst the game isn't quite as prolific or varied as further west, what's around is becoming increasingly relaxed. The team here conduct both day & night game drives. Walks are usually part of the menu, & for these you usually cross the river to explore the wilderness area to the west. This part of the Kafue has no roads, & is a lovely area to walk around — whilst the energetic can arrange a rendezvous with one of the lodge's boats. Within a kilometre of the camp is a marvellous natural hot spring, within which the team have used the area's natural stone to section off a sand-bottomed 'jacuzzi'.

Boat trips are a major feature, with fishing & birdwatching favourite activities, though there are a number of offbeat possibilities for the more adventurous. For example, if you want to sleep out on one of the islands at night, then the team will arrange for a fly-camp to be set up for you. When arriving at the camp, it's possible to be met at the Lubungu pontoon & boated downstream from there, stopping to camp on islands on the way. Or, if you want to continue to Lufupa some 20km downstream after staying here, a boat transfer can be arranged. A trip to the Busanga Plains can also be organised. *US$420 pp sharing (30% sgl supplement), inc FB, most alcoholic drinks, activities & park fees, but exc return vehicle transfers from Lusaka (US$240 pp).* ☼ *all year (though airstrip closed around late Nov–end Apr).*

🏠 **McBrides' Camp** (7 chalets) e mcbrides.camp@ uuplus.com; www.mcbridescamp.com (✪ MCBRID 14°41.537'S; 26°23.107'E). Chris & Charlotte McBride started their camp in July 2002, in the style of a small 'walking' bushcamp like those in the Luangwa Valley. To get there, see *Driving from Mumbwa to the Lubungu pontoon, Via Kabulushi gate,* pages 410–11.

Five of the thatched, 2-person chalets each have a dbl & a sgl bed, whilst the other 2 are smaller, with just 2 sgls each. All are carefully furnished with mosi nets over the beds, a solid wooden chest of drawers, chairs on a small private veranda, & some thoughtful touches. At the back of each chalet is an open-air bathroom, with a hot shower, washbasin, & flush toilet under its own small thatched roof. The camp's lighting is by candlelight, paraffin lanterns & solar power. There's also a simple reed-&-thatch open dining room & lounge.

Moored alongside are the camp's boats, the *Fish Eagle* (a large pontoon used for cruises on the river), the *River Lion,* used for drifts, and a banana boat for fishing. Otherwise activities major around walking safaris, although game drives are available on request. Alternatively it's possible to make a trip to their new fly-camp, 14km downstream. All safaris are led by Charlotte & Chris, who have spent most of their lives in the bush: indeed, Chris's MSc thesis was on lions, & he went on to write 3 books on the subject, including *The White Lions of Timbavati. US$330 pp, inc FB, activities & park fees, exc transfers & alcohol.* ☼ *Apr–Jan.*

🏠 **Leopard Lodge** (6 rooms) ☏ +27 82 416 5894; e info@leopard-lodge.com; www.leopard-lodge.com (✪ 14°33.003'S; 26°29.118'E). In the GMA outside the national park's northeast boundary, about 3.5km upstream of the Lubungu pontoon, Leopard Lodge was set to reopen at the end of 2007. You can reach it by turning off the main track (D181) at ✪ TULOEP 14°32.700'S; 26°28.050'E & following this to the camp.

The lodge is on the banks of the Kafue River. Most of the thatched brick-built chalets sleep 2 people, with en-suite facilities, but extra beds can be placed on the veranda; just 1 has 2 rooms sharing a (hot) shower, toilet & washbasin. Mosquito nets are provided for all beds, & there are braai facilities, a gas stove, fridge & freezer. Plans for a bar & restaurant should materialise in 2008, when it will be possible to stay on an FB basis. For now, flexibility is the watchword; beer & wine can be bought in with advance notice, as can meat for the BBQ.

As you might expect, activities focus on fishing, boat cruises, birdwatching & game viewing on foot or by vehicle (inc night drives). Some 4km from the camp is a natural hot spring, while the hill behind affords views over the surrounding area. There are also plans for scenic flights, microlights, sunset cruises & a mini health spa. *Chalet €35 pp self-catering (until 2008 only); €150 pp inc FB & 1 activity/day; camping €20 for 2 people (€5 for each additional person, up to 6). Activities extra.* ☼ *all year, but must be pre-booked.*

Camping Camping in the park is easily arranged at Lufupa, and Kafwala is only a little more expensive than a campsite. It may be possible to camp up at Treetops; ask the scouts for the latest information on this, and possibly for permission. Note – there are no campsites on the Busanga Plains, and you are not allowed to just camp anywhere. This rule is both wise and effectively enforced.

SOUTHERN KAFUE South of the main road, the park is long and thin; and stretches about 190km southwards, although it is only about 85km wide at its broadest point.

THE DEMISE OF THE TEAK FORESTS

Between two junctions (⊕ J07 15°55.583'S; 25°54.910'E and ⊕ J08 15°57.076'S; 25°56.872'E) is a fairly clearly signposted track that is seldom driven. This is a shame, as it weaves its way through the beautiful and intriguing Ngoma Forest. This is a dense stand of mature trees which are largely Zambezi teak, *Baikiaea plurijuga* (previously called Rhodesian teak) – a tree that occurs only in undisturbed areas of Kalahari sand in northern Botswana, northern Namibia, southern Angola and southwest Zambia.

These reach up to 20m in height, with a dense, spreading crown of leaves, and smooth, grey-brown bark. The trees flower from December to March, bearing lovely pinky-mauve flowers. Seedpods follow, from June to September, cracking open explosively to catapult their seeds a distance to the ground.

The tree's wood is dense and hard, but also very even-grained and strong. It's never had many traditional uses, as it was too hard to cut, but was a sought-after timber that was (and sadly is) commercially very valuable. It's been widely used for bridge-building and railway sleepers, and Palgrave (see *Appendix 3*, page 512) reports that 'when the London corn exchange was rebuilt in 1952 a special grooved floor was designed to take the grain thrown down by the merchants, and *B. plurijuga* was selected for the parquet blocks because of its ability to withstand abrasion without splintering'.

Stands of this forest probably covered fairly large areas of the Kalahari, and certainly of southwestern Zambia. Now it's severely threatened, and its demise is typical of that of several other hardwood species that were once common here, like mukwa, *Pterocarpus angolensis*, and rosewood, *Guibourtia coleosperma*.

Baikiaea plurijuga has been commercially logged in Zambia since around the start of the 20th century. Zambian timber production probably peaked in the 1930s, but by the 1960s huge tracts of teak forest had been lost. Now the export of *Baikiaea* logs is banned. However, licences are still being given out to sawmills to export *Baikiaea* timber, predicated on (difficult to enforce) promises to leave a minimum number of the trees, and then not log the same area for 20 years.

Meanwhile, experts suggest that a 300-year cycle would be needed to allow the forests to regenerate. They note that fire is often used as a tool by loggers, to open up the dense under-storey of vegetation (known as mutemwa) in *B. plurijuga* forests, and that the debris left behind after logging will often lead to fires. *Baikiaea plurijuga* is particularly sensitive because its thin bark renders it very susceptible to fire; once burnt, these forests degrade forever and don't recover.

In recent years the poverty in the area, combined with major commercial pressures, has led to many of Zambia's remaining 'forest reserves' being degazetted, which then opens them up for commercial logging. So, sadly, a beautiful teak forest like Ngoma is an increasingly rare sight.

On the park's eastern boundary is the Kafue River and the Itezhi-Tezhi Dam: 300km² of water. Itezhi-Tezhi differs from many dams as, apparently, it is not made of continuous concrete but instead is filled with earth, in order to render it less vulnerable to tremors and minor earthquakes.

The vegetation and geography of the southern side are similar to the north – see the *Geography, flora and fauna* section on page 414 – although there's more Kalahari sand in the south, and it's notable for a few really beautiful teak forests.

Route directions for 4x4s Chunga and Mukambi are very near the main road, and so are clearly signposted around the main bridge over the Kafue in the centre of the

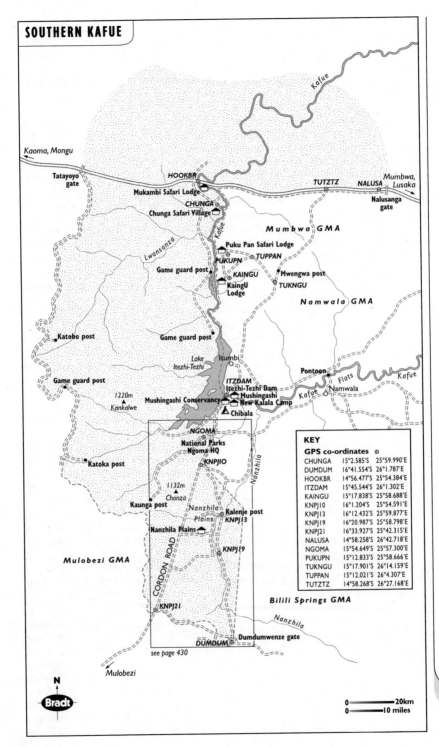

SOUTHERN KAFUE

Kaoma, Mongu

Tatayoyo gate

HOOKBR

Mukambi Safari Lodge

CHUNGA

Chunga Safari Village

Lwansanza

Kafue

Puku Pan Safari Lodge

PUKUPN *TUPPAN*

Game guard post

KAINGU

KaingU Lodge

Mwengwa post

TUKNGU

Katobo post

Game guard post

Game guard post

1220m
▲
Kankalwe

Lake Itezhi-Tezhi

Itumbi

ITZDAM

Itezhi-Tezhi Dam

Mushingashi

Mushingashi Conservancy

New Kalala Camp

▲ Chibala

NGOMA

National Parks
Ngoma HQ

KNPJ10

Katoka post

1132m
▲
Chonza

Kaunga post

Nanzhila Plains

Kalenje post

KNPJ13

Nanzhila Plains

KNPJ19

Mulobezi GMA

CORDON ROAD

Nanzhila

KNPJ21

Bilili Springs GMA

Nanzhila

Dumdumwenze gate

DUMDUM

see page 430

Mulobezi

Mumbwa a GMA

TUTZTZ *NALUSA*

Mumbwa, Lusaka

Nalusanga gate

Namwala GMA

Pontoon *Flats* *Kafue*

Namwala

Kafue

KEY

GPS co-ordinates ⊕

CHUNGA	15°2.585'S	25°59.990'E
DUMDUM	16°41.554'S	26°1.787'E
HOOKBR	14°56.477'S	25°54.384'E
ITZDAM	15°45.544'S	26°1.302'E
KAINGU	15°17.838'S	25°58.688'E
KNPJ10	16°1.204'S	25°54.591'E
KNPJ13	16°12.432'S	25°59.877'E
KNPJ19	16°20.987'S	25°58.798'E
KNPJ21	16°33.927'S	25°42.315'E
NALUSA	14°58.258'S	26°42.718'E
NGOMA	15°54.649'S	25°57.300'E
PUKUPN	15°12.833'S	25°58.666'E
TUKNGU	15°17.901'S	26°14.159'E
TUPPAN	15°12.021'S	26°4.307'E
TUTZTZ	14°58.268'S	26°27.168'E

N

Bradt

0 ——— 20km
0 ——— 10 miles

park. To reach the heart of the southern section of the park you must either take the road through the GMA, which leaves the Great West Road about 65–70km west of Mumbwa, or alternatively approach from the south from Monze, Choma or Kalomo on the Lusaka–Livingstone road.

Only the first of these approaches is practical in the wet season, and all require a 4x4 throughout the year.

From the Lusaka–Mongu road – west of Lake Itezhi-Tezhi
Despite a fiction perpetrated by distant cartographers, the 'road' south from Chunga to the Itezhi-Tezhi Dam, which follows the western bank of the Kafue, is not passable any more. It was built sometime before the 1920s, and then improved in 1976. It was said to be a lovely road, with many bridges (as it crossed 11 rivers). Most of these seem to have been intact when the Itezhi-Tezhi Dam was built in 1978, and some were repaired in 1979. However, in the 1980s it seems to have been totally neglected and now, having fallen into disuse, it's simply unnavigable.

When approaching from the north, the only way into the southern section of the park is through the Mumbwa and Namwala GMAs, east of the lake. Both of these have safari camps, where the game is increasingly good.

From the Lusaka–Mongu road: the 'GMA road'
Heading west from Lusaka, Mumbwa is almost 150km away. Bypass Mumbwa and continue for about 37km until you reach Nalusanga scout post (⊕ NALUSA 14°58.258'S; 26°42.718'E), the entry gate to the Kafue National Park.

The turning (⊕ TUTZTZ 14°58.268'S; 26°27.168'E) into the south of the park leaves this Lusaka–Mongu road about 28km west of this, or 65km from Mumbwa. If you're approaching from the west, that's a fraction more than 51km from the main Hook Bridge over the Kafue River. It is clearly signposted to Itezhi-Tezhi.

Until recently this road has been appalling, earning it the title of the country's worst tar road: 120km of pot-holes taking five to six hours in a good, sturdy 4x4, even in the dry season. Whole sections were popular with tsetse flies, making air conditioning a valuable accessory for your vehicle. Since then the remaining tar areas have been removed and graded, and in 2007 there were promises that the whole road would be regraded soon. In the meantime, you'll still need to drive very carefully.

Whatever the surface, about 45km after turning, you will pass the Mwengwa scout post (⊕ MWEENG 15°16.539'S; 26°14.950'E) which is a game scout checkpoint. You must stop here to sign in. About 2km south of that, there's a turning clearly marked for KaingU Safari Lodge and Puku Pan (⊕ TUKNGU 15°17.901'S; 26°14.159'E).

About 39km from the scout post you'll stop at a veterinary control post; then a further 22km and you reach the crossroads at Itezhi-Tezhi village (⊕ ITEZHI 15°44.252'S; 26°2.202'E). This is about 106km from the main Lusaka–Mongu road. Continue across the junction for about 5km until you pass a police post. If you then turn right at the police station and left at the top of the hill, you will pass a post office, a bank, a school and the ZESCO offices, where you can arrange for fuel supplies (⊕ 08.00–12.30 & 14.00–16.30). By this time, you'll be high up and overlooking the lake. If you don't need fuel, or want a view of the lake, then go left past the police station, and drive below the dam wall (⊕ ITZDAM 15°45.544'S; 26°1.302'E) to get to the lodges, which are well signposted on the right-hand side of the road. Then it's just a couple of kilometres further to Musa gate (⊕ MUSAGA 15°47.802'S; 25°59.938'E), to continue back into the southern section of Kafue National Park.

A few waypoints for this route, after KALBRI and before DUMDUM, in sequence south to north, might include:

⊕ KAF028   16°58.807'S; 26°26.871'E
⊕ KAF025   16°54.895'S; 26°21.610'E
⊕ KAF022   16°46.474'S; 26°18.875'E
⊕ KAF019   16°44.210'S; 26°10.162'E
⊕ KAF016   16°41.628'S; 26°05.948'E

From Kalomo to Dumdumwenze gate There's a ZOT station in Kalomo, and you should fill up there. From Kalomo (which is about 126km from Livingstone on the way to Lusaka) there is an old sign to Kafue and Musungwa pointing roughly north. You will drive past the Kalomo Hotel and turn left at the next T-junction. Within 20m the road becomes a dirt track. Continue on this to another T-junction, turn right and follow the road as it curves left (ignoring right-hand turn-off).

Continue over a railway bridge, and shortly afterwards a river bridge (⊕ KALBRI 17°0.915'S; 26°29.468'E), and then take the next left fork. Continue following the main track, ignoring any turnings and keeping left at forks. After a few kilometres you should be travelling northwest. About 40km after the main road, you will start leaving the rural villages behind to climb through some hills. Eventually, after about 74km, you drop down gradually to Dumdumwenze gate (⊕ DUMDUM 16°41.554'S; 26°1.787'E), where the game scouts will sign you into the park. (Note that Dumdumwezi is the local spelling and pronunciation.) The road is not in good condition, and you should take particular care at the river crossings closer to Dumdumwenze.

North from Dumdumwenze From here, you should always ask the scouts for advice – if only to determine how wet the roads are, and so if it's safe to go on the much more interesting Nanzhila River route.

Between about December and July, there's little choice: you will have to take the **Cordon route**, which skirts around the southwest side of the park through woodlands. This gets to Ngoma without crossing any substantial rivers, and so while it does have the odd sticky dambo, an experienced driver with a 4x4 should be able to get through even in the rains.

For this route you go into the park, heading north for about 2.3km, then take a left turn at your first junction (⊕ J20 16°40.332'S; 26°1.722'E). From here you proceed about 40km, through fairly thick forest, heading slightly north of west, until you reach a junction (⊕ KAFU01 16°33.927'S; 25°42.314'E), which indicates the southwestern tip of the park. There you turn right, to head north and slightly east on a basically straight road that passes through the heart of the southern end of the park. This ultimately meets other roads near Ngoma at junction ⊕ J10 16°1.204'S; 25°54.591'E.

During the dry season, consider taking the **Nanzhila River route**, which is much more interesting. This shadows the river north, crossing it several times and skirts around the eastern edge of the Nanzhila Plains. For this go to the junction (⊕ J20 16°40.332'S; 26°1.722'E) 2.3km north of Dumdemwenze, then continue straight ahead. The vegetation along this route can be exceedingly thick even in June, so it's best to wait until at least July to drive along here.

From that first junction it's about 19km until you cross to the east bank of the Nanzhila River at ⊕ NANRV2 16°30.905'S; 26°0.164'E. Although the river isn't

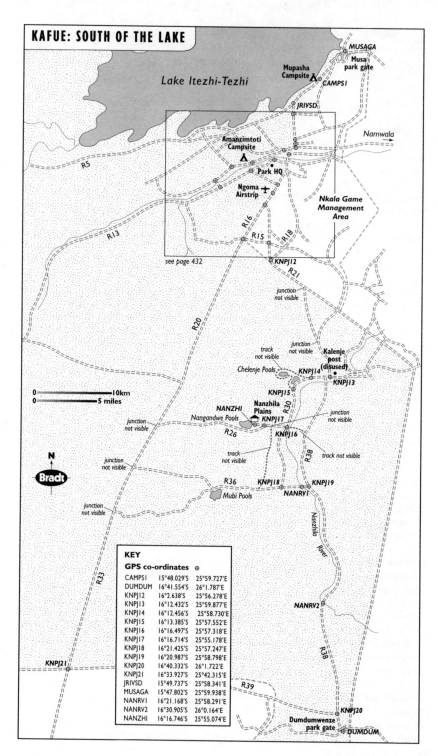

KAFUE: SOUTH OF THE LAKE

Lake Itezhi-Tezhi

MUSAGA

Musa park gate

Mupasha Campsite

CAMPS1

JRIVSD

Namwala

Amanzimtoti Campsite

Park HQ

Ngoma Airstrip

R5

R13

R16

R15

R18

Nkala Game Management Area

see page 432

KNPJ12

R21

junction not visible

R20

junction not visible

Kalenje post (disused)

track not visible

Chelenje Pools

KNPJ14

KNPJ13

KNPJ15

R30

NANZHI

Nanzhila Plains

Nangandwe Pools

KNPJ17

junction not visible

R26

KNPJ16

R38

track not visible

junction not visible

track not visible

junction not visible

R36

KNPJ18

KNPJ19

Mubi Pools

NANRV1

junction not visible

N

Bradt

0 ——————— 10km
0 ——————— 5 miles

KNPJ21

Nanzhila River

NANRV2

R38

R33

R39

KEY

GPS co-ordinates ⊕

CAMPS1	15°48.029'S	25°59.727'E
DUMDUM	16°41.554'S	26°1.787'E
KNPJ12	16°2.638'S	25°56.278'E
KNPJ13	16°12.432'S	25°59.877'E
KNPJ14	16°12.456'S	25°58.730'E
KNPJ15	16°13.385'S	25°57.552'E
KNPJ16	16°16.497'S	25°57.318'E
KNPJ17	16°16.714'S	25°55.178'E
KNPJ18	16°21.425'S	25°57.247'E
KNPJ19	16°20.987'S	25°58.798'E
KNPJ20	16°40.332'S	26°1.722'E
KNPJ21	16°33.927'S	25°42.315'E
JRIVSD	15°49.737'S	25°58.341'E
MUSAGA	15°47.802'S	25°59.938'E
NANRV1	16°21.168'S	25°58.291'E
NANRV2	16°30.905'S	26°0.164'E
NANZHI	16°16.746'S	25°55.074'E

KNPJ20

Dumdumwenze park gate

DUMDUM

very deep, its banks are steep and can be slippery, so if there's any danger of you getting stuck, make sure that you have a back-up plan. Continue north, and after about 19km you may spot a very faint track heading west, to your left, at ⊕ J19 16°20.987'S; 25°58.798'E. There might be a concrete sign marker still there.

In 2003, this track had virtually disappeared – but don't let that put you off. Turn left as if it were there (it should be!), across the vegetation if necessary! In about 800m you'll reach a river crossing (⊕ NANRV2 16°30.905'S; 26°0.164'E). Continue over this and for a further 2km on a better track until you meet a road junction (⊕ J18 16°21.425'S; 25°57.247'E). Turn right to take a really lovely road north. It passes the Nanzhila Plains, and bends east at the Chelenje Pools, and then leads to Kalenje scout post. If you didn't go west at J19, then continuing straight would also bring you to Kalenje.

From Kalenje there's a variety of game drive roads which will lead you slightly west of north to Ngoma.

From Monze on the Lusaka–Livingstone Road From Monze take a turning on the north side of town towards Chongo, heading northwest towards Lochinvar National Park. You may need to ask local directions to get on the right track, but it passes through waypoint ⊕ TULOCH 16°15.465'S; 27°28.632'E. After 7–8km you will pass Chongo – keep left there as the track divides after the village. About 8km after Chongo the road forks (⊕ T2LOCH 16°10.054'S; 27°23.610'E): right leads to Lochinvar National Park; left leads to Namwala and thence the Ngoma area of Kafue.

About 35km later, on a dusty (or, if wet, muddy) and rather pot-holed track, you will reach Chitongo, and a T-junction. Here you find an implausibly good tarred road! (If you turn left onto this, you would find the tar turn into poor gravel about 60km before Choma.)

For the Kafue take a right turn at Chitongo onto the tar, and follow this as it turns from heading slightly west of north, to heading due west. About 50km after Chitongo you will reach the larger village of Namwala, on the southern edge of the Kafue's floodplain (where, incidentally, there's a pontoon over the Kafue). From there, the track leads about 60km west, into the park. This is bumpy and pot-holed gravel, but is passable during the rains. It enters the park past the site of the old Nkala Mission, joining the road network at ⊕ TUNAMW 15°53.894'S; 25°57.854'E, about 2km north of Ngoma.

Places to visit Southern Kafue does suit exploration in your own 4x4 well, and so to concentrate on a few places to visit is really to miss the point. However, a few notable highlights are:

Ngoma Ngoma (⊕ NGOMA 15°54.649'S; 25°57.300'E) is the national park's headquarters in the south side of the park, about 20km from the Itezhi-Tezhi Dam wall. There are various offices and houses for the park's staff, and you can drop in, but it's not in great condition, and isn't really set up for visitors. About 5km south of here is an all-weather airstrip (⊕ AIRNGO 15°57.867'S; 25°56.422'E).

Riverside Drive Home to some of the best game in the south, which is protected by the proximity of Ngoma HQ and, in the dry season, enticed by lush grassy plains next to the lake.

Chilenje Pools Further south, several pools lie at the heart of two large, neighbouring grassy dambos. In theory there's a track going round this area; in practice you may have to make your own across the bumpy expanse of solidified mud. It's a major attraction for game during the drier months.

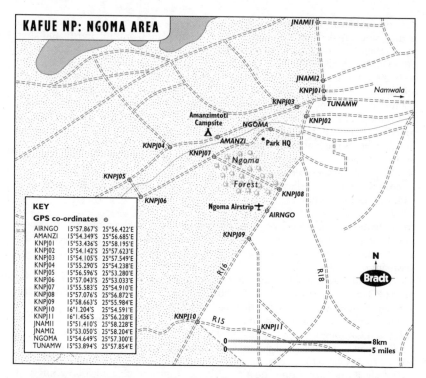

KAFUE NP: NGOMA AREA

KEY

GPS co-ordinates ⊕

AIRNGO	15°57.867'S	25°56.422'E
AMANZI	15°54.349'S	25°56.685'E
KNPJ01	15°53.436'S	25°58.195'E
KNPJ02	15°54.142'S	25°57.623'E
KNPJ03	15°54.105'S	25°57.549'E
KNPJ04	15°55.290'S	25°54.238'E
KNPJ05	15°56.596'S	25°53.280'E
KNPJ06	15°57.043'S	25°53.033'E
KNPJ07	15°55.583'S	25°54.910'E
KNPJ08	15°57.076'S	25°56.872'E
KNPJ09	15°58.663'S	25°55.984'E
KNPJ10	16°1.204'S	25°54.591'E
KNPJ11	16°1.456'S	25°56.228'E
JNAMI1	15°51.410'S	25°58.228'E
JNAMI2	15°53.050'S	25°58.204'E
NGOMA	15°54.649'S	25°57.300'E
TUNAMW	15°53.894'S	25°57.854'E

Nanzhila Plains/Nangandwe Pools If you're travelling through the south of the park, then two tracks run east–west. Be aware that both may be quite indistinct in places. Take these towards the start of the dry season, and you'll often find yourself in plains with grass several metres tall, which is lovely but doesn't make for good game viewing. It's surprisingly easy to get lost here! (Beware of inflammable seeds in your radiator – see *Driving through high grass*, on page 107.)

Within this area you'll also find woodland sections, tree-islands and even the odd lone baobab tree, *Adansonia digitata*. One area to aim for is around Nanzhila Plains Safari Camp (⊕ NANZHI 16°16.746'S; 25°55.074'E). where the Nangandwe Pools attract relatively large herds of game.

🏠 **Where to stay** If you're just passing through the park on the main Lusaka–Mongu road, then perhaps you might consider stopping for a night or two in the Mukambi/Chunga area – although if you have more time, then it's certainly worth penetrating deeper into the park. The southern Itezhi-Tezhi area, and around Ngoma, certainly has the most spectacular game on the southern side, whilst KaingU Safari Lodge is not only exceptionally promising, but also built beside a unique and very lovely part of the river.

If you're driving and taking camping kit then you can probably afford to turn up at the lodges in the Itezhi-Tezhi area and find somewhere that suits you. If you're arranging a fly-in trip, on a flexible budget, then there's nothing in southern Kafue which is perfect for what you want, though (again) KaingU is probably the one to watch most closely, as it has the potential to be a good fly-in destination. The Nanzhila Plains were a great destination as late as the 1990s, but with the closure of the camps, the tracks were beginning to fall into disuse. Now, though, a new camp has opened on the same site, and access to the area is being restored.

Considering the southern Kafue's camps, I'll split them up into three distinct areas: 'Near the Lusaka–Mongu Road', 'In the GMA' and 'Around Itezhi-Tezhi Dam and south'. Taking these area by area:

Near the Lusaka–Mongu Road There are several choices on or very near the road, but for most people one of Mukambi's options is probably going to be the best bet.

⌂ **Mukambi Safari Lodge** (9 chalets)
e info@mukambi.com; www.mukambi.com
(✇ MUKAMB 14°58.656'S; 25°59.599'E). Mukambi is run by Edjan & Robyn van der Heide, who have built it up considerably in the past few years, & are working hard to raise its standards still further. It's a well-built lodge that appears to have concentrated, successfully, on being comfortable. They claim the food is the best for 270km — which may be an exaggeration, but shows what they're striving for. The turn-off to Mukambi is signposted on the main Lusaka–Mongu tar road, about 9km east of the main Hook Bridge over the Kafue. The camp is 2km from the main road, & is easily accessed in a normal 2WD.

The thatch-on-brick chalets (3 twin & 4 dbl, plus a family chalet & a family villa) are solidly built with beautifully carved wooden doors. Inside, the décor is consciously ethnic with murals & the odd *objet d'art*. Four-poster beds have mosquito nets, & the windows are netted, too. Showers in the clean, recently re-tiled bathrooms are solar-heated, with a geyser in the villa.

The central dining/bar area is well designed & quite smart, like a hotel. It overlooks the Kafue River & the national park from the GMA, a view shared by the accommodation, the swimming pool, & a large sundeck.

A range of walking, boating and 4x4 game-viewing trips is available — as is a conference room for work trips! Overall game densities in the Chunga area (where they drive) have improved considerably since the camp was opened & anti-poaching measures put in place. In addition to some lovely herds of elephant, there are now regular sightings of lion, leopard, cheetah & wild dog. Fishing is also possible, with rods & tackle for hire & a large, stable pontoon-type boat for use as a moving platform. Mukambi's houseboat was sold in 2007 & is currently not operational.

(A short wander downstream from the lodge, the present campsite will be closed in 2008. For now, there are campfire areas, with staff on hand to help with fires or anything else. Guests here are welcome to eat at the lodge when it is not busy, & with advance notice.) US$180/210 pp sharing,
chalet/villa, FB. Activities (walking, boating & game drives) US$30 pp, fishing US$35 pp, all exc park fees. ⊕ all year.

⌂ **Mukambi Bushcamp** (7 tents) Contact via Mukambi, above. Mukambi also has a bushcamp on the Kafue River, a short wander upstream from the main lodge. This can accommodate 14 people in large dome-like tents with sewn-in groundsheets. Each tent has 2 proper beds, mosquito-mesh windows, bedside tables & mats on the floor — & is sheltered by a large thatched sunshade. All of these share an ablution block. There are full braai facilities & camp staff are on hand to help if required. US$110 pp sharing, FB. ⊕ all year.

⌂ **Mukambi Plains Camp** (4 tents) Contact via Mukambi, above. Mukambi's more exclusive plains camp was opened in 2006, but for 2008 will be operating from a new location on the eastern side of the Lufupa River, well away from other operators & said to be 'teeming with game'. Individual tents are set up on platforms, each with an en-suite open-air bathroom & bush shower. And the team promises 4-star cuisine! US$400 pp sharing, inc FB, drinks, activities, park fees & transfers to Mukambi (max 8 people). ⊕ mid-Jul–end Oct.

Å **Chunga Safari Lodge** (4 rondavels, family bungalow, camping) m 097 9427589, 097 7148987; e bobmalambo@yahoo.com. Turn south off the main road about 6.7km west of the main Kafue Hook Bridge (✇ TUCHGA 14°56.832'S; 25°51.222'E). A good gravel road heads south for about 21km until the road splits: carry straight on for the Wildlife Training College, or bend right for a further 4km to the National Parks & Wildlife Service Headquarters at Chunga and the adjacent lodge (✇ CHUNGA 15°2.585'S; 25°59.990'E). You are now about 7.5km due south of Mukambi Safari Lodge, but on the opposite side of the river, the west bank.

This old-style self-catering village is next to the wildlife HQ, although nowadays meals can be provided with advance notice at around Kw10,000–25,000. Its whitewashed thatch-on-brick rondavels were being refurbished in 2007, to include en-suite showers & toilets. It's also possible to camp here.

14

If you are self-catering, & have your own camping kit, then it might be worth looking in here — if only for the delightful bushbuck that wander nonchalantly around the camp. In theory it's possible to do walking safaris game drives and boat cruises, at US$25 pp each, but facilities are very limited. That, & the fact that it's far from any game-driving roads, means that few people feel it's worth the effort. *Rondavel US$40 pp, bungalow US$50 pp, camping US$10 pp. Park fees extra.* ⊕ *all year.*

In the GMA There are two lodges beside the river in the GMA. They're too far from the Mongu–Lusaka road to be mere stop-overs, and whilst the game is reasonable – the river is stunning!

🛖 **KaingU Safari Lodge** (4 tents, 1 family unit) e tomh@kaingu-lodge.com, reservations@kaingu-lodge.com; www.kaingu-lodge.com (⊕ KAINGU 15°17.838'S; 25°58.688'E). The relatively new KaingU Safari Lodge stands on the east bank of the Kafue River, within the Namwala GMA; as the bee-eater flies it's about 10km south of Puku Pan. To get here see *From the Lusaka–Mongu road: the 'GMA road'* on page 428. Turn west at the signpost to KaingU, leaving this road at ⊕ TUKNGU 15°17.901'S; 26°14.159'E, just a few kilometres south of the Mwengwa scout post. This bush track twists & winds through dense miombo woodlands for about 23.5km until you fork left at ⊕ TUPPAN 15°12.021'S; 26°4.307'E. From there it's just under 18km to the lodge, during which you cross a small pole bridge.

The lodge comes as a delightful surprise. Its design is broadly very traditional, using large, green Meru-style tents beside the river, each with a large veranda at the front. What's surprising is the amount of care (verging on perfectionism) that's gone into the construction of these. The tents are on carefully laid wooden decking under thatch, with a stone bathroom at the back which has not only an indoor & outdoor shower, but also lots of clever touches like the towel rail of knurled wood built into the wall. Each tent has hot water (heated by wood) & small 12v solar-powered lights. Large, high-quality beds stand on hand-woven rugs, & it's possible to open up the whole of the front of the tent to be one big mesh window. The addition of a family unit with its own plunge pool adds flexibility to the options.

A small team led by Tom Heineken, & his wife Viviane, built the lodge, but Tom's main passion is the wildlife & the natural environment. Thus activities emphasise walking & river trips, though day & night game drives (& fishing excursions) are also an option, & there's a pool for those seeking to relax. There are also walking trails across the river in the park, for which a park entry fee of US$15 pp is payable, or you can meander down the Kafue

to Itezhi-Tezhi Dam in an inflatable rubber boat. With such a small lodge, & a high degree of enthusiasm, the activities are fairly flexible, lasting pretty much as long as you want them to.

There has long been game in the area around Puku Pan, effectively protected from poaching by the presence of that lodge, so having 2 lodges adjacent to each other is widening the safe area. That said, although the game is building up, it isn't as good as in the park's best corners.

In recompense, the river beside the lodge is most unusual, & as lovely as any stretch of African river that I know: it's worth coming here just to spend a few days afloat. KaingU stands beside an area where the river broadens to accommodate a scattering of small islands, each consisting of vegetated sandy banks & huge granite rocks interspersed with rapids. Imagine someone throwing half of Zimbabwe's Matobo Hills into a wide, shallow river & you'll get the picture. So to potter round here with a canoe, or a motorboat, or even just to go fishing, is a real journey of discovery — endless side channels & islands to explore. There's something different around every corner, plenty of vegetation everywhere — & birds all around. It's a real gem of an area. *US$320 pp sharing (sgl US$384 May–Oct), inc FB & activities, exc imported drinks & park fees (although the lodge is in the GMA, so park fees are not always payable).* ⊕ *all year.*

▲ **KaingU Campsite** (2 private campsites, 1 shared site) Contact via KaingU Safari Lodge, above. KaingU has one 'large' campsite, which can take up to 16 people (max 4 vehicles) using shared ablutions. It also has 2 private riverside pitches, set apart from the main site, each with its own reed-walled ablutions (flush toilet, hot shower & washbasin), a cooking grid, a fireplace, a tap & a table for washing up. These private sites can each take up to 8 people & 2 vehicles. All the sites are pleasant & grassy, under trees, & firewood is provided. However, you must bring all your food as meals are not usually available at the lodge unless you've arranged them well in advance. *US$20 pp.* ⊕ *all year.*

Puku Pan Safari Lodge (8 chalets, camping) \ 021 1266927; m 097 7780080; e pukupan@zamnet.zm; www.pukupan.com (✆ PUKUPN 15°12.833'S; 25°58.666'E). Puku Pan overlooks the park from the GMA beside the Kafue River, north of Itezhi-Tezhi Dam. As the fish eagle flies, it's about 30km south of the main Lusaka–Mongu road, & 10km north of KaingU. Puku Pan has an airstrip nearby (✆ AIRPUK 15°12.202'S; 26°1.989'E), so it's possible to fly in, but most people drive.

To get here by road see *From the Lusaka–Mongu road: the 'GMA road' on page 428*. Turn west at the signpost, leaving this road at ✆ TUKNGU 15°17.901'S; 26°14.159'E, just a few kilometres south of the Mwengwa scout post. This bush track twists & winds through dense miombo woodlands for about 23.5km until you fork right at

✆ TUPPAN 15°12.021'S; 26°4.307'E. From there it's just under 14km to the lodge, passing the airstrip on the way.

The lodge has a lovely situation on a 200m stretch of the river. One of the few Zambian-managed safari lodges, it has been renovated recently, but remains simple with no frills. Each of its cottages, built of mud-finished blocks & wood under thatch, has its own veranda, plus flush toilet & inside bath or shower with hot water; there is also electric power. Alternatively there's a basic campsite with shared ablutions, inc hot showers. If you are coming here then you'd be very wise to book in advance, & not just to turn up. Guests can take part in game drives or boat trips (US$20 pp), or fishing & game walks (US$17 pp). US$180 pp FB. Self-catering (Zambian residents only) US$40 pp. Camping US$7 pp. ⊕ all year.

Around Itezhi-Tezhi Dam and south Grouped around the small village in the GMA, just east of the Itezhi-Tezhi Dam wall, are three camps: all are fairly old-style places catering more to Zambian tastes than overseas visitors. They're not expensive – and some would regard them as good value. Further south, the old Nanzhila Restcamp has recently been rebuilt, which makes this remote area of the park accessible once again to adventurous visitors.

Mushingashi m 097 7846978; e darrell@mushingashi.co.zm. The Mushingashi Conservancy runs for 18km along the river and shares a 37km boundary with the national park. Around half of visitors come for the fishing, and are accommodated in one of 3 strictly self-catering camps (bring *all* your own supplies), each with en-suite facilities: Kanonga Waloba (15 chalets), the most upmarket of the 3; Delai Camp (7 chalets); & Khosi Koto Camp (7 chalets). In addition to fishing, guests can do game drives & walking safaris, or hire boats (US$100 per day, but bring your own fuel). US$30 pp.

New Kalala Camp (13 chalets, camping) \ 021 3263179, 1265375; f 021 1290162; e info@newkalala.com; www.newkalala.com (✆ NEWKAL 15°46.583'S; 26°0.538'E). New Kalala is just south of the dam wall, overlooking the lake from a stunning perch on a rock kopje. The camp is built around large granite rocks where you'll see the odd rock dassie scurry. A complete refurbishment in recent years has brought a new lease of life. Today, small round chalets, dotted around the rocks, all have en-suite tiled bathrooms, minibars, & AC, albeit with somewhat corporate furnishings. It is also possible to camp on the lake shore. Meals are available at the lodge – lunch & dinner are a fixed

US$12 pp. Chalet US$140/180/200 dbl B&B/HB/FB. Camping US$6 pp. Game drive US$20 pp & park fees; boat cruise US$20 pp; boat hire US$120–170 per day, plus fuel.

Chibala Camp (3 chalets, camping) \ 097 7794036; e 890121@zm.celtelplus.com; www.wcsz.com; or book via WECSZ in Lusaka (see page 51). A little less than a kilometre north of the old Musungwa Safari Lodge, or 6km from the South Park gate, Chibala – formerly known as the David Shepherd Camp – stands between large granite boulders on the shores of Lake Itezhi-Tezhi. It was built for members of the Wildlife Conservation Society of Zambia (the forerunner of the present WECSZ), and has recently been reopened – though it remains available to members only. Each of the chalets has 4 beds, en-suite shower & toilet, & a private veranda. It's a self-catering camp, but staff are on hand and there's a fully equipped kitchen & BBQ area. US$20 pp; camping US$2.50.

Nanzhila Plains Safari Camp (4 chalets, camping) \/f +267 2413740; e info@nanzhila.com; www.nanzhila.com (✆ NANZHI 16°16.746'S; 25°55.074'E). Newly built on the site of the old Nanzhila Restcamp, which dates back to the 1950s, Nanzhila Plains lies in the remote south of the park, characterised by woodland & plains. The camp overlooks the Nangandwe Pools, which attract relatively large herds of game, inc roan & sable, reedbuck, defassa waterbuck, oribi, hartebeest & eland as well as all the major carnivores, inc wild dog & cheetah. Birdlife is good year round; look out in particular for the endemic black-cheeked lovebird.

To access the camp by road you'll need a 4x4, & plenty of time: the roads from north or south are equally poor. From the Musa gate, continue 22km to the park HQ at Ngoma, then follow the Cordon rd, turning left after the airstrip for a further 35km to the disused Kalenji scout post; a right turn here will lead after 15km to the camp. From the Dumdumwenze gate, follow the track for 3km to a fork; if it's dry, continue straight ahead to the east of the river, but when wet you *must* turn left & continue north for 65km on the Cordon rd, eventually turning right to the camp. For fly-in visitors it's a 2hr game drive to the airstrip.

Guests are accommodated in solidly built thatched chalets, with hardwood furniture, & en suite shower, toilet & twin washbasins. There's also a simple campsite with a long-drop toilet, bucket shower, water & firewood, but you'll need to bring in everything else.

Central to the camp is a huge jackalberry tree, *Diospyros mespiliformis*, under which is a thatched boma incorporating a lounge, dining area, bar & veranda. A firepit, the focal point of evenings in camp, sits on an adjoining kopje.

The camp is owner managed, & its activities are flexible. In addition to game drives (day & night) & guided walks, visitors can be taken to Lake Itezhi-Tezhi or – by arrangement – to visit Shezongo village. *US$395 pp sharing, fully inc (except imported wines & spirits); US$315 pp sharing self-drive; US$220 pp sharing FB. Camping US$15 pp, all exc park fees.* ⊕ *May–Nov.*

National Parks campsites In this southern side of the park there are a couple of marked, organised campsites where you can camp inside the park. Facilities are minimal – usually zero – and they're certainly your wildest option in the area if you've arrived with a self-contained vehicle and your own food and water.

⚑ **Mupasha Campsite** (✪ CAMPS1 15°48.029'S; 25°59.727'E). As you head south from the park's Musa gate, on the southeast side of Lake Itezhi-Tezhi, Mupasha is the first campsite you come to: on the right, barely 600m from the gate, in a lovely spot beside a rock kopjie on the shores of the lake. The site itself is tucked away behind a reed screen in vegetation, although there is an adjacent thatched

hide from which to view the lake. *US$5 pp, plus park fees.*

⚑ **Amanzimtoti Campsite** (✪ AMANZI 15°54.349'S; 25°56.685'E). This is further south, about 1km northwest of Ngoma, very clearly signposted off the road in a fairly open area. Despite this I couldn't find any trace of a place where anyone had camped. *US$5 pp, plus park fees.*

LOCHINVAR AND BLUE LAGOON NATIONAL PARKS

(*Park fees Lochinvar US$10 pp, Blue Lagoon US$5 pp per night, plus US$15 per vehicle per night*) Further down the Kafue's course, east of Ngoma, are two small national parks that encompass opposite sides of the Kafue River's floodplain. Their geography and ecosystems are very similar, although Lochinvar's wildlife has probably fared better over the past few decades than that of Blue Lagoon – despite continuing efforts to rejuvenate both parks.

Historically, both Blue Lagoon and Lochinvar have had populations of people living and farming around their borders, and often inside the park. Most are poor cattle herders, and probably aren't averse to supplementing their diets with (technically illegal) subsistence hunting. Their ancestors probably hunted here before these areas were either taken over as farms, or declared national parks; hence it could easily be argued that these lands belong more to these people than they do to ZAWA (Zambia Wildlife Authority). Clearly any long-term solution needs to include these people – which is not an easy task.

Neither park receives many visitors, and those who do visit should arrive with their own supplies, unless they're booked into Lechwe Plains Tented Camp, in Lochinvar.

GEOGRAPHY, FLORA AND FAUNA

Geography Both parks are very flat, and the sections nearer the river are seasonally flooded. The resulting watery grassland reflects the sky like a mirror, for as far as you can see. It is quite a sight, and a remarkable environment for both animals and waterfowl.

In both parks you'll find a variety of quite clearly defined environments, as you move away from the waterways to the dry, permanent woodlands. Immediately beside the water, you'll find very large areas of open grassland which are seasonally flooded – a classic **floodplain** environment. On the drier side of this, where the grassland does not receive a regular annual flooding, termitaria can exist – with high solid mounds (often looking like chimneys) to keep their occupants safe from drowning in the occasional exceptional flood. This is a very distinct area in the grasslands, known as the **termitaria zone**.

Further away still, where there's absolutely no risk of flooding, you'll find a variety of trees in the woodlands which extend across the south of Lochinvar and the north of Blue Lagoon.

Flora The landscapes in both parks change with proximity to the river, especially above the 'high flood' line. Within parts of the termitaria zone you'll find some low bushes like the paperbark acacias (*Acacia sieberana*), zebrawoods (*Dalbergia melanoxylon*), fever trees (*Acacia xanthophloea*) and rough-leaved raisin bushes (*Grewia flavescens*). Drier patches here, such as the area around the tented camp, often have pretty acacia glades with large and shady white thorns (*Acacia polyocantha*) and smaller blue thorns (*Acacia erubescens*).

As the plains gradually merge into woodland, you'll find some of the typical species from munga woodlands (see *The Natural Environment*, page 34) including sickle-leafed albezias (*Albezi harveyi*), pepper-leafed commiphoras (*Commiphora mossambicensis*) and the distinctive woolly caper-bushes (*Caparis tormentosa*).

Slightly higher and further from the water, the tree-belt becomes more established and varied, containing different bands of mixed woodlands. The belts of mopane woodland are particularly distinctive, dominated by *Colophospermum mopane*, but also including leadwoods (*Combretum imberbe*), raintrees (*Lonchocarpus capassa*), and even the occasional knobthorn (*Acacia negrescens*).

Finally, well away from the water, you find stands of classic miombo woodland becoming the dominant environment – for example, as you travel south out of Lochinvar. (As an aside, it was interesting to see some notable specimens of Natal mahogany, *Trichilia emetica*, in this particular woodland.)

Fauna The very different bands of vegetation in these parks give rise to a wide variety of birds and animals – although this also means that some of the species found here are restricted to fairly small areas of the parks and so you need to move around if you're to have a chance of seeing a good range of them.

Animals The parks are home to huge herds of Kafue lechwe – a little-known subspecies of the red lechwe, endemic to the Kafue's floodplain. Historically the Kafue lechwe used to occur here in enormous numbers. In the 1930s, population estimates suggested about 250,000 Kafue lechwe lived across the whole Kafue Flats area. By the 1950s an aerial survey put the population at about 95,000 lechwe. By 1988 this was revised down to 65,000, and the most recent survey in 1999 estimated the population as down to about 45,000. However, wander around Lochinvar or Blue Lagoon and you'll still see thousands of them – but look at the change over the last century and you'll see that we have to move swiftly to conserve them, and their habitat.

14

Alongside the Kafue lechwe, many other species occur here – although all have reduced in numbers drastically over the last few decades. Typical of this area are buffalo, eland, roan, Burchell's zebra, Lichtenstein's hartebeest, blue wildebeest, puku, reedbuck and the delightful, diminutive oribi antelope; whilst in the thickets on the edge of the plains you'll find kudu, baboon and vervet monkeys. That said, last reports were that reedbuck had disappeared from Blue Lagoon, and that bushbuck numbers were in single digits.

Birds The best season for birds on the Kafue's floodplain is probably around April/May, when the waters are at their highest levels. Then the resulting lagoons attract a great variety of migrant birds – giving a staggering spectacle of waterfowl. Often you'll find large numbers of just a couple of species in one area. This may be dominated by fulvous ducks, pratincoles, sandgrouse, or waders like sandpipers, avocets, ruff, Kittlitz's plovers, little stints and black-winged stilts. In the last ten years, Lochinvar has become a major wintering ground for black-tailed godwits, 3,000 or more of them. Plovers are usually plentiful, including long-toed, crowned, white-crowned and the ubiquitous blacksmith.

Pelicans are always around, both white and pink backed, and sometimes so are small numbers of flamingos. Cranes, both wattled and crowned, are there, usually in flocks of a hundred or more, plus spoonbills and a variety of storks and ibises (notably sacred and glossy). In both parks the best areas for watching waterbirds are unpredictable. They depend on the water levels, which in turn depend on the flood regime of the Itezhi-Tezhi Dam upstream.

However, during the early rains, the grasslands are always full of harlequin quails, Luapula cisticolas, Ethiopian snipe, yellow-crowned bishops and a sprinkling of streaky-breasted flufftails. Later in the season when the plains are dry, secretary birds pace around in pairs, whilst in the air are plenty of raptors – bateleur, martial and African hawk eagles, plus brown and black-breasted snake eagles. Amongst the thousands of lechwe there are always recent deaths, so there are four species of vulture present, plus large numbers of marabou storks.

LOCHINVAR NATIONAL PARK Lochinvar's northern boundary is the Kafue River. The land on which the park stands was originally obtained from local chief, Hamusonde, in around 1908 by a Mr Horne, a man known locally as 'the Major'. Horne was a Scottish cattle farmer from Botswana who registered the land on behalf of the British South Africa Company, and built the old Lochinvar Lodge as his farmhouse.

Previously little of this land had been used for farming because of the game here, including lion and leopard. To convert the land into a cattle ranch, Horne set about exterminating these. In a ruthless programme of annihilation, populations of sable, roan, eland, warthog and wildebeest were wiped out, as well as lion – the last of which is thought to have been killed in 1947.

However, in 1966 Lochinvar Ranch (as it was then called) was bought by the Zambian government with the help of a grant from the WWF, and converted into a GMA; but the extra protection afforded to the wildlife by this designation was not enough to prevent its numbers from diminishing further, and so in 1972 Lochinvar was upgraded to a national park.

Subsequently the park has been designated by the WWF as a 'Wetland of International Importance', and a WWF team have been working with the local people on a project to manage the park on a sustainable basis for the benefit of both the people and the wildlife. Details of the project are available within the park.

There are a lot of settlements around Lochinvar, and local people still come into the park – as they have done for centuries. Many were unhappy with Lochinvar Ranch – and have always felt that this is their land. They come to gather wild foods

The Kafue River was dammed in two stages. Initially, in 1971, a dam was built in the Kafue Gorge, just south of Lusaka, which permanently flooded 800–1,100km² of land on the eastern side of the Kafue Flats. However, the gradient of the river above this point had always been very low (about 8m drop in over 200km of river), so the result was a huge, shallow reservoir with a relatively low volume (785 million cubic metres). The Kafue Dam's primary purpose was to provide hydro-electric power: it supplies up to 75% of Zambia's electricity. To guarantee this it needed a reservoir which was effectively larger than this.

Thus a second dam was built and closed in 1977: the Itezhi-Tezhi Dam. This is about 450km upstream of the Kafue Dam, and flooded only 300km² of land with a much deeper lake – holding about 4,925 million cubic metres of water. Hence the flow from Itezhi-Tezhi could be regulated to provide the constant flow needed by the Kafue Dam to generate electricity. When the dams were constructed, ZESCO (Zambia Electricity Supply Corporation) was obliged to ensure that there was a continuous flow out of Itezhi-Tezhi, in order to preserve the Kafue Flats habitat, and service the other users of the water. (The largest of these are the sugar industry around Mazabuka, and the municipality of Lusaka, which extracts water for the city.) However, this was a very difficult task – made all the more complex because the flood takes about six weeks to get from Itezhi-Tezhi to the Kafue Dam.

Before the dams, the river's flow varied enormously with the season: the Kafue Flats flooded every year and the floodplains experienced a long dry season. Since the dams, ZESCO has released a four-week artificial 'flood' in March, but clearly it has failed to simulate the natural situation. The UK's Department for International Development (DFID) reported in 2001 on *Managed Flood Releases from the Itezhi-Tezhi Reservoir*, and within that noted:

> Since the dams, the flooding pattern has changed considerably. There has been a reduction in the seasonal fluctuations. The annual minimum flood area has increased from about 300km² to approximately 1,500km². In places permanent lagoons have formed where ephemeral aquatic habits had existed before. In broad terms, the western half of the Flats is drier, whilst the eastern half is wetter than they were prior to dam construction.

This altered flood pattern has knock-on effects to the whole ecosystem. Old-time visitors to Lochinvar will tell you that the vegetation there has changed enormously over the last 30 years, and not for the better. With the change in vegetation come changes in the grazing – for both wildlife and cattle. Then, of course, the breeding cycles of the fish are affected and there's no longer any movement of fish upriver past the dams. When fish populations change, so do those of many bird species.

There is much further research to be done, and the WWF are already involved in a project to simulate the river's old flood regime using new computer models to control the Itezhi-Tezhi Dam outflow. Many people are now starting to make strenuous efforts to ensure that whilst maximising the benefits provided by these dams, they also minimise the inevitable environmental problems caused by them.

and fish, and even to drive their cattle from one side to the other; so although major conservation efforts are being made in Lochinvar, building up the diversity and number of game species here is not an easy task.

Getting there Lochinvar is easiest to approach from Monze, on the Livingstone–Lusaka road – about 287km from Livingstone and 186km from

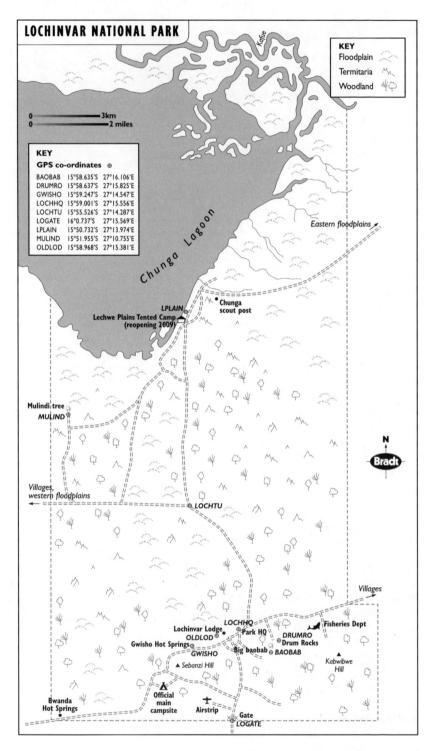

LOCHINVAR NATIONAL PARK

KEY
Floodplain
Termitaria
Woodland

0 ————— 3km
0 ————— 2 miles

KEY
GPS co-ordinates ⊕

BAOBAB	15°58.635'S	27°16.106'E
DRUMRO	15°58.637'S	27°15.825'E
GWISHO	15°59.247'S	27°14.547'E
LOCHHQ	15°59.001'S	27°15.556'E
LOCHTU	15°55.526'S	27°14.287'E
LOGATE	16°0.737'S	27°15.569'E
LPLAIN	15°50.732'S	27°13.974'E
MULIND	15°51.955'S	27°10.755'E
OLDLOD	15°58.968'S	27°15.381'E

Kafue

Chunga Lagoon

Eastern floodplains →

LPLAIN
Lechwe Plains Tented Camp
(reopening 2009)

• Chunga
scout post

Mulindi tree
MULIND

*Villages,
western floodplains* ←

⊕ **LOCHTU**

N

Bradt

Villages →

Lochinvar Lodge •   **LOCHHQ**
OLDLOD   ⊕ Park HQ   ▲ Fisheries Dept
Gwisho Hot Springs ⊕   **DRUMRO**
GWISHO   Big baobab   Drum Rocks
▲ Sebanzi Hill   ⊕ **BAOBAB**
*Kabwibwe
Hill* ▲

Bwanda
Hot Springs   ⚑
**Official
main
campsite**   ✈
Airstrip   ⊕ Gate
LOGATE

440

Lusaka. The road that heads northwest from Monze, signposted for Namwala, is just north of the grain silos on the Lusaka side of town. From town head for the point ✪ TULOCH: 16°15.465'S; 27°28.632'E.

It passes Chongo village and forks (✪ T2LOCH: 16°10.054'S; 27°23.610'E) about 8km afterwards. Ask local advice to find this junction if necessary. Take the right fork, or you will end up in Kafue. Follow this road for about 10km and then turn left at another sign (✪ TULV14 16°3.718'S; 27°22'E). It is then about 14km to the park gate. This last section of the track twists and turns, but all the tracks that split off eventually rejoin each other and lead to the park. There are also a few more signs so, if you become unsure, ask a local person and they'll show you the way. The gate to Lochinvar (✪ LOGATE 16°0.737'S; 27°15.569'E) is about 48km from Monze.

Maps An excellent (albeit very out-of-date) 1:50,000 visitors' map to Lochinvar was published by the surveyor general in 1986, and is still available at their main office in Lusaka. It indicates the vegetation types and also gives photographs and short descriptions of some of the park's interesting features and wildlife. Most of the 'camps' depicted are now disused, and some of the roads now seem as if they were figments of a cartographer's imagination.

Where to stay The original state-run, red-brick Lochinvar Lodge, built in the colonial style of 1912, was used as a farmhouse until 1966, when it was sold to the government. As the state of the park gradually deteriorated, the lodge was put up for tender to private safari operators in 1996. Eventually, Star of Africa agreed to take it as part of a 'package' of old government properties around the country. Renovating it would have been a huge job, so instead they built a tented camp which, today, is the only camp or lodge in the park. In 2007, the camp was taken over by Sanctuary Lodges & Camps.

Lechwe Plains Tented Camp (6 tents) Contact via Sanctuary Lodges & Camps, page 261 (✪ LPLAIN 15°50.732'S; 27°13.974'E). Following the recent takeover, Lechwe Plains Tented Camp will not be reopened until 2009.

Camping Until Lechwe Plains Tented Camp is reopened, your only option is to camp, for which you will need all your own supplies. There have been several sites here, but it's best to ask the scouts at the gate for the latest news. To reach what was the official campsite, drive about 2km past the gate into the park, and take the second left turning. Continue for about 5km. This site has water, a long-drop toilet and a simple cold shower. Firewood and a barbecue are provided. This is close to the hot springs at Bwanda, near the old Lupanda Wildlife Camp. If you wish to pick up a scout from the gate to guide you, then it's advisable to arrange this in advance.

What to see and do Although there is some game here, and the large herds of Kafue lechwe can be totally spectacular, the birds are the main attraction at Lochinvar. The best birding is generally close to the water, on the floodplain. For this it's probably best to walk north and east from Mulindi Tree or north of Chunga towards Hippo Corner. It's vital to avoid driving anywhere that's even vaguely damp on the floodplain as your vehicle will just slip through the crust and into the black-cotton soil – which will probably spoil and extend your stay in equal measure. A few sites to note include:

Lochinvar Lodge This is the site of the old farmhouse (✪ OLDLOD 15°58.968'S; 27°15.381'E) built by Horne, and later the old government-run lodge. There are plans to renovate this dilapidated, crumbling old building. It does have superb views over the park, and with a lot of work, and money, a lodge here would contrast perfectly with the seasonal tented camp of Lechwe Plains. However, until enough people come to Lochinvar to make a second lodge economically viable, it's likely to remain an evocative old ruin.

Gwisho Hot Springs Gwisho Hot Springs (⊕ GWISHO 15°59.247'S; 27°14.547'E) are near the southern edge of the park. To get here drive from the main gate to the old lodge, and then turn sharp left immediately in front of the old lodge's gates. From the campsite, drive north out of the camp and turn right towards Sebanzi Hill, following the edge of the plain. After about 2.5km turn left at a stone cairn and palms. The springs are signposted, and just a few kilometres further on, about 2km west of the old lodge.

The springs' hot waters vary from about 60°C to 94°C, and contain a high concentration of sodium, chlorine, calcium and sulphates. The thick vegetation around them is surrounded by a picturesque stand of real fan palms, *Hyphaene petersiana*, which have small fruits – when opened, these are seen to have a hard kernel known as 'vegetable ivory'. In the thick, wet vegetation here keep a lookout for birding 'specials' including black coucal and Fülleborn's longclaw. Also look out for the stand of knarled old trees on the rocks at the top of the small rise beside the springs. These may look a little like deformed baobabs, but they are in fact African star-chestnut trees, *Sterculia africana*.

Excavated in the early 1960s, the remains of late Stone-Age settlements were uncovered here; it was described as one of the best-preserved and oldest sites in southern Africa. (Some artefacts discovered here are on display at Livingstone Museum.) It seems that the local inhabitants had traded the salt collected here far and wide, possibly as far as east Africa, as Arab-style trading beads were found here.

Talk to the local people and they will tell you that the Gwisho area was the location for several fierce battles between the Tonga/Ila people and the Batwa, with hundreds of men being killed at a time – hence the existence of several mass burial sites nearby.

Looking even further back, into geological history, the springs were formed by a geological fault which stretches along the southern end of the park, on the edge of the Kafue Flats Basin. Associated with this is a deposit of gypsum, the mineral used to make plaster of Paris, which was mined at Gwisho from 1973 to 1978. You can follow the white rocks which mark this fault from Bwanda Hot Springs past the old campsite and Sebanzi Hill through Gwisho Hot Springs to the lodge, and past Drum Rocks.

The water which wells up into these springs has been heated far below the surface, and thus is independent of the rainfall or local surface water conditions.

Bwanda Hot Springs Bwanda Hot Springs lie in the southwest of the park, and are surrounded by a large area of reed beds. They're quite close to Limpanda Scout Camp, and so are often used for bathing and washing by the local people – and even sometimes as a place to water their cattle.

Sebanzi Hill This national monument marks the position of an Iron-Age village on the top of the hill, which was excavated during the 1960s. Archaeologists say it has been inhabited for most of the last millennium. Originally known as Ko-Banza, the village continued to exist right up to the first half of the 20th century when the villagers were evicted, presumably by the ranch owners. Looking out from this site you have an excellent view over the park and the springs, and hence realise why it was a strategically important site in times of turmoil.

The giant baobab on Sebanzi is said to be 2,500 years old, and is often used by nesting white-backed vultures. There are also said to be some caves in the side of the hill, though these are now hidden behind deep, impenetrable thicket. The hill is still probably home to some threatened southern African species, including pangolin and aardvark, as well as hyenas, jackals, bush pig, bushbuck and small wildcats. Notable birds often seen here include the African broadbill.

Drum Rocks Close to the lodge, in the south of the park, is an outcrop of rocks (⊕ DRUMRO 15°58.635'S; 27°16.106'E) that echo when tapped, producing a curious, resonant, almost metallic sound. These are the Drum Rocks, or Ibbwe Lyoombwa in the local language. Ask the scouts to direct you to these: they are fascinating. (Similar rocks, on the farm called Immenhof, in Namibia, were originally discovered by San/Bushmen and are now known locally as the 'singing rocks'.)

Considered sacred by the locals, these rocks are actually just the remnants of much larger boulders that were dynamited by the ranch's owners, curious to know the secret of their sound. They play an important part in the local religious calendar. As part of an elaborate rite of passage, it is traditional for a young man to come with his cattle to the rocks, chant 'Ibbwe Lyoombwa' and then perform a dance and various rituals designed to prove his manliness. At the end, he should leave with his cattle without turning back, for fear of seeing his dead ancestors, and then stay away from his village until the beginning of the rains. If he had proved himself sufficiently, he would then be considered an adult and would be able to take a bride on his return. Even today, visitors are supposed to chant 'Ibbwe Lyoombwa' to prevent bad luck befalling them.

Nearby is a large baobab (⊕ BAOBAB 15°58.637'S; 27°15.825'E) with a completely hollow trunk that can be entered from a crack in the side (which is the size of a small doorway). According to Chief Hamusende, the cave was formed by an old man who, given a magic club, decided to try it out by bashing it against a nearby baobab; a broken tree and the formation of the cave were the result of his experiment. It was actually used as a shelter by the district commissioner during the 1800s, and local legend has it that anybody who refuses to believe in the customs and beliefs of the villagers will enter into the cave and never return, the tree sealing up and closing behind them.

Chunga This group of large winterthorn trees, *Acacia albida*, is roughly where the main track meets the lagoon. It's the site of the old wildlife camp, and a good spot to camp provided you don't mind being disturbed by the odd vehicle.

MWANACHINGWALA CONSERVATION AREA Although east of the national park boundary, Mwanachingwala lies in a similar environment to Lochinvar National Park, and is normally accessed from Mazabuka. For details, see pages 210–11.

BLUE LAGOON NATIONAL PARK (*US$5 pp per day, plus US$5 per vehicle*) Blue Lagoon is on the north side of the river. It was originally owned by a farming couple turned conservationists, the Critchleys, but more recently, especially during KK's reign, the Ministry of Defence restricted access to the military, plus a few privileged politicians and generals who used the old farmhouse intermittently as a hunting retreat – with predictable impact on the local wildlife.

Now it's much more relaxed and the team from Mukambi Safari Lodge in Kafue have been working with the WWF to try and resuscitate the park. Given that the environment is still in reasonable shape, and the natural flooding regime of the river can be re-established, it is hoped that there is every chance of success in the long term. However, the park's Nakeenda Lodge was up for sale in 2007, so the future remains uncertain. Reports suggest that many of the park's trails are very overgrown and that, while the birding is excellent, and antelope are to be seen near the lagoons, other wildlife is little in evidence.

Getting there Note that it's not possible to reach Blue Lagoon from the south, unless you're arriving by boat in the floods!

From Lusaka Blue Lagoon is reasonably well signposted, and there are several ways to reach it. From Lusaka, the easiest is probably to take the Great West Road towards Mumbwa then turn left after about 22km, opposite the Farmer's filling station. This all-weather gravel road will lead you to the national park's scout camp at Naleeza. Alternatively, if you're heading for Nakeenda Lodge (currently closed) then follow the sign left.

From the west If coming from the west, pass through Mumbwa and look for a Total garage near Nangoma, around 81km east of Kafue's Nalusanga gate. Fill up here. Then continue towards Lusaka for a few hundred metres, taking the first right turn after this filling station, following the power lines. In less than a kilometre, turn right at the crossroads and keep following those power lines! This junction is on a local bus route, so if you ask directions you will probably end up with a guide and their luggage. (A fair deal all round!) Continuing for 9km brings you to Myooye village, where you should take the left fork that passes the clinic on the right-hand side.

Follow this track for 31km to a T-junction, ignoring smaller side tracks. (If the group of huts on the left, halfway along this road, has a flag flying, it means that the Tonga chief who lives here is in residence.) At this T-junction turn right. To reach Nakeenda Lodge, continue straight on for about 10km then turn left at the signpost.

If you're not going to Nakeenda, then turn right at the T-junction, and continue for 22km, ignoring a right-hand turn, passing through the first gate and finally reaching the scout post. At the post, sign in, pay the park and camping fees, and check the current camping rules with the scouts. You may end up turning around to retrace your tracks for 11km, before passing through the gate and turning right at the road signposted to 'Nakeenda Wildlife Police Unit'. This road quickly passes a derelict entry and after 7km reaches Nakeenda Lodge.

⌂ **Where to stay** The only campsite here, Nakeenda Lodge, was closed in 2007 and up for sale, but details have been left in case it should be taken over. In the meantime, it may be worth asking one of the scouts at the gate if you can use one of the old national park sites.

⌂ **Nakeenda Lodge** (4 chalets) Closed in 2007. This old-style self-catering lodge behind the Critchleys' simple farmhouse is right next to the old causeway, with lovely views over the flats. Thatched chalets each have a bedroom & en-suite flush toilet, washbasin & shower. Water is heated by wood-fired boilers &, although there's a small generator, most of the lighting is by paraffin lamps. Visitors must bring their own food, but cooking utensils, crockery, cutlery & (borehole) water are provided, along with bedding & towels.

What to see and do The park is dominated by the Kafue Flats, which are flooded in the rainy season. This is certainly the best time for birdwatching here; and the park is generally at its best. In the dry season the view is not so stunning but still worth a visit.

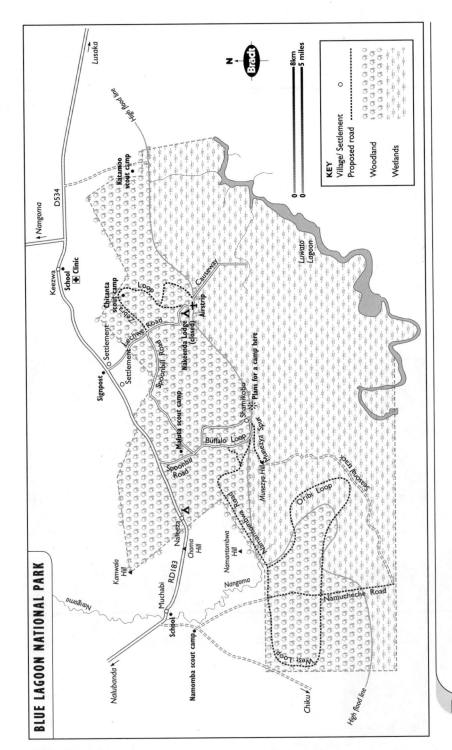

BLUE LAGOON NATIONAL PARK

KEY

Village/ Settlement

Proposed road

Woodland

Wetlands

N

Bradt

8km

5 miles

Lusaka

High flood line

Katambo
scout camp

Luwato
Lagoon

Nangoma

D534

Keezwa

School
Clinic

Causeway

Chitanta
scout camp
Settlement
Loop
Lechwe Road
Nakeenda Lodge
(closed)
Airstrip

Signpost
Settlement

Plans for a camp here

Spoonbill Road

Mafuta scout camp
Shamikobo

Buffalo Loop

Spoonbill Road

Munezya Hill
Munezya Spur

Orlbi Loop

Naleeza

Namutomba Road

Kamwala
Hill

Choma
Hill

Namantombwa
Hill

Nangoma

Leopard track

RD183

Nangoma

Muchabi

School

Namomba scout camp

Nalubanda

West Loop

Namucheche Road

Chiku

High flood line

The Critchleys built a causeway here that extends for about 5km over the marshy flats, enabling a vehicle to drive out onto the flats for a wonderful view of the stunning birdlife. There's even a turning circle at the end, and several memorial stones along this causeway. One reads:

> Erica Critchley 1910–1976.
> To the memory of the
> one who loved Zambia
> So much she cared for
> human and natural resources.
> Let what she stood for
> not be forgotten by Zambians
> especially by its youth.
>
> Kenneth Kaunda
> President of Zambia
> March 30 1976

In the dry season the end of the causeway doesn't usually reach the water so you need a ranger from the scout post, who will take you on walks around the flats. Aside from the wildlife, do visit the old farmhouse that used to be owned by the Critchleys, even if you're not staying there. It's fascinating.

15

Western Zambia

This remote area of western Zambia is difficult to visit but can reward intrepid travellers with some of the country's most interesting experiences. The Barotseland floodplains, near Mongu, offer a glimpse of rural Zambian life that is still largely untouched by the 21st century, while the Liuwa Plain National Park has excellent game and few visitors. It may be the venue for one of Africa's last great wildlife migrations, which has remained largely unknown because of the difficulty of getting into the area. Other parks, Sioma Ngwezi and West Lunga, do not have the same reputation for wildlife, but are still very wild places to explore with a well-prepared group of 4x4 vehicles.

Common to the whole region are the related problems of supplies and transport. Much of the region stands on deep Kalahari sand where vehicles need a high-clearance 4x4 capability. If you are going off the main roads, then a small expedition is needed consisting of several vehicles, in case one runs into problems. During the rainy season, many of the roads are impassable, and even the pontoons (ferries) across the rivers will often stop working. Being stranded is a very real possibility. Thus the area's paucity of visitors is largely explained by the sheer difficulty of getting around.

The Christian missions have a very well-established network here. On the whole, these do remarkable work for the communities in the area, being involved with schools, hospitals, churches, development projects and many other aspects of local life. The courteous traveller can learn a lot about the region from these missions, and they are also good places to find English-speaking guides to accompany you on your travels – who will prove invaluable for just a few dollars per day.

I've divided this chapter up into three sections: southwestern Zambia, Barotseland and northwestern Zambia. These don't slavishly follow provincial divisions; rather they reflect the differences between the areas as I understand them and are a convenient way to organise this chapter. I have also written the first half of the chapter, through southwestern Zambia, as a tour, starting from the border towns of Kazungula and Sesheke, and continuing north up the Zambezi to Lukulu and beyond.

TOUR OPERATORS

Few companies operate in this region, but one that is currently running a few trips is the South African Umkulu Safari & Canoe Trails (+27 21 853 7952; f +27 21 853 8391; e info@umkulu.co.za; www.umkulu.co.za). They organise excursions to this area from Livingstone, covering the Ngonye Falls, the Barotse floodplains, Liuwa Plain and West Lunga national parks, and the source of the Zambezi.

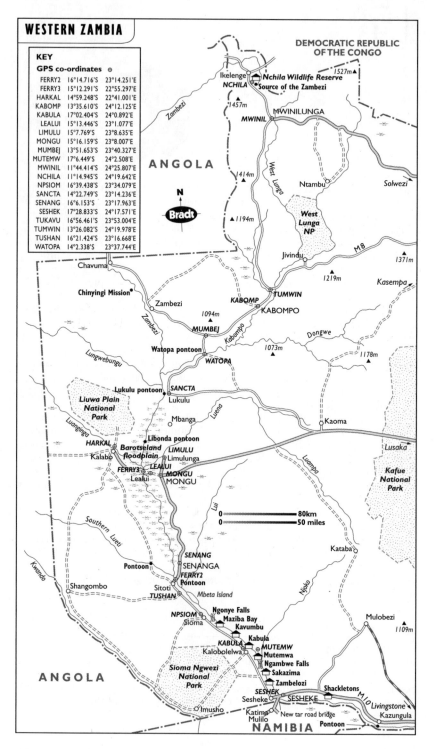

The southwest of the country has been largely neglected, with few roads (which are generally poor) and no major towns. This does mean that its sights, like the marvellous Ngonye Falls, are very quiet.

KAZUNGULA There's an excellent tarred road, the M10, leading from Livingstone to the small border town of Kazungula, a journey of just under an hour. Here, there's a ferry over the Zambezi into Botswana (⊕ *06.00–18.00*). This is reliable and large enough to take several trucks at a time, and can get very busy. The crossing costs about US$20 per vehicle, depending on the vehicle's size.

Just before the ferry, down a short road to the left, are a few shops, a small market (⊕ *early–18.00 daily*) and a simple restaurant. This is also where local buses stop.

Getting there and away A daily bus service links Mongu and Livingstone, via Sesheke, so if you're heading for Botswana, then hop on one of these and get off at Kazungula. The ferry to Botswana is a good place to hitchhike. After that, to get into Kasane or to head for Nata, you should walk the short distance to the disease control post, which makes a perfect hitchhiking spot as vehicles have to stop here anyway.

Where to stay and eat Before you reach the ferry terminus, there are a couple of places to stop for a quick lunch, or even to stay overnight.

ⓧ **Kazungula Resthouse** On the left of the main M10, close to the river, this has a large restaurant boma where snacks & more substantial dishes are on offer ($). There are pre-erected tents for camping (Kw75,000 pp), or you could pitch your own (around Kw20,000 pp).

ⓧ **Kazungula Restaurant** (6 rooms) A little closer to the ferry, accessed through the marketplace, this restaurant with rooms (& a pool table) is right on the river, & gets pretty noisy. Rooms are built in a sgl block, with bare concrete floors, but there are mosquito nets, & a very basic shower block. $

SESHEKE Sesheke actually consists of two small towns located on opposite sides of the Zambezi, linked in 2004 by a new bridge (see box, page 450). In the bigger town, on the east side (✦ 17°28.599'S; 24°17.208'E), there are a few stores, a small branch of the Finance Bank, a simple hospital, a police station (listen for their marching songs at 04.30 if you're staying overnight!), a post office and a few small guesthouses. If you have a mobile phone you can get coverage here from the Namibian 'MTN' network; if you're heading north, this could be your last chance to use it for a while!

The smaller western section of Sesheke town, located next to the border with Namibia, has a police post and a small local store. Across the border in Namibia's Katima Mulilo fuel is cheaper and supplies are more plentiful, so Sesheke can be very quiet.

Getting there and away Sesheke is easily reached from either Livingstone or Katima Mulilo, in Namibia, on excellent tarred roads. There's a daily bus service from Livingstone, costing Kw40,000 one way.

If you're driving from Livingstone to Sesheke then read *Driving west* in *Chapter 8*, page 163.

Where to stay Sesheke has a handful of places to sleep on both sides of the river, all them very unsophisticated and basic, and correspondingly inexpensive. These

In May 2004 the Zambian and Namibian presidents, Levy Mwanawasa and Sam Nujoma, opened this new bridge which connects Namibia to central Africa. They enthused that it would unlock the potential for trade and transport between their two countries, whilst opening up vital access to the Namibian port of Walvis Bay for central Africa.

The bridge is 900m long and lies about 5km inside Zambian territory. It was financed largely by Germany, who provided 32 million euros to build the bridge and improve the Sesheke–Livingstone road in Zambia as part of an infrastructure aid programme.

German and South African companies took only two years to build what is still only the fifth bridge to span the width of the Zambezi – the others being the road bridges at Chirundu, Tete and Livingstone, and the footbridge at Chinyingi Mission.

include **Sisheke Lodge** (⊶ *021 1481086;* f *021 1481165*), and Brenda's Baobab, described below.

If you're driving yourself, then your options widen considerably with at least one lodge (Shackletons, see below) beside the river to the east of town, and several other places just north of town, on the way to Ngonye Falls (see pages 455–6).

🏠 **Brenda's Baobab** (4 chalets, camping) Mulambwe St; ⊶ 021 1481228 (⊕ SESHES 17°28.833'S; 24°17.571'E). Popular with backpackers, this unexpected gem sits behind St Kizito Roman Catholic Church, just over a kilometre from the centre of town. It's run by Brenda & her husband, a Dutch GP, who travel regularly to Europe, & their dbl-storey en-suite chalets are certainly the best rooms in town. Down by the river are grassy lawns dotted with shady picnic tables & a campsite. Nearby are clean toilets & showers, & a large expanse of wooden decking around the large baobab which dominates the camp. They'll serve food, drinks, & an eclectic range of beers drawn from Namibia, Zambia & South Africa, & kayaks can be rented. $$. *Camping US$5 pp.*

East of Sesheke

🏠 **Shackletons Upper Zambezi Lodge** (6 chalets) m 097 7934149; e info@shackletons.co.za; www.shackletons.co.za (⊕ SOKACA 17°29.793'S; 24°46.519'E; the turn-off from Livingstone–Sesheke road is ⊕ TUSOKA 17°28.010'S; 24°46.948'E). Formerly known as Soka Fishing Camp, Shackletons is around 55km east of Sesheke, some 3km down an easily navigable approach road. It overlooks a side channel of the Zambezi, & beyond are wide floodplains, typical of the seasonally flooded eastern end of Namibia's Caprivi Strip.

Newly built thatched, en-suite chalets with twin beds overlook the river from their wooden verandas. At the heart of the lodge is a modern building that incorporates a lounge, dining area & riverside bar, with a swimming pool & deck nearby. While the change of name has taken the lodge upmarket, the emphasis remains the same: on fishing – although there are plenty of birding opportunities, too, as well as river cruises, mokoro excursions & cultural visits. *US$250pp sharing, inc FB & fishing, exc drinks & transfers.* ⊕ *all year.*

Driving north from Sesheke to Ngonye
The route north from Sesheke to Senanga is fairly straightforward, following the western bank of the river for the first 190km to Sitoti along an intermittently good all-weather gravel road. This should be navigable with a high-clearance 2WD all year, although sections do get washed away sometimes and there's very little traffic on the road – so I'd feel happier travelling this way with at least a 4x4, if not two. On the way you'll pass several fishing camps on islands in the river which make convenient bases for those wishing to spend some time in the area. These are clearly signposted from the road.

Camps to the north of Sesheke The following are listed in the order in which they are encountered when driving north from Sesheke:

⌂ **Zambelozi Island Lodge** (3 tents, 3 chalets) +27 82 775 4888; e zambelozi@yahoo.com; web: http://zambelozi.phathost.co.za. The well-signposted turning to Zambelozi (⊕ TUZAML 17°19.919'S; 24°8.184'E) is just over 18km from Sesheke. From there the track leads east for about 1km to the banks of the Zambezi, from where you can see the lodge on the southern end of a small island in the river. (On the northern end is a lovely little 'glade' of baobabs.) Reached by boat, it is a comfortable lodge & there are plans to take it upmarket. Much of the lodge is laid out as decking – with a small swimming pool, several secluded corners in which you can relax, & a thatched bar & sitting area on the camp's eastern side.

The accommodation consists of standard Meru-style tents with sturdy twin beds, a wardrobe, & an en-suite bathroom with flush toilet, shower & washbasin; water is heated by individual gas boilers. There are also 3 more spacious reed chalets with thatched roofs, solid wooden dbl beds, walk-in mosquito nets, big showers, toilets & washbasins. However, these only have relatively small windows, so are rather dark. The owners also plan to construct a couple of larger, luxury chalets.

Zambelozi has always been sold as a fishing camp, & it is certainly that, with boats specially designed for fly-fishing. It would, though, also make a comfortable stop for a few nights of birdwatching on the way north – provided you are not put off by their very slow communications or unreasonably high rates. *US$400 pp sharing, inc FB, activities & equipment.*

⌂ **Sakazima Island Camp** (7 bungalows, camping) ⌕/f +27 11 469 4980, 3413; m +27 83 277 1413; f +27 11 469 3415; e ebonyplace@ yebo.co.za, sakazima@tiscali.co.za.(⊕ TUSAKA 17°17.868'S; 24°8.230'E). About 28km north of Sesheke, & 2hrs' drive from Livingstone, this small fishing camp is located on a group of 5 islands in the Zambezi. It is co-owned, & was constructed by Ian Lowe & Dave Telford. When I talked to Ian at the lodge, he was at pains to stress how careful they were not to remove any of the island's trees when building the lodge, & there's still a lush, tropical feel about the place – lots of wild date palms (*Phoenix reclinata*), African mangosteens (*Garcinia livingstonei*), ebonies (*Diospyros mespiliformis*), knobthorns (*Acacia nigrescens*) & the occasional pod mahogany (*Afzelia quanzensis*).

Each of the camp's bungalows has an en-suite bathroom with shower, toilet & washbasin, with water heated by individual gas boilers. Visitors can also camp on the riverbank opposite the lodge. The main deck has a river-water swimming pool. The lodge caters mainly for fully catered birding & fishing parties – with great fly-fishing opportunities on the rapids. When whole groups book the lodge then it's possible to do so on a self-catering basis. Mokoro rides, short nature drives in the nearby bush, guided birding walks & day trips to Ngonye Falls & Livingstone can be booked in advance. *R1,100 pp sharing, inc FB & sunset cruise. Self catering R360 pp. Camping R72 pp (all in South African rand).* ⊕ all year.

⌂ **Mutemwa Lodge** (6 tents) ⌕ (South Africa) +27 11 234 1747; f +27 11 234 1748; e mutemwa.lodge@mweb.co.za; www.mutemwa.com (⊕ MUTEMW 17°6.449'S; 24°2.508'E). On the Upper Zambezi, a little over 50km north of Sesheke, Mutemwa opened in 1996 & is well known in South African sporting circles as it is owned & run by Gavin Johnson, the former Springbok rugby player, & his wife, Penny.

From the neatly signposted turn-off (⊕ TUMUTE 17°7.056'S; 24°1.861'E), it is just 1.6km to the lodge.

Built on the riverbank, this is the smartest lodge in the area. Its clientele is mainly upmarket groups (up to 12 people, & usually of South African origin) coming on fishing trips. Although it's possible to drive here, most groups charter 14-seater planes from Livingstone to Mutemwa's own landing strip, near the lodge. Its remote location makes transfers like this relatively cheap for a large group, but sadly rather more expensive for smaller numbers of people thinking of flying in themselves. An added option is to combine a trip here with the sister lodge, Maziba Bay, which is close to Ngonye Falls.

Mutemwa's smart, Meru-style tents are spread out on individual teak decks along the water's edge. They are shaded by the remaining tall trees in the riverine forest, & surrounded on the banks by clipped lawns. Each 2-person tent has a flush toilet & (gas-heated) shower in its en-suite bathroom, & a small sitting area at the front overlooking the Zambezi. Under a large central thatched roof, Mutemwa shelters a bar, lounge, dining area & small curio shop; nearby is a swimming pool. Dinner is served in the boma area, where individual guest tables are set around the fire; b/fast & lunch are served on the lower deck overlooking the river. Expect a good standard of food.

Activities centre on guided fishing trips, though birding trips & sundowner cruises are also on the menu (the camp has 6 good motorboats & guides available), as are canoeing excursions. US$320 pp sharing, inc FB & activities; exc drinks & lost or broken fishing tackle! Closed during heavy rains (Jan–Feb).

About 60km out of Sesheke, and just after Mutemwa Island Lodge, you pass through Kalabolelwa, where a track leads off left into Sioma Ngwezi National Park (about which, see pages 452–5) – although I couldn't find this when I last passed this way. Several further camps lie off the road north of here, including:

🏠 **Kabula Lodge** (8 chalets, camping) ☎ +27 82 550 8642, +27 82 672 5168; f +27 88 012 811 1000; e info@kabulalodge.com; www.kabulalodge.com (⊕ KABULA 17°02.404'S; 024°00.892'E). From its riverside location on the Zambezi, this self-catering lodge is primarily geared to families coming in search of the fishing & birding. It is clearly signposted about 58km from the border post at Katima Mulilo, along a challenging 4x4 road; alternatively, the lodge has its own airstrip (⊕ KABAIR 17°03.281'S; 024°00.125'E). Accommodation is in dbl or 4-bed reed chalets (linen provided), each en suite & with its own deck overlooking the river. Lights that operate off your vehicle battery are provided, but there is no other power. A communal kitchen is equipped with gas fridges, a cooker & basic utensils. For campers, there's a tree-shaded campsite with ablution facilities in individual rondavels rather than a block. Each pitch has a tap & its own washing-up area, with water heated by wood-fired boilers, & there's a thatched lapa with tables & benches.

In addition to the fishing that draws most visitors (equipped boats are available for hire), there are opportunities for walking & birding on Kabula Island, just upstream of the lodge, where over 200 species of birds have been recorded, as well as canoeing & rafting on the river. Chalet R450 dbl; camping R85pp (South African rand) ⊕ all year.

🏠 **Kavumbu River Camp** (3 bungalows) ☎ +1 858 794 0294; f +1 858 794 8870; e vacationenquiries@kavumburivercamp.com; www.kavumburivercamp.com. Kavumbu stands in riverine forest beside the Zambezi river, within a GMA. The turn-off to the camp (⊕ TUKAVU

16°56.461'S; 23°53.004'E) is about 27km north of the Mutemwa turn-off, or 87km north of Sesheke, marked by the Kavumbu Camp store. Alternatively, it's possible to fly in from Livingstone.

Accommodation is in 4-bed thatched bungalows, each with 2 bedrooms & en-suite hot water shower & flush toilet, & a river view. A central area comprises a lounge & kitchen; most guests stay on a full-board basis, but self-catering prices can be quoted on request. Prime attractions are fly-fishing & birdwatching, but it's quite possible simply to explore the river. US$220–420 pp sharing, inc FB, drinks, boat hire & river guide; sgl supplement US$80. ⊕ all year.

🏠 **Maziba Bay** ☎ +27 11 234 1747; m +27 829 902405; f +27 11 234 1748; e mutemwa.lodge@mweb.co.za; www.mutemwa.com/maziba.htm About 127km north of Sesheke, and less than 10km south of Zambia's spectacular Ngonye Falls, Maziba Bay (⊕ MAZIBA 16°40.594'S; 23°37.647'E) has a superb location on the western bank of the Zambezi River. It used to be a spectacular camp, and has recently been reopened as a sister to Mutemwa Lodge.

Individual thatched chalets with en-suite bathrooms line a spectacular beach of fine white sand which (but for the local crocodile population) would put it on a par with the best of the Indian Ocean islands. Unlike many of the other river camps in the area, Maziba Bay is close enough to the Ngonye Falls to offer white-water rafting, kayaking & canoe safaris on the river, as well as fishing trips & even microlight flights! Rates on application. Closed during heavy rains (Jan–Feb).

SIOMA NGWEZI NATIONAL PARK (Park fees US$5 pp, plus US$15 per vehicle per day)

Of all of Zambia's remote and seldom-visited parks, Sioma Ngwezi would probably be one of the easiest to regenerate. It is really very close to the Victoria Falls/Livingstone area, which has a huge reservoir of visitors keen to do short safari trips. Tourism to Namibia's Caprivi Strip is rapidly taking off, and with the main road across the Strip now completely tarred, access to the vicinity of the park is very good. Also mooted has been its inclusion in a trans-frontier conservation area, or 'peace park' as they're widely known.

However, despite all this, the park remains largely unvisited, whilst its game is persecuted and the local communities around it subsist in poverty.

Geography Positioned in the far southwestern corner of Zambia, Sioma Ngwezi National Park shares a long border with Angola, along the Kwando River, and also a short border with Namibia in the south. This corner is less than 50km from northern Botswana, and its vegetation and landscape owe much to the Kalahari sand that lies beneath it.

Most of the park is flat, dry and quite densely wooded – covered with a mosaic of miombo and acacia woodland, with the occasional area of teak forest. There are a few open dambos and sometimes these surround the occasional pool in the bush – but surface water is rare here during the dry season.

Geographical problems Angola has had a civil war for many years; it has only recently showed signs of starting on the long road back to peace, let alone prosperity. Namibia's Caprivi Strip is a far-flung corner of that country, which has had its security problems also in recent years. Sioma Ngwezi borders both these areas – and so was always going to be a difficult park to keep secure and well managed. Cross-border poaching is rarely as prevalent as many in Africa will claim (people from 'over there' always make easy scapegoats for crimes), but it certainly is a problem in this area.

Looking at the park's geography, you'll realise that most of the animals must either survive entirely without surface water, or need to drink from one of the two rivers nearby: the Kwando on the western border, or the Zambezi which is east, outside of the park. Study a detailed map and you'll realise that what settlements there are in this area are strung out on the banks of these same rivers. So after around July, by which time the park's few dambos have dried out, much of the game needs to run a daily (or more likely, nightly) gauntlet of the riverside villages to drink.

A further problem is how much the logging, which has decimated the oldest hardwood trees in most of Zambia's western provinces, has encroached illegally into this park.

Flora and fauna Sioma Ngwezi is the only Zambian park, outside the Luangwa Valley and the Mosi-oa-Tunya National Park, where giraffe have historically been found. These are certainly not of the same subspecies as those in Luangwa (Thornicroft's giraffe). It is claimed that they are an 'Angolan' subspecies, which is different again from the normal 'southern' variety found throughout the subcontinent.

Some of the other native antelope species here include roan, sable, eland, tsessebe, blue wildebeest, zebra, reedbuck, kudu, steenbok, oribi and possibly lechwe on the Kwando River. The major predators are lion, leopard and spotted hyena.

Current game populations Sioma Ngwezi's game populations are not in a healthy state. Poaching (aka subsistence hunting) is common, and made much easier by the trek to water that much of the game makes – thus bringing it into close contact with the settlements beside the two main rivers. The predators have also suffered, as they're attracted to the easy meat of grazing cattle from nearby local villages, which then bring them into direct conflict with the local people.

That said, it seems that small populations of most of the main game species still occur here, including elephants – which frequently come down to the Zambezi to drink in the dry season.

In Buk's report on the status of wild dog (see *Appendix 3*, page 512), he observes that there had been several sightings of wild dog there in 1993–94, whilst local game scouts told me, in 2003, that wild dog are still seen here occasionally. However, these are quite possibly packs visiting from the strong population in northern Botswana.

In short, Sioma Ngwezi's game is scarce and skittish, so it's likely that the casual visitor will see virtually no game here at all.

Future possibilities Left on its own, ZAWA (Zambian Wildlife Authority) doesn't have the finances or probably the capacity to revitalise Sioma Ngwezi. The park's only long-term hope is the intervention of an organisation with the finance and patience to engage both ZAWA and the local population, and push conservation and development here over the long term. In 2003 there were plans for African Parks (see page 473) to do just that. However, by the time that all the agreements were signed in 2004 – by African Parks, ZAWA and the Barotse Royal Establishment – Sioma Ngwezi had been dropped. They cited settlement along the Kwanda, and very low game densities, amongst their reasons for this. This was sad; although perhaps, pragmatically, if they can save Liuwa and get that back on its feet, then perhaps they'll be able to look at Sioma at a later date. (They are now actively looking for a second park to help in Zambia.)

A second possibility that could help is a plan to create a huge Transfrontier Conservation Area (TCA) in the Okavango/Upper Zambezi area. This is being considered by the Peace Parks Foundation (*www.peaceparks.org*), which has already been successful in creating six TCAs in southern Africa. Such an area would include Botswana's Okavango and Chobe National Park, Zimbabwe's Zambezi National Park and Zambia's Kafue National Park, as well as Sioma Ngwezi, and many areas and game corridors between these parks.

This would open up this corner of Africa to much wider game movements – and be a step towards ending the absurd situation where Chobe has too many elephants … yet just over the border, this corner of Zambia has too few!

Getting there and getting organised This is difficult and requires the backing of a couple of 4x4s. The Kalahari sand can be slow going, and there is only one decent road through the park. The driving is also very heavy on fuel – so remember that this is available only at Sesheke or Katima Mulilo in the south, or Senanga and Mongu to the north.

If you intend to explore this area independently, then get a scout from the National Parks and Wildlife Service office at Sioma to guide you. Even the scouts probably won't know the park that well, but their presence will make exploring much safer and more productive. Permits are available from the national park office (⊕ NPSIOM 16°39.438'S; 23°34.079'E) at Sioma Falls.

The main route through the park is the track that comes from the northwest, keeping close to the Kwando from Shangombo. A little north of the Namibian border, this turns sharply left and heads northeast through the middle of the park. Around the park's eastern boundary, at Ngwezi Pools, there is a poor track southeast to the Zambezi, via Cholola, and another track leading northwest, roughly along the park's boundary – as well as the continuation of the original track which leads directly to the Zambezi at Kalabolelwa. You may need local assistance to find these, but there are villagers in the area who can help. There are no specific campsites within the park, but a scout will show visitors good sites for camping.

When to go The best time to visit Sioma Ngwezi is probably just after the end of the rains, when the dambos inside the park still have a little water and are attracting the game. Alternatively, spend time beside the Kwando later in the year, when it's the only water source around.

Security note Note that there is some question over the precise location of the border as pre-1970s it used to be the eastern edge of the Kwando floodplain. Then Zambia 'moved' it to the middle of the river. Wherever it is, you don't want to stray over it accidentally.

THE NGONYE FALLS AREA As it lies about 132km north of Katima Mulilo, the main reason for visiting this area of southwest Zambia is for the Ngonye Falls (often referred to as the Sioma Falls) and the Sioma Ngwezi National Park. The falls are spectacular, although the park is not easy for the casual visitor to enjoy. With travel in the area often taking much time, these are also good places at which to rest for a few days if you are travelling between Sesheke and Mongu. Livingstone passed this way, having come north through what is now Botswana. He noted:

> 30th November, 1853 – At Gonye Falls. No rain has fallen here, so it is excessively hot. The trees have put on their gayest dress, and many flowers adorn the landscape, yet the heat makes all the leaves droop at mid-day and look languid for want of rain. If the country increases as much in beauty in front, as it has done within the last four degrees of latitude, it will indeed be a lovely land.
>
> For many miles below, the river is confined in a narrow space of not more than one hundred yards wide. The water goes boiling along, and gives the idea of great masses of it rolling over and over, so that even the most expert swimmer would find it difficult to keep on the surface. Here it is that the river when in flood rises fifty or sixty feet in perpendicular height. The islands above the falls are covered with foliage as beautiful as can be seen anywhere. Viewed from the mass of rock which overhangs the fall, the scenery was the loveliest I had seen.

This was about two years before Livingstone journeyed further down the Zambezi and saw the Victoria Falls for the first time.

Getting there and away The Ngonye Falls are a short walk from the road, about 120km as the crow flies from Sesheke, and 57km southeast of the Sitoti Ferry. Driving to them, you should first stop at the national park office at Ngonye (⊕ NPSIOM 16°39.438'S; 23°34.079'E), which is clearly marked beside the road. Here you can pay the entry fees, leave your vehicle safely, and find a guide to take you down to the falls themselves.

Where to stay If you stop at the National Parks and Wildlife Service office near the falls, then they'll point you to a basic campsite nearby (*US$10 pp*), although it's not run by the national park's staff. They'll also give you advice on the best way to see the falls.

What to see and do Although not as impressive as Victoria Falls, the Ngonye Falls are still impressive, and if the former didn't exist then they would certainly draw visitors. The geology of the area is the same as that of Victoria Falls, and these falls were formed by a similar process, with erosion taking advantage of cracks in the area's basalt rock.

Ngonye's main falls form a rather spectacular semicircle of water, with lots of smaller streams and falls around the edges. Some of these create little pools, ideal for bathing, though be careful to remain at this point as the main river has too many crocodiles to be safe. They are at their most beautiful when full, from January to around July,

A guide at the national park office will escort you on a 15-minute walk to the falls. Seeing the falls is easy, though getting a really good view of them in their entirety is much harder. Your guide may simply walk you to the nearest viewing point on the western bank, and tell you that's all there is to see. S/he has a point. However, most of the main falls cannot be seen from the bank, and you certainly won't appreciate them fully. To get a really good view, you must cross onto an island in the river in front of the falls – which requires you to go a little downstream, and to find a boat.

There used to be a small metal boat/ferry, which had been made by Brother Hugh at the Sioma Mission, but on my last visit that seemed to have gone. There was certainly a new motorboat moored nearby, owned by Mutemwa Lodge – although that seemed only to be for the use of their guests.

A few years ago some local families started a mokoro service across the river, and would guide visitors on a beautiful one-hour walk (each way) to the best views of the Ngonye Falls. Assuming their initiative is still operational, you can reach the right point on the riverbank by turning off the road at ⊕ 16°40.468'S; 23°34.800'E or ⊕ 16°39.482'S; 24°34.311'E. You could expect the ferry and guide to cost around Kw10,000 per adult.

White-water rafting The rapids below the falls are graded as a class III white-water run (see *Livingstone*, page 201–2, for an explanation of these gradings), and Maziba Bay used to take rafting trips here which run them in a couple of hours. It's not really very serious rafting, especially after a trip below Victoria Falls, but it is fun and makes a lovely afternoon activity.

Fishing The *raison d'être* of coming to the camps on the Upper Zambezi always used to be fishing – for bream and tigerfish. Now the area has a wider attraction, but still many visitors are attracted here by the excellent fishing. The Zambezi River here is generally wide, although in parts of its course between Senanga and Sesheke it becomes shallow, is broken by forested islands and rocky outcrops and you'll also find waterfalls and rapids. So there are conditions suitable for challenging fly-fishing and spinning. Tigerfish are the most sought-after challenge, whilst various bream species, particularly the predatory yellow-belly and the thin-face breams, make good sport fishing in the faster sections. In the slower sections, fishermen find the more sedentary three-spot, red-breast and greenhead bream.

Birding For a more gentle interaction with some of the wildlife, this area has some excellent, undisturbed birdwatching – with various species frequenting different areas of the river and the surrounding vegetation. A few of the area's 'specials' include rock pratincoles, seen darting about the rocks of many sections of rapids; African finfoots, which lurk at the water's edge in areas of thick, overhanging vegetation; African skimmers, which nest on some of the river's exposed sandbanks; and Pel's fishing owls resting in some of the old riverine trees. You'll also have chance to spot Schalow's and Lady Ross's turacos, yellow-spotted nicator, narina trogon and wood owls (Mutemwa Lodge area is particularly good for these).

DRIVING NORTH FROM NGONYE TO SENANGA
From Ngonye to Sitoti From the park's office at Ngonye Falls it's about 61km northwest to the Sitoti pontoon. On the way you'll pass the turn-off west to the Nangweshi Refugee Camp (⊕ TUNANG 16°27.904'S; 23°23.205'E) and a second turn-off, this time to the east, for **CB Riverside Lodge** (⊕ turning to CB Riverside Lodge TUCBRI 16°24.370'S; 23°19.795'E), a very, very basic establishment. There is a toilet here, but no obvious showers.

About 45km north of Ngonye, and 16km south of the ferry, there's a substantial road junction (⊕ TUSHAN 16°21.424'S; 23°16.668'E) with a road heading west to Shangambo, which is on the Kwando (aka Cuando) River. A sign here points to **Cuando Lodge**, which proudly advertises that it has 'showers and lights', and the Shangambo Mission. This turning is beside a small settlement known as Matebele, where there's a small bridge over a tributary to the Zambezi. Just north of this, the road forks and the right fork drops down onto the lower-lying grasslands of the Zambezi's floodplains – and thence to the Sitoti pontoon.

The left fork here probably leads to what, in theory, is a very difficult and sandy track along the western side of the Zambezi floodplain to Kalabo; see page 466 under *Driving from Kalabo to Sitoti* for details.

Sitoti pontoon The pontoon across the Zambezi (⊕ FERRY2 16°14.716'S; 23°14.251'E) is a little over 20km (40 minutes) south of Senanga. It's a good, large pontoon which can take several vehicles at a time, setting off when it's full; there's no set schedule. During the dry season it runs from 06.00 to 18.00, and costs around Kw25,000 for a typical Land Rover. In the wet season it has a similar schedule, though the crossing is longer, and the fare is considerably higher.

SENANGA Coming from the south, this is the first 'proper' town since Sesheke, and you're now back on tarmac. Bliss! Approaching from Lusaka, however, Senanga lies beside the Zambezi and right at the end of a very long stretch of (very pot-holed) tar. It's a pleasant place, very linear in layout with a tall radio mast near the centre. Here you'll also find a vital BP fuel station (which usually even has fuel), a hospital (almost opposite the BP garage), a post office and a handful of shops and small bottle stores – but you still can't shake off the feeling that it's out on a limb. Senanga has a Catholic church (☏ 021 7230090), with radio communications to other missions; it's looked after by Franciscans.

Getting there and away There is no navigable road on the east side of the Zambezi south of the Sitoti pontoon, so you've got to cross to the west bank to head further south. For a description of that road, read *From Ngonye to Sitoti*, above.

🏠 **Where to stay** Senanga's choice is limited. There are several basic resthouses in town, of which the Mwanambinyi is arguably the best, though a better bet is the Senanga Safaris Lodge:

🏠 **Senanga Safaris Lodge** (32 rooms, camping) ☏/f 021 7230156; f 021 7230051 (⊕ SENANG 16°6.153'S; 23°17.963'E). The obvious place to stay in town is this passable small hotel which has reasonable rooms, with AC, fridge & TV, all laid out on a sloping grassy bank down to the side of the Zambezi. The views across the wide river to the floodplains opposite are excellent. If you ask nicely they may allow you to camp. There is a lively bar & a quieter dining room which serves edible, but very unexciting, meals. Visiting one year in September, we arrived during the annual fishing competition, when the place was buzzing with large 4x4s & very serious fishermen; there wasn't a room to be had, & flat ground on which to pitch a tent was also difficult to find. *Chalets $$, camping around Kw20,000 pp.*

🏠 **Mwanambinyi Resthouse** ☏ 021 7230094. On the main road, next to Senanga Safaris, this would make a reasonable second choice of place to stay. $

NORTH TO MONGU Heading north to Mongu is tarmac all the way – about 110km. Although it was tarred in the late 1990s, it seems this was very poorly done as the road has degenerated badly. When last I drove here, it had become pot-holed to the point of being very painful and slow to drive on; the kind of road that you'd prefer was just gravel!

The former British protectorate of Barotseland, now usually referred to as simply the Western Province (WP), covers the floodplains which surround some of the upper reaches of the Zambezi. It is the homeland of the Lozi king, the Litunga, and his people – a group who have retained much of their cultural heritage despite the ravages of the past century. They were granted more autonomy by the colonial authorities than most of the ethnic groups in Zambia's other regions, and perhaps this has helped them to preserve more of their culture. The Litunga has winter and summer palaces nearby, and a hunting lodge in Liuwa Plain. (Chapter 47 of John Reader's excellent *Africa: A Biography of the Continent* covers some of the history of this area in fascinating detail. See *Appendix 3*, page 510, for details.)

For the traveller this means that some aspects of life here have altered relatively little since pre-colonial times. Most of the local people still follow lifestyles of subsistence farming, hunting and gathering, and when rains are good they must still move to higher ground to escape the floodwaters.

BAROTSE FLOODPLAINS The area bordering the Zambezi River as it runs through Mongu represents the second-largest wetland in Zambia, and was designated as a Ramsar site in 2007. After the rains, the Barotse or Zambezi floodplains are transformed with small islands of vegetation dotted through the expanse of water. Ramsar (*www.ramsar.org*) notes that 'there is sparse riparian vegetation, small stands of *Acacia albida* in the floodplains, *Syzygium guineens* along the main river channel and patches of *Diplorhynchus* scrub and *Borassus* forest in the northern areas. Semi-evergreen woodlands found on the Kalahari sands have economically important species like *Baikiaea plurijuga* and *Pterocarpus angolensis*'.

MONGU Perched high above the eastern edge of the Zambezi's floodplains, Mongu is the provincial centre for western Zambia – and the only large town this side of Livingstone or Lusaka. Very few tourists reach here, so there are few people who aren't Zambian, and almost all of those work with or for the fairly permanent contingent of NGO personnel. The areas around Mongu are amongst Zambia's poorest and many are isolated by seasonal floods, so there is often need for relief workers here.

If you're visiting, then there is little to really attract you to Mongu, apart from perhaps the phenomenally good baskets and weaving to be found here. However, you're highly likely to need the bank, fuel station, supplies, communications or relative comforts here – as there are precious little of any of these outside Mongu. It is linked to Lusaka by a tar road that starts by crossing a raised causeway across the Zambezi's floodplains. As a result of this road, Mongu is easily reached from Lusaka and is the best place in the region to get fuel or supplies.

Geography Mongu is set on a ridge overlooking the north of the Barotse Plains. It's about 25km from the dry-season course of the Zambezi, or immediately adjacent to the water when in full flood. The town is spread out, following the ridge, with no real centre but several quite different busy areas. The views west over the floodplain are spectacular when the water is fairly high: myriad channels snaking through apparently endless flat plains. By contrast, small villages and cattle dot the dusty plains during the dry season, but when wet it is all transformed into a haze of green grass on a mirror of water that reflects the sky.

Orientation The tar road west from Lusaka meets the tar road heading south to Senanga at a central crossroads (✪ MONGU 15°16.159'S; 23°8.007'E). North of

MONGU

KEY

GPS co-ordinates ⊕

AIRMON	15°15.227'S 23°9.376'E
BP	15°15.474'S 23°8.308'E
CALTEX	15°15.949'S 23°8.054'E
CROSSR	15°15.939'S 23°9.118'E
GREENV	15°13.960'S 23°8.721'E
HARMON	15°16.293'S 23°7.180'E
MONGU	15°16.159'S 23°8.007'E
OASISR	15°15.573'S 23°8.267'E
POMONG	15°16.256'S 23°7.566'E
SHOPRT	15°17.186'S 23°9.047'E
TOTAL	15°16.180'S 23°8.415'E

↑ *Limulunga*

● Water tower

GREENV ⊕
⊡ Green View

Falcon
Teachers'
College ●

New
market ▢

Zambian
Army HQ
● Mongu
✈ Mongu
Airport

⊕ AIRMON

↑ *Kaoma, Lusaka*

0 ■■■■ 200m
0 ■■■■ 200yds

⊠ Kanyonyo
Post office

DHL ●

BP ⊕
● BP
Bus station ⊡
⊕ OASISR
✗ Oasis

Old
market ◇

$ Standard
Chartered

⊕ CALTEX

Kambule
Reformed
Baptist
Church ✝

Our Lady of
Lourdes
Cathedral
Parish ✝

● Mumwa
Craft
Association

⊕ TOTAL
⊡ Total

Kambule
Technical
High School ●

CROSSR ⊕

Prison ●
⊡ Crossroads Lodge

✚ Zambian
Red Cross
Society

⊡ Caltex
⊕ Caltex

Provident
House ●

ZNC
$

MONGU ⊕

School ●

✝

▢ Ngulu-ta-Utoya

● Shoprite
● SHOPRT

Office of the
President ●
POMONG ⊕

⊠ Mongu
Post office

↓ *Senanga*

HARMON ⊕
● Mongu
Harbour
▢ Lyambai

Lealui,
Zambezi River

N ⊕ **Bradt**

Contracts signed in March 2002 started the construction of a 74km tar road from Mongu, via Kalabo, to the Angolan border which, it was envisaged, would completely open up wet-season access to impoverished areas west of the Zambezi and into Angola.

The project planned to connect Mongu and Kalabo, and ultimately Lusaka, with Angola – spanning not only the Zambezi River, but also the width of the Zambezi floodplain, about 35km of raised causeway above low-lying plains that are seasonally inundated when the river breaks its banks. Initially it was scheduled for completion by February 2004, but exceptional flooding washed away part of the structure, prompting a major reassessment of the design. Even then, a hydrologists' report suggested that the section to the east of the Zambezi River (from the Zambezi to the canal) wasn't strong enough to support a road, and funds for the project started to run seriously short.

Despite these problems, the 22km section of the road running east from Kalabo to the edge of the floodplain was opened, but the rest of the project has been abandoned. Perhaps the road's builders have finally realised what their predecessors at Kariba Dam already knew – that Nyaminyami, the old river god of the Zambezi Valley's Tonga people, is very hard to tame.

this is a vibrant, packed old town area with shops, a heaving market, a bus station and an army barracks; and if you pass these, then ultimately you'll find a tar road to Limulunga. West of the crossroads lies a small hill, upon which you'll find most of the government buildings. On the other side of this hill, you drop down to the harbour, and to the road across the river, to Kalabo and Liuwa Plain. If you're only passing through, then do use this book's map for Mongu – it may save you a lot of time trying to find your way around!

Getting there and away

By air Mongu Airport (✪ AIRMON 15°15.227'S; 23°9.376'E) used to be served twice a week by the old Eastern Air. However, there are no services that I know of now – and chartering a plane (Livingstone or northern Kafue would be closest) to get here would be very expensive.

By bus Several buses link Lusaka to Mongu every day – expect a minibus to cost around Kw75,000 and a larger, slower bus to be about Kw60,000. There is also a regular daily service run by Mazhandu Family Bus service between Livingstone and Mongu, via Sesheke, stopping at several villages along the way. The bus station is beside the old market.

Hitchhiking Hitching to Mongu on the Great West Road is possible for the determined. Hitching to get around the surrounding countryside is very slow and difficult – but it is how most of the local population travel.

Driving west to Sandaula on the Zambezi Much of the promised new tar road to Kalabo, which was to head west along a causeway across the floodplains, has been abandoned (see box above). It'd be wise to ask around in Mongu about the road's current state before you leave, and expect travel to be very difficult (or impossible) when the floodplains are wet, between about December and July.

To get to this road, head west from the main Mongu crossroads, over the hill, past the post office and turn left down towards the harbour. There you'll clearly see the road dropping down onto the Barotse floodplain in front of you. Remember to fill up with fuel at Mongu before you leave; there are no fuel stations west of here.

If the conditions are dry, then you'll find sections where you have to drop down off the causeway and onto parallel tracks on the floodplain. There are plenty of people to ask, all heading roughly between Mongu and the ferry, so it's difficult to get lost. However, the sand can be very deep and troublesome – so a high-clearance 4x4 remains essential.

About 12.3km northeast of Mongu's harbour area, you'll reach Lealui (✪ LEALUI 15°13.446'S; 23°1.077'E). This would have been a ten-minute drive when the tar was finished, but is more likely be a two-hour slalom.

Lealui is the location of the isolated summer palace of the Litunga, the Lozi king (see page 464 for more details), and a centre for the Lozi administration. Visitors are advised to show courtesy and respect, even if it doesn't appear to be different from any other small African village. With the accessibility brought by the new road, Lealui will probably lose a little of its mystique – and the convoys of swish black Mercedes with darkly tinted windows that whisk unseen royalty past you on this road will probably change from 4x4s to saloon limousines!

A little over 10km northwest of Lealui, you'll reach the ferry (✪ FERRY3 15°12.291'S; 22°55.297'E) across the Zambezi, at Sandaula – although when the bridge over the river is completed, this is likely to disappear. See *Kalabo*, pages 464–6, for more details of the route west.

Driving south to Senanga This clear wide tarmac road was badly pot-holed when I last drove along it; let's hope that it's repaired to a higher standard than it was built to in the first place!

Driving north to Lukulu There's a good tarred road for 15km north of Mongu, basically as far as the Litunga's winter palace. Then there's nothing more than vanishing local tracks across the Barotse floodplains between there and Lukulu. These are passable in the dry season – see the Lukulu sections, pages 467–70, for directions – but otherwise consider driving to Lukulu on all-weather roads via Kaoma.

Getting around Mongu has a reputation for theft, so visitors should take great care of their belongings and vehicles here. The police appear to be vigilant, as there are often several roadblocks around the town where they will check your vehicle and its papers. Make sure that you're wearing your seatbelts and driving slowly through town. Options for getting around are:

By boat Boat transport is the best way to see the immediate area around Mongu, and it is the only way if the flood is high. For a few dollars you can hire a mokoro to take you out on the waterways, and perhaps down towards Lealui and the main channel. Spend a few hours like this, on the water, and you will appreciate how many of the locals transport themselves around. You will see everything from people to household goods, supplies, live animals and even the occasional bicycle loaded onto boats and paddled or poled (punted) from place to place.

For rather more, larger boats with outboard motors will take 20 or so people on longer journeys; there's typically one of these per day between Mongu and Kalabo.

By 'postboat' Given that boats are the only way to reach some settlements in this area during the wet season, there is a privately run 'postboat' on the Zambezi that carries passengers, cargo (including the occasional vehicle) and even the mail. Ask at the Mongu District Council offices (☎ 021 7221039), for more details – but note that ferrying a vehicle is likely to be a very expensive option, costing over US$100 one way for a vehicle from Mongu to Kalabo.

Driving Apart from the main roads from Lusaka to Mongu and Lukulu, most of the area's roads are little more than vehicle tracks, and they degenerate into patches of deep sand quite frequently. You really need a 4x4 here even in the dry season, and the worst of these tracks will require almost constant low-range driving through long sections of Kalahari sand.

During the wet season, the whole area north of the Ngonye Falls is subject to flooding. Then the Barotse floodplain becomes a large, shallow lake – much of the population moves to higher ground to live, and boats are the only option for getting around. Don't even think about trying to drive anywhere off the tarred roads then.

Where to stay

Where to stay There's a choice of accommodation in Mongu, most of it of fairly poor quality. There are a few relatively large, old-style hotels, like the Ngulu and the Lyambai, of which the latter has recently had a long-overdue facelift. To fill the gap, a rash of small guesthouses has sprung up, privately owned and run. These cater mainly to top local businesspeople, foreign aid workers and expats – people who will usually try to find the best place in town. Thus the best of these do have reasonable standards of accommodation and security, although even then they're nothing special. Note that price is seldom a useful guide to quality here – and as new places spring up they will often be better than what is here already. Try to book something in advance if you need it, as the better places are often full – although sadly many won't take bookings unless you pay them in advance.

Given Mongu's bad reputation for theft, you should take maximum precautions against losing your belongings, even when staying in one of the hotels. It is not generally safe to camp randomly around here. If you can't make it into town, and need to stay in the area, then it's better to ask at a village than to camp alone.

Ngulu-ta-Utoya Hotel (18 rooms) ☎ 021 7221414, 7221286, 7221957; e nguluhot@zamtel.zm. A few kilometres south of the centre, on the left as you head towards Senanga & just before the turning to Shoprite, this old-style hotel is used for a lot of local conferences – though it could do with being refurbished. Rooms all have en-suite bathrooms with toilets & baths. The car park is at the front, set above the main road (with a good view of the floodplains), & has a guard on duty. They can arrange laundry. $, inc cont b/fast.

Lyambai Hotel (17 rooms) ☎/f 021 7221138; m 097 7826953; e comacs@coppernet.zm. This old-style hotel, fairly near the harbour, has recently been privatised, and was being renovated in 2007. Its rooms are laid out in one long row, each with en-suite shower & toilet. When completed, all rooms will have TV & a fan, while suites will boast AC & a fridge as well. There's a restaurant & bar, while outside is secure parking. Rates will go up when renovations are complete, but are unlikely to exceed this category. $–$$, inc cont b/fast.

Green View Guesthouse (6 rooms, camping) (✪ GREENV 15°13.960'S; 23°8.721'E). This small, quiet guesthouse belongs to the New Apostolic Church, beside which it is located. To reach it head north on the tar road to Limulunga, & look for the sign to the left – about 2km after the turning to Sir Mwanawina III Hotel. Being attached to a church seems to lend this a very happy, relaxed air – & it's sufficiently outside town for security to be less of an issue. The small sgl rooms share separate toilets & showers, whilst the dbl room is a lot bigger & has an en-suite toilet, bath & shower. All are very simply furnished & have mosquito nets, but none is sparklingly clean. The chalets, by contrast, are really much nicer – tiled from floor to ceiling & with en-suite showers & toilets that work well. These chalets are certainly one of the better options in Mongu. They will also allow camping here, although facilities for campers are limited. Chalet $. Camping around Kw20,000 pp. No meals.

Crossroads Lodge (13 rooms) ☎ 021 7221199 (✪ CROSSR 15°15.939'S; 23°9.118'E). On the south side of the road from Kaoma/Lusaka, about 2km from the main crossroads at the centre of Mongu, this overlooks the floodplain & is currently about the best place in town. It has fairly small but very clean & functional rooms – all with en-suite shower & flush toilet, remote-control TV & AC. There's a pleasant bar in the courtyard, & the parking is very secure behind an electric gate. Note that they're keen on having the bills for rooms paid in advance, & that smoking in rooms is not allowed. $$, inc cont b/fast.

✗ Where to eat

The hotels will sometimes serve food if requested but for the town's best food try the **OK restaurant** in the centre of town, or the reliable:

✗ **Oasis Restaurant** ✎ 021 7221931 (⊕ OASISR 15°15.573'S; 23°8.267'E). On the road behind the old market (turn off opposite the Total garage & head directly to the BP garage). Here you'll find dishes such as pepper or T-bone steaks with chips & salad. The Oasis doesn't have a licence for alcohol – but ask nicely & they'll send someone out to buy drinks for you. $

Otherwise you could just go to Shoprite, below, and put together your own picnic.

Other practicalities There are three main fuel stations in town: Caltex just 400m north of the crossroads; BP another kilometre further on, past the old market; and Total just 700m east of the crossroads.

There's a ZNC Bank beside the crossroads with a reasonably reliable ATM machine taking Visa credit cards (but not Mastercard). On the other side of the road is a Standard Chartered Bank. The post office (⊕ POMONG 15°16.256'S; 23°7.566'E) is west of the banks, high on the hill above the harbour; it also houses the Western Union money transfer office. For sending anything apart from money, there's a DHL office (✎ 021 7221013) just north of the BP station. The town also has an internet café.

Shopping Mongu is the obvious place in the Western Province to buy supplies and get organised. The best place to head for is the large and well-stocked Shoprite (⊕ SHOPRT 15°17.186'S; 23°9.047'E; ⊕ 08.00–18.00 Mon–Fri, 08.00–17.00 Sat, 09.00–13.00 Sun & public holidays), by far the biggest and best store in town. It is reached by heading about 3km south of town towards Senanga, and then taking the signposted turning left. Note that Shoprite accepts only kwacha cash – they don't take travellers' cheques or credit cards.

The huge old market in town is a good place to buy locally produced fresh fruit and vegetables (and, I'm told, bread also). Between this and the BP garage (⊕ BP 15°15.474'S; 23°8.308'E) you'll find the taxi rank and bus station.

For **handicrafts**, take the main road to Lusaka from the crossroads, and on the south side, just before the Total garage (⊕ TOTAL 15°16.180'S; 23°8.415'E), you will find the Mumwa Craft Association (✎ 021 7221263, f 021 7221262; e mundiakk@yahoo.com). This non-profit-making society was established in 1994 to improve the economic, social and cultural well-being of the local communities by representing a network of several hundred local producers spread throughout the Western Province. They concentrate on wood carvings, weaving, pottery and metalwork, as well as some of the very best basket-weaving in Africa. Items such as large and very beautiful linen baskets are woven using skills developed over the centuries by the Lozi people in making their woven fishing traps. You won't find better baskets supporting a more worthy cause, or at lower prices.

Excursions from Mongu Aside from wandering around the local market, in the town centre, there are no specific sights in Mongu. You may, though, like to visit the lively and very traditional harbour (⊕ HARMON 15°16.293'S; 23°7.180'E) or

15

take a wander around the market. The two obvious attractions, however, are both excursions from town:

The Litunga's summer palace at Lealui About 13km west from Mongu, amidst the floodplains, the summer palace is set in a large grove of trees, which is easily seen from the escarpment on which Mongu stands. If there is no road here, then you can hire a mokoro to bring you out here from Mongu.

Don't expect a Western-style palace, as the Litunga's will appear to be a normal small African village with thatched huts. However, this is not only the king's summer residence, but also the main Lozi administration centre. Visitors are warmly welcomed, though are strongly advised to show the utmost courtesy and respect to their hosts. Indeed, until very recently it was normal to introduce yourself to the Kuta (the traditional court) as a courtesy, especially if you planned to continue on to Liuwa. See *Driving west to Sandaula on the Zambezi* on page 460 for directions of how to get here from Mongu, and *The Ku-omboka* in *Chapter 2*, pages 26–7, for information about the famous annual ceremony that's held here.

The Litunga's winter palace and the Nayuma Museum and Heritage Centre 15km north of Mongu, near the Litunga's main winter palace, is the Nayuma Museum and Heritage Centre (⊕ *08.00–17.00 Mon–Fri, entry Kw2,000*), which houses some interesting exhibits on the history and culture of the Lozi people, with a strong focus on conserving and promoting the region's heritage. Its director, Manyando Mukela, is also *Ngambela* (prime minister) to the Litunga.

A small craft shop sells some really beautiful basketwork from the area, at very reasonable prices.

To get here, take the tar road north from Mongu's new market to Limulunga then turn left down a tarred side road opposite the water tower at the centre of town. Follow this round and after a kilometre or so you reach a barrier, with the museum on the left, and the Lozi palace on the right. This royal complex is all fairly grand and impressive, complete with keen security guards from about March to June, when the Litunga is in residence.

TRADITIONAL CEREMONIES

The Ku-omboka If the rains have been good, and the floodwaters are rising, then around February or March, often on a Thursday, just before full moon, the greatest of Zambia's cultural festivals will take place. The Ku-omboka is the tradition of moving the Litunga, the Lozi king, plus his court and his people, away from the floodwaters and onto higher ground.

This spectacular ceremony is described in detail in *Chapter 2*, pages 26–7. It involves a flotilla of boats for most of the day, plus an impromptu orchestra of local musicians and much celebration. Don't miss it if you are travelling in western Zambia at the time.

KALABO This small town by the Luanginga River is the gateway to Liuwa Plain National Park. Kalabo is a rambling group of dwellings. The name is derived from the Lozi word *silambo*, meaning 'paddling stick'.

Coming from Mongu, you'll first enter a wide main street lined by grand old buildings with verandas, most in various states of decay. It usually seems very quiet, though clearly the shopkeepers have active imaginations with the originally named 'Just Imagine Restaurant' and the 'Hard Work Makes Dreams Come True Restaurant'.

Drive down the main tar road to reach Kalabo's harbour, where there is a small pontoon (⊕ HARKAL 14°59.248'S; 22°41.001'E) over the Luanginga. The fare is

Kw25,000 one way, or Kw40,000 return, plus a Kw5,000 carbon tax. (Alternatively, late in the dry season, the river can be forded – with local guidance on where to cross.)

Kalabo has a mission with a large hospital (⊕ HOSPKA 14°59.111'S; 22°40.654'E), and a basic government resthouse. African Parks also plans to open a campsite just outside the town. Note there is no fuel available in Kalabo – and although you can get the basics in the market or in local shops, you'd be well advised to buy all your supplies in Mongu before you arrive.

There's a convenient general store entitled 'Manel Restaurant' on the right as you enter the harbour area, and opposite that is a small basic café overlooking the harbour – ideal for those long waits whilst people fetch the pontoon owner for you!

Kalabo has its own airstrip (⊕ KALAIR 14°59.501'S; 22°38.484'E), so it is at least possible – albeit very expensive – to charter a plane into the area.

National Parks office and immigration Of vital importance to most visitors is the African Parks office, which is conveniently beside the harbour   in Kalabo (⊕ HARKAL 14°59.248'S; 22°41.001'E). This is where most people get their permits for Liuwa Plain National Park or organise to camp.

The immigration office book is also held in the parks office, so you can fill out all the necessary paperwork while buying your permits for the park. The official immigration office is behind some of the shops near the harbour, on the left of the Luanginga pontoon. Even if you're not entering or leaving the country, he will usually collar you to check your passports, and to ask you questions about your movements. In my case, he was also curious to find out if I wanted to surreptitiously buy diamonds or gemstones! (The correct answer to this was an emphatic 'no' – as I was keen to see Liuwa, rather than the inside of a local police station.)

Getting there and away With the tar road from Mongu no longer likely to be completed (see box on page 460), Kalabo is not easy to reach, and is inaccessible from that direction outside of the months from July to December. In fact, anywhere west of the Zambezi remains expedition territory. 'Roads' here are usually just tracks in the Kalahari sand, which need days of low-range driving. They require not only a 4x4 (preferably several, in case of emergency), but also large quantities of fuel. This cannot be replenished outside of Mongu, so long-range extra fuel tanks and lots of jerrycans are the normal solution. See *Driving in sand*, pages 106–7, for more advice – and note especially the points on higher fuel consumption and misleading milometer readings.

Water is also a problem, as it tends to seep through the Kalahari sand rather than forming pans on the surface. Hence no potable water can be relied upon outside Kalabo, so if you're heading west, take some good containers and fill up at Mongu and Kalabo.

Driving from Mongu via Sandaula See the directions for *Driving west to Sandaula on the Zambezi* on page 460 for the route from Mongu to the Sandaula Ferry across the Zambezi. (Completion of the major tar road from Mongu via Kalabo to the Angolan border has now been abandoned.)

The ferry (⊕ FERRY3 15°12.291'S; 22°55.297'E) operates from sunrise to sunset and is large enough for three vehicles – although it will often leave with just one or two. During the dry season, the Zambezi is confined within its banks, only a hundred metres or so wide; the ferry is about 22km from Mongu and costs around Kw40,000 per vehicle.

15

On the western bank, the tracks used to diverge as they crossed the floodplains, which was marvellously confusing. With the construction of the new road, it was envisaged that most tracks would disappear, but that's no longer a reality and the tracks remain.

Kalabo is about a 42km drive northwest of the ferry in the dry season. At first, the road from the ferry heads in a westerly direction across the floodplains, before climbing up onto a ridge after about 20km. Then it turns more northerly, and reaches Kalabo in a further 22km. The final 40km of this road are tar.

Driving from Mongu via the Libonda pontoon In theory it should be possible in the dry season to cross the Zambezi higher up the river, at the Libonda pontoon – and then to head westwards, and slightly south, on small paths and tracks across the floodplains. However, we have reports that the pontoon is no longer operational, presumably put out of business by the now abandoned plans for the new road.

If you do try this way, then you should certainly take a local guide (hitchhiker) to help you navigate – and you will see plenty of these throughout the area. You will pass men, women and children carrying everything from luggage to mattresses and supplies on their heads. Given the area's lack of transport, it you have room in your vehicle then you should offer lifts whenever possible.

Driving to Liuwa See *Getting there*, under *Liuwa Plain National Park*, for details, on page 475.

Travelling anywhere else If you're planning on going anywhere else besides Liuwa, then your best source of information is either the African Parks office or the mission station in Kalabo, which is effectively the last outpost of civilisation. They have radio communications with various mission stations established nearby, and can advise on ferries and the logistics of your trip. They can also be your last contact point so that, should you fail to return by a certain time, they will contact the authorities. In return, do offer donations and help in the form of taking letters or goods or providing transport.

Wet-season travel In the absence of the new tarred road to Mongu, Kalabo remains cut off during the wet season. Then your options for getting here or away are: a) wait for the Zambezi ferry to start up again after the floods; b) use the expensive 'postboat' from Mongu, which takes one vehicle at a time – enquire locally to find out if it can be arranged; or c) use the sandy track on the west side of the Zambezi, between Kalabo and Sitoti, discussed below.

Driving from Kalabo to Sitoti There is a track on the western side of the Zambezi between Kalabo and Sitoti, but it is thick sand with no fuel (or much else) on the way. You'd probably be wise to take local hitchhikers as guides. The route heads south and slightly west (average bearing of about 157°) from Kalabo to the Sitoti pontoon (see page 457); aim for GPSTUSHAN 16°21.424'S; 23°16.668'E.

This is 164km as the heron flies, and a lot more on the ground. I haven't driven this route, but am reliably informed that it's about 12 hours of driving. If you were forced to do this, it would take much more time and fuel than going via Mongu and Senanga. So if you cross from Mongu west of the Zambezi during the wet season, bear in mind that this could be your only way out.

LUKULU The riverside town of Lukulu is the main town in the district, hence it has a collection of government offices and local council offices in the boma (the central area; see map). There is also a district hospital, which includes two doctors from the Netherlands (as do many such hospitals in the Western Province, which is being helped by a Dutch aid programme). However, medical facilities and supplies here are very limited.

Lukulu is a typical rural town. It has a ZESCO plant (Zambia's electricity supply company), and hence has erratic supplies of electricity. It also has a public water pumping and distribution system, which means running water some of the time. It's also sufficiently rural to make visitors – especially those with fair skins – something of a novelty.

Getting there and away There are good all-weather roads linking Lukulu (✪ SANCTA 14°22.749'S; 23°14.236'E) with Kaoma, which is just off the Lusaka–Mongu road, Kabompo and Zambezi. Despite its proximity, the route to Mongu is nothing but a series of inter-village footpaths across the Barotse floodplain. There are no reliable roads on the west side of the Zambezi, though crossing the river and finding a route through to Liuwa Plain is possible.

From Mongu – across the Barotse floodplain By far the quickest and best route to Lukulu starts near the Kaoma turn-off, on the Lusaka–Mongu road. However, if it is well into the dry season, then there is another possibility described here: heading cross country across the floodplains.

Leaving Mongu past the new market, the tar ends after the shops at Limulunga (✪ LIMULU 15°7.769'S; 23°8.635'E) and shortly the track forks. Head down the hill, towards the small river. Fording the first shallow channel of this, take a hard right onto a motorable track and follow this. There are lots of people down here, and if you can pick up a hitchhiker to guide you, then do so. You'll probably give lifts to several before the day is out!

As you head north the tracks split and fork, getting smaller all the time, until about midway to Lukulu. Then there appear to be no good tracks. However, gradually, as you continue, they get clearer again as you approach Lukulu. Think about it and you'll realise that they are all made by the local people, travelling from village to

15

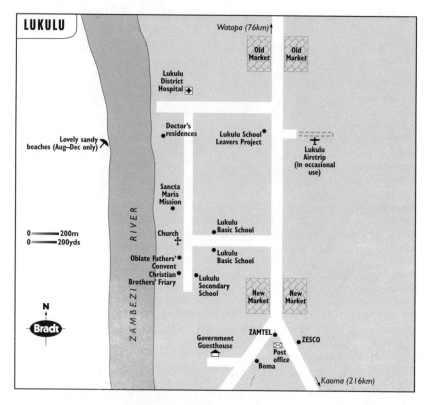

village, and (crucially) to their nearest town – so they radiate out from the towns. This is the typical pattern made by the smallest thoroughfares in most rural areas.

There's little point my trying to describe the precise route here, as every vehicle will end up on slightly different track – which is half the fun! Instead I'll list a few waypoints, south to north, so that those travelling with a GPS can keep track that they're heading roughly in the right general direction:

- ⊕ NANGIL 14°52.659'S; 23°4.478'E Nangili School where an engaging headteacher presides over about 350 children, from grades one to nine.
- ⊕ AIRNGU 14°36.687'S; 23°6.977'E Ngulwana Airstrip, which is occasionally used by fishermen coming on private trips up to this corner of the Zambezi.
- ⊕ KAWYA 14°28.827'S; 23°13.999'E Near the school at Kawaya. If coming south towards Mongu, this point marks where you deviate from the track to Mbanga, turning right down a steep bank. Coming north, you join a better track here.
- ⊕ TUMONG 14°24.515'S; 23°15.588'E Where the bush track from Mongu/Mbanga meets the good Kaoma–Lukulu road.
- ⊕ SANCTA 14°22.749'S; 23°14.236'E The Sancta Maria Mission at Lukulu.

The countryside is lovely here, with open fields and plenty of patches of various interesting palm trees. You'll pass through a variety of tiny villages and settlements – mostly subsistence farming of rice and maize. On very rural routes like this it's important that you give lifts to other travellers; they're often poor people for whom there probably isn't any other form of transport. Conveniently, they'll often be able to direct you to the nearest town, making the second half of your journey much easier than the first. It's about 99km as the stork flies between Mongu and Lukulu, and going over the floodplains will take you about five to six hours.

From Kaoma to Lukulu This is a reasonable, all-weather gravel road, and the most reliable way to reach Lukulu. When the Barotse Plains are flooded, then travellers from Mongu will reach Lukulu either by boat, or by driving east to Kaoma and then northwest to Lukulu.

If you are backpacking, there are buses that ply between Kaoma and Lukulu. However, they don't run to a fixed schedule; rather the driver waits (possibly for several days) for the bus to fill up enough to make the trip worthwhile. Karun Thanjavur (a VSO volunteer working in Lukulu) described the road as 'an axle breaker … the buses creak and groan from abuse'. She advises travellers coming this way on public transport to travel with a good stock of food and water (at least for two days), and a sleeping bag (with mosquito net/coils) etc – just in case the bus breaks down. Most people will hitch a ride on any vehicle rather than wait for a bus, and van drivers charge about US$2–4/Kw10,000–20,000 for the trip.

From Lukulu to Kasempa Heading north-northwest you pass the Sancta Maria Mission and then the old market before leaving town. This is a reasonable gravel road through the bush, for which you'd want a high-clearance vehicle, and 4x4 in the rains – but otherwise it is a main artery by local standards on which you can reach 50–60km/h. Either side of you is a mix of bush and settlements, with plenty of mango trees and cassava crops being grown.

It's about 62km to the slow, manually operated Watopa pontoon (✛ WATOPA 14°2.338'S; 23°37.744'E), which didn't appear to cost anything – though clearly the guys that operated it appreciated a tip for their efforts. There are a few small shops around the ferry, and the road continued southeast from the ferry back to meet the road to Kaoma.

Continue directly for about 21km, heading slightly east of north, from Watopa and you'll reach a road junction with the east–west 'M8' road.

This is Mumbeji (✛ MUMBEJ 13°51.653'S; 23°40.327'E), which isn't a place to linger in – it's little more than a T-junction with a range of small stalls and shops around it. Look out for the 'Strugglling Grocery' (*sic*) here and the 'Slow by Slow Restaurant and Grocery'.

From here the good all-weather M8 gravel road (50–60km/h when dry!) goes west to Zambezi, and east about 67km to Kabompo (✛ KABOMP 13°35.610'S; 24°12.125'E). Although there has clearly been some logging here, much of this road goes through thick woodlands with very few settlements.

Without your own vehicle, the only means of public transport around these areas are private local 4x4s, assorted lorries and vans. The charge varies (depending whether you wish to ride in the cab or in the open back braving the elements) but you can get from Lukulu to Watopa or Kabompo, for example, for about US$4/Kw20,000. Some drivers will inevitably charge more if you are fair-skinned, as you are perceived to be a wealthy *makuwa* (white person). On average, this is probably a fair assumption – so pay and smile, and don't complain!

West from Lukulu There is a pontoon crossing here, but no real roads on the other side – just a series of paths that link the small villages there. Crossing here and then driving south to Kalabo or Liuwa would be possible in the dry season, but a local guide and a GPS would be essential. Kalabo is much easier to reach by crossing the river further south.

If you do want to use the pontoon at Lukulu, then Sue Grainger commented: 'The pontoon at Lukulu is an adventure. The pontoon is owned by the hospital, the engine by the veterinary service and fuel is a matter of local negotiation. Therefore time, patience and the services of a guide are much appreciated. It is a one-car pontoon and the steep sandy east bank of the Zambezi is perceived to be better than the west bank. It is best to get off the pontoon on the west bank in a forward gear. You therefore back onto the pontoon – which can be quite daunting when you are looking at a 1-in-3 slope of sand on the east bank!'

🏠 **Where to stay** Lukulu has a **government guesthouse** ($), reached by turning southwest off the main road, just west of the post office and Zamtel office, and then taking the first right turn. There's also a private **hotel** ($), near the old market on the right of the road as you head north to Watopa. Both are very simple and basic.

There are no campsites, but in the dry season there are many lovely spots along the river (especially just across from Lukulu on the far bank) where a well-equipped traveller can camp in peace. Ask whoever owns the nearest homestead for permission.

🍴 **Where to eat** There are several basic restaurants here, mostly in the old and new markets. All usually offer rather meagre fare of nshima and some form of relish ($). Fernando's Butchery, in the old market, can serve slightly more elaborate meals for a little more, if you give them a few hours' notice.

The shops in the old and the new markets have only the most basic essentials. The chances of finding even canned food here are slim. Both soft drinks and beer depend on a truck supplying them from Lusaka; news of its arrival spreads like wildfire through the town.

The local people live by subsistence farming and fishing, each eating just what s/he cultivates or catches. Hence, not much fresh produce reaches the market. You'll probably find just one or two varieties of seasonal fresh fruits and vegetables, dried fish, roller meal for nshima, etc. Visitors should arrive with a good stock of food and drink – and the locals will probably be grateful for anything that you leave behind.

What to see and do Lukulu doesn't have many obvious attractions, though the nearby Zambezi River and floodplains are very scenic. As with many of the area's smaller places, privacy can be a problem as an outsider is regarded as a source of free entertainment by some of the local community. Karun, a VSO volunteer living here, commented: 'If the visitor is willing to offer to the local people the same right to watch that s/he has assumed, then we have a happy relationship; if not, we have an unhappy visitor but content locals. Except for an occasional visit by a group of Makishi dancers, there are no other festivals that take place in Lukulu.'

Perhaps, for sanctuary or interest, you might like to stop at one of the country's loveliest mission stations:

Sancta Maria Mission The peaceful Sancta Maria Catholic Mission (✪ SANCTA 14°22.749'S; 23°14.236'E) at Lukulu was founded in the 1930s and has a stunning setting high on one bank of the Zambezi, overlooking palm-fringed woodlands opposite. It is a beautiful place from which to watch the sunset. The mission is run by the Sisters of the Holy Cross whose projects include community education and a leprosy clinic.

There is a Sunday service in Lozi that offers a fascinating blend of Catholicism and Lozi culture – with lots of singing and dancing. Being just over the river from Liuwa Plain, the sisters tell of one day, in the 1950s, when the bell in the tower started ringing wildly. On investigation the bell ringer proved to be a spotted hyena which had seized the rawhide rope in its jaws, and was trying to pull it off and eat it.

LIUWA PLAIN NATIONAL PARK (*Park fees US$40 pp per day; camping US$10 pp. Cost to hire a scout about US$10*) Liuwa Plain is as wild and remote as virtually any park in Africa; at the right time of year, its game is also as good as most of the best. The cliché 'best-kept secret' is applied with nauseating frequency to many places in Africa by copywriters who can't think of anything original; this is perhaps one of the few places which would deserve it.

Liuwa Plain has long been a very special place. It was declared a 'game reserve' as early as the 19th century, by the king of Barotseland, and subsequently administered by the Litunga. or Lozi king. Traditionally, the park was the Litunga's private hunting ground, and the villagers were charged with looking after the animals for him. Then in 1972 it became a national park, and its management was taken over by central government, although the local people retain utilisation rights of the park, grazing their animals, fishing in the rivers and pools, and harvesting plants for use in traditional crafts.

The word *liuwa* means 'plain' in the local Lozi language. Legend relates how one Litunga planted his walking stick here on the plain, where it grew into a large *mutata* tree. The tree in question can still be seen from the track which leads from Minde to Luula: after leaving the first tree belt, look in the distance on your left side when you are halfway to the next tree belt. Liuwa Plain is certainly the most fascinating park in the region, but getting here currently requires an expedition. There isn't another way.

For this reason, visitor numbers are tiny: from January to October 2002 only about 121 visitors entered the park (52 South Africans, 44 Zambians, seven British, a similar number of Germans, five Japanese, three French, two Namibians and one American!) Yet even these figures dwarf those in some of the previous years: only 50 tourists visited in the whole of 2000. Now that African Parks (see box page 473) are putting it on the map, numbers are increasing, but in order to preserve the park's fragile ecosystem the number of vehicles admitted at any one time is limited to 25.

Geography Although a network of sand game-viewing tracks has been established in the 3,660km² park, it remains largely untouched. Most of it is a vast honey-coloured grass plain, stretching about 70km long and 30km wide. Within this there's just the occasional open pan, cluster of raffia palms, or small tree-island interrupting the flatness. In places you can look 360° around you and see nothing but a flat expanse. The environment is unlike any other park in Zambia – the most similar places are probably Katavi, in western Tanzania, and, possibly, the much smaller Kazuma Pan in Zimbabwe.

Large areas of this plain are totally flooded from around December to April, with the waters rising in the north and spreading southwards. It's this flooding which drives the migration, as the herds move out of the woodlands to the north, and onto the open plain for new, fresh grazing.

In the centre, and especially the southern side, of this enormous grassy plain, you'll find a scattering of open pans, many of which hold their water well into the dry season. These are well worth investigating. Although in the dry season some will appear almost lifeless, others will have great concentrations of birds or antelope.

Flora and fauna

Flora Liuwa Plain's main plant life, on first glance, appears to be vast areas of grasslands, within which species like *Vossia cuspidate* and *Echinocloa stagnina* are

15

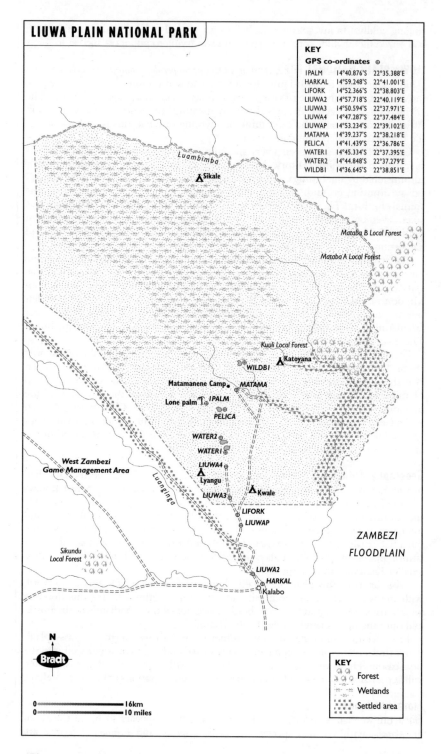

LIUWA PLAIN NATIONAL PARK

Luambimba

Sikale

Mataba B Local Forest

Mataba A Local Forest

Kuuli Local Forest

Katoyana

WILDB1

Matamanene Camp

MATAMA

Lone palm IPALM

PELICA

WATER2

WATER1

**West Zambezi
Game Management Area**

Luanginga

LIUWA4

Lyangu

LIUWA3

Kwale

LIFORK

LIUWAP

*Sikundu
Local Forest*

*ZAMBEZI
FLOODPLAIN*

LIUWA2

HARKAL

Kalabo

N

Bradt

0 ————— 16km
0 ————— 10 miles

African Parks (*www.african-parks.org*) is a company that was founded by a group of businesspeople and conservationists who recognised that African governments had limited resources to pay for conservation or the social development which is needed to accompany it. Their first major venture required about US$15 million to buy the land for, and completely redevelop, Marakele National Park, in South Africa's Waterberg Mountain – in an amazingly short time.

Backed by finance and expertise from multi-millionaire Dutch businessman, Paul Fentener van Vlissingen, that first project was a huge success. Van Vlissingen's family own the multi-national SHV – one of the Netherlands' largest companies. (It controls numerous companies worldwide, including the Makro chain of wholesale stores.)

African Parks is now concerned with the long-term sustainability of some of Africa's national parks by forming commercial agreements with governments to manage and finance national parks. They aim to work with the inclusion of local communities, to safeguard the flora and fauna and to relieve local poverty. Ultimately, they aim to make their parks into sustainable, self-financing business units. However, they are willing to provide substantial funds to 'kick start' failing parks and areas – and also act as a channel for grants received for this from other donors.

The lease agreement for the 3,662km² Liuwa Plain National Park was finally signed in Lusaka on 31 May 2004. The event was attended by the Litunga, the Ngambela, the minister of tourism, representatives from the Barotse Royal Establishment and the Libonda Royal Establishment, the ambassadors of the USA and Netherlands, and various ZAWA personnel.

African Parks committed the sum US$2 million to Liuwa Plain over a five-year period – and signs that poaching was coming under control (eg: wildebeest meat is no longer available in local markets) were swift to follow. Since then the picture for the park's wildlife is at last beginning to look more positive.

amongst the most important for the herds of grazing herbivores. On tree-islands, and around the edges of the plain, you'll find the small false mopane, or copalwood (*Guibourtia coleosperma*); the silver cluster-leaf (*Terminalia sericea*), which is so typical of the Kalahari; stands of Zambezi teak (*Baikiaea plurijuga*); weeping wattle (*Peltophorum africanum*); and occasional stands of palms including the odd tall *Hyphaene* stand around the pans.

Mammals and reptiles As is common in vast open areas, many of Liuwa's larger mammals tend to group together into great herds when on the plain – and these are much of the park's attraction. The 1991 wildlife census estimated populations at 30,000 blue wildebeest, 8,000 tsessebe, 1,000 zebra and 10,000 other large mammals which would have included herds of buffalo, red lechwe, eland, Lichtenstein's hartebeest and roan antelope as well as assorted pairs of reedbuck and the delightful, diminutive oribi which are so common here. The scouts say that sitatunga are still found in some of the rivers on the edge of the park.

Later surveys suggested that game numbers had declined by around a third, with buffalo, eland, Lichtenstein's hartebeest and roan antelope possibly wiped out completely. However, with more active protection, numbers are building up again; the 2007 count revealed 33,500 wildebeest, and increasing populations of all herbivore species. Both roan antelope and wild dogs have returned to the park, and the population of red lechwe is recovering well. There were plans to move eland

Western Zambia BAROTSELAND

15

and possibly buffalo here at the end of 2007, with lion and perhaps Lichtenstein's hartebeest to be reintroduced during 2008.

The largest herds currently seen in the park are the blue wildebeest which mass here in their thousands during the rains. Amongst them, you'll find zebra and tsessebe. Though widely regarded as a 'migration', some suggest that it may in fact just be a gathering on the plain of all the game that has previously been in the surrounding bush, rather than an actual migration from, say, Angola. Regardless, if you can catch it at the right time, it's a stunning sight: flat, open plain with animals as far as the eye can see.

That said, I think it's quite wrong to concentrate on the sights in November and, in effect, dismiss the rest of the year. I last visited for a few days in the month of September which yielded plenty of wildebeest on the plain, including one herd of over a thousand; several smaller herds of zebra, tsessebe and red lechwe, one of the last numbering over 120 individuals; and some of the most spectacular birding that I'd ever seen in southern Africa.

Predators have also been well represented in Liuwa. Lion, leopard, cheetah, wild dog and hyena all occur here, although by 2007 there was just one remaining lioness; there are plans to reintroduce lion during 2008. Liuwa's prides of lion, which blend superbly into the golden grass, have a reputation for aggression and even for charging vehicles, so be careful. It may simply be that they are unfamiliar with humans – although if this were the case excessive timidity might be a more normal reaction. They also climb trees.

Leopard occur within the national park, though the surrounding forest is a better habitat for them than the plain itself. Hyenas are fairly commonly seen, and are cheeky enough to come to the edge of your firelight's glow. Buk's survey of wild dogs (see *Appendix 3*, page 512) suggested that in 1993–94 the size of the packs was larger than average.

With sharp eyes you're also likely to spot smaller curious omnivores like side-striped jackal, troops of banded mongooses, and possibly porcupines. I've had reports of some particularly large snakes living here – though (thankfully) been unable to verify these.

Birds Liuwa boasts a total of about 319 bird species which, even when I visited during a dry month like September, were amazing: spectacular groups of crowned cranes often numbered several hundred birds; wattled cranes, so endangered in many places, thrive here with numerous pairs and smaller groups of up to 30 individuals; while one particular flock of pelicans included several hundred individuals. I saw all of these in just a few days in early September – and so when it rains, the park's birding must be quite unbelievable.

Then, when the pans fill up, open-billed, yellow-billed, marabou and saddle-billed storks arrive, with spoonbills, grey herons, egrets, three-banded and lots of blacksmith's plovers, pygmy and spur-winged geese, and many other waterbirds. Slaty egrets are seen in groups, a rare occurrence elsewhere.

Bob Stjernstedt, a Zambian birding expert, comments that Liuwa is relatively rarely visited, and so many more birds are sure to be added to this list. Secretary birds and Denham's and white-bellied bustards are common; and the park is famous for huge numbers of the migrant black-winged pratincoles, a finely-marked swift-like bird which is rare further east. Other 'specials' here include the pink-billed and clapper larks, rosy-breasted longclaw, swamp boubou, long-tailed widow, sharp-tailed starling and white-cheeked bee-eater. The plain is also a great area for raptors from the greater kestrel to bateleur and martial eagles, fish eagles and palmnut vultures. Pel's fishing owl is found along the rivers, the Luanginga to the south and the Luambimba to the north.

When to go – the migration The park is accessible by vehicle from about June to November – and it's worth visiting whenever you can get there; there's always some amazing wildlife to be seen! However, before you visit it's important to understand the weather and the game movements in the park.

From January to about May, a large area of the plain is covered in shallow water, and all the pans in the south of the park are full – perfect for the large herds of herbivores which gather there, and the large numbers of birds which also arrive. However, **around June/July** the plains dry up, the waters recede northwards, and gradually the herds move that way also. They desert the waterholes of the southern side of the plain, and move back northwest, eventually melting back into the woodlands which surround the park. Plenty of resident wildlife remains, relying on a scattering of pans which retain their water for most of the year.

From August to October the herds start drifting southwards again. At first, in September, you'll find just a few herds, typically just a few hundred wildebeest, venturing south onto the northern areas of the plain – but gradually as the rains approach these increase in number and move further south into the park.

In November and December the first rains are falling, and the plains are teeming with game. November is classically the best time to visit the park – a balance between catching the best of the game, and yet avoiding any danger of getting permanently stuck in deep mud.

For those who are feeling seriously adventurous, the park is accessible from around February to May by walking and canoeing. If you're thinking of this then you should contact the park's team in advance to arrange boats and local guides. (Don't underestimate what a serious trip this would be!)

Getting there

From Kalabo First head to the office on the 'harbour' (✪ HARKAL 14°59.248'S; 22°41.001'E) to get your permits, then take the pontoon across the Luanginga River. This manual pontoon costs Kw25,000 per crossing, plus Kw5,000 tax; there's usually an adjacent rowing boat which ferries pedestrians.

On the north side of the pontoon, the track splits and you should head for route markers, ✪ LIUWAP 14°59.044'S; 22°40.900'E, which you'll pass after barely 500m, and then for ✪ LIUWA2 14°57.718'S; 22°40.119'E, which is a further 3km away. You'll then be on the right track. There are a few small villages, but little game along the early part of this drive. The route is frequented by many lilac-breasted rollers, which brighten up the tops of trees along the roadside, giving dazzling flashes of blue as they fly.

Beneath you is deep Kalahari sand, and the driving is a very steady, slow plod in low-range third or fourth gear, with an average speed of about 15km/h. From the pontoon it's about 13km north and slightly east to the park entrance (✪ LIUWAP 14°53.234'S; 22°39.102'E) – which consists of a simple signboard.

Shortly afterwards there is a small fork in the track (✪ LIFORK 14°52.366'S; 22°38.803'E), from which both branches continue into the park. The right branch takes you on a track which continues all the way to Matamanene Camp – and given the increased traffic that is likely to travel this way, this might be the best one to follow.

However, on my last visit I took the left branch, which continues towards waypoint ✪ LIUWA3 14°50.594'S; 22°37.971'E. As you get further into the park the trees start to spread out, grouping themselves into small, slightly raised islands, surrounded by a sea of knee-to-thigh-deep golden grass. Carry on for a further 10km or so after the entrance board to ✪ LIUWA4 14°47.287'S; 22°37.484'E, by which time you're basically out of the trees, and onto the southern edge of the plain. Here, the track into the park starts to become much less distinct – and ultimately vanishes. (If you're coming back out of the park, then head for this point to pick up the track out.)

Whichever fork you take, you should expect two or three hours of rough, sandy driving after you leave the pontoon before you are well into the park. The good news is that although getting into the park is a slow slog through deep sand, most of the tracks within the park are generally much firmer, easier and more pleasant to drive. Enjoy!

🏠 **Where to stay** Over the years, several operators have tried to set up permanent camps in Liuwa. All have failed; it's just too remote. There was also a time when a few companies operated mobile safaris here – notably Robin Pope Safaris, Chilongozi and the nearby Tiger Camp. All have now given up.

Now, however, several campsites have been established as a joint venture between the community and African Parks, thus making the park accessible if you are in a position to drive yourself in a small expedition. Remember, though, that you must be totally self-sufficient, and that you should bring sufficient food for your scout as well as for your own party. Water is provided from wells at the three main campsites.

Campsites (m *097 7158733;* e *liuwa@africanparks.co.zm; www.liuwaplain.com; US$10 pp*) There are four designated community campsites around the park, three of them within a 15km radius of Matamenene Camp, along the wildebeest migration route.

Each of the sites, except Sikale, has two showers, two toilets, a washbasin (all upgraded in 2006) and water from a well, as well as a small craft shop stocking baskets, mats, carvings and other traditional items. No more than 5 vehicles can be accommodated on each site at any one time. You can pick up plastic bags from African Parks in Kalabo, so bring all your rubbish out; you're not allowed to collect firewood in the park, so buy firewood and/or charcoal in as you pass though Kalabo. Note that half of the fee for camping goes to the African Parks Community Fund, with the rest going towards the running of the camp.

It is sometimes possible to arrange for traditional dances to take place at the campsites or for visitors to be invited to a nearby village. For those interested in fishing, traditional techniques can be demonstrated or even taught, while other options include boat trips or guided walks, the latter with an armed scout.

⚔ Kwale (⊕ KWALE 14°49.03'S; 022°41.01'E). Situated 22.1km (1hr) from Kalabo in the southeast of the park, Kwale is a shady site bordering open grassland. The wildlife is at its best from the end of Oct.

⚔ Lyangu (⊕ LYANGU 14°46.49'S; 022°34.44'E). 26.4km (1½hrs) from Kalabo, in the southwest of the park. This woodland site with plenty of indigenous flora is within easy distance of the Lone Palm & several self-drive loops affording excellent birding & game viewing.

⚔ Katoyana (⊕ KATOYA 14°36.42'S; 022°42.08'E) Central location 49.9km (2½hrs) from Kalabo.

⚔ Sikale (⊕ SIKALE 14°17.56'S; 022°33.15'E). The newest of the park's campsites, 81km (3½hrs) from Kalabo, Sikale is an isolated spot at the northern edge of the park, in an area that is 'teeming with wildebeest & zebra' between Aug & Oct. There are no facilities here at all.

Getting around independently Game drive loops have been designated for independent visitors, and there's a tourism liaison officer on hand to guide visitors around the park.

If you register with African Parks at Kalabo on the way in, then there's no real need to take a scout as a guide – provided that you're fully equipped with a reliable GPS and have a back-up plan in case of an emergency (see *Safety precautions* below).

However, if you do take a guide, then you may learn quite a bit from him, as well as helping the park with a valuable extra source of employment.

Safety precautions A GPS system is just about essential for anyone planning to visit the park as landmarks are few and the tall grass can obscure views. Early in the year it's important to have netting on your vehicle to stop grass seeds which will clog up your radiator and may combust (see *Driving through high grass*, on page 107). It's also wise in a park that's this remote to travel in convoy, with a reliable satphone in case of emergency.

Useful spots in Liuwa Plain Liuwa is all about exploring on your own – and although you're requested to stick to existing roads where possible you're still allowed to head off on your own into areas where there are no roads. That said, there are a couple of spots worth noting:

- ⊕ WATER1 14°45.334'S; 22°37.395'E This great waterhole seemed to be a magnet for cranes, with a huge flock of crowned cranes always around it, augmented by parties of wattled cranes.
- ⊕ WATER2 14°44.848'S; 22°37.279'E Another lovely spot which was generally quieter, though did seem to be visited daily by a herd of red lechwe.
- ⊕ 1PALM 14°40.876'S; 22°35.388'E This is the spot known as 'Lone Palm', for obvious reasons. There's also a huge waterhole here where the general birding was excellent.

NORTHWESTERN ZAMBIA

West of the Copperbelt, squeezed between Angola and DRC, this area is distant from most of Zambia. This is reflected in its flora and fauna which, in parts, are much more like those of the wet tropical forests which occur to the north than those of the drier areas of the Kalahari to the south.

Despite being out on a limb, the roads here generally work well, with a tar road from the Copperbelt to Mwinilunga and another being constructed over the top of the good gravel road known as the M8, which links Solwezi with Zambezi.

KABOMPO This small town built beside the surging Kabompo River, in the sparsely-populated northwest, is at the centre of Zambia's remaining teak forests – but otherwise fairly unremarkable. There is a long-established Catholic mission here, a hospital, a post office, a branch of the Finance Bank, several small shops and a handful of resthouses. As for fuel, diesel is generally available, but petrol only occasionally, though it's probably wise not to rely on it.

Getting there and away Navigating to and from Kabompo (⊕ KABOMP 13°35.610'S; 24°12.125'E) is very easy, as it's on the main M8 road. However, if you're heading from here northwards, to Mwinilunga, then that turning is easy to miss. First drive northeast about 27km towards the busy roadside town of Manyinga (⊕ MANYIN 13°25.095'S; 24°19.901'E). The main road through this spread-out settlement crosses two bridges – over the Kabompo River on the east side, and over the Manyinya River to the west.

The turn-off north to Mwinilunga (⊕ TUMWIN 13°26.082'S; 24°19.978'E) is west of both of these bridges – and not between them, as the maps suggest. (There's no ferry here either, as marked on some maps; I think the bridges have replaced it!) It's a good gravel road but there's no signpost so it's easy to miss; you may need to ask for local help to find it.

After about 4.5km this splits; the road to Mwinilunga takes the right fork over the tributary, and then bends back to the left, heading roughly north-northwest with the Manyinya River on its left. See the section on getting to Mwinilunga, page 485, for more about this road.

Where to stay and eat Aside from the mission's own accommodation, there are three guesthouses in town. The government resthouse and the district resthouse are exceedingly basic. If you need to pick up some food, you might try the appropriately named 'Last Resort Restaurant', in town.

ZAMBEZI The road from Kabompo, the M8, is a remarkably good gravel road (gradually being tarred), with relatively few villages and lots of thick teak forests along it. In the dry season the smoke from occasional bush fires will be seen drifting in the sky, above areas of scorched and blackened ground. Note that, like many regional centres in Zambia, Zambezi is referred to locally as 'the boma'.

Zambezi is a small town with a few very basic shops, a mission, a telecommunications centre (Zambia's PTC) and a small local market. There is just one fuel station, with erratic supplies. Diesel is more reliable than petrol, albeit at a very expensive Kw80,000–10,000 per litre. There are disturbing reports from this area of watered-down petrol from illicit sources – known as 'bush fuel' – being sold to unsuspecting travellers. This makes it even more essential, if you're driving into this area, to do so with very large reserves of fuel.

Note on security Because tourists are rare, and the border with Angola is a sensitive one, travellers going west or north from Zambezi should report to the local police – just to let them know that they're here. Perhaps going into the police station to inquire 'if it is safe to proceed' is the easiest way to do this. It will allow them to ask you questions if they wish, and reassure them that you mean no harm and are not there to cause problems.

Getting there and away
From Lukulu See *From Lukulu to Kasempa*, on page 469, for the road to Watopa pontoon (⊕ FERRY4 14°2.338'S; 23°37.744'E), and note that this pontoon is incorrectly marked on the ITM map of Zambia. Then it is 20km north to the M8 road at Mumbeji (⊕ MUMBEJ 13°51.653'S; 23°40.327'E), and a further 75km west and northwest to Zambezi.

This good M8 road continues to the Angolan border, at Chavuma, and there are plans to tar it.

 Where to stay There is one simple hotel here, the **Zambezi Motel** (✆ *021 8371123*; $), and an even more basic (and cheaper) **government resthouse**, but a new guesthouse was under construction in 2007.

What to see and do
Traditional dancing A few kilometres north of town are the palaces of the Lunda and the Luvale senior chiefs, on the east and west sides of the road respectively – as you might predict from the rough distribution of languages mapped out in *Chapter 2*, page 21. The Luvale chief's palace is not only the venue for the Likumbi Lya Mize (see page 27), but also for traditional dancing which is held here several times a week.

MAKISHI DANCERS

Judi Helmholz

Sometimes in Mongu, or whilst travelling in the north of the western provinces, you will encounter colourfully clad characters adorned with fearsome costumes – Makishi dancers. For the uninitiated (defined as women and children in Luvale society), these are traditionally believed to be female spirits from the dead, and most will talk in high voices and even have 'breasts' made of wire.

The creative and artistic skills of the Luvale people are reflected in the wide variety of mask styles worn by the Makishi. These are huge constructions, often made of bark and wood and frequently coloured with red, white and black. Even helicopter blades are sometimes spotted in the designs – a memory of the war in Angola.

Each Likishi (the singular of Makishi) dancer is distinctive and plays a specific role within the various ceremonies and festivals. For example, the Mungali, or hyena, depicts menacing villains, whilst the Chikishikishi, a monster with a boiling pot, represents discipline – and will consume mischievous members of society.

Apart from their occasional appearances throughout the land, the Makishi dancers play central roles during two of the most important ceremonies of Luvale culture: the Mukanda and the Wali. These are the initiation rites for boys and girls respectively.

The Mukanda, also known as circumcision camps, are traditional 'schools' for local boys, aged from 12 to 17, where they are introduced to adult life and circumcised. The dancer known as 'Chileya cha Mukanda', which literally means 'the fool of the school', serves as a jester by mimicking the participants so as to relieve tension and anxiety before the circumcision ceremony. The girls attend a similar ceremony, though there is no physical clitoridectomy operation, as occurs in other cultures.

CHINYINGI SUSPENSION BRIDGE

with thanks to Richard Miller, Cheshire, Connecticut, USA

The Chinyingi Mission was founded to minister to villagers on both sides of the Zambezi, bringing them education and health care. However, at this point the river is over 210m wide, and subject to annual flooding, yet the only means of crossing it in the early days of the mission was by dugout canoe.

When he first arrived at the mission, Brother Crispin was responsible for transport, maintenance and cooking, and in order to help bring heavy supplies as well as people over the river he introduced a pontoon ferry. However, in 1971 four people were drowned while bringing a woman to hospital in a dug-out canoe, and he vowed to prevent any further accident by building a bridge over the river. While his was an unlikely background for the engineering feat he had undertaken, Brother Crispin didn't lack faith. From a picture of a suspension bridge in India that he had seen in *National Geographic*, he set to work, identifying people who could help him in the design of the bridge, sourcing the materials, and securing funds to pay for the project. He pulled together a team of just five young labourers, then spent all his free time working alongside them; for safety reasons, no work was undertaken unless he was present.

The project was not without significant setbacks. At just 6m high, the original towers at each end of the bridge proved to be too low for the cables to span the river at the right height, and had to be rebuilt twice to reach the necessary 18m. The suspension cables, when first hung, swung wildly, until Brother Crispin was advised to install guy wires to hold them in place. And every element of the supplies had to be trucked up to 800km across unforgiving terrain in all weathers. Little wonder that it took over five years for the bridge to be completed.

The result, though, has stood the test of time. Since its opening in 1977, the 300m bridge has continued to provide a lifeline to people on the opposite side of the river to the mission, and a supply line for the mission itself. While Brother Crispin has now returned to his native Italy, as many as 500 people a day continue to cross the 1m wide metal walkway (the original wood was replaced by Brother Crispin before he left), that he and his team suspended some 13m above the waters. They come on foot, on bicycles, and even on mopeds, up to 60 at a time, taking for granted the work of a Capuchin monk who built their bridge on faith.

Chinyingi Mission About a third of the way from Zambezi to Chavuma, just after the Makondu River, is a major track heading west and leading to the Chinyingi Mission. If you miss this turning then there is another, better-signposted turning a few kilometres later.

The mission is located on the west side of the river, and runs a school and a rural health centre. It is perhaps most famous for the Chinyingi suspension bridge – one of only four bridges to span the width of the Zambezi anywhere along its length at the time of its construction (see box above), though a fifth, at Sesheke, has since been built. The mission is run by Capuchin brothers. They are helpful and usually jovial, and will happily tell you more about the area and the mission if you ask them.

CHAVUMA Chavuma stands about 6km south of the Angolan border and the place where the Zambezi re-enters Zambia. The land around here is arid, and the soil mostly grey in colour, which makes villages in this area look dull compared with those further south. Proximity to the border means that the town has attracted a number of illegal Angolan diamond sellers.

As in the town of Zambezi, paying your respects to the local police is a wise move, just so that they know who you are and what you are doing in their area. The same goes for the Brethren Missionaries, who will also be able to help you with advice on camping or accommodation. They are found in a large compound up on the hill by the town. They have their own camping spot by the river, which they may allow you to use, and they will certainly be able to direct you to other suitable places.

Fuel supplies are very intermittent, so it's important not to rely on filling up here.

Getting there The M8 road here from Solwezi via Kabompo and Zambezi is a decent gravel road. If you're approaching from the south via Lukulu then it's best to cross the Kabompo River at the Watopa pontoon (✪ FERRY4 14°2.338'S; 23°37.744'E) and then join this road from there. See *From Lukulu to Kasempa* on page 469.

What to see and do
Chavuma Falls This is not nearly so spectacular as the Zambezi's drops at Ngonye and Victoria Falls, but makes a good picnic site for an afternoon – the falls are found by taking the footpath near the pontoon.

No man's land Every morning there is a small market here in no man's land, between the territories of Zambia and Angola. Both Zambians and Angolans come to barter for goods, under the watchful eyes of the armed border guards. It is a fascinating occurrence. As a foreigner, make sure you have very clear permission from the border guards before you even consider joining in, and don't take any photographs without permission.

WEST LUNGA NATIONAL PARK Some 150km northwest of Kafue, as the pied crow flies, West Lunga is another of Zambia's parks which is very wild and little visited. It was originally gazetted as a game reserve in the late 1940s, mainly to preserve its population of yellow-backed duiker. Then elephants were also abundant, along with a multitude of antelope species including Angolan (giant) sable and Lichtenstein's hartebeest. There was big game here – including buffalo, lion and leopard – but probably never in the volumes found in the Luangwa or Kafue. However, in the last few decades it's been used very little, except as an area for hunting and fishing by the local communities, and so has been off the map for most visitors.

There are signs that, possibly, with a lot of dedication and hard work, it might be coming back to life. In 2002, several local stakeholders formed the West Lunga Development Trust, to try to conserve some of this pristine corner of Zambia. The advantage that they have here is that the surrounding population density is relatively low, and it is almost entirely adjacent to the main roads. So with the help and drive of the local chiefs, they've been able to mobilise many of the local communities into 'Village Action Groups' to help patrol and monitor the environment. Community Resource Boards (CRBs) are currently being formed which will eventually control the natural resources in each of the surrounding areas, and derive a financial benefit from any operations there.

Game counting is now under way, and together with ZAWA there are signs that a new era might be starting here.

Geography, flora and fauna West Lunga National Park covers 1,684km² of forests, dambos, open grasslands and papyrus swamps. It is bounded by the Kabompo River to the east and south (adjacent to which are most of the park's swamps) and

15

CRYPTOSEPALUM FORESTS AND THE WHITE-CHESTED TINKERBIRD

Almost exclusive to Zambia, *Cryptosepalum* forests are distinctive dry evergreen forests which occur in the area of the Kabompo River. They are regarded by botanists as forming the largest area of tropical evergreen forest in Africa outside the equatorial zone.

Dominating these forests is the mukwe tree, *Cryptosepalum pseudotaxus*, which grows on relatively infertile Kalahari sand, where there is no permanent surface water. This lack of water means that these areas remain relatively uninhabited. Other trees often found here include the much-exploited rosewood, *Guibourtia coleosperma*, and, further south, the character of these forests gradually changes and they become dominated by Zambezi teak trees, *Baikiaea plurijuga* (see *The demise of the teak forests*, page 426). Hence logging is a serious threat to them.

The under-storey in *Cryptosepalum* forests is usually dense and tangled, including *Liana* and *Combretum* species which form impenetrable thickets. Epiphytic lichens are common, and the forest floor is mainly covered in mosses. It's very difficult to walk through unless a path has already been cleared.

The avifauna is usually particularly rich, with a mixture of bird species which frequent moist evergreen forests, woodlands and riverine forests. Amongst specials found in these forests are gorgeous bush shrikes, crested guineafowls, purple-throated cuckoo-shrikes, Margaret's batises and square-tailed drongos. However, the area is famous amongst ornithologists for the controversy surrounding its one and only endemic species: the white-chested tinkerbird. Only one of these birds has ever been found, and that was the 'type specimen' netted in 1964. Numerous subsequent attempts to find more have failed.

Some feel that they have simply been defeated by the dense foliage, and that a population of these birds exists deep within the thickets. Others argue that the one specimen found was probably an aberrant individual of the similar golden-rumped tinkerbird, which also occurs in these forests. Whatever the truth, it makes these forests a magnet for birdwatchers, all keen to catch a glimpse of the world's second white-chested tinkerbird!

by the West Lunga River to the west. The environment is still pristine miombo, interspersed with large grassland plains, flooded dambos and some particularly attractive *Cryptosepalum* forests.

It's very beautiful and wild, but the grass and vegetation are thick and difficult even to walk through. The rivers that flow through the park are great for canoeing and boating – with some sections of rapids, and some where you canoe beside rock walls.

Buk's 1993–94 survey (see *Appendix 3*, page 512) reported two sightings of wild dog in West Lunga, although noted that poaching remained heavy and the species was probably declining here. Rob Munro reports that he saw buffalo, impala, puku and warthog in the park on a trip in mid-1999.

More recently, in mid-2004, Dorian Tilbury (a first-class guide with a long history in Zambia's more remote areas) reported confirmed sightings of puku, hippo, crocodile, vervet monkey, yellow baboon and numerous excellent sightings of samango monkey, plus spoor of bushbuck, bush pig, cane rat, thick-tailed bushbaby, civet and genet. The scouts at Jivundu believe that there are also buffalo, roan, sable, hartebeest, impala, eland and elephant here. It's also quite likely that there will be a few sitatunga, blue, common and yellow-backed duiker and defassa waterbuck around. There are probably no lion or leopard remaining, though both certainly used to occur here.

Of course with an untouched environment, the birding remains excellent – and even a short visit along the rivers should yield sightings of half-collared kingfishers, African finfoots and large numbers of black saw-wing swallows amongst many more common species. Zambia's turacos do well here, with Schalow's and Ross's more common than the grey lourie.

Getting there The easiest ways to get to West Lunga are either to approach from the Copperbelt or to skirt Kafue National Park's eastern boundary and proceed through Kasempa. Approaching from Mongu is very time-consuming and slow-going – with a good 4x4 essential even in the dry season.

From the Copperbelt Take the tar road through Kitwe and Chingola to Solwezi (✪ SOLWEZ 12°10.931'S; 26°23.960'E), from where it turns south until crossing the Mutanda River at Mwelemu (✪ MWELEM 12°23.661'S; 26°14.276'E). On the other side of the river, there's a good tar road on the right, which heads west to Mwinilunga. The road continues south, towards Kabompo and Kasempa – so take this road. After almost 90km it is joined from the east by a road coming from Kitwe (which would have made a shorter, but more time-consuming, approach), via the village of Ingwe.

About 16km later there is a road left to Kasempa, and one straight on to Kabompo (✪ KABOMP 13°35.610'S; 24°12.125'E). Take the road going straight. This is the section of the M8 where tarring has been started, and by July 2004 it had reached about 20km west of that junction – and is a super road. The tar is gradually moving west of here, but the remainder of the M8 to Kabompo is a good gravel road, albeit with a few pot-holes. Driving carefully, you can average 50–60km/h on this.

After 140km there is a signpost to turn right to the small village of Jivundu, which is 12km away on a good sand track, on the south bank of the Kabompo River. Jivundu is the local headquarters for West Lunga's ZAWA, and that's where you pay entrance fees, and arrange for a scout to accompany you. There is an airstrip here, and nearby is the ferry across to the north bank of the Kabompo, and into the park.

From Kafue Follow the directions in *Chapter 14*, pages 408–9, to approach Kasempa from Mumbwa via the Lubungu and Lunga pontoons, then head north from Kasempa onto the road from Mwelemu to Kabompo. (Note there is never fuel at Kasempa!) Alternatively, take the tar road to Kitwe and Solwezi, and then cut southwest; this is likely to be easier and probably faster.

What to see and do Check with the National Parks and Wildlife Service for the latest news about the park (there is an office at Solwezi if you are approaching from the north), and also possibly with Mwinilunga Ventures (see below). It's still an exceptionally wild park – so you will require an independent streak to get here, and get around.

On dry land If you want to just drop in on your own then it's probably best to leave your vehicle at Jivundu, under the watchful eyes of the scouts, and take a scout/guide from there to walk with you into the park for a few days. The pontoon across the river is working, and ZAWA have cleared about 20km of road through the park from the south. This is part of an effort to open the road from Jivundu through the park to Ntambu, in the north, which is then within reach of the Solwezi–Mwinilunga road.

Canoeing The rivers here are in stunning condition. For water-based exploration, Charles Rae of Mwinilunga Ventures (✆ *021 8361076;* f *021 8361033;* e *crea@*

A personal view of canoeing the West Lunga, from Dorian Tilbury

> Twisting and turning, your feelings are burning,
> You're breaking the girl … she loves no one else …

The song rolls around my head like the incessant chant of some rhythmic revolution; and it's not from listening to the Red Hot Chili Peppers either. We've been on the road around Zambia for some time and don't have the track in our collection but we spent the night with a Peace Corps volunteer in a village outside Kasempa and he played us a tune one night … strummed his guitar around the dancing firelight and sang the Chili Peppers song. It stuck.

This mission is an odd one. There are two girls involved, one whom I would love to break, the other I would most definitely not. The latter is my wife, newly wed and the single most important person in my life; the former is the West Lunga River down which we are canoeing for the next six days … twisting and turning … my fears are returning … I'm breaking the girl …

There is no road for resupply or extraction, no radio communication, no boat, no village, no Burger King drive-through if it all gets too much. Once we launch our canoe we are committed to the river, to the exit point six days and more than 70km away. But we are well prepared and once we're in and drifting with the oscillating current, we're twisting and turning … our senses enduring … we're breaking the girl …

The water is crystal clear, cutting its snaking path through this emphatic and wild terrain. The banks are high, sometimes even carved from black rock, sheer and straight, almost overbearing in grace and stature. Freaky euphorbias and silver figs emerge from the granite, their roots entwined through crags and crevices, creeping and drifting down secret passages until somewhere their food source is found. When there are no rocks, the banks bulge and swell with matted trees all clambering for a front-row seat, a room with a view, a perch on the edge of this marvellous show. Everything, it seems, was caught suspended in time making a rush for this river. It is so outlandishly beautiful that to miss any part of the spectacle is to miss life itself.

We cannot see through the trees, the world no longer exists outside the river. We creep down this mystic rhythm with just the noise of our paddles gliding the surface and a multitude of birds flashing blues and yellows, scarlets and purples, every colour of every rainbow on temporary display. Schalow's lourie, half-collared kingfisher, African finfoot and black saw-wing swallows provide the entertainment and make up the pixels within this big picture charade. And all the while, pyjama-clad samango monkeys dance through the trees, turn and look, then sheepishly disappear.

We don't know what awaits us with this girl … we hit rapids and rock pools, hippos and croc dives. We catch glimpses of memories … just a flash then they're gone … evidence of poachers in the shadows of a distant past, long since departed along with the game. There are times when it is almost silent and eerie, the forgotten relic of a time gone by, a time of animal crowding. One day perhaps the forests will again echo and cry with the howl of territory calls, the crack of feeding branches, the whistles of alarm. But for now, the silent majesty flows her irrefutable path down a million years of creation. She carries her life blood and snakes her course, relinquishing the secrets of her past, oblivious to the prospect of her future … twisting and turning … her feelings are burning … we're breaking the girl …

zamtel.zm) used to organise a variety of canoeing and camping trips from one-, two- or three-days to two weeks. Charles Rae grew up in the area, visiting the park since he was a child, and originally ran canoeing trips just for his family (some of whom have been right down the West Lunga, Kabompo and Zambezi rivers to Victoria Falls by canoe – taking 52 days!). We have been unable to contact Charles for this edition, but it's always worth a try.

Canoeists need to bring their own bedding and drinks. It's important that you can swim and take care of yourself, since the guides here are not veteran white-water guides and there are some Class 3 rapids (so it's almost certain that you'll find yourself out of the canoe at some point!). Trips run from about May to the end of October.

One long trip on this river starts about 30km south of Mwinilunga, and takes six days of hard paddling to get to Jivundu. Note though that these are organised in a fairly ad hoc way; they're not regular fixtures, and won't have all the back-up and experience of, for example, the Zambezi's highly experienced canoe operators. Once you start canoeing down this almost 'virgin' river, it would be exceedingly difficult to get you out before the end, even in case of an emergency. There is virtually no road access, and you're miles from anyone who could help. So if you come to canoe, expect a mini-expedition: bring your own safety equipment and a sense of adventure.

MWINILUNGA Mwinilunga is a large, thriving outpost of a town, raised up in the remote northwest corner of Zambia. In the town you'll (usually) find fuel, as well as shops with basic supplies and a sizeable local market, several banks, including a Finance Bank, a large post office, a few outposts for aid agencies, a small Franciscan mission, and a choice of basic local resthouses.

Getting there and away By far the easiest way to get to Mwinilunga is via the Copperbelt, Chingola and Solwezi. To reach it, travel through Chingola and then take the turn to Solwezi. This is tarmac, but in a variable state of repair.

About 28km after Solwezi there's a junction at Mwelemu (✈ MWELEM 12°23.661'S; 26°14.276'E). Mwinilunga is signposted to the right, and from there it's about 288km of largely reasonable tarmac away. Eventually you'll descend a hill, cross the West Lunga River, and drive into town. Beyond the tar, a good gravel road leads north into DRC via Ikelenge. Alternatively, head for Angola via Kalene Hill, and the border at Jimbe Bridge just over 100km away.

From Kabompo See Kabompo's section on *Getting there and away* (pages 477–8) to locate the turn-off for Mwinilunga from the M8 (✈ TUMWIN 13°26.082'S; 24°19.978'E). Then after 4.5km, take the right fork, and bend around left. It's a beautiful drive here along a good but narrow road on which you can average about 30–40km/h in the dry season. On either side are occasional subsistence farming communities, and large areas of forest. It does cross one or two large dambos, which could be very sticky during the rainy season.

Note that this route does go relatively close to Angola, and you'd be well advised to check the security situation locally before coming this way. Equally, don't be tempted to divert off to the west of the road unless you know exactly where you're going.

After about 49km it passes the village of Lunsongwe (✈ LUNSON 13°2.068'S; 24°13.385'E), where there's a school and a small grocery shop. (It is spelled 'Lusongwa' on some maps.) Around 54km later, you pass the very spread-out village of Kanyilambi, notable mainly for its church and beautiful silvery fields of rice – and then you're almost halfway to Mwinilunga.

Continuing north, the forests and other vegetation start to get thicker whilst the atmosphere becomes perceptibly warmer and more humid – despite the slight but steady rise in altitude. In places the forest is thick enough for the canopy of trees over the track to interlock – and for some of the birding 'specials' found in Mwinilunga to occur here too.

Eventually you reach a T-junction (✪ TUKABO 11°45.158'S; 24°26.114'E) with the main Mwinilunga–Solwezi tar road, and the centre of town is a few kilometres west. In the dry season it takes about five hours to cover this 219km from Kabompo.

🏠 **Where to stay** Mwinilunga has an assortment of very unremarkable places to sleep and/or eat, all fairly inexpensive, though most visitors will simply stop to refuel then proceed straight to Hillwood Farm and Nchila Reserve.

If you do wish to stay, you could try the **Muzina Guest House** (☏ *021 8361002*). For campers, a better alternative would be the new campsite at the source of the Zambezi (see page 490), or perhaps:

🏠 **Mwinilunga Riverside Guesthouse** Opposite the turning from the tar road to go south to Kabompo, open-sided rondavels are spread out on a grassy bank down to the river. As this is on the edge of town, campers should beware of petty theft.

HILLWOOD FARM AND NCHILA WILDLIFE RESERVE
Hillwood Farm is an improbable place. It's an oasis of peace and order in a corner of Zambia which the world's media might expect, given its position between Angola and the DRC, to be under permanent siege. What's more, within its bounds, Hillwood has a very special reserve, Nchila, which has flora and fauna that are unique to Zambia: it contains a slice of equatorial forest that's been preserved and nurtured. The family who own this farm, the Fishers, have been working in close partnership with the local communities here for generations.

In short, although it's exceedingly 'out of the way' by anyone's standards, Hillwood is a totally fascinating place that's delightful to visit and contains some amazing wildlife. If you're anywhere near here, don't miss it!

Getting there and away To reach here from Mwinilunga, continue through town on the main road, past the turn-off to the airport. After about 7km, the road changes from tar to well-maintained gravel road. Over its course it then crosses a series of rivers, and you'll drive over four bridges. (Whilst you don't need a 4x4 for this in the dry season, there are several steep sections that could become tricky in the wet season.) In sequence, the rivers include Luakela, the Chitunta and the Kaseki.

About 47km from Mwinilunga there's a right turn that is clearly marked (✪ TUZAMB 11°23.321'S; 24°16.632'E). After about 4.6km, this leads to the source of the Zambezi (see page 490 for details). Then about 3km after that turning, you cross the final river, the Sakeji. About 9km after this there is a clear signpost to the right (✪ TUHILL 11°17.040'S; 24°16.663'E) proclaiming that Hillwood Farm and Nchila Wildlife Reserve are about 7km away. This final road felt a little like a local footpath through a village to us, but eventually you do reach Hillwood Farm (✪ HILLWO 11°14.989'S; 24°18.852'E) – an oasis of order.

Note that on the way from Mwinilunga to Hillwood you pass (although may not notice) the Luakela Forest Reserve and later Chitunta Plain, both of which have some of the birds which attract ornithologists to this corner of the country. Luakela Forest Reserve is noted for lots of bar-winged weavers, whilst Chitunta

Plain is very important for many species, including the Angola lark, Grimwood's longclaw, the dambo (black-tailed) cisticola, the black and rufous swallows and short-tailed pipits. Venture several kilometres up the stream there, and you've a good chance of seeing another very uncommon bird, Bocage's weaver.

Hillwood is about 68km from Mwinilunga and, if you don't stop for any birdwatching, will take a bit less than two hours to drive. Alternatively, Nchila can be reached by a short (though not very cheap) charter flight from Lusaka or (marginally less costly) from Lunga River Lodge in northern Kafue.

Where to stay Both the bushcamp and campsite are on the reserve, and reservations for both are virtually obligatory, otherwise they may not have the space, staff or supplies to accommodate you. Your two options are:

Nchila Bushcamp (3 chalets) e nchila@nchila-wildlife-reserve.com, nchilawildlife@iwayafrica.com; www.nchila-wildlife-reserve.com (✪ NCHILA 11°14.945'S; 24°19.642'E). Nchila's small bushcamp overlooks a large plain & dambo from the edge of riverine forest & miombo woodland. Recently upgraded, it can take a maximum of 6 people (8 if squeezed!) in well-furnished chalets with solid wooden furniture, stylish fabrics & imaginative touches. One stunning chalet, which wouldn't be out of place in the most stylish of lodges, has a king-size bed & a big en-suite bathroom, incorporating a large, slightly sunken bath beside the window, & a good shower. A good 2nd chalet has 2 twin rooms which share a bathroom, inc a flush toilet, shower & a bath with another shower over it. Both are spacious, built of stone with thatched roofs, & with water heated by wood-fired boilers. A smaller chalet (comfortable for 1 person, or 'cosy' for 2) has its own en-suite shower & toilet.

At the camp's heart is a thatched dining & lounge area, the two separated by a large log fire. With a lovely view over the dambo, it makes a pleasant place to sit & watch the wildlife. Behind, in a separate building, is the kitchen which is staffed by Nchila if you're on a fly-in trip & they are catering for you. The food is good but simple: very fresh wholesome farm fare. If you are driving yourself & can bring your own food & drink, then you can stay on a self-catering basis, & cook for yourself. While limited amounts of fresh produce are sometimes available from the farm (milk, cream, eggs, butter, beef & pork products, as well as lamb & game), all are dependent upon availability, so you must bring most of your own supplies, inc any packet or canned foods that you need. It's best to agree in advance with Nchila what you'd like them to provide if they can.

If you're self-catering, then a guide is available on request, & a 4x4 with driver can be hired with advance notice. A 90-min game drive costs about US$30 pp. US$75 pp sharing self-catering; US$250 pp inc FB & activities, both inc entry fee. ⏲ 15 May–15 Nov.

Å Nchila Campsite For contact details, see above. The tented camp, in a lovely shady spot next to the Sakeji River, has been completely rebuilt with new ablution block to include showers & flush toilets. There's also a dining area & a kitchen with a small stove, hot water, & lighting if required. Firewood is provided & a staff member is available to draw & heat water for showers. Some items of fresh produce may be available (see above). US$15 pp camping. ⏲ 15 May–15 Nov.

What to see and do Although most people will stay on the reserve, there is lots to see around the farm. Most people will also detour to the source of the Zambezi, and keen ornithologists will frequently head into the surrounding area in search of the 'specials' found in this corner of Zambia.

Hillwood Farm Zambian farms don't come much more remote or well established than Hillwood. Relatively speaking, it's had a lot of time to build up a very self-sufficient yet interdependent community of people.

Of interest here are the farm itself, which these days relies on beef and dairy cows, cereal and, increasingly, tourism to generate income. The orphanage and the school are also fascinating; the boarding school is used by some of Zambia's more affluent residents, so it's not at all impoverished by local standards.

15

Pete Fisher is Zambian – part of the fourth generation of Fishers in Zambia. Lynn, his wife, is Californian, but has always lived in Zambia. They live in the oldest house on Hillwood Farm with their two sons, Sonny and Christopher. Pete's father, Paul Fisher, and his sister Melanie, and her family, also live and work at Hillwood.

The history of the Fisher family is an interesting one, and inextricably linked with the development of the local area. The story begins in the late 19th century. Inspired by David Livingstone's and Fred Arnott's aspirations to end the slave trade in Africa by establishing Christianity and legitimate commerce in its place, Walter Fisher was a willing recruit to the missionary quest. In 1889, freshly qualified as a doctor and with a gold medal for surgery at Guy's Hospital, Walter Fisher left the UK with a party of seven other men and women, bound for the Angolan coast. Suffering from various hardships on arrival, the party moved out of Portuguese territory to Kalene Hill in Northern Rhodesia. Indeed, the ruins of the houses and store rooms they built in the Angolan style, with bricks made of baked anthill, can still be found there.

Kalene Hill eventually became the home of a mission hospital and an orphanage after Walter's wife, Anna Fisher, rescued a newborn baby. She found the child after it had been lying on its mother's grave for two days – where it had been placed as it was believed to have caused her death (the mother had died in childbirth). The orphanage is now on Hillwood Farm, in the care of Paul and Eunie Fisher, and its emphasis is on keeping a traditional African way of life so that the children can return to their village at about six years old. Until then, they are taught, fed and clothed to give them a good start. As has always been the case here, each baby comes with a female family member to assist with its care. There are currently 30 orphans; visitors are warmly welcomed. Esther Townsend and Helen Finney, two English orphanage mothers, currently manage the day-to-day needs of the orphanage.

In addition to the orphanage, Anna Fisher was also responsible for establishing the Nyamuweji village for old ladies, where they cultivated the land and were protected by the Fishers from customary witch-hunts. Such women, too old to work hard, often came for refuge. There remain six to eight women at Kalene, and they are more or less self-supporting.

Sakeji School started in 1925, next to Hillwood. It has a very wide catchment area for its size, made possible by road links and the well-maintained Sakeji Airstrip. The school teaches Grades 1 to 7 (Junior) and is funded and staffed by mainly Canadian and American missionary workers from an organisation called 'Christian Churches in Many Lands' (CCML). In 1962 the Bible was translated into Lunda by Singleton Fisher. A new version by Paul Fisher and Joan Hoyt is under way for the Zambian Bible House.

If you have the opportunity to chat with Pete, Lynn or Pete's father, Paul – do so. You'll get a fascinating insight into the area's past and present. They have always worked closely with the surrounding communities – Pete meets with the local village headmen once a month to inform, involve and share out the maintenance and development work on the reserve fairly between the villages. Roads, bridges, fences and shelters are all built and maintained with local labour and materials wherever possible. This 'Nchila Committee' also helps a great deal to prevent poaching, kept to a minimum thanks to the excellent rapport within the community as a whole. This is built on many years of talking together, mutual trust and help.

Nchila Wildlife Reserve (*www.nchila-wildlife-reserve.com*; ⊕ *15 May–15 Nov; entrance US$10 pp*). Nchila Wildlife Reserve is a 40km² area of virgin bush within the boundaries of Hillwood Farm. It's a great area for game drives and walks, always accompanied by a guide from Nchila (hence the need to book in advance). See below for more on the flora and fauna, but note that even if you're not a keen 'twitcher', the rolling country is very pleasant walking, with patches of evergreen forests adding a welcome touch of shade.

The prime time to visit is August to end-October for the birding.

Flora and fauna Nchila attracts a steady stream of ornithologists, herpetologists, zoologists and other keen observers of the natural world. Most come for the reserve's pockets of pristine wet, evergreen forest (rainforest). These are typical of large areas of its neighbouring countries – so you'll find species here which you can't see anywhere else, unless you're prepared to brave the instability of either Angola or the DRC.

Note that you'll find some exceedingly comprehensive details of Nchila's flora and fauna on the reserve's website so here I'll just mention a few of the more obvious highlights.

Flora This beautiful, rolling and hilly area has large areas of moist open plains dotted with termitaria. These are veined by miombo woodland and, in the lower areas, patches of wet, evergreen (mishutu) forest which surround many permanent streams.

Animals The larger wildlife here includes possibly Zambia's largest herd of sable antelope (some of which appear to have some genes in common with Angolan giant sables, given their appearance), and very good numbers of roan and eland that are generally very relaxed and approachable. In addition, there are Burchell's zebra, defassa waterbuck, impala, Lichtenstein's hartebeest, Kafue lechwe, puku and kudu. Oribi are very common on the plains, warthog are sometimes seen grubbing around, and there's a herd of blue wildebeest.

Sitatunga frequent the denser, wetter patches of forest – and, like the bushbuck which are found here, sometimes venture out along the edge of the open plains; it's here that I had one of the clearest sightings of these shy antelope that I've ever experienced. The Nchila team say that there are two different subspecies of sitatunga here: 'normal' sitatunga such as are found to the south in Zambia and the rest of southern Africa, and an 'Angolan' subspecies.

In the forest patches you'll find vervet and blue monkeys, as well as common and blue duiker. (With some luck and much skill, the guides can sometimes call the curious blue duiker in to approach you!)

Birdlife The birdlife here is a real draw; it's a very special place. The forests contain 30 species not found anywhere outside of the DRC, Angola and this area – most of which do not even occur around Mwinilunga (only 70km south of Nchila). However, for some of this area's 'specials' you may have to go a further 50km north to the very tip of Zambia – around the source of the Salujinga and the Jimbe. The borders with Angola and Congo are very sensitive – so take local advice before you venture that far.

The source of the Zambezi and the Sakeji River, which runs through Hillwood, is a microcosm of the DRC forests. Many of the birds which occupy ecological niches south of here are replaced by different, but closely related, species. The area's 'specials' often need work to spot, and a fair amount of searching with one of Nchila's guides who knows where to look. They include afep and bronze-naped pigeons; black-collared bulbuls; grey-winged robins; rufous ant thrushes; Fülleborne's and rosy-breasted longclaws; honeyguide greenbuls; shining blue, white-bellied and blue-breasted kingfishers; olive long-tailed cuckoos; orange-tufted, green-throated and Bates' sunbirds; buff-throated apalises; Laura's and bamboo warblers; white-cheeked bee-eaters; red-bellied paradise flycatchers; and splendid glossy starlings.

Excursions from Nchila The **Zambezi rapids** near to Hillwood are a very popular day trip – as a lovely spot to play in the water and float down on inflatable inner tubes. This is a particularly good place for birdwatchers to search for the rare Forbes plover, which hunts for insects on the bare rocks.

Further north, around the **source of the Jimbe River**, is the best place to look for the compact weaver and white-spotted flufftails; a recent sighting of the shrike flycatcher was a new discovery for Zambia.

Source of the Zambezi About 12km south of the entrance road to Nchila is a turn-off (⊕ TUZAMB 11°23.321'S; 24°16.632'E) to the official spot at Kalene Hill where the mighty Zambezi begins its 2,700km journey to the Indian Ocean. Though unexceptional, the site has been declared a national monument and the surrounding dense forest canopy, part of a 36.8ha reserve, is impressive.

At present, a copper plaque, unveiled in 1964 to celebrate Zambia's independence, marks the site, at an altitude of about 1,500m. In September 2007, however, it was announced that work was nearing completion on a US$300,000 visitor centre which is being built to attract tourists to the region. In addition to the centre, there will be a campsite (expect the rate to be US$10 per person, in line with other National Heritage Commission sites).

The short access road to the source is, in part, the boundary between Zambia and the DRC.

Appendix I

WILDLIFE GUIDE

This wildlife guide is designed in a manner that should allow you to name most large mammals that you see in Zambia. Less common species are featured under the heading *Similar species* beneath the animal to which they are most closely allied, or bear the strongest resemblance.

CATS AND DOGS

Lion *Panthera leo* Shoulder height 100–120cm. Weight 150–220kg.
Africa's largest predator, the lion is the animal that everybody hopes to see on safari. It is a sociable creature, living in prides of five to ten animals and defending a territory of 20–200km². Lions often hunt at night, and their favoured prey is large or medium antelope such as wildebeest and impala. Most of the hunting is done by females, but dominant males normally feed first after a kill. Rivalry between males is intense and takeover battles are frequently fought to the death, so two or more males often form a coalition. Young males are forced out of their home pride at three years of age, and cubs are usually killed after a successful takeover.

When not feeding or fighting, lions are remarkably indolent – they spend up to 23 hours of any given day at rest – so the anticipation of a lion sighting is often more exciting than the real thing. Lions naturally occur in any habitat, except desert or rainforest. They once ranged across much of the Old World, but these days they are all but restricted to the larger conservation areas in sub-Saharan Africa (one residual population exists in India).

Lions occur throughout Zambia, and are very common in the larger parks with better game densities – Luangwa (North and South), Kafue and Lower Zambezi. Spend a week in any of these with a good guide and you'd be unlucky not to see at least some lion! They occur in smaller numbers in the more marginal parks and GMAs, and more sparsely in areas with more human population.

Leopard *Panthera pardus* Shoulder height 70cm. Weight 60–80kg.
The powerful leopard is the most solitary and secretive of Africa's big cats. It hunts at night, using stealth and power, often getting to within 5m of its intended prey before pouncing. If there are hyenas and lions around then leopards habitually move their kills up into trees to safeguard them. The leopard can be distinguished from the cheetah by its rosette-like spots, lack of black 'tearmarks' and more compact, low-slung, powerful build.

The leopard is the most common of Africa's large felines. Zambia's bush is perfect for leopard, which are common throughout the country, as they favour habitats with plenty of cover, like riverine woodlands. Despite this, a good sighting in the wild during the day is unusual. In fact there are many records of individuals living for years, undetected, in

close proximity to humans. Sightings at night are a different story and, because Zambia's national parks allow night drives, it's probably Africa's best country for seeking leopard.

South Luangwa National Park was recently chosen by the BBC for the filming of their remarkable documentary, *Night of the Leopard*. Leopard sightings often become the main goal of night drives there. Your chances of spotting them are equally good in the Lower Zambezi, whilst consistently first-class sightings are also reported from Lufupa Lodge in Kafue. Remarkably they usually seem unperturbed by the presence of a vehicle and spotlight, and will often continue whatever they are doing regardless of an audience. Watching a leopard stalk is captivating viewing.

Cheetah *Acynonix jubatus* Shoulder height 70–80cm. Weight 50–60kg.

This remarkable spotted cat has a greyhound-like build, and is capable of running at 70km per hour in bursts, making it the world's fastest land animal. Despite superficial similarities, you can easily tell a cheetah from a leopard by the former's simple spots, disproportionately small head, streamlined build, diagnostic black tearmarks, and preference for relatively open habitats. It is often seen pacing the plains restlessly, either on its own or in a small family group consisting of a mother and her offspring. Diurnal hunters, cheetah favour the cooler hours of the day to hunt smaller antelope, like steenbok and duiker, and small mammals like scrub hares.

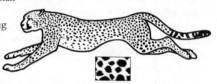

Zambia has a small but growing population of cheetah, centred on Kafue National Park. They're very rare in the Luangwa, and have recently been reintroduced into the Lower Zambezi (though with mixed success).

Similar species: The **serval** (*Felis serval*) is smaller than a cheetah (shoulder height 55cm) but has a similar build and black-on-gold spots giving way to streaking near the head. Seldom seen, it is widespread and quite common in moist grassland, reed beds and riverine habitats throughout Africa, including Zambia. It does particularly well in some of the swampier areas, and Lechwe Lodge reports a particularly high number of them, attracted by the prevalence of cane rats in the Kafue River. Servals prey on mice, rats and small mammals, but will sometimes take the young of small antelope.

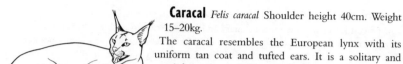

Caracal *Felis caracal* Shoulder height 40cm. Weight 15–20kg.

The caracal resembles the European lynx with its uniform tan coat and tufted ears. It is a solitary and mainly nocturnal hunter, feeding on birds, small antelope and young livestock. Found throughout the subcontinent, it easily adapts to a variety of environments and even occurs in some of Zambia's populated areas. Despite this, being nocturnal it is rarely seen. Caracals normally stalk their prey as closely as possible, before springing with surprise.

Similar species: The smaller **African wild cat** (*Felis sylvestris*) is found from the Mediterranean to the Cape of Good Hope, and is similar in appearance to the domestic tabby cat and a little larger. It has an unspotted torso, a ringed tail and a reddish-brown tinge to the back of its ears. Wild cats are generally solitary and nocturnal, often utilising burrows or termite mounds as daytime shelters. They prey upon reptiles, amphibians and birds as well as small mammals.

African wild dog *Lycaon pictus* Shoulder height 70cm. Weight 25kg.

Also known as the painted hunting dog, the wild dog is distinguished from other African dogs by its large size and mottled black, brown and cream coat. Highly sociable, living in packs of up to 20 animals, wild dogs are ferocious hunters that literally tear apart their prey on the run. They are now threatened with extinction, the most endangered of Africa's great predators. This is the result of relentless persecution by farmers, who often view the dogs as dangerous vermin, and their susceptibility to diseases spread by domestic dogs. Wild dogs are now extinct in many areas where they were formerly abundant, like the Serengeti, and they are common nowhere. The global population of fewer than 3,000 is concentrated in southern Tanzania, Zambia, Zimbabwe, Botswana, South Africa and Namibia.

Wild dogs prefer open savanna with only sparse tree cover, if any, and packs have enormous territories, typically covering 400km² or more. They travel huge distances in search of prey and so few parks are large enough to contain them. In Zambia wild dogs have their strongest base in Kafue, closely followed by the Luangwa, though even in these parks they are regarded as an uncommon sight. They are sometimes seen in Liuwa, Lower Zambezi and Sumbu areas. Elsewhere their existence is less certain.

Side-striped jackal *Canis adustus* Shoulder height 35–40cm. Weight 8–12kg.

Despite its prevalence in other areas of Africa, the side-striped jackal is common nowhere in Zambia although occurring throughout the country. It is greyish in colour and has an indistinct pale horizontal stripe on each flank and often a white-tipped tail. These jackals are most often seen singly or in pairs at dusk or dawn. They are opportunistic feeders, taking rats, mice, birds, insects, wild fruits and even termites. The side-striped jackal is Zambia's only species of jackal.

Spotted hyena *Crocuta crocuta* Shoulder height 85cm. Weight 70kg.

Hyenas are characterised by their bulky build, sloping back, rough brownish coat, powerful jaws and dog-like expression. Contrary to popular myth, spotted hyenas are not exclusively scavengers; they are also adept hunters, which hunt in groups and kill animals as large as wildebeests. Nor are they hermaphroditic, an ancient belief that stems from the false scrotum and penis covering the female hyena's vagina. Sociable animals, hyenas live in loosely structured clans of about ten animals, led by females who are stronger and larger than males, based in a communal den.

Hyenas utilise their kills far better than most predators, digesting the bones, skin and even teeth of antelope. This results in the distinctive white colour of their faeces – which is an easily identified sign of them living in an area.

The spotted hyena is the largest hyena, identified by its light brown, blotchily spotted coat. It is found throughout Zambia, though is increasingly restricted to the national parks and GMAs. Although mainly nocturnal, spotted hyenas can often be seen around dusk and dawn in the Luangwa, Kafue and Lower Zambezi. Their distinctive, whooping calls are a spine-chilling sound of the African night. Note that neither of the spotted hyena's close relatives, the brown hyena and aardwolf, are thought to occur in Zambia.

PRIMATES

Common baboon *Papio cynocaphalus cynocaphalus* Shoulder height 50–75cm. Weight 25–45kg. This powerful terrestrial primate, distinguished from any other monkey by its much larger size, inverted U-shaped tail and distinctive dog-like head, is fascinating to watch from a behavioural perspective. It lives in large troops that boast a complex, rigid social structure characterised by a matriarchal lineage and plenty of inter-troop movement by males seeking social dominance. Omnivorous and at home in almost any habitat, the baboon is the most widespread primate in Africa, frequently seen in most game reserves. With their highly organised defence system, the only predators that seriously affect baboons are leopard, which will try to pick them off at night, whilst they are roosting in trees.

There are three African races, regarded by some authorities as full species. The chacma baboon (*P. c. ursinus*) is grey and confined largely to areas south of the Zambezi. The yellow baboon (*P. c. cynocephalus*) is the yellow-brown race occurring in Zambia, northern Mozambique, Malawi, southern and eastern Tanzania and eastern Kenya. The olive or anubis baboon (*P. c. anubis*) is a hairy green-to-brown baboon found in Ethiopia, Uganda, northern Tanzania and Kenya.

Vervet monkey *Cercopithecus aethiops* Length (excluding tail) 40–55cm. Weight 4–6kg. Also known as the green or grivet monkey, the vervet is probably the world's most numerous monkey and certainly the most common and widespread representative of the *Cercopithecus* guenons, a taxonomically controversial genus associated with African forests. An atypical guenon in that it inhabits savanna and woodland rather than true forest, the vervet spends a high proportion of its time on the ground. It occurs throughout Zambia, preferring belts of tall trees and thicker vegetation within easy reach of water.

The vervet's light grey coat, black face and white forehead band are distinctive – as are the male's garish blue genitals. Vervets live in troops averaging about 25 animals; they are active during the day and roost in trees at night. They eat mainly fruit and vegetables, though are opportunistic and will take insects and young birds, and even raid tents at campsites (usually where ill-informed visitors have previously tempted them into human contact by offering food).

Blue monkey *Cercopithecus mitis* Length (excluding tail) 50–60cm. Weight 5–8kg. The blue monkey is known also as moloney's monkey in Zambia, the samango monkey throughout southern Africa, the golden monkey in southwest Uganda, Sykes' monkey in Kenya and the diademed or white-throated guenon in some field guides. This most variable monkey is divided by some authorities into several species. It is unlikely to be confused with the vervet monkey, as blue monkeys have a dark blue-grey coat, which becomes reddish towards its tail. Its underside is lighter, especially its throat.

These monkeys live in troops of up to ten animals and associate with other primates where their ranges overlap. They live in evergreen forests, and so are most likely to be seen around the Copperbelt and North Western Provinces, or north of Kasanka. However, they occur as far south as the Lower Zambezi National Park and are resident along the Luangwa's Muchinga Escarpment.

Angola black-and-white colobus monkey *Colobus angolensis* Length (excluding tail) 65cm. Weight 12kg.

This beautiful jet black monkey has bold white facial markings, a long white tail and white sides and shoulders. Almost exclusively arboreal, it is capable of jumping up to 30m, a spectacular sight with its white tail streaming behind. Several races have been described, and most authorities recognise this Angolan variety as a distinct species. In Zambia they are very rare, but have been reported from the forests north of Mwinilunga.

Bushbaby *Galago crassicaudatus* Length (excluding tail) 35cm. Weight 1–1.5kg.

The bushbaby is Zambia's commonest member of a group of small and generally indistinguishable nocturnal primates, distantly related to the lemurs of Madagascar. In Zambia they occur throughout the country, though are very seldom seen during the day. At night their wide, endearing eyes are often caught in the spotlight during night drives,

Bushbabies are nocturnal and even around safari camps they can sometimes be seen by tracing a cry to a tree and shining a torch into the branches; their eyes reflect as two red dots. These eyes are designed to function in what we would describe as total darkness, and they feed on insects – some of which are caught in the air by jumping – and also by eating sap from trees, especially acacia gum.

They inhabit wooded areas, and prefer acacia trees or riverine forests. I remember once being startled, whilst lighting a barbecue, by a small family of bushbabies. They raced through the trees above us, bouncing from branch to branch whilst chattering and screaming out of all proportion to their modest size.

Similar species: Lesser bushbaby *Galago senegalensis* Length (excluding tail) 17cm. Weight 150g. The lesser bushbaby, or night ape, is half the size of the bushbaby and seems to be less common than its larger cousin. Where it is found, it is often amongst acacia or terminalia vegetation, rather than mopane or miombo bush.

LARGE ANTELOPE

Sable antelope *Hippotragus niger* Shoulder height 135cm. Weight 230kg.

The striking male sable is jet black with a distinct white face, underbelly and rump, and long decurved horns – a strong contender for the title of Africa's most beautiful antelope. The female is chestnut brown and has shorter horns, whilst the young are a lighter red-brown colour. Sable are found throughout the wetter areas of southern and east Africa.

They are not common in Zambia. However, Kafue is probably the best park for sable, with Kasanka also worthy of note. They're confined to the foothills of the Muchinga Escarpment in the Luangwa, and so very rarely seen by visitors. Sumbu has a small population, as is reported from Sioma Ngwezi and West Lunga.

Sable are normally seen in small herds: either bachelor herds of males, or breeding herds of females and young which are often accompanied by the dominant male in that territory. The breeding females give birth around February or March; the calves remain hidden, away from the herd, for their first few weeks. Sable are mostly grazers, though will browse, especially when food is scarce. They need to drink at least every other day, and seem especially fond of low-lying dewy vleis in wetter areas.

Roan antelope *Hippotragus equinus* Shoulder height 120–150cm. Weight 250–300kg.

This handsome horse-like antelope is uniform fawn-grey with a pale belly, short decurved horns and a light mane. It could be mistaken for the female sable antelope, but this has a well-defined white belly, and lacks the roan's distinctive black-and-white facial markings. The roan is a relatively rare antelope; common almost nowhere in Africa (the Nyika Plateau being one obvious exception to this rule). In Zambia small groups of roan are found in South Luangwa, Kafue, Kasanka, Sumbu, Liuwa Plains and (probably) Sioma Ngwezi.

Roan need lots of space if they are to thrive and breed; they don't generally do well where game densities are high. Game farms prize them as one of the most valuable antelope (hence expensive to buy). They need access to drinking water, but are adapted to subsist on relatively high plateaux with poor soils.

Waterbuck *Kobus ellipsiprymnus* Shoulder height 130cm. Weight 250-270kg.

The waterbuck is easily recognised by its shaggy brown coat and the male's large lyre-shaped horns. The common race of southern Africa (*K. e. ellipsiprymnus*) and areas east of the Rift Valley has a distinctive white ring around its rump, seen on the left of the sketch. The defassa race (known as *K. e. defassa* or *K. e. crawshayi*) of the Rift Valley and areas further west has a full white rump, as indicated on the right.

In Zambia, the common waterbuck populates the Luangwa and Lower Zambezi valleys, whilst the defassa race occurs throughout most of the rest of the country, including Kafue National Park. They need to drink very regularly, so usually stay within a few kilometres of water, where they like to graze on short, nutritious grasses. At night they may take cover in adjacent woodlands. It is often asserted that waterbuck flesh is oily and smelly, which may discourage predators.

Blue wildebeest *Connochaetes taurinus* Shoulder height 130–150cm. Weight 180–250kg.

This ungainly antelope, also called the brindled gnu, is easily identified by its dark coat and bovine appearance. The superficially similar buffalo is far more heavily built. When they have enough space, blue wildebeest can form immense herds – as perhaps a million do for their annual migration from Tanzania's Serengeti Plains into Kenya's Masai Mara. One such gathering occurs on the Liuwa Plains around November, when tens of thousands of animals gather here as the rains arrive.

In Zambia wildebeest naturally occur from around the Kafue National Park area westwards, to Angola. There's also a subspecies, Cookson's wildebeest, *Connochaetes taurinus cooksoni*, which is endemic to the Luangwa Valley. It's found commonly on the north side, in North Luangwa, but only rarely further south. It differs from the main species by having cleaner colours including slightly reddish bands and being a little smaller and more compact.

Lichtenstein's hartebeest *Alcelaphus lichtensteini* Shoulder height 125cm. Weight 120–150kg.

Hartebeests are awkward antelopes, readily identified by the combination of large shoulders, a sloping back, a smooth coat and smallish horns in both sexes. Numerous subspecies are recognised, all of which are generally seen in small family groups in reasonably open country. Though once hartebeest were found from the Mediterranean to the Cape, only isolated populations still survive. Hartebeests are almost exclusively grazers and they like access to water.

The only one native to Zambia is Lichtenstein's hartebeest, which used to be found throughout the country, except for the extreme south and west. They are seen frequently in Kafue, and also occur in Sumbu and Kasanka. The Luangwa has a good population, but they generally stay away from the river, and so remain out of view for most visitors.

Similar species: The **tsessebe** (*Damaliscus lunatus*) is basically a darker version of the hartebeest with striking yellow lower legs. (A closely related subspecies is known as *topi* in east Africa.) These are very sparsely distributed in Zambia, occurring in the Kasanka–Bangweulu area, and to the far west of the Zambezi, in Liuwa and Sioma Ngwezi. Its favourite habitat is open grassland, where it is a selective grazer, eating the younger, more nutritious grasses. The tsessebe is one of the fastest antelope species, and jumps very well.

Kudu *Tragelaphus strepsiceros* Shoulder height 140–155cm. Weight 180–250kg.
The kudu (or, more properly, the greater kudu) is the most frequently observed member of the genus tragelaphus. These medium-size to large antelopes are characterised by their grey-brown coats and up to ten stripes on each side. The male has magnificent double-spiralled corkscrew horns. Occurring throughout Mozambique, Zimbabwe, Zambia, Botswana and Namibia, kudu are widespread and common, though not in dense forests or open grasslands. They are normally associated with well-wooded habitats. These browsers thrive in areas with mixed tree savannah and thickets, and the males will sometimes use their horns to pull down the lower branches of trees to eat, with mahogany, *Trichelia emetica*, being a particular favourite.

In Zambia they occur throughout the country except for the far northern areas. Normally they're seen in small herds, consisting of a couple of females and their offspring, sometimes accompanied by a male. Otherwise the males occur either singly, or in small bachelor groups.

Sitatunga *Tragelaphus spekei* Shoulder height 85–90cm. Weight 105–115kg.
The semi-aquatic antelope is a widespread but infrequently observed inhabitant of west and central African papyrus swamps from the Okavango in Botswana to the Sudd in Sudan. In Zambia sitatunga are very widespread. Good populations are found in Bangweulu, the Busanga Swamps, Sumbu and Kasanka.

Because of its preferred habitat, the sitatunga is very elusive and seldom seen, even in areas where it is relatively common. They are also less easy to hunt/poach than many other species, although they are exceedingly vulnerable to habitat destruction. Kasanka National Park's tree hide is commended, at least to the more agile of visitors, as one of Africa's very best places to see these antelope. It provides a superb vantage point above a small section of papyrus swamp, and sightings are virtually guaranteed in the early morning or late afternoon. Sitatunga are noted for an ability to submerse themselves completely, with just their nostrils showing, when pursued by a predator.

Eland *Taurotragus oryx* Shoulder height 150–175cm. Weight 450–900kg.
Africa's largest antelope, the eland is light brown in colour, sometimes with a few faint white vertical stripes. Relatively short horns and a large dewlap accentuate its somewhat bovine appearance. It was once widely distributed in east and southern Africa, though the population

has now been severely depleted. Small herds of eland frequent grasslands and light woodlands, often fleeing at the slightest provocation. (They have long been hunted for their excellent meat, so perhaps this is not surprising.)

Eland are opportunist browsers and grazers, eating fruit, berries, seed pods and leaves as well as green grass after the rains, and roots and tubers when times are lean. They run slowly, though can trot for great distances and jump exceedingly well. In Zambia they occur widely but sparsely, and are largely confined to the country's protected areas.

MEDIUM AND SMALL ANTELOPE

Bushbuck *Tragelaphus scriptus* Shoulder height 70–80cm. Weight 30–45kg.

This attractive antelope, a member of the same genus as the kudu, is widespread throughout Africa and shows great regional variation in its colouring. It occurs in forest and riverine woodland, where it is normally seen singly or in pairs. The male is dark brown or chestnut, while the much smaller female is generally a pale reddish brown. The male has relatively small, straight horns and both sexes are marked with white spots and sometimes stripes, though the stripes are often indistinct.

Bushbuck tend to be secretive and very skittish, except when used to people. They depend on cover and camouflage to avoid predators, and are often found in the thick, herby vegetation around rivers. They will freeze if disturbed, before dashing off into the undergrowth. Bushbuck are both browsers and grazers, choosing the more succulent grass shoots, fruit and flowers. In Zambia they are very widely distributed and fairly common.

Impala *Aepeceros melampus* Shoulder height 90cm. Weight 45kg.

This slender, handsome antelope is superficially similar to the springbok, but in fact belongs to its own separate family. Chestnut in colour, and lighter underneath than above, the impala has diagnostic black-and-white stripes running down its rump and tail, and the male has large lyre-shaped horns. One of the most widespread and successful antelope species in east and southern Africa, the impala is normally seen in large herds in wooded savannah habitats. It is the most common antelope in the Luangwa Valley, and throughout much of the central and southern areas of Zambia. However, in more northerly areas, puku are sometimes more common. As expected of such a successful species, it both grazes and browses, depending on what fodder is available.

Reedbuck *Redunca arundinum* Shoulder height 80–90cm. Weight 45–65kg.

Sometimes referred to as the southern reedbuck (as distinct from mountain and Bohor reedbucks, found further east), these delicate antelope are uniformly fawn or grey in colour, and lighter below than above. They are generally found in reedbeds and tall grasslands, often beside rivers, and are easily identified by their loud, whistling alarm call and distinctive bounding running style. In Zambia they occur widely, though seem absent from the very bottom of the Zambezi and Luangwa valley floors. (They do occur in both Luangwa and Lower Zambezi national parks, but usually on slightly higher ground, away from the rivers.)

Klipspringer *Oreotragus oreotragus* Shoulder height 60cm. Weight 13kg.

The klipspringer is a strongly built little antelope, normally seen in pairs, and easily identified by its dark, bristly grey-yellow coat, slightly speckled appearance and unique habitat preference. Klipspringer means 'rock jumper' in Afrikaans and it is an apt name for an antelope which occurs exclusively in mountainous areas and rocky outcrops from Cape Town to the Red Sea.

They occur throughout most of Zambia, except for the extreme western areas, but only where rocky hills or kopjes are found. Given Zambia's generally rolling topography, this means only the odd isolated population exists. They are seen occasionally on the escarpments of the main valleys, but usually away from the main game areas. Klipspringers are mainly browsers, though they do eat a little new grass. When spotted they will freeze, or bound at great speed across the steepest of slopes.

Lechwe *Kobus leche* Shoulder height 90–100cm. Weight 80–100kg.

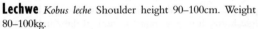

Lechwe are sturdy, shaggy antelope with beautiful lyre-shaped horns, adapted to favour the seasonal floodplains that border lakes and rivers. They need dry land on which to rest, but otherwise will spend much of their time grazing on grasses and sedges, standing in water if necessary. Their hooves are splayed, adapted to bounding through their muddy environment when fleeing from the lion, hyena and wild dog that hunt them, making them the most aquatic of antelope after sitatunga.

Lechwe are found in DRC, Angola, northern Botswana and Namibia's Caprivi Strip, but their stronghold is Zambia. Wherever they occur, the males are generally larger and darker than the females, and in Zambia there are three subspecies (though none occurs in the Luangwa or Lower Zambezi valleys).

The **red lechwe** (*K. l. leche*) is the most widespread subspecies. It's the only one found outside Zambia and has a chestnut-reddish coat, darker on the back and much lighter (almost white) underneath. Its legs have black markings, as does the tip of its tail. Inside Zambia red lechwe are found in large numbers (about 5,000 probably) on the Busanga Plains, with smaller populations in the Western Province and the Lukanga Swamps.

The **Kafue lechwe** (*K. l. kafuensis*) are slightly larger animals, with bigger horns, and are restricted to the Kafue Flats area, between Lake Itezhi-Tezhi and Lusaka. This race is more light brown than red, with black patches on their shoulders that run into the black on their legs. Most of the 40,000–50,000 that remain are confined to the Lochinvar and Blue Lagoon national parks.

The **black lechwe** (*K. l. smithemani*) used to occur in huge numbers, perhaps as many as half a million animals, centred on the plains to the south of the Bangweulu Swamps. They are now restricted to about 30,000–40,000 animals in the same area, and a small population have been reintroduced into the Nashinga Swamps to the west of Chinsali. Black lechwe are much darker and the older males have almost black backs and brownish undersides.

Puku *Kobus vardoni* Shoulder height 80cm. Weight 60–75kg.

Unless you see them beside each other, puku can be hard to distinguish from red lechwe – though the adults are generally slightly smaller than the lechwe. They are also stocky, orangey-red antelope with shaggy coats. Male pukus have stout, ribbed horns which curve forwards at the tips, though are shorter and spread out less than a lechwe's horns.

Puku are grazers, typically inhabiting open plains adjacent to rivers or marshes, or woodland fringes. They are always found close to water, although are not as fond of completely flooded areas as lechwe. Puku usually feed early or late in the day, and will often lie down in the shade during the heat of the day.

They are one of Zambia's most common antelope, found throughout western and northern Zambia, and the Luangwa Valley, although they are noticeably absent from the Lower Zambezi Valley. South of Zambia, puku are exceedingly rare, occurring only in one small corner of northern Chobe; to the north they are native to areas of Malawi and the DRC, and common in Tanzania.

Young males form bachelor groups, from which prime animals break away to form territories. The more dominant the buck, the more attractive are the feeding resources within these territories, into which they attract females. Breeding takes place between April and July and thus calves are born in the green season when food resources are abundant.

Steenbok *Raphicerus cempestris* Shoulder height 50cm. Weight 11kg.

This rather nondescript small antelope has red-brown upper parts and clear white underparts, and the male has short straight horns. It is very common south of the Zambezi, but only occurs in southwestern Zambia (Mazabuka seems to be about the limit of their distribution). They like grasslands and open country with a scattering of cover, and seem to do very well in the drier areas. Like most other small antelopes, the steenbok is normally encountered singly or in pairs and tends to 'freeze' when disturbed, before taking flight.

Similar species: **Sharpe's grysbok** (*Raphicerus sharpei*) is similar in size and appearance, though it has a distinctive white-flecked coat. It occurs widely throughout Zambia, and appears to be absent only from the far northwest (Liuwa/Mwinilunga area). It is almost entirely nocturnal in its habits and so very seldom seen.

The **Oribi** (*Ourebia ourebi*) is also a widespread but generally uncommon antelope. It is usually found only in large, open stretches of dry grassland, with the termitaria zones of the Busanga Plains, Lochinvar and Bangweulu area standing out as good places to spot them. It looks much like a steenbok but stands about 10cm higher at the shoulder and has an altogether more upright bearing.

Common duiker *Sylvicapra grimmia* Shoulder height 50cm. Weight 20kg.

This anomalous duiker holds itself more like a steenbok or grysbok and is the only member

of its (large) family to occur outside of forests. Generally grey in colour, the common duiker can most easily be separated from other small antelopes by the black tuft of hair that sticks up between its horns. They occur throughout Zambia, and tolerate most habitats except for true forest and very open country. They are even found near human settlements, where shooting and trapping is a problem, and are usually mainly nocturnal. Duikers are opportunist feeders, taking fruit, seeds and leaves, as well as crops, small reptiles and amphibians.

OTHER LARGE HERBIVORES

African elephant *Loxodonta africana* Shoulder height 2.3–3.4m. Weight up to 6,000kg.

The world's largest land animal, the African elephant is intelligent, social and often very entertaining to watch. Female elephants live in close-knit clans in which the eldest female plays matriarch over her sisters, daughters and granddaughters. Their lifespans are comparable to those of humans, and mother–daughter bonds are strong and may last for up to 50 years. Males generally leave the family group at around 12 years to roam singly or form bachelor herds. Under normal circumstances, elephants range widely in search of food and water, but when concentrated populations are forced to live in conservation areas their habit of uprooting trees can cause serious environmental damage.

Elephants are widespread and common in habitats ranging from desert to rainforest. In Zambia they were common everywhere except for the Upper Zambezi's floodplains, but have now become more restricted by human expansion. However, individuals often wander widely, turning up in locations from which they have been absent for years.

Zambia's strongest population is in the Luangwa, where there are now about 15,000. As recently as 1973 estimates put the Luangwa's population at more than 100,000, but the late 1970s and '80s saw huge commercial poaching for ivory, which wiped out a large proportion of this. Outside of a small, protected area in South Luangwa National Park, Zambia's elephants fared even worse. The populations in Kafue and even North Luangwa are still small, and the individuals are very nervous and skittish near people. (The exception here is possibly the Lower Zambezi, where the elephants regularly swim between Zimbabwe and Zambia, because the Zimbabwean parks were, on the whole, better protected from poaching than the Zambian parks. Hence the Lower Zambezi's elephant population is also fairly relaxed and numerous.)

Black rhinoceros *Diceros bicornis* Shoulder height 160cm. Weight 1,000kg.

This is the more widespread of Africa's two rhino species, an imposing and rather temperamental creature. (White rhino are not thought to have been native to Zambia.) In the 1960s, the black rhino was recorded in the Kafue, Luangwa, Lower Zambezi and in the far north around Sumbu and Mweru Wantipa. However, by the late 1990s it had probably been poached to extinction in Zambia, whilst becoming highly endangered in many of the other countries within its range. (There were a handful of reports of isolated individual animals existing in very remote areas; none was ever confirmed.) However, in mid-2003 black rhino were reintroduced into a subsection of North Luangwa National Park, and there are plans to bring more in.

Black rhinos exploit a wide range of habitats from dense woodlands and bush, and are generally solitary animals. They can survive without drinking for four to five days. However, their territorial behaviour and regular patterns of movement make them an easy target for poachers. Black rhinos can be very aggressive when disturbed and will charge with minimal provocation. Their hearing and sense of smell are acute, whilst their eyesight is poor (so they often miss if you keep a low profile and don't move).

Hippopotamus *Hippopotamus amphibius* Shoulder height 150cm. Weight 2,000kg.

Characteristic of Africa's large rivers and lakes, this large, lumbering animal spends most of the day submerged but emerges at night to graze. Strongly territorial, herds of ten or more animals are presided over by a dominant male who will readily defend his patriarchy to the death. Hippos are abundant in most protected rivers and water bodies and are still quite common outside of reserves.

Hippos are widely credited with killing more people than any other African mammal, but I know of no statistics to support this. John Coppinger (one of the Luangwa Valley's most experienced guides) suggests that crocodile, elephant and lion all account for more deaths in that area than hippos – despite the valley having one of Africa's highest

A1

concentrations of hippos. So whilst undoubtedly dangerous, perhaps they don't quite deserve their reputation.

In Zambia they are exceptionally common in most of the larger rivers, where hunting is not a problem. The Kafue, the Luangwa and the Zambezi all have large hippo populations.

Buffalo *Syncerus caffer* Shoulder height 140cm. Weight 700kg.
Frequently and erroneously referred to as a water buffalo (an Asian species), the African, or Cape, buffalo is a distinctive, highly social ox-like animal that lives as part of a herd. It prefers well-watered savanna, though also occurs in forested areas. Common and widespread in sub-Saharan Africa, in Zambia it is widely distributed. The Luangwa, and especially the north park, seems to have some particularly large herds, hundreds of animals strong. Buffalo are primarily grazers and need regular access to water, where they swim readily. They smell and hear well, and it's often claimed that they have poor eyesight. This isn't true, though when encountered during a walking safari, they won't be able to discern your presence if you keep still and the wind is right.

Huge herds are generally fairly peaceful, and experienced guides will often walk straight through them on walking safaris. However, small bachelor herds, or even single old bulls (known in the Luangwa as 'kakuli'), can be very nervous and aggressive. They have a reputation for charging at the slightest provocation, often in the midst of thick bush, and are exceedingly dangerous if wounded. Lion often follow herds of buffalo, their favourite prey.

Giraffe *Giraffa camelopardis* Shoulder height 250–350cm. Weight 1,000–1,400kg.
The world's tallest and longest-necked land animal, a fully grown giraffe can measure up to 5.5m high. Quite unmistakable, giraffe live in loosely structured herds of up to 15, though herd members often disperse, when they may be seen singly or in smaller groups. Formerly distributed throughout east and southern Africa, these great browsers are now found only in the southern side of the Luangwa Valley and the far southwest of Zambia.

About eight subspecies of giraffe have been identified in Africa, and the Luangwa Valley contains one such distinct population, **Thornicroft's giraffe** (*G. c. thornicroftii*). These are generally regarded as having dark body patches and lighter neck patches than the normal 'southern' race of giraffe, and their colour patches don't normally extend below the knees, leaving their lower legs almost white. Their faces are also light or white. The vast majority of these live on the east side of the Luangwa River, in the GMA outside the park. They have been protected from hunting by a local taboo.

Much further west, the pocket of giraffe which are thought to still survive around the Sioma Ngwezi National Park are **Angolan giraffe** (*G. c. angolensis*), although so little is known of what survives in Sioma Ngwezi that their current status there is uncertain.

Burchell's zebra *Equus burchelli* Shoulder height 130cm. Weight 300–340kg.
Also known as common or plains zebra, this attractive striped horse is common and widespread throughout most of east and southern Africa, where it is often seen in large herds alongside wildebeest. It is common in most conservation areas from northern South Africa all the way up to the southeast of Ethiopia.

Most southern races, although not those found in Zambia, have paler brownish 'shadow-stripes' between their bold black stripes. In Zambia, the subspecies in the Luangwa Valley is **Crawshay's zebra** (*E. b. crawshaii*), which also occurs on Nyika Plateau and possibly in

Malawi's Vwaza Marsh. Norman Carr comments in his book on the Luangwa's wildlife (see *Appendix 3*, page 512) that the zebra found to the west of the Muchinga escarpment belong to the *E. b. zambeziensis* subspecies.

Regardless of these minor taxonomic differences, zebra are widely distributed throughout Zambia, though they tend to be restricted by human activity to the more remote or protected areas. They lack the brown shadow-stripes of their cousins further south, but otherwise are very similar.

Warthog *Phacochoerus aethiopicus* Shoulder height 60–70cm. Weight up to 100kg.

This widespread and often conspicuously abundant resident of the African savanna is grey

in colour with a thin covering of hairs, wart-like bumps on its face, and rather large upward-curving tusks. Africa's only diurnal swine, the warthog is often seen in family groups, trotting around with its tail raised stiffly (a diagnostic trait) and a determinedly nonchalant air. They occur in most areas of Zambia, except in the extreme northwest, and are very common in most of the national parks. They don't usually fare well near settlements, as they are very susceptible to subsistence hunting/poaching. Wherever they occur, you'll often see them grazing beside the road, on bended knee, with their tails held high in the air as soon as they trot away.

Similar species: Bulkier, hairier and browner, the **bushpig** (*Potomochoerus larvatus*) is known to occur throughout Zambia, and even in the vicinity of cultivated land where it can do considerable damage to crops. However, it is very rarely seen due to its nocturnal habits and preference for dense vegetation.

SMALL MAMMALS

African civet *Civettictis civetta* Shoulder height 40cm. Weight 10–15kg.

This bulky, long-haired, rather feline creature of the African night is primarily carnivorous, feeding on small animals and carrion, but will also eat fruit. It has a similar-coloured coat to

a leopard: densely blotched with large black spots becoming stripes towards the head. Civets are widespread and common throughout Zambia in many habitats, and make frequent cameo appearances on night drives. Though occasionally called 'civet cats', this is misleading because they are far more closely related to the mongooses than the felines.

Similar species: The smaller, more slender **tree civet** (*Nandinia binotata*) is an arboreal forest animal with a dark brown coat marked with black spots. It is really a resident of the equatorial forests, although is found in a few mountain areas on Zambia's Malawi border (including Nyika) as well as north of Mwinilunga. It is nocturnal, solitary and largely arboreal – and so is very seldom seen.

The **small-spotted genet** (*Genetta genetta*), **large-spotted genet** (*Genetta tigrina*) and **rusty-spotted genet** (*Genetta rubignosa*) are the most widespread members in Zambia of a large group of similar small predators (which even the experts often can't tell apart without examining their skins by hand). All the genets are slender and rather feline in appearance (though they are not cats), with a grey to gold-brown coat marked with black spots (perhaps combining into short bars) and a long ringed tail.

You're most likely to see them on nocturnal game drives or occasionally scavenging around game reserve lodges. They are found all over Zambia, even in urban areas if there is a plentiful supply of rodents. They are excellent climbers and opportunists, eating fruit, small birds, termites and even scorpions.

Banded mongoose *Mungos mungo* Shoulder
height 20cm. Weight around 1kg.
The banded mongoose is probably the most
commonly observed member of a group of small,
slender, terrestrial carnivores. Uniform dark grey-
brown except for a dozen black stripes across its

back, it is a diurnal mongoose occurring in playful family groups, or troops, in most habitats
throughout Zambia. It feeds on insects, scorpions, amphibians, reptiles and even carrion and
bird's eggs, and can move through the bush at quite a pace.

Similar species: Another eight or so mongoose species occur in Zambia; some are social and
gather in troops, others are solitary. Several are too scarce and nocturnal to be seen by casual
visitors. Of the rest, the water or **marsh mongoose** (*Atilax paludinosus*) is large, normally
solitary and has a very scruffy brown coat; it's widespread in the wetter areas. The **white-
tailed mongoose** (*Ichneumia albicauda*), or white-tailed ichneumon, is a solitary, large brown
mongoose with long, coarse, woolly hair. It is nocturnal and easily identified by its bushy
white tail if seen crossing roads at night. It's not uncommon in cattle-ranching areas, where
it eats the beetle-grubs found in the manure.

The **slender mongoose** (*Galerella sanguinea*) is as widespread and also solitary, but it is
very much smaller (shoulder height 10cm) and has a uniform brown or reddish coat and
blackish tail tip. Its tail is held up when it runs, and it is common throughout Zambia where
there is lots of cover for it. The **dwarf mongoose** (*Helogate parvula*) is a diminutive (shoulder
height 7cm), highly sociable light brown mongoose often seen in the vicinity of the termite
mounds where it nests. This is Africa's smallest carnivore, occurring in a higher density than
any other, and is widespread throughout Zambia. Groups of 20–30 are not unknown,
consisting of a breeding pair and subordinate others. These inquisitive little animals can be
very entertaining to watch.

The **large grey mongoose** (*Herpestes ichneumon*), also called the Egyptian mongoose, is a
large mongoose with course, grey-speckled body hair, black lower legs and feet, and a black
tip to its tail. It's found all over Zambia, but is common nowhere, is generally diurnal and is
solitary or lives in pairs. It eats small rodents, reptiles, birds and also snakes – generally killing
rather than scavenging. The **bushy-tailed mongoose** (*Bdeogale crassicaude*) is a small, mainly
nocturnal species that looks mainly black, especially its legs and tail. It is found throughout
Zambia, though appears relatively uncommon south of the Zambezi.

Meller's mongoose (*Rhynchogale melleri*) is a variable shaggy, grey colour with dark legs
and a large muzzle. Its distribution is patchy and somewhat uncertain, but it is thought to
occur throughout western Zambia and the Luangwa, but not north of the Serenje–Mbala
road. It is solitary and nocturnal, eating a large proportion of termites as well as reptiles,
amphibians and fruit. **Selous's mongoose** (*Paracynictis selousi*) is smaller, with fine, speckled
grey fur, and a white tip at the end of its tail. It likes open country and woodlands, occurring
in many areas of southern and western Zambia, even including the Luangwa. It is nocturnal
and solitary, eating mainly insects, grubs, small reptiles and amphibians – it seems especially
fond of the larvae of dung beetles, and so is sometime found in cattle country.

Honey badger *Mellivora capensis* Shoulder height 30cm. Weight 12kg.
Also known as the ratel, the honey badger is black with a puppyish face and grey-white
back. It is an opportunistic feeder best known for its allegedly symbiotic relationship with

a bird called the honeyguide which leads it to a
beehive, waits for it to tear it open, then feeds on
the scraps. The honey badger is among the most
widespread of African carnivores, and also
amongst the most powerful and aggressive for its
size; it occurs all over Zambia. However, it is thinly

distributed and infrequently seen, except when it has lost its fear of people and started to scavenge from safari camps.

Similar species: Several other mustelids occur in the region, including the **striped polecat** (*Ictonyx striatus*), a widely distributed but rarely seen nocturnal creature with black underparts and a bushy white back, and the similar but much scarcer **striped weasel** (*Poecilogale albincha*). This has been reported from several locations in Zambia, but only rarely.

The **Cape clawless otter** (*Aonyx capensis*) is a brown freshwater mustelid with a white collar, whilst the smaller **spotted-necked otter** (*Lutra maculicollis*) is darker with light white spots on its throat. Both occur fairly commonly throughout the rivers, swamps and lakes of Zambia.

Aardvark (*Orycteropus afer*) Shoulder height 60cm. Weight up to 70kg.

This singularly bizarre nocturnal insectivore is unmistakable with its long snout, huge ears and powerful legs, adapted to dig up the nests of termites, on which it feeds. Aardvarks occur throughout southern Africa, except the driest western areas of the Namib. Though their distinctive three-toed tracks are often seen, and they are not uncommon animals, sightings of them are rare.

Aardvarks prefer areas of grassland and sparse scrub, rather than dense woodlands. They are absent from Zambia's floodplains and marshes, but otherwise occur throughout the country where termites are found.

Pangolin *Manis temmincki* Total length 70–100cm. Weight 8–15kg.

Sharing the aardvaak's diet of termites and ants, the pangolin is another very unusual nocturnal insectivore – with distinctive armour plating and a tendency to roll up in a ball when disturbed. (Then it can swipe its tail from side to side – inflicting serious damage on its aggressor.) Sometimes known as Temminck's pangolins, or scaly anteaters, these strange animals walk on their hindlegs, using their tail and front legs for balance. They are both nocturnal and rare – so sightings are exceedingly unusual and their distribution is uncertain. However, they are thought to occur in Kafue National Park and southern Zambia, as well as in the Luangwa Valley. (Evidence of their occurrence in the Luangwa is limited to about two sightings over the last few decades.)

In some areas further south, particularly Zimbabwe, local custom is to make a present of any pangolin found to the paramount chief (often taken to mean the president). This has caused great damage to their population.

Porcupine *Hystrix africaeaustralis* Total length 80–100cm. Weight 15–25kg.

This is the largest rodent found in the region, and occurs throughout Zambia and all over southern Africa. It easily identified by its black-and-white striped quills, generally black hair, and shambling gait. If heard in the dark, then the slight rattle of its quills augments the rustle of its foraging. These quills drop off fairly regularly, and are often found in the bush.

The porcupine's diet is varied, and they are fairly opportunistic when it comes to food. Roots and tubers are favourites, as is the bark of certain trees; they will also eat meat and small reptiles or birds if they have the chance.

Similar species: Also spiky, the **southern African hedgehog** (*Erinaceus frontalis*) has been recorded in a few locations in Zambia, including the Lusaka, Mumbwa and Chipata areas. It's likely to occur elsewhere, though is small and nocturnal, so rarely seen even where it does occur. Hedgehogs are about 20cm long (much smaller than porcupines), omnivorous and uncommon.

Yellow-spotted rock hyrax *Heterohyrax brucei* Length 35–50cm. Weight 2.5–3.5kg.

Rodent-like in appearance, hyraxes (also known as dassies) are claimed to be the closest living relative of elephants. Yellow-spotted rock hyraxes are often seen sunning themselves in rocky habitats, and become tame when used to people.

They are social animals, living in large groups, and largely herbivores, eating leaves, grasses and fruits. Where you see lots of dassies, watch out for black eagles and other raptors which prey extensively on them.

Similar species: Very similar, the **tree hyrax** (*Dendrohyrax arboreus*) has been recorded in a few locations on the eastern side of the country, including South Luangwa.

Scrub hare *Lepus saxatilis* Shoulder height 45–60cm. Weight 1–4.5kg.

This is the largest and commonest African hare, occurring throughout Zambia. In some areas a short walk, or drive, at dusk or after nightfall might reveal three or four scrub hares. They tend to freeze when disturbed.

Tree squirrel *Paraxerus cepapi* Total length 35cm. Weight 100–250g.

This common rodent is a uniform grey or buff colour, with a long tail that is furry but not bushy. It's widely distributed all over southern and east Africa, and occurs throughout Zambia in most woodland habitats, although not wet evergreen or montane forests. It's often so common in mopane woodlands that it can be difficult to avoid seeing it, hence its other common name – the mopane squirrel.

Tree squirrels can live alone, in pairs or in small family groups, usually nesting in a drey of dry leaves, in a hole in a tree. They are diurnal and venture down to the ground to feed on seeds, fruit, nuts, vegetable matter and small insects. When alarmed they will usually bolt up the nearest tree, keeping on the side of the trunk away from the threat and so out of sight as much as possible. If they can attain a safe vantage point with a view of the threat, then they'll sometimes make a loud clicking alarm call.

Similar species: The **sun squirrel** (*Heliosciurus rufobrachium*) is the largest of Zambia's squirrels, and is found everywhere north of a rough line between Kabwe and Lukulu. It has similar habits to those of the more common tree squirrel, though will lie in the sun more often. Its colour varies considerably between individuals, and seasons, from light fawn to greyish brown, though its long bushy tail is consistently crossed by numerous whitish, longitudinal stripes.

The **red and black squirrel** (*Heliosciurus lucifer*) is a very pretty species with flame-red upper parts, a black patch in the middle of its back, and whitish underside. It occurs only in montane forest and in Zambia is thought to be restricted to the Nyika Plateau.

Boehm's squirrel (*Paraxerus boehmi*) has a similar size, shape and greyish colouring to the tree squirrel. However, it has two very distinct white stripes, bordered by black, down the side of its back from nape to tail. It inhabits riverine evergreen forest, and has a limited distribution in Zambia, restricted to the country's far north, around the Sumbu and Lusenga Plain areas.

The **flying squirrel** (*Anomalurus derbianus*) is quite unmistakable as there's a membrane of skin linking the fore and hind legs, and also the base of the tail. It uses this to glide with, when jumping from a higher branch to a lower one. It's a solitary, arboreal species that prefers miombo woodlands. It occurs from the Liuwa area east across Mwinilunga and the Copperbelt, and into the western side of northern Zambia, but is seldom seen.

Appendix 2

LANGUAGES

Zambia's main language groups are briefly outlined in *Chapter 3*, pages 20–5. This section will try to note down just a few useful phrases, and give their local translations in six of the most frequently encountered languages: Nyanja, Bemba, Lozi, Lunda, Tonga and Luvale. The visitor will probably find Nyanja or Bemba the most useful of these: Nyanja is the language that visitors are most likely to hear in the parks, while Bemba is more widely spoken countrywide. However, in the more remote areas – like the Western Province – where Nyanja and Bemba are not spoken, the other languages will prove invaluable.

Space is too short here, and my knowledge too limited, to give a detailed pronunciation guide to these six languages. However all are basically phonetic and by far the best way to learn the finer nuances of pronouncing these phrases is to find some Zambians to help you as soon as you arrive. Asking a Zambian to help you with a local language is also an excellent way to break the ice with a new local acquaintance, as it involves them talking about a subject that they know well, and in which they are usually confident.

There may be several ways of saying goodbye, depending on the circumstances. In Nyanya, for example, one form may be said by the person leaving, and the other by the person staying behind – translating as 'go well' and 'stay well'. An alternative is to use the more informal 'see you later'.

Note that there is no specific word for 'please'; rather the meaning is incorporated into the word structure, so in Lozi, for example, 'please' is expressed by adding an 'a' to the subjunctive of the verb.

As noted in *Cultural guidelines*, pages 22–3, learning a few simple phrases in the local language will go a long way towards helping the independent traveller to have an easy and enjoyable time in Zambia. Just remember to laugh at yourself, and have fun. Most Zambians will be very impressed and applaud your efforts to speak their language, no matter how hard they may laugh!

	Nyanja	**Bemba**	**Lozi**
Good morning. How are you?	*Muli bwanji?* (formal) *Muli shani?* (informal)	*Mwashibukeni?* (formal) *Muzuhile?* (informal)	*Muzuhile cwani?* (formal) *Mucwani?* (informal)
I am fine	*Nile bwino* (formal) *Bwino* (informal)	*Eyamukwayi, Ndifye bwino* (formal) *Bwino* (informal)	*Lu zuhile hande* (formal), *Hande* (informal)
Goodbye	*Salani bwino*	*Shaaleenipo*	*Muzamave hande*
See you later (*ciao*)	*Tisau onana*	*Twalaamonana*	*Lukabonana*
yes	*inde*	*eya ye*	*kimona*
no	*iyayi*	*awe*	*baatili*
thank you	*zikomo*	*twa to te la*	*nitumezi*
hey you!	*iwe!*	*iwe!*	*wena!*
I want	*ndifuna*	*ndefwaya*	*nabata*

507

Judi Helmholz

During your travels you may have the good fortune to meet a Wireless, a Handbrake or an Engine. If you are really lucky, you may encounter a Cabbage. These are names of people I have met in Zambia.

Looking for Fame and Fortune? Look no further than twin boys living in the Western Province. Beware of Temptation though, he is a money-changer known for calculating exchanges solely to his advantage.

Working with Sunday and Friday got rather amusing, 'Sunday, can you work on Saturday with Friday?' Working with Trouble was another matter entirely, as we had frequently to enquire, 'Where can I find Trouble?' Gift, true to his namesake, felt compelled to ask for one, while Lunch took on a whole new meaning and Clever is a friend who is true to his name.

Unusual names aren't limited solely to English. For example, there is Mwana Uta which literally means 'son of a gun', and Saka Tutu meaning 'father of an insect'. Pity the local man named Mwana Ngombe or 'child of a cow'!

	Nyanja	**Bemba**	**Lozi**
there	*kunja*	*kulya* (also 'food')	*kwale*
here	*apa*	*hapa* (silent 'h')	*faa*
stop	*imilira*	*yema*	*iminina*
let's go	*tiyeni or tye*	*aluye*	*natuleya*
help me	*niyetizipita*	*ngafweniko*	*nituse kwteni*
how much?	*zingati?*	*shinga?*	*kibukayi?*
it is too much!	*yadula!*	*fingi!*	*kihahulu!*
where can I find … ?	*alikuti…?*	*kwisa…?*	*uinzi kai…?*
the doctor	*sing'ang'a doctoro*	*shinganga*	*mualafi*
the police	*kapokola*	*kapokola*	*mupokola*
the market	*kumusika*	*ekobashita fyakulya*	*kwamusika*
drinking water	*mazi akumwa*	*amenshi ayakunwa*	*mezi a kunwa*
some food	*chakudya*	*ichakulya*	*sakuca*

	Lunda	**Tonga**	**Luvale**
How are you?	*Mudi nahi?*	*Mwabuka buti?*	*Ngacili?*
		Muli buti?	
I am fine	*Cha chiwahi*	*Kabotu*	*Kanawa*
Goodbye	*Shalenuhu*	*Muchale kabotu*	*Salenuho mwane*
See you later (*ciao*)	*Tuualimona*	*Tulabonana*	*Natulimona*
yes	*ena*	*inzya*	*eawa*
no	*inehi*	*pepe*	*kagute*
thank you	*kusakililaku*	*twalumba*	*gunasakulila*
hey, you!	*enu!*	*yebo!*	*enu!*
I want	*nakukena*	*ndiyanda*	*gikutonda*
there	*kuna*	*okuya*	*haaze*
here	*kunu*	*aano or awa*	*kuno*
stop	*imanaku*	*koyima or ima*	*imana*
let's go	*tuyena*	*atwende*	*tuyenga*
help me	*kwashiku*	*ndigwashe*	*gukafweko*
how much?	*anahi?*	*ongaye?*	*jingayi?*
it is too much!	*yayivulu!*	*chadula! or zinji!*	*yayivulu!*
where can I find...?	*kudihi...?*	*ulikuli...?*	*ali kuli...?*

	Lunda	**Tonga**	**Luvale**
the doctor	*ndotolu*	*mun'g'anga*	*ndotolo*
the police	*kapokola*	*kappokola*	*kapokola*
the market	*chisakanu*	*musika*	*mushika*
drinking water	*meji akunwa*	*maanzi akunywa*	*meya a kunwa*
some food	*chakuda*	*chakulya*	*kulya*

Appendix 3

FURTHER INFORMATION

BOOKS

History and culture

Africa: A Biography of the Continent by John Reader. Penguin Books, London, 1997. Over 700 pages of highly readable history, interwoven with facts and statistics, make a remarkable overview of Africa's past. Given that Zambia's boundaries were imposed from Europe, its history must be looked at from a pan-African context to be understood. This book can show you that wider view; it is compelling and essential reading. Chapter 47 is largely devoted to the Lozi people.

The Africa House by Christine Lamb. Viking, London, 2nd edition 2004. This fascinating book pieces together the life and times of Sir Stewart Gore-Browne from diaries, correspondence and memories. It's a spellbinding tale, eloquently told. If this can't convey the fascination of Shiwa, and make you want to see it, then nothing can.

Black Heart: Gore-Browne and the Politics of Multiracial Zambia by Robert I Rotberg. University of California Press, Berkeley, 1977.

David Livingstone and the Victorian Encounter with Africa. National Portrait Gallery, London, 1996. Six essays on Livingstone's life, concentrating on not only what he did, but also on how he was perceived in the UK.

A History of Zambia by Andrew Roberts. Africana Publishing, New York, 1976. A detailed and complete history of Zambia, from prehistory to 1974.

The Lake of the Royal Crocodiles by Eileen Bigland. Hodder and Stoughton, London, 1939.

Lusaka and its Environs ed Geoffrey J Williams. ZGA Handbooks, Lusaka.

Makishi: Mask Characters of Zambia by Manuel Jordan. Fowler Museum of Cultural History, Los Angeles, 2007.

Missionary Travels and Researches in Southern Africa by David Livingstone. 1857. Over a century after it was written, this classic still makes fascinating reading.

Tales of Zambia by Dick Hobson. Zambia Society Trust, London, 1996. This is a lovely book, cataloguing big moments in Zambia's history, as well as some of its quirkier incidents and characters. It has sections on legends, mining and the country's flora and fauna and is very readable. Dick Hobson's knowledge and love of Zambia shine through.

Zambia's Ancient Rock Art: The Paintings of Kasama by Benjamin W Smith. National Heritage Conservation Commission, Livingstone, 1997.

Guidebooks

Kasanka: A Visitor's Guide to Kasanka National Park by Lucy Farmer. Kasanka Trust, July 1992. This superb little 36-page guide is now out of print, but it is well worth trying to find a copy, although its map of the park's roads is now inaccurate. It includes comprehensive sections on the geography, vegetation, wildlife, birdlife and facilities for visitors at Kasanka.

A Guide to Little-Known Waterfalls of Zambia by Quentin Allen, Ilse Mwanza & Heather Chalcraft. Published privately, Lusaka, 2005. A mine of useful information, this detailed guide offers an excuse to head off the beaten track as well as detailed information relating to Zambia's innumerable waterfalls. Illustrated with line drawings, paintings and photographs, it also has plenty of practical information, including GPS coordinates.

National Monuments of Zambia by D W Phillipson, revised by N M Katanekwa. National Heritage Conservation Commission, Livingstone, 1972 (4th printing 1992). Look for this small, green paperback around Lusaka, and buy it if you see one as they're quite scarce. It describes all of Zambia's national monuments, including many historical monuments, archaeological sites and even places of great scenic beauty – with some great old black-and-white photos.

A Visitor's Guide to Nyika National Park, Malawi by Sigrid Anna Johnson. Mbabazi Book Trust, Blantyre. Length 150 pages. Available at most good bookshops in Blantyre and Lilongwe, and at the park reception at Chelinda. The book provides a detailed historical and ecological background to Nyika, 20 pages of special-interest sites and notes on recommended walks - and hikes, as well as complete checklists of all mammals, birds, butterflies and orchids which are known to occur in the park. In short, an essential purchase.

Travelogues and biography

Billy The Hippo by Sheila Siddle. Mission Press, Ndola, 2006. A children's book telling the story of an orphaned hippo raised by the author at Chimfunshi.

In My Family Tree: A Life with Chimpanzees by Sheila Siddle, with Doug Cress. Grove/Atlantic, New York, 2002, and Double Storey, Cape Town, 2004. Sheila Siddle's story of the establishment of Chimfunshi Wildlife Orphanage makes inspirational – if sometimes shocking – reading.

Just Driving Around in the North by C A Quarmby. Health Rescue International, Zambia.

Kakuli: A Story about Wild Animals by Norman Carr. CBC Publishing, 1996. A collection of Norman Carr's tales from his time in the Luangwa Valley. Excellent light reading whilst on safari.

Pole to Pole by Michael Palin. BBC Consumer Publishing, London, 1999. This has an excellent section on Zambia, and Shiwa Ng'andu in particular is covered well.

Survivor's Song: Life and Death in an African Wilderness by Mark & Delia Owens. HarperCollins, London, 1993. Published as *The Eye of the Elephant* in the USA. This relates the authors' struggles to protect the wildlife of North Luangwa National Park from poachers, and their efforts to develop viable alternatives to poaching for the local people. It is excellent reading, though insiders complain of sensationalism, and that it ignores valuable contributions made by others.

General reference

An Explorer's Handbook: Travel, Survival and Bush Cookery by Christina Dodwell. Hodder and Stoughton, London, 1984. Over 170 pages of both practical and amusing anecdotes, including chapters on 'unusual eatables', 'building an open fire', and 'tested exits from tight corners'. Practical advice for both plausible and most unlikely eventualities – and it's a great read.

Zambia: Condemned to Debt World Development Movement (*www.wdm.org.uk*), London, May 2004. The WDM is a charity which researches into global trade and debt trends, and campaigns for policies to reduce injustice and tackle poverty.

Zambia: Debt & Poverty by John Clark. Oxfam, Oxford, 1989. This slim volume looks with clarity at Zambia's international debt, its causes and its consequences.

Wildlife and natural history
Field guides

Books published in Lusaka by the Wildlife and Environmental Conservation Society of Zambia (WECSZ) and Zambian Ornithological Society are usually obtainable from bookshops in Lusaka, or direct from the WECSZ office.

A Field Guide to Zambian Birds not found in Southern Africa by Dylan Aspinwall and Carl Beel. Zambian Ornithological Society, Lusaka, 1998. This excellent small guide is designed to complement a book covering Africa south of the Zambezi, such as Newman's guide, by describing only the birds occurring in Zambia which aren't included in Newman's guide. It's widely available in Zambia, but difficult to find elsewhere.

'African Wild Dog Survey in Zambia' by Kenneth Buk (Zoological Museum, University of Copenhagen), *Canid News*, vol 3, 1995. This piece of academic research looked at the distribution of wild dogs in Zambia in 1994, the reasons for their decline, and their possibilities for long-term survival.

A Guide to Common Wild Mammals of Zambia. WECSZ, 1991. A small field guide to the more common species.

A Guide to Reptiles, Amphibians & Fishes of Zambia. Wildlife Conservation Society of Zambia, Lusaka, 1993. Another good guide to the more common species.

A Guide to the Common Wild Flowers of Zambia and Neighbouring Regions. Macmillan Educational, London, 1995. This is a good small field guide to the more common species, obtainable from bookshops in Lusaka, or direct from the WECSZ.

A Guide to the Snakes of the Luangwa Valley by Patrick Nyerenda. WECSZ, reprinting 2007.

A Guide to the Wildlife of the Luangwa Valley by Norman Carr. Montford Press, Malawi, 1st edition, 1985. This small paperback (70 pages) was written by the valley's most famous guide and conservationist. It's not comprehensive, but is fascinating for the author's personal insights into the Luangwa area and its wildlife.

Birds of Africa south of the Sahara by Ian Sinclair and Peter Ryan. Struik, Cape Town, 2003. The field guide used by many of Zambia's birders as it incorporates both central African and southern African species, though it's a hefty tome to cart around.

Birds of Southern Africa by Ber van Perlo. Collins Illustrated Checklist, 1999. The only concise field guide that covers both Zambia and the rest of the region.

Common Birds of Zambia Zambian Ornithological Society, Lusaka, revised 1993. A good small field guide to the more common species, obtainable from the Wildlife Shop in Lusaka, or direct from the WECSZ.

Common Trees, Shrubs and Grasses of the Luangwa Valley by P P Smith. Trendrine Press, Zennor, 1995. This small, practical field guide has pictures to aid identification at the back, and includes a small section on the value to wildlife of the various plants.

Important Bird Areas in Zambia by Peter Leonard. Zambian Ornithological Society, Lusaka, 2005. The most comprehensive survey of the country's top birding areas – complete with a lot of other useful detail about Zambia's ecology, flora and fauna.

Minerals of Zambia by Gerald Cooray and Andrew Lane. Nchanga Consolidated Copper Mines Ltd.

Newman's Birds of Southern Africa by Kenneth Newman. Southern Books, South Africa, first edition 1988. This has been republished numerous times since its first edition and has become the standard field guide to birds in southern Africa, south of the Kunene and Zambezi rivers. It also covers most species found in Zambia.

Tanganyika Cichlids in their Natural Habitat by Ad Konings. Cichlid Press (*www.cichlidpress.com*), El Paso, 1998.

Trees of Southern Africa by Keith and Meg Coates Palgrave (eds). Struik, South Africa, 2003.

Health

Bugs, Bites & Bowels by Dr Jane Wilson-Howarth. Cadogan Books, London, 2006. An amusing and erudite overview of the hazards of tropical travel which is small enough to take with you.

Your Child Abroad: A Travel Health Guide by Dr Jane Wilson-Howarth and Dr Matthew Ellis. Bradt Travel Guides, Chalfont St Peter, 2nd edition 2005. An invaluable resource for all those travelling with children.

WEBSITES Website addresses seem to change frequently, especially in Zambia, but some of the more interesting ones include:

Tourist information sites

www.zambia.co.zm Bills itself as 'The National Homepage of Zambia', and has some useful links.

www.zambiatourism.com The official website of the Zambia National Tourist Board.

www.zambia-travel-guide.com An online version of this guide.

Media sites

www.lowdown.co.zm An electronic version of *The Lowdown*, Lusaka's monthly magazine (see page 153). It's topical, informative and fun.

www.postzambia.com For a more independent view, look at this site from *The Post* newspaper. It usually takes a more objective, critical and questioning approach.

www.times.co.zm The extensive side of the *Times of Zambia*. Featuring the main stories of the day, plus a searchable (but not listed) archive containing selected stories from June 2001 to the present day.

Index

Page numbers in **bold** indicate main entries; those in *italics* indicate maps.

aardvark 505
Abercorn 339
abseiling 199–200
accidents, motoring 70
accommodation 51, **74–5** *see also* places
Administrator's House (Kalomo) 207
adventure activities 198–204
Adventure City (Lusaka) 154
African Parks 454, **473**
African Queen 189, **193**
agriculture 17
AIDS 19, 82, 97
airlines 52–3, **67**, **122**, 161–2, 384
air travel 52–3, 66–7
  to/from Livingstone 161–2
  to/from Lusaka 121–2
  to/from Mfuwe 261–2
airports
  Kitwe 390
  Livingstone 161
  Lusaka 122
  Mfuwe 262–3
  Ndola 384
Albida Suite 239
Albidon nickel mine 211
alcohol 28, 75–6
Amanzimtoti Campsite 436
Ana Tree Lodge 241
Angelo 389
Angola 5, 9, 53, 453, 478, 481
animals *see* wildlife
antelope 495–500
Arcades complex (Lusaka) 146
Arnott, Fred 488
arrest 101–2
Asian Zambians 25

baboon, common 494
Baines' River Camp 238
balancing rocks 355
Banda, Abraham 254
Bangweulu, Lake *296*, **324–32**
Bangweulu Wetlands 65, 295, *296*, *326*, **324–32**
banks and banking **65**, 148
Bantu 4, 19
Barotseland 447, **458–77**
baskets 77, 148, 156, 184, 195, 209, 212, 214, 263, 388, 463, 476
Batoka 209
Batoka Gorge 160, 194, 202
BaTonga 211
bats, fruit 310, **315**
Batwa 442
bazaars 154
Bechuanaland, Protectorate of 6
beer 64, **75**, 77
Bell, Grace 298
Bemba 5, 20, 306, 340, 507–8

Berry, Phil 254
bicycle hire 166, 373
Big Lagoon Camp 268
bilharzia **98–9**, 212–13
Bilimungwe Bushcamp 268
binoculars 60
birds and birdwatching **35–6**
  Bangweulu 327, 328–9
  Jimbe River 490
  Kafue National Park 416–17
  Kasanka National Park 315–16
  Lake Tanganyika 344
  Liuwa Plain National Park 474
  Livingstone area 194
  Lochinvar and Blue Lagoon National Parks 438
  Lower Zambezi Valley 231, 234
  Nchila Wildlife Reserve 489–90
  Nyika Plateau National Park 369–70
  seasons for **43–4**, 328–9
  Shiwa Ng'andu 310
  South Luangwa National Park 257–8
  Sumbu National Park 351, 355
  Upper Zambezi 456
  Victoria Falls 194
  West Lunga National Park 482, 483
Bisa 322, 323
Blue Lagoon National Park 407, **443–6**, *445*
boats
  Lake Tanganyika 346–8, 353
  Mongu area 461
Boers 6
border posts 53–4, 192, 220, 228, 248, 297, 346, 388, 448, 454, 478, 480, 484
Botswana 53, 448
bribery 102
Bridge Camp 245–6
British 6–7
British Council 150
British South Africa Company 6–7, 8, 306, 375
Broken Hill Man 3, 155, 378
budgeting 61–4
buffalo 113, **502**
Buffalo Camp 289–90
bungee jumping 199
bureaux de change **65**, 149
Burundi 375
bus travel 68
  to/from Chipata 246
  to/from Kasama 334
  to/from Kitwe 390
  to/from Livingstone 162–3, 170

bus travel *continued*
  to/from Lusaka 123–4
  to/from Mpika 298
  to/from Mpulungu 346
  to/from Mumbwa 410
  to/from Ndola 384
  to/from Nyika 370
  to/from Solwezi 402
Busanga Bushcamp 423
Busanga Plains 407, 414, 415–18, 420, 425
Busanga Swamps 414, 420
bushbaby 495
bushbuck 498
Bushbuck Camp 239–40
bushcamps 75 *see also* fly-camping
Bushfront Lodge 177
bushpig 503
bush travel, lessons in 262–3
Bwana Mkubwa 375, 378
Bwanda Hot Springs 442

Cabora Bassa, Lake 204
cameras 58, 59, 60, **62**, 112, 148
campfires 109
camping 70, 94, **108–12**, 116, 138, 316, 338, 418 *see also* places by name
  equipment 110–11
canoeing **115–16**
  Lower Zambezi 220
  Lower Zambezi Valley 234–6
  Mutinondo Wilderness Area 305
  Shiwa Ng'andu 309
  Upper Zambezi 200–1
  West Lunga River 483–5
Cape Colony 6
Caprivi Strip 452, 453
Captain Solo 11–12
car hire **70–3**, 128–9, 164–6, 384, 395, 398
car repairs 150, 188, 394, 398
caracal 492
Carr, Norman 37, 112, 250, **252**, 253, 254
carvings 77, 148, 155, 184, 194, 221, 226, 463, 476
cat, African wild 492–3
Central African Federation 8
Chakwenga Mine 234
Chama 24, 248
Chambeshi Monument 339
Chambeshi River 339
Chamilandu Bushcamp 268
Chaminuka Lodge 139–40
Changwena Falls 297
Chaplin's Barbet (lodge) 378
charities **82–3**, 118, 246, 254, 259
charter planes **66–7**, 162
Chavuma 496, **480–1**

Chavuma Falls 481
cheetah 492
Chembe Bird Sanctuary 395
Chete Island 223–4
Chete Island Safari Lodge 224
Chewa 5, 28, 314
Chiawa Camp 240
Chiawa GMA 228, 234, 237
Chibala Camp 435
Chibembe Lodge 252, **268–9**
Chibesakunda, Lombe 12
Chichele Presidential Lodge 269
chiefs 4–5
Chifunda Community Bushcamp 288
Chifungwe Plain 253, 257, 293
Chikanka Island 225
Chikanka Island Camp 225
Chikaya Plain 253
Chikoko Trails 252, **269**
Chikoko Bushcamp 269
Chikufwe Plain 319
Chikuni 329–31
Chikwa Bushcamp 288
Chilanga 49, 157
Chilengwa, Lake 390
Chilenje Pools 431
Chelinda Camp 371
Chelinda Lodge 371
Chilindi Chipususha Falls 320
chilli fences 318
Chiluba, Frederick 10–13
Chimfunshi Wildlife Orphanage 398–401
chimpanzees 398–400, 401
Chindeni Bushcamp 269–70
Chinengwe 270
Chingola 375, **395–98**, *397*
Chinsali 325
Chinyangale Plain 319
Chinyingi Mission 463, **480**
Chinzombo Safari Lodge 252
Chipata 47, 245, **246–8**, *247*
Chipembele Wildlife Education Centre 259
Chipepo Harbour 209
Chipoma Falls 302
Chipundu 320
Chirundu 53, 212, **227–8**
Chirundu Forest Reserve 227
Chisala River 356
Chisekesi 209
Chisenga, Freddy 320
Chisengu 265
Chishimba Falls 339
Chitambo 318
chitenje 77–8
Chitipa 370
Chitongo 431
Chitoshi 338
Chitunta Plain 486
Chiundaponde 322–3
Cholilo 320

Cholola 454
Choma 207–8
Chongo 431, 441
Chongwe River Camp 239
Chongwe River House 240
Chowo Forest 372
Chrismar Hotel (Livingstone) 176
Chunga (Lochinvar) 443
Chunga (Kafue) 426
Chunga Safari Lodge 433–4
Chusa Falls 311
China 9
cigarettes 77
cichlids 345
cinema 146
civet 503
climate 29–32, *31*, 41–2
clothing 23, **57–8**, 72, 93, 185, 375
coach travel 68
to/from Livingstone 162–3
to/from Lusaka 123–5
coal 16
cobalt 2, **16**, 375
colonisation, Western 7–7
communications 79–81
conservation **36–40**, 258–60, 285, 317, 325, 439, 443, 453
Conservation Lower Zambezi (CLZ) 232–3
constitution 11, 13
copper 2, 7, 9, 10, **16**, **375–8**, 376
Copperbelt 7, 8, 28, **375–405**, 376
Copperbelt Museum 388
Coppinger, John 254
Corbeil, Father 341
Coulter, Dr George 218
coup d'état 11–12
courier services 150, 187
crafts **77**, 148, 195–6, 209, 215, 225, 261, 262, 263, 290, 388, 395, 463
credit cards 50, 54, **64–5**, 183
Croad, Hector 339
Crocodile Bushcamp 252, **269**
crocodile farms (Lake Kariba) 221
crocodile ponds 395
Crocodile Park (near Livingstone) 197
crocodiles 116
Cryptosepalum forest 482
cultural guidelines **22–3**, 63
cultural tourism 196, 228, 282–3, 323
culture 26–8
curios **77–8**, 148, 184–5, 195–6
currency 2, **61**

dambo **34–5**
dancing, traditional 27, 479
David Livingstone Safari Lodge 177
David Shepherd Camp *see* Chibala Camp
debt, national 9, 10–11, 12, **14–15**
deep vein thrombosis (DVT) 90–1
Democratic Republic of Congo (DRC) 12, 53–4, 100, 297, 358, 361, 366, 376, 384, 388, 395, 477
dengue fever 97
dentists 91
departure tax 52, 122
dialling codes 2, **79–80**
diarrhoea 95–6
disabled travellers 50–1
distances, flying 68

distances, driving 72
diving 345, 354
dress *see* clothing
drink 75–7
drink driving 73
driving **69–73**, **103–8**, 116, 129, 164–5
drumming 196, 246
Drum Rocks 443
duiker, common 500
Dumdumwenze gate 429

economy 9–11, **14–18**, 377–8
education 9, 10, **25–6**, 82, 423
Edward VII, King 27
eland 497–8
elections 9, 10–11, 12, 13
electricity **59**
elephant 108, 114, 143–4, **500–1**
elephant-riding 203–4
email 81
embassies 55–6, 151
emergencies, medical **91**, 152, 187, 395, 398, 405
Enhanced Structural Adjustment Facility (ESAF) 14–15
entry requirements 54–5
environment, physical 29-32
etiquette **22–3**, 101, 113
evergreen forest 34, 482
exchange rates 61
expatriates 25
exports 78, 377
eye problems 93

fauna *see* birds; wildlife
fax services 81
Federation of African Societies 8
ferries and pontoons
Kafue River 234
Lake Kariba 213
Lake Mweru 362
Lake Tanganyika 346–7
Luanginga River 475
Luangwa River 288
Luapula River 358
Lubungu River 410
Lunga River 409
Zambezi River 53, 448, 457, 465
festivals 26–8
field guides 36, **511–12**
Field Museum (Livingstone) 195
Fingira Rock 372
fires, camp 109
fish 218-19, 344–5
Fisher family 488
fishing 44, 467
Kafue River 227
Kasanka National Park 317
Lake Kariba 220
Lake Tanganyika 345–6
Livingstone/Victoria Falls 194
Lower Zambezi Valley 234
Nyika Plateau National Park 373
Upper Zambezi 456
flag 2
Flatdogs Camp 278
Flight of Angels 198–9
flights, over Victoria Falls 198–9
floodplains 34
flora 32, **33–5**, 51
Kafue National Park 414
Kasanka National Park 312–14

flora *continued*
Lake Tanganyika 344
Liuwa Plain National Park 471–2
Lochinvar and Blue Lagoon National Parks 437
Lower Zambezi Valley 229–30
Luambe National Park 293
Mutinondo Wilderness Area 303
Nchila Wildlife Reserve 489
North Luangwa National Park 286
Nyika Plateau National Park 368
South Luangwa National Park 255
Sumbu National Park **351**, 355
West Lunga National Park 481–2
fly-camping 281, 317
flyinig fox 200
fly-in trips 48–9
food **75–6**
hygiene and storage 92
shopping for 75, 78, 147, 183–4
subsidies 14
footwear 58
forests 34, 482
Fort Elwes 297–8
Fort Monze 210
4x4 vehicles 63, **71–2**, 101
driving techniques 106–8
trips 49
Frankfurt Zoological Society 285
Freedom Statue (Lusaka) 156
Fringilla Lodge 378
fuel **70**, 103, 107

game
driving near 108
seasons for 42–3
see also wildlife
game management areas (GMAs) 32, 38–40 *see also* named GMAs
Gamitto, Antonio 250
GDP 2, 14, 16, 17, 377
gemstones 2, 16
genet 503
geology 29
Copperbelt 377
Luangwa Valley 255
Victoria Falls 160–1
George VI, King 193, 306, 307
Germans 6, 339–40
getting around Zambia 66–75
getting to Zambia 52–4
giraffe 502
golf 197
Gore-Browne, Stewart 8, **305–6**, 307–8
gorge swing 199–200
Gough, Mary 293
government 13
GPS systems x, **60**
grass, driving through 107
grasslands 34–5
Great East Road 245–49
Great North Road 295–302, 333–42, 378–82
Great Rift Valley 3, 333, 341, 377
greetings 22–3
grysbok, Sharpe's 500
guesthouses 74 *see also places by name*

guides
canoeing 115–16, 235
national parks 51
South Luangwa National Park 254
walking safaris 112
Gwabi River Lodge 228
Gwala Walking Camp 270
Gwembe Safari Lodge 208
Gwisho Hot Springs 442

Hammarskjoeld, Dag 389
handshaking 23
Hankin, Peter 252
hare, scrub 506
hartebeest, Lichtenstein's 496–7
Harvey, Lorna 315, 306
Harvey, Major John 314, 306
health 51, **85–100**, 212–13, 512
returning home 99–100
heatstroke 92–3
hedgehog, southern African 505–6
helicopter flights 199
Henry Tayali Visual Art Centre (Lusaka) 156
hepatitis 86, **97**
high wire 200
Hillwood Farm 486–90
Hippo Lodge 431, **424–5**
hippopotamus 114–5, 116, **501–2**
history **3–13**, 121, 159–60, 250–3, 284–85, 305–6, 312, 378
hitchhiking 53, 54, **73–4**, 228, 266, 336, 346, 370, 382, 384, 390, 449, 460
HIV 70, 97
honey 478
honey badger 504–5
horseriding 203, 305, 310, 373
hospitals 91 *see also* emergencies, medical
host communities 117
hotels 74 *see also places by name*
houseboats 220, 222
humanism 9
hunting 37–40, 208, 258, 259, 292, 293, 331, 350, 417 *see also* poaching
Hwange 160
hydro-electricity 2, 16, 211, 339, 360, 414, 439
hyena, spotted 493
hygiene 92, 117
hyrax 506

Ibis Gardens 378–9
Ikelenge 54, 485
Ila 28, 442
immunisations 85–6
impala 498
imports and exports 78
independence 8–9
industry 10, 16–17, 377
infant mortality 19
inflation 14, 61
inoculations 67–8
insect repellents 94
insect bites 93–4
insurance 85, 101
camera 60
disabled travellers 51
International Monetary Fund (IMF) 10, 11, 14–15
internet access 81
Iron Age **3–4**, 207, 302, 321, 341, 375, 442
Isanga Bay Lodge 349
Isangano National Park 332

Island Bushcamp 270
Islands of Siankaba 175–6
Isoka 24, 249, 299
Isokwe 362
Itezhi-Tezhi Dam and Lake 414, 416, 426, 428, 435, **439**, 499
itineraries 48–9
It's Wild 290
ivory 78, 501

jackal, side-striped 493
Jalawe Rock 372
jet boats 203
Jimbe Bridge 484
Jimbe River 490
Jivundu 483, 485
judicial system 13
Jumbe 265

Kabanga Scout Post 409
Kabompo **477–8**, 483, 485–6
Kabompo River 481–2
Kabula Lodge 452
Kabwata Cultural Centre (Lusaka) 77, **155**
Kabwe 3, 327, 375, **379–381**, *380*
Kabwelume Falls 364, **365–6**
Kafue (town) 211, **226–7**
Kafue Dam 227, **439**
Kafue Flats 3, 30, 327, 407, 437, 439, 442, **444–6**
Kafue Lodge 387
Kafue National Park 34, 36, 48–9, 204, *406*, 407, **413–36**, *419*, *427*, *430*, *433*, 454
Kafue Queen 227
Kafue River 30, 226, 227, 229, 234, 398–9, 414, 416, 418, 426,,**439**
Kafue River Basin *406*, **407–46**
Kafunta River Lodge 270
Kafwala 414, 418
Kafwala Camp 422
Kafwala Rapids Camp 421, **422**
Kaingo Camp 270–1
KaingU Campsite 434
KaingU Safari Lodge 428, 432, **434**
Kakuli Bushcamp 252, **271**
Kalabo 5, 460, **464–6**, 474
Kalabolelwa 452, 454
Kalahari Desert 3, 29
Kalambo Falls 3, **341–2**, 347
Kalambo Falls Lodge 349
Kalamu Lodge 271
Kalene Hill 484, 490
Kalimba Reptile Park 156
Kalomo **207**, 429
Kalundu Mound 207
Kalungwishi River 362, **364–6**
Kanona 321
Kansanshi Mine 378
Kanyemba Lodge 237
Kanyilambi 485
Kaoma 408, **411–12**, *412*, 467, 468–9
Kaonde 22
Kapabi Swamp 312, 315
Kapamba Bushcamp 271–2
Kapani Safari Lodge 93, 252, 272
Kapatu Mission 368
kapenta fishing **218–19**, 221, 225
Kapinga Bushcamp 423–4
Kapiri Mposhi 68, 69, 375, **381–2**
Kapishya Hot Springs 309
Kapuma Falls 367
Kaputa 362, **363**

Kariba Bush Club 222
Kariba Dam 46, 205, **211–12**, 220–1
Kariba Gorge 212-13, 221, 236
Kariba, Lake 205, *206*, **211–25**
Kasaba Bay Lodge 366, 379, 353, 355
Kasaka River Lodge 238
Kasakalawe Lodge 349
Kasama **335–38**, *336*
rock paintings 338–9
Kasane 163, 198, 449
Kasanga 342, 346
Kasanka National Park 34, 295, **312–19**, *313*
Kasansanya 252
Kasaramba Viewpoint 372
Kaseki River 486
Kasempa 22, 403, **407–9**, 413, 420, 469
Kashiba, Lake 390
Kasonso-Busanga GMA 420
Katete 246
Katima Mulilo 449, 454
Kaudina Falls 320
Kaulime, Lake 371–2
Kaunda, Kenneth **9–10**, 11, 26, 155, 274, 307, 355, 390, 446
Kavumbu River Camp 452
Kawambwa 360, **364**
Kawaza Village 253, **282–3**
kayaking 202
Kayila Lodge 237
Kazungula 53, 163, **449**
Khama, King 6
Kiambi Lower Zambezi 236–7
Kifubwa Stream Rock Shelter 405
Kilwa 362
Kitwe 375, **390–5**, *391*
klipspringer 499
Ku-omboka **26–7**, 464
kudu 497
Kufukwila 28
Kulamba 28
Kunda 28
Kundabwika Falls 364, **366**
Kundalila Falls 297, **320–1**
Kutandala Camp 290–1
Kuyenda 272
kwacha 11, 14, **61**, **65**
Kwando River 453, 457
Kwena Lagoon Camp 272

Lake Tanganyika Lodge 348–9
Lake View 222
language 20, *21*, **22–3**, **507–8**
language groups 20–5
Lavushi Manda National Park **323–4**
lead 16, 375, 379
Lealui 26–7, 461, **464**
lechwe 499
Lechwe Lodge 141, **226–7**
Lechwe Plains Tented Camp 441
leopard 114, **491–2**
Leopard Lodge 425
Libonda pontoon 466
life expectancy 19
light aircraft, Victoria Falls 198
Likumbi Lya Mize **27**, 479
Lilayi Lodge 141–2
Limulunga 26–7, **467**
Linyanti 159
lion 114, **491**
Lion Camp 273
Lion Plain 253
literacy 19
Litunga 5, **26–7**, 461, **471**
palaces 464

Liuwa Plain National Park 43, 447, **473–7**, *472*
Livingstone 17, 22, 24, 28, 48–9, 74, 121, 123, **159–204**, *165*, *168–9*, 205
Livingstone, David **6**, **159–60**, 193, 195, 198, 211, 250, 295, 310, **319–20**, **455**
Livingstone Island 193
Livingstone Memorial 319–20
Livingstone Museum 195
Livingstone Safari Lodge 179–80
Livingstonia 371, 372, 373
Lobengula 6
local payments 117–18
location 2, 29
Lochinvar Lodge 441–3
Lochinvar National Park 49, 210, 407, **436–43**, *440*
lodges 75 *see also individual lodges by name*
London Missionary Society 362
Lowden Lodge 386–7
Lowdown, The 153
Lower Zambezi National Park 48–9, 228, **229–42**
Lower Zambezi Valley 48–9, 205, *206*, **229–43**
Lozi 5, 20, 22, 458, 461, 464, 507–8
Luakela Forest Reserve 486
Luakela River 486
Luambe National Park 245, 287, **291–4**
Luangwa River 250, 252, **253–5**, 292, 367, 502
Luangwa River Lodge 273
Luangwa Safari House 273
Luangwa Valley 3, 48–9, 112, 229, *244*, **245–94**, 502, 505
Luangwa village 242, 245
Luangwa Wilderness Lodge 293
Luapula River 357, 360–1
Lubi River 253
Lubuji River 416
Lubungu pontoon 409, 410, 411, 421, 424
Lubwe 358
Luchazi 22
Lufubu River 351, 352
Lufupa Tented Camp 416, 420, **421–2**
Lufupa River 418, 420
luggage 57
Lukanga Swamps 407, 499
Lukulu 49, 413, 447, 461, **466–71**, *468*
Lukulu River 324, 329
Lukuni Luzwa Buuka 28
Lukusuzi National Park 245, **294**
Lumangwe Falls 364, **365**
Lunda 23, 361, 479, 507–9
Lundazi 245, **248–9**
Lundazi Castle Hotel 249
Lundu Plain 253
Lunga River 418
Lunga River Lodge 417, **424**
Lungu, Stepehen 11
Lunsemfwa River 298
Lunsemfwa Wonder Gorge **298**, 380
Lunsongwe 485
Luombe River 368
Lupande GMA 259–60
Lupupa Falls 368
Lusaka 3, 19, 20, 24, 32, 49, **121–57**, *126–7*, *134–5*, *144*, 417

Lusenga Plain National Park 333, **364**
Luunda 22, 27
Luvale 23, 479, 508–9
Luwi Bushcamp 273
Luwingu 367
Luwombwa Fishing Lodge 316–17
Luyana 23
Lwiinda 28
Lwitikila Falls 302
Lwitikila River 299

Maaze Island 223
Malaila 28
Machel, Samora 355
magazines 81–2
Makishi dancers 27, 470, 155, **479**
Makololo 159
Malaila 28
Malambo 250
Malambo Women's Craft Centre 209
malaria **86–7**, **96**, 99–100
Malawi 7, 8, 54, 249, 368, 372
Mambilima Falls 361
Mambwe-Lungu 24
mammals 35
man, early 3, 195, 379
Manda Hill Shopping Centre (Lusaka) 146
Mansa 383, **358–60**, *359*
Manshya River 309
Manyinga 477
maps **59**, 60, 103, **125**, 267, 287, 388, 441
list of vi
Maramba River Lodge 179
markets 208, 211–12, 498
Lusaka 153–4
Livingstone 195–6
Marula Lodge 273
Mashapi Island 223
Mashi 24
Masuku Lodge 209
Matebele 457
Matesi River 163
Mazabuka **210–11**, 439, 443
Maziba Bay 452
Mbala 335, **339–41**, *340*, 352, 399
Mbereshi 362–3
Mbunda 24
Mbwela 24
McBride's Camp 425
Mchenja Camp 273–4
media 81–2
medical kit 89–90
medical services **91**, 152, 187, 395, 398, 405
meningitis 86, **97**
Mfuwe 30, **261–3**, *264*, 266
Mfuwe Lodge 274
microlighting 198
migration, wildlife 474, 475
Mindolo Dam 395
mineral resources 16–17, 375–8
minibuses 128
minimum impact 116–18
mining 7, 8, 10, **16–17**, 375–8
miombo woodland 33–4
Mishembe Bay – Luke's Place 349
missionaries 6, 160, 372, 338, 350, 447, 480–1, 488
Mize 26
Mkushi 295–6
Mkushi River 380
mobile phones 80–1
mobile safaris 281

Mokuni, Chief 28
money 61–6
mongoose 504
Mongu 420, 421, 428, 433, 457, **458–64**, *459*, 465, 466, 467
monkey 494–5
montane forest 34
montane grasslands 35
Monze 209–10, 431
Moorings Campsite 209
mopane woodland 33
Moshi Camp **422**
Mosi-oa-Tunya National Park 35, 160, **204**
mosquitoes 93–4
Moto Moto Museum (Mbala) 341
motto 2
Movement for Multiparty Democracy (MMD) 10–11, 12, 138
Mozambique 5, 9, 54
Mpata Gorge 242
Mpika 266, 287, 292, **299–302**, *301*
Mporokoso 363, **366–7**
Mpulungu 335, **346–50**, *347*
Mtanda Plain 253
Muchinga Escarpment 253, 284, 298, 320, 381, 495
mud, driving in 107
Mukambi Bushcamp 433
Mukambi Plains Camp 433
Mukambi Safari Lodge 426, **433**
Mukinge Hospital (Kasempa) 408
Mukuni village 196
Mukuyu Camp 386
Mulembo Falls 299
Mumbeji 469
Mumbuluma Falls 360
Mumbuluma Falls II 366
Mumbuluma Falls III 367
Mumbwa 407, **409–10**
Mumwa Craft Association 463
Munali Hills 211
Munda Wanga Wildlife Park & Sanctuary 157
munga woodland 34
Mununga 380, 362
Munyamadzi GMA 292
Mupamadzi River 253, 292
Mupasha Campsite 436
Musanza Tented Camp 423
museums 155, 194–5, 208, 341, 388, 464
Mushingashi Conservancy 435
Mushroom Lodge & Presidential House 274
Musonda Falls 361
Musumpu River 320
Mutanda River 405, 483
Mutanda Falls 405
Mutemwa Lodge **451–2**, 456
Mutenguleni 28
Mutinondo Wilderness Area 49, 295, **302–5**
Mutinondo Wilderness Lodge 304
Mutomboko 27–8, **361**
Muwele 331
Muyombe 249
Mvuu Lodge 237–8
Mwaleshi Camp 291
Mwaleshi River 313
Mwamba Bushcamp 252, **274–5**
Mwambashi River Lodge 241
Mwanachingwala Conservation Area **210–11**, 443

Mwanawasa, Levy Patrick 12–13
Mwandi 194
Mwansabombwe 27, **361**
Mwanya Bushcamp 278
Mwata Kazemba 5
Mwelemu 483, 485
Mwense 360
Mweru, Lake 5, 250, 325, 362
Mweru Wantipa, Lake 352, 362
Mweru Wantipa National Park 333, **363**
Mwinilunga 34, 477, **485–6**
Mzuzu 370

Nachikufu Cave 301–2
Nachipala Bareback Hill 310
Nakapalayo Village **323**, 331
Nakeenda Lodge 444
Nakonde 123, 299, 336
names 508
Namibia 6, 53, 442, 448
Namundela Falls 312
Namwala 430
Namwane Art Gallery (Lusaka) 156
Nangandwe Pools 432
Nanzhila Plains 429, **432**
Nanzhila Plains Safari Camp 432, **435–6**
Nanzhila River 429
Nata 448
Natangwe Community Campsite 288
National Assembly buildings (Lusaka) 156
National Heritage Conservation Commission (NHCC) 38
National Museum (Lusaka) 155
national parks 38–40, *39*, 49–52 *see also by name*
entry fees 49–50
National Redemption Council 11
Natural Mystic Lodge 175
natural resources 2, 16–17
navigation **59–60**, 103
Nayuma Museum and Heritage Centre 464
Nchelenge 352, 356, 360, **362**
Nchila Bushcamp 487
Nchila Wildlife Reserve 49, **486–90**
Nc'wala 28
Ndebele 159
Ndola 375, **382–90**, *383*
Ndole Bay Lodge 353, **354**
Ndolwa, Lake 319
New Kalala Camp 435
newspapers 81
Nganda Peak 372
Ng'andu 5
Ngoma 415, 417, **431**, *432*
Ngoma Forest 414, 426
Ngombe Ilede 4, 215
Ng'ona River 27
Ngoni 298
Ngonye Falls 447, **455–6**
Ngwezi Pools 454
Niamkolo Church 350
nightclubs 145–6, 183, 387, 394
Nkamba Bay Lodge 353, **354–5**
Nkanga River Conservation Area 208–9
Nkoya-Mbwela 24
Nkwali 275
North Luangwa National Park 35, 40, 48–9, 245, **284–91**, *289*

Northern Rhodesian African Mineworkers Union 8
Northern Rhodesian African National Congress 8, 9
Nsalu Cave 297, **321**
Nsama 352
Nsefu Camp 252, 254, **275**
Nsefu, Chief 252, 253, 283
Nsefu Sector 43, 252, 255, 258, *280*, 282,
Nsendamila Cultural Village 283
Nsenga 24, 28
Nsobe Game Camp 386
Nsolo Bushcamp 275–6
Ntanta Plain 253
Ntemwa Camp 423
Ntemwa River 418, 420
Ntendere 249
Nthunta Escarpment 293
Ntumbachushi Falls 363–4
Nundo Head Peninsula 355
Nyaminyami 460
Nyamuweji village 488
Nyanja 24, 507–8
Nyao dancers 28
Nyasaland *see* Malawi
Nyausa 366
Nyerere, Julius 9
Nyika 24
Nyika Plateau 29, 34, 35, 54, 110, 368, *369*, 370, 496, 502, 506
Nyika Plateau National Park 333, **368–73**, *369*

Old Drift 160, 204
Old Mondoro 241
Operation Noah 212
oribi 500
otter 505
overheating, engine 108
overland travel 53–4
Owens, Mark and Delia 285

paintballing 204
pan 35
pangolin 505
Paris Club 15
Peace Parks Foundation 454
Pemba 209
people 19–24
Perekani 250
Petauke 24, **246**, 265–6
pharmacies 51, 88, **91–2**, 148, 185, 388, 395, 408
photography 22, 26, **44**, **60–1**, **62–3**, 101
Pioneer Camp 140
poaching 35, **40**, 78, **232–3**, 256, **258–9**, 285, 312, 314, 317, 325, 332, **417**, 436, 453, 473, 488
polecat, striped 505
police 69, 101, 104–5
politics **8–13**
pontoons 108 *see also* ferries
Pope, Robin and Jo 254, 261
population 19
porcupine 505
Portuguese 5, 250
postal services **79**, 150, 187
postboats **69**, 358, 461–2
postbuses 68, **124**
pottery 4, 342
poverty 15, 18, 82
precious stones, fake 77
press, the 81–2
privatisation 14, **15**
Protea Hotel Lusaka Safari Lodge **140–1**, 378
provinces 13, *13*

public holidays 2, 45
puku 499–500
Puku Pan Safari Lodge 435
Puku Ridge Tented Camp 276
Pule Falls 367

quad-bike excursions 204

rabies 86, **98**
radio 82
rafting 201–2
rail travel 54, 67, 68, 125, 281–2, 300, 335, 384, 390
to/from Kapiri Mposhi 381–2
to/from Livingstone 163
to/from Lusaka 124–5
Railway Museum (Livingstone) 195
rainfall 30–2, *31*
Reader, John 26, 458
Redcliff Zambezi Lodge 242
reedbuck 498
religion 25
restaurants 64 *see also places by name*
resthouses, government 74–5
rhinoceros 232, 258
black 114, 233, 258, 286, 416, 417, **501**
white 204, 501
Rhodes, Cecil 6–7
Rhodesia
Northern 7–9, 121, 160, 377
Southern 7, 8, 9
rift valley 3, 229, 245, 255, 333, 341, 373
riparian forest 34
Riverane Guesthouse 393
riverboarding 202–3
River Club, The 173
river cruises 193–4
river safaris 282
rivers, crossing 108
roadblocks 104–5
road travel 104–6
roads, quality of 69, **104–6**
rock art 3, 301, 338–9, 366, 405
rocky terrain, driving on 108
Royal Chundu Zambezi River Lodge 176
Royal Livingstone 177
Royal Zambezi Lodge 238–9
rubbish 117
Rumphi 371

sacred lake 390
safaris
around Livingstone 204
elephant-back 203
mobile 281
operators 46–7, 260–1, 418
organising 45–52
prices 45, 61–4
river 282
walking 44, 93–4, 112–13, 234, 236, 252, 284, 317
safety 73–4, **100–2**, 213–15, 345
sailing 223
Sakazima Island Camp 451
Samfya 357, 357–8
San/Bushmen 3, 4, 159, 301, 321
Sancta Maria Mission (Lukulu) 470–1
sand, driving in 106–7
Sandaula 460, 461, 465
Sata, Michael 12
Sausage Tree 240–1
schistosomiasis 98–9
Schultz, Bert 253

scorpions 94–5
Scramble for Africa 6–7
Sebanzi Hill 455, **442–3**
segway tours 204
Sekula Island 223, 225
Senanga **457**, 461
Senga 233
Senga Hill 338
Senkele Falls 311–12
Serenje 294, **298–9**, 356
serval 492
Sesheke **449–50**, 454, 480
sexually transmitted diseases 97
Shackletons Upper Zambezi
   Lodge 450
Shamabinga Retreat 393
Shangambo Mission 457
Shangombo 454
Shimunenga 28
Shiwa Ng'andu 8, 47–8, 284,
   295, **305–11**
Shoebill Island Camp 331
shoebills 295, 327, **328**
shopping **77–8**, 146–8, 153–4,
   183–6, 387–8, 394, 462 *see
   also* bazaars; markets
Showgrounds (Lusaka) 156
Shumba Bushcamp 431, **422–3**
Siameja 209
Sianzovo 209
Siavonga 205, **213–21**, *214*
Siddle, Sheila and David 398–9
Simonga village 196
Sinazongwe 205, 213, **221–3**
Sindabezi Island 174
Sioma Falls *see* Ngonye Falls
Sioma Ngwezi National Park
   447, **452–5**
sitatunga 497
Sitoti pontoon 456, 457
skin infections 93
slave trade 5, 6, 243, 488
Slave Tree (Ndola) 388–9
sleeping sickness 99
snakes **94–5**, 112, 115
snorkelling 345
Solwezi 328, 375, **401–05**, *402*,
   408
Songwe village 196
Songwe Village (lodge) 178
South Africa 7, 8, 52, 53
South African Nationalist Party
   8
South Luangwa Conservation
   Society 259
South Luangwa National Park
   40, 42, 48–9, 58, 232, 245,
   249–83, *251*, *264*, *280*
South West Africa 6, 9 *see also*
   Namibia
souvenirs 78, 148, 184–5, 221,
   261, 263 *see also* crafts; curios
spa services 198
spare parts, vehicle 103, 150,
   188, 380, 394, 398
speed limits 69
spiders 94
sport 154
squirrel 506
Stanley Safari Lodge 180
state of emergency 11
steenbok 500
Stone Age 3, 178, 250, 301,
   321, 338, 341, 343, 405, 442
Sumbu National Park 333,
   349, *350*, **350–6**
Sumbu town 356
Sun International 74, 176
sunburn 92–3
sunken lakes 389–90
Sussi & Chuma (lodge) 172–3
swamps 34, 35

swimming 345
   dangers of 99, 215, 345

Tafika 252, **276–7**
Taita Falcon Lodge 178–9
Tangala House 174–5
Tanganyika, Lake 42, 44, 49,
   218-19, 333, **342–6**, *343*,
   378, 379, 381–3
Tanzania 9, 54, 200, 341
taxis **68–9**, 128, 164
TAZARA trains 54, 67, 68,
   125, **381–2**
teak forest 34, **426**
telephone codes 2, 79–80
telephone services 79–80
television 82
temperatures 32
Tena Tena 277
tents 110
termites 76
Tete 250, 450
textiles 17, 148, 261, 263, 388
theatre, Lusaka 146
theft 100–1
Thornicroft 279
Thorntree River Lodge 173
tickbite fever 98
Tiger Camp 467
Tikondane 246
tinkerbird, white-chested 482
tipping 65–6
toilets 117
Toka-Leya 28, 159
Toka Leya (lodge) 172
Tondwa GMA 350, 351
Tonga 20, 204, 209, 442, 444,
   460, 507–9
Tongabezi 174
topography 29, *30*
tour operators **46–8**, 189–90,
   260–1, 333, 418–18, 447
   disabled travellers 51
tourism **17–18**, **38**, 41
   cultural 196, 228, 282–3, 323
   minimum impact 116–18
   responsible 117
   seasons 41–4
   sustainable 38, 252
tourist information 44, 153,
   161
Track and Trail Rivercamp
   279
trade 4, 5, 9, 19–21
trains 54, 67–8, 124–5, 163,
   281–2, 300, 335, 381–2, 384,
   390
Transfrontier Conservation
   Areas (TCAs) 454
transport 52–4
   disabled travellers 50–1
travel agents 152–3, 188, 388,
   395, 398
travel clinics 87–9
travellers' cheques 5, 65, 149
Treetops Conservation School
   Camp 423
Tribal Textiles 261
'tribes' 19–20
trypanosomiasis 99
tsetse flies 94, *99*
Tumbuku 25
Tunduma 46
Tuwimba 28

Undi 5
Unilateral Declaration of
   Independence (UDI) 9
United National Independence
   Party (UNIP) 9, 10–11, 155,
   274

vaccinations 85–6
vanadium 375
vegetation 33–4, 42
vehicle hire 70–3
vehicle repairs 150, 188, 394,
   398
Victoria Falls 33, 46, **159–60**,
   190–2, *191*
   activities and excursions
   194–204
Victoria Falls (town) 163, 192
Victoria Falls National Park
   204
visas **54–5**, 163
Vlissingen, Paul Fentener van
   473
voluntary work 246
von Lettow-Vorbeck, General
   339

Waka Waka, Lake 49, **321–2**
walking
   etiquette 42
   in the bush 112–15
   Lower Zambezi Valley 234
   Mutinondo Wilderness Area
   304–5
   Nyika Plateau National Park
   371, 372, 373
   safaris 44, 93–4, 112–13,
   234, 236, 252, 284, 317
   Shiwa Ng'andu 309–10
   south of Lusaka 227
   Sumbu National Park 355
warthog 503
Wasa Lodge 316
water **76–7**, 92, 110
Waterberry Zambezi Lodge 175
waterbuck 496
Watopa pontoon 468, 481
weasel, striped 505
weaving 395, 458, 463
websites 512–13
weights and measures 2
welfare associations 7–8
West Lunga National Park 447,
   481–6
West Lunga River 482, 485
weather 41–2 *see also* climate
   dry season 41–2
   wet season 42
what to take 57–9
when to go 41–4
white Zambians 25
white-water kayaking 203
white-water rafting **201–2**, 456
wild dog, African 232, 493
wildebeest, blue **496**
   migration 474, 475
wildlife **35–40**, **491–506**
   Bangweulu 325–7
   dangers for campers 111–12
   encounters with 108,
   113–15, 116
   Kafue National Park 414–17
   Kasanka National Park
   314–15
   Lake Tanganyika 344–5
   Liambe National Park 293
   Liuwa Plain National Park
   473–5
   Lochinvar and Blue Lagoon
   National Parks 437–8
   Lower Zambezi Valley 230–1
   Mutinondo Wilderness Area
   303
   Nchila Wildlife Reserve 489
   North Luangwa National
   Park 286
   Nyika Plateau National Park
   368–9
   seasons for 42–4

wildlife *continued*
   Shiwa Ng'andu 309–10
   Sioma Ngwezi National
   Park 453–4
   South Luangwa National
   Park 255–8
   Sumbu National Park 351,
   355
   West Lunga National Park
   482
   see also birds; conservation
Wildlife Camp 279–81
Wildlife and Environmental
   Conservation Society of
   Zambia (WECSZ) **51–2**, 511
Witch Doctor's Falls 363–4
women travellers 101
woodland 33–4
World Bank 11, 14–15, 209
World War I 339, 375
World War II 7
World Wide Fund for Nature
   (WWF) 38, 40, 324, 438,
   439, 443

Yangumwila Falls 366

Zaire *see* Democratic Republic
   of Congo (DRC)
Zambelozi Island Lodge 450
Zambezi (town) 478–9
Zambezi Breezers 228
Zambezi Kulefu Camp 241–2
Zambezi National Park 204
Zambezi River 26, 29, 35, 44,
   159, 160, 172, 205, 212-13,
   224, 225, 229–30, 250, 458,
   460, 461, 485, 490
   bridges 449, **450**, **480**
   ferries 53, 212, 457, 461,
   466, 470
   Lower *230–1*
   source 489, **490**
   Upper 22, 26, 69, 160,
   193–4, 200–1
   watersports 115, 200–3, 220,
   221, 235–6, 483–5 *see also*
   Kariba Dam; Lower
   Zambezi Valley; Ngonye
   Falls; Victoria Falls
Zambezi Sun 178
Zambezi Waterfront 176
Zambia
   facts and figures 2
   northern **333–74**, *334*
   southern *158*
   western **447–90**, *448*
Zambia African National
   Congress (ZANC) 9
Zambia Consolidated Copper
   Mines (ZCCM) 10, 14, 16
Zambia Development Agency
   (ZDA)
zebra 502
Zambia National Tourist Board
   (ZNTB) 44, 153, 160, 513
Zambia Wildlife Authority
   (ZAWA) 40, **49**, 225, 223,
   338, 356, 362, 417, 454, 482
Zebra Island 224
Zebra Pans Bushcamp 277
Zimba 205
Zimbabwe 7, 24, 53, 55, 163,
   164, 190, 200, 211, 220,
   222–4, 228–9
zinc 16, 375, 378
ZOCS project 82
Zombe 342
Zovo Chipola Forest 372
Zulu, Isaac 254
Zumbo 250
Zungulila Walking Camp 270